Essential Dutch dictionary

Dutch–English/English–Dutch dictionary

Gerdi Quist & Dennis Strik

For UK order enquiries: please contact Bookpoint Ltd,
130 Milton Park, Abingdon, Oxon OX14 4SB.
Telephone: +44 (0) 1235 827720. Fax: +44 (0) 1235 400454.
Lines are open 09.00–17.00, Monday to Saturday, with a 24-hour
message answering service. Details about our titles and how to
order are available at www.teachyourself.com

For USA order enquiries: please contact McGraw-Hill
Customer Services, PO Box 545, Blacklick, OH 43004-0545, USA.
Telephone: 1-800-722-4726. Fax: 1-614-755-5645.

For Canada order enquiries: please contact McGraw-Hill
Ryerson Ltd, 300 Water St, Whitby, Ontario L1N 9B6, Canada.
Telephone: 905 430 5000. Fax: 905 430 5020.

Long renowned as the authoritative source for self-guided
learning – with more than 50 million copies sold worldwide –
the **teach yourself** series includes over 500 titles in the fields of
languages, crafts, hobbies, business, computing and education.

British Library Cataloguing in Publication Data: a catalogue record
for this title is available from the British Library.

Library of Congress Catalog Card Number: on file.

First published in UK 2003 as *Teach Yourself Dutch Dictionary*
by Hodder Education, part of Hachette UK, 338 Euston Road,
London NW1 3BH.

First published in US 2003 as *Teach Yourself Dutch Dictionary* by
The McGraw-Hill Companies, Inc,

The **teach yourself** name is a registered trade mark of Hodder
Headline.

This edition published 2010.

Copyright © 2003, 2010 Gerdi Quist & Dennis Strik

Typeset by MPS Limited, A Macmillan Company.

Printed in Great Britain for Hodder Education, a Hachette UK
Company, 338 Euston Road, London NW1 3BH, by CPI Group
(UK) Ltd, Croydon, CR0 4YY.

The publisher has used its best endeavours to ensure that the URLs
for external websites referred to in this book are correct and active
at the time of going to press. However, the publisher and the
author have no responsibility for the websites and can make no
guarantee that a site will remain live or that the content will remain
relevant, decent or appropriate.

Hachette UK's policy is to use papers that are natural, renewable
and recyclable products and made from wood grown in sustainable
forests. The logging and manufacturing processes are expected to
conform to the environmental regulations of the country of origin.

Impression number   10 9 8 7 6 5 4 3
Year   2014 2013 2012

Contents

Meet the authors

Gerdi Quist and Dennis Strik are highly experienced language teachers and authors. Gerdi is lecturer in Dutch at University College London (UCL), and conducts research into language teaching in general, and Dutch in particular, focusing on intercultural communication. Dennis worked as a lecturer in Dutch at UCL for ten years, before moving back to the Netherlands, where he continues to write language books, teaches Dutch and works as a professional translator.

Together Gerdi and Dennis have written a whole range of language course books for learners at all levels, from beginners to advanced learners at an academic level, both for self-study purposes and classroom environments. Amongst the titles Gerdi and Dennis have produced are *Get Started in Dutch*, *Complete Dutch* and *Essential Dutch Grammar*, published by Hodder Education, which are aimed at beginners and students at intermediate level, and Routledge Intensive Dutch Course, which is intended for academic learners.

Only got a minute?

Dutch is a West Germanic language, closely related to German and English, and is spoken by around 23 million people, mainly in the Netherlands, Belgium, Surinam (South America) and the Dutch Antilles and Aruba.

Dutch spelling is officially regulated by law. De Nederlandse Taalunie (the Dutch language union) publishes **het Groene Boekje** (literally, *the little green book*) which contains the official spelling of words in the Dutch language.

Looking up words

Verbs are listed under the infinitive form. Remember that separable verbs come with a prefix which may be separated from the verb. Adjectives are entered in the dictionary under their basic form, without the extra **-e** which is sometimes added. Nouns are entered in the dictionary under their singular form.

Don't forget the various spelling rules which apply, for instance, to the doubling of consonants or vowels, or the rules which mean that **s** and **f** sometimes change into **z** and **v**, and vice versa.

To help you understand the meaning of abbreviations, and what they stand for, for most abbreviations the full Dutch form is given after a colon: **a.s.: aanstaande**, *coming:* **9 juli a.s.**, *9 July next.*

5 Only got five minutes?

Dutch is a West Germanic language and is spoken by around 23 million people in the Netherlands, Belgium, Surinam (South America) and the Dutch Antilles and Aruba (both in the Caribbean), and in very small pockets of Northern France and along Germany's Western border. Within Western Europe, Dutch is a medium-sized language. To give an idea of what this means, Dutch is spoken by more people than the Scandinavian languages Swedish, Norwegian, Danish and Icelandic combined.

Dutch is closely related to German and English and shares many features with these languages, making it a relatively easy language to learn for speakers from these language areas. However, grammatically, Dutch is considerably less complex regarding its system of verb declensions, cases, and the gender system of nouns than its closest relation, German.

Dutch spelling is officially regulated by law. The first official spelling rules in the Netherlands date back to 1804. In Belgium, a different official spelling was adopted in 1841. In 1851 Flanders and the Netherlands decided to publish **het Woordenboek der Nederlandsche Taal** (*dictionary of the Dutch language* – note the spelling of **Nederlands** as **Nederlandsch**), which required the two countries to adopt a joint spelling. This spelling was completed and published in 1863 and adopted as law in Belgium and, quite a few years later, in the Netherlands. All spelling reforms have subsequently been based on this spelling. Simplification has been the main aim of these reforms, i.e. it is attempted to simplify the spelling rules and to make written Dutch more phonetic, so that the written word more closely resembles spoken language.

In 1980 the Flemish and Dutch governments founded **de Nederlandse Taalunie** (*the Dutch language union*), a kind of joint governmental language department which, since 2004, also has ties with Surinam, the former Dutch colony in South America. De Nederlandse Taalunie publishes **het Groene Boekje** (literally, *the little green book*) which contains the official spelling of words in the Dutch language. Its official title is **Woordenlijst Nederlandse Taal** (*word list [of the] Dutch language*) and can been found online on the following website: http://woordenlijst.org.

In 1994 it was decided to publish a revised edition of **het Groene Boekje** every ten years, following the publication of a new edition in 1995. The first revision appeared in 2005, and became law in 2006. However, a number of Dutch newspapers and magazines strongly criticized the revisions adopted for the new spelling – which attempted to iron out confusions, complexities and ambiguous rules in the 1995 spelling – and founded **Platform de Witte Spelling** (*the white spelling platform*) which, together with **het Genootschap Onze Taal** (literally, *the our language association*, an organization of language experts and aficionados) devised an alternative spelling, **de Witte Spelling**, which was published in **het Witte Boekje** (*the little white book*). The platform claims that this spelling more closely ties in with how native speakers of Dutch use their language. The present dictionary follows the official spelling from **het Groene Boekje**.

Using the dictionary

This dictionary contains the most frequently used Dutch words, which are given translated from Dutch into English, and also from English into Dutch. It is intended for learners of Dutch from beginner's level to intermediate and advanced.

DIFFERENT FORMS

Dictionaries are wonderful books for looking up all sorts of words, but unfortunately not all the words you may want to look up appear in the dictionary exactly as you come across them. When using language, words change and can have many different forms. Here are some of the main word categories and how to look them up.

Regular verbs

Verbs are listed under only one of their many forms, the infinitive, so it is important that you know how to find the infinitive. For most verbs this is quite easy because all their forms consist of the stem of the verb plus one or more letters added at the end (a suffix) or beginning (a prefix). The stem of regular verbs is usually the infinitive minus **-en**, so once you've found the stem, simply add this **-en** back on and you'll know where to look in the dictionary. Some examples:

	stem	infinitive
Je <u>kookte</u> *you were cooking*	kook	koken
Het heeft <u>gewaaid</u> *there was a strong wind*	waai	waaien

Separable verbs

With separable verbs you should remember that they come with a prefix which may be separated from the verb, and can normally be found at the end of the sentence. With past participles, the prefix comes before **ge-**. So, in the sentence **Je stelt me teleur** *you disappoint me*, you should look up **teleurstellen**.

Irregular verbs

Irregular verbs often don't base their forms on the stem. The best advice is to try and learn their forms by heart. Most language or grammar books, such as *Essential Dutch Grammar* in the Teach Yourself series, contain a list of irregular verbs.

Adjectives

Adjectives are entered in the dictionary under their basic form. Sometimes an **-e** is added to this basic form when the adjective is used in a sentence, so all you have to do is chop off the extra **-e** to find the basic form which is listed in the dictionary.

Nouns

Nouns are entered in dictionaries under their singular form. If you have a plural noun, simply take away **-en** or **-s** to get the singular form. However, don't forget that there are some irregular forms as

well. **Kinderen** should be looked up under its singular form **kind,**
and **politici** is the plural of **politicus** or **politica**.

SPELLING

Don't forget the various spelling rules which apply, for instance, to
the doubling of consonants or vowels, or the rules which mean that
s and f sometimes change into z and v, and vice versa.

As you can see it is important to gain a good understanding of
Dutch grammar in order to make full use of a dictionary and really
set you on your way to acquire a greater knowledge of Dutch.

ABBREVIATIONS

To help you understand the meaning of abbreviations – and what
they stand for – for most abbreviations the full Dutch form is given
after a colon:

    a.s.: aanstaande, *coming*: **9 juli a.s.,** *9 July next*

10 Only got ten minutes?

Dutch is a West Germanic language which is spoken by around 23 million people in the Netherlands, Belgium, Surinam (South America) and the Dutch Antilles and Aruba (both in the Caribbean), and in very small pockets of Northern France and along Germany's Western border. Within Western Europe, Dutch is a medium-sized language. To give an idea of what this means, Dutch is spoken by more people than the Scandinavian languages Swedish, Norwegian, Danish and Icelandic combined.

Dutch is closely related to German and English and shares many features with these languages, making it a relatively easy language to learn for speakers from these language areas. However, grammatically, Dutch is considerably less complex regarding its system of verb declensions, cases and the gender system of nouns than its closest relation, German.

Dutch spelling is officially regulated by law. The first official spelling rules in the Netherlands date back to 1804. In Belgium, a different official spelling was adopted in 1841. In 1851 Flanders and the Netherlands decided to publish **het Woordenboek der Nederlandsche Taal** (*dictionary of the Dutch language* – note the spelling of **Nederlands** as **Nederlandsch**), which required the two countries to adopt a joint spelling. This spelling was completed and published in 1863 and adopted as law in Belgium and, quite a few years later, in the Netherlands. All spelling reforms have subsequently been based on this spelling. Simplification has been the main aim of these reforms, i.e. it is attempted to simplify the spelling rules and to make written Dutch more phonetic, so that the written word more closely resembles spoken language.

In 1980 the Flemish and Dutch governments founded **de Nederlandse Taalunie** (*the Dutch language union*), a kind of joint governmental language department which, since 2004, also has ties with Surinam, the former Dutch colony in South America. **De Nederlandse Taalunie** publishes **het Groene Boekje** (literally, *the little green book*) which contains the official spelling of words in the Dutch language. Its official title is **Woordenlijst Nederlandse Taal** (*word list [of the] Dutch language*) and can been found online on the following website: http://woordenlijst.org.

In 1994 it was decided to publish a revised edition of **het Groene Boekje** every ten years, following the publication of a new edition in 1995. The first revision appeared in 2005, and became law in 2006. However, a number of Dutch newspapers and magazines strongly criticized the revisions adopted for the new spelling – which attempted to iron out confusions, complexities and ambiguous rules in the 1995 spelling – and founded **Platform de Witte Spelling** (*the white spelling platform*) which, together with **het Genootschap Onze Taal** (literally, the our language association, an organization of language experts and aficionados) devised an alternative spelling, **de Witte Spelling**, which was published in **het Witte Boekje** (*the little white book*). The platform claims that this spelling more closely ties in with how native speakers of Dutch use their language. The present dictionary follows the official spelling from **het Groene Boekje.**

Using the dictionary

HOW TO LOOK UP WORDS IN THE DICTIONARY

This dictionary contains the most frequently used Dutch words, which are given translated from Dutch into English, and also from English into Dutch. It is intended for learners of Dutch from beginner's level to intermediate and advanced. In order to ensure that this dictionary matches the needs of learners of Dutch today, words from a wide variety of different contexts – including the media and IT – have been included.

Dictionaries are a very important and useful tool for understanding a foreign language and improving your language skills. However, it is important that you do not simply take a given translation from a dictionary and use it without further thought. Never assume, for instance, that a particular translation is always applicable.

Most words have various different meanings depending on the context in which they are used, i.e. the meaning of a word can change from one situation to another. The English word *hard*, for instance, can refer to the hardness of a material (**hard** in Dutch), or it can mean *difficult* (**moeilijk** in Dutch). Similarly, the Dutch word **hard** also has more than one meaning. It can mean *hard* (referring to the hardness of a material), but it can also mean *fast*. Another Dutch example is **bank**, which can mean *bank* (where you put your savings) or **sofa**.

Some entries display more than one translation or meaning, but others are given with only one translation. Wherever the latter is the case, there may still be other meanings, but these are not frequently used. In allowing as many entries as possible, we have often included only the dominant meaning of a word.

More subtle differences also exist between different translations, where different words carry different stylistic values. The English word *man*, for instance, can be translated as **man**, but also as **kerel** (besides various other possible translations). However, **kerel** is much more informal than **man** and generally is not used in formal situations. Such information has been included wherever possible.

GENERAL

Each entry is given in bold, followed by a comma and the translation: **auto (de)**, *car*.

Multiple meanings are separated by a semi-colon: **daverend**, *thunderous; resounding*.

Translations which are close in meaning are separated by a comma: **com'mercie (de)**, *commerce, trade*.

When different forms of a word exist, this is indicated by brackets: *girlfriend*, **vriendin(netje)** indicates **vriendin** or **vriendinnetje**.

Where deemed helpful, entries which belong to different grammatical categories are listed separately, otherwise they are separated by a colon:

kussen, *to kiss*
kussen (het), *pillow, cushion*
lijden, *to suffer: suffering*

ARTICLES

Dutch nouns are accompanied by one of the articles **het** or **de**. This is indicated in brackets straight after the entry. Articles are only given in the Dutch–English section: e.g., **bankoverval (de)**, *bank robbery*.

Occasionally a noun takes either **de** or **het**, in which case both articles are listed:

de'bacle (het, de), *disaster, failure*

When a noun has a different meaning depending on which article it takes, they are listed as separate entries:

bal (de), *ball (e.g. football)*
bal (het), *ball (dance)*

STRESS

The stress in most words in Dutch is on the first syllable. When another syllable is stressed, this is indicated by an apostrophe in front of the stressed syllable: **fi'nesses**, *details*.

CONTEXT

When translated meanings could cause confusion, an explanation is given in brackets after the translation:

hé, *hey, hello, oh (really)?* (greeting/pleasant surprise)

If a word has a particular stylistic value, for example, if it is vulgar or informal (inf), this is indicated in brackets before the translation:

boob, **flater, blunder; borst,** (inf) **tiet**

EXPRESSIONS

Frequently used expressions are included after the translation.
The keyword is then substituted by –:

haarfijn, *minutely:* **iets – uitleggen**, *to explain something in great detail*

When keywords are used mainly as part of an expression,
no separate translation is given of the keyword alone:

aanklampen: iemand – *to accost someone*

DIFFERENT FORMS OF WORDS

Dictionaries are wonderful books for looking up all sorts of words,
but unfortunately not all the words you may want to look up appear
in the dictionary exactly as you come across them. When using
language, words change and can have many different forms. Here
are some of the main word categories and how to look them up.

Regular verbs
Verbs are listed under only one of their many forms, the infinitive,
so it is important that you know how to find the infinitive. For most
verbs this is quite easy because all their forms consist of the stem
of the verb plus one or more letters added at the end (a suffix) or
beginning (a prefix). The stem of regular verbs is usually the infinitive
minus -en, so once you've found the stem, simply add this -en back
on and you'll know where to look in the dictionary. Some examples:

	stem	infinitive
Je <u>kookte</u> *you were cooking*	kook	koken
Het heeft <u>gewaaid</u> *there was a strong wind*	waai	waaien

Separable verbs
With separable verbs you should remember that they come with
a prefix which may be separated from the verb, and can normally
be found at the end of the sentence. With past participles,

the prefix comes before **ge-**. So, in the sentence **Je stelt me teleur**
you disappoint me, you should look up **teleurstellen**.

Irregular verbs

Irregular verbs often don't base their forms on the stem. The best
advice is to try and learn their forms by heart. Most language or
grammar books, such as *Essential Dutch Grammar* in the Teach
Yourself series, contain a list of irregular verbs.

Adjectives

Adjectives are entered in the dictionary under their basic form.
Sometimes an -e is added to this basic form when the adjective is
used in a sentence, so all you have to do is chop off the extra **-e** to
find the basic form which is listed in the dictionary.

Nouns

Nouns are entered in dictionaries under their singular form. If you
have a plural noun, simply take away **-en** or **-s** to get the singular
form. However, don't forget that there are some irregular forms as
well. **Kinderen** should be looked up under its singular form **kind**,
and **politici** is the plural of **politicus** or **politica**.

SPELLING

Don't forget the various spelling rules which apply, for instance, to
the doubling of consonants or vowels, or the rules which mean that
s and **f** sometimes change into **z** and **v**, and vice versa.

As you can see it is important to gain a good understanding of Dutch
grammar in order to make full use of a dictionary and really set you
on your way to effectively acquire a greater knowledge of Dutch.

ABBREVIATIONS

To help you understand the meaning of abbreviations – and
what they stand for – for most abbreviations the full Dutch
form is given after a colon: **a.s.: aanstaande**, *coming*: **9 juli a.s.**,
9 July next.

Introduction

This dictionary contains the most frequently used Dutch words, which are given translated from Dutch into English, and from English into Dutch. It is intended for learners of Dutch from beginner's level to intermediate and advanced. The selection of words is based on the original edition by Peter and Margaretha King but has been extensively adapted and revised to make it more up to date and reflect contemporary usage of the Dutch language. In order to ensure that this dictionary matches the needs of learners of Dutch today, words from a wide variety of different contexts – including the media and IT – have been included, while terminology of a highly specialized technical nature, such as nautical and scientific terminology, has been omitted.

A

aaien to stroke
aak (de) (Rhine) barge
aal (de) eel
aalbes (de) red, black or white currant
aalmoes (de) alms
aambeeld (het) anvil
aambeien piles
aan at; on; to
aan on, at, by, of: **– het hoofd staan** to head, to manage (an institution or company) **ik woon – zee** I live by/near the sea; **zij heeft een leuke rok –** she's wearing a nice skirt **ik heb daar niets –** that's of no use to me
aanbeeld (het) anvil
aanbellen to ring the bell
aanbesteden to put out to contract
aanbevelen to recommend
aanbeveling (de) recommendation
aan'bidden to worship, to adore
aanbieden to offer
aanbieding (de) offer
aanbinden to tie on
aanblik (de) sight, spectacle
aanbod (het) offer
aanbouw (de): in – under construction
aanbranden to burn (in cooking)
aanbreken to come; break into (money or supplies); break, dawn **een nieuw tijdperk is aangebroken** a new age has begun/dawned
aandacht (de) attention
aan'dachtig attentive
aandeel (het) share, portion
aandeelhouder (de) shareholder
aandenken (het) memory; memento
aandienen to announce
aandikken to thicken; to lay it on

aandoen to put on; to move; to affect; to call at a place **hoe kun je me dat –?** how can you do such a thing to me?
aandoening (de) infection (of the throat, etc.)
aan'doenlijk moving
aandrang (de) insistence; urgency; impulse
aandringen op to press for; to insist on **op – van** at the insistence of
aanduiden to indicate
aan'een together; consecutively
aanfluiting (de) mockery
aangaan to begin; to enter into; to concern: **dat gaat jou niks aan** that's none of your business!
aan'gaande concerning
aangapen to gape at
aangeboren innate
aangedaan moved, affected
aange'legenheid (de) affair, concern
aangenaam agreeable, pleasant
aangenomen adopted; assumed
aangeschoten tipsy
aangetrouwd connected by marriage
aangeven to give; to hand; to indicate; to register (luggage); to notify; to inform the police
aangezien seeing that, since
aangifte (de) notification, declaration
aan'grenzend adjacent
aangrijpen to grasp; to seize, to assail
aan'grijpend moving, touching
aangroeien to increase, to grow
aanhalen to tighten; to quote; to fondle, to paw
aan'halig physically demonstrative

aanhalingsteken (het) inverted comma

aanhang (de) following; supporter

aanhangen to follow, support

aanhanger (de) follower, supporter

aan'hangig pending, *sub judice*

aanhangsel (het) appendix

aanhangwagen (de) trailer

aan'hankelijk affectionate

aanhebben to have on, to wear

aanhef (de) opening words

aanheffen to start, to strike up

aanhoren to listen to, to hear out

aanhouden to keep on; to persist; to arrest

aan'houdend constant; persistent

aanhouding (de) arrest, detention

aanjagen: schrik – to give a fright

aankijken to look at

aanklacht (de) charge, accusation

aanklagen to charge, to accuse

aanklager (de) plaintiff, prosecutor

aanklampen to accost

aankleden to dress

aankloppen to knock at the door; to appeal

aanknopen to tie on; to enter into **een gesprek –** to start a conversation

aanknopingspunt (het) point of contact

aankomen to arrive **daar komt het juist op aan** that is just the point

aankomst (de) arrival

aankondigen to announce

aankondiging (de) announcement

aankoop (de) purchase

aankopen to purchase

aankoppelen to couple

aankunnen to be a match for, to cope (with)

aankweken to cultivate, to grow; to foster **een gewoonte –** to foster/cultivate a habit

aanleg (de) layout; (natural) aptitude **in –** under construction

aanleggen to lay out; to build; to moor; to manage

aanlegplaats (de) berth (at a wharf)

aanlegsteiger (de) landing stage

aanleiding (de) occasion **naar – van** with reference to

aanlengen to dilute

aanleren to learn, to acquire

aanleunen to lean against

aan'lokkelijk tempting, attractive

aanloop (de) preliminary run; preamble **veel –** many callers

aanlopen tegen to collide with; to come across

aanmaken to manufacture; to light (a fire)

aanmanen to urge, to exhort, to press

aanmatigen zich – to presume

aan'matigend arrogant, presumptuous

aanmelden to announce **zich –** to present oneself

aan'merkelijk considerable

aanmerken op to find fault with

aanmerking (de) critical remark **in – nemen** to take into consideration

aanmoedigen to encourage

aanmoediging (de) encouragement

aan'nemelijk acceptable, plausible

aannemen to accept; to assume; to adopt; to contract for

aannemer (de) contractor

aanpakken to take hold of; to tackle

aanpappen to chum up

aanpassen to try on **zich – bij** to adapt oneself to

aanpassingsvermogen (het) adaptability

aanplakbiljet (het) poster

aanplanten to plant

aanpraten to talk (a person) into

aanprijzen to recommend strongly
aanraden to advise
aanraken to touch
aanraking (de) contact
aanranden to assault
aanrander (de) assailant
aanrecht (het) draining board
aanreiken to hand
aanrekenen to account **iemand iets −** to hold something against a person
aanrichten to cause, to do
aanrijden to run into **komen −** to drive up
aanrijding (de) collision, crash
aanroeren to touch (on); to mix
aanschaffen to procure, to purchase
aan'schouwen to behold
aanschrijven to notify officially **hij staat goed aangeschreven** he is well thought of
aanslaan to strike (a note); to assess (for tax); to catch on (a trend)
aanslag (de) attack; (tax) assessment; fur, scale
aanslibben to silt (up)
aansluiten to connect, to link up **zich − bij** to join
aansluiting (de) connection
aansmeren to foist on
aansnijden to start cutting; to broach
aanspannen to tighten up **een proces −** institute legal proceedings
aanspoelen to drift ashore
aansporen to urge on
aanspraak (de) claim; contacts **− maken op geld** claim money **hij heeft weinig −** he has few contacts, not many people talk to him
aan'sprakelijk answerable
aanspreken to address
aanstaan to please

aanstaande next; prospective **mijn aan'staande** my *fiancé(e)*
aanstalten maken to get ready
aan'stekelijk infectious
aansteken to light; to infect
aansteker (de) (cigarette) lighter
aanstellen to appoint **zich −** SARA to put on airs
aanstelle'rij (de) affectation, showing off
aanstelling (de) appointment
aansterken to recuperate
aanstichten to instigate
aanstippen to touch (on)
aanstoot (de) offence
aan'stotelijk offensive
aansturen op to head for, to aim at
aantal (het) number
aantasten to attack; to impair
aantekening (de) note
aantonen to demonstrate
aan'toonbaar demonstrable
aantreffen to meet, to find
aan'trekkelijk attractive
aantrekken to attract; to put on **trek je daar maar niets van aan!** forget it!
aan'vaarden to begin; to assume; to accept
aanval(len) (de) (to) attack
aanvaller (de) assailant
aanvang (de) beginning, start
aanvangen to begin, to start
aan'vankelijk initial
aanvaren to collide
aan'vechtbaar debatable
aanvechting (de) sudden impulse
aanvoelen to feel; to sense
aanvoer (de) supply
aanvoerder (de) leader
aanvoeren to supply; to command
aanvraag (de) application
aanvragen to apply for
aanvullen to supplement

aanwakkeren to rouse; to fan
aanwenden to apply
aanwennen: zich – to acquire (a habit)
aanwerven to recruit
aan'wezig present
aanwijzen to point out
aangewezen obvious
aan'wijzend voornaamwoord (het) demonstrative pronoun
aanwijzing (de) indication
aanwinst (de) acquisition, asset
aanwippen to drop in
aanwrijven to rub against; to impute, to blame **iemand iets –** to pin something on someone
aanzetten to put on; to hone; to tighten up; to egg on
aanzien to look at: **(het)** distinction, reputation
aanzien voor to (mis)take for
aan'zienlijk notable; considerable
aanzoek (het) request, proposal
aanzwellen to swell
aap (de) monkey **de – uit de mouw** the cat out of the bag
aardappel (de) potato
aardbei (de) strawberry
aardbeving (de) earthquake
aarde (de) earth; soil
aarden to thrive **– naar** to take after
aardewerk (het) earthenware
aardgas (het) natural gas
aardig nice, pleasant **– wat** a fair amount

aardigheid (de) joke, fun
aardrijkskunde (de) geography
aardrijks'kundig geographical
aards earthly
aardschok (de) earth tremor
aard(ver)schuiving (de) landslide
aarts- arch-
aarzelen to hesitate
aarzeling (de) hesitation
aas (het) ace; bait; carrion
ab'ces (het) abscess
ab'dij (de) abbey
ABN: Algemeen Beschaafd Nederlands (het) Standard Dutch
abnor'maal abnormal
abomi'nabel abominable
abon'nee (de) subscriber
abonne'ment (het) subscription; season ticket
abon'neren: zich – op to subscribe to
abri'koos (de) apricot
ab'sent absent(-minded)
ab'sentie (de) absence
absoluut absolute, absolutely
absor'beren to absorb
ab'stract abstract(ed)
abstra'heren to abstract
absurdi'teit (de) absurdity
abt (de) abbot
a'buis (het) (in) error
abu'sievelijk erroneously
aca'demie (de) university; academy
aca'demisch academic
accent (het) accent; stress
het – leggen op to stress

Insight

Aardig means *nice* and *pleasant*, but it is also frequently used in Dutch as an adverb of degree. In this case, it means *pretty, fairly, quite*: **aardig duur** is *pretty expensive* and **het is hier aardig warm** means *it's quite warm here*. To express that someone is *quite nice*, you can say **hij/zij is vrij aardig**.

accentu'eren to accent(uate)
accep'teren to accept
ac'cijns (de) excise duty
ac'countant (de) chartered
  accountant, auditor
accu (de) accumulator, battery
accu'raat accurate
ach! ah! oh! alas!
acht eight **acht slaan op** to heed
  in acht nemen to observe
achtbaan (de) rollercoaster
achteloos negligent
achten to consider; to esteem
achtens'waardig estimable
achter behind **van achter(en)** from
  behind
achter'aan last, in the rear
achter'af on second thoughts **zich —**
  houden to keep in the background
achterbak (de) boot
achter'baks underhand
achterblijven to stay, to lag behind
achterblijver (de) straggler
achterdocht (de) suspicion
achter'dochtig suspicious
achter'een at a stretch
achtereen'volgend consecutive
achtereen'volgens successively
achtergrond (de) background
achter'halen to overtake; to recover
achterhoede (de) rearguard
achterhouden to keep back
achter'in at, in the back
achterkleinkind (het) great-
  grandchild
achterklep (de) lid of the boot,
  hatchback, tailgate
achterlaten to leave behind
achterlijk backward
achter'nalopen to run after
achternaam (de) surname
achterneef (-nicht) (de) great-
  nephew (-niece), second cousin
achter'om round the back

achter'op behind
achter'over back(wards)
achterstaan to be inferior to;
  to be behind
achter'stallig in arrear
achterstand (de) arrears
  een — hebben to trail behind
achterstellen bij to discriminate
  against
achter'uit (de) reverse gear
achter'uit back(wards)
achter'uitgaan to move backwards;
  to fall (off); to deteriorate
achter'uitgang (de) decline;
  deterioration
achtervoegsel (het) suffix
achter'volgen to pursue
achter'volging (de) pursuit
achter'wege laten to omit
achthoek (de) octagon
achtste eighth, quaver
ac'quit discharge
acro'baat (de) acrobat
acroba'tiek (de) acrobatics
a'cryl (het) acrylic
ac'teren to act
ac'teur (de) actor
actie (de) action, campaign
ac'tief active
activi'teit (de) activity
ac'trice (de) actress
actuali'teit (de) topic(ality)
actu'eel topical
adder (de) viper
adel (de) nobility
adelaar (de) eagle
adem(loos) breath(less) **buiten —**
  out of breath **op — komen** to
  recover one's breath
ademen, ademhalen to breathe
ader (de) vein
aderverkalking (de) hardening of
  the arteries
administra'teur (de) manager

admini'stratie (de) book-keeping; management

administra'tief administrative

admini'stratiekosten (de) administrative costs, service charges

a'dres (het) address; petition **je bent aan het goede –** you've come to the right place

a'dresboek (het) directory

arbeidsduurverkorting (de) reduction of working hours

adver'tentie (de) advertisement

adver'teren to advertise

ad'vies (het) advice

advi'seren to advise

advi'seur (de) adviser

advo'caat (de) lawyer

af off; down; finished **– en aan** to and fro **– en toe** now and then

afbakenen to buoy; to stake out; to define

afbeelden to depict

afbeelding (de) picture

afbellen to ring off

afbetalen to pay off

afbetaling (de) hire purchase, credit

afboeken to write off

afbraak (de) demolition, rubble

afbreken to demolish; to break off

afbrengen to put off, to get off **het er goed –** to make a good job of it

afbreuk doen aan to injure; to detract from

afbrokkelen to crumble (away)

afdak (het) lean-to

afdalen to descend

afdammen to dam

afdanken to discard; to dismiss, to disband

afdankertje (het) hand-me-down

afdeling (de) division, section, detachment, department

afdingen to haggle

afdoen to take off; to settle **die theorie heeft afgedaan** that theory is quite exploded

afdoend conclusive

afdrogen to dry (up)

afdruipen to drip off; to slink off

afdruk (de) copy, print; imprint

afdrukken to print (off)

afdwalen to stray; to digress

afdwingen to extort; to compel

af'faire (de) affair

af'fiche (het) poster

afgaan to go down; to go off; to flop **van school –** to leave school **het gaat hem goed af** it comes easily to him **op iemand –** to go up to a person **afgaande op de feiten** judging by the facts

afgang (de) flop, embarrassing moment

afgelegen remote

afgemeten measured; formal

afgescheiden van apart from

afgevaardigde (de) deputy

afgeven to hand over; to hand in; to emit **de verf geeft af** the paint comes off

afgezaagd hackneyed

afgezant (de) envoy

afgezien van apart from

afgietsel (het) (plaster) cast

afgifte (de) delivery; issue

afgod (de) idol

af'grijselijk horrible

afgrond (de) abyss

afgunst (de) jealousy

afhalen to take down; to collect; to strip; to string (beans)

afhandelen to settle (business)

af'handig: iemand iets – maken to con someone out of something

afhangen to hang down; to depend

af'hankelijk van dependent on

afhebben to have finished
afhelpen to rid of, to relieve of;
  to help off; to help down
afhouden to keep off; to deduct
afkammen to disparage
afkeer (de) aversion
af'kerig van averse to
afketsen to glance off; to reject;
  to come to naught
afkeuren to disapprove of; to reject
  as unfit, to condemn
afkeurens'waardig reprehensible
afkijken to crib; to look down
afkloppen to beat off; to 'touch
  wood'
afkomen to come down **er –** to get
  off **ergens van –** to get rid of a
  thing
afkomst (de) origin, birth
af'komstig van originating from
afkondigen to proclaim
afkondiging (de) proclamation
afkooksel (het) decoction
afkoopsom (de) ransom
afkopen to buy off
afkorten to abbreviate
afkrijgen to get off; to get finished
afkunnen to be able to manage
afleggen to cover (a distance);
  to take (an oath) **het – tegen
  iemand** be no match for someone
afleiden to distract; to deduce;
  to derive
afleiding (de) distraction; derivation
afleren to unlearn; to break off a
  habit
afleveren to deliver
aflevering (de) delivery; number,
  instalment, episode
afloop (de) end, outcome; expiry
aflopen to run down; to slope; to
  end; to expire **ik heb alle winkels
  afgelopen** I have been to every
  shop in town

af'losbaar redeemable
aflossen to redeem; to relieve
afluisteren to eavesdrop
afmaken to finish; to kill; to
  break off
af'mattend exhausting
afmeten to measure (off)
afmeting (de) dimension
afnemen to take off; to take down;
  to clear away; to decrease
afnemer (de) customer
afpakken to snatch out of one's
  hand
afpersen to extort
afpoeieren to send packing
afraden to dissuade
afraffelen to rush through (a task
  or a speech)
afranselen to thrash
afrastering (de) (wire) fence
afreageren to work off (one's
  emotions)
afrekenen to settle accounts
afrekening (de) settlement
afremmen to slow down, to break;
  to curb
afroepen to call
afronden to round off
afruimen to clear away
afschaffen to abolish
afschaffing (de) abolition
afscheid (het) parting **– nemen**
  to take one's leave
afscheuren to tear off
afschepen to fob off
afschilderen to depict
afschrift (het) copy **afschrijven**
  to copy; to write off; to cancel
afschrikken to frighten away
afschrikkingsmiddel (het) deterrent
afschuw (de) loathing
af'schuwelijk loathsome, hideous
afslaan to beat off; to decline
  rechts – to turn to the right

afslachten to butcher

afslag (de) exit (on motorway); Dutch auction; erosion

afsloven: (zich) – to wear (oneself) out

afsluitboom (de) gate, barrier

afsluitdijk (de) dam; causeway

afsluiten to lock; to close; to turn off; to cut off; to balance; to conclude

afsnauwen to snap at

afsnijden to cut off

afspelen to play (a CD on a CD player) **zich –** to occur, to happen

afspiegelen to reflect

afspoelen to rinse (off)

afspraak (de) appointment, date, arrangement

afspreken to agree, to arrange

afstaan to cede

afstammen to descend

afstamming (de) descent

afstand (de) distance

afstappen to step down

afsteken bij to contrast with

afstemmen to tune (a radio); to attune, to gear towards

afstempelen to stamp

afsterven to die off

afstoffen to dust

afstompen to blunt

afstormen op to rush at

afstoten to push off; to repel

af'stotelijk repellent

afstraffen to punish; to reprimand

afstraffing (de) punishment, dressing-down

afstudeerrichting (de) main subject (of study)

afstuderen to graduate, to complete one's studies

afsturen op to head for; to unleash

aftakelen to dismantle; to age badly

af'tands worn out

aftappen to tap; to draw off

aftekenen to outline **zich – tegen** to stand out against

aftocht (de) retreat

aftrap (de) kick-off

aftrappen to kick off; to kick down

aftreden to resign

af'trekbaar (tax) deductible

aftrekken: zich – to masturbate (men)

aftroeven to trump

aftroggelen to wheedle out of

aftuigen to give a hiding

afvaardigen to delegate

afvaart (de) departure, sailing

afval (het) refuse; waste

afvalbak (de) dustbin, rubbish bin

afvallen to fall down, to fall away; to lose weight

af'vallig disloyal

afvalprodukt (het) by-product, waste product

afvaren to (set) sail

afvegen to wipe (off)

afvloeien to flow down; to be discharged

afvoer (de) removal; discharge; waste (pipe)

afvoeren to carry away

afvragen: zich – to wonder

afwachten to await, to wait and see (about)

afwachting (de) expectation

afwas (de) washing-up, dishes

afwasbak (de) washing-up bowl

afwassen to wash up or off

afwateren to drain

afweergeschut (het) anti-aircraft guns

afwegen to weigh up

afwenden to avert **zich –** to turn away

afwennen to break a habit

afweren to ward off

afwerken to finish off

af'wezig absent
af'wezigheid (de) absence
afwijken to deviate
afwijking (de) deviation
afwijzen to turn down or away, to reject
afwikkelen to unroll; to wind up
afwisselen to alternate, to vary **elkaar –** to take turns
af'wisselend alternating; varied
afzakken to come down
afzeggen to cancel
afzetgebied (het) market
afzetten to take off; to depose; to amputate; to trim; to cordon off; to cheat **een ge'voel van zich –** to shake off a feeling
afzette'rij (de) swindle
af'zichtelijk hideous
afzien van to give up **afgezien van** apart from **binnen af'zienbare tijd** within the not too distant future
af'zijdig aloof
afzonderen to isolate, to segregate
afzondering (de) seclusion
af'zonderlijk separate
afzweren to abjure
a'genda (de) agenda; diary
a'gent (de) agent; policeman
a'gentschap (het) agency, branch (bank)
a'geren to agitate
air (het) air, demeanour
akelig nasty, unpleasant; unwell
akker (de) (arable) field
ak'koord (het) agreement; chord: agreed!
akoes'tiek (de) acoustics
akte (de) deed; contract **– van geboorte** birth certificate
aktentas (de) briefcase
al all: already; even though **– te** too
a'larmcentrale (de) emergency centre, emergency number

alarmeren alert; to startle, to frighten
alcoholhoudend alcoholic
alcoholvrij non-alcoholic
aldoor all the time
al'dus thus
alge'meen general, common **over het –** in general
alhoe'wel although
a'linea (de) paragraph
Allah Allah
alle'bei both
alle'daags commonplace, of daily occurrence
al'leen alone; only
al'leenspraak (de) soliloquy
al'leenstaand single
alle'gaartje (het) hotchpotch
alle'maal all; altogether **– tegelijk** all together
alle'machtig terrific, fantastic; **wel –** I'll be damned
allen all
al'lengs gradually
aller'liefst most charming
aller'eerst first of all
aller'lei, aller'hande all sorts of
aller'minst (the) very least; not in the least
alles everything **van –** all sorts of things **van – en nog wat** anything and everything
al'licht quite likely; I should think so! **we kunnen het – proberen** no harm in trying!
allochtoon (de) (im)migrant, alien; foreign(er)
al'lure (de) air, style **iemand met –** someone with a certain presence
al'machtig almighty
almanak (de) almanac
al'om everywhere
alomtegen'woordig ubiquitous
als as; like; if; when

alsje'blieft please; here you are
als'mede as well as
als'nog as yet
als'of as if
alstu'blieft (*see* alsje'blieft)
alt (de) alto
altaar (het) altar
al'thans at least
altijd always
al'vast meanwhile
al'vorens before
al'wetend omniscient
a'mandel (de) almond
a'mandelen (de) tonsils
amanu'ensis (de) laboratory
  assistant
ambacht (het) trade
ambas'sade (de) embassy
ambassa'deur (de) ambassador
ambi'ëren to aspire to
am'bitie (de) ambition
ambiti'eus ambitious
ambt (het) function; office
ambtelijk official
ambtenaar (de) official, civil servant
ambtena'rij (de) red tape
ambu'lance (de) ambulance
amfi'bie (de) amphibian
ampel ample
amper scarcely
ampu'teren to amputate
amu'seren to amuse
ana'loog analagous
ana'lyse (de) analysis
analy'seren to analyse
ana'lytisch analytical
ananas (de) pineapple
ander different; other **om de
  andere dag** every other day **onder
  andere (o.a.)** *inter alia*
anderhalf one and a half
anders different; else **net als –** just
  as usual
anders'om the other way round

anders'talige non-native speaker
anderzijds on the other hand
an'dijvie (de) endive
ane'moon (de) anemone
angel (de) sting; fishhook
an'gina (de) tonsillitis
angst (de) fear, terror
angstig afraid, fearful
angst'vallig scrupulous, timid
angst'wekkend alarming
angstzweet (het) cold sweat
a'nijszaad (het) aniseed
ani'matiefilm (de) animation film
animo (het, de) zest
anker (het) anchor
ankeren to anchor
an'nex (de) annexe; enclosed,
  attached
an'nexeren to annex, incorporate
anno in the year **– 1876** in the
  year 1876
annu'leren to cancel
annu'lering (de) cancellation
ano'niem anonymous
ansicht(kaart) (de)
  picture postcard
an'sjovis (de) anchovy
an'tenne (de) aerial
anti'climax (de) anticlimax
an'tiek (de) antique(s)
antipa'thiek antipathetic
antiquari'aat (het) secondhand
  bookshop, antique shop
antiqui'teiten antiques
antivries (de) antifreeze
antropolo'gie (de) anthropology
antwoord (het) answer
antwoordapparaat (het) answering
  machine, ansaphone
antwoorden to answer
AOW (abbrev) **(de)** state pension
a'part apart, separate **iets zeer –**
  something very special
a'pathisch apathetic

apegapen: op – liggen to be at one's last gasp
apenstaartje (het) @ sign
a'postel (de) apostle
apo'theek (de) (dispensing) chemist('s)
apo'theker (de) pharmacist
appa'raat (het) apparatus
appartement (het) flat, apartment
ap'pel (het) appeal, rollcall
appel (de) apple
appelgebak (het) apple pie
appel'leren to appeal
appelsap (de) apple juice
appelstroop (de) apple spread
ap'plaus (het) applause
applaudiss'eren to applaud
april April
apro'pos (het): van zijn – raken to be unnerved
aqua'rel (de) watercolour
arbeid (de) labour
arbeiden to labour
arbeider (de) labourer
arbeidsduurverkorting (de) reduction of working hours
arbeidsinten'sief labour-intensive
arbeidsonge'schikt unable to work **– verklaard worden** be declared as unable to work
arbeidstijdverkorting (de) reduction of working hours
arbeidsvoorwaarde (de) condition of employment
ar'chief (het) archives; record office
archi'tect (de) architect
architec'tuur (de) architecture
are (de) 100 square metres
arend (de) eagle
argeloos unsuspecting
arg'listig crafty
argwaan (de) suspicion
arg'wanend suspicious
arm poor

arm (de) arm; branch (of a river)
armband (de) bracelet, armlet
armleuning (de) elbow rest
armoe (de) poverty
ar'moedig needy; shabby
arm'zalig pitiful
armslag (de) elbow room
ar'rest (het) arrest, detention
arres'tant (de) prisoner
arres'teren to arrest
arrondise'mentsrechtbank (de) district court, county court
ar'senicum (het) arsenic
ar'tiest (de) variety artist
artille'rie (de) artillery
arti'sjok (de) artichoke
arts (de) doctor
a.s.: aanstaande coming: **9 juli a.s.** 9 July coming
as (de) ash(es): axle; axis
asbakje (het) ashtray
as'best (het) asbestos
a'siel (het) asylum; refuge
asjemenou well, I never!
as'perge (de) asparagus
astro'loog (de) astrologer
astro'noom (de) astronomer
ate'lier (het) studio, workshop
at'leet (de) athlete
atle'tiek (de) athletics
at'tent attentive; considerate
at'tentie (de) attention; act of courtesy
at'test (het) certificate, testimonial
at'tractie (de) attraction
at'tractiepark (het) theme park, amusement park
ATV (abbrev), reduction of working hours
au pair (de) au pair
auber'gine (de) aubergine, eggplant
auditie (de) audition, screentest
au'gurk (de) gherkin
augustus August

aula (de) auditorium
au'teur (de) author
au'teursrecht (het) copyright
auto (de) car
autobiogra'fie (de) autobiography
autochtoon (de) autochthonous,
  indigenous; aboriginal
autodi'dact (de) self-taught (person)
autogordel (de) seatbelt
autokaart (de) roadmap, road atlas
auto'maat (de) automaton; slot
  machine

auto'noom autonomous
autori'seren to authorize
autori'tair high-handed;
  authoritarian
autoweg (de) motorway
averechts wrong
avond (de) evening
avondeten (het) supper
avon'tuur (het) adventure
avon'tuurlijk adventurous
azen op to prey on
a'zijn (de) vinegar

B

baai (de) bay
baal (de) bale, bag
baaldag (de) (inf) day off, sickie
baan (de) way, track; orbit; (tennis)
  court; job
baanbreker (de) pioneer
baard (de) beard **hij heeft de – in
de keel** his voice is breaking
baarmoeder (de) womb
baas (de) master; boss
baat (de) benefit **– hebben/vinden
bij** to benefit from **ten bate van**
  for the benefit of
baatzucht (de) selfishness
babbelen to chatter; to gossip
babysit (de) babysitter
bad (het) bath
baden to bath, to bathe **zich in
weelde –** to wallow in luxury
badkleding (de) bathing costume,
  swimwear
badkuip (de) bathtub
ba'gage (de) baggage, luggage
baga'tel (het, de) trifle
bagger (de) mud
baggeren to dredge; to squelch
bak (de) tray; bin; pan
bakbeest (het) huge thing
bakermat (de) birthplace

bakkebaarden side whiskers
bakken to bake; to roast; to fry
  versgebakken broodjes freshly
  baked rolls
bakker (de) baker
bakke'rij (de) bakery
baksteen (de) brick **zakken als
een –** to fail (an exam) utterly
bal (de) ball (e.g. football)
bal (het) ball (dance)
ba'lans (de) balance(sheet),
  scales
bal'dadig wanton, destructive
balen to be fed up
balie (de) railing, counter
balk (de) beam, rafter
  over de – gooien to squander
bal'kon (het) balcony
bal'let (het) ballet, dance
balling(schap) (de) exile
bal'lon (de) balloon
ba'lorig refractory; ill-tempered
balpen (de) ballpoint pen
balsemen to embalm
ban (de) excommunication; spell
  in de – zijn van iets to be/fall
  under the spell of something
ba'naal banal
ba'naan (de) banana

band (de) band, tape; ligament; waveband; tyre; bond **aan banden leggen** to put under restraint **uit de – springen** to let one's hair down

bandje (het) band; cassette, tape

ban'diet (de) bandit

bandrecorder (de) tape recorder

banen: de weg – voor to pave the way for **zich een weg –** to force one's way (through)

bang afraid

bangmake'rij (de) intimidation

bank (de) bench, settee; bank

bankbiljet (het) banknote

ban'ket (het) banquet; fancy cakes

ban'ketbakker (de) pastry cook

ban'kier (de) banker

bankkluis (de) safe-deposit box

bankoverval (de) bank robbery

bankpas (de) bankcard; debit card

bank'roet (het) bankrupt(cy)

bankstel (het) sitting-room suite

bannen to banish

bar (de) bar **– slecht** very bad **hij maakt het al te –** he is going too far

ba'rak (de) hut, barracks

bar'baars barbaric

baren to give birth to

ba'ret (de) cap, beret

barm'hartig charitable, merciful **de –e Samaritaan** the Good Samaritan

barrevoets barefoot

bars gruff, stern

barst (de) crack

barsten to burst, to crack; to explode

bas (de) bass

ba'seren to base

basis (de) basis, base; footing

basisonderwijs (het) primary education

basisschool (de) primary/elementary school

bast (de) bark

basterdsuiker (de) moist (brown) sugar

baten to avail

batig saldo (het) credit balance

batikken to do batik

batte'rij (de) battery

bavi'aan (de) baboon

ba'za(a)r (de) bazaar; sale of work

bazelen to talk nonsense

bazig bossy

ba'zuin (de) trumpet, trombone

be'ambte (de) official; employee

be'amen to assent

be'angstigen to alarm

be'antwoorden to answer; to return; to correspond

be'bloed bloody

be'boeten to fine

be'bossen to afforest

be'bouwen to cultivate; to build on (or up)

be'cijferen to calculate

bed (het) bed

be'daard calm, composed

be'dacht op alive to, mindful of

be'dachtzaam circumspect

be'danken to thank; to decline; to resign

be'dankje (het) word of thanks

be'daren to calm down

beddengoed (het) bedding

bede (de) prayer, request

be'deesd timid; coy

be'dekken to cover

bedelaar (de) beggar

bedelen to beg

be'delen to endow; to distribute relief

be'delven to bury

be'denkelijk grave; precarious; questionable

be'denken to recollect; to consider; to think up **zich –** to change one's mind
be'derf (het) corruption; decay
be'derven to spoil; to go bad
bedevaart (de) pilgrimage
be'diende (de) servant
be'dienen to serve; to (ad)minister (to)

be'drijf (het) industry, business, undertaking; act
be'drijfscultuur (de) corporate culture
be'drijfseconomie (de) business economics
be'drijfskapitaal (het) working capital
be'drijfsleider (de) manager
be'drijfsvoering (de) management

Insight

De bedrijfsvoering is the Dutch word for *management*. However, in many of areas of life English terminology is adopted more and more. This is particularly true of business life, the economy and finance, where **het management** is used frequently, as are, for instance, **de manager, de managementbuy-out, managen** (*to manage*), **de managementtraining** and **de managing director.**

be'diening (de) service
be'dieningspaneel (het) control panel
be'ding (het): onder geen – not in any circumstances
be'dingen to stipulate
be'disselen to see to
be'doelen to mean
be'doeling (de) intention
be'dompt close; stuffy
be'donderen to bamboozle **ben je bedonderd?** are you crazy?
be'dotten to fool, take in
be'drading (de) (electric) wiring
be'drag (het) amount
be'dragen to amount to
be'dreigen to threaten
be'dremmeld shy, confused
be'dreven proficient
be'driegen to deceive
bedriege'rij (de) deception
be'drieg(e)lijk deceptive, deceitful

be'drijvigheid (de) bustle, activity
be'drinken: zich – to get drunk
be'droefd sad **– weinig** precious little
be'droevend sad, depressing; miserable
be'drog (het) deceit, trickery
be'drukt depressed; printed
be'ducht apprehensive
be'duidend significant, considerable
be'dwang (het) restraint **zich in – houden** to restrain oneself
be'dwelmen to stun; to drug; to intoxicate
be'dwingen to suppress, to curb
be'ëdigen to swear in
beek (de) brook
beeld (het) image; picture; statue; beauty **zich een – vormen van** to visualize
beeldbuis (de) television screen **voor de – zitten** sit in front of the box
beeldhouwen to sculpt

beeldhouwer (de) sculptor
beeldmerk (het) logo
beeldspraak (de) metaphor
been (het) leg; bone
beenbreuk (de) fracture
beer (de) bear; boar; buttress
beerput (de) cesspit
beest (het) animal, beast
beestachtig beastly
beestenboel (de) filthy mess, pigsty
beet (de) bite, sting
beet hebben to have got hold of
beetje (het) (little) bit
beetnemen to take in
beetpakken to take hold of
be'faamd famous, notorious
be'gaafd gifted
be'gaan to tread; to commit
  (a murder or blunder)
be'gaan zijn met to feel sorry for
be'gaanbaar passable
be'gane grond (de) ground level
be'geerte (de) desire
bege'leiden to accompany
bege'leiding (de) supervision,
  support; accompaniment,
  accompanying
bege'nadigen to pardon, to bless
be'geren to desire, to covet
be'gerig desirous, covetous
be'geven to give way; to bestow
  zich – to go, to proceed
be'gin (het) beginning
be'ginneling (de) beginner
be'ginnen to start, to begin **wat
  moet ik nu –?** whatever shall I do
  now? **er is niets met hem te –**
  there is no doing anything with him
be'ginpunt (het) starting point
be'ginsel (het) principle
be'ginstadium (het) initial stage
be'graafplaats (de) cemetery
be'grafenis (de) funeral
be'graven to bury

be'grenzen to bound, to limit
be'grijpelijk understandable
be'grijpen to understand; include
be'grip (het) concept(ion); notion;
  comprehension **vlug van –** quick on
  the uptake
be'groeid overgrown
be'groeten to greet
be'groten to estimate
be'groting (de) estimate, budget
be'gunstigen to favour
be'ha (de) bra
be'haaglijk pleasant, comfortable
be'haard hairy
be'halen to gain, to win
be'halve except, apart from
be'handelen to treat, to deal with
be'handeling (de) treatment
be'hang(sel) (het) wallpaper
be'hangen to paper, to drape
be'hartigen to have at heart,
  to look after
be'heer (het) management
be'heerder (de) manager,
  administrator
be'heersen to rule; to control;
  to command (a language);
  to dominate
be'helpen: zich – to make do,
  to rough it
be'hendig dexterous
be'hept met afflicted with
be'heren to manage, to administer
be'hoedzaam cautious
be'hoefte (de) need
be'hoefte (hebben) aan (to have a)
  need for
be'hoeve: ten – van for the sake of,
  in aid of
be'hoorlijk proper; decent
be'horen to belong; to be fitting
  naar – properly
be'houd (het), preservation
be'houden to retain; to preserve

be'houdend conservative
be'hulp: met — van with the aid of
be'hulpzaam helpful
beide(n) both; two geen van —
neither (of them)
be'ijveren: zich — to do one's utmost
be'invloeden to influence
beitel (de) chisel
beits (de) (wood) stain
beitsen to stain (wood)
be'jaard aged
be'jaarde (de) old-age pensioner
be'jaarden(te)huis (het) old
people's home, home for
the elderly
be'jammeren to lament
be'jegenen to treat
bek (de) mouth, beak
be'kaaid: er — afkomen to come
off badly
bekaf dog tired
be'kakt snooty, affected
be'kend (well-)known; acquainted
ik ben hier niet — I'm a stranger
here: I don't know the area
be'kende (de) acquaintance
be'kendheid (de) acquaintance;
reputation, notoriety van
algemene — generally known
be'kendmaken to announce; to
make public; to familiarize (with)
be'kendmaking (de) announcement
be'kennen to admit, to confess;
to follow suit
be'kentenis (de) admission,
confession
beker (de) cup, mug
be'keren to convert
be'keuring (de) charge, fine
be'kijken to look at; to look into
be'kijk(s) hebben to attract
attention
bekken (het) basin; pelvis
be'klaagde (de) accused

be'kladden to besmirch
be'klagen to pity zich — to complain
be'kleden to cover; to upholster een
ambt — to hold an office
be'kleding (de) covering, upholstery;
lagging
be'klemd oppressed; stressed
be'klemdheid (de) oppression;
constriction
be'klimmen to climb
be'klinken to rivet; to settle
be'kneld locked, jammed
be'knopt concise
be'kocht cheated
be'koelen to cool down
be'kogelen to pelt
be'kokstoven to wangle
be'komen to recover; to agree with
be'kommeren: zich — om to bother
about
be'konkelen to scheme
be'kopen (met de dood) to pay
(with one's life)
be'korten to curtail
be'kostigen to pay for
be'krachtigen to confirm, to ratify
be'krassen to cover with scratches
bekriti'seren to criticize, to find
fault with
be'krompen narrow-minded;
restricted
be'kronen to crown, to award a prize
be'kruipen to take by surprise het
gevoel bekroop me the feeling
came over me
bekvechten to wrangle noisily
be'kwaam capable
be'kwaamheid (de) ability
bel (de) bell; bubble
be'labberd rotten
be'lachelijk ridiculous
be'landen to land (up)
be'lang (het) interest; importance
be'langeloos disinterested

be'langrijk important
belang'stellend interested
be'langstelling (de) interest
belangwekkend interesting
be'lastbaar taxable, dutiable
be'lasten to burden; to tax; to
charge; to debit **zich – met** to take
upon oneself
be'lasteren to slander; to libel
be'lasting (de) tax(ation); load
be'lastingaangifte (de) tax return
be'lastingaanslag (de) tax
assessment
be'lastingdienst (de) Inland
Revenue, Internal Revenue
Service (Am)
be'lastingheffing (de) taxation
be'lastingontduiking (de) tax
evasion
be'lazeren to bamboozle **ben je
belazerd?** are you mad?
be'ledigen to insult
be'lediging (de) insult
be'leefd(heid) (de) polite(ness)
beleefdheids'halve out
of politeness
be'leg (het) siege
be'legen mature (cheese)
be'leggen to cover; to call
(a meeting); to invest
be'leid (het) administration;
prudence
be'lemmeren to hamper
be'lendend adjacent
be'letsel (het) obstacle, hindrance
be'letten to prevent
be'leven to experience, to live
through **avonturen –** to have/
experience adventures
be'lezen well-read
be'lichamen to embody
be'lichten to throw light on;
to expose
be'lijden to confess; to profess

be'lijdenis (de) confession, creed;
confirmation
belknop (de) bell-pull; bell-push
bellen to ring (the bell)
belletje (het) call, buzz, ring
be'loeren to spy upon
be'lofte (de) promise
be'lonen to reward
be'loop: op zijn – laten to let
(something) take its course
be'loven to promise
be'luisteren to listen to
be'lust op eager for
be'machtigen to secure
be'mannen to man
be'manning (de) crew; garrison
be'merken to perceive
be'mesten to manure
be'middelaar (de) intermediary
be'middeld well-to-do
be'middelen to mediate
be'middeling (de) mediation
be'mind much loved
be'moedigen to encourage
be'moeial (de) busybody
be'moeien: zich – met to concern
oneself with, to meddle with
be'moeienis (de) concern
be'moeilijken to hinder
be'moeiziek meddlesome
be'nadelen to harm
be'naderen to estimate; to get near
be'nadering: bij – approximately
be'nard critical; perilous
be'nauwd close, stuffy; constricted;
afraid **ik heb het –** I can't breathe
be'nauwdheid closeness;
constriction; fear
bende (de) gang; mess
be'neden below, downstairs; under,
beneath
be'nedenhuis (het) bottom flat
be'nedenverdieping (de)
ground floor

be'nemen to take away **de moed —** to discourage
be'nepen cramped; narrow-minded; timid
be'nevelen to befog, to fuddle
bengelen to dangle
be'nieuwen: het zal me — I wonder
be'nieuwd curious to know
be'nijden to envy
benijdens'waard(ig) enviable
be'nodigd required
be'noemen to appoint; to nominate
be'nul (het) notion **ik heb geen flauw —** I haven't got a clue
be'nutten to make use of
ben'zine (de) petrol
ben'zinepomp (de) petrol station; fuel pump
be'oefenen to study, to practise
be'ogen to have in view
be'oordelen to judge, to review
be'oordeling (de) assessment, evaluation, judgement
bepaald positive; definite; appointed
in een — geval in a given case
niet — beleefd not exactly polite
be'pakken to pack
be'palen to determine, to define
zich — tot to confine oneself to
be'paling (de) definition; regulation; stipulation
be'perken to limit, to confine
be'planten to plant
be'pleiten to plead
be'praten to talk over **zich laten —** to be persuaded
be'proefd well-tried
be'proeven to try, to put to the test; to afflict
be'raad (het) deliberation, consideration
be'raadslagen to deliberate
be'raden: zich — (op) to consider
be'ramen to devise

berde: te — brengen to broach
be'rechten to adjudicate
be'redderen to arrange
be'reden mounted
berede'neren to reason out
be'reid ready, prepared
be'reiden to prepare
bereid'vaardig, bereid'willig ready to help
be'reik (het) reach; range
be'reiken to reach, to achieve
be'reikbaar attainable
be'rekenen to calculate; to charge
niet berekend voor het werk not equal to the work
be'rekening (de) calculation
berg (de) mountain
bergachtig mountainous
berg'afwaarts downhill
bergen to store; to salvage; to accommodate
bergingswerk (het) salvage operations
bergkam (de), bergrug (de) mountain ridge
bergkloof (de) ravine, gorge
bergruimte (de) storage space
bergwand (de) mountain face
be'richt (het) news, report; notice
be'richten to inform
be'rispen to rebuke, to reprimand
berk (de) birch
berm (de) shoulder (roadside)
be'roemd famous
be'roemdheid (de) fame, celebrity
be'roemen: zich — op to pride oneself on
be'roep (het) profession; appeal
in hoger — gaan to appeal
beroepen: zich — op to appeal to, to plead, to refer to
be'roeps- professional
beroeps'halve in one's professional capacity

be'roerd rotten
be'roeren to stir, to disturb
be'roerte (de) stroke, fit
be'rokkenen to cause iemand
  schade – to cause damage
  to someone
be'rooid penniless
be'rouw (het) repentance
be'rouwen: het zal je – you will
  be sorry (for it)
be'rouwvol repentant
be'roven to rob, to deprive
be'rucht notorious
be'rusten in to be resigned to
be'rusten op to rest on; to be due to
  dit moet op een misverstand –
  this must be due to a
  misunderstanding
bes (de) berry, (red) currant
be'schaafd well-bred; civilized
be'schaamd ashamed
be'schadigen to damage
beschamen to shame; to dash
  (hope); to betray (confidence)
  beschamend humiliating
be'schaving (de) culture, civilization
be'scheiden modest, retiring
be'schermeling (de) protégé(e)
be'schermen to protect
be'schermengel (de) guardian angel
be'scherming (de) protection,
  patronage
be'schikbaar available
be'schikken over to have at one's
  disposal
be'schikking: ter – available
be'schilderde ramen stained glass
  windows
be'schimmelen to go mouldy
be'schouwen to regard, to
  contemplate wel beschouwd all
  things considered
be'schrijven to describe; to cover
  with writing

be'schrijving (de) description
be'schroomd timid
be'schuldigde (de) accused,
  defendant
be'schuldigen to accuse
be'schuldiging (de) accusation
be'schutten to shelter
be'sef (het) realization; notion
be'seffen to realise, to be aware of
be'slaan to take up (space); to
  mount (with silver, etc.); to shoe;
  to get blurred; to tarnish
beslag (het) batter; fitting zijn –
  krijgen to settle, to be put into
  effect – leggen op to take up;
  to secure; to claim
be'slissen to decide
be'slist decided, for certain
be'sloten private; close
be'sluipen to steal up on
be'sluit (het) conclusion; decision
be'sluiteloos irresolute
be'sluiten to conclude, to decide
be'smettelijk contagious, infectious
be'smetten to infect, to
  contaminate
be'sneeuwd snow-covered
be'snijden to circumcise
be'snoeien to lop, to prune;
  to cut down
be'sparen to save
be'spatten to bespatter
be'spelen to play
be'speuren to perceive
be'spieden to spy on
be'spiegelend contemplative
be'spiegeling (de) contemplation
be'spoedigen to speed up
be'spottelijk ridiculous
be'spotten to ridicule
be'spraakt never at a loss for words
be'spreken to book, to reserve;
  to discuss, to review
be'sprenkelen to sprinkle

be'springen to pounce upon
be'sproeien to spray
best best; very good; dear; very well
 het is mij – it is all right by me **ten**
 beste geven to contribute
be'staan (het) existence, livelihood
bestaan to exist **– uit** to consist of
 – van to subsist on
be'staanbaar possible
be'staansmiddel (het) means
 of support
be'staansminimum (het)
 subsistence level
be'staansrecht (het) right to exist
be'stand (het) truce
be'stand tegen be immune to
be'standdeel (het) ingredient,
 component
be'steden to spend; to devote
be'stedingspatroon (het) pattern
 of spending
be'steedbaar disposable
be'stelen to rob
be'stellen to order; to deliver
be'stelwagen (de) (delivery) van
be'stemmen to destine; to intend
be'stempelen to stamp;
 to designate
be'stendig constant; lasting;
 steady
be'sterven: hij bestierf het van
 schrik he nearly died of fright **dat**
 woord ligt in zijn mond bestorven
 he is always using that word
be'stijgen to mount, to ascend
be'stormen to storm
be'straffen to punish
be'straten to pave
be'strijden to combat; to defray
be'strijdingsmiddel (het)
 pesticide; weed killer
be'strijken to cover
be'strooien to strew, to sprinkle
bestu'deren to study

be'stuiven to (cover with) dust;
 to pollinate
be'sturen to govern; to drive;
 to steer
be'stuur (het) government,
 administration; committee
bèta science subjects
be'taalpasje (het) cheque card,
 debit card
be'talen to pay (for) **ik zal het**
 hem betaald zettten I'll get even
 with him
be'tamelijk seemly
be'tasten to feel
be'tegelen to tile
be'tekenen to mean **het heeft**
 niets te – it is of no consequence
be'tekenis (de) meaning;
 significance
beter better
beterschap (de) recovery
be'teugelen to curb
be'teuterd taken aback
be'tichten to accuse
be'timmeren to panel with wood
be'titelen to style
be'togen to argue
be'toging (de) demonstration,
 march
be'ton (het) concrete
be'tonmolen (de) concrete mixer
be'tonnen concrete
be'toog (het) argument;
 exposition
be'toveren to bewitch, to fascinate
be'traand tear-stained
be'trachten to do, to show
be'trappen to catch **iemand op**
 heterdaad – to catch someone
 red-handed
be'treden to tread; to set foot on
be'treffen to concern **wat mij**
 betreft as far as I am concerned
be'trekkelijk relative

be'trekken to move into; to involve; to cloud over

be'trekking (de) post, job **met – tot** with reference to

be'treuren to regret

betreurens'waardig regrettable

be'trokken overcast **be'trokken bij** concerned (with, in)

be'trouwbaar reliable

be'tuigen to express; to protest; to profess

betweter (de) knowall

be'twijfelen to doubt

be'twistbaar contestable

be'twisten to dispute, to contest

beu fed up

beuk (de) beech

beuken to beat, to pound

beul (de) executioner; brute

beunhaas (de) bungler

beunhazen to dabble, to moonlight

beurs overripe; bruised

beurs (de) purse; scholarship; exchange

beurt (de) turn **een goede – maken** make a good impression, earn brownie points; **jij bent aan de –** it's your turn

be'vallen to please; to be confined

be'valllig graceful

be'vatten to contain; to comprehend

be'veiligen to safeguard

be'vel (het) order, command

be'velen to command

be'velhebber (de) commander

beven to tremble

bever (de) beaver

beverig shaky

be'vestigen to fasten; to consolidate; to confirm; to induct

be'vinden to find **zich –** to be (situated)

be'vlekken to stain

be'vlieging (de) sudden impulse, whim

be'vochtigen to moisten

be'voegd competent, qualified

be'volking (de) population

be'volkingsdichtheid (de) population density

be'volkingsgroep (de) section of the population

be'voordelen to benefit

be'vooroordeeld prejudiced

be'voorrechten to privilege

be'vorderen to promote

be'vorderlijk voor conducive to

be'vredigen to satisfy; to appease

be'vreesd voor afraid of

be'vriend on friendly terms

be'vriezen to freeze, to get frost-bitten

be'vrijden to liberate, to release

be'vrijdingsdag (de) liberation day

be'vruchten to fertilize

be'vuilen to soil

be'waken to guard

be'wapenen to arm

be'waren to keep, to preserve

be'waring (de) keeping, custody **in – geven** to deposit

be'weegbaar movable

be'weeglijk mobile, fidgety

be'weegreden (de) motive

be'wegen to move; to induce

be'weging (de) movement, motion **uit eigen –** of one's own accord

be'weren to assert, to contend

be'werkelijk laborious

be'werken to till; to work on or up; to adapt; to bring about

bewerk'stelligen to bring about

be'wijs (het) proof; certificate; evidence

be'wijsgrond (de) argument

be'wijzen to prove; to show

be'wind (het) government, rule

be'wolken to cloud over
be'wolking (de) cloud(s)
be'wonderen to admire
be'wonen to inhabit
be'woner (de) resident, occupant, inhabitant
be'woonbaar liveable, habitable
be'wust conscious; concerned **zich – zijn van** to be aware of **de bewuste brief** the letter in question
be'wusteloos unconscious
be'wustzijn (het) consciousness **buiten –** unconscious
be'zaaien to strew; to dot; to litter **het is bezaaid met bloemen** it is strewn/dotted with flowers
be'zadigd sober-minded
be'zegelen to seal
bezem (de) broom
be'zeren to hurt
be'zet occupied, engaged; set
be'zeten possessed
be'zetten to occupy; to set
be'zetting (de) occupation; cast (of a play)
be'zichtigen to view
be'zielen to inspire **wat bezielt je?** what has come over you?
be'zien to look at **dat staat nog te –** that remains to be seen
bezig occupied, busy **druk –** hard at work
bezigheid (de) occupation
bezighouden to keep occupied
be'zinken to settle (down); to sink in
be'zinksel (het) sediment
be'zinnen: zich – to reflect; to change one's mind
bezinning (de): tot – komen to come to one's senses
be'zit (het) possession(s), estate
be'zittelijk voornaamwoord (het) possessive pronoun
be'zitten to possess

be'zittingen (de) property, possessions
be'zoedelen to defile
be'zoek (het) visit **we krijgen –** we are expecting visitors
be'zoeken to visit; to afflict
be'zondigen: zich – aan to be guilty of
be'zopen tipsy; crazy
be'zorgd anxious; provided for
be'zorgen to procure; to give; to deliver
be'zuinigen to economize
be'zuren to suffer for
be'zwaar (het) objection; drawback
be'zwaard weighted; burdened, oppressed
be'zwaarlijk scarcely **bezwaarlijk vinden** to object to
be'zwaarschrift (het) petition
be'zwarende omstandigheden aggravating circumstances
be'zweet sweating
be'zweren to adjure; to exorcise
be'zwijken to succumb, to collapse
be'zwijmen to faint
bibberen to shiver
bibliothe'caris (de) librarian
biblio'theek (de) library
bidden to pray, to say grace
biecht (de) confession
biechten to confess; to go to confession
bieden to offer; to bid
biefstuk (de) rump steak
bier (het) ale, beer
biet (de) beet **rode –** beetroot
bietsuiker (de) beet sugar
biezen (made of) rushes
big (de) piglet
bij near, at, with, by; present; in addition; bee **hij is goed –** he is all there **er staat me iets van –** I seem to remember something about it

bij- secondary, in addition
bijbedoeling (de) ulterior motive
bijbel (de) bible
bijblijven to keep pace with; to stick in the memory
bijbrengen to impart; to bring round
bijde'hand smart
bijdraaien to heave to; to come round
bijdrage (de) contribution
bijdragen to contribute; to tend
bij'een together
bij'eenkomen to come together
bij'eenkomst (de) meeting, gathering
bij'eengenomen: alles – all things considered
bijenkorf (de) beehive
bijgaand enclosed
bijgedachte (de) implication; association
bijgeloof (het) superstition
bijge'lovig superstitious
bijhouden to keep up to date; to keep up with
bijkeuken (de) utility room
bijknippen to trim
bijkomen to come to, to revive **er komt nog bij** what is more
bijkomend, bij'komstig attendant; incidental
bijl (de) hatchet, axe **het bijltje erbij neerleggen** to chuck it (in)
bijlage (de) enclosure; appendix
bijleggen to make up (a quarrel); to add (money) to
bijna almost **– niet** hardly
bijnaam (de) nickname
bijpassen to pay the difference
bijpassend matching
bijschenken to fill up
bijscholen to get/give further training

bijschrijven to include
bijslag (de) bonus, extra allowance; extra charge; **kinderbijslag** child benefit
bijsluiter (de) information/ instruction leaflet
bijsmaak (de) trace, tang
bijspijkeren to brush up (skills), to catch up
bijspringen to help
bijstaan to assist
bijstand (de) assistance; social security, welfare
bijstandsmoeder (de) (single) mother on social security
bijstandsuitkering (de) social security payment
bijstelling (de) readjustment
bijster: het spoor – zijn to have lost one's way **niet –** not particularly
bijten to bite **van zich af –** to bite back
bijtend caustic; cutting; corrosive
bij'tijds in good time
bijtrekken to pull up; to improve
bijvak (het) subsidiary subject
bijval (de) approbation; applause
bijvallen to back up
bijverdienen to earn a little on the side
bijvoegen to add
bij'voeglijk naamwoord (het) adjective
bijvoegsel (het) supplement
bij'voorbeeld for instance
bijwerken to touch up; to bring up to date; to give extra coaching
bijwonen to attend
bijwoord (het) adverb
bijzaak (de) matter of secondary importance
bijzettafeltje (het) occasional table
bij'ziend short-sighted
bijzijn (het) presence

bijzin (de) subordinate clause
bij'zonder special, particular; private **niets bijzonders** nothing out of the ordinary
bij'zonderheden (de) particulars
bil (de) buttock
bil'jart (het) billiard table, billiards
bil'jet (het) (bank)note; ticket
billijk fair
binden to bind, to tie (up); to thicken
binnen within, inside, in **het schoot me te —** it (suddenly) struck me
binnenband (de) inner tube
binnen'door gaan to take a short cut
binnengaan to go in
binnenkomen to come in
binnen'kort shortly
binnenlands internal, home … **Ministerie van Binnenlandse Zaken** Home Office
binnens'huis indoors
binnens'monds under one's breath, indistinctly
binnenste'buiten inside out
binnenvaart inland navigation
bio'loog (de) biologist
bios'coop (de) cinema
bisschop (de) bishop
bitter bitter **bitter weinig** next to nothing
bitterkoekje (het) macaroon
bivak (het) bivouac
blaadje (het) petal; leaflet; tray **ik sta bij hem in een goed —** I am in his good books
blaar (de) blister
blaas (de) bladder; bubble
blaasinstrument (het) wind instrument
blad (het) (pl bladen) leaf; sheet of paper; newspaper; tray: **(pl bladeren)** leaf of a tree **hij neemt geen — voor de mond** he does not mince his words

bladgroente (de) greens
bladzij(de) (de) page
blaffen to bark
bla'mage (de) disgrace, blunder
blanco blank
blank white; pure; naked; flooded
blaten to bleat
blauw blue
blauwe'regen (de) wisteria
blazen to blow; to spit (cat) **hoog van de toren —** to brag
bleek pale
bleken to bleach
bles'sure (de) wound, injury (in sport)
blij(de) glad
blijdschap (de) gladness
blijk: — geven van to show signs of
blijkbaar apparently
blijken to appear, to transpire **'t moet nog —** it remains to be seen
blijspel (het) comedy
blijven to stay, to remain
blijvend lasting, permanent
blik (de) glance, look
blik (het) tin, can; dustpan
blikgroente (de) tinned vegetables
blikken: zonder — of blozen without turning a hair
blikopener (de) tin opener
blikschade (de) bodywork damage (to a car)
bliksem (de) lightning
blikvanger (de) eyecatcher
blind blind **zich — staren op** to be obsessed by
blinddoeken to blindfold
blinde'darmontsteking (de) appendicitis
blindelings blindly
blindheid (de) blindness
bloed (het) blood
bloedarmoede (de) anaemia
bloedbad (het) carnage, bloodbath

bloeden to bleed
bloederig bloody
bloedneus (de) nose bleed
bloedsomloop (de) circulation
(of the blood)
bloei (de) bloom, blossom(ing);
prosperity
bloeien to bloom; to flourish
bloeitijd (de) blossom time; heyday
bloem (de) flower; flour **de**
bloemetjes buiten zetten
to paint the town red
bloembol (de) bulb
bloe'mist (de) florist
bloemkool (de) cauliflower
bloemlezing (de) anthology
bloemrijk florid
bloemstuk (het) bouquet
bloesem (de) blossom
blok (het) block; log
blokfluit (de) recorder
blokje (het) cube; square
blok'kade (de) blockade
blokken to swot, to grind
blok'keren to block; to blockade
blond fair
bloot bare, naked; sheer
blootgeven: zich – to lay oneself
open (to attack)
blootje: in je – in the nude
blootleggen to reveal
blootshoofds bareheaded
blootstaan aan to be exposed to
blootstellen to expose
blos (de) blush; bloom
blozen to blush
blubber (de) mud
bluffen to brag
blunder (de) blunder
blussen to extinguish; to quell
blut broke
bobbel (de) bump; bubble
bobbelig lumpy
bobslee (de) bob (sleigh)

bochel (de) hump; hunchback
bocht (de) bend
bochtig winding
bod (het) bid
bodem (de) bottom; soil; territory
bodemloos bottomless
boed'dhisme (het) Buddhism
boedel (de) household goods;
personal estate
boeg (de) bow (s) **veel werk voor**
de – a lot of work on hand
boei (de) buoy
boeien (de) fetters; to fetter; to hold
the attention
boeiend fascinating
boek (het) book **te – staan als**
to have the reputation of **je**
gaat buiten je boekje you are
overstepping the mark
boekdeel (het) volume
boekenlegger (de) bookmark
boeken to book
boekenkast (de) bookcase
boekenwijsheid (de) book learning
boekhandel (de) bookshop
boekhouden to keep accounts
boeking (de) booking, reservation;
caution (in football)
boel: een – a lot **een armoedig**
boeltje a shoddy outfit
boemeltrein (de) slow train
boenen to scrub
boenwas (de) wax polish
boer (de) farmer; knave (at cards);
boor; belch
boerde'rij (de) farm
boeren to belch
boeren'jongens brandy and raisins
boeren'kool (de) kale
boerenverstand (het)
common sense
boe'rin (de) farmer's wife
boers boorish
boete (de) penalty, fine; penance

boeten voor to atone for
boet'seren to model
boezem (de) bosom
bof (de) stroke of luck; mumps
boffen to be lucky
bok (de) buck; billy goat
bokkensprong (de) caper, prank
boksen to box
bol (de) globe, sphere; crown (of hat); bulb; head: convex, bulging
bolhoed (de) bowler hat
bollen to bulge
bollenteelt (de) bulb-growing (industry)
bollentijd (de) bulb season
bolletje (het) little ball; roll
bolletjesslikker (de) someone who smuggles drugs by swallowing them
bolster (de) shell, husk
bolwerk (het) bulwark
bolwerken: hij kon het niet – he could not manage it
bom (de) bomb
bomaanslag (de) bomb attack
bombar'deren to shell; to bomb(ard)
bom'melding (de) bomb alert
bon (de) voucher; coupon
bond (de) alliance, union
bondgenoot (de) ally
bondig terse
bondscoach (de) national (football) coach
bondselftal (het) national (football) team
bonne'fooi: op de – ergens heen gaan go somewhere on the off chance
bons (de) bump, thud **de – geven** to sack, to throw over
bont (het) fur
bont many-coloured; gaudy; piebald; varied; motley **je maakt het te –** you are going too far
bonzen to throb; to pound; to bump

boodschap (de) message, errand
boodschappen doen to go shopping
boog (de) arch, arc; bow
boogschieten (to do) archery
Boogschutter (de) Sagittarius
boom (de) tree; barrier; pole
boomgaard (de) orchard
boomstam (de) tree trunk
boon (de) bean
boor (de) drill, gimlet
boord (het, de) collar; (ship)board **aan –** on board
boordevol brim-full
booreiland (het) oilrig
boormachine (de) (electric) drill
boos angry; evil
boos'aardig malicious
boosheid (de) anger
boot (de) boat
bootreis (de) voyage, cruise
bord (het) plate; board
bor'deel (het) brothel
bor'des (het) (flight of) steps
bordkrijt (het) chalk
bor'duren to embroider
boren to drill, to bore
borg (de) surety, security, bail
borgsom (de) deposit; security (money)
borgstelling (de) security; bail
borgtocht (de) security, bail
borrel (de) dram, shot (of an alcoholic drink); a social occasion
borrelen to (have a) drink; to bubble
borst (de) breast, chest **tegen de – stuiten** to go against the grain
borstbeeld (het) bust
borstel (de) brush; bristle
borstelen to brush
borstelig bristly
borstkanker (de) breast cancer
borstkas (de) chest
borstplaat (de) fondant

borstvoeding (de) breastfeeding
borstzak (de) breast pocket
bos (de) bunch, bundle, tuft
bos (het) bundle, bunch; forest
bosachtig wooded
bosbes (de) bilberry, blueberry
bosbouw (de) forestry
boswachter (de) (forest)keeper
bot (het) bone **bot** blunt **– vangen** to meet with a curt refusal
botvieren to give rein to
boter (de) butter
boterbloem (de) buttercup
boterham (de) slice of bread; sandwich
botsen to collide, to bump
botsing (de) collision
botweg flatly
boud bold
bou'gie (de) sparking plug
bouil'lon (de) beef tea, stock
bout (de) bolt; wooden pin; leg cut of meat
bouw (de) build, construction; cultivation; structure
bouwen to build
bouw'kundig architectural
bouwkunst (de) architecture
bouwterrein (het) building site
bouwval (de) ruin
bouw'vallig tumble-down, dilapidated
boven above, over **te – gaan** to exceed **te – komen** to get over
bovenaan at the top
boven'dien moreover
bovenmodaal above average
boven'menselijk superhuman
bovenna'tuurlijk supernatural
bovenop on (the) top of
bovenste topmost
boventoon (de) overtone **de – voeren** to (pre)dominate
bovenverdieping (de) top floor

bowl (de) punch
box (de) playpen
braaf good, decent, upright
braak fallow
braaksel (het) vomit
braam (de) blackberry
Brabançonne (de) 'Brabançonne' (national anthem of Belgium)
braden to roast
braille (de) Braille
brak brackish
braken to vomit
brallen to brag
bran'card (de) stretcher
branche (de) sector (of industry or business), branch, department
brand (de) fire **in – vliegen** to catch fire
brandbaar inflammable
brandblusser (de) fire extinguisher
branden to burn
brandgevaar (het) fire hazard, fire risk
brandkast (de) safe
brandmerken to brand
brandnetel (de) stinging nettle
brandpunt (het) focus
brandschoon spotless
brandstapel (de) stake; funeral pile
brandstof (de) fuel
brandweer (de) fire brigade
bra'voure (de) bravado
breed broad, wide
breed'sprakig long-winded
breedte (de) breadth, width; latitude
breed'voerig detailed
breekbaar breakable, fragile
breekijzer (het) crowbar
breien to knit
brein (het) brain
breiwerk (het) knitting
breken to break
brengen to bring, to take **er toe –** to induce

bres (de) breach
bre'tels (de) braces
breuk (de) fracture, fraction, rupture
bre'vet (het) (flying) certificate
brief (de) letter
briefkaart (de) postcard
briefwisseling (de) correspondence
bries (de) breeze
briesen to snort
brievenbus (de) letterbox
brij (de) pulp; porridge
bril (de) glasses
brilmontuur (het) glasses frame
Brits British
broche (de) brooch
bro'chure (de) brochure; prospectus
broeden to brood
broeder (de) brother
broeien to brood; to brew; to heat
broeierig sultry
broeikas (de) greenhouse
broeikaseffect (het) greenhouse
   effect
broeinest (het) hotbed
broek (de) (pair of) trousers,
   knickers
broekje (het) panties, knickers
broekspijp (de) trouser leg
broer (de) brother
brok (het) fragment; lump
bro'kaat, bro'caat (het) brocade
brokkelen to crumble
brommen to growl, to grumble
bromvlieg (de) bluebottle
bron (de) spring, source
brons (het) bronze
bronzen bronze
brood (het) bread, loaf **zijn –**
   verdienen to earn one's living
broodbeleg (het) sandwich filling
broodje (het) (bread)roll
broodjeszaak (de) sandwich bar
broos brittle, fragile, frail
brouwen to brew

brouwe'rij (de) brewery **leven in**
   de – brengen to liven things up
brug (de) bridge **over de – komen**
   to pay up
brui (de): er de – aan geven to
   chuck it
bruid (de) bride
brui(de)gom (de) bridegroom
bruidsjapon (de) wedding dress
bruidsmeisje (het) bridesmaid
bruidspaar (het) bride and
   bridegroom
bruidsschat (de) dowry
bruikbaar usable
bruikleen: in – on loan
bruiloft (de) wedding (feast)
bruin brown
bruisen to effervesce; to seethe
brullen to roar
bru'taal impudent
bru'taalweg calmly
brutali'teit (de) insolence
bruto gross (weight)
brutosalaris (het) gross salary
bruusk brusque
bruut brutish
bruut (de) brute
btw (de) VAT
buffel (de) buffalo
buf'fet (het) sideboard; buffet
bui (de) shower (of rain); fit
buigbaar flexible
buigen to bend, to bow; to submit
buiging (de) bow, bend; inflexion
buigtang (de) (pair of) pliers
buigzaam pliable; yielding
buiig showery
buik (de) belly
buikje (het) tummy
buikpijn (de) stomach ache
buikspreker (de) ventriloquist
buil (de) bump (on someone's head)
   daar kun je je geen – aan vallen
   you can't go far wrong with that

buis (de) tube, pipe; jacket
buiten outside; beyond; without; in the country **het ging – mij om** it occurred without my knowledge **van – kennen** to know by heart
buitenband (de) tyre
buitenbeentje (het) odd one out, outsider
buitenge'meen, buitenge'woon uncommon, extraordinary
buite'nissig odd
buitenkansje (het) stroke of luck
buitenkant (de) outside
buitenland: in het – abroad
buitenlander (de) foreigner
buitenlands foreign
buitenlucht (de) open air
buitens'huis out of doors
buiten'spel (de) off-side
buiten'sporig excessive
buitenstaander (de) outsider
buitenste outermost
buitenwijk (de) suburb
bukken to duck, to stoop **gebukt gaan onder** to be weighed down by
bul (de) bull; diploma
bulderen to roar

bulken to bellow **– van het geld** to roll in money
bult (de) hump, lump
bundel (de) bundle; collection (of poems etc.)
bungelen to dangle
burcht (de) castle, citadel
bu'reau (het) office; desk
bureaucra'tie (de) bureaucracy
bureaulamp (de) desk lamp
burger (de) citizen, civilian
burger- civil(ian), civic
burgerlijk bourgeois, civil
burgelijke stand (de) registry of births, marriages and deaths
burgeroorlog (de) civil war
bus (de) tin, canister; bus
buschauffeur (de) bus driver
busdienst (de) bus service
buurman (de), buurvrouw (de) neighbour
buurt (de) neighbourhood
buurtbewoner (de) local resident
buurthuis (het) community centre
buurtvereniging (de) residents' association
b.v.: bijvoorbeeld e.g.

C

ca'cao (de) cocoa
ca'deau (het) present
ca'deaubon (de) gift voucher
calcu'leren to calculate, to compute
ca'mee (de) cameo
camou'fleren to camouflage
cam'pagne (de) campaign
camper (de) camper
camping (de) campsite
capaci'teit (de) capacity; ability
capitu'leren to capitulate
capri'ool (de) caper, prank; antics
carbu'rator (de) carburettor
carri'ère (de) career

cas'setteband (de) cassette, tape
cas'settedeck (de) tape deck
cassis (de) cassis, sparkling blackcurrant drink
casta'gnetten (de) castanets
cas'treren to castrate
catalogi'seren to catalogue
ca'talogus (de) catalogue
catechi'satie (de) confirmation class, religious instruction
cate'gorie (de) category
cate'gorisch categorical
cd (de) CD
ceder (de) cedar

Insight

The Dutch translation of *CD* is the same word as in English, but written in lower case: **de cd**. The Dutch are much less keen on using capital letters than speakers of English. A *CD-ROM* is **een cd-rom**, for instance, a *DVD* is **een dvd**, and *VAT* is **de btw**.

cein'tuur (de) belt, sash
cel (de) cell
celi'baat (het) celibacy
celiba'tair celibate
cel'list (de) violoncellist
cello (de) cello
Celsius Centigrade
censu'reren to censor
cen'suur (de) censorship
cent (de) cent **eurocent** eurocent
  (1/100 of one euro)
cen'traal central
cen'trale (de) power station
centrum (het) centre
ceremoni'eel ceremonial
cere'moniemeester (de) master
  of ceremonies
certifi'ceren to certify
cha'grijn (het) chagrin
cha'grijnig cantankerous
champi'gnon (de) mushroom
chan'tage (de) blackmail
cha'otisch chaotic
char'mant charming
char'meren to charm
chef (de) head, manager, chief
chemi'caliën chemicals
chemicus (de) (analytical) chemist
che'mie (de) chemistry
chemisch chemical
cheru'bijn (de) cherub
chip (de) chip
chipknip (de) smart card
chips (de) crisps, chips (Am)
chi'rurg (de) surgeon
chirur'gie (de) surgery

chi'rurgisch surgical
chloor chlorine
choco'laatje (het) chocolate
  (drop)
choco'la(de) (de) chocolate
choco'la(de)melk (de) cocoa
christelijk Christian
christen (de) Christian
Christus Christ
chromo'soom (het) chromosome
chronisch chronic
chronolo'gie (de) chronology
chry'sant (de) chrysanthemum
cider (de) cider
cijfer (het) figure, digit, mark
ci'linder (de) cylinder
ci'lindrisch cylindrical
cim'baal (de) cymbal
ci'pier (de) warder
ci'pres (de) cypress
circa approximately
circu'latie (de) circulation
circu'leren to circulate
cirkel (de) circle
cirkelen to circle
cirkel'vormig circular
ci'taat (het) quotation
ci'teren to quote
ci'troen (de) lemon
ci'troenpers (de) lemon
  squeezer
ci'viel civil; moderate
claim (de) claim
claimen to (file a) claim
clande'stien clandestine; illicit;
  bootleg

clau'sule (de) clause; proviso
cle'ment lenient
cle'mentie (de) clemency
clo'set (het) water-closet, toilet
club (de) club
coa'litie (de) coalition
co'con (de) cocoon
codi'cil (het) codicil
cogni'tief cognitive
cohe'rent coherent
co'hesie (de) cohesion
coke (de) coke; snow (cocaine)
col (de) rollneck, polo neck; mountain (pass)
col'bert (het) jacket
collec'tant (de) person collecting money
col'lecte (de) collection
collec'teren to collect money
col'lega (de) colleague
col'lege (het) board; college; university lecture **– geven** to lecture
collegi'aal friendly, harmonious
col'loquiem (het) symposium
co'lonne (de) column (of soldiers)
comeback (de) comeback
comfor'tabel comfortable
comi'té (het) committee
comman'dant (de) commandant, commander, ship's captain
comman'deren to command, to order about
com'mando (het) command
commen'taar (het) commentary
com'mercie (de) commerce, trade
commerci'eel commercial
commissari'aat (het) directorate
commis'saris (de) chief inspector of police
com'missie (de) committee, commission
com'mune (de) commune

communi'catie (de) communication
communica'tief communicative
communi'ceren to communicate
communi'qué (het) statement, bulletin **een – uitgeven** to put out a statement
com'pact compact, dense
compact disc (de) compact disk
compa'gnon (de) (business) partner
comparti'ment (het) compartment
compen'satie (de) compensation
compen'seren to compensate
compe'tent competent, capable
compi'latie (de) compilation
compi'leren to compile
com'pleet complete
comple'teren to complete
compli'catie (de) complication
compli'ment (het) compliment
complimen'teren met to compliment on,
complimen'teus complimentary
com'plot (het) conspiracy
compo'neren to compose (music)
compo'nist (de) composer
compromit'teren to compromise
com'puter (de) computer
com'puteren to work/play on the computer
concen'tratievermogen (het) power of concentration
concen'treren to concentrate
con'cept (het) draft (document)
con'cert (het) concert, recital; concerto
con'certgebouw (het) concert hall
con'certzaal (de) concert hall; auditorium
con'cessie (de) concession
con'ciërge (de) caretaker, hall porter
con'creet concrete(ly)
concur'rent (de) competitor
concur'rentie (de) competition
concur'reren to compete

concur'rerend competitive
conden'sator (de) condenser
conden'seren to condense
con'ditie (de) condition **in conditie** fit
condo'leren to offer one's condolences
conduc'teur (de) guard, tram, or bus conductor
con'fectie (de) ready-made (clothes)
con'fessie (de) confession
confessio'neel confessional, denominational
confidenti'eel confidential
con'flict (het) conflict
con'form in accordance with
confor'meren: zich – to conform (to), to comply (with)
confron'tatie (de) confrontation
confron'teren to confront
con'gres (het) conference, congress
conjunc'tuur (de) market conditions
con'fuus confused, abashed
conse'quent consistent
conse'quentie (de) consequence, consistency
conser'vator (de) curator
con'serven (de) preserves
con'sorten (de) confederates
consta'teren to establish
constru'eren to construct
consulaat (het) consulate
consu'lent (de) expert adviser
con'sult (het) consultation
consul'tatie (de) consultation
consul'tatiebureau (het) clinic, health centre
consu'ment (de) consumer
consu'mentenbond (de) consumers' organization
con'sumptie (de) consumption, food and/or drink(s)

con'tact (het) contact, connection, touch
con'tactadvertentie (de) personal ad
con'tactdoos (de) socket; appliance inlet
con'tant (in) cash, ready money
context (de) context
continu'eren to continue
continuï'teit (de) continuity, continuation
contra contra, against, versus
contra'ceptie (de) contraception
con'tract (het) contract, agreement
contrac'teren to contract
contramine: in de – in a contrary mood
con'trole (de) check, supervision
contro'leren to check, to inspect
contro'leur (de) inspector
cor'rect correct; right
cor'rectie (de) correction, adjustment; marking
cor'rectiewerk (het) marking, correcting
correspon'deren to correspond
correspon'dentie (de) correspondence
corri'geren to correct
cou'lant obliging, accommodating
cou'lissen (de) wings (theatre)
cou'pé (de) compartment
cou'veuse (de) incubator
cre'peren to perish; to suffer: **– van de pijn** to be racked with pain
cricketen to play cricket
crisis (de) crisis
cri'terium (het) criterion
crois'sant (de) croissant
cru crude
culi'nair culinary
culmi'neren to culminate
cultfiguur (de/het) cult figure

cultu'reel cultural
cul'tuur (de) culture
cum laude: – geslaagd zijn to pass with a distinction/credit/a first
cura'tele (de) guardianship; legal restriction **onder – staan** be under legal restriction, in receivership
cur'ator (de) curator
curiosi'teit (de) curio
cur'riculum (het) curriculum;

curriculum vitae (CV, cv) CV, résumé (Am)
cur'sief italicized
cur'sist (de) learner, student
cursus (de) school year, course of studies
cursusboek (het) textbook, course book
cynicus (de) cynic
cynisch cynical

D

daad (de) deed, act(ion)
daad'werkelijk actual
daags daily
daar there; as, because
daar'achter behind it
daar'aan on (to) that **wat heb je –?**, what good is that?
daarbe'neden down there, below
daarbij near it; moreover
daar'binnen in there, inside
daar'door through it, as a result
daaren'tegen on the other hand
daar'ginds over there
daar'heen there
daargelaten (quite) apart from
daar'net just now
daarom therefore
daarom'trent thereabouts
daar op on that; on top of that
daarop'volgend subsequent, next
daarover over it, about it
daar'tegen against that, next to that
daarvan'daan from there
daar'voor in front of it, before that; that's why
dadel (de) date
dadelijk immediate
dader (de) perpetrator
dag (de) day(light)
dag! hello!, goodbye **om de drie dagen** every third day

dagblad (het) daily paper
dagboek (het) diary
dagdeel (het) part of the day; shift
dagelijks daily
dagen to summon; to dawn
dageraad (de) dawn
dagkaart (de) day ticket
dagkoers (de) current rate (of exchange)
dagloner (de) day labourer
dagopvang (de) day nursery
dagretour (het) day return
dagschotel (de) today's special
dagtekenen to date
dagtocht (de) day trip
dagvaarden to summon
dagvaarding (de) summons
dagverblijf (het) day nursery, crèche; outside pen (for animals)
dak (het) roof
dakgoot (de) gutter
dakkapel (de) dormer (window)
dakloos homeless
dakkamer (de) attic room
dakloze (de) homeless person
dakpan (de) tile
dakraam (het) skylight
dal (het) valley
dalen to go or come down
daling (de) descent; drop
daluren (de) off-peak hours

dam (de) dam, causeway; king (in draughts)
dambord (het) draught board
dame (de) lady
damesmode (de) ladies' fashion
damhert (het) fallow deer
dammen to play draughts
damp (de) vapour
dampkring (de) atmosphere
dan then; still; than — **ook** so (consequence) **(hoe, wat, wie)** — **ook** (how-, what-, who-) ever
danig exceeding; greatly
dank thanks **dank zij** thanks to
dankbaar grateful, gratifying
dankbaarheid (de) gratitude
danken to thank, to say grace
dans (de) dance
dansen to dance
dapper brave
darm (de) intestine
dartel frisky
dartelen to frolic, to gambol
das (de) (neck)tie, scarf; badger
dat that; which
data (de) data; dates
databank (de) data bank
da'teren to date
datgene that (one)
datum (de) date
dauw (de) dew
daveren to thunder, to resound
daverend thunderous; resounding
de the
de'bacle (het, de) disaster, failure
de'bat (het) debate
debat'teren to debate
debet (het) debit; overdrawn
de'biel (de) (term of abuse) moron, cretin
debi'teren to debit
debi'teur (de) debtor
de'buut (het) début
december December

decentrali'seren to decentralize
decla'meren to recite
decla'ratie (de) expenses claim
de'cor (het) décor, scenery, setting
decora'tief decorative
de'creet (het) decree
decre'teren to decree
deeg (het) dough; mixture
deel (het) part, share; volume
deel'achtig participating in
deelbaar divisible
deelgenoot (de) participant; partner
deelgenootschap (het) partnership
deelnemen (aan) to participate (in)
deelnemer (de) participant
deelneming (de) participation; sympathy
deels partly
deelteken (het) division sign
deeltijdbaan (de) part-time job
deeltje (het) particle
deelwoord (het) participle
dee'moedig meek
Deen(se) (de) Dane, Danish woman
deernis (de) compassion
deernis'wekkend pitiable
de'fect (het) faulty, out of order; defect, fault
de'fensie (de) (national) defence
defi'lé (het) parade, procession
defi'leren to march past
defini'ëren to define
defini'tief definite, definitive
de'flatie (de) deflation
deftig dignified; distinguished
degelijk sound; substantial **hij weet het wel** — he knows (it) perfectly well
degen (de) sword
de'gene die the one who
degra'deren to degrade, to downgrade
deinen to heave; to bob
deining (de) swell; commotion

dek (het) cover; bedclothes; deck
deken (de) blanket; dean
dekhengst (de) stallion
dekken to cover; to lay (the table); to serve (a mare) **zich –** to take cover
dekking (de) cover **– zoeken** to take cover
deksel (het) lid, cover
dekzeil (het) tarpaulin
delen to divide, to share, to split
deling (de) division
delin'quent (de) delinquent, offender
delfstof (de) mineral
delica'tesse (de) delicacy
delven to dig
de'ment demented
demo'craat (de) democrat
democra'tie (de) democracy
demon'stratie (de) demonstration, display; march
demonstra'tief demonstrative
demon'streren to demonstrate; to protest (against)
demon'teren to dismantle
dempen to fill in (with earth); to subdue
den, denneboom (de) pine(-tree)
Den Haag the Hague

denderend smashing
Denemarken Denmark
denkbaar conceivable
denkbeeld (het) idea
denk'beeldig imaginary; fictitious; hypothetical
denkelijk probably
denken (aan) to think (of)
  doen – aan to remind of
denkvermogen (het) intellectual capacity
dennenappel (de) fir cone
dennenhout (het) pinewood
depo'neren to deposit, to file, to register
de'pot (het) depot; branch establishment
depri'meren to depress
derde third **– wereld (de)** Third World **–'wereldwinkel (de)** Third World shop **ten –** thirdly
derdemachtswortel (de) cube root
derde'rangs third rate
deren to harm
dergelijk such (like) **iets dergelijks** something of the sort
der'halve hence
dermate to such a degree
dertien(de) thirteen(th)

Insight

The Dutch seat of government and royal residence is called **Den Haag** *The Hague*. However, this name is a short form of the longer name **'s-Gravenhage**. The **'s** indicates the genitive case (possessive). The name is often understood to mean the wood (**haag** or **hage**) of the count (**graaf**); however, it seems in the past **hage** may actually have referred to a small stream. Note that place names in Belgium often have two names, one Dutch and one French. Examples are **Antwerpen/***Anvers***, Brussel/***Bruxelles***, Brugge/***Bruges***.

dertig thirty
derven to lack
des of the **des te (meer)** all the (more)
desalniette'min nevertheless
desas'treus disastrous
desbe'treffend relating to this
desge'lijks likewise
desge'wenst if desired
desillusie (de) disillusionment
des'kundig(e) (de) expert
des'noods if need be; at a pinch
deson'danks nevertheless
des'poot (de) despot
des'sin (het) design
des'tijds at the time
de'tail (het, de) detail; retail
de'tailhandel (de) retail trade
de'tentie (de) detention, custody
determi'neren to determine; to identify
deti'neren to detain
deto'neren to detonate; to be out of tune, to be out of keeping
deugd (de) virtue
deugdelijk reliable
deugdzaam virtuous
deugen: niet – to be no good
deugniet (de) rascal, good-for-nothing
deuk (de) dent **ik lag in een –** (inf) I was laughing my head off
deuken to dent
deuntje (het) tune
deur (de) door **met de – in huis vallen** to come straight to the point
deurwaarder (de) bailiff
de'vies (het) motto, device
de'viezen (de) (foreign) currency
deze this, these **– of gene** (some) one or other
de'zelfde the same
dhr.: de heer Mr
diag'nose (de) diagnosis

diago'naal diagonally
di'aken (de) church worker; deacon
dia'loog (de) dialogue
dia'mant (de) diamond
dia'manten (made of) diamond
dia'mantslijper (de) diamond cutter
diameter (de) diameter
diar'ree (de) diarrhoea
dicht closed; dense
dicht'bij near (to), close by
dichtbevolkt densely populated
dichten to write poetry; to stop a leak
dichter('es) (de) poet(ess)
dichterlijk poetic(al)
dichtkunst (de) (art of) poetry
dichtstbij'zijnd nearest
dichtvriezen to freeze over (of a canal, lake)
dic'taat (het) dictation; lecture-notes; notebook
dictatori'aal dictatorial
dicta'tuur (de) dictatorship
dic'tee (het) dictation
die that, those; who, which; he, she, it, they
di'eet (het) diet
dief (de) thief
diefstal (de) theft
die'gene he, she
dienaar (de) servant
diender (de) cop(per)
dienen to serve **waar dient dit voor?** what is the use of this? **daar ben ik niet van gediend** I take exception to that
dienovereen'komstig accordingly
dienst (de) service, duty
dienstbode (de) (house)maid
dienstensector (de) services sector
dienstplicht (de) compulsory (military) service
dienstregeling (de) timetable

dienstverlening (de) services; caring profession

dienstweigeraar (de) conscientious objector

dientenge'volge in consequence

diep deep; profound

diepgaand searching

diepgang (de) depth; profundity

diepte (de) depth

diepvries (de) freezer **spinazie uit de –** frozen spinach

diep'zinnig profound; abstruse

dier (het) animal

dierbaar dearly loved

dierenbescherming (de) prevention of cruelty to animals

dierenmishandeling (de) cruelty to animals

dierenriem (de) zodiac

dierenwinkel (de) pet shop

dierlijk animal; bestial

die'vegge (de) female thief

digi'taal digital

dij (de) thigh

dijbeen (het) thighbone

dijk (de) dike, embankment; dam **aan de – zetten** to sack someone

dik thick; fat; dense

dikkerd (de) fatty

dikte (de) thickness

dikwijs often

dimmen to dim, to dip

di'neren to dine

ding (het) thing

dingen to bargain **– naar** to compete for, to sue for

dinsdag Tuesday

diplo'maat (de) diplomat(ist)

diplo'matenkoffertje (het) attaché case

diploma'tie (de) diplomacy

direc'teur (de) director, manager, head(master)

di'rectie (de) management

diri'gent (de) conductor

diri'geren to conduct

discu'teren to discuss, to argue

dis'puut (het) dispute; debating society

disser'tatie (de) thesis for a doctorate

distel (de) thistle

distilla'teur (de) distiller

distilleerde'rij (de) distillery

distri'butie (de) distribution, (food) allocation; radio-diffusion

dit this, these

ditmaal this time

di'versen (de) miscellaneous, sundries

diversi'teit (de) diversity, variety

divi'dend (het) dividend

di'visie (de) division; league (in sport)

dobbelaar (de) gambler, dice player

dobbelen to play dice

dobbelstenen (de) dice

dobber (de) float **een harde – hebben** to be hard put to it

dobberen to bob up and down

do'cent (de) teacher

do'ceren to teach

doch but; however

dochter (de) daughter

docto'raal (e'xamen) (het) examination for master's degree

docto'randus person who has passed the *doctoraalexamen*

docu'ment (het) document, paper

documen'taire (de) documentary

dode (de) dead (wo)man, deceased

dodelijk mortal, deadly

doden to kill

dodenherdenking (de) commemoration of the (war) dead

doedelzak (de) bagpipes

doel (het) target, goal; aim

doe-het-zelfzaak (de) DIY shop

doelbe'wust purposeful
doeleinde (het) purpose
doelen op to allude to
doelloos aimless, pointless
doel'matig appropriate; efficient
doel'treffend effective
doemdenken (het) doom-mongering
doemen to doom
doen to do, to make; to ask; to put **ik kan er niets aan –** I can't help it **ik heb met je te –** I am sorry for you **het doet er niet(s) toe** it makes no difference **– in** to deal in **– en laten** behaviour, doings
doetje (het) softy
doezelen to drowse
dof dull, dim
dok (het) dock
dokken to dock; to fork out **je zult moeten –** you'll have to fork out
dokter (de) doctor
doktersbehandeling (de) medical treatment
doktersrecept (het) medical prescription
dol mad, frantic
dolblij overjoyed
dolen to wander
dol'fijn (de) dolphin
dolgraag only too gladly
dolheid (de) frenzy
dolk (de) dagger
dolleman (de) madman
dollen to romp
dom stupid; **(de)** cathedral, dome
do'mein (het) domain
domheid (de) stupidity
dominee (de) minister, clergyman
domi'neren to dominate; to play dominoes
domkop (de) blockhead
dommelen to doze
dompelaar (de) diver (bird); plunger

dompelen to plunge
dona'teur (de) donor, supporter
donder (de) thunder **iemand op zijn – geven** to give a person a good hiding **het kan me geen – schelen** I don't give a damn
donderbui (de) thunderstorm
donderdag Thursday
donderen to thunder
donderjagen to be a nuisance, to mess about
donderslag (de) thunderclap
do'neren to donate
donker dark
donor (de) donor
donorcodocil (het) donor card
dons (het) down
donzig downy
dood (de) death
dood dead
doodbloeden bleed to death
doodeen'voudig perfectly simple
doodgaan to die
doodgraver (de) gravedigger
doodop dead beat
doods deathly, mortally
doodsbang scared to death
doodskist (de) coffin
doodslag (de) homicide
doodsnood: in – in the throes of death
doodstraf (de) capital punishment
doodsstrijd (de) death struggle, throes of death
doodzwijgen to hush up, to keep quiet
doof deaf
doof'stom deaf mute
dooi (de) thaw
dooien to thaw
dooier (de) yolk
doolhof (het) labyrinth
doop (de) baptism
doopsge'zind Baptist

doopvont (het) font
door through; by **– de week** on weekdays
doorbladeren to glance through
doorbrengen to spend
door'dacht carefully considered, well thought-out
door'dat owing to
doordraaien to keep going; to remain unsold
doordrammen to nag, to go on about something
doordrijven to get one's own way
doordringen to penetrate
door'eenmengen to mix together
dooreten to go on eating, to eat up
doorgaan to go on **– voor** to pass for **er van doorgaan** to bolt
doorgaande trein (de) through train
doorgaans usually
doorgang (de) passage, way through
doorgeven to pass (on)
doorgewinterd seasoned, experienced
door'gronden to fathom
doorhalen to strike out (words); to pull through
door'heen through
door'kneed in well-versed in
doorkomen to get through
door'kruisen to traverse
doorleren to stay at school, to continue with one's education
doorlichten to screen; to X-ray; to investigate
door'lopen to complete, to pass through
doorlopen to walk to run on; to get a move on; to run (of colours); to walk through
door'lopend continuous, continual
doormaken to go through
door'midden in half

doorn (de) thorn
doornat wet through
door'schijnend translucent
doorslaand bewijs convincing proof
doorslag (de) dip, turn; carbon copy **de – geven** to turn the scale
doorslaggevend decisive
doorsnede (de) cross-section; diameter
doorsnee average
doorsneemens (de) the average person
door'staan to stand, to endure
door'tastend vigorous, thorough-going, go-ahead
door'trapt cunning; villainous
door'trokken soaked; imbued
doorvertellen to pass on (a secret or information)
door'voed well-fed
door'waadbare plaats ford
doorzakken to make a night of it
doorzetten to persevere
door'zichtig transparent
doos (de) box, case **uit de oude –** antiquated
dop (de) shell, husk, pod; top
dopen to baptize, to dip
doperw (de) (green) pea
doppen to shell
dor dry, arid
dorp (het) village
dorpeling (de) villager
dorsen to thresh
dorst (de) thirst
dosis (de) dose
dos'sier (het) file, document, records
dot (de) tuft; pet
dou'ane (de) Customs
dove (de) deaf person
doven to extinguish, to dim
do'zijn (het) dozen
draad (de) thread, wire
draadloos wireless

draagbaar stretcher; portable
draagkracht (de) carrying capacity,
  range
draaglijk tolerable
draagmoeder (de) surrogate mother
draagstoel (de) sedan chair
draagvlak (het) basis, support **het
  maatschappelijk –** the public
  support
draai (de) turn, twist **een – om
  de oren** a box on the ears **zijn –
  vinden** to find one's niche
draaibaar revolving
draaibank (de) lathe
draaiboek (het) scenario, script
draaideur (de) revolving door
draaien to turn, to revolve;
  to prevaricate
draaierig dizzy
draaikolk (de) whirlpool
draaimolen (de) roundabout
draaiorgel (het) barrel organ
draaitafel (de) turntable
draak (de) dragon **de – steken met**
  to make fun of
drab (de) dregs
dracht (de) dress, wear
draderig stringy
draf (de) trot
dragen to bear; to wear; to carry
dralen to tarry
drang (de) pressure; urge
drank (de) drink **aan de – zijn** to be
  addicted to drink
dra'peren to drape
drassig marshy
drastisch drastic
draven to trot
dreef (de) avenue, lane; mead (ow)
  op – in/on form
dreggen to drag
dreige'ment (het) threat
dreigen to threaten
dreinen to whine

drempel (de) threshold
drenkeling (de) drowning person
drentelen to saunter
drenzen to whine
dres'seren to train (animals)
dres'soir (het) sideboard
dreumes (de) toddler
dreun (de) drone; blow
dreunen to drone, to rumble
drie three
drie'delig tripartite; three-piece
driedimensio'naal
  three-dimensional
drie'dubbel triple
driehoek (de) triangle
driekwart three-quarter(s)
drieling (de) triplet(s)
drieluik (het) triptych
driepoot (de) tripod
drietjes: met z'n – the three of
  us/them
drievoud treble; triplicate
driewieler (de) tricycle
drift (de) passion; drift
driftig hot-tempered; in a temper
driftkop (de) hothead
drijfhout (het) driftwood
drijfkracht (de) drive
drijfnat sopping wet
drijfveer (de) mainspring; incentive;
  motive
drijfzand (het) quicksand(s)
drijven to float, to drift; to drive;
  to run (a business)
dringen to crowd, to jostle; to press
  de tijd dringt time presses
dringend urgent
drinken to drink
droef sad
droefenis (de) sorrow
droef'geestig mournful
droefheid (de) sadness
droevig sad
droge (het) dry land

drogen to dry
drogiste'rij (de) chemist's (shop)
dromen to dream
dromerig dreamy
dronk (de) drink, draught, toast
dronkaard (de) drunkard
dronken drunk(en)
droog dry
droogleggen to drain, to reclaim
droogrek (het) clotheshorse
droogte (de) dryness; drought
droogtrommel (de) tumble dryer
droom (de) dream
droomprins (de) Prince Charming
droomwereld (de) dreamworld
drop (de) liquorice; drop
drug (de) drug, narcotic
drugsbeleid (het) drug policy
drugshandel (de) dealing (in drugs)
drugsverslaafde (de) drug addict
druif (de) grape
druilerig: het is – weer there is rain in the air
druipen to drip
druipsteen (het, de) stalactite, stalagmite
druisen to roar, to churn
druk busy; fussy; gaudy; pressure; print **maak je niet –** be calm **een – bezochte vergadering** well-attended meeting
drukfout (de) misprint
drukken to (de)press; to oppress; to print; to shake (hands)
drukkend oppressive
drukker'ij (de) printer('s works)
drukletters (de) type
drukte (de) bustle; pressure of business; fuss
drukwerk (het) printed matter
druppel (de) drop, drip
druppelen to drip
dubbel double
dubbeldekker (de) double-decker

dubbelganger (de) double
dubbeltje (het) ten-cent piece
dubbel'zinnig ambiguous
dubbel'zinnigheid (de) ambiguity
dubi'eus doubtful
dubio: in – in doubt
duchten to dread
duchtig thorough, strong
duf musty
duidelijk clear, obvious
duidelijkheidshalve for clarity's sake
duiden op to point to
duif (de) dove, pigeon
duikboot (de) submarine
duikelen to tumble
duiken to dive; to plunge
duim (de) thumb
duin (het) dune
duister (de) dark: darkness
duisternis (de) darkness
Duitser (de) German
Duitsland Germany
duivel (de) devilish
duivels devilish
duiventil (de) dovecote(e)
duizelen to get dizzy or giddy
duizelig dizzy, giddy
duizeling (de) (fit of) dizziness, giddiness
duizeling'wekkend dizzy
duizend a thousand
duizendpoot (de) centipede
dulden to bear, to endure
dumpen dump
dun thin
dunk (de) opinion
dunken be of the opinion **me dunkt** indeed! **het dunkt mij...** I am of the opinion...
dunnen to thin
duo (het) duo, pair
duobaan (de) job share
du'peren to hit; to let down
dupli'caat (het) duplicate

duplo: in – to duplicate
duren to last
durven to dare
dus so
dus'danig (in) such (a way)
dusver: tot – thus far
dutje (het): een – doen to have a nap
dutten to doze
duur expensive; duration **op de(n) –** in time
duurzaam durable
duw (de) push, shove
duwen to push, to shove
dwaalspoor (het) wrong track
dwaas (de) fool: foolish
dwaasheid (de) foolishness
dwalen to wander; to err
dwaling (de) error
dwang (de) compulsion
dwangarbeid (de) hard labour
dwangarbeider (de) convict
dwangbuis (de) straightjacket
dwarrelen to whirl
dwars transverse; cross- grained **het zit me –** it worries me, it annoys me

dwarsbomen to thwart
dwars door straight through
dwarsdoorsne(d)e (de) cross-section
dwarsfluit (de) flute
dwarsliggen to be obstructive
dwarsligger (de) sleeper; troublemaker
dwarsschip (het) transept
dwarsstraat (de) side street: **neem maar een –** just an example
dweepziek fanatic
dweil (de) floorcloth; slut
dwepen met to think the world of; to rave about
dweper (de) zealot; fan(atic)
dwerg (de) dwarf, midget
dwingeland (de) tyrant; bully
dwingen to force
d.w.z.: dat wil zeggen i.e.
dyna'miek (de) dynamics, vitality
dy'namisch dynamic
dy'namo (de) dynamo
dys'lectisch dyslexic
dys'lexie (de) dyslexia

E

e.a.: en andere(n) et al.
eb (de) ebb (tide)
ebbenhout (het) ebony
echo (de) echo; ultrasound
echt real, genuine, thorough
echtelijk matrimonial
echter however
echtgenoot (de) husband
echtgenote (de) wife
echtheid (de) genuineness
echtpaar (het) married couple
echtscheiding (de) divorce
e'clips (de) eclipse
ecolo'gie (de) ecology
econo'mie (de) economy; economics

eco'nomisch economic; economical(ly)
eco'noom (de) economist
ec'zeem (het) eczema
e.d.: en dergelijke and the like
edel noble
Edel'achtbare Your Honour
edelgesteente (het) precious stone(s)
edel'moedig generous
edelsteen (de) gem
e'ditie (de) edition
educa'tief educational
eed (de) oath
eekhoorn (de) squirrel
eelt (het) hard skin

Insight

The word **een** has two different meanings, depending on the pronunciation. It means *a* or *an* when the double e is pronounced as the *a* in English *about*. However, it means *one* when the double e is pronounced as the *a* in English *late*. In this case, **een** may also be written with accents on the e's (**één**), although this is not compulsory.

een a(n); one **– en al** all; nothing but

eend (de) duck

eender the same

een'drachtig united

eenge'zinswoning (de) (small) family home

eenheid (de) unit(y)

eenheidsprijs (de) unit price; uniform price

eenhoorn (de) unicorn

een'jarig yearling

een'kennig shy

eenletter'grepig monosyllabic

eenmaal once **het is nu – zo** but there it is

eenper'soonskamer (de) single room

een'richtingsverkeer (het) one-way traffic

eens once, one day; just **het – zijn** to agree

eensge'zind as one, unanimous

eensge'zindheid (de) harmony, unanimity

eensklaps suddenly

eensluidend similar, true

een'stemmig in unison; with one accord

een'stemmig unanimous

eentje one **in je –** on your own

een'tonig monotonous

een'voudig simple

eenvoud (de) simplicity

eenzaam lonely, solitary

eenzaamheid (de) solitude

een'zelvig self-contained

een'zijdigheid (de) one-sidedness, bias

eer (de) honour **– aandoen** to do credit to

eerbetoon (het), eerbewijs (het) mark of honour, homage

eerbied (de) respect

eer'biedig respectful

eer'biedigen to respect

eerder before, sooner; rather

eer'gisteren (de) the day before yesterday

eerlijk honest, fair

eerst first, former **de eerste de beste** the first (man, opportunity) that comes along **ten eerste** in the first place **voor het –** for the first time

Eerste Kamer (de) Upper Chamber/House (of the Dutch parliament)

eersteklas first-rate, first-class

eervol honourable

eerzaam respectable

eerzucht (de) ambition

eer'zuchtig ambitious

eetbaar edible

eetgelegenheid (de) eating place

eetkamer (de) dining room

eetlepel (de) tablespoon
eetlust (de) appetite
eetservies (het) dinner service
eetstokje (het) chopstick
eetwaren (de) provisions
eetzaal dining hall
eeuw (de) century, age
eeuwfeest (het) centenary
eeuwig eternal, everlasting
eeuwigheid (de) eternity
ef'fecten stocks (and shares)
effec'tief effective
effen level, smooth
effenen to level, to smooth (down)
effici'ënt efficient
e'gaal smooth, uniform
egel (de) hedgehog
ego (het) ego
ego'centrisch egocentric,
 self-centred
EHBO (de) first aid
ei (het) egg
eicel (de) ovum
eierdooier (de) eggyolk
eierdopje (het) eggcup
eierstok (de) ovary
eigen (of one's) own; private
eigenaar (de) owner
eigen'aardig peculiar, strange
eigen'aardigheid (de) peculiarity
eigenbaat (het) egoism
eigenbelang (het) self-interest
eigendom (het) property
eigendomsbewijs (het) title-deeds
eigendunk (de) self-conceit
eigenge'maakt home-made
eigenge'reid opinionated
eigenlijk actual, proper, real
eigennaam (de) proper name
eigenschap (de) quality, property
eigenwaarde (de) self-respect
eigen'wijs self-opinionated,
 pig-headed, cocky
eigen'zinnig self-willed

eik (de) oak
eikel (de) acorn; glans (penis); oaf
eiland (het) island
eind (het) end(ing); length, distance
 ten einde raad at one's wits' end
einddiploma (het) school-leaving
 certificate
eindelijk at last
eindeloos endless, superb
eindexamen (het) school-leaving
 exam; final exam
eindigen to finish (off)
eindje (het) piece, bit; short distance
eindproduct (het) finished article
eindpunt (het) eindstation (het)
 terminus
eindsignaal (het) final whistle
 (in sport)
eis (de) demand, claim **aan de eisen
 voldoen** to satisfy the requirements
eisen to demand, to claim
eiser (de) plaintiff, prosecutor
eiwit (het) white of egg; protein
**EK: Euro'pees Kampi'oenschap
 (het)** European Championship
ekster (de) magpie
e'lan (het) élan
eland (de) elk
elas'tiek (het) elastic
elas'tiekje (het) rubber band
elders elsewhere
electo'raat (het) electorate
elektri'ciën (de) electrician
electrici'teit (de) electricity
e'lectrisch electric
elektro'cutie (de) electrocution
elek'tronisch electronic
ele'ment (het) element, component
elemen'tair elementary, basic
elf eleven; elf **op zijn elf-en-dertigst**
 at a snail's pace
elfde eleventh
elf'stedentocht (de) skating
 marathon in Friesland

elftal (het) eleven, team
elimi'neren to eliminate, to remove
eli'tair elitist
e'lite (de) elite
elk each, any
el'kaar, el'kander each other, one another **alles bij – genomen** all things considered **ik kan ze niet uit – houden** I can't tell one from the other **alles is voor –** everything has been arranged
elleboog (de) elbow
el'lende (de) misery
el'lendeling (de) rotter
el'lendig wretched, miserable; rotten
e-mail (de) e-mail
e-mailen to send an e-mail
e'mail (het) enamel
e'maillen enamelled
emanci'patie (de) emancipation, liberation
embleem (het) emblem
emi'greren to emigrate
emmer (de) pail
e'motie (de) emotion
emotio'neel emotional
em'pirisch empirical
emplo'yé (de) employee
en and **– ... –** both ... and
encyclope'die (de) (en)cyclopaedia
end (het) distance
enenmale: ten – absolutely
ener'gie (de) energy
ener'giek energetic
ener'giebedrijf (het) power company
ener'giebesparing (de) energy-saving
enerlei of the same kind
enerzijds on the one hand
en'fin in short **maar –** but there (it is)
eng narrow; horrible, creepy
engel (de) angel

Engeland England
Engels English
enig only, unique; marvellous; some, any, a few **zij is de enige** she is the only one
enigs'zins somewhat, in a way
enkel (de) ankle
enkel single, only
enkeling (de) individual
enkelvoud (het) singular
e'norm enormous
en'quête (de) poll, survey
en'quêteformulier (het) questionnaire
ensce'neren to stage(manage)
enten to graft
enthousi'ast enthusiastic
en'tree (de) entrance; entrée; admission
en'treegeld (het) admission charge
enz(ovoort) etc(etera), and so on
epide'mie (de) epidemic
epi'loog (de) epilogue
epos (het) epic
equivalent (het) equivalent
er there: of it, of them **– zijn –, die ...** there are those who ... **wat is –?** what's the matter?
er'aan on (it) **ik kom eraan** I'm on my way
er'achter behind (it)
er'barmelijk pitiable
er'bij there, included at; at it
erboven'op on top of it
ere- honorary, of honour
e'rectie (de) erection
eredienst (de) divine worship
eren to honour
erf (het) (farm)yard
erfelijk hereditary
erfelijkheid (de) heredity
erfenis (de) heritage, legacy
erfgenaam (de) heir
erfgename (de) heiress

erfgoed (het) inheritance
erfstuk (het) heirloom
erg bad; very (much) **zonder –** unintentionally **ik had er geen – in** I was not aware of it
ergens somewhere, anywhere
ergeren to annoy; to scandalize **zich – to** be vexed, to take offence **het is om je dood te –** it's infuriating
ergerlijk annoying, offensive
ergernis (de) annoyance, offence
er'kend recognized; acknowledged
er'kennen to recognize; to acknowledge, to admit
er'kentelijk grateful
erker (de) bay window
ernst (de) seriousness
ernstig serious
ertegen'aan on to it; **we gaan –** we're going for it/to tackle it
ertussen'in in between; in the middle
ertussen'uit out of it **een dagje –** a day out
er'uitzien to look; to look like; **ze ziet er niet goed uit!** she looks awful!
er'varen experienced
er'varen to experience
er'varing (de) experience
erven to inherit
erwt (de) pea
es (de) ash tree
esca'leren to escalate
esdoorn (de) maple tree
es'kader (het) eska'dron (het) squadron
es'sentie (de) essence
essenti'eel essential
esta'fette (de) relay race
e'tage (de) floor, storey
e'tagewoning (de) flat
eta'lage (de) shop window
e'tappe (de) stage, lap
eten (het) food; meal

eten to eat, to have a meal
etenstijd (de) dinnertime
etentje (het) dinner, (special) meal
e'thiek (de) ethics
ethisch ethical
eti'ket (het) label
etmaal (het) (space of) 24 hours
ets (de) etching
etsen to etch
ettelijke several
etter (de) pus; a pain in the neck, a nasty piece of work
etteren to fester
é'tui (het) pencil case
EU: Euro'pese Unie (de) European Union
euro (de) euro
eurocent (de) eurocent
Eu'ropa (het) Europe
europarlement (het) European Parliament
Europe'aan (de) European
euthana'sie (de) euthanasia
euvel (het) evil
evacuatie (de) evacuation
evacu'eren to evacuate
evalu'atie (de) evaluation, assessment
evalu'eren to evaluate, to assess
evan'gelisch evangelical
even even, equally; just (as) **het is mij om het –** it's all the same to me **– ... als** as ... as
evenaar (de) equator
evenals just as
eve'naren to equal
evenbeeld (het) image; likeness
even'eens likewise
evene'ment (het) event
evengoed (just) as well
evenmin ... als no more ... than
even'redig proportional
eventjes just (for) a moment
eventu'eel possible; by any chance

evenveel as much, as many
even'wel however
evenwicht (het) balance
evenwichtig (well-)balanced, level-headed
evenwichtstoestand (de) equilibrium
even'wijdig parallel
even'zeer as much
even'zo likewise
everzwijn (het) wild boar
e'xamen (het) examination
  een – afnemen to examine
excentrek eccentric
excu'seren to excuse
ex'cuus (het) excuse, apology

exem'plaar (het) specimen; copy
expe'ditie (de) expedition
exploi'tatie (de) operation; exploitation
expo'sitie (de) exhibition
e'xotisch exotic
experimen'teel experimental
ex'pres express
ex'tase (de) ecstasy
exteri'eur (het) exterior
ex'tern non-resident; external
extra extra; special
extraatje (het) bonus
ezel (de) ass, donkey; easel
ezelsbrug (de) mnemonic
ezelsoor (het) dog ear, donkey's ear

F

f., fl. (=florijn) guilder(s)
faam (de) fame, repute
fabel (de) fable, fabrication
fabelachtig fabulous
fabri'ceren to manufacture
fa'briek (de) factory
fabri'kaat (het) manufacture
fabri'kant (de) manufacturer
fa'cet (het) aspect, facet
facili'teit (de) facility, amenity
fac'tuur (de) invoice
facul'teit (de) faculty
fa'got (de) bassoon
fail'liet bankrupt
faillisse'ment (het) bankruptcy
fakkel (de) torch
falen to fail
fal'set (het) falsetto
fa'meus famous, wonderful
familiair familiar, informal
fa'milie (de) family, relation(s)
fa'miliekwaal (de) hereditary disease
fa'naticus (de) fanatic
fanatiek fanatical

fana'tisme (het) fanaticism
fanta'seren to indulge in fantasies
fanta'sie (de) fantasy, fancy, imagination
fan'tastisch fantastic, fabulous
fas'cisme (het) fascism
fasci'neren to fascinate, captivate
fase (de) phase
fa'taal fatal
fat'soen (het) decency, good manners **houd je –** behave yourself
fat'soenlijk decent, respectable
fau'teuil (de) armchair
faxen to fax
fa'zant (de) pheasant
febru'ari February
fee (de) fairy
feeë'riek fairy-like
feeks (de) shrew
feest (het) feast, festival, fête
feestelijk festive
feestje (het) party
feestmaal (het) banquet
feestvarken (het) person giving a party

feestvieren to celebrate, to go on a spree
feilbaar fallible
feilloos faultless
feit (het) fact
feitelijk actual
fel fierce
felici'tatie (de) congratulation
felici'teren met to congratulate on
femi'nistisch feminist
fenome'naal phenomenal
ferm firm; brave
fes'tijn (het) feast
fê'teren to fête
feuille'ton (de) serial story
fi'asco (het) disaster, failure, flop
fiche (het) counter; token (in a game)
fic'tief fictitious
fier proud, undaunted
fiets (de) bicycle
fietsen to cycle
figu'rant (de) extra (films); super (numerary)
figu'reren to figure
fi'guur (het, de) figure; character
  een gek – slaan to cut a ridiculous figure
fi'guurlijk figurative, metaphorical
fijn fine; subtle
fijnge'voelig sensitive
fijnproever (de) connoisseur
fijntjes nicely, subtly
fik (de) (inf) fire

fikken (inf) to burn
fiks robust, vigorous; brave
fiksen to fix (something); manage
file (de) line, row; traffic jam
fi'leren to fillet
fi'let (het, de) fillet, filet (of meat)
  – américain steak tartare
filhar'monisch philharmonic
fili'aal (het) branch (establishment)
filmkeuring (de) film censorship, board of film censors
filmopname (de) film shot; to make a film of
filter (de, het) filter; percolator
filteren to filter
fi'naal final; quite
financi'eel financial
fi'nanciën (de) finance(s)
finan'cieren to finance
fi'neer (het) veneer
fi'neren to veneer; to refine
fi'nesses (de), details
finishen to finish
fin'geren to feign; to invent
firma (de) firm
fiscus (de) treasurer, treasury
fit fit, fresh
fix'eren to fix; to look intently at
fladderen to flutter; to flit
flakkeren to flicker
fla'neren to saunter, to parade, to stroll

Insight

Besides the meanings *fine* and *subtle*, **fijn** also frequently means *nice* or *lovely*. You can ask someone **heb je een fijne dag gehad?** *did you have a nice day?* Or you can wish someone **een fijn weekend!** *have a nice weekend*. And coming back from holiday you can tell your friends and family **het was een fijne vakantie** *it was a great holiday*.

flan'keren to flank
flappen: eruit – to blurt out
flapuit (de) blabber
flarden (de) tatters **aan –** in rags; to shreds
flater (de) blunder **een – slaan** to make a blunder
flat'teren to flatter, to be becoming
flat'teus flattering
flauw insipid, feeble, faint
flauwe'kul (de) nonsense, rubbish
flauwte (de) fainting fit
flauwtjes faintly
flensje (het) thin pancake
fles (de) bottle
flesopener (de) bottle opener
flesvoeding (de) bottle feeding; baby milk/formula
flets lacklustre, pale
fleurig colourful
flikkeren to flicker
flink tough, capable; considerable
flits (de) flash
flitsend stylish, snappy
flodderig shapeless, flimsy
flonkeren to sparkle, to twinkle
floppen to flop
floppydisk (de) floppy disk
flo'reren to flourish
floris'sant flourishing
fluisteren to whisper
fluit (de) flute
fluiten to whistle
fluitje (het) whistle
fluitketel (de) whistling kettle
flu'weel (het) velvet
fnuiken to break, to ruin
fnuikend fatal
foefje (het) trick, dodge
foei'lelijk as ugly as sin
foelie (de) mace
foeteren to rage, to grumble
föhn (de) hair dryer, blow dryer
fokken to breed

folder (de) leaflet, brochure
folie (de) (tin) foil
folteren to torture
fonds (het) fund
fonkelen to sparkle
fon'tein (de) fountain
fon'teintje (het) small handbasin
fooi (de) tip
foppen to hoax
fopspeen (de) baby's dummy
for'ceren to force; to strain
fo'rel (de) trout
fo'rens (de) season ticket holder, commuter
for'maat (het) size; stature
formali'teit (de) formality
formateur (de) person charged with forming a new government
for'meel formal
formi'dabel formidable
for'mule (de) formula
formu'lier (het) form
for'nuis (het) cooker
fors robust, strong, vigorous
fort (het) forte; fort(ification)
for'tuin (het) fortune
for'tuinlijk fortunate
fos'siel (het) fossil
fotogra'feren to photograph, to take a photograph (of)
fouil'leren to search (a person)
fourni'turen (de) haberdashery
fout (de) mistake, fault, error
fou'tief wrong, erroneous
fraai nice; handsome
fractie (de) fraction; group
fractieleider (de) leader of a parliamentary party
fragmen'tarisch fragmentary
fram'boos (de) raspberry
franje (de) fringe
fran'keren to stamp
Frankrijk France
frap'pant striking

frase (de) phrase
fratsen (de) pranks
fraude (de) fraud
fraudu'leus fraudulent
fre'gat (het) frigate
fre'quent frequent
friemelen to fumble
fries (het, de) frieze
Fries Frisian
friet (de) chips, fries
fris (het, de) soft drink
fris fresh, refreshing; airy;
  chilly, cool **het is frisjes vanavond**
  it's chilly this evening
frisdrank (de) soft drink
fri'turen to deep-fry

fruitautomaat (de) slot machine
fri'vool frivolous
frommelen to crumple
fronsen to frown
fruiten to fry, to sauté
frus'tratie (de) frustration
functie (de) to function
functio'naris (de) functionary
functio'neren to function
fun'dering (de) foundation
fu'nest fatal
fun'geren to function
fu'seren to merge (with)
fusie (de) merger, fusion
fut (de) spirit, go
futloos lifeless

G

gaaf sound, whole; great
gaai (de) jay
gaaies (het) riffraff
gaan to go **hoe gaat het?** how are
  you (getting on)? **het gaat om ...**
  it is a question of ...; it is about
gaande afoot, going
gaandeweg gradually
gaar cooked, done
gaarkeuken (de) communal kitchen
gaarne gladly
gaas (het) gauze; wire netting
gaatje (het) small hole **ik heb nog**
  een – op donderdag I can just fit
  (that) in on Thursday
gabber (de) mate, pal
gade spouse
gadeslaan to watch
gading (de) liking **iets van je –**
  vinden to find something you like
gal (de) bile, gall
gal'lant courteous
gale'rie (de) (art) gallery
gale'rij (de) gallery, walkway
galg (de) gallows

galmen to resound, to reverberate
ga'lop (de) gallop
gammel ramshackle
gang (de) passage; gait; way **aan**
  de – going, working **op –** in form;
  (in) working (order) **ga je –** go
  ahead; help yourself
gangbaar current, available
gans (de) goose
gapen to yawn; to gape
gappen to pinch
ga'rage (de) garage
garan'deren to guarantee
ga'rantie (de) guarantee, warranty
garde (de) guard(s); whisk
garde'robe (de) wardrobe;
  cloakroom
ga'reel (het) horse collar, harness
  in het – lopen to toe the line
garen (het) thread
garen to gather
gar'naal (de) shrimp
gasfabriek (de) gasworks
gasleiding (de) gas pipe(s),
  gas main(s)

gasmeter (de) gas meter
gaspedaal (het, de) accelerator
gaspit (de) gasring, gas jet
gasstel (het) gas ring(s)
gast (de) guest
gastarbeider (de) immigrant worker
gastheer (de) host
gastvrij hospitable
gast'vrijheid (de) hospitality
gastvrouw (de) hostess
gat (het) hole **in de gaten krijgen**
  to spot **in de gaten houden**
  to keep an eye on
gauw quick
gave (de) gift
ga'zon (het) lawn
ge'aardheid (de) disposition
ge'acht: Geachte Heer/Mevrouw
  Dear Sir/Madam
geaffec'teerd affected
gealli'eerd allied
geani'meerd animated, lively
ge'armd arm in arm
ge'baar (het) gesture
ge'baard bearded
ge'bak (het) fancy cake(s)
ge'barentaal (de) sign language
ge'bed (het) prayer
ge'bergte (het) mountain range
ge'beten zijn op to have a grudge
  against
ge'beuren to happen
ge'beurtenis (de) event
ge'bied (het) territory; field, realm
ge'bieden to order
ge'bit (het) set of teeth
ge'bladerte (het) foliage
ge'bod (het) command(ment)
ge'boorte (de) birth
ge'boortecijfer (het) birth rate
ge'boortekaartje (het) birth
  announcement card
ge'boorteland (het) native country
ge'boren born

ge'bouw (het) building
ge'brek (het) lack; failing; infirmity
ge'brekkig defective, faulty;
  deformed
ge'broeders (de) brothers
gebrouil'leerd not on speaking
  terms
ge'bruik (het) use; custom
ge'bruikelijk customary
ge'bruiken to use; to partake of
gebruikers'vriendelijk user-friendly
ge'bruiksaanwijzing (de) directions
  for use
gechar'meerd: ik ben niet zo — van
  I am not that keen on/I am not
  really taken with
gecompli'ceerd complicated
ge'daagde (de) defendant
ge'daante (de) form, shape
ge'daanteverwisseling (de)
  metamorphosis
gedachte (de) thought
ge'dachteloos thoughtless
ge'dachtengang (de) train of
  thought
ge'dagvaarde (de) person
  summoned
ge'deelte (het) part
ge'deeltelijk partly
gedele'geerde (de) delegate
ge'dempt subdued, muffled, hushed
ge'denkdag (de) anniversary
ge'denken to commemorate
ge'denkteken (het) monument
gedenk'waardig memorable
gedepu'teerde (de) deputy
ge'dicht (het) poem
ge'dienstig obliging
ge'dijen to thrive
ge'ding (het) lawsuit; issue
gediplo'meerd qualified
gedistil'leerd distilled
gedistin'geerd distinguished-
  looking

ge'doe (het) fuss; business
ge'dogen to permit
ge'donder (het) thunder; trouble; messing around
ge'drag (het) behaviour
ge'dragen: zich – to behave
ge'dragslijn (de) policy
ge'drang (het) crowd, crush
ge'drocht (het) monstrosity
ge'drongen thick-set; impelled
ge'druis (het) rumbling, roaring
ge'ducht formidable
ge'duld (het) patience
ge'duldig patient
ge'durende during
ge'durfd daring; risky
ge'dwee submissive
geel yellow
geelzucht (de) jaundice
geen not a, not any, no
geënga'geerd zijn to be committed
geenszins by no means
geest (de) spirit; mind; wit
geest'dodend soul-destroying
geestdrift (de) enthusiasm
geestelijk spiritual, mental
geestelijke (de) priest
geestig witty
geestigheid (de) wit, witticism
geestkracht (de) fortitude
geestverruimend mind-expanding; hallucinogenic
geestverwant (de) kindred spirit
geeuw(en) (to) yawn
gefortu'neerd wealthy
ge'gadigde (de) prospective buyer; applicant
ge'gevens (de) data
ge'goed well-off
ge'grond well-founded
ge'haaid canny
ge'hakt (het) minced meat (beef)
ge'halte (het) content; quality

ge'hard seasoned; injured; tempered
ge'harrewar (het) bickering
ge'havend battered
ge'heel (het) whole, all, quite **in het – niet** not at all
ge'heelonthouder (de) teetotaller
ge'heim (het) secret
ge'heimschrift (het) (secret) code
geheim'zinnig mysterious
ge'hemelte (het) palate
ge'heugen (het) memory
ge'hoor (het) hearing, ear; audience, congregation
ge'hoorapparaat (het) hearing aid
ge'hoorzaal (de) auditorium
ge'hoorzaam obedient
ge'hoorzaamheid (de) obedience
ge'hoorzamen to obey
ge'horig far from sound-proof, noisy
ge'hucht (het) hamlet
ge'huichel (het) hypocrisy
ge'huisvest housed
gehu'meurd: goed – good-tempered
ge'ijkt standard, traditional, common
geil horny, randy; rank
gein (de) fun
geinig funny
geintje (het) joke
geïrri'teerd irritated; irritable
geiser (de) geyser
geit (de) goat
ge'jaagd agitated
gek mad, foolish; idiot **voor de – houden** to make a fool of
gekheid (de) foolishness, joke
gekkekoeienziekte (de) BSE, mad cow disease
ge'kleurd coloured **je staat er – op** you look silly
ge'klungel (het) bungling
gekostu'meerd in fancy dress

Insight

Sometimes you will find two dots on a Dutch vowel, such as in geïrriteerd *irritated*. The two dots are called de **trema** and are used to help your pronunciation, i.e. the trema indicates the start of a new syllable. Without the trema on the i in geïrriteerd, we would have had to pronounce **geir** as one syllable, but with the trema we know that a new syllable starts on the i. This means the word breaks down into syllables as follows: **ge-ir-ri-teerd**, with the stress on the final syllable, indicated with an apostrophe in the dictionary.

ge'knipt voor cut out for
gekscheren to joke
ge'kunsteld artificial
ge'laat (het) countenance; face
ge'laatskleur (de) complexion
ge'laatstrek (de) feature
ge'lang: naar – van according to
ge'lasten to order
ge'laten resigned
geld (het) money
gelden to apply, to count **zich doen – ** to assert oneself **de algemeen geldende mening** the generally accepted view
geldig valid
geldstuk (het) coin
geldwolf (de) money grubber
geldzuivering (de) currency reform
ge'leden ago
ge'leerd learned
ge'leerde (de) scholar, scientist
ge'legen situated; convenient **er is veel aan – ** much depends on it
ge'legenheid (de) occasion, opportunity; place
ge'leide (de) escort
ge'leidelijk gradually
ge'leiden to conduct
ge'letterd lettered
ge'lid (het) rank, file, order
ge'liefd beloved, popular

ge'liefkoosd favourite
ge'lieven to please
ge'lijk equal, alike; level **je hebt – ** you are right **iemand – geven** to agree with a person
ge'lijkenis (de) resemblance; parable
gelijkge'zind like-minded
ge'lijkheid (de) equality
gelijk'matig equable; even
gelijk'tijdig simultaneous
gelijk'vloers on the ground floor; on the same floor
ge'lofte (de) vow
ge'loof (het) belief, faith
geloof'waardig credible
ge'loven to believe, to think
ge'lovig faithful
gelovige (de) believer
ge'luid (het) sound
ge'luidloos noiseless
ge'luidshinder (de) noise pollution
ge'luidsinstallatie (de) sound equipment
ge'luk (het) luck, good fortune; happiness
ge'lukkig happy; fortunate, lucky
ge'luksvogel (de) lucky one
ge'lukwens (de) congratulation

ge'lukwensen to congratulate
ge'maakt affected, feigned; ready-
made
ge'maal (het) pumping engine
ge'mak (het) ease; comfort;
convenience
ge'makkelijk easy, comfortable;
convenient
ge'makshalve for the sake
of convenience
gemak'zuchtig lazy
ge'matigd temperate; moderate
gember (de) ginger
ge'meen (in) common; foul, nasty
ge'meend sincere
ge'meenplaats (de) platitude
ge'meenschap (de) community;
(sexual) intercourse
gemeen'schappelijk common, joint
ge'meenschapsgevoel (het) public
spirit
ge'meente (de) municipality;
congregation; parish
ge'meentebelasting (de) (local)
rates
ge'meentelijk municipal
ge'meenteraad (de) council
ge'meenteraadsverkiezing (de)
council elections
ge'meentereiniging (de)
environmental health department
of the council
gemelijk peevish
ge'middeld average
ge'mis (het) lack, want, loss
ge'moed (het) heart, mind,
feeling(s)
ge'moedelijk kindly, informal
ge'moedsrust (de) peace of mind
ge'moeid involved
gems (de) chamois
ge'mutst: goed — in a good mood
ge'naamd named
ge'nade (de) grace; mercy; pardon

ge'nadeloos merciless
ge'nadeslag (de) finishing stroke
gen (het) gene
gene that; the other deze en —
several people
ge'neesheer (de) physician
genees'krachtig curative
ge'neeskunde (de) medicine
ge'neesmiddel (het) remedy;
medicine
ge'negen willing; inclined, disposed
ge'negenheid (de) affection
ge'neigd inclined, prone
gene'raal (de) general
generale repetitie (de) dress
rehearsal
generen to embarrass zich —
to feel embarrassed
ge'netisch genetic
ge'nezen to cure, to heal; to recover
ge'nezing (de) cure; recovery
geni'aal brilliant
ge'nie (het) military; engineers;
(man of) genius
ge'niepig underhand
ge'nieten (van) to enjoy
ge'nodigden (de) invited guests
ge'noeg enough
ge'noegdoening (de) satisfaction,
reparation
ge'noegen (het) pleasure
ge'noeglijk pleasant
ge'noegzaam sufficient
ge'nootschap (het) society,
association
ge'not (het) joy, delight
genuan'ceerd subtle
geo'graaf (de) geographer
geo'loog (de) geologist
ge'oorloofd permitted
ge'ordend regulated, orderly
georgani'seerd organized
georiën'teerd (op) with leanings
towards, minded

ge'paard gaan met to be accompanied by

ge'past fitting, seemly **– geld** the exact amount

ge'peins (het) pondering

ge'peperd peppered, pungent

gepi'keerd offended, piqued, nettled

ge'prikkeld irritated, irritable

gepromo'veerd promoted; holding a doctor's degree

ge'raamte (het) skeleton

ge'raden advisable

geraffi'neerd refined; unmitigated; artful

ge'raakt offended, moved

ge'raken to become, to get

ge'raspt grated

ge'recht (het) dish (food)

ge'rechtelijk judicial, legal

ge'rechtigd entitled

ge'rechtigheid (de) justice

ge'rechtshof (het) court of justice

ge'reed ready

ge'reedschap (het) tools

gerefor'meerd Dutch Reformed, Calvinist(ic)

ge'regeld regular

ge'remd inhibited

gerenom'meerd renowned

ge'rief(e)lijk comfortable

ge'ring small, slight

ge'roezemoes (het) buzz, bustle

gerouti'neerd experienced

ge'rucht (het) rumour; noise

ge'ruchtmakend sensational

ge'ruim ample

ge'ruisloos noiseless

ge'ruit checked

ge'rust easy **neem (het) maar –** you're welcome (to it)

ge'ruststellen to reassure

ge'schater (het) peals of laughter

ge'schenk (het) present

ge'schieden to happen, to come about

ge'schiedenis (de) history; story; affair

geschied'kundig historical

ge'schiedschrijver (de) historian

ge'schift nuts, crazy

ge'schikt suitable; decent

ge'schil (het) dispute

ge'schoold trained, skilled

ge'schrift (het) writing

ge'schut (het) artillery

gesel (de) whip

geselen to whip, to lash

gesterili'seerd sterilized

ge'situeerd: goed – well-off

ge'slaagd successful

ge'slacht (het) stock; generation; sex; gender

ge'slachtsdelen (de) genitals

ge'slachtsziekte (de) venereal disease

ge'slepen cunning; sharpened **– glas** cut glass

ge'sloten close(d); uncommunicative

ge'sluierd veiled

gesp (de) buckle, clasp

ge'spannen tense, strained

gespen to buckle

ge'spierd muscular

ge'spikkeld speckled, dotted

ge'sprek (het) conversation

ge'spuis (het) rabble

ge'stadig steady

ge'stalte (de) figure; stature

ge'stel (het) constitution

ge'steldheid (de) condition; nature, character

ge'stemd tuned; disposed

ge'sticht (het) institution

ge'streept striped

ge'strest stressed

ge'stroomlijnd streamlined

getai'lleerd tailored, close-fitting

ge'tal (het) number
ge'tand toothed, cogged
ge'tij (het) tide
ge'tikt crazy
ge'tint tinted
ge'tob (het) worry(ing)
ge'tralied barred, latticed
ge'troosten: zich veel moeite –
  to take great pains
ge'trouw faithful
ge'trouwd married
ge'tuige (de) witness
ge'tuigen to testify
ge'tuigenis (de) testimony, evidence
ge'tuigschrift (het) certificate;
  testimonial
geul (de) channel; gully
geur (de) scent **iets in geuren**
  en kleuren vertellen to go into
  elaborate details about something
geuren to smell
geurig fragrant
ge'vaar (het) danger
ge'vaarlijk dangerous
ge'vaarte (het) huge object
ge'val (het) case **in geen –**
  on no account
ge'vangene (de) prisoner
ge'vangenis (de) prison
ge'vangenschap (de) imprisonment
gevari'eerd varied
ge'vat quick-witted
ge'vecht (het) fight
gevel (de) façade
geven to give **het geeft niets**
  it does not matter; it is no use
gever (de) donor
ge'vestigd settled, established
ge'vleugeld winged
ge'vlij: bij iemand in het – komen
  to worm oneself into a person's
  favour
ge'voel (het) feeling, sense
ge'voelig sensitive; tender

ge'voelloos numb; unfeeling
ge'voelsmens (het) emotional
  person
ge'vogelte (het) birds, poultry
ge'volg (het) consequence; retinue
  – geven aan to comply with
ge'volgtrekking (de) conclusion
ge'waad (het) garment
ge'waagd bold, *risqué* **aan elkaar –**
  well-matched
ge'waarworden to become aware of
ge'waarwording (de) sensation
gewapender'hand by force of arms
ge'was (het) vegetation, crops
ge'weer (het) gun, rifle
ge'wei (het) antlers
ge'weld (het) violence, force
  – aandoen to violate
geweld'dadig violent
ge'weldig terrific
ge'welf (het) vault
ge'welfd vaulted, domed
ge'wennen to accustom
ge'west (het) region
ge'westelijk regional
ge'weten (het) conscience
ge'wetenloos unprincipled
ge'wetensbezwaar (het)
  conscientious objection
ge'wezen late, ex-
ge'wicht (het) weight; importance
ge'wichtig weighty; important
  – doen to be pompous
ge'wiekst smart
ge'wild in demand
ge'willig willing
ge'wond wounded, injured
ge'woon usual, ordinary,
  accustomed
ge'woonlijk usually
ge'woonte (de) custom, habit
ge'woonweg simply
ge'wricht (het) joint
ge'wrongen laboured; twisted

ge'zag (het) authority, command
ge'zaghebbend authoritative
ge'zagvoerder (de) captain, pilot
ge'zamenlijk joint; complete
ge'zang (het) singing; hymn
ge'zant (de) ambassador, minister
ge'zapig slow, lethargic
ge'zegde (het) (old) saying;
  predicate
ge'zel (de) mate, companion
ge'zellig cosy; pleasant; sociable
ge'zelschap (het) company, party
ge'zet corpulent; set
ge'zicht (het) sight; face
ge'zichtsbedrog (het) optical
  illusion
ge'zichtsvermogen (het) (eye)sight
ge'zichtspunt (het) point of view
ge'zichtsveld (het) field of vision
ge'zien seen; highly thought of;
  in view of
ge'zin (het) family
ge'zind disposed, minded
ge'zocht sought (after), far-fetched
ge'zond healthy, sound
gezondheid (de) health
ge'zwel (het) tumour, swelling
ge'zwollen swollen; bombastic
gids (de) guide
giechelen to giggle
gier (de) vulture
gierig miserly
gierigheid (de) avarice
gietbui (de) downpour
gieten to pour; to cast
gieter (de) watering can
gietijzer (het) cast iron
gif(t) (het) poison
gift (de) donation, contribution
giftig poisonous; venomous
gi'gantisch gigantic, huge
gij thou, ye, you
gijzelaar (de) hostage
gijzelen to take as a hostage

gil (de) scream, shriek
gilde (de) guild
gillen to yell
ginder, ginds over there
ginnegappen to giggle
gips (het) gypsum, plaster (of Paris)
gipsafgietsel (het) plaster cast
gi'reren to pay by giro
giro (de) giro; giro account;
  bank/giro transfer
girobe'taalkaart (de) giro cheque
gissen to guess
gissing (de) guess
gist (de) yeast
gisten to ferment
gisteren yesterday
gister'avond last night
gisting (de) ferment(ation)
gi'taar (de) guitar
gitzwart jet-black
glaasje (het) small glass
glad smooth, slippery; glib, cunning
gladheid (de) slipperiness
glans (de) gloss, sheen, lustre
glansrijk brilliant
glanzen to shine, to gleam
glanzig glossy
glas (het) glass
glashelder crystal clear
glazen (made of) glass
glazenwasser (de) window-cleaner
glazenwisser (de) squeegee
glazig glassy, waxy
gla'zuren to glaze, to ice
gletscher gletsjer (de) glacier
gleuf (de) groove, slit, slot
gleufhoed (de) trilby
glibberen to slither
glijbaan (de) slide
glijden to slide; to glide
glimlach (de) smile
glimlachen to smile
glimmen to shine, to gleam
glimp (de) glimpse

glimworm (de) glow-worm
glinsteren to glitter, to glisten
glippen to slip
glo'baal rough, broad
gloed (de) glow; blaze; ardour
gloednieuw brand-new
gloeidraad (de) filament
gloeien to glow **gloeiend heet** burning hot
gloeilamp (de) electric light bulb
glooien to slope
glooiing (de) slope
glorie (de) glory
glorierijk glori'eus glorious
gluiper(d) (de) sneak
gluiperig sneak
glunderen to beam (with joy)
gluren to peer
gniffelen, gnuiven to laugh in one's sleeve
goddelijk divine
goddeloos godless
godgeklaagd crying (to heaven)
godgeleerdheid (de) theology
go'din (de) goddess
godsdienst (de) religion
godsdienstwaanzin (de) religious mania
godslasteraar (de) blasphemer
gods'lasterlijk blasphemous
goed good; well
goe'daardig good-natured; benign
goederen (de) goods
goed'geefs generous
goedge'lovig credulous
goedge'zind well-disposed
goed'hartig kind-hearted
goedheid (de) kindness
goedig sweet-natured
goedje (het) stuff
goedkeuren to approve of
goedkeuring (de) approval, assent
goed'koop cheap
goed'lachs easily amused

goed'moedig good-natured
goedpraten to explain away
goedschiks of kwaadschiks willing or unwilling
goedvinden to approve
goeierd (de) kind soul
gokken to gamble, to chance
gokker (de) gambler
golf (de) wave; bay; gulf
golfbreker (de) breakwater
golflengte (de) wave-length
golfslag (de) dashing of the waves
golven to wave, to undulate
gom (de) gum; rubber
gondel (de) gondola
gonzen to buzz
goochelaar (de) conjurer, juggler
goochela'rij (de) conjuring, juggling
goochelen to conjure, to juggle
goochem smart
gooi (de) throw
gooien to fling, to throw
goor dingy; rank
goot (de) gutter; drain
gootsteen (de) (kitchen) sink
gordel (de) belt; girdle
gordelroos (de) shingles
gor'dijn (het) curtain
gorgelen to gargle
gort (de) pearl barley
gortig: het te – maken to go too far **dat is me toch te –** that's more than I can take
gotisch gothic
goud (het) gold
gouden gold(en)
goudmijn (de) goldmine
graad (de) degree, rank, grade
gradenboog (de) protractor
graaf (de) count, earl
graafschap (het) county
graafwerk (het) excavation(s)

graag eager; gladly **(ja)** – yes please
  ik zou – willen weten I would
  (dearly) like to know
graaien to rummage; to grab
graan (het) grain, corn
graanschuur (de) granary
graansoorten (de) cereals
graat (de) fishbone
grabbel: te – gooien to throw away
grabbelen to scramble; to win
  in lucky dip
grabbelton (de) lucky dip
gracht (de) (town) canal; moat
graf (het) grave, sepulchre
gra'fiek (de) graph
grafkelder (de) (family) vault
grafschrift (het) epitaph
grafstem (de) sepulchral voice
grafzerk (de) tombstone
gram (het) gram
gram'matica (de) grammar
gra'naat (de) shell, grenade
gra'naatappel (de) pomegranate
gra'naatscherf (de) (piece of)
  shrapnel
gra'niet (het) granite
grap (de) joke **voor de –** for fun
grapjas (de), grappenmaker
  (de) wag
grappig funny
gras (het) grass
grasduinen to browse
grashalm (de) grasspriet (de)
  blade of grass
graszode (de) turf, sod
gratie (de) grace; free pardon; favour
  uit de – zijn being out of favour
grati'eus graceful
gratifi'catie (de) bonus
grauw grey, drab
grauwen to snarl, to growl
graven to dig
gra'veren to engrave
gra'vin (de) countess

gra'vure (de) engraving
grazen to graze **iemand te –**
  nemen to take someone for a ride
greep (de) grip; grasp; hilt
grendel (de) bolt
grendelen to bolt
grenen (de) deal; pinewood
grens (de) bound(ary), frontier, limit
grensgeval (het) borderline case
grensrechter (de) linesman
grenzen aan to border on
grenzeloos boundless
greppel (de) field drain;
  narrow ditch
gretig eager
Griekenland Greece
Griek(s)(se) (de) Greek (woman)
grienen to sniffle
griep (de) flu
griezel monstrosity
griezelen to shudder
griezelig gruesome
grif readily
grif'fier (de) clerk of the court
grijns (de) grin, sneer
grijnzen to sneer, to grin
grijpen to seize
grijs grey
grijsaard (de) old man
gril (de) caprice
grillig capricious
gri'mas (de) grimace
grime (de) (stage) make-up
grimmig grim
grinniken to chuckle, to snigger
grint (het) gravel
grissen to snatch
groef (de) groove; furrow
groeien to grow
groeistuipen (de) growing pains
groen green
groente(n) (de) vegetables
groenteboer (de) greengrocer
groep (de) group

groe'peren to group, to cluster (around)

groepsgewijze in groups

groet (de) salute, greeting **de groeten doen** to give one's kind regards

groeten to greet, to nod good-day

groezelig grubby

grof coarse; rude; gross **– geld verdienen** to earn big money

grommen to growl, to grumble

grond (de) ground, earth, soil **in de – van de zaak** basically **te gronde gaan** to go to pieces

grondbeginsel (het) basic principle

grondbelasting (de) land tax

grondbezitter (de) landowner

grondgebied (het) territory

grondig thorough

grondslag (de) foundation

grondstof (de) raw material

grondverf (de) undercoat

grondwet (de) constitution

grond'wettelijk constitutional

groot large, big, great, tall **in het –** on a large scale

grootbrengen to bring up

groothandel (de) wholesale trade

grootheid (de) magnitude

grootheidswaanzin (de) megalomania

groothouden: zich – to put a brave face on it

grootmoeder (de) grandmother

groot'moedig magnanimous

grootouders (de) grandparents

groots grand(iose)

grootscheeps large-scale

grootsheid (de) grandeur

grootspraak (de) boasting

grootte (de) size

grootvader (de) grandfather

gros (het) gross; majority

gros'sier (de) wholesaler

grot (de) grotto, cave

grotendeels for the greater part

gruis (het) grit, slack

gruizele'menten (de) smithereens

grut: klein – little ones

gruwel (de) atrocity, horror

gruweldaad (de) atrocity

gruwelijk horrible

gruwen to shudder; to abhor

guitig mischievous

gul open-handed

gulden (de) guilder

gulheid (de) generosity

gulp (de) fly

gulzig greedy

gum (de) rubber, eraser

gunnen to grant **het is je gegund** you're welcome to it

gunst (de) favour

gunstig favourable

gutsen to gush

guur bleak, raw

gym (de) gymnastics; **gym'nasium (het)** grammar school

gymnas'tiek (de) gymnastics

gymnas'tiekzaal (de) gymnasium

gympen gym shoes, trainers

H

haag (de) hedge

(Den) Haag The Hague

haai (de) shark

haak (de) hook **niet in de –** not all that it should be **tussen haakjes** in brackets; by the way

haaknaald (de), haakpen (de) crochet hook

haal (de) (pen) stroke; pull

haalbaar attainable, feasible

haan (de) cock **daar kraait geen – naar** nobody will be any the wiser

haar (het) hair **het scheelde maar een –** it was touch and go
haar her
haard (de) stove; centre; hotbed
  open – (de) fireplace
haardos (de) head of hair
haarfijn minutely **iets – uitleggen** to explain something in great detail
haarklove'rij (de) hair-splitting
haarspeld (de) hairclip
haarspeldbocht (de) hairpin bend
haarspoeling (de) hair colouring
haaruitval (de) hair loss
haas (de) hare
haast almost; haste
haasten: zich – to hurry
haastig hasty
haat (de) hatred
haat'dragend vindictive
hachelijk precarious
hachje (het): bang voor zijn – afraid to risk one's life
hage'dis (de) lizard
hagel (de) hail; shot
hagelen to hail
hagelwit white as snow
hak (de) (shoe)heel **van de – op de tak springen** to jump from one subject to another **iemand een – zetten** to play a person a dirty trick
hakblok (het) chopping block
haken to crochet; to hook
hakenkruis (het) swastika
hakkelen to stammer
hakken to chop, to hack
hakmes (het) cleaver
hal (de) hall
halen to fetch, to get; to catch
  hij haalt het nooit he will never manage it **dat haalt er niet bij** there's no comparison
half half, semi- **– zes** half past five
half'gaar underdone; half-witted
halfgod (de) demigod

halfrond (het) hemisphere
half'slachtig half-hearted
half'stok at half mast
halm (de) stalk, blade
hals (de) neck
halsband (de) (dog)collar
halssnoer (het) necklace
hals'starrig stubborn
halte (de) stop(ping place)
hal'veren to halve
halverwege half-way
hamer (de) hammer, mallet
hameren to hammer
hamsteren to hoard
hand (de) hand **handen thuis!** hands off! **de handen uit de mouw steken** to get down to it **er is niets aan de –** there is nothing wrong **met de handen in het haar** at one's wits' end **op handen dragen** to worship **van de – doen** to dispose of **voor de – liggen** to be obvious
handbagage (de) hand luggage
handboeien (de) handcuffs
handdoek (de) towel
handdruk (de) handshake
handel (de) trade **in de –** in business; on the market
handelaar (de) dealer
handelbaar handy; pliant
handelen to act; to trade
handeling (de) act(ion)
handelsakkoord (het) trade agreement
handelsbetrekkingen (de) trade relations
handelsrecht (het) commercial law
handelswaren (de) merchandise
handelswijze (de) method(s) (of dealing), behaviour
handgemeen worden to come to blows
handgreep (de) grip, handle

handhaven to maintain
handig handy, deft
handlanger (de) accomplice
handleiding (de) manual
handrem (de) hand break
handschoen (de) glove
handschrift (het) manuscript; handwriting
hand'tastelijk aggressive, violent **– zijn** to touch up
handtastelijkheden (de) blows, fighting; pawing
handtekening (de) signature; autograph
handvat (het) handle
handvest (het) charter
handwerk (het) (handi)craft; needlework
handwerken to do needlework
hangen to hang
hangend(e) drooping; pending
hanger (de) (coat)hanger; pendant
hangerig listless
hangmat (de) hammock
hangslot (het) padlock
han'teerbaar manageable
han'teren to handle, to operate
hap (de) mouthful, bite
haperen to falter **er hapert iets** there is a hitch somewhere
happen to take a mouthful
happig keen, eager
hard hard **– nodig** very necessary **ik heb er een – hoofd in** I have my doubts (about the result)
harden to harden, to temper **ik kon het niet langer –** I couldn't stand it any longer
hard'horig hard of hearing
hardlopen to run
hard'nekkig stubborn
hardop aloud
hard'vochtig callous
harig hairy

haring (de) herring; tent peg
hark (de) rake; gawk
harken to rake
harlekijn (de) harlequin
har'monica (de) accordion, mouth organ
harmo'nie (de) harmony
harmoni'ëren to harmonize
har'monisch harmonious; harmonic
harnas (het) armour **iemand in het – jagen** to put a person's back up
harrewarren to squabble
hars (het, de) resin, rosin
hart (het) heart **heb het – niet!** don't you dare!
hart-en vaatziekten (de), cardiovascular diseases
hartaanval (de) heart attack
hartelijk cordial, hearty
harteloos heartless
hartelust: naar – to one's heart's content
hart'grondig whole-hearted
hartig savoury; forthright
hartinfarct (het) heart attack
hart'roerend touching
hartstikke (inf) very, terribly, completely **ik heb het – druk** I'm incredibly busy
hartstocht (de) passion
harts'tochtelijk pasionate
hartverlamming (de) heart failure
hartver'scheurend heartbreaking
hatelijk spiteful
hatelijkheid (de) spite(ful remark)
haten to hate
haveloos ragged; shabby
haven (de) harbour
havenarbeider (de) dock worker
havenstad (de) port
haver (de) oats **van – tot gort kennen** to know inside out
haverklap: om de – at the slightest provocation; every other minute

havermout (de) porridge (oats)
havik (de) hawk
haviksneus (de) aquiline nose
hazelnoot (de) hazelnut
hazenlip (de) harelip
hbo: hoger be'roepsonderwijs
(het) higher vocational education
hé hey, hello, oh (really)? (greeting/
pleasant surprise)
hè oh, what? (unpleasant surprise)
leuk hè? great, isn't it?
hebben to have **hoe laat heb je**
het? what time do you make it?
wat heb ik eraan? what's the good
of it to me? **het – over** to talk about
hebberig greedy
hebzucht (de) greed
heb'zuchtig grasping
hecht firm, solid
hechten to attach; to stitch (up)
ge'hecht aan fond of, attached to
hechtenis (de) custody
hechting (de) stitch
hechtpleister (de) adhesive plaster
heden today **– ten dage** nowadays
hedendaags present-day
heel whole, entire; quite, very
heelhuids unscathed
heen gone; on the way out **daar**
kun je niet – you can't go there
– en weer to and fro **waar wil je –?**
where do you want to go? what are
you driving at?

heengaan to go away
heenweg: op de – on the way there
heer (de) gentleman; master; lord
heerlijk delicious; delightful
heerschap'pij (de) dominion, rule
heersen to rule; to prevail
heerser (de) ruler
heers'zuchtig ambitious
hees hoarse
heester (de) shrub
heet hot
heetge'bakerd quick-tempered
hefboom (de) lever
heffen to raise
heffing (de) levy
heft (het) handle, haft
heftig violent; vehement
heg (de) hedge
heibel din, racket
heide (de) moor, heath(er)
heiden (de) heathen, pagan
heidendom (het) paganism, pagan
world
heidens heathen(ish), pagan
heien (het) pile-driving
heiig hazy
heilbot (de) halibut
heilig holy, sacred
heiligdom (het) sanctuary, sanctum
heilige (de) saint
heiligen to hallow; to keep holy
heiligschennis (de) sacrilege
heiligverklaring (de) canonization

Insight

In the meaning of *very*, **heel** is synonymous with **erg** in
Dutch. You can say **het is heel koud** *it is very cold* or
het is erg koud; mijn oma is heel rijk *my grandmother is*
very rich or **mijn oma is erg rijk**. However, you can also
combine the two to intensify the meaning, although in this
case **heel** always precedes **erg: mijn oma is heel erg lief** *my*
grandmother is incredibly sweet.

heilloos evil; disastrous, fatal
heilzaam salutary
heimelijk secret, furtive
heimwee (het) homesickness, nostalgia
heinde en ver near and far
heining (de) fence
heipaal (de) (concrete) pile
hek (het) railings; gate
hekel (de) hackle **ik heb er een —
aan** I dislike it intensely **over de —
halen** to criticize sharply
hekelen to heckle, to satirize
hekkensluiter (de) last comer
heks (de) witch; hag
heksenketel (de) cacophony
heksentoer (de) insuperable task
hel (de) hell
he'laas alas
held (de) hero
helder clear, lucid; bright; clean
helder'ziend clairvoyant
held'haftig heroic
hel'din (de) heroine
helemaal completely **hele'maal
niet** not at all
helen to receive stolen goods; to heal
helft (de) half
hellen to slope, to slant
helling (de) slope, incline, slipway
helm (de) helmet; beach-grass
helpen to help, to be effective
hels infernal, hellish **— zijn** to be wild
(with rage)
hem him
hemd (het) vest, shirt
hemel (de) heaven, sky; canopy
hemellichaam (het) celestial body
hemels heavenly **hemelsbreed
verschil** all the difference
in the world
hemelsvaartdag (de) Ascension Day
hen them
hengel (de) fishing rod

hengelaar (de) angler
hengelen to angle, to fish
hengsel (het) handle; hinge
hengst (de) stallion
hennep (de) hemp
her: van eeuwen — from times
immemorial **van oudsher** of old
her- re-, again
her'ademen to breathe again
heral'diek (de) heraldry
herberg (de) inn
herbergen to accommodate;
to harbour
herber'gier (de) inn keeper
her'denken to commemorate;
to recall
her'denking (de) commemoration
herder (de) shepherd; herdsman
herdershond (de) sheepdog
her'drukken to reprint
her'enigen to reunite
herfst (de) autumn
her'haald(elijk) repeated(ly)
her'halen to repeat; to revise
her'haling (de) repetition; revision
herinneren remember; remind **— aan**
to remind of **zich —** to remember
her'innering (de) recollection,
memory
herintreden return to work (a
woman after a childcare break)
her'kauwen to chew the cud; to
ruminate
her'kenbaar recognizable
her'kennen to recognize
her'kiezen to re-elect
herkomst (de) origin
her'leiden to convert, to reduce
her'leven to revive; to live again
her'nemen to resume; to take again
her'nieuwen to renew
hero'ïne (de) heroin
herontdekken to rediscover
her'overen to recapture

herrie (de) row, hullabaloo
her'roepen to revoke
hersenen (de) brain(s)
hersenpan (de) cranium
hersenschim (de) chimera
hersenschudding (de) concussion
her'stel (het) recovery, convalescence
her'stellen to mend; to restore; to recover
her'stellingsoord (het) convalescent home
hert (het) deer, stag
hertenkamp (de) deer park
hertog (de) duke
hertogdom (het) duchy
herto'gin (de) duchess
her'trouwen to remarry
her'vatten to resume
her'vormd reformed; protestant
her'vorming (de) reform(ation)
her'winnen to regain
her'zien to revise; to review
het it: the
heten to be called
hetero'geen heterogeneous
heteroseksu'eel heterosexual
het'geen (that) which
het'zelfde the same
het'zij ... of (or dan wel) either or whether ... or
heugen: dat zal je – you won't forget that in a hurry
heuglijk joyful
heulen met to be in league with
heup (de) hip
heus real; courteous
heuvel (de) hill
hevig violent
hi'aat (het) hiatus
hiel (de) heel
hier here
hierheen this way
hier'naast next to this; next door

hier'namaals (het) (life) hereafter
hieruit out (of) here; from this
hij he
hijgen to pant
hijsen to hoist
hijskraan (de) crane
hik (de) hiccups
hikken to have hiccups
hilari'teit (de) hilarity, mirth
hinderen to hinder; to annoy
hinderlaag (de) ambush
hinderlijk annoying; inconvenient
hindernis (de), hinderpaal (de) obstacle
hinken to limp; to hop
hinniken to neigh
his'torisch historic(al)
hitte (de) heat
hobbel (de) bump
hobbelen to jolt
hobbelig bumpy
hobbelpaard (het) rocking horse
hobo (de) oboe
hoe how – **eerder – beter** the sooner the better – **dan ook** however
hoed (de) hat
hoe'danigheid (de) quality
hoeden to guard
hoef (de) hoof
hoefijzer (het) horseshoe
hoegenaamd niets nothing whatever
hoek (de) angle; corner, nook
hoekig angular
hoenderhok (het) hen coop
hoepel (de) hoop
hoer (de) whore
hoes (de) loose cover; dustsheet
hoest (de) cough
hoesten to cough
hoeveel how much, how many
hoe'veelheid (de) quantity

hoeveelste: de – is het vandaag?
what is the date today?
hoeven to need
hoe'ver how far **in hoeverre**
to what extent
hof (het) court **het – maken** to court
hoffelijk courteous
hofhouding (de) royal household
hoge'school (de) institution of
higher education
hok (het) kennel, pen, sty, hutch
hokken to shack up with
hol (het) den, cave
hol hollow, concave
Hollands Dutch
hollen to run
holte (de) cavity
hommel (de) bumble bee, drone
homoseksu'eel homosexual
homp (de) lump, chunk
hond (de) dog, hound **rode –**
German measles
hondeweer (het) foul weather
honderd a hundred **honderduit**
praten to talk nineteen to the
dozen
honds'dolheid (de) rabies
honen to scoff at
Honga'rije Hungary
honger (de) hunger
hongerig hungry
hongerloon (het) starvation wage
hongersnood (de) famine
honing (de) honey
honingraat (de) honeycomb
honk (het) base, home
hono'rair honorary
hono'rarium (het) fee
hono'reren to honour; to pay
hoofd (het) head; principal, chief
hoofdartikel (het) leading article
hoofdbreken (het) brain racking
hoofddoek (de) scarf; veil
hoofdgetal (het) cardinal number

hoofdkussen (het) pillow
hoofdkwartier (het) headquarters
hoofdletter (de) capital letter
hoofdpijn (de) headache
hoofdstad (de) capital, principal
town
hoofdstraat (de) main street
hoofdstuk (het) chapter
hoofdzaak (de) main thing
hoofd'zakelijk mainly
hoofs courtly
hoog high, tall **drie –** on the third
floor
hoogachten to esteem
hoogachtend yours faithfully, yours
sincerely
hoog'dravend bombastic
hoog'hartig haughty
Hoogheid (de) Highness
hooghouden to uphold
hoog'leraar (de) professor
hoogmoed (de) pride
hoog'moedig proud
hoogmoedswaanzin (de)
megalomania
hoog'nodig very necessary
hoogoven (de) blast furnace
hoogst highest; extremely **ten**
hoogste at most
hoogseizoen (het) high season
hoogspanning (de) high voltage
hoogstaand of high moral character
hoogstens at most
hoogstnodig absolutely necessary
hoogte (de) height, altitude **op de –**
well-informed **uit de –** supercilious
hoogtepunt (het) acme, zenith
hoogtezon (de) sun-lamp; ultra-
violet light
hoogtij vieren to be rampant
hoogtijdag (de) heyday; high day
hoogvlakte (de) plateau
hoogvlieger (de): hij is geen –
he's no genius

hoog'waardigheidsbekleder (de) (high) dignitary
hoog'water (het) high tide
hooi (het) hay **teveel – op zijn vork nemen** to bite off more than one can chew **te – en te gras** haphazardly
hooiberg (de) haystack
hooien to make hay
hooivork (de) pitchfork
hoon (de) scorn
hoop (de) hope; heap, stack
hoopvol hopeful
hoorbaar audible
hoorn (de) horn, bugle; telephone receiver
hoornvlies (het) cornea
hoorspel (het) radio play
hopeloos hopeless
hopen to hope
hor (de) gauze screen
horde (de) horde, mass; hurdle: **hordeloop (de)** hurdle race
horen to hear; to belong (to); to be right (and proper), ought
horizon'taal horizontal
hor'loge (het) watch
horrelvoet (de) clubfoot
hort: met horten en stoten jerkily
horzel (de) horsefly
hospes (de), hospita (de) landlord, landlady
hossen to sing and dance arm in arm
hotsen to jolt
houdbaar: – tot best before
houden to hold; to keep **– van** to like, to love **– voor** to take for **zich goed –** to control oneself
houding (de) position, pose; attitude, manner **zich geen – weten te geven** feel awkward
hout (het) wood
houten wooden
houterig wooden, stiff

houtje (het) bit of wood **iets op eigen – doen** do something on your own (initiative)
houtskool (de) charcoal
houtsne(de)e (de) woodcut
houtsnijwerk (het) wood carving
houvast (het) hold
hou'weel (het) pickaxe
hozen to bale/bail; to pour (with rain)
huichelaar (de) hypocrite
huichela'rij (de) hypocrisy
huichelen to be hypocritical; to feign
huid (de) skin, hide
huidig present-day
huifkar (de) covered wagon
huilebalk (de) cry baby
huilen to cry, to howl
huis (het) house, home
huisarts (de) family doctor
huisbaas (de) landlord
huisdier (het) pet
huiselijk domestic(ated); homely
huisgenoot (de) member of the household
huis'houdelijk domestic, household
huishouden (het) household; housekeeping
huishouden to keep house **vreselijk – to play havoc
huishoudkunde (de) domestic science
huishoudster (de) housekeeper
huiskamer (de) living room
huisraad (het) household goods
huis-tuin-en-keuken suburban, common
huisvesten to house
huiswerk (het) homework
huiveren to shudder
huiverig voor wary of
huivering (de) shudder
huivering'wekkend horrible
hulde (de) homage

huldigen to pay tribute to
hulp (de) help
hulpbehoevend in need of help, infirm, invalid
hulpeloos helpless
hulpmiddel (het) remedy; aid; means
hulptroepen (de) auxiliaries
hulp'vaardig(heid) (de) helpful(ness)
hulpverlening (de) assistance; caring profession
hulpwerkwoord (het) auxiliary verb
huls (de) pod; case; cover
hulst (de) holly
humeur (het) mood; temper
hu'meurig moody
hummel (de) tiny tot
humor (de) humour
hun their; (to) them
hunkeren naar to hanker after
huppelen to hop
huren to hire, to rent
hurken to squat

hut (de) cabin, hut
hutkoffer (de) trunk
hutspot (de) traditional Dutch stew; hotpot
huur (de) rent
huurder (de) tenant
huurling (de) hireling, mercenary
huurmoordenaar (de) assassin
huurovereenkomst (de) rental agreement
huursubsidie (de) rent subsidy
huwbaar marriageable
huwelijk (het) marriage
huwelijksaanzoek (het) proposal (of marriage)
huwelijksreis (de) honeymoon
huwelijksvoltrekking (de) marriage ceremony
huwen to marry
hygi'ëne (de) hygiene
hypermodern ultramodern
hypo'theek (de) mortgage
hy'sterie (de) hysteria
hys'terisch hysterical

I

ide'aal (het) ideal
ideali'seren to idealize
idea'lisme (het) idealism
i'dee (het, de) idea
ide'ëel imaginary; idealistic
idem ditto
iden'tiek identical
identifi'ceren to identify
identi'teit (de) identity
identi'teitsbewijs (het) ID card
idi'oom (het) idiom
idi'oot (de) idiot
idi'oot idiotic
ido'laat van infatuated with
ieder every, each, any
ieder'een everyone, anyone
iemand someone, anyone

iep (de) elm
Ier (de) Irishman
Iers Irish
Ierland Ireland
iets something, anything
ietsje, ietwat somewhat
ijdel vain
ijdelheid (de) vanity
ijdeltuit (de) vain person
ijken to calibrate, to verify
ijl: in aller – hastily
ijl thin; rarefied
ijlen to be delirious; to hasten
ijs (het) ice
ijsbaan (de) skating rink
ijsbeer (de) polar bear
ijsberen to pace up and down

ijsberg (de) iceberg
ijsblokje (het) ice cube
ijselijk horrible
ijskast (de) refrigerator
ijskoud icy, (cold), iced
IJsland Iceland
ijsschots (de) ice floe

impo'neren to impress
impo'sant impressive
imperia'lisme (het) imperialism
im'perium (het) empire
impli'ceren to imply
impor'teren to import
improviseren to improvise

Insight

In Dutch the letter **i** is often used in combination with the letter **j**. So much so, in fact, that many Dutch speakers consider the combination **ij** a separate letter. When the combination appears at the start of a word which should begin with a capital letter, for instance, both letters are written in upper case, such as in **het IJsselmeer**, the large lake (inland sea) north of Amsterdam. The combination **ij** is pronounced the same way as the diphthong **ei**, i.e. similar to *i* in the English *wise*, but with the lips spread.

ijstijd (de) ice age
ijver (de) diligence
ijverig diligent, keen
ijzel (de) ice on the roads
ijzen to shudder
ijzer (het) iron
ijzerdraad (het) wire
ijzerhoudend ferrous
ijzig icy; frightful
ijzing'wekkend ghastly
ik I **het –** the ego
ille'gaal illegal
il'lusie (de) illusion
illus'treren to illustrate
i'mago (het) image
imam (de) imam
imker (de) beekeeper
immer ever
immers surely; after all
immi'grant (de) immigrant
immi'gratie (de) immigration
immo'reel immoral
im'muun immune

impul'sief impulsive, impetuous
in in, at, to, into, on, inside
in'achtneming (de) observance
inademen to breathe in
inbeelden: zich – to imagine
inbeelding (de) imagination; conceit
inbegrepen including
inbegrip: met – van inclusive of
inbe'slagneming (de) seizure (of goods)
inbinden to bind **je moet je wat –** you must climb down
inboedel (de) household effects
inboeten to forfeit **hij heeft er het leven bij ingeboet** the attempt cost him his life
inboezemen to inspire
inbraak (de) burglary
inbreken to burgle, to break in
inbreker (de) burglar
inbrengen to bring in; to put forward **hij heeft niets in te –** he has no say in the matter

inbreuk (de) infringement
inburgeren to naturalize;
to settle down
inburgeringscursus (de) integration
course
incas'seren to cash; to collect
in'cluis included
inclu'sief including, inclusive (of)
incom'pleet incomplete
inconse'quent inconsistent
indampen to evaporate
indelen to class(ify), to allocate
indeling (de) classification, grouping
indenken: zich — to imagine,
to visualize, to conceive
inder'daad indeed
inder'tijd at one time, at the time
indeuken to dent
India India
Indië Dutch East Indies
in'dien if
indienen to introduce, to submit
indijken to surround with dikes
indivi'du (het, de) indiviual
individu'eel individual
indommelen to doze off
Indo'nesië Indonesia
indringen: zich — to intrude
in'dringend penetrating
indroevig very sad
indrogen to dry up
indruisen tegen to run counter to
indruk (de) impression
indruk'wekkend impressive
industriali'seren to industrialize
indus'trie (de) industry
indu'striebond (de) industrial union
industri'eel industrial
indu'strieterrein (het) industrial
zone
indutten to doze off
in'een together
in'eengedoken hunched up
in'eenkrimpen to cower, to double up

in'eens at once
in'eenstorten to collapse, to come
crashing down
in'eenzakken, in el'kaar zakken
to collapse, to cave in
inenten to inoculate, to vaccinate
infante'rie (de) infantry
inferi'eur inferior
influisteren to whisper in a person's
ear
informateur (de) politician charged
with investigating a proposed
cabinet formation
infor'matie (de) information
infor'meren (naar) to inquire
(about)
in'fuus (het) drip; infusion
ingaan to enter; to take effect
niet — op to ignore
ingang (de) entrance **met — van**
as from
ingebeeld imaginary; conceited
ingeboren innate
ingehouden restrained
ingeni'eur (de) (qualified) engineer
ingeni'eus ingenious
ingenomen met pleased with
ingespannen strenuous; intent
ingetogen modest, subdued
inge'val in case
ingeven to prompt; to administer;
to inspire
ingeving (de) inspiration
inge'volge in accordance with
ingewanden (de) intestines
ingewijde (de) old hand; insider
inge'wikkeld complicated
ingeworteld deep-seated
ingezetene (de) inhabitant
ingezonden stuk (het) letter to the
editor
ingooien to throw in(to); to smash
ingreep (de) intervention
ingrijpen to intervene

in'grijpend far-reaching
inhalen to catch up, to overtake; to take in
inha'leren to inhale
in'halig grasping
inham (de) creek
in'hechtenisneming (de) arrest
in'heems indigenous
inhoud (de) content(s); capacity
inhouden to contain; to restrain; to dock
inhoudsmaat (de) cubic measure
inhoudsopgave (de) table of contents
inhuldigen to inaugurate
inkeer: tot – komen to repent
inkleden to put into words
inkomen (het) income
inkomen to come in **dar kan ik –** I can understand that **daar komt niets van in** that's out of the question
inkomsten (de) income, revenue
inkopen to buy, to purchase
inkorten to shorten, to curtail
inkrimpen to shrink, to cut down
inkt (de) ink
inktvis (de) squid
inkwartieren to billet
inlassen to fit in, to insert
inlaten to let in **zich – met** to have dealings with
inleiden to introduce
inleiding (de) introduction
inleven: zich – in to imagine oneself as
inleveren to hand in
inlichten to inform
inlichting (de) information
inlijsten to frame
inlijven to incorporate
inlossen to redeem
inluiden to ring in
inmaak (de) preserving; preserves

inmaken to preserve
inmenging (de) interference
in'middels meanwhile
innemen to take (in, up); to capture; to please
innen to collect
innerlijk inner; intrinsic
innig heartfelt, intimate
inpakken to pack (up), to wrap up
inpalmen to grab; to inveigle
inpikken to grab; to tackle
inpolderen to reclaim (land)
inpompen to pump in; to cram
inprenten to instil, to imprint
inrichten to arrange, to rig up, to furnish
inrichting (de) institute; institution; arrangement, furnishing
inrijden to ride, or drive into; to break or run in
inrit (de) entrance
inroepen to call in, to invoke
inruilen to trade in, to exchange
inruimen to clear, to vacate; to put back
inschakelen to switch on; to put into gear
inschenken to pour out
inschepen: zich – to embark
inschieten: erbij – to go by the board
in'schikkelijk accommodating
inschikken to move in closer
inschrijven to register; to tender; to subscribe
insge'lijks likewise
in'signe (het) badge
inslaan to smash (in); to stock up on; to turn into (a street)
inslapen to fall asleep
insluiten to enclose, to surround; to include, to comprise
inspannen to exert, to strain
in'spannend strenuous

inspanning (de) exertion
inspec'teur (de) inspector
inspi'rerend inspiring
inspraak (de) involvement,
 having a say
inspreken: iemand moed –
 to put heart into a person
inspringen to stand in (for a
 colleague)
inspringende regel (de)
 indented line
inspuiten to inject
instaan voor to vouch for
instal'leren to install; to induct
in'standhouden to maintain
in'stantie (de) authority **in laatste
 instantie** in the last resort
instellen to institute; to focus **er op
 ingesteld zijn** to be used to it
instelling (de) institution
instemmen to agree
instemming (de) approval
instinc'tief instinct'matig
 instinctive
instoppen to tuck in
instorten to collapse
instru'eren to instruct
instuderen to practise; to study
inteelt (de) inbreeding
in'tegendeel on the contrary
inte'grerend integral
intekenen op to subscribe to
in'tentie (de) intention
interen to live on one's capital
interes'sant interesting
interes'seren: zich – voor
 to be interested in
in'tern internal
inter'naat (het) boarding school
inter'neren to intern
internetten to work/surf
 on the internet
interpre'tatie (de) interpretation
inter'punctie (de) punctuation

interrum'peren to interrupt
interviewen to interview
in'tiem intimate
intimi'teit (de) intimacy
intocht (de) (ceremonial) entry
intoetsen to key in
intomen to curb; to rein in
intrappen to kick open;
 to tread down
intreden to enter (upon), to set in
intrek: zijn – nemen in to take
 up residence at
intrekken to draw in; to move in;
 to withdraw; to retract
in'trige (de) intrigue
intuïtie (de) intuition
intuï'tief intuitive, instinctive
in'tussen meanwhile
inval (de) invasion; raid; brainwave
inva'lide (de) disabled person
invalidi'teit (de) disablement
invallen to fall in; to deputize;
 to enter, to raid
inven'taris (de) inventory
inventari'satie (de) stock taking
inves'teren to invest
investering (de) investment
invetten to grease
invliegen: er – to fall for a trick
invloed (de) influence
invloedrijk influential
invoegen to insert
invoer (de) import(s)
invorderen to collect (debts)
in'vrijheidstelling (de) release
in'wendig internal, inward
inwerken op to act on
inwijden to consecrate; to initiate
inwilligen to comply with
inwinnen to obtain
inwisselen to (ex)change, to cash
inwrijven to rub in(to)
inzage: ter – for inspection,
 on approval

in'zake with reference to
inzakken to collapse
inzamelen to collect
inzegenen to consecrate
inzender (de) contributor; exhibitor
inzending (de) contribution;
  exhibit(s)
inzepen to soap
inzet (de) stake(s)
in'zetbaar usable, available
  (e.g. for work)
inzetten to put in; to start; to stake
inzicht (het) insight, understanding
inzien to glance through; to realize
  iets ernstig – to take a grave view
  of something **bij nader –**
  on second thoughts **mijns inziens**
  in my opinion

inzinken to subside; to decline
inzinking (de) subsidence; relapse
inzitten: erover – to be worried
  about something **de inzittende**
  the occupant
iro'nie (de) irony
i'ronisch ironical
irre'ëel unreal
irrele'vant irrelevant
irri'tant irritating, annoying
irri'teren to irritate
ischias (de) sciatica
isla'mitisch Islamic
iso'latie (de) insulation
isole'ment (het) isolation
iso'leren to isolate, to insulate
i'voor (het) ivory
I'vriet (modern) Hebrew

J

ja yes
jaagpad (het) towpath
jaap (de) gash
jaar (het) year
jaarbeurs (de) industrial fair
jaargang (de) a year's issue
  (of a periodical), volume

jaargenoot (de) classmate
jaargetij (het) season
jaarkaart (de) annual season ticket
jaarlijks annual
jaartal (het) date
jaartelling (de) era
jaarwisseling (de) turn of the year

Insight

Jaar or *year* is not normally used in its plural form in Dutch, so *ten years* is **tien jaar**. Dag *day*, week *week* and **maand** *month* are used in the plural, i.e. dagen, weken, maanden. **Uur** *hour* and **kwartier** *quarter of an hour*, on the other hand, aren't (**het is twee uur rijden** *it's a two hour drive*), but **seconde** *second* and **minuut** *minute* are, i.e. **seconden** or **secondes** and **minuten**. For weights and measures the plural forms are not generally used either: **gram** *gram*, **ons** *100 grams*, **pond** *500 grams*, **kilo, liter, millimeter, centimeter, meter, kilometer** (**twee ons kaas, graag** *200 grams of cheese, please*).

jacht (de) hunt(ing); shoot(ing), pursuit
jacht (het) yacht
jachten to hurry
jachthaven (de) marina
jachthond (de) hound
jachtschotel (de) hotpot
jagen to hunt; to shoot; to race
jager (de) hunter, sportsman
jakhals (de) jackal
jakkeren to hustle
ja'loers jealous
ja'loersheid (de) jealousy
jaloe'zie (de) jealousy; Venetian blind
jammer (de, het) distress **– genoeg** unfortunately **wat –!** what a pity!
jammeren to lament
jammerlijk miserable
Jan en alle'man every Tom, Dick and Harry
Jan met de pet the (ordinary) man in the street
janboel (de) muddle
janken to whine; to badger
ja'pon (de) dress
jarenlang for years
jarig one year old **ik ben –** it is my birthday
jarige (de) birthday boy or girl
jarre'telle (de) suspender, garter
jas (de) coat
jasje (het) jacket
jas'mijn (de) jasmine
jassen to peel (spuds)
ja'wel certainly
jawoord (het) consent
je you; your
jegens towards
je'never (de) Dutch gin
je'neverbes (de) juniper berry or tree
jengelen to whimper
jeugd (de) youth
jeugdherberg (de) youth hostel

jeugdig youthful, young
jeuk (de) itch
jeuken to itch; to scratch
je'zelf yourself
jihad (de) jihad
jij you
j.l.: jongst'leden last **15 maart j.l.** 15th of March last
jochie (het) kid, lad(die)
jodendom (het) Jews; Judaism
jodium (het, de) iodine
joelen to cheer; to howl
jokken to fib
jokkebrok (de) fibber
jol (de) yawl, dinghy
jolig jolly
jonassen to swing a child by its arms and legs
jong young
jonge'lui (de) young people
jongen (de) boy
jongen to give birth (animals)
jongensachtig boyish
jong'leur (de) juggler
jongs: van – af aan right from childhood
jongst'leden last
jood (de) Jew
joods Jewish
Joost: – mag het weten (I have) no idea, search me
jota (de) iota
jou you
jour'naal (het) logbook; journal; newsreel
journalis'tiek (de) journalism
jouw your
jouwen to hoot
jubelen to shout for joy
jubi'laris (de) man celebrating some personal anniversary
jubi'leren to celebrate some anniversary in one's life
jubi'leum (het) jubilee, anniversary

juf (de) female teacher, Miss
juffrouw Miss, Madam
juichen to shout for joy
juist correctly; exactly; right; just
  daarom – for that very reason
juk (het) yoke
jukbeen (het) cheekbone
juli July
jullie you (people)

juni June
ju'ridisch juridical, legal
ju'rist (de) lawyer
jurk (de) dress
jury (de) jury
jus (de) gravy
jus'titie (de) judicature; justice, law
ju'weel (het) jewel; gem
juwe'lier (de) jeweller

K

kaak (de) jaw **aan de – stellen**
  to expose
kaakje (het) biscuit
kaal bald; bare; threadbare
kaalslag (de) deforestation
kaap (de) cape
kaars (de) candle
kaarsrecht bolt upright
kaarsvet (het) candle grease
kaart (de) card; map, chart; hand
  (at cards)
kaarten to play cards
kaartenbak (de) index box
kaartje (het) card; ticket
kaartsysteem (het) card index
kaas (de) cheese **ik heb er geen –**
  van gegeten I don't know
  the first thing about it
kaasschaaf (de) cheese slicer
ka'baal (het) racket, din
kabbelen to lap, to ripple
kabel (de) cable
kabelbaan (de) cable lift
kabel'jauw (de) cod
kabi'net (het) cabinet
ka'bouter (de) goblin, gnome
kachel (de) stove
ka'daster (het) land registry
kade (de) quay
kader (het) cadre, framework, scope
ka'detje (het) soft roll
kaf (het) chaff

kaft (de) (book) cover, book jacket
kaftan (de) kaftan
kajak (de) kayak
ka'juit (de) saloon, cabin (of a ship)
kakelbont gaudy, motley
kakelen to cackle, to chatter
kake'toe (de) cockatoo
kakkerlak (de) cockroach
kale'bas (de) gourd
ka'lender (de) calendar
kalf (het) calf
kalfsvlees (het) veal
ka'liber (het) calibre
kalk (de) lime; mortar
kalkaanslag (de) limescale
kal'koen (de) turkey
kalm calm
kal'meren to calm
kalmerend calming **– middel**
  (het) sedative
kalmpjes calmly
kalmte (de) calm(ness), composure
ka'lotje (het) skullcap
kalven to calve
kalverliefde (de) puppy love
kam (de) comb; crest; bridge
  (of a violin) **over één – scheren**
  to treat alike
ka'meel (de) camel
kamer (de) room, chamber
kame'raad (de) comrade
kameraad'schappelijk friendly

kamergenoot (de) roommate
kamerjas (de) dressing gown
kamerlid (het) member of
  parliament
kamerscherm (het) screen
ka'mille (de) camomile
kammen to comb
kamp (het) camp; contest
kam'peerterrein (het) campsite
kam'peerwagen (de) camper;
  campervan
kampen to fight; to contend
kam'peren to camp

kanni'baal (de) cannibal
kano (de) canoe
ka'non (het) gun
kans (de) chance
kans'arm deprived
kansel (de) pulpit
kansspel (het) game of chance
kant (de) side, edge; lace **dat raakt
  – nog wal** that is quite irrelevant
  iets over zijn – laten gaan to
  put up with something **zich van
  – maken** to do oneself in **op 't
  kantje af** only just

Insight

Dutch can be a very literally descriptive language. *A coaster*
is called **een onderzetter** (literally an 'under putter') and
black pudding is called **bloedworst** (literally 'blood sausage'),
for instance. And so it is with most cuts of meat. *Veal* is **het
kalfsvlees** ('calf meat'), *pork* is **het varkensvlees** ('pig meat'),
beef is **het rundvlees** ('cow meat', although **koe** is the more
common word for *cow*) and *lamb* is **lamsvlees**. Just to show
that Dutch has more figurative expressions too, *puppy love* is
called **de kalverliefde** ('calf's love').

---

kamper'foelie (de) honeysuckle
kampi'oen (de) champion
kampi'oenschap (het)
  championship
kan (de) jug, can
ka'naal (het) canal; channel
Ka'naaltunnel (de) Channel
  Tunnel
ka'narie (de) canary
kandelaar (de) candlestick
kandi'daat (de) candidate
kan'dijsuiker (de) sugar candy
ka'neel (de) cinnamon
kanjer (de) whopper
kanker (de) cancer
kankeren to grumble
kankerver'wekkend carcinogenic

kant-en-klaar ready-to-use
kan'teel (het) battlement
kantelen to topple over; to tilt
kanten (made of) lace **zich – tegen**
  to oppose
kan'tine (de) canteen
kantklossen (het) lace making
kantlijn (de) margin
kan'tongerecht (het) district
  court
kan'toor (het) office
kan'toorbaan (de) office job
kan'toorbenodigdheden (de)
  (*pl*) stationery
kap (de) cap; hood; bonnet;
  lampshade
ka'pel (de) chapel; band

kape'laan (de) curate
kapen to hijack
kaper (de) hijacker; privateer
  kapers op de kust rivals
kapi'taal (het) capital
kapitaal'krachtig financially strong
kapitali'seren to capitalize
kapita'lisme (het) capitalism
kapi'tein (de) captain
kaplaars (de) top boot, wellington
ka'pot broken
kappen to cut or chop down;
  to dress hair
kapper (de) hairdresser
kapsalon (de) hairdresser's,
  barbershop
kapseizen to capsize
kapsel (het) hairstyle/cut
kapstok (de) hallstand, coathooks
kar (de) cart
ka'raat (het) carat
kara'bijn (de) carbine
ka'raf (de) carafe, decanter
ka'rakter (het) character
karakteri'seren to characterize
karakteris'tiek characteristic
kara'vaan (de) caravan
karbo'nade (de) chop
kardi'naal (de) cardinal
karig parsimonious; sparing, scanty
karnemelk (de) buttermilk
karnen to churn
karper (de) carp
kar'tel (het) cartel, trust
kar'ton (het) cardboard; carton
kar'wei (het) job (of work)
kar'wijzaad (het) caraway seed
kas (de) socket; greenhouse; cash
  (desk) **goed bij kas** in funds
kassa (de) pay desk, box office; till
kas'sier (de) cashier
kast (de) cupboard; case
kas'tanje (de) chestnut
kaste (de) caste

kas'teel (het) castle
kaste'lein (de) publican
kas'tijden chastise
kastje (het) locker **van het –**
  naar de muur from pillar to post
kastpapier (het) lining paper
kat (de) cat **de – uit de boom**
  kijken to play a waiting game
kater (de) tomcat; hangover
ka'theder (de) lectern
kathe'draal (de) cathedral
katho'liek (Roman) Catholic
katje (het) kitten; catkin
ka'toen (de) cotton
ka'trol (de) pulley
kattenbak (de) litter tray (of a cat)
kattenkwaad (het) mischief
kattenpis: dat is geen – no kidding!
kattig catty
katzwijm (de) feigned swoon
kauwen to chew
kauwgom (het, de) chewing gum
ka'zerne (de) barracks
keel (de) throat **het hangt me**
  de – uit I'm sick and tired of it
keelpijn (de) a sore throat
keer (de) turn; time(s) **een**
  doodenkele – once in a blue moon
  te – gaan to storm
keerkringen (de) tropics
keerpunt (het) turning point
keerzijde (de) reverse side
keet (de) shed, hut
keet trappen (inf) to kick up a racket
keffen to yap
kegel (de) cone; skittle
kegelen to play skittles
kei (de) boulder, cobblestone,
  set; 'wizard'
keihard rock-hard
keilen to fling
keizer (de) emperor
keize'rin (de) empress
keizerlijk imperial

keizerrijk (het) empire
keizersnede (de) caesarian
kelder (de) cellar, vault
kelderen to go to the bottom; to slump
kelk (de) chalice; calyx
kelner (de) waiter
kemphaan (de) fighting cock
kenau (de) amazon
kenbaar distinguishable **– maken** to make known
kenmerk (het) characteristic
kenmerken to characterize
kennelijk apparent, clear
kennen to know **te – geven** to intimate **men heeft mij er niet in gekend** I was not consulted
kenner (de) connoisseur
kennis (de) knowledge; acquaintance **– geven van** to announce **buiten –** unconscious
kennisgeving (de) notification
kenschetsen to characterize
kenteken (het) registration/ licence number (of a car)
kentekenplaat (de) number/ licence plate
kerel (de) fellow
keren to turn, to stem
kerf (de) notch
kerfstok (de): hij heeft veel op zijn – he has a lot to answer for
kerk (de) church
kerkbank (de) pew
kerkdienst (de) (divine) service
kerkelijk ecclesiastical; church (going)
kerker (de) dungeon
kerkhof (het) churchyard
kermen to moan
kermis (de) fair
kern (de) kernel, core; crux, gist
kernachtig pithy
kerncentrale (de) nuclear power station

kerngezond fit as a fiddle
kernwapen (het) nuclear weapon
kerrie (de) curry
kers (de) cherry
kerst (de) Christmas **eerste kerstdag** Christmas Day; **tweede kerstdag** Boxing Day
kers 'vers quite fresh
kerven to carve, to notch, to cut
ketel (de) kettle, boiler
ketelsteen (de) scale, fur
keten (de) chain(s)
ketenen to chain
ketjap (de) soysauce
ketsen to misfire
ketter (de) heretic
ketteren to swear, to rage
ketting (de) chain; necklace
keu (de) (billiard) cue
keuken (de) kitchen; cuisine
keukenfornuis (het) kitchen range
keukengerei (het) kitchen utensils
keuren to examine; to inspect; to sample
keurig trim, very nice
keuring (de) medical examination; inspection
keurslijf (het) bodice; straitjacket
keus (de) choice
keutel (de) dropping
keuvelen to chat(ter)
keuze (de) choice
kever (de) beetle
kibbelen to squabble
kicken to get a kick (out of)
kidnappen to kidnap
kiepen to topple (over)
kieken to take a snapshot of
kielzog (het) wake
kiem (de) germ; seed
kiemen to germinate
kier (de) chink **op een –** ajar
kies (de) molar
kiesbaar eligible

kiesdistrict (het) constituency
kies'keurig fastidious
kiespijn (de) toothache
kiesrecht (het) franchise
kietelen to tickle
kieuw (de) gill
kievit (de) lapwing
kiezelsteen (de) pebble
kiezen to choose, to elect
kiezer (de) voter; (pl) electorate
kijf: buiten – beyond dispute
kijk (de) outlook, insight
kijk- en luistergeld (het) TV and
　radio licence fee
kijken to (have a) look
kijker (de) telescope, binoculars;
　viewer
kijkgat (het) peephole
kijven to quarrel
kik: hij gaf geen – he did not
　utter a sound
kikken: je hebt maar te – you've
　only to say the word
kikker (de) frog; cleat
kikvors (de) frog
kil chilly
kilo(gram) (het, de) kilogram
kin (de) chin
kind (het) child
kinderachtig childish
kinder'bijslag (de) child benefit
kinder'dagverblijf (het) crèche, day
　nursery
kinderlijk childlike
kinderloos childless
kinderopvang (de) crèche, day
　nursery; childcare
kindersterfte (de) infant mortality
kinderwagen (de) pram
kinds infantine
kindsbeen: van – af ever since
　childhood
kink (de) kink **een – in de kabel**
　a hitch

kinkhoest (de) whooping cough
kip (de) chicken, hen
kippengaas (het) chicken wire
kippenhok (het) hen house
kippenvel (het) goose bumps
kippig short-sighted
kirren to coo
kist (de) (packing), case, chest; coffin
kittig spirited
klaaglied (het) lamentation, dirge
klaar clear; ready, finished **– wakker**
　wide awake
klaar'blijkelijk evident
klaarkomen to (be) finished,
　to complete; to come (sex)
klaarlichte dag (de) broad daylight
klaarspelen: het – to manage it
klacht (de) complaint
klad (het) rough draft **iemand bij**
　de kladden pakken to grab hold
　of a person
kladden to daub, to scrawl
kladpapier (het) scribbling paper
klagen to complain
klakkeloos groundless,
　off-hand, rash
klam clammy
klampen to clamp
klan'dizie (de) custom(ers)
klank (de) sound
klankbord (het) sounding board
klankloos toneless
klant (de) customer, client
klantenservice (de) customer service
klap (de) blow, smack, crack
klappen: in de handen – to clap
klappertanden to shiver
klaproos (de) poppy
klapstoel (de) tip-up seat,
　folding chair
klapwieken to flap the wings
klari'net (de) clarinet
klas, klasse (de) class(room),
　form (grade)

klassenstrijd (de) class war
klas'siek classic(al)
klateren to splatter, to cascade
klauteren to clamber
klauw (de) claw, talon
klave'cimbel (de, het) harpsichord
klaver (de) clover
kla'vier (het) keyboard
kleden to dress; to clothe
klederdracht (de) local costume
kle'dij (de), kleding (de) clothes, attire
kledingstuk (het) garment
kleed (het) carpet; cloth; gown
kleedje (het) rug, (table)cloth
kleedkamer (de) dressing room, changing room
kleermaker (de) tailor
klei sticky, soggy
klef (de) clay
kleimasker (het) mudpack
klein little, small **– geld** small change
kleindochter (de) granddaughter
klei'neren to belittle
klein'burgerlijk narrow-minded, petty bourgeois
klein'geestig narrow- minded
kleinigheid (de) trifle
kleinkind (het) grandchild
kleinkrijgen to break (a person)
kleintje (het) baby, little one
klein'zerig easily hurt, soft
klein'zielig petty(-minded)
kleinzoon (de) grandson
klem (de) trap; clip; emphasis
klemmen to pinch, to clench **een klemmend betoog (het)** a convincing argument
klemtoon (de) stress
klep (de) valve; flap; peak
klepel (de) clapper
kleppen to clang, to clatter
klepperen to rattle, to bang to and fro
kleren (de) clothes

klerenkast (de) wardrobe
klerk (de) clerk
kletsen to chatter; to talk rubbish
kletskous (de) gossip, chatter-box
kletteren to clatter, to patter
kleur (de) colour; suit (cards)
– bekennen to follow suit; to show one's colours
kleur'echt colour-fast (dyed)
kleuren to colour; to blush
kleurenpracht (de) blaze of colour
kleurloos colourless
kleurstof (de) colouring matter
kleuter (de) toddler
kleven to cleave, to stick
kleverig sticky
kliederen to make a mess
kliek (de) clique
kliekje (het) leftovers (of food)
klier (de) gland **wat een –** he is a real pain in the neck
klieven to cleave
klif (het) cliff
klikspaan (de) telltale
kli'maat (het) climate
klimato'logisch climatic
klimmen to climb
klimop (de) ivy
klingelen to tinkle
kli'niek (de) clinic
klink (de) latch
klinkbout (de) rivet
klinken to sound, to ring (out); to clink glasses, to rivet
klinker (de) vowel; riveter
klinkklaar utter, pure
klinknagel (de) rivet
klip (de) rock, reef
klis (de), klit (de) burr, burdock; tangle
klodderen to clot; to daub
kloek brave; stout; substantial
klok (de) clock; bell **alles wat de – slaat** all one hears about

klokhuis (het) core
klokkenspel (het) carillon, chimes
klokslag (de) stroke (of the clock)
klomp (de) clog; lump; nugget
klompvoet (de) clubfoot
klont(er) (de) lump, clod, clot
klonteren to clot
klonterig lumpy
kloof (de) cleft, crevice; rift
klooster (het) monastery, convent
klop (de) knock, throb
klopjacht (de) round-up
kloppen to knock, to tap, to beat;
  to tally **dat klopt als een bus** that
  tallies all along the line
klos (de) bobbin, reel; coil
klotsen to slosh, to splash
kloven to cleave, to split
klucht (de) farce
kluif (de) knuckle of pork; (meaty)
  bone **een hele –** quite a job
kluis (de) safe, safe-deposit box
kluisteren to fetter
kluit (de) clod, lump **flink uit de
  kluiten gewassen** strapping
kluiven to gnaw a bone
kluizenaar (de) hermit
klungel (de) bungler
klungelen to bungle
klus (de) job, chore **een hele –**
  a tough job
kluts (de): de – kwijtraken to lose
  one's head
klutsen to whisk
knaagdier (het) rodent
knabbelen to nibble
knagen to gnaw
knakken to snap, to break
knakworst (de) Frankfurt sausage
knal (de) bang
knallen to bang, to ring out
knalpot (de) silencer
knap handsome, pretty; clever; neat
knappen to snap; to crackle

knarsen to grate; to crunch
knarsetanden to gnash one's teeth
knauwen to gnaw, to munch;
  to damage or hurt seriously
knecht (de) (man)servant
knechten to enslave
kneden to knead; to mould
kneedbaar malleable
kneep (de) pinch; dodge
knel: in de – zitten to be in a fix
knellen to pinch
knetteren to crackle
kneuzen to bruise
kneuzing (de) bruise
knevelen to gag, to pinion
knibbelen to haggle
knie (de) knee **onder de knie
  krijgen** to master
kniebuiging (de) curtsey
knielen to kneel
knieschijf (de) kneecap
kniezen to mope
knijpen to pinch **ik knijp 'm**
  I've got the wind up
knijper (de) clothespeg
knik (de) crack; buckle; twist
knikkebollen to nod (with sleep)
knikken to nod
knikker (de) marble
knip (de) snap; trap; catch;
  clasp; purse
knipogen to wink; to blink
knippen to cut (off/out), to clip
  geknipt voor cut out for
knipperen to flicker
knipsel (het) cutting
knobbel (de) bump
knobbelig gnarled
knoei: in de – zitten
  to be in difficulties
knoeiboel (de) mess; swindle
knoeien to make a mess; to bungle
knoeie'rij (de) corruption; bungling
knoeiwerk (het) shoddy work

knoest (de) knot (in wood)
knoflook (het, de) garlic
knok(kel) (de) knuckle
knokken to scrap
knokploeg (de) gang of thugs, henchmen
knol (de) tuber; turnip
knolraap (de) swede
knoop (de) knot; button; node
knooppunt (het) junction
knoopsgat (het) buttonhole
knop (de) button
knopje (het) (push)button, switch
knopen to tie, to knot
knorren to grunt; to grumble
knorrig peevish
knot (de) knot
knotwilg (de) pollard willow
knuffelen to cuddle
knuist (de) fist
knul (de) fellow
knuppel (de) cudgel
knus(jes) snug
knutselen to make things (for a hobby)
koe (de) cow **oude koeien uit de sloot halen** to rake up the past
koek (de) gingerbread
koeke'loeren (inf) to stare inquisitively
koekenpan (de) frying pan
koekje (het) sweet biscuit
koekoek (de) cuckoo
koel cool
koel'bloedig cool-headed
koelen to cool (down) **zijn woede –** to vent one's anger
koelkast (de) fridge
koelte (de) cool(ness)
koepel (de) dome
koe'rier (de) courier
koers (de) course; price (of stocks); rate of exchange
koesteren to cherish **zich –** to bask

koetjes en kalfjes (de) trifling matters
koets (de) coach
koffer (de) suitcase
kofferbak (de) boot, trunk
koffie (de) coffee
koffiemelk (de) coffee cream, evaporated milk
kogel (de) bullet; ball
kogellager (het) ball bearing
kok (de) cook
koken to cook; to boil
koker (de) (long) case
kokette'rie (de) flirtation
kokhalzen to retch
kokosmat (de) coconut mat(ting)
kokosnoot (de) coconut
kolen (de) coal(s) **op hete –** on tenterhooks
kolendamp (de) carbon monoxide
kolenhok (het) coalshed
kolf (de) (rifle) butt; retort
kolk (de) whirlpool
ko'lom (de) column
koloni'aal colonial
kolonia'lisme (het) colonialism
ko'lonie (de) colony
kolos'saal colossal
kom (de) basin, bowl; the populous part, centre
kom'af (de) descent, birth
komedi'ant (de) (play-) actor, comedian
ko'medie (de) comedy play; theatre; comedy
ko'meet (de) comet
komen to come **hoe komt dat?** how did that happen?
komisch comic(al)
kom'kommer (de) cucumber
komma comma, (decimal) point
kommer (de) sorrow, distress
kom'pas (het) compass
kom'plot (het) plot

komst (de) coming
ko'nijn (het) rabbit
koning (de) king
koning'in (de) queen
Koning'innedag (de) Queen's birthday
koningsgezind royalist
koninklijk royal, regal
koninkrijk (het) kingdom
konkelen to scheme
kon'vooi (het) convoy
kooi (de) cage, pen; bunk
kook (de) boil **water aan de – brengen** bring water to the boil
kookboek (het) cookery book
kool (de) cabbage; coal(s); carbon
koolhydraat (het) carbohydrate
koolmees (de) great tit
koolzaad (het) rape seed
koolzuur (het) carbonic acid
koop (de) purchase **te –** for sale **te – lopen met** to show off **op de – toe** into the bargain
koopakte (de) title deed
koopcontract (het) contract of sale, title deed
koophandel (de) commerce
koopje (het) bargain
koopkracht (de) purchasing power
koopman (de) merchant
koopvaar'dij (de) merchant service
koopwaar (de) merchandise
koor (het) choir, chorus; chancel
koorbank (de) choir stall
koord (het) cord
koorddansen (het) tightrope walking
koorts (de) fever **– hebben** to have a temperature
koorts(acht)ig feverish
kop (de) head; large cup; bowl (of a pipe) **de – indrukken** to nip in the bud **op de – tikken** to pick up, to find (a bargain) **op de – af** precisely

kopen to buy
koper (de) purchaser
koper (het) copper, brass
kopergroen (het) verdigris
ko'pie (de) copy
kopi'ëren to copy
ko'pij (de) copy, manuscript
kopje (het) (tea)cup **kopje duikelen** to turn somersaults
koplamp (de) headlight
koploper (de) leader, frontrunner
koppel (de) leash
koppel (het) couple
koppelaar (de) matchmaker
koppelen to couple, to join
koppeling (de) coupling; clutch
koppelteken (het) hyphen
koppig obstinate
kopstuk (het) head/big man
kopzorg (de) worry
ko'raal (het) choral(e); coral
kor'daat resolute
koren (het) corn
korenschuur (de) granary
korf (de) basket; hive
korfbal (het) korfball
korrel (de) grain; pellet
korrelig granular
korst (de) crust, rind; scab
korstdeeg (het) short pastry
kort short, brief **– en bondig** terse **– maar krachtig** short and snappy
kort'ademig short of breath
kort'af curt
kortheids'halve for the sake of brevity
korting (de) discount, deduction
kor'tom in short
kortsluiting (de) short circuit
kort'stondig short-lived
kortweg without wasting words
kortwieken to clip the wings of
kort'zichtig short-sighted
korzelig grumpy

kost (de) food; living; board **– en inwoning (de)** board and lodging
kostbaar expensive; precious
kostbaarheden (de) valuables
kostelijk superb; priceless
kosteloos (cost-)free
kosten (de) expense(s), cost, charges: to cost
koster (de) verger
kostganger (de) boarder
kostgeld (het) board
kostschool (de) boarding school
kostwinner (de) breadwinner
kotsen to puke
kou (de) cold **– vatten** to catch cold
koud cold
koukleum (de) chilly person
kous (de) stocking
kouwelijk sensitive to cold
ko'zijn (het) windowsill, windowframe
kraag (de) collar, ruff
kraai(en) (to) crow
kraakbeen (het) cartilage
kraakstem (de) grating voice
kraal (de) bead
kraam (de) booth, stall
kraambed (het) childbed, confinement
kraan (de) tap; crane
kraanwagen (de) breakdown truck
krab (de) crab
krabbel (de) scratch, scrawl
krabbelen to scratch, to scrawl
krabben to scratch
kracht (de) force, strength, power **volle – vooruit** full speed ahead **op krachten komen** to regain strength
kracht'dadig vigorous
krachteloos powerless
krachtens by virtue of
krachtig powerful
krachtsinspanning (de) exertion
kra'kelen to quarrel

kraken to crack; to creak; to crunch
kramp (de) cramp; spasm
kramp'achtig desperate; taut
kranig smart; brave; brilliant
krank'zinnig insane
krans (de) wreath
krant (de) newspaper
krap tight; short of money
kras scratch; strong (for one's age)
krassen to scratch; to screech
krat (de) crate
krater (de) crater
kreeft (de) lobster
kreek (de) creek
kreet (de) cry, scream
kregel peevish
kreng (het) carrion; rotter, bitch
krenken to offend
krent (de) currant; skinflint
krenterig niggardly
kreukel (de) crease
kreukelen to crease
kreunen to groan
kreupel lame
kreupelhout (het) thicket
krib(be) (de) manger, crib
kribbig testy
kriebelen to itch, to tickle; to write a niggling hand
kriebelig itchy
kriek (de) black cherry
krieken: bij het – van de dag at the crack of dawn
krielkip (de) bantam hen
krijgen to get **te pakken –** to get hold of
krijger (de) warrior
krijgertje (het) hand-me-down
krijgsgevangene (de) prisoner of war
krijgs'haftig warlike
krijgslist (de) stratagem
krijgsmacht (de) armed forces
krijgsraad (de) council of war; court martial

krijgstocht (de) campaign
krijgstucht (de) military discipline
krijgs'zuchtig bellicose
krijsen to screech
krijt (het) chalk
krijtrots (de) chalk cliff
krimp: geen – geven to not falter
krimpen to shrink; to back
krimpvrij unshrinkable
kring (de) circle
kringloop (de) cycle
kri'oelen to swarm
kris'tal (het) crystal
kri'tiek (de) criticism; review
kritisch critical
kriti'seren to criticize
kroeg (de) pub
kroegbaas (de) landlord; inn-keeper
kroep (de) croup
kroepoek (de) prawn crackers
kroes (de) mug, crucible
kroeshaar (het) frizzy/curly hair
krokusvakantie (de) spring half-
  term/semester break
krols on heat
krom crooked, bent, curved **je –**
  lachen to double up with laughter
kromliggen to pinch and scrape
kromtrekken to warp
kronen to crown
kro'niek (de) chronicle
kroning (de) coronation, crowning
kronkel (de) twist, kink
kronkelen to twist, to wind
kronkelig winding
kronkeling (de) convolution
kroon (de) crown; corolla, chandelier
  dat spant de – that beats
  everything
kroongetuige (de) crown witness
kroonlijst (de) cornice
kroos (het) duckweed
kroost (het) progeny
kropsla (de) lettuce

krot (het) hovel
kruid (het) herb
kruiden to season
kruide'nier (de) grocer
kruidenthee (de) herbal tea
kruide'rijen (de) spices
kruidnagel (de) clove
kruien to wheel (in a barrow); to
  break up, to drift (of ice)
kruier (de) (luggage) porter
kruik (de) stone bottle; hot water
  bottle
kruimelig crumbly
kruin (de) crown, top
kruipen to creep; to crawl; to cringe
kruiperig cringing
kruis (het) cross; sharp (in music);
  croup, crupper, crutch; seat
  – of munt head or tails
kruisbeeld (het) crucifix
kruisbes (de) gooseberry
kruiselings crosswise
kruisen to cross; to cruise
kruisigen to crucify
kruispunt (het) point of intersection,
  crossroads
kruisraket (de) cruise missile
kruistocht (de), kruisvaart (de)
  crusade
kruit (het) (gun)powder
kruiwagen (de) (wheel)barrow;
  influential friend
kruk (de) crutch; doorhandle; crank;
  stool
krul (de) curl; scroll
krullebol (de) curly-head
kubiek cubic
kubus (de) cube
kuch (de) dry cough
kuchen to give a slight cough
kudde (de) herd, flock
kuieren to stroll
kuif (de) quif, crest
kuiken (het) chicken

kuil (de) pit; (pot)hole
kuiltje (het) dimple
kuip (de) tub
kuis chaste
kuisheid (de) chastity
kuit (de) calf (of the leg); spawn; roe
kuitschieten to spawn
kul (de): flauwe – nonsense, rubbish
kundig able; knowledgeable **ter zake
– expert**
kundigheden (de) accomplishments
kunnen to be able to, may **dat kan
(wel)** that is (quite) possible, maybe
kunst (de) art; trick **daar is geen –
aan** there's nothing to it
kunst- artificial; art
kunstenaar (de) artist
kunstgeschiedenis (de) history
of art
kunstgreep (de) trick, manoeuvre
kunstig ingenious
kunstijsbaan (de) skating rink
kunstkenner (de) connoisseur
kunst'matig artificial
kunstmest (de) fertilizer
kunst'nijverheid (de) applied art
kunstrijden (het) figure skating
kunstschaatsen figure skating
kunststof (de) man-made/synthetic
material
kunststuk (het) work of art
kunst'vaardig skilful
kunst'zinnig artistic
kurk (de) cork
kurkentrekker (de) corkscrew
kus (de) kiss
kussen (het) pillow, cushion
kussen to kiss
kussensloop (het) pillow case
kust (de) coast, shore **te – en te
keur** in plenty
kustvaart (de) coastwise trade
kut (de) (vulg) cunt
kuur (de) whim; cure

kwaad bad; angry **– geweten** guilty
conscience **het te – krijgen**
to break down
kwaad (het) evil; harm
kwaad'aardig malicious
kwaad'denkend suspicious
kwaadschiks with an ill grace
kwaadspreke'rij (de) scandal-
mongering
kwaad'willig malevolent
kwaal (de) complaint, ailment
kwabbig flabby
kwa'draat (het) square
kwa'jongen (de) (young) rascal
kwa'jongensachtig mischievous
kwak (de) thud; blob
kwaken to quack; to croak
kwakkelen to have poor health
kwakkelwinter (de) mild winter
kwakzalver (de) quack
kwal (de) jellyfish; jerk
kwalifi'ceren to describe
kwalijk evil **– nemen** to blame **neem
me niet –** I am sorry
kwanti'teit (de) quantity
kwark (de) cottage cheese, soft
curd cheese
kwart (het) quarter
kwar'taal (het) quarter, term
kwartel (de) quail
kwartje (het) 25 cents of a guilder
kwar'tier (het) quarter of an hour;
quarter(s)
kwarts (het) quartz
kwast (de) brush, tassel; knot (in
wood); coxcomb; smart alec
kwebbelen to chatter
kweek (de) cultivation, growth,
culture
kweken to grow; to foster
kweker (de) nurseryman
kweke'rij (de) nursery
kwekken to yap; to chatter
kwelen to warble

kwellen to torment
kwelling (de) torment
kwestie (de) question
kwetsbaar vulnerable
kwetsen to wound, to injure
kwet'suur (de) wound
kwetteren to twitter
kwiek spry
kwijlen to dribble

kwijnen to languish
kwijt rid (of) **– zijn** to have lost
kwijtraken to lose
kwijten: zich – van to discharge
kwijtschelden to remit, to forgive
kwik (het) mercury
kwispel(staart)en to wag the tail
kwistig lavish
kwi'tantie (de) receipt

L

la(de) (de) drawer, till
laadvermogen (het) loading
  capacity
laag (de) layer, stratum **hij gaf me
  de volle –** he let me have it **lager
  onderwijs** primary education
laag low(-pitched)
laag-bij-de-'gronds crude
laag'hartig base
laagseizoen (het) low season,
  off-season
laagte (de) low level, dip
laag'water (het) low tide
laaien to blaze
laan (de) avenue
laantje (het) path, lane
laars (de) boot
laat late
laat'dunkend arrogant
laatst last, latest; recently
laatstge'noemde (de) latter
la'biel unstable
labora'torium (het) laboratory
lach (de) laugh
lachen to laugh
lachlust: de – opwekken
  to raise a laugh
lachspiegel (de) distorting mirror
lach'wekkend laughable
la'cune (de) gap
ladder (de) ladder
laden to load, to charge

ladenkast (de) chest of drawers
lading (de) load, cargo; charge
laf cowardly
lafaard (de), lafbek (de) coward
laf'hartig cowardly
lafheid (de) cowardice
lager (de) bearing(s)
Lagerhuis (het) Lower House,
  House of Commons
la'gune (de) lagoon
lak (het, de) sealing wax; lacquer
  ik heb er – aan a fat lot I care
laken (het) cloth, sheet **de lakens
  uitdelen** to rule the roost **hij kreeg
  van hetzelfde – een pak** he was
  treated in just the same way
lakken to lacquer; to seal
laks(heid) (de) lax(ity)
lam (de) lamb
lam paralysed; nasty
lam'lendig wretched, indolent
lammeling (de) wretch
lammetje (het) little lamb
lamp (de) lamp, bulb, valve **tegen
  de – lopen** to get into trouble
lampi'on (de) Chinese lantern
lamstraal (de) wretch
lamsvlees (het) lamb (meat)
lan'ceren to launch
land (het) land, country, field **ik heb
  er het – aan** I hate it **aan – gaan**
  to go ashore

landaanwinning (de) l land
reclamation
landarbeider (de) agricultural
labourer
landbouw(kunde) (de) agriculture
landbouw'kundige (de)
agriculturalist
landelijk rural; nation-wide
landen to land
landengte (de) isthmus
landerig in the dumps
landgenoot (de) compatriot
landgoed (het) estate
landingsbaan (de) runway
landkaart (de) map
landmacht (de) army, land forces
landmijn (de) landmine
landschap (het) landscape
landverraad (het) high treason
lang long, tall **– van stof**
long-winded **– niet** not nearly
lang'dradig long-winded
lang'durig lengthy
langge'rekt protracted
langs along, past **– elkaar heen
praten** to talk at cross purposes
langskomen to come past; to drop by
lang'uit at full length
lang'werpig oblong, elongated
langzaam slow
langzamerhand gradually
lank'moedig long-suffering
lans (de) lance
lan'taarn (de), lan'taren (de)
lantern; skylight; lamp
lan'taarnpaal (de) lamppost
lanterfanten to loaf
lap (de) piece (of cloth), rag;
patch; steak
lapmiddel (het) makeshift
lappen to patch; to wipe; to manage
lappendeken (de) patchwork quilt
larie (de) stuff and nonsense
larve (de) larva

lassen to weld
last (de) load, burden;
instruction(s); trouble
lasteren to slander
lasterlijk slanderous
lastig difficult, tiresome **lastig
vallen** to trouble
lastpost (de) nuisance
lat (de) lath, slat
laten to let; to leave (off) **ik kan het
niet –** I can't help it **iets – doen**
to have something done
later afterwards, later
La'tijn (het) Latin
latwerk (het) trellis
lau'rier (de) laurel
lauw tepid
lauweren (de) laurels
la'vendel (de) lavender
la'waai (het) din
la'wine (de) avalanche
la'xeermiddel (het) laxative
la'xeren to purge
lbo: lager beroepsonderwijs
(abbrev) lower vocational education
lebberen to lap, to sip
lector (de) university lecturer
lec'tuur (de) reading (matter)
ledematen (de) limbs
ledig empty
ledi'kant (het) bed(stead)
leed (het) sorrow
leedvermaak (het) pleasure
at other people's misfortune
leedwezen (het) regret
leefbaar liveable, endurable
leefgemeenschap (de) commune;
community
leeftijd (de) age **op –** elderly
leeftijdsgenoot (de) peer
leeftijdsgrens (de) age limit
leefwijze (de) manner of living
leeg empty
leeggieten to empty/pour (out)

leegte (de) emptiness, void
leek (de) layman
leem (het) loam
leemte (de) gap, hiatus
leep cunning
leer (de) doctrine **in de – bij** apprenticed to
leer (het) leather
leerboek (het) textbook
leergang (de) course of study
leer'gierig studious
leerjongen (de) apprentice
leerkracht (de) teacher
leerling (de) pupil
leerlooien to tan (leather)
leermeester (de) teacher
leerplan (het) curriculum
leerplicht (de) compulsory education
leerrijk instructive
leerstoel (de) chair
leerstof (de) subject matter
leertje (het) washer (in a tap)
leerzaam instructive
leesbaar readable, legible
leesblind dyslexic
leesteken (het) punctuation mark
leeszaal (de) reading room; public library
leeuw('in) (de) lion(ess)
leeuwerik (de) (sky)lark
lef (het, de) guts, nerve

le'gaal legal
le'gaat (het) legacy
legbatterij (de) battery (cage)
legen'darisch legendary
le'gende (de) legend
leger (het) army **Leger des Heils** Salvation Army
leggen to lay, to put
legio (de) countless
legi'oen (het) legion, army
legiti'matiebewijs (het) identification paper
legiti'meren: zich – prove one's identity
legpuzzel (de) jigsaw
lei (de) slate
leiden to lead
leider (de) leader
leiding (de) guidance, direction, lead; pipe(line)
leidingwater (het) tap water
leidraad (de) guideline
leien: alles ging van een – dakje everything went smoothly
lek (het) leak(y) **een lekke band** a puncture
lekken to leak
lekker nice **ik ben niet –** I am not very well **iemand – maken** to rouse a person's expectations
lekkerbek (de) gourmet
lekker'nij (de) delicacy

Insight

Lekker first and foremost refers to food which tastes nice (**de soep is lekker!** *the soup tastes great!*), but this meaning is frequently also used in different contexts. Just look at the following examples: **de rozen ruiken lekker** *the roses smell great*; **wat een lekker weer** *such (a) nice weather*; **heb je lekker gezwommen?** *did you have a nice swim?*; **wat een lekker stuk, zeg!** *my, what a gorgeous hunk/woman!* (note: this last example is very informal).

lel (de) lobe; clout
lelie (de) lily
lelijk ugly; badly **dat treft –** that's awkward
lende (de) small of the back, loin
lendenen (de) loins
lenen to lend; to borrow
lengte (de) length, height; longitude
lenig supple, lithe
lening (de) loan
lente (de) spring
lepel (de) spoon, ladle
lepra (de) leprosy
leraar (de) (male) teacher
lera'res (de) (female) teacher
leren to teach; to learn **de tijd zal het –** time will tell
leren (made of) leather
les (de) lesson
les'bienne (de) lesbian
lesbisch lesbian
lesgeld (het) tuition fee
lesgeven to teach
lesrooster (het) timetable
lessen to quench, to slake
letsel (het) injury
letten op to pay attention to; to look after **let wel!** mark you!
letter (de) letter, type
letteren literature
lettergreep (de) syllable
letterkunde (de) literature
letterlijk literal
letterteken (het) character
leugen (de) lie
leugenaar (de) liar
leugenachtig mendacious
leuk nice, cute, amusing
leukweg coolly
leunen to lean
leuning (de) (hand)rail; parapet; back, arm(rest)
leunstoel (de) armchair
leuren met to hawk

leus (de), leuze (de) slogan, device
leut (de) fun
leuteren to talk drivel; to loiter
leven (het) life; noise
leven to live, to be alive
levend (a)live, living
levendig lively
levenloos lifeless
levensbehoefte (de) necessity of life
levensbeschouwing (de) philosophy of life
levensbeschrijving (de) biography
levensge'vaarlijk perilous
levensgroot life-size(d)
levenslang lifelong
levensloop (de) course of life; curriculum vitae
levenslust (de) *joie de vivre*
levensmiddelen (de) provisions
levensonderhoud (het) subsistence
levensstandaard (de) standard of living
levensstijl (de) lifestyle
levens'vatbaar viable
levensverzekering (de) life insurance
lever (de) liver
leveran'cier (de) purveyor, retailer
leve'rantie (de) delivery, supply
leveren to supply, to deliver
levertraan (de) codliver oil
leverworst (de) liver sausage
lezen to read; to gather
lezer('es) (de) reader
lezenaar (de) lectern
lezing (de) lecture; version
li'bel (de) dragonfly
libe'raal liberal
lichaam (het) body
lichaamsbeweging (de) exercise
lichaamsbouw (de) physique
li'chamelijk bodily, physical
licht (het) light

licht light, mild, slight; easily
lichtbundel (de) beam of light
lichtelijk slightly
lichten to weigh, to lift
lichte(r)laaie: in – ablaze
lichtge'raakt touchy
lichtgevend luminous
lichting (de) draft, class, levy; collection (of mail)
lichtpunt (het) point of light; lighting point; ray of hope
lichtsignaal (het) light signal
licht'vaardig rash, lightly
licht'zinnig frivolous, flighty
lid (het) limb, finger joint; member; sub-section; term **uit het –** dislocated
lidmaatschap (het) membership
lidwoord (het) article
lied(eren) (het) song(s)
lieden people
liedje (het) ditty, song **het is het oude –** it's the same old story
lief dear, sweet, nice **meer dan me – is** more than I care for **voor – nemen** to put up with
lief'dadig charitable
lief'dadigheid (de) charity
liefde (de) love
liefdeloos loveless
liefderijk loving
liefdeslied (het) love song
lief(e)lijk charming, sweet
liefhebben to love
liefhebber (de) lover, enthusiast
liefhebbe'rij (de) hobby
liefkozen to fondle
liefst dearest; preferably
lief'tallig sweet, winsome
liegen to tell lies
lies (de) groin
lieve'heersbeestje (het) ladybird
lieveling (de) darling
liever rather, sooner

lieverd darling
liften to hitch-hike
liggen to lie **waar ligt het aan?** what is the cause of it?
ligging (de) situation
ligplaats (de) berth
lijden to suffer **ik mag hem wel –** I rather like him **lijdend voorwerp (het)** direct object
lijdzaam submissive
lijf (het) body; bodice **het heeft weinig om het –** it is of little importance
lijfsbehoud (het) self-preservation
lijfspreuk (de) motto
lijfwacht (de) bodyguard
lijk (het) corpse
lijken (op) to resemble; to seem
lijkschouwer (de) coroner
lijkschouwing (de) post-mortem
lijm (de) glue
lijmen to glue
lijn (de) line; route
lijndienst (de) scheduled service (of transport)
lijnen to diet
lijnolie (de) linseed oil
lijnrecht straight; diametrically
lijnvlucht (de) scheduled flight
lijnzaad (het) linseed
lijst (de) list; frame
lijster (de) thrush
lijsterbes (de) mountain ash
lijvig corpulent, bulky
lijzig drawling
lik (de) lick; swipe
likdoorn (de) corn
li'keur (de) liqueur
likkebaarden to lick one's lips
likken to lick
lila lilac(-coloured)
li'miet (de) limit
limo'nade (de) (fruit) cordial
linde (de) lime tree

lini'aal (de) ruler
linie (de) line **over de hele –**
  all round
linker- left
links (to the) left; left-handed;
  gauche **– laten liggen** to cold-
  shoulder
linksaf, linksom to the left
linnen (het) linen
lint (het) ribbon
lintje (het) ribbon **een – krijgen**
  to be decorated
lintworm (de) tapeworm
linzen (de) lentils
lip (de) lip
lippenstift (de) lipstick
liqui'deren to wind up (a business)
lispelen to lisp
list (de) ruse
listig cunning
lite'rair literary
lite'rator (de) man of letters
litera'tuur (de) literature
litera'tuurlijst (de) reading list;
  bibliography
litteken (het) scar
lobbes (de) big good-natured person
  or animal
lobbyen to lobby
locomo'tief (de) (railway) engine
lodderig drowsy
loden lead(en)
loeder (het, de) swine, bitch
loeien to low; to roar
loempia (de) spring roll
loensen to squint
loep (de) magnifying glass **iets
  onder de – nemen** to scrutinize
  something
loer: op de – liggen to lie in wait
  iemand een – draaien
  to play a dirty trick on a person
loeren to peer; to spy
lof (de) praise

log unwieldy; log
loge (de) lodge; (theatre) box
lo'gé(e) (de) guest
lo'geerkamer (de) spare room
loge'ment (het) inn
lo'geren to stay
logica (de) logic
lo'gies (het) accommodation
  – met ontbijt bed and breakfast
logisch logical
logischer'wijs logically
logo (het) logo
logope'die (de) speech therapy
lok (de) lock (of hair)
lo'kaal (het) room
lokaas (het) bait
lo'ket (het) counter, booking office
lokken to (al)lure
lokmiddel (het) lure, bait
lokvogel (de) decoy
lol (de) lark, fun
lollig funny
lommer (het) shade; foliage
lomp boorish, clumsy
lompen (de) rags
lomperd (de) lout
lonen to (re)pay
long (de) lung
longontsteking (de) pneumonia
lonk(en) (to) ogle
lont (de) fuse **– ruiken** to smell a rat
loochenen to deny
lood (het) lead **– om oud ijzer** six of
  one and half a dozen of the other
  uit het – geslagen bewildered
loodgieter (de) plumber
lood'recht perpendicular, vertical
loods (de) shed; pilot
loodsen to pilot
loodvrij unleaded
loodwit (het) white lead
loofboom (de) deciduous tree
loom languid
loon (het) wages

loonbelasting (de) income tax
loondienst (de) salaried
  employment
loop (de) gait; course; (gun) barrel
loopbaan (de) career
loopgraaf (de) trench
loopjongen (de) errand boy
loopneus (de) runny nose
loopplank (de) gangway
loops on heat
loor: te – gaan to be lost
loos cunning; false
lootje (het) lottery ticket, raffle
  ticket **– s trekken** draw names
  (out of a hat)
lopen to walk, to go, to run
lopend running; current
loper (de) walker; carpet strip;
  bishop (in chess); master key
los loose, detachable **er op –**
  recklessly
los'bandig dissolute
losbarsten to burst out
losbinden to untie
los'bladig loose-leaf
losgeld (het) ransom
losjes loosely
loskopen to ransom
loskoppelen to disconnect
loslaten to let go
los'lippig indiscreet
loslopen to run free **het zal wel –**
  it won't be all that bad
lossen to discharge, to unload
loszinnig frivolous
lot (het) fate; lottery ticket
loten to draw lots
lote'rij (de) lottery
lotgenoot (de) partner in adversity
lotgevallen (de) adventures
louche shady
loupe (de) magnifying glass
louter pure, sheer
louteren to purify

loven to praise **– en bieden** to
  haggle
lo'yaal loyal
lozen to get rid of; to drain
lucht (de) air; sky; smell **– geven
  aan** to vent
luchtaanval (de) air raid
luchtafweer (het) anti-aircraft
  defence
luchtalarm (het) air raid alarm
luchtballon (de) (hot-air) balloon
luchtbed (het) inflatable bed
luchtdruk (de) atmospheric pressure
luchten to air, to vent(ilate) **ik kan
  hem niet –** I can't abide him
luchter (de) candelabrum, chandelier
lucht'hartig light-hearted
luchthaven (de) airport
luchtig airy
luchtje (het) odour
luchtkoker (de) ventilating shaft
lucht'ledig vacuum
luchtmacht (de) airforce
luchtpijp (de) windpipe
luchtvaart (de) aviation
luchtverfrisser (de) air freshener
luchtvervuiling (de) air pollution
lucht'vochtigheid (de) humidity
lucifer (de) match
lucra'tief profitable
lu'guber lugubrious
luiaard (de) sloth
lui (*pl*) people
lui lazy
luid loud
luiden to ring **de brief luidt als
  volgt** the letter reads as follows
luidkeels at the top of one's voice
luid'ruchtig noisy
luidspreker (de) loudspeaker
luier (de) nappie
luieren to laze
luifel canopy
luiheid (de) laziness

luik (het) hatch; trapdoor; shutter
luilak (de) lazybones
luilakken to (be) idle
luis (de) louse
luister (de) splendour
luisteraar (de) listener
luisteren to listen
luisterrijk splendid, glorious
luister'vaardigheid (de) listening skill
luistervink (de) eavesdropper
luitenant (de) lieutenant
luiwammes (de) lazybones
lukken to succeed **het lukt me nooit** I shall never manage it
lukraak haphazard
lul (de) (inf) prick; (term of abuse) dickhead
lullen (inf) to talk (drivel)

lumi'neus luminous **een – idee** a brainwave
lummel (de) lout
lummelen to loiter
lurven: bij de – pakken to take by the scruff of the neck
lus (de) loop; noose
lust (de) inclination, liking **een – voor het oog** a sight for sore eyes
lusteloos listless
lusten to like, to fancy
lustig lusty
lustobject (het) sex object
luttel little
luwte (de) sheltered (from the wind)
luxaflex (de) Venetian blinds
luxe (de) luxury
luxu'eus luxurious
lyrisch lyrical

M

maag (de) stomach
maagd (de) virgin, maid(en)
maagdelijk(heid) (de) virgin(ity)
maagpijn (de) stomach ache
maagzuur (het) gastric acid; heartburn
maagzweer (de) gastric ulcer
maaien to mow
maal (het) meal **tienmaal** ten times
maalstroom (de) whirlpool
maaltijd (de) meal
maan (de) moon **loop naar de –** go to hell
maand (de) month
maandag Monday
maandblad (het) monthly periodical, magazine
maandelijks monthly
maandenlang for months on end
maandverband (het) sanitary towel
maanjaar (het) lunar year

maansverduistering (de) eclipse of the moon
maar but; only; just
maarschalk (de) marshal
maart March
maas (de) mesh; loophole
maat (de) measure, size; time, bar; mate, partner
maatje (het) decilitre; pal
maatregel (de) measure
maat'schappelijk social
maatschap'pij (de) society; company
maatstaf (de) criterion
maatwerk (het) clothing made to measure; bespoke work
machi'naal mechanical
ma'chine (de) engine, machine
ma'chinegeweer (het) machine gun
machine'rieën (de) machinery
machi'nist (de) ship's engineer; engine driver

macht (de) power, might **– der ge'woonte** force of habit **niet bij machte** unable

machteloos powerless

machtig mighty, terrific; rich (food) **een taal – zijn** to have command of a language

machtigen to authorize

machtiging (de) authorization

machtspositie (de) position of authority

made'liefje (het) daisy

maffen (*inf*), to snooze

maga'zijn (het) store(s), storehouse; magazine

mager thin, lean, meagre

ma'gie (de) magic

magisch magic(al)

magi'straal imposing

mag'naat (de) magnate

mag'neet (de) magnet

mag'netisch magnetic

magneti'seren to magnetize; to mesmerize

magne'tron (de) microwave

magni'fiek magnificent

maïs (de) maize

maïskolf (de) cob of corn

maï'zena (de) cornflour

majesteit (de) majesty

majestu'eus majestic

ma'joor (de) major

mak tame, gentle

makelaar (de) broker, estate agent

maken to make; to mend **dat heeft er niets mee te –** that has nothing to do with it **hoe maakt u het?** how do you do?

makkelijk easy

makker (de) comrade, mate

ma'kreel (de) mackerel

mal (de) mould, template; stencil: foolish

malen to grind

maling: – hebben aan to not give a damn/hoot **in de – nemen** to make a fool of

mal'loot (de) silly creature, fool

mals tender; lush; gentle (rain)

man (de) man; husband **aan de – brengen** to sell **op de – af** point blank

man'chet(knopen) (de) cuff (links)

mand (de) basket **door de – vallen** to fail as

man'daat (het) mandate

manda'rijn (de) mandarin; tangerine

ma'nege (de) riding school

maneschijn (de) moonlight

man'haftig manly

ma'nie (de) mania

manier (de) manner, way

mani'fest (het) manifesto, manifest

manifes'tatie (de) manifestation, demonstration

manipu'leren to manipulate

mank lame, crippled

man'keren to be lacking or absent; to fail **wat mankeert je?** what's come over you?

man'moedig manful

man(ne)lijk male, masculine, manly

mannetje (het) little man; male (animal)

manoeu'vreren to manoeuvre

mans: niet veel – not very strong

manschappen (de) men

mantel (de) coat, cloak

mantelpak (het) (woman's) suit

manusje van alles (het) odd job man

manziek man-made

map (de) folder, file

ma'quette (de) model

mar'cheren to march

marechaus'see (de) military constabulary

marge (de) margin
ma'rine (de) navy
mari'neren to marinate, to marinade
mari'nier (de) marine
mar'kant striking
mar'keren to mark
mar'kies (de) marquis; sun-blind
markt(plein) (het) market(place)
marktkraam (de) stall
marmer (het) marble
mar'mot (de) marmot; guinea pig
mars (de) march **hij heeft heel wat in zijn –** he has a lot to offer
marse'pein (het) marzipan
martelaar, martela'res (de) martyr
martelen to torture, to torment
marteling (de) torture
masker (het) mask
mas'keren to camouflage
massa (de) mass, crowd
mas'saal massive
mas'seren to massage
mas'sief solid
mast (de) mast
mat weary; matt; dim
mat (de) mat; checkmate
mateloos boundless
materi'aal (het) material(s)
ma'terie (de) matter
materi'eel (het) material
matglas (het) frosted glass
matig moderate
matigen to moderate
matje (het) (table)mat; mullet (hairstyle) **op het – roepen** to be called to account
ma'tras (de) mattress
ma'troos (de) sailor
mattenklopper (de) carpet beater
mazelen measles
mecani'cien (de) mechanic
me'chanica (de) mechanics
mecha'niek (het, de) mechanism

me'chanisch mechanical
me'daille (de) medal
medail'lon (het) medallion; locket
mede with, also: fellow-
mede'deelzaam communicative
mededelen to inform
mededeling (de) communication; information
mededingen to compete
mede'klinker (de) consonant
me(d)eleven to sympathize
me(d)elij(den) (het) pity
mede'plichtig accessory
me(d)evoelen met to feel for
me(d)ewerken to cooperate
medewerker (de) co-worker
medewerking (de) active support, co-operation
medeweten (het) knowledge
medezeggenschap (de) say (in the matter)
medi'cijn (het) medicine
medisch medical
mee with
meebrengen: met zich – to bring with one; to entail
meedoen to take part
mee'dogenloos merciless
meegaan to go, to come (along)
mee'gaand accommodating
meekomen to come (along); to keep pace
meel (het) meal, flour
meemaken to experience
meenemen to take (along)
meepraten to join in the conversation; to go along with, to parrot
meer (het) lake
meer more
meerdere (de) superior; several
meerderheid (de) majority
meerder'jarig of age
meerekenen to include

meerijden to drive with, to be given a lift
meermalen more than once
meermin (de) mermaid
meervoud (het) plural
mees (de) titmouse
meeslepen to drag along; to carry away
meest(al) most(ly)
meester (de) master
meeste'res (de) mistress
meesterstuk (het) masterpiece
meeuw (de) seagull
meevallen to be better than one expected **dat valt niet mee** that is not easy
meevaller (de) bit of luck
mei May
meid (de) young woman, girl
meineed (de) perjury
meisje (het) girl, girlfriend
meisjesachtig girlish
meisjesnaam (de) maiden name; girl's name
me'juffrouw (de) Madam, Miss
mekk(er)en to bleat
me'lange (de) blend
melden to report; to announce
meldens'waard(ig) worth mentioning
melding maken van to mention
melig corny
melk (de) milk
melkboer (de) milkman
melken to milk
melkweg (de) Milky Way
me'loen (de) melon
men one, people, they, you
me'neer (de) Sir; (gentle)man
menen to think, to mean **'t wordt menens** it's getting serious
mengelmoes (de) jumble
mengen to mix, to mingle, to blend **zich – in** to meddle with

mengsel (het) mixture, blend
menig many a
menigeen many a person
menigmaal many a time
menigte (de) crowd
menig'vuldig manifold
mening (de) opinion
mennen to drive (a carriage)
mens man; human being **het is een goed –** she is a good soul
mensdom (het) mankind
menselijk human
menselijkheid (de) humanity
mensenkenner (de) judge of character
mensheid (de) mankind
mep (de) smack, whack
meppen to smack
meren to moor
merendeel (het) greater part
merendeels mostly
merk (het) mark, brand, brandname
merkbaar noticeable
merrie (de) mare
mes (het) knife
Mes'sias (de) Messiah
mest (de) dung, manure
mesten to fatten; to manure
mesthoop, mestvaalt (de) dunghill
met with, of; plus, and; by, through, in; at **tot en –** up to and including **– wie spreek ik?** who am I speaking to? (on the phone) **ik kom – de trein** I'm coming by train **hij komt – zijn vriendin** he's coming with (bringing) his girlfriend
me'taal (het) metal
meta'foor (de) metaphor
me'teen straight away; presently
meten to measure
meter (de) metre; meter
metgezel('lin) (de) companion
me'thodisch methodical
metselaar (de) bricklayer

metselen to build (using mortar)
metselwerk (het) masonry
metten: korte – maken met
to make short work of
meubel (het) piece of furniture
meubelmaker (de) cabinet maker
meubi'lair (het) furniture
meubi'leren to furnish
me'vrouw (de) Mrs; Madam; lady
middag (de) midday; afternoon
middageten (het), middagmaal
(het) midday meal
middel (het) waist; remedy, means
middelbaar average, medium
middelbaar onderwijs (het)
secondary education
middeleeuwen (de) Middle Ages
middeleeuws medieval
Middellandse Zee (de)
Mediterranean
middellijn (de) diameter
middel'matig mediocre, average
middelpunt (het) centre, pivot
middelste middlemost, centre
midden (het) middle, midst
midden'in in the middle (of)
middenstand (de) self-employed;
middle classes
midder'nacht (de) midnight
mier (de) ant
mierenhoop (de) anthill
miezerig drizzly; puny
mijden to shun
mijl (de) mile; kilometre
mijlpaal (de) milestone
mijmeren to muse
mijn my
mijn (de) mine: pit
mijnenveger (de) mine sweeper
mijnenveld (het) minefield
mijn'heer (de) Sir; Mr; (gentle)man
mijnwerker (de) miner
mijter (de) mitre
mikken (op) to aim (at)

mikpunt (het) aim, target, butt
mild liberal; mild
mili'tair (de) soldier; military
mil'joen (het) million
mille (het) (one) thousand (euros)
millimeter (de) millimetre
millimeteren to crop (hair) close
min minus; little, few
minachten to regard with disdain
minachting (de) contempt
minder less(er), fewer
minderen inferiors; to decrease
minderheid (de) minority
minder'jarig under age
minder'waardig inferior
minder'waardigheidscomplex (het)
inferiority complex
mini'maal minimum
mi'nister (de) minister, secretary
(of state) **president (de)** prime
minister
mini'sterie (het) ministry, office
minnaar (de) (male) lover
minna'res (de) (female) lover
minnen to love
minnetjes poorly
minst least
minstens at least
minuti'eus meticulous
mi'nuut (de) minute
minzaam affable
mis wrong
mis (de) Mass
misbruik (het) abuse **misbruik**
maken van to abuse
mis'bruiken to abuse, to misuse
misdaad (de) crime
mis'dadig criminal
misdadiger (de) criminal
mis'dragen: zich – to misbehave
misdrijf (het) offence
mis'gunnen to begrudge
mis'handelen to maltreat
miskraam (de) miscarriage

mis'leiden to mislead
mislopen to go wrong
mis'lukken to fail
mis'lukking (de) failure
mis'maakt deformed
mis'plaatst misplaced, out of place
mis'prijzen to disapprove of
mis'schien perhaps
misselijk sick; disgusting
missen to miss; to lack
missie (de) mission
missio'naris (de) (RC) missionary
misstand (de) abuse
misstap (de) false step, slip
mist (de) fog
misten to be foggy
misvatting (de) misunderstanding
misverstaan misunderstand
misverstand (het)
  misunderstanding
mis'vormd misshapen
mitrail'leur (de) machine gun
mits provided (that)
modder (de) mud
mode (de) fashion
mo'del (het) model; pattern
modeshow (de) fashion parade
modi'eus fashionable
moe tired
moed (de) courage
moedeloos dejected
moeder (de) mother; matron
moederlijk motherly
moederschap (het) motherhood
moedertaal (de) mother tongue
moedervlek (de) birthmark, mole
moederziel alleen quite alone
moedig courageous
moed'willig wilful
moeien: de politie in een zaak –
  to call in the police **er is een week
  mee ge'moeid** it will take a week
moeilijk difficult, with difficulty
moeilijkheid (de) difficulty

moeite (de) trouble; difficulty
  de – waard worthwhile
moeizaam laborious
moer (de) nut
moe'ras (het) marsh
moe'rassig marshy
moes (de, het) mash, pulp
moesson (de) monsoon
moestuin (de) kitchen garden
moeten must, to have to **wat moet
  dat?** what's going on (there)? **je
  moest je schamen** you ought
  to be ashamed of yourself
moffelen to smuggle away
mogelijk possible
mogelijker'wijs possibly
mogelijkheid (de) possibility
mogen to be allowed, may; to like
mogendheid (de) power
mokka (de) mocha
mokken to sulk
mol (de) mole; flat, minor (key)
molen (de) mill
molenaar (de) miller
molenwiek (de) sail of a windmill
mollen to do (a person) in, to destroy
mollig chubby
molshoop (de) molehill
momen'teel momentary; at present
mo'mentopname (de) snapshot
mompelen to mutter
mond (de) mouth; muzzle **met de
  – vol tanden** tongue-tied **iemand
  naar de – praten** to play up to a
  person
mon'dain fashionable
mondeling oral
mond-en-'klauwzeer (het) foot
  and mouth disease
mondig of age
mondje (het) mouthful, taste **zij is
  niet op haar – gevallen** she gives
  as good as she gets, she has a
  ready tongue

mondjes'maat (de) bare minimum
monnik (de) monk
monnikenwerk (het) drudgery, donkey work
mono'toon monotonous
monster (het) monster; (free) sample
monsterachtig monstrous
monstru'eus monstrous
mon'tage (de) assembly, mounting
monter lively
mon'teren to assemble, to set (up)
mon'teur (de) fitter, mechanic
mon'tuur (het) (spectacle) frame
mooi beautiful, fine
moord (de) murder
moordaanslag (de) murderous attempt
moord'dadig murderous
moordenaar (de) murderer
moordpartij (de) massacre
moors moorish
moot (de) fillet (of fish)
mop (de) joke **een schuine –** a dirty joke
mopperen to grumble
mo'raal (de) moral(s)
morali'seren to moralize
mo'reel (het) moral; morale
mores (de) manners, customs
morgen (de) morning; tomorrow **'s morgens** in the morning, every morning **morgen'ochtend** tomorrow morning
mormel (het) freak **verwend –** spoiled brat
mor'fine (de) morphine
morrelen to fumble
morren to grumble
mors'dood stone-dead
morsen to spill, to make a mess
mos (het) moss
mos'kee (de) mosque
Moskou Moscow

mossel (de) mussel
mosterd (de) mustard **(als) – na de maaltijd** a bit late in the day
mot (de) moth; bust-up
motie (de) motion, vote
mo'tief (het) motive; motif
moti'veren to justify, to defend
motor (de) motor, engine
motorpech (de) engine trouble
motregen (de) drizzle
mous'seren to effervesce
mouw (de) sleeve **ergens een – aanpassen** to manage somehow **iemand iets op de – spelden** to fool a person
moza'ïek (het) mosaic
muf musty
mug (de) gnat
muggenzifte'rij (de) hair splitting
muilkorf (de) muzzle
muis (de) mouse; ball of the thumb
muisjes (de) aniseed comfits
muiten to mutiny
muite'rij (de) mutiny
muizenval (de) mouse trap
mul loose, sandy
multiplex (het) plywood
mummie (de) mummy
mu'nitie (de) ammunition, munitions
munt (de) coin(age); currency; mint **kruis of –** heads or tails
munteenheid (de) monetary unit
munten to mint **dat was op mij gemunt** that (remark) was aimed at me
muntstuk (het) coin
murmelen to babble
murw soft, tender **iemand – maken** break someone's spirit
mus (de) sparrow
musi'ceren to make music

> ## Insight
>
> The Dutch word **museum** is not going to pose speakers of English with any problems. However, be aware that, besides the plural form **museums**, the plural **musea** also exists. Both forms are used and can be interchanged freely, although sometimes the two are mixed up, resulting in the incorrect form **musea's**. Other words with similar plural forms are **catalogus** *catalogue* which has the plural forms **catalogi** and **catalogussen**; **datum** *date* has the plural forms **datums** and **data**; and **politicus**, which has the feminine form **politica** (*female politician*) and the plural **politici**.

musicus (de) musician
mus'kiet (de) mosquito
muts (de) hat
muur (de) wall
muurschildering (de) mural
muurvast firm as a rock
mu'ziek (de) music
mu'ziekkorps (het) band

mu'ziektent (de) bandstand
muzi'kaal musical
muzi'kant (de) street musician; bandsman
mys'terie (het) mystery
mysteri'eus mysterious
mythe (de) myth

N

na after; close **op één –** all but one **de op één – duurste**, the second most expensive one **iedereen komt, op mijn moeder –** everyone is coming, except for my mother
naad (de) seam **het naadje van de kous willen weten** to want to know every detail
naaien to sew; to screw (vulg)
naaister (de) needlewoman
naakt naked, nude
naald (de) needle
naaldbos (het) pinewood
naam (de) name
naambord (het) nameplate
naamgenoot (de) namesake
naamloze vennootschap (de) limited company

naamval(suitgang) (de) case (ending)
naäpen to ape
naar to, for **we gaan – Rome** we're going to Rome **ik ben op zoek –** I'm looking for
naar'mate (according) as
naarstig diligent
naast next to; nearest
nabestellen to put in a further order
na'bij near, close
na'bijgelegen neighbouring
nablijven to stay behind
nabootsen to imitate
na'burig neighbouring
nacht (de) night **bij – en ontij** at all hours of the day and night
nachtbraken to make a night of it

nachtegaal (de) nightingale
nachtelijk nocturnal
nachtgoed (het) nightwear
nachtmerrie (de) nightmare
nachtploeg (de) night shift
nachtpon (de) nightdress
nachtverblijf (het) lodging
  for the night
nadat after
nadeel (het) disadvantage,
  detriment
na'delig disadvantageous,
  detrimental
nadenken to reflect
nader nearer; further **bij – inzien**
  on second thoughts
nader'bij nearer **van –** more closely
naderen to approach
nader'hand afterwards
na'dien since (then)
nadoen to imitate
nadruk (de) emphasis; reprint
na'drukkelijk emphatic
nagaan to examine, to trace
nagedachtenis (de) memory
nagel (de) nail
nagellak (de) nail varnish
nagelriem (de) cuticle
nagemaakt imitation, spurious
nagenoeg almost
nagerecht (het) dessert
nageslacht (het) posterity
nageven: dat moet ik hem – I'll say
  that for him
nahouden: er op – to maintain
na'ïef naïve
najaar (het) autumn
nakijken to gaze after; to check
na'komeling (de) descendant
nakomen to carry out
nalaten to leave (behind); to omit
  ik kon niet – u te vertellen I could
  not help telling you
na'latig negligent, remiss

naleven to observe;
  to comply with
nalezen to read over or again
nalopen to run after; to be slow
namaak (de) imitation
namaken to imitate, to forge
namelijk namely, i.e.; because
namens on behalf of
namiddag (de) afternoon
naoorlogs post-war
napluizen to examine in detail
napraten to parrot; to stay behind
  talking
napret (de) fun after the event
nar (de) jester
nar'cis (de) daffodil
nar'cose (de) narcosis
narekenen to check
narigheid (de) unpleasantness
na'saal nasal
naschrift (het) postscript
naslaan to look up
nasleep (de) aftermath
nasmaak (de) aftertaste
nastaren to (turn round and) stare
nastreven to strive after
nat wet
natafelen to linger at the dinner
  table
natellen to check, to count (again)
natie (de) nation
nationali'seren to nationalize
nattigheid (de) moisture **– voelen**
  to smell a rat
na'tura: in – in kind
natu'rel natural
na'tuur (de) nature; scenery **van**
  nature by nature
na'tuurgetrouw true to nature
na'tuurkunde (de) physics
natuur'kundige (de) physicist
na'tuurlijk natural; of course
na'tuurverschijnsel (het) natural
  phenomenon

nauw narrow, tight, close **hij neemt het niet te –** he is not very particular
nauwelijks scarcely
nauwge'zet conscientious
nauw'keurig accurate
nauw'sluitend close-fitting
navel (de) navel
navelstreng (de) umbilical cord
navertellen to repeat
navraag (de) enquiries
naweeën (de) aftereffects
nawerken to make its effect felt
nazien to check
nazomer (de) late summer
neder down
nederig humble
nederlaag (de) defeat
Nederlander (de) Dutchman
Nederlands Dutch
Nederlandse (de) Dutch woman
nederpop (de) Dutch pop music
nederzetting (de) settlement
neef (de) cousin, nephew
nee no
neer down
neer'buigend condescending
neerhalen to haul down; to run down

neerkomen to come down **het komt hierop neer** it boils down to this
neerleggen to put down; to resign
neerslaan to strike down; to precipitate **de ogen –** to cast down one's eyes
negen nine
negende ninth
negentien(de) nineteen(th)
negentig ninety
neger (de) negro
negeren to bully
ne'geren to ignore
nege'rin (de) negress
neigen to incline
neiging (de) inclination, tendency
nek (de) (nape of the) neck **met de – aankijken** to cold-shoulder
nekken to break, to ruin
nemen to take **we zullen het er eens van –** let's enjoy ourselves
nergens nowhere **ik weet – van** I know nothing about it
ner'veus nervous
nest (het) nest; minx
nestelen to nest **zich –** to ensconce oneself; to nestle
net (het) net(work); system **achter het – vissen** to miss the boat

Insight

The Netherlands is a plural term in English, but note that in Dutch the country's name is singular, **Nederland**. Don't be confused with **Nederlands** which means *Dutch* (both the language and the adjective), but remember that, as an adjective, **Nederlands** can get an extra -e when used before a noun: **dit is Nederlandse wijn** *this is Dutch wine*. A *Dutchman* is **een Nederlander** and *a Dutchwoman* is **een Nederlandse**. So you could say **Isa is Nederlandse** *Isa is a Dutchwoman*, although **Isa is Nederlands** *Isa is Dutch* is also possible.

net tidy, neat; respectable, decent; just, exactly **we waren – op tijd** we were just in time
netel (de) nettle
netjes tidily, neat, nice, decent
netto nett
netvlies (het) retina
neuriën to hum
neu'rose (de) neurosis
neus (de) nose, nozzle **het is maar een wassen –** there is nothing to it **met de – in de boter vallen** to come at the right moment
neusgat (het) nostril
neushoorn (de) rhinoceros
neusvleugel (de) nostril
neu'traal neutral
neuzen in to pry into
nevel (de) mist, haze
nicht (de) niece, cousin; fairy, queen, poofter, faggot
niemand nobody
nier (de) kidney
niet not
nieten to staple
nietig null and void; diminutive; trivial
nietje (het) staple
nietmachine (de) stapler
niets nothing
nietsbe'duidend, nietsbe'tekenend insignificant
nietsnut (de) good-for-nothing
niets'zeggend meaningless
niette'min nevertheless
niet'waar is(n't) it?, do(n't) you?, does(n't) she? etc. **jij spreekt Japans, –?** you speak Japanese, don't you?
nieuw new
nieuw'bakken new-fangled
nieuweling (de) novice
nieuws (het) news
nieuwsblad (het) newspaper

nieuws'gierig inquisitive
nieuwtje (het) piece of news
niezen to sneeze
nihil nil
nijdig angry
nijlpaard (het) hippopotamus
nijptang (de) (pair of) pliers
niks nothing
nimf (de) nymph
nimmer never
nippertje: op het – in the nick of time
nis (de) niche, alcove
ni'veau (het) level
nivel'leren to level
n.l. (namelijk) i.e.; you see
nobel noble-minded
noch ... noch neither ... nor
nochtans nevertheless
nodig necessary **– hebben** to need
noemen to name, to call; to mention
noemens'waard(ig) worth mentioning
nog still, yet **vandaag –** this very day **– vele jaren!** many happy returns!
nogal rather, fairly
nogmaals once again
nok (de) ridge of the roof
no'made (de) nomad
non (de) nun
nonsens (de) nonsense
nood (de) need, emergency; distress
noodge'dwongen from necessity
noodgeval (het) emergency
nood'lijdend destitute
noodlot (het) fate
nood'lottig fatal
noodrem (de) safety brake
noodtoestand (de) state of emergency; untenable situation
noodweer (het) deluge
noodgebouw (het) temporary building
noodzaak (de) necessity

nood'zakelijk necessary
nooit never
Noor (de) Norwegian
noord north
noordelijk northern, northerly
noorden (het) North
noorderlicht (het) northern lights
noorderzon: met de – vertrekken
  to cut and run
noordpool (de) north pole
noordwaarts northward(s)
Noors (het) Norwegian
Noorwegen Norway
noot not
noot (de) not: nut **hele, halve –,**
  kwartnoot etc breve, minim, crotchet
  etc **hij heeft veel noten op zijn**
  zang he is hard to please, pretentious
nootmus'kaat (de) nutmeg
nor (de) (vulg), clink
nor'maal normal
nor'maliter normally
nota (de) note; bill, account
no'taris (de) notary
notendop (de) nutshell

notenkraker (de) nut cracker
no'teren to note (down)
notie (de) notion
no'titie (de) note; notice
no'tulen (de) minutes
nou now: you bet!
no'velle (de) short story
nu now (that) **van – af aan**
  from now on
nuchter sober, level-headed **op de**
  nuchtere maag on an
  empty stomach
nukkig wayward
nul (de) nought, nil, zero; nonentity
nulpunt (het) zero
nummer (het) number; issue
  iemand op zijn – zetten
  to put a person in his place
nummeren to number
nurks grumpy
nut (het) use, benefit
nutteloos useless
nuttig useful
nuttigen to partake of
N.V. ltd (company)

O

o.a.: onder andere *inter alia*;
  including
o'ase (de) oasis
o-benen (de) bandy legs
ober (de) waiter
ob'ject (het) object(ive)
obli'gatie (de) bond
ob'sceen obscene
obser'vator (de) observer
oce'aan (de) ocean
och ah!, oh
ochtend (de) morning **'s ochtends**
  in the morning(s)
oc'taaf (de) octave
oc'trooi (het) patent; charter
oefenen to train, to practise

oefening (de) exercise, practice
oer- primal
Oeral (de) Urals
oermens (de) prehistoric man
oerwoud (het) virgin forest, jungle
oester (de) oyster
oever (de) bank, shore
of or; whether, if **– ... –** either ....
  or; whether ... or
offer (het) sacrifice, victim
offeren to sacrifice; to offer up
of'ferte (de) offer; tender
offici'eel official
offi'cier (de) officer **– van justitie**
  public prosecutor
offici'eus semi-official

of'schoon although
ogen to eye; to be attractive
ogenblik (het) moment
ogen'blikkelijk immediate
ogen'schijnlijk seemingly
ogenschouw: in – nemen
  to look over
oksel (de) armpit
olie (de) oil
oliën to oil
olifant (de) elephant
o'lijf (de) olive
om round, about; at **– de andere**
  dag every other day **– te** in order
  to **de tijd is –** time is up
oma (de) grandma
om'armen to embrace
ombrengen to kill
omdat because
omdoen to put on, to wrap round
omdraaien to turn (round), to twist
omduwen to knock over
omgaan to go round; to associate;
  to manage/deal **het hoekje –**
  to peg out
omgaande: per – by return (of post)
omgang (de) social intercourse,
  dealings; procession; gallery
omgangstaal (de) everyday speech
omgangsvormen manners
omgekeerd upside-down; reverse(d)
om'geven to surround
om'geving (de) surroundings
omgooien to knock over
omhakken to cut down
om'heen round (about)
om'heinen to fence in
om'heining (de) fence, enclosure
om'helzen to embrace
om'hoog up(wards)
om'hulsel (het) cover,
  wrapping, casing
omkantelen to topple over
omkeren to turn (round)

omkijken to look round
omkleden to change clothes
omkomen to perish
omkopen to bribe
om'laag down (below)
om'lijnen to outline
om'lijsten to frame
omloop (de) circulation,
  course; gallery
omlopen to walk round
ommekeer (de) change; turn
omploegen to plough up
ompraten to talk round
omrekenen to convert, to work out
om'ringen to surround
omroep (de) broadcasting service
omroepen to broadcast
omroeper (de) announcer
omroeren to stir
omruilen to exchange
omschakelen to switch over
om'schrijven to define; to
  circumscribe
om'schrijving (de) definition;
  paraphrase
om'singelen to encircle
omslaan to turn (over); to knock over
omslag (de) cuff; cover
om'sluiten to enclose
omsmelten to melt down
omspitten to dig (over)
omspoelen to rinse
omspringen met to handle,
  to manage
omstander (de) bystander
om'standigheid (de) circumstance,
  condition
om'streden contested
omstreken (de) environs
omstreeks about
omtoveren to transform as
  if by magic
omtrek (de) outline, contour;
  neighbourhood; circumference

omvallen to fall over
omvang (de) extent, girth
om'vangrijk extensive
om'ver down; over
om'verwerpen to overthrow
omwaaien to (be) blow(n) down
omweg (de) detour, roundabout way
omwenteling (de) revolution, rotation
omwerken to remodel, to rewrite
omwisselen to (ex)change
om'zeilen to get round
omzet (de) turnover
omzetbelasting (de) sales tax
omzetten to transpose; to convert; to sell
om'zichtig circumspect
omzien to look after
on'aangenaam unpleasant
onaan'nemelijk unacceptable, implausible
onaan'tastbaar unassailable
onaan'zienlijk insignificant
on'aardig: niet – not at all bad
on'afgebroken continuous
onaf'hankelijk independent, irrespective
onaf'scheidelijk inseparable
onbe'dorven unspoilt
onbe'duidend trivial
onbe'gonnen werk (het) hopeless task
onbe'heerd unattended
onbe'holpen awkward
onbe'kend unfamiliar
onbe'kwaam incapable
onbe'lemmerd unrestricted
onbe'nullig inane
onbe'paald indefinite
onbe'perkt unrestricted
– vert'rouwen implicit faith
onbe'rekenbaar incalculable
onbe'schaafd ill-mannered; uncivilized

onbe'schaamd shameless; brazen
onbe'schoft impertinent
onbe'schrijfelijk indescribable
onbe'slecht onbe'slist undecided
onbe'streden uncontested
onbe'suisd reckless
onbe'taalbaar priceless
onbe'tekenend insignificant
onbe'twist undisputed
onbe'twistbaar indisputable
onbe'vangen unbiased
onbe'voegd not qualified; unauthorized
onbe'vredigend unsatisfactory
onbe'waakt unguarded
onbe'weeglijk motionless, immovable
onbe'werkt untreated
onbe'wogen unmoved
onbe'woonbaar uninhabitable
onbe'woond uninhabited
onbe'wust unconscious
onbe'zorgd carefree
on'breekbaar unbreakable
on'bruikbaar useless
on'dankbaar ungrateful, thankless
ondanks despite
on'denkbaar unthinkable
onder under(neath); among; during
onder'aan at the foot of
onder'in at the bottom (of)
onder'aards subterranean
onderafdeling (de) subdivision
onderbewust subconscious
onder'breken to interrupt
onderbrengen to accommodate, to place
onderbroek (de) (under)pants
onderdak (het) shelter, accommodation
onder'danig submissive
onderdeel (het) part
onderdoen: niet – voor to be in no way inferior to

onderdompelen to immerse
onder'door under, through
onder'drukken to oppress,
to suppress
onderduiken to dive; to go
into hiding
onder'gaan to go down; to perish
onder'gaan to undergo
ondergang (de) downfall, ruin
ondergeschikt subordinate;
secondary
onderge'tekende (de) (the)
undersigned
ondergoed (het) underwear
onder'graven to undermine
ondergrond (de) subsoil; foundation
onder'handelaar (de) negotiator
onder'handelen to negotiate
onder'handelingen (de)
negotiations
onderhoud (het) maintenance;
interview
onder'houden to maintain,
to support
onder'houdend entertaining
onder'huids subcutaneous,
hyperdermic
onderjurk (de) slip
onderkant (de) underside
onderkin (de) double chin
onderkomen (het) shelter
onderkoning (de) viceroy
onderling mutual
onderlopen to get flooded
onder'mijnen to undermine
onder'nemen to undertake
onder'nemend enterprising
onder'nemer (de) employer;
contractor
onder'neming (de) enterprise;
company
onder'onsje (het) friendly get-
together
onderpand (het) pledge, security

onder'schatten to underestimate
onderscheid (het) difference,
distinction
onder'scheiden to distinguish
onder'scheiding (de) distinction,
honour
onder'scheidingsvermogen (het)
discrimination
onder'scheppen to intercept
onderschrift (het) caption
onderspit: het – delven to get
the worst of it
onderstaand (mentioned) below
onderste bottom(most)
onderste'boven upside down; upset
onder'steunen to support
onder'steuning (de) support, relief
onder'strepen to underline
onder'tekenen to sign
ondertrouw (de) registration
of intended marriage
onder'tussen meanwhile
onderverhuren to sub-let
onder'vinden to experience
onder'voed under-nourished
onder'vragen to interrogate
onder'weg on the way
onderwerp (het) subject
onder'werpen to subject; to
subdue; to submit
onder'wijl meanwhile
onderwijs (het) education
onder'wijzen to teach
onder'wijzer (de) schoolteacher
onder'worpen submissive
onder'zeeboot (de) submarine
onderzoek (het) enquiry,
investigation, examination, research
onder'zoeken to investigate,
to examine
onder'zoekingstocht (de)
exploratory expedition
on'deugend naughty
on'diep shallow

ondoor'dacht thoughtless
ondoor'dringbaar impenetrable
ondoor'grondelijk inscrutable
ondoor'schijnend opaque
ondoor'zichtig not transparent
on'draaglijk unbearable
ondubbel'zinnig unequivocal
on'duidelijk indistinct
onecht spurious; illegitimate
on'eens: het – zijn to disagree
oneer'biedig disrespectful
on'effen uneven
on'eindig infinite
on'enigheid (de) discord
oner'varen inexperienced

ongeëvenaard unequalled
onge'frankeerd unstamped, carriage forward
onge'hinderd unimpeded
onge'hoord unheard of
onge'huwd unmarried
on'geldig invalid
onge'legen inopportune
onge'lijk uneven, unequal
ongelijk (het) (hebben) (to be) wrong
ongelikte beer (de) rough customer
ongelimiteerd unlimited
onge'lofelijk incredible
ongeloof'waardig improbable

Insight

Ongelofelijk *incredible* can also be spelt **ongelooflijk**. The word also knows two different pronunciations, one with the extra e-sound after the **f**, and one without (the latter spelling and pronunciation are generally considered a little more formal). Don't forget, however, that there is no difference in spelling between adjectives and adverbs in Dutch, so **ongelofelijk** (or **ongelooflijk**) means both *incredible* and *incredibly*, just as **zacht** means both *soft* and *softly*, **snel** means *quick* and *quickly*, and **goed** means both *good* and *well*: **een goed boek** *a good book*; **goed gedaan!** *well done!*

oneven odd
oneven'redig disproportionate
onfat'soenlijk improper
on'feilbaar infallible
ongeacht irrespective of
onge'bonden unbound; dissolute
onge'daan maken to undo
onge'deerd unhurt
ongedierte (het) vermin
ongeduld (het) impatience
onge'duldig impatient
onge'durig restless
onge'dwongen unconstrained

ongeluk (het) accident, misfortune
onge'lukkig unhappy, unfortunate, unlucky
ongemak (het) inconvenience, discomfort
onge'makkelijk uncomfortable; hard to please; awkward
ongemeubi'leerd unfurnished
onge'moeid laten to leave in peace
onge'naakbaar unapproachable
ongenade (de) disgrace, disfavour
onge'nadig merciless
onge'neeslijk incurable

onge'nietbaar unpalatable;
unbearable
ongenoegen (het) displeasure
onge'past improper
onge'regeld irregular
onge'regeldheden (de)
disturbances
onge'rust anxious, uneasy
onge'schikt unfit, unsuitable
onge'schonden undamaged;
unimpaired
onge'schoold untrained
onge'steld: zij is – she's having
her period
onge'stoord undisturbed
onge'straft unpunished;
with impunity
onge'trouwd single, unmarried
onge'twijfeld undoubtedly
ongeval (het) accident
onge'veer approximately
onge'voelig unfeeling
onge'wapend unarmed
onge'wenst undesirable
onge'wijzigd unaltered
onge'wild unintentional
onge'woon unusual
onge'zellig unsociable;
cheerless
onge'zouten unsalted; plain
on'gunstig unfavourable
on'guur sinister, unsavoury
on'handelbaar intractable
on'handig clumsy; awkward
onheil (het) calamity
onheil'spellend ominous
onher'bergzaam inhospitable
onher'roepelijk irrevocable
onher'stelbaar irreparable
on'houdbaar untenable
on'juist inaccurate
onkosten (de) expenses
onkostendeclaratie (de) expenses
claim

onkostenvergoeding (de) payment/
reimbursement of expenses;
mileage allowance
onkruid (het) weed(s)
onlangs recently
on'leesbaar illegible
onlusten (de) disturbances
onmacht (de) impotence,
powerlessness
onmens (de) brute
on'menselijk inhuman
on'merkbaar imperceptible
on'metelijk vast
on'middellijk immediate
on'misbaar indispensable
onmis'kenbaar unmistakable
on'mogelijk impossible, not possible
onna'volgbaar inimitable
on'nodig unnecessary
on'noembaar, on'noemelijk
immeasurable
on'nozel silly; innocent
onom'stotlelijk incontestable
onom'wonden frank
ononderbroken uninterrupted
onont'beerlijk indispensable
onont'koombaar inescapable
on'ooglijk unsightly
onop'houdelijk incessant
onop'lettend inattentive
onover'gankelijk intransitive
onover'troffen unsurpassed
onover'winnelijk invincible
onpar'tijdig impartial
on'passelijk sick
onper'soonlijk impersonal
onrecht (het) injustice **ten onrechte**
wrongly
onrecht'matig unlawful
on'redelijk unreasonable
onroerende goederen (de)
immovable property
onrust (de) unrest
onrust'barend alarming

on'rustig restless
onruststoker (de), onrustzaaier (de) troublemaker
ons (het) 100 grams
ons us
onsamen'hangend incoherent
on'schadelijk harmless
on'schatbaar priceless; invaluable
on'schendbaar inviolable
onschuld (de) innocence
on'schuldig innocent
on'smakelijk unsavoury
on'sterfelijk immortal
onsympa'thiek uncongenial, unpleasant
ont'aard(en) (to) degenerate
on'tastbaar intangible
ont'beren to lack
ont'bieden to summon
ont'bijt (het) breakfast
ont'bijten to have breakfast
ont'binden to undo; to decompose, to disintegrate, to dissolve; to disband
ont'binding (de) decomposition, disintegration, dissolution
ont'bloot bare; devoid
ont'bloten to bare, to uncover, to strip
ont'brandbaar inflammable
ont'branden to catch fire; to flare up
ont'breken to be missing **het ontbrak me aan moed** I lacked the courage
ont'cijferen to decipher
ont'daan cut up, shaken
ont'dekken to discover
ont'dekking (de) discovery
ont'dekkingsreiziger (de) explorer
ont'dooien to thaw (out)
ont'duiken to elude, to evade
ont'eigenen to expropriate
on'telbaar innumerable
on'tembaar indomitable

ont'eren to dishonour
ont'erend degrading
ont'erven to disinherit
onte'vreden discontented, dissatisfied
ont'fermen: zich – over to take pity on; to take care of
ont'futselen to filch
ont'gaan to elude
ont'ginnen to reclaim (land); to cultivate
ont'glippen to slip (out); to escape
ont'groeien to outgrow; to become estranged to
ont'groenen to initiate
ont'haal (het) reception
ont'halen to regale
ont'haren to depilate
ont'heffen to relieve; to exempt
ont'heiligen to desecrate
ont'hoofden to behead
ont'houden to remember; to withhold **zich – van** to abstain from
ont'hullen to unveil; to reveal
ont'hutst disconcerted
ont'kennen to deny
ont'kenning (de) denial, negation
ont'ketenen to unchain; to unleash
ont'kiemen to germinate
ont'kleden to undress
ont'knoping (de) denouement
ont'komen to escape
ont'kurken to uncork
ont'lasten to unburden, to relieve, to discharge
ont'leden to analyse; to dissect
ont'lenen to borrow, to derive
ont'lokken to elicit
ont'lopen to evade
ont'luiken to open, to blossom (out)
ont'mantelen to dismantle
ont'maskeren to unmask, to expose
ont'moedigen to discourage
ont'moeten to meet

ont'moeting (de) encounter, meeting
ont'nemen to deprive of
ont'nuchteren to disillusion
ontoe'gankelijk inaccessible
ontoe'geeflijk unaccommodating
ontoe'laatbaar inadmissible
ontoe'reikend inadequate
ontoe'rekenbaar not responsible for one's actions
on'toombaar uncontrollable
on'toonbaar not fit to be seen
ont'plofbare stof explosive
ont'ploffen to explode
ont'plooien to develop; to display; to unfold
ont'poppen: zich – als to turn out to be
ont'raden to advise against
ont'rafelen to unravel
ont'roeren to move, to touch
ont'roering (de) emotion
on'troostbaar inconsolable
ontrouw (de) disloyal(ty)
ont'roven to rob of
ont'ruimen to vacate, to evacuate
ont'rukken to snatch away from
ont'schepen to disembark
ont'schieten to escape (one's memory)
ont'sieren to disfigure, to mar
ont'slaan to discharge
ont'slag (het) discharge **– nemen** to resign
ont'sluieren to unveil
ont'sluiten to open up
ont'smetten to disinfect
ont'smettingsmiddel (het) disinfectant
ont'snappen to escape
ont'spannen to relax
ont'spanning (de) relaxation, recreation
ont'sporen to (be) derailed

ont'springen to have its source **de dans –** to have a narrow escape
ont'spruiten to sprout; to arise from
ont'staan to originate, to come into being; **(het)** origin **doen –** to bring about
ont'steken to kindle, to ignite; to inflame
ont'steking (de) inflammation; ignition
ont'steld alarmed
ont'stemd upset, put out
ont'trekken to withdraw **zich – aan** to shirk
ontuig (het) riffraff
ont'vangstbewijs (het) receipt
ont'vangen to receive
ont'vanger (de) recipient
ont'vangst (de) reception, receipt
ont'vankelijk susceptible
ont'vlambaar inflammable; excitable
ont'vlammen to inflame
ont'vluchten to escape from
ont'voeren to abduct
ont'vouwen to unfold
ont'vreemden to steal
ont'waken to wake up
ont'wapenen to disarm
ont'warren to disentangle
ont'wennen to lose the habit of
ont'werp (het) project; design
ont'werpen to design, to plan
ont'wijken to evade, to avoid
ont'wijkend evasive
ont'wikkeld educated, developed
ont'wikkelen to develop, to generate
ont'wikkeling (de) development, education
ont'wortelen to uproot
ont'wrichten to dislocate
ont'zag (het) awe
ont'zaglijk tremendous
ontzag'wekkend awe-inspiring

ont'zeggen to deny, to refuse
ont'zenuwen to unnerve; to disprove
ont'zet appalled
ont'zetten to relieve; to deprive; to put out
ont'zettend terrible, appalling: awfully
ont'zien to spare, to save
on'uitgesproken unspoken
onuit'puttelijk inexhaustible
onuit'spreekbaar unpronounceable
onuit'staanbaar intolerable
onuit'voerbaar impracticable
onuit'wisbaar indelible
onvast unstable, unsteady
onver'anderd unaltered
onver'anderlijk invariable
onver'antwoord irresponsible
onverant'woordelijk irresponsible, inexcusable
onver'beterlijk incorrigible
onver'biddelijk inexorable
onver'bloemd plain
onver'brekelijk indissoluble
onver'deeld undivided, unqualified
onverdiend undeserved
onver'dienstelijk undeserving
onver'draagzaam intolerant
onver'droten indefatigable
onver'enigbaar incompatible
onver'gankelijk imperishable
onver'geeflijk unpardonable
onver'getelijk unforgettable
onver'hinderd unimpeded
onver'klaarbaar inexplicable
onver'kort unabridged
onver'krijgbaar unobtainable
onver'mijdelijk unavoidable
onver'minderd undiminished
onver'moed unsuspected
onver'moeibaar indefatigable
onver'moeid untiring
onvermogen (het) inability; powerlessness

onver'murwbaar inexorable, unyielding
onverrichter zake with nothing accomplished
onver'schillig indifferent, unconcerned
onver'schrokken intrepid
onver'slijtbaar indestructible, very hard-wearing
onver'staanbaar unintelligible
onver'standig unwise
onver'stoorbaar imperturbable
onver'togen unseemly
onver'wacht unexpected
onver'wijld immediate
onver'woestbaar inextinguishable
onver'zettelijk stubborn
onver'zoenlijk irreconcilable
onver'zorgd unattended; careless, untidy
onvol'daan unsatisfied; unpaid
onvol'doende (de) unsatisfactory mark, fail
onvol'doende insufficient, unsatisfactory
onvol'prezen beyond praise
onvol'tooid unfinished; imperfect (tense)
on'voorbereid unprepared
onvoor'delig unprofitable, uneconomical
onvoor'waardelijk unconditional
on'vriendelijk unkind
on'vrij not free, without any privacy
on'vruchtbaar infertile, fruitless
onwaarde: van — null and void
on'waardig unworthy, undignified
onwaar'schijnlijk improbable
onweer (het) thunder storm
onweer'staanbaar irresistible
on'wel unwell
on'wennig ill at ease
onweren to thunder
on'wetend ignorant

on'wettig unlawful, illegal, illegitimate
on'wezenlijk unreal
on'wijs fabulously, terrifically, unbelievably — **gaaf** unbelievably fab/cool/fantastic
onwil (de) unwillingness
onwille'keurig involuntary
on'willig unwilling, obstinate
on'wrikbaar unshakable
onze our(s)
on'zedelijk immoral
on'zeker uncertain
onze-lieve-'heersbeestje (het) ladybird
on'zichtbaar invisible
on'zijdig neutral, neuter
onzin (de) nonsense
on'zinnig absurd
on'zuiver impure, inaccurate, out of tune
oog (het) eye
oogarts (de) ophthalmologist
ooggetuige (de) eye witness
oogharen eyelashes
oogholte (de), oogkas (de) eye socket
oogkleppen blinkers
ooglid (het) eyelid
oogluikend toelaten to turn a blind eye (to something)
oogopslag (de) glance, look
oogpunt (het) point of view
oogst (de) harvest, crop
oogvlies (het) cornea
oogwenk (de) twinkling of an eye
ooievaar (de) stork
ooit ever
ook also, too; either **wat (dan) —** whatever **waar (dan) —** wherever
oom (de) uncle
oor (het) ear; handle
oorbel (de) earring
oord (het) place, region, resort

oordeel (het) opinion, judgement
oordelen to judge
oorkonde (de) charter, (ancient) document
oorlel (de) earlobe
oorlog (de) war(fare)
oorpijn (de) earache
oorsprong (de) origin, source
oor'spronkelijk original
oorver'dovend deafening
oorzaak (de) cause
oost east, Orient
oostelijk easterly, east (of)
oosten (het) east
Oostenrijk Austria
oosters eastern, oriental
oostwaarts eastward(s)
Oost'zee (de) Baltic
op on; at; in; up **het bier is —** the beer is finished **ik heb veel met hem —** I like him a lot
opa (de) grandad
opbellen to ring up
opbergen to put away
opbeuren to lift up; to cheer up
opbiechten to own up
opblazen to inflate
opbloei (de) revival
opbouwen to build up
opbreken to break up
opbrengen to yield
opbrengst (de) yield, proceeds
opdagen to turn up
op'dat in order that
opdienen to dish up, to serve
opdissen to dish up
opdoeken to close down, to clear out
opdoemen to loom (up)
opdonderen: donder op! get the hell out of here!
opdracht (de) instruction(s), commission; dedication
opdragen to instruct, to order; to dedicate

opdrijven to force up; to drive
opdringen to thrust on (a person)
op'dringerig obtrusive
opduiken to bob up, to crop up
op'een together, on top of one another
op'eens all at once
opeen'volgend successive
opeisen to claim, to demand
open open
open'baar public
open'baren to reveal
open'baring (de) revelation
opendoen to open; to answer the door
openen, opengaan to open
open'hartig frank
open('hartig)heid (de) frankness
opening (de) opening
openlijk public, open
openmaken to open, to undo
openrijten to rip open
openslaan to open **openslaande deur (de)** folding door(s), French window **– raam (het)** casement window
openstaande rekening (de) unsettled account
openstellen to (throw) open (to the public)
openvouwen to open out
ope'ratie (de) operation
ope'ratiekamer (de) operating theatre
ope'reren to operate (on)
ope'rette (de) operetta
opeten to eat (up), to finish (up)
opfrissen to refresh
opgaaf, opgave (de) statement, return; task, problem, (examination) paper
opgaan to rise, to go up; to be absorbed; to come off **dat gaat niet altijd op** that does not always hold good

opgeblazen puffed-up, bumptious
opgelucht relieved
opgeruimd cheerful
opgesloten locked up; implied
opgetogen enraptured
opgeven to give (up); to cough up; to state **hoog – van** to speak highly of
opgevreten eaten away, consumed
opgewassen tegen a match for
opgewekt cheerful
opgewonden excited
opgezet swollen; stuffed **groot(s)**
opgezet ambitious
opgooien to toss (up)
opgraven to dig up
ophaalbrug (de) drawbridge
ophalen to draw up; to pick up; to shrug; to sniff (up)
ophef (de) fuss
opheffen to lift up; to abolish, to close (down)
ophelderen to elucidate; to clear
ophemelen to extol
ophitsen to incite, to set on
ophopen to pile up; to accumulate
ophouden to hold up; to uphold; to cease; to delay
o'pinie (de) opinion
opkikkeren to perk up
op'klapbaar folding
opklapbed (het) tip-up bed
opklaren to clear up
opknappen to smarten up; to cope with; to get well
opkomen to come up, to (a)rise; to come on; to stick up (for) **het kwam bij me op** it occurred to me
opkomst (de) rise; attendance
opkrassen to clear out
opkroppen to bottle up
oplaag (de), oplage (de) number of copies printed
oplaaien to flare up
oplaten to fly

oplawaai (de) wallop
opleggen to impose; to lay on; to store
opleiden to train
opleiding (de) training, education
opletten to pay attention
op'lettend attentive
opleven to revive
opleveren to produce, to present
oplichten to lift (up); to swindle
oplichter (de) swindler
oplopen to run up; to rise; to mount; to incur
op'losbaar soluble
oplossen to (dis)solve
oplossing (de) solution
opluchting (de) relief
opluisteren to add lustre to
opmaak (de) layout
opmaken to make (up); to gather
op'merkelijk remarkable
opmerken to observe
opmerking (de) remark
op'merkzaam maken op to call attention to
opname (de) recording, photograph; admission
opnemen to take/lift (up); to take in; to record; to answer (telephone)
op'nieuw anew
opnoemen to enumerate; to call (out)
opofferen to sacrifice
oponthoud (het) delay
oppas (de) babysitter, childminder
oppassen to take care (of); to beware
oppasser (de) caretaker, attendant
opper'best excellent
opperbevel (het) supreme command
opperbevelhebber (de) commander-in-chief
opperen to propose
opperhoofd (het) chief(tain)

oppervlak (het) (outer) surface
opper'vlakkig superficial
oppervlakte (de) surface, area
oppikken to pick up
opprikken to pin up
oprakelen to poke (up); to rake up
oprapen to pick up
op'recht sincere
oprichten to erect; to establish
oprichter (de) founder
oprijlaan (de) drive
oprit (de) drive
oproep (de) summons, call
oproepen to call (up)
op'roerig rebellious
oproerkraaier (de) agitator
opruien to incite to rebellion
opruimen to clear (away)
opruiming (de) clearance sale
oprukken to press onward
opscharrelen to dig up
opschepen met to saddle with
opscheppen to serve; to brag
opschepper (de) braggart
opschieten to get (a move) on **met elkaar –** to get on (well) together
opschorten to suspend
opschrift (het) inscription, caption
opschrijven to note down
opschrikken to start, to be startled
opschrokken to gobble up
opschudding (de) commotion
opschuiven to push up, to move up
opslaan to raise; to turn up; to lay in; to rise (in price)
opslag (de) rise; storage
opslorpen, opslurpen to drink noisily; to absorb
opsluiten to lock (up)
opsommen to enumerate, to recount
opspelen to kick up a row
opsporen to track (down)
opspraak (de) disrepute
opstaan to rise

opstand (de) rising; elevation
 in – komen to rebel
opstandeling (de) rebel
op'standig rebellious
opstap (de) step
opstapelen: zich – to accumulate
opstappen to go away; to go up
opsteken to put up; to light;
 to get up **– van** to profit by
opstel (het) essay
opstellen to draft; to place
opstijgen to rise; to climb up,
 to mount
opstoken to stir up (animosity)
opstootje (het) disturbance
opstrijken to run an iron over; to
 rake in
opstropen to roll up
optekenen to note down
optellen to add up
optocht (de) procession
optreden (het) action; performance,
 show
optreden to appear; to act
optrekken to pull up; to raise
 – tegen to march against
 – met to go about with
optrommelen to round up
optuigen to decorate
opvallen to be conspicuous, to strike
op'vallend conspicuous
opvangen to catch; to overhear
opvatten to take (up), to interpret,
 to conceive
opvatting (de) conception, opinion
opvoeden to educate
opvoeding (de) upbringing
 lichamelijke – physical training
opvoeren to raise; to perform
opvoering (de) performance
opvolgen to succeed; to carry out
opvolger (de) successor
op'vouwbaar collapsible
opvreten to devour

opvrolijken to cheer up
opwaarts upward(s)
opwachten to wait for
opwegen tegen to offset
opwekken to arouse, to stimulate,
 to generate
op'wekkend encouraging
opwerken: zich – to work
 one's way up
opwinden to wind (up), to excite
opwinding (de) excitement
opzeggen to recite; to terminate,
 to cancel **zijn baan –** to give notice
opzet (de) plan, intent(ion)
op'zettelijk, met opzet deliberate
opzetten to set up; to put on;
 to turn (against); to swell
opzichter (de) superintendent
op'zichtig flashy
opzien tegen to look up to; to dread
opzien'barend sensational
opzoeken to look up
o'ranje (het) orange
orchi'dee (de) orchid
orde (de) order **aan de –**
 up for discussion
ordelijk orderly
ordenen to (put in) order
order (de) order, command
ordi'nair (de) vulgar
ordner (de) file
or'gaan (het) organ
organi'seren to organize
orgel (het) organ
orgeldraaier (de) organ grinder
oriën'teren zich – to find
 one's bearings
origi'neel original
or'kaan (de) hurricane
or'kest (het) orchestra
os (de) ox, bullock
oud old, ancient **bij het oude laten**
 to leave (things) as they were
oud'bakken stale

oude van dagen (de) aged
oudejaars'avond (de) New Year's Eve
ouder (de) older, elder; parent
ouderdom (de) (old) age
ouderlijk parental
ouder'wets old-fashioned
oudheid (de) antiquity
oudje (het) old (wo)man
oudoom (de) great-uncle
oudsher: van — (from) of old
oudst oldest, elder; senior
oudtante (de) great-aunt
ouwel (de) wafer
ouwelijk elderly
o'vaal oval
oven (de) oven, furnace, kiln
over over, across; via; past; about;
left (over) **— en weer** mutually **tijd
te —** time to spare **ik heb veel voor
hem —** I would do anything
for him **— een paar dagen**
in a few days' time
over'al everywhere
overbekend widely known
overbelasten to overburden; to
overload
overbelicht over-exposed
overblijfsel (het) remains, relic
overblijven to be left; to stay
(at school for lunch)
over'bodig superfluous
over'boord overboard
overbrengen to convey
over'bruggen to bridge
overbuur (de) neighbour across the
road
overdaad (de) excess
over'dadig excessive
over'dag during the day
over'dekt covered
over'denken to consider
overdoen to do again; to pass on
over'donderen to overwhelm
overdracht (de) transfer

over'drachtelijk metaphorical
overdragen to transfer, to convey
over'dreven exaggerated
over'drijven to exaggerate
over'duidelijk obvious
over'dwars across, athwart
over'eenkomen to agree
over'eenkomst (de) agreement,
similarity
overeen'komstig corresponding (to)
over'eenstemmen to agree
over'eind upright, on end
overgaan to cross over; to pass (on);
to go up (to a higher form)
overgang (de) transition, change;
crossing; menopause
overgangsmaatregel (de)
temporary measure
over'gankelijk transitive
overgave (de) surrender
overgelukkig over-joyed
overgeven to hand over, to
surrender; to vomit
overge'voelig hypersensitive
overgieten to transfer, to decant
overgooier (de) tunic
overgordijn (het) (running) curtain
over'goten met bathed in
overgrootmoeder (de) great-
grandmother
overgrootvader (de) great-
grandfather
overhalen to pull over; to persuade
overhand (de) upper hand
over'handigen to hand (over)
over'heen across, over **er gaan
jaren —** it takes years
overheerlijk exquisite
over'heersen to (pre)dominate
overheid (de) authorities
overhellen to incline, to lean over
overhemd (het) shirt
overhevelen to siphon
over'hoop in a mess

over'horen to test
overhouden to have left
overig remaining
overigens for the rest; anyway
overkant (de) opposite side
over'kapping (de) roof(ing)
over'koepelend coordinating
over'komen to happen to
overkomen to come over (to visit); to come across
overladen to transfer
over'langs lengthwise
overlast (de) inconvenience, nuisance
overlaten to leave
over'leden deceased
over'leg (het) deliberation, consultation
over'leggen to deliberate
over'leven to survive
over'levende (de) survivor
overleveren to hand down; to deliver up
over'levering (de) tradition
overlezen to read through, to read again
over'lijden to die
overloop (de) landing
overlopen to run over; to go over
overloper (de) deserter, traitor
overmaat excess **tot – van ramp** to crown it all
overmacht (de) superior force; force majeure
overmaken to do again; to transfer
over'mannen to overpower; to overcome
over'meesteren to overpower
over'moedig overconfident
over'morgen the day after tomorrow
over'nachten to stay the night
overnemen to take over; to adopt
overplaatsen to transfer

overplanten to transplant
over'reden to persuade
over'rijden to run over
over'rompelen to take by surprise
overschenken to decant
overschot (het) remainder, surplus
over'schreeuwen to shout down
over'schrijden to exceed; to step across
overschrijven to copy (out); to transfer
overslaan to skip; to estimate; to crack
over'spannen overwrought, suffering from severe stress
overspel (het) adultery
overstaan: ten – van in the presence of
overstappen to change
oversteekplaats (de) (pedestrian) crossing
oversteken to cross
over'stelpen to overwhelm
over'stemmen to drown, to shout down
over'stromen to flood, to in-undate
over'stuur upset
overtocht (de) crossing, passage
over'tollig superfluous
over'treden to transgress; to infringe
over'treffen to surpass
    overtreffende trap (de) superlative
overtrek (de) (loose) cover
over'tuigen to convince
over'tuiging (de) conviction
overuren (de) overtime
overval (de) surprise attack
over'vallen to surprise
over'vleugelen to surpass; to outflank
overvloed (de) abundance
over'vloedig abundant
over'vragen to overcharge
overwaaien to blow over
overweg (de) level crossing

over'weg kunnen to get on well
over'wegen to consider
over'wegend preponderant
over'weging (de) consideration
over'weldigen to overpower
over'weldigend overwhelming
overwerken to work overtime
over'werken to overwork
overwicht (het) preponderance, authority
over'winnaar (de) victor

over'winnen to conquer
over'winning (de) victory
overzicht (het) summary
over'zichtelijk well organized; clearly set out
over'zien to survey
overzijde (de) opposite side
OV-'jaarkaart (de) annual season ticket/travel card
oxi'deren to oxidize
ozon (de) ozone

P

paadje (het) (foot)path
paal (de) pole, pile, post **als een — boven water** as clear as daylight
paar (het) pair, couple; few
paard (het) horse
paardenbloem (de) dandelion
paardenkracht (de) horsepower
paars violet, purple
paarsgewijs in pairs
paartijd (de) mating season
paasdag (de): de eerste — Easter Day **de tweede —** Easter Monday
paasvakantie (de) Easter holidays
pachter (de) tenant farmer
pad (de) toad
pad (het) path
paddestoel (de) toadstool, mushroom
padvinder (de) boy scout
padvindster (de) girl guide
paf staan to be dumbfounded
pafferig puffy
pagina (de) page
pais en vree (de) peace and quiet
pak (het) pack(age); suit **— slaag** thrashing
pakhuis (het) warehouse
pakje (het) parcel, packet
pakken to pack; to seize; to hug **iemand te — krijgen** to get hold of

a person **ik heb het erg te —** I've got it badly
pakkend fascinating; catchy
pakkerd (de) hug and kiss
pakpapier (het) brown paper
pal (de) catch: directly; due **— oost** due east
pa'leis (het) palace
Pales'tijn (de) Palestinian
Pales'tijns Palestinian, Palestine
Pales'tina Palestine
paling (de) eel
palm (de) palm
Palm'pasen Palm Sunday
pam'flet (het) pamphlet lampoon
pan (de) pan; tile; shindy **in de — hakken** to make mincemeat of
pand (het) forfeit; premises; (coat)tail
pandjeshuis (het) pawn shop
pa'neel (het) panel
pa'neermeel (het) breadcrumbs
pa'niek (de) panic
panne (de) breakdown
pannenkoek (de) pancake
panta'lon (de) trousers
panter (de) panther
pan'toffel (de) slipper
pan'toffelheld (de) henpecked husband

pantser (het) armour
pantserdier (het) armadillo
pantseren to armour; to brace
pap (de) milk pudding, porridge
pa'paver (de) poppy
pape'gaai (de) parrot
pa'pier (het) paper **pa'pieren** papers; stocks and shares; credentials
papje (het) paste
pappie (de) daddy
paprika (de) (sweet) pepper
pa'raaf (de) initials
pa'raat ready
para'chute (de) parachute
pa'rade (de) review, parade
para'dijs (het) paradise
para'feren to initial
para'graaf (de) paragraph, section
paral'lel parallel
parano'ïde paranoid
paranor'maal paranormal
para'plu (de) umbrella
para'siet (de) parasite
par'cours (het) course
par'does slap(bang)
par'don (het) pardon; mercy
parel (de) pearl
parel'moer (het) mother of pearl
paren to mate **zich – aan** to be coupled with
par'fum (het) scent
parfu'meren to scent
park (het) park
par'keerautomaat (de) (car park/ parking lot) ticket machine
par'keerboete (de) parking fine
par'keerbon (de) parking ticket
par'keergarage (de) (underground) car park, parking garage
par'keergeld (het) parking money
par'keerplaats (de) parking place/ space, parking lot, car park
par'keerterrein (het) car park

par'keerverbod (het) parking ban, no parking (on signs)
par'keren to park
par'ket (het) public prosecutor's office; parquet **in een lastig –** in a predicament
par'kiet (de) parakeet
parle'ment (het) parliament
parlemen'tair parliamentary
parlemen'tariër (de) member of parliament, representative
pa'rochie (de) parish
paro'die (de) parody
parodi'ëren to parody
par'terre (de) pit; ground floor
particu'lier private
par'tij (de) part(y); game; consignment **– kiezen** to take sides
par'tijdig biased
pas (de) step; pass, passport
pas only (just) **te – en te onpas** at random **te –, van –** (be)fitting
Pasen Easter
pasfoto (de) passport photo
pasge'boren new-born
pasge'trouwd newly wed
paskamer (de) fitting room
pasklaar ready for fitting
paspoort (het) passport
paspoortcontrole (de) passport control
pas'sage (de) passage; arcade
passa'gier (de) passenger
passen to fit; to try on; to match; to be fitting; to pass **ik pas ervoor** I won't do it **– op** to take care (of)
passend fitting, appropriate
passer (de) pair of compasses
pas'seren to pass (over); to happen
passie (de) passion
pas'sief passive
passievrucht (de) passion fruit
pasta (de) paste, pasta
pas'tei (de) patty; paste

pas'toor (de) parish priest
pasto'rie (de) parsonage
pa'tat (de) chips, fries **– met** chips
with mayonnaise

peer (de) pear; light bulb **met de
gebakken peren zitten** to be left
holding the baby
pees (de) tendon; gristle

Insight

Patat met is *chips with mayonnaise*, but Dutch speakers like
nothing so much as a diminutive, so more often than not,
people will ask for **een patatje met**. It is important to realize
that the diminutive form doesn't mean that it is a small
portion of chips – diminutives frequently indicate a positive
attitude (in this case that someone likes chips and is looking
forward to eating them). People also say: **lekker weertje!**
great weather! However, funnily enough, diminutives can
also express the opposite: **wat een akelig mannetje** *what a
horrible little man.*

pa'tatje (het) (portion of) chips/fries
pa'tent (het) licence; patent
patisse'rie (de) pastries; pastry shop
pa'trijs (de) partridge
pa'trijspoort (de) porthole
pa'troon (de) cartridge
pa'troon (het) pattern, design
pa'trouille (de) patrol
pats (de) smack; bang!
patser (de) show-off
patserig macho
pauk (de) kettledrum
paus (de) pope
pauselijk papal
pauw (de) peacock
pauze (de) interval, pause
pavil'joen (het) pavilion; marquee
pech (de) bad luck
pechvogel (de) unlucky person
pe'daal (het) pedal
pe'daalemmer (de) pedal bin
pe'dant pedant(ic)
peddelen to pedal; to paddle
pedi'cure (de) chiropodist
peen (de) carrot

peet (de) godparent
peetoom (de) godfather
peil (het) gauge, level **er is op hem
geen – te trekken** he is quite
unpredictable
peilen to gauge, to sound
peinzen to muse
peinzend thoughtful
pelgrim (de) pilgrim
pelgrimstocht (de) pilgrimage
pellen to peel, to shell
pelo'ton (het) platoon;
pack, bunch
pels (de) pelt; fur coat
pen (de) pen, nib, quill; peg, pin
penalty (de) penalty (kick, shot)
pe'narie: in de – in a fix
pendelen to commute
pe'nibel grim
peni'tentie (de) penitence; ordeal
pennen to pen
penning (de) medal; official badge
penningmeester (de) treasurer
pens (de) paunch; tripe
pen'seel (het) (artist's) brush

pen'sioen (het) pension **met – gaan** to retire (on a pension)
pen'sion (het) guesthouse; board
peper (de) pepper
peperduur very expensive
peperkoek (de) gingerbread
peper'munt (de) peppermint
pepernoot (de) ginger nut
per'ceel (het) plot; premises
percen'tage (het) percentage
per'centsgewijze proportional
perfectio'neren to perfect
peri'ode (de) period
perio'diek periodical
perk (het) flower bed; limit
perka'ment (het) parchment
permit'teren to permit
per omgaand by return (of post)
per'plex perplexed
per'ron (het) platform
per se at all cost
pers (de) press; Persian (rug)
persbureau (het) press agency
persen to press, to squeeze
persfotograaf (de) press photographer, newspaper photographer
perso'neel (het) staff, personnel
perso'neelschef (de) personnel manager, staff manager
perso'neelszaken (de) personnel/ staff matters; personnel department
per'sonenauto (de) private car, passenger car
per'soon (de) person
per'soonlijk personally, private, individual
per'soonlijkheid (de) personality
per'soonsbewijs (het) identity card
perspec'tief (het) perspective
perti'nent emphatic, positive
per'vers perverse
perzik (de) peach

Perzisch Persian
pest (de) plague, pest(ilence)
pesten to bait, to tease the life out of
pestkop (de) bully
pet (de) cap **dat gaat boven mijn –** it beats me
petekind (het) godchild
peter'selie (de) parsley
pe'troleum (de) paraffin
peukje (het) cigar(ette) butt
peultjes (de) mange tout peas
peulvruchten (de) legumes
peuter (de) tiny tot
peuteren to fiddle, to tinker
peuterwerk(je) (het) finicky job
pi'anokruk (de) music stool
pi'as (de) clown
piccolo (de) piccolo; pageboy
picknick (de) picnic
picknicken to picnic
picknickmand (de) picnic hamper
piek (de) peak, spike
piekeren to puzzle, to brood
piekfijn smart, posh
pienter bright, smart
piepen to squeak, to cheep
piepjong very young
pier (de) pier, jetty; (earth)worm **ik ben altijd de kwaaie –** I get the blame for everything
pierenbad (het) paddling pool
piet'luttig petty
pietsje (het) wee bit
pijl (de) arrow
pijler (de) pillar
pijn (de) pain, ache **– doen** to hurt
pijnigen to torture, to rack
pijnlijk painful
pijn'stillend sedative, soothing
pijnstiller (de) painkiller
pijn (de) pipe; tube; funnel; trouser leg
pik (de) (vulg) penis, dick **een stijve –** a hard-on
pi'kant piquant, spicy

pik'donker (het) pitch blackness, pitch darkness
pikhouweel (het) pickaxe
pikken to peck; to pinch, steal; to put up with
pil (de) pill; chunky book
pi'laar (de) pillar
pi'loot (de) pilot
pimpelaar (de) tippler
pin (de) peg, pin
pin'cet (het) tweezers
pinda(kaas) (de) peanut (butter)
pindasaus (de) peanut sauce
pingelen to haggle
pinguïn (de) penguin
pink (de) little finger **bij de pinken** all there
Pinksteren Whitsun(tide)
pinnen to pay by bankcard; withdraw money from a cashpoint
pinpas (de) cash card, bankcard
pi'oenroos (de) peony
pi'on (de) pawn
pio'nieren to pioneer
pi'pet (de) pipette
pips off colour
pi'raat (de) pirate
pis'tool (het) pistol
pit (de) kernel, stone, pip; burner; pith
pittig pithy, spicy; tough
pizza (de) pizza
pk (paardenkracht) (de) horsepower
plaag (de) nuisance, plague
plaat (de) plate; slab; (gramophone) record; picture
plaats (de) place; room; yard; seat **in – van** instead of **ter plaatse** on the spot
plaatsbewijs (het) ticket
plaatselijk local
plaatsen to place
plaatsvervanger (de) deputy
pla'fond (het) ceiling

plagen to tease, to worry
plage'rij (de) teasing
plagi'aat (het) plagiarism
plak (de) slice; slab **onder de – zitten** to be under a person's thumb
plakband (het) adhesive tape
plakboek (het) scrapbook
plakken to stick
pla'muren to fill cracks
plan (het) plan, project **van – zijn** to intend
pla'neet (de) planet
plank (de) plank, board; shelf
plankenkoorts (de) stage fright
plant (de) plant
plant'aardig vegetable
plan'tage (de) plantation
planten to plant
plantengroei (de) vegetation
plantkunde (de) botany
plant'soen (het) gardens, flower bed
plas (de) pool, puddle; lake
plassen to go to the loo/toilet, to (have a) pee
plat flat; vulgar
pla'taan (de) plane tree
platenspeler (de) record player
platenzaak (de) record shop
platina (het) platinum
platte'grond (de) (ground)plan
platte'land (het) country(side)
platte'lands country, rural
plattrappen to trample down
plat'vloers coarse, crude
platzak penniless, empty-handed
pla'veien to pave
pla'vuis (de) flagstone
plebs (het) hoi polloi
plecht('stat)ig solemn
plechtigheid (de) ceremony, solemnity
pleeg- foster-
plegen to commit **overleg –** to consult together

plei'dooi (het) plea, (address for the) defence
plein (het) square, open space
pleister (de) plaster, bandaid
pleiten to plead **dat pleit voor hem** that's a point in his favour
plek (de) spot
pletten to roll out, to crush
pletter: te – slaan to smash to smithereens
plexiglas (het) plexiglass
ple'zier (het) pleasure
ple'zierig pleasant
plicht (de) duty
plicht(s)getrouw plicht'matig dutiful
plint (de) plinth; skirting board
ploeg (de) plough: gang, shift, team
ploegen to plough
ploegendienst (de) shift work
ploegleider (de) team manager
ploeteren to splash; to plod; to drudge
plof(fen) (de) (to) thud, (to) plop
plomp plump, squat
plons (de) splash
plonzen to (s)plash
plooi (de) fold, pleat, crease **uit de – komen** to unbend
plooibaar pliable
plooien to fold, to pleat
plotseling sudden
pluche (de) plush
pluim (de) plume, feather; tuft
pluimpje (het) compliment
pluimvee (het) poultry
pluis: niet – fishy
pluisje (het) piece of fluff
plukken to pick, to pluck
plunderen to plunder
plunjezak (de) kitbag
plus'minus approximately
pluspunt (het) plus, asset

pochen to boast
podium (het) stage, platform
poedel (de) poodle
poedel'naakt stark naked
poeder (de, het) powder
poedersuiker (de) icing sugar
poe'ha (de) fuss, la-di-da
poeieren to powder
poel (de) pool, puddle
poe'lier (de) poulterer
poen (de) dough, dosh
poep (de) crap, shit
poepen to (have a) crap
poes (de) (pussy)cat **niet voor de –** no chicken feed
poeslief honey-lipped, smooth
poespas (de) fuss about nothing
poetsen to polish, to brush
poë'zie (de) poetry
poffen to puff; to pop; to roast
poffertjes (de) small pancakes
pogen to endeavour
poging (de) attempt
pokken (de) smallpox
pokkewerk (het) nasty/unpleasant work
polderpop (de) Dutch pop music
Polen Poland
po'lijsten to polish
polikliniek (de) out-patients' clinic
polis (de) insurance policy
po'liticus (de) politician
po'litie (de) police
po'litieagent (de) policeman
po'litiebureau (het) police station
poli'tiek (de) politics
poli'tiek political
pollepel (de) wooden spoon
pols (de) pulse, wrist
polsen to sound someone out about
polsslag (de) pulse, pulsation
polsstokspringen (het) pole vaulting
pomp (de) pump

pompen to pump
pom'peus pompous
pom'poen (de) pumpkin
pompstation (het) petrol/service station
pond (het) (British) pound, 500 grammes
pont (de) ferry boat
pony (de) pony; fringe
pooier (de) pimp
pook (de) poker
pool (de) pole
poolcirkel (de) polar circle
Pools Polish
poolshoogte nemen to see how the land lies
poolster (de) pole star
poolzee (de) (ant)arctic sea
poort (de) gate(way)
poos(je) (het, de) (little) while
poot (de) paw, leg
pootjebaden to paddle
pop (de) doll; puppet; dummy
   nu heb je de poppen aan het dansen! now we're in for it!
popelen to quiver, to itch
poppenhuis (het) doll's house
poppenkast (de) puppet show, Punch and Judy show
popperig diminutive
popu'lair popular
populari'teit (de) popularity
popu'lier (de) poplar
popzanger(es) (de) pop/rock singer
por (de) prod
po'reus porous
porie (de) pore
porno(gra'fie) (de) porno(graphy)
porren to poke, to prod
porse'lein (het) china(ware)
por'taal (het) porch; hall
porte'feuille (de) portfolio; wallet
portemon'nee (de) wallet, purse
portie (de) share, helping

por'tiek (de, het) porch, doorway
por'tier (de) (hall) porter; (car) door
por'tierraampje (het) car window
porto (de) postage
por'tret (het) portrait
po'seren to pose, to sit
po'sitie (de) position, situation
posi'tief positive
po'sitiekleding (de) maternity clothes
posi'tieven (de) wits
post (de) post; mail; item; picket
   op – on duty
postbode (de) postman
postbus (de) post office box
postcode (de) postal code, ZIP code (Am)
posten to post; to picket
poste'rijen (de) postal service
postkantoor (het) post office
postorderbedrijf (het) mail-order company
pos'tuum posthumous
pos'tuur (het) figure; posture
postwissel (de) money order
postzegel (de) postage stamp
pot (de) pot, jar; (chamber) pot; saucepan, pot; kitty, pool; (inf) lesbian, dyke/dike
pot'dicht shut tight
poten to plant, to dibble
poten'tieel potential
potig hefty
potlood (het) pencil; black lead
potten to pot; to hoard
pottenbakker (de) potter
pottenkijker (de) nosy parker, snooper
potvis (de) sperm whale
pover poor, meagre
praal (de) pomp, splendour
praat(je) (het, de) talk, chat, gossip
   veel praats hebben to talk big
praatgraag, praatziek garrulous

praatpaal (de) emergency telephone
pracht (de) splendour
prachtig splendid, magnificent
practicum (het) practical (work)
prak (de) hash
prakken to mash (up)
prak'tijk (de) practice
praktisch practical
prakti'seren to practise
pralen to shine; to flaunt
prat gaan op to pride oneself on
praten to talk
pre'cair precarious
pre'cies precise, exact
predi'kant (de) minister, vicar
prediken to preach
preek (de) sermon
preekstoel (de) pulpit
prefe'reren to prefer
prei (de) leek
preken to preach
premie (de) premium
pre'mier (de) prime minister
prent (de) print, picture
prenten to imprint
presen'teren to offer; to present
pre'sentielijst (de) attendance list
pressen to press
presse-pa'pier (de) paper weight
pressie uitoefenen to bring pressure to bear
pres'tatie (de) achievement
pres'teren to achieve
pret (de) fun
pre'tentie (de) pretension **zonder pretenties** unassuming
preten'tieus pretentious
pretje (het) bit of fun
prettig pleasant, nice **– vinden** to like
preuts prudish, squeamish
preva'leren to prevail
prevelen to mutter

priester (de) priest
prijken to (be) display(ed)
prijs (de) price; prize **op prijs stellen** to appreciate
prijsbe'wust cost-conscious
prijsdaling (de) fall in price
prijsgeven to abandon, to give up
prijskaartje (het) price tag
prijsklasse (de) price range, price bracket
prijslijst (de) price list
prijsopgave (de) estimate, quotation, tender
prijsuitreiking (de) distribution of prizes, prize-giving ceremony
prijsverhoging (de) rise, price increase
prijsverlaging (de) price cut/ reduction
prijsvraag (de) competition
prijzen to praise; to price, to mark
prijzig expensive
prik (de) prick, stab; pop, fizz
prikbord (het) noticeboard, bulletin board
prikkel (de) sting, goad; spur
prikkelbaar irritable
prikkeldraad (het) barbed wire
prikkelen to prickle; to irritate, to provoke; to stimulate
prikken to prick; to tingle
pril tender, vernal
prima first-rate
pri'mair primary
pri'meur (de) scoop
primi'tief primitive, crude
prin'cipe (het) principle
principi'eel fundamental, of or on principle
prins (de) prince **van de – geen kwaad weten** to be as innocent as an unborn babe
prinselijk princely
prin'ses (de) princess

printen to print
printer (de) printer
priori'teit (de) priority
privati'seren to privatize
privé private
pro'beren to try (out)
pro'bleem (het) problem
pro'bleemloos trouble-free,
uncomplicated, smooth
procé'dé (het) process
proce'deren to take it to court
pro'cent (het) percent
pro'ces (het) lawsuit; process
iemand een – aandoen to bring
an action against a person
pro'ces-ver'baal (het) official report
procu'reur (de) attorney
pro deo voluntarily, for love
produ'cent (de) producer
produ'ceren to produce
pro'duct (het) product(ion)
pro'ductie (de) production
pro'ductiekosten (de) cost(s) of
production
productivi'teit (de) productivity
proef (de) test; proof
proefkonijn (het) laboratory rabbit;
guinea pig
proefschrift (het) thesis
proeftijd (de) apprenticeship;
probation
proefwerk (het) test (paper)
proesten to splutter
proeven to taste
pro'feet (de) prophet(ess)
pro'fessor (de) professor
pro'fiel (het) profile; cross-section
pro'fijt (het) profit, advantage
profi'teren van to profit by, to take
advantage of
prog'nose (de) prognosis; forecast
pro'gramma (het) programme
program'meertaal (de) computer
language

program'meren to program
(computers); to programme,
to schedule
progres'sief progressive
projec'teren to project, to plan
pro'jectie (de) projection
prole'tariër (de) proletarian
prolon'geren to continue
pro'loog (de) prologue
pro'motie (de) promotion,
graduation (ceremony)
promo'veren to obtain a
doctor's degree
pronk: te – staan to be on show
pronken to show off
pronkstuk (het) show piece
prooi (de) prey
proost! cheers!
prop (de) plug, wad **met
een voorstel op de proppen
komen** to come out with a
suggestion
propa'geren to propagate
proper clean and tidy
propvol chock-full
prostitu'ee (de) prostitute
prosti'tutie (de) prostitution
prote'ïne (de) protein
protes'teren to protest
pro'these (de) artifical teeth
(or limb etc.)
protserig ostentatious
provi'and (de) provisions
provinci'aal provincial
pro'vincie (de) province
pro'visie (de) provision;
commission
provi'sorisch provisional
provo'ceren to provoke
proza (het) prose
pruik (de) wig
pruilen to pout
pruim (de) plum
prul (het) trash

prullenmand (de) wastepaper
  basket
prut (de) mud, mire, grounds
prutsen to mess about, to
  botch
pruttelen to simmer; to
  grumble
pseudo'niem (het) pseudonym
psychi'ater (de) psychiatrist
psychi'atrisch psychiatric
psychisch psychological,
  mental
psycho'loog (de) psychologist
puber (de) adolescent
pube'raal adolescent
puber'teit (de) adolescence
publi'ceren to publish
pu'bliek (het) public, audience
pu'bliekstrekker (de) crowd puller,
  box-office hit
puffen to puff
puin (het) rubble

puinhoop (de) ruins; mess
puist (de) spot, pimple
puistje (het) pukkel,
  pimple
pulken to pick
pu'naise (de) drawing pin,
  thumbtack
punctu'eel punctual
punt (de) (het) point, tip; full stop
  dubbel(e) – colon **– komma** semi-
  colon **als puntje bij paaltje komt**
  when push comes to shove **geen –**
  no problem
puntig pointed, jagged
pu'pil (de) pupil
put (de) pit, well **in de – zitten**
  to be depressed
putten to draw, to derive
puur sheer, neat
puzzelen to do puzzles;
  solve crosswords, jigsaw
  puzzles

Q

qua as regards, as far as … goes
quaran'taine quarantine
quitte quits

quiz (de) quiz
quizleider (de) quiz master
quota (de) quota, share

Insight

Qua *as regards...* or *with regards to...* is perhaps more
frequently expressed with **met betrekking tot,** which is often
abbreviated to **m.b.t.** Other frequently used abbreviations
are **i.v.m.** for **in verband met** *in connection with*; **a.u.b.** for
alstublieft *please*; **enz.** for **enzovoort** or **etc.**, both meaning
et cetera; **bijv.** for **bijvoorbeeld** *for example*; and **blz.** for
bladzijde *page*. The abbreviation **t/m** for **tot en met** *up to*
(and including) is used to differentiate from **tot** *up to*, so
blz. 1 **tot** 5 means *pages 1 through 4*, but **blz.** 1 **t/m** 5 means
pages 1 through 5.

R

raad (de) advice; council, board
raadgevend advisory
raadhuis (het) council offices
raadplegen to consult
raadsel (het) riddle, puzzle; enigma
raadselachtig mystifying
raadslid (het) councillor
raadsman (de) adviser
raadsverkiezingen (de) municipal election
raadzaam advisable
raaf (de) raven
raak well-aimed, to the point
  maar raak at random
raam (het) window; frame
raamkozijn (het) window frame, window sill
raar strange, funny, odd
ra'barber (de) rhubarb
rab'bijn (de) rabbi
race (de) race **nog in de –** still in the running
raceauto (de) racecar
racebaan (de) (race)track
racefiets (de) racing bicycle
racen to race
ra'cisme (het) racism
ra'cist (de) racist
rad (het) wheel
radbraken to wreck, to mangle

radeloos at a loss, distraught
raden to guess; to advise
radi'caal radical, fundamental
ra'dijs (de) radish
radioac'tief radioactive
rafelen to fray
raffinade'rij (de) refinery
rage (de) craze
ragfijn (de) gossamer(y)
rakelings langs gaan to skim past
raken to hit, to touch; to concern; to get
ra'ket (de) rocket, missile
rakker (de) rascal
ram (de) ram
Ram Aries, the Ram
ramadan (de) Ramadan
ramen (op) to estimate
rammelaar (de) rattle
rammelen to rattle, to clank **door elkaar –** to give a thorough shaking to
rammen to ram
ramp (de) disaster
ramp'zalig disastrous, wretched
ran'cune (de) rancour
rand (de) edge, (b)rim
randgemeente (de) suburb
randgroep'jongere (de) young dropout
Randstad (de): de – Holland urban area in western Holland

Insight

De Randstad or De Randstad Holland is an area in the west of the Netherlands (largely, although not exclusively, in the provinces of Noord- and Zuid-Holland) where a number of cities are slowly growing into a large urban conglomerate. De Randstad consists of the four largest cities of The Netherlands – Amsterdam, Utrecht, Rotterdam, Den Haag – plus a number of smaller cities like Leiden and Haarlem. The non-urbanized centre of the area, where a lot of green still exists, is called **het groene hart**, literally *the green heart*.

rang (de) rank, grade
rangschikken to arrange
rangtelwoord (het) ordinal
  number
ranja (de) orange squash,
  orangeade
rank (de) slender, sleek-lined:
  (de) tendril
ranselen to thrash
rans(ig) rancid
rant'soen (het) ration
rap nimble
rapen to gather
rap'port (het) report
rap'portcijfer (het) report mark
rappor'teren to report
rari'teit (de) curio(sity)
ras (het) race, breed, variety
ras quick, soon
rasartiest (de) born artist
rasecht true-born
rasp (de) grater, rasp
raspen to grate, to rasp
rassendiscriminatie (de) racial
  discrimination
rasta (de) Rasta(farian)
rat (de) rat
ratel (de) rattle; tongue
ratelen to rattle, to roll
rationali'seren to rationalize
ratio'neel rational
ratje'toe (de) hotchpotch
rauw raw; raucous **dat valt me –
  op het lijf** that's an unexpected
  blow
rauwkost (de) uncooked vegetables
  or fruit
ra'vage (de) ravage(s), havoc;
  debris
ra'vijn (het) ravine
ra'votten to romp
ra'yon (het) district, territory
razen to roar, to rage
razend furious, wild, frantic

razer'nij (de) frenzy
re'actie (de) reaction
rea'geerbuis (de) test tube
rea'geerbuisbaby (de) test tube
  baby
rea'geren to react, to respond
reali'seerbaar realizable,
  feasible
reali'seren to realize
rea'lisme (het) realism
reali'teit (de) reality
reani'matie (de) resuscitation,
  reanimation
reani'meren to resuscitate, revive
re'bel (de) rebel
rebel'leren to rebel
recen'sent (de) reviewer
re'censie (de) review
re'cept (het) recipe; prescription
re'ceptie (de) reception
re'cherche (de) criminal
  investigation department
recher'cheur (de) detective
recht (het) straight; right; law
rechtbank (de) (law) court(s)
rechter (de) judge
rechter- right **rechterhand (de)**
  right hand (side)
rechtelijk judicial
rechthoek (de) rectangle
recht'hoekig rectangular, right-
  angled
recht'op upright, erect
rechts (on) the right; right-handed;
  right
rechts'af to the right
rechtsom'keert! about turn!
rechtspositie (de) legal status
rechtspraak (de) administration of
  justice
rechtspreken to administer
  justice
rechtstreeks direct
rechtzaak (de) lawsuit

rechtzaal (de) court room
recht'uit straight (on)
recht'vaardig just
recht'vaardigen to justify
reci'teren to recite
re'clame (de) advertisement
  – maken voor to advertise
re'clameaanbieding (de)
  special offer
re'clameblaadje (het) advertising
  leaflet, pamphlet
re'clameboodschap (de)
  commercial
re'clamefolder (de) advertising
  brochure, pamphlet
re'clamespot (de) commercial
reclas'sering (de) (prisoner)
  rehabilitation
reconstru'eren to reconstruct
recre'atie (de) recreation, leisure
recrea'tief recreational
recru'teren to recruit
rector (de) principal, master
  – mag'nificus vice-chancellor
re'çu (het) receipt, ticket
re'cyclen to recycle
redac'teur (de) editor
re'dactie (de) editorial staff
reddeloos irretrievable
redden to save, to rescue **ik kan me**
  wel – I can manage (all right)
reddingsboot (de) lifeboat
reddingspoging (de) rescue attempt
rede (de) reason; speech
  in de – vallen to interrupt
redelijk reasonable; rational
reden (de) reason
rede'natie (de), rede'nering (de)
  reasoning
rede'neren to reason; to hold forth
reder(ij) (de) ship owner(s)
redetwisten to dispute
redevoering (de) speech, oration
redi'geren to edit

redu'ceren to reduce, to decrease
re'ductie (de) reduction
ree(bok) (de) roe(buck)
reeds already
re'ëel real(istic)
reeks (de) series, row, string
reep (de) strip, bar; rope
reet (de) (vulg) crack, arse/ass,
  backside
refe'rentie (de) reference
refe'reren to refer
refor'matie (de) reformation
re'frein (het) refrain
regel (de) rule; line
regelen to arrange; to regulate
  zich – naar to conform to
regeling (de) arrangement
regelmaat (de) regularity
regel'matig regular
regelrecht straight
regen (de) rain **van de – in de drop**
  from the frying pan into the fire
regenachtig rainy
regenbui (de) shower (of rain)
regenen to rain
regenkleding (de) rainproof clothing
regenjas (de) raincoat
regenpijp (de) drainpipe
re'gent (de) regent, governor
regenval (de) rain fall
re'geren to govern, to rule
re'gering (de) government, reign
re'geringsbeleid (het) government
  policy
re'geringspartij (de) party in office/
  power, government party
re'gie (de) production
regis'seur (de) producer
re'gister (het) register; index;
  organ stop
regis'treren to register
regle'ment (het) regulation(s)
reglemen'tair regulatory; regulation
regu'leren to regulate

reiger (de) heron
reiken to reach, to stretch
reikhalzend longingly
rein clean; chaste **je reinste** utter **in het reine brengen** to straighten out
reinigen to clean(se)
reinigingsmiddel (het) detergent
reis (de) journey, voyage
reisbureau (het) travel agency
reischeque (de) traveller's cheque
reisgids (de) travel brochure; guidebook, (travel) guide (both book and person)
reiskosten (de) travelling expenses
reisorganisatie (de) travel organization, tour operator
reisverzekering (de) travel insurance
reizen to travel
reiziger (de) traveller, passenger
rek (de) elasticity
rek (het) rack, shelves
rekbaar elastic
rekenen to reckon, to count; to charge **reken maar!** you bet!
rekenfout (de) (mathematical) error
rekening (de) bill, account **– houden met** to take into consideration
rekening-cou'rant (de) current account
rekenmachine (de) calculator
rekensom (de) sum; problem, question
rekken to stretch; to protract
rekstok (de) horizontal bar
rel (de) riot
re'latie (de) (business) relation, connection
rela'tief relative
re'ligie (de) religion
reling (de) (ship's) rail(s)
relletje (het) disturbance
relschopper (de) rioter, hooligan
rem (de) brake

remmen to brake; to restrain; to retard
remspoor (het) skid mark
remweg (de) braking distance
renbaan (de) race course; speedway
ren'dabel profitable, paying
rende'ment (het) return, yield, output; efficiency, output, performance
ren'deren to pay (its way)
rendier (het) reindeer
rennen to run
renpaard (het) racehorse
rentabili'teit (de) productivity, cost effectiveness, profitability
rente (de) interest
renteloos free of interest
rente'nieren to live on private means
rentevoet (de) interest rate
reorgani'satie (de) reorganization
reorgani'seren to reorganize
rep en roer (de) uproar
repa'ratie (de) repair(s)
repa'reren to repair, to mend
repatri'ëren to return home, to repatriate
repe'teren to repeat; to rehearse; to coach (for an examination)
repe'titie (de) (revision) test; rehearsal
repor'tage commentary
reppen: – van to make any mention of **zich –** to hurry (up)
representa'tief representative, typical (of); presentable
rep'tiel (het) reptile
repub'liek (de) republic
republi'kein (de) republican
repu'tatie (de) reputation
reser'vaat (het) reserve
re'serve (de) reserve(s)
reser'veren to reserve, put aside; book, reserve **een tafel –** to book a table

reser'vering (de) booking, reservation
re'servesleutel (de) spare key
re'servewiel (het) spare wheel
resi'dentie (de) royal residence; residency
reso'luut resolute
respec'tievelijk respectively
rest (de) rest, remainder
res'tant (het) remnant
restau'ratie restoration, renovation; refreshment room, dining car
restau'reren to restore
resten to remain
res'teren to be left, to remain
res'terend remaining
resul'taat (het) result
resu'meren to summarize
re'torisch rhetorical
re'tour (het) return
re'tourtje (het) return, round trip
reuk (de) smell, scent, odour
reukwater (het) scent
reuma rheumatism
reü'nie (de) reunion
reus (de) giant
reus'achtig gigantic; great
reuze enormous, wizard
reuzenrad (het) Ferris wheel
re'vanche (de) revenge
re'visie (de) revision
revolutio'nair revolutionary
re'vue (de) review; revue
riant ample, spacious
rib (de) rib
ribbel(ig) (de) rib(bed)
ribbenkast (de) rib cage
richel (de) ledge, ridge
richten to direct, to aim; to address
  zich – naar to conform to
richting (de) direction, trend
  iets in die – something of the sort
richtingaanwijzer (de) (direction) indicator

richtinggevoel (het) sense of direction
richtlijn (de) guiding principal
ridder (de) knight
ridderlijk chivalrous
ridderorde (de) order of knighthood
rieken to smell
riem (de) strap, belt; oar; ream
riet (het) reed; cane
rieten dak (het) thatched roof
rietje (het) (drinking) straw
rietsuiker (de) cane sugar
rif (het) reef
rij (de) row
rijbaan (de) riding track; carriageway
rijbewijs (het) driving licence
rijbroek (de) riding breeches
rijden to ride, to drive, to run
rijdier (het) mount
rijexamen (het) driving test
rijk (het) state, kingdom, empire; government, state
rijk rich, wealthy, sumptuous
rijkdom (de) riches, wealth
rijkelijk richly, amply
rijke'lui (de) rich people
rijksambtenaar (de) civil servant
rijksuniversiteit (de) state university
rijks'waterstaat (de) Department/ Ministry of Waterways and Public Works
rijksweg (de) trunk road
rijkswege: van – on government authority
rijles (de) driving lesson, riding lesson
rijm (het) rhyme
rijmen to rhyme; to tally, to reconcile
rijmpje (het) rhyme, short verse
Rijn (de) Rhine
rijpen to ripen, to mature **het heeft gerijpt** there has been a hoar frost
rijschool (de) riding school
rijst (de) rice

rijstebrij (de), rijstepap (de) rice
 pudding
rijstrook (de) (traffic) lane
rijsttafel (de) meal of savoury
 dishes with rice
rijtjeshuis (het) terrace(d) house
rijtuig (het) carriage
rijweg (de) carriage way
rijwiel (het) (bi)cycle
rijwielhandel (de) bicycle shop
rijwielstalling (de) bicycle
 parking area
rijzen to (a)rise
rijzig tall
riksja (de) rickshaw
rillen to shiver, to shudder
rilling (de) shiver, shudder, tremble
rimboe (de) jungle
rimpel (de) wrinkle; ripple
rimpelen to wrinkle, crinkle
ring (de) ring
rinkelen to jingle, to tinkle
rio'lering (de) sewerage
ri'ool (het) sewer, drain
risico (het) risk
ris'kant risky
ris'keren to risk
rit (de) (tram, bus) ride, drive, rally
ritme (het) rhythm
ritmisch rhythmic(al)
rits (de) zipper, zip; string,
 batch, battery
ritselen to rustle
ritssluiting (de) zip fastener
ritu'eel (het) ritual
rivali'teit (de) rivalry
ri'vier (de) river
rob (de) seal
ro'bijn (de) ruby
ro'buust robust
rochelen to rattle, to ruckle
roddel (de) gossip
roddelblad (het) gossip magazine
roddelen to gossip

roddelpers (de) gutter press,
 gossip papers
rode'hond (de) German measles
Rode 'Kruis (het) Red Cross
roe(de) (de) rod, birch; **rood**
roeiboot (de) rowing boat
roeien to row
roeispaan (de) oar
roekeloos reckless
roem (de) glory; renown
roemen to praise; to boast
Roe'menië Rumania
roemrijk, roemvol glorious
roep (de) call, cry; fame
roepen to call (out)
roeping (de) calling, vocation
roer (het) rudder, helm
roerbakken to stir fry
roerei (het) scrambled egg
roeren to stir; to move
roerend moving, pathetic
 roerende goederen movables
roerig restless, lively
roerloos motionless: rudderless
roes (de) intoxication, fever
 of excitement
roest (de) rust, blight **oud –**
 scrap iron
roesten to rust
roestig rusty
roestvrij rustproof, stainless
roet (het) soot **– in het eten gooien**
 to throw a spanner in the works
roezemoezig rowdy
roffel (de) (drum) roll
rogge (de) rye
roggebrood (het) rye bread,
 pumpernickel
rok (de) skirt; tails
roken to smoke
roker (de) smoker
rokerig smoky
rokkostuum (het) dress suit
rol (de) roll; part, role

rolgordijn (het) blind
rol'lade (de) rolled meat
rollen to roll
rollenspel (het) role playing
rolletje (het) roll, packet; castor
rolluik (het) roller shutter
rolschaats (de) roller skate/blade
rolschaatsen to roller skate/blade
rolstoel (de) wheelchair
roltrap (de) escalator
rolverdeling (de) cast; division
  of roles
roman (de) novel
roman'tiek (de) romanticism
romantisch romantic
Ro'mein(s) Roman
rommel (de) mess, rubbish, junk
rommelen to rummage; to rumble
rommelig untidy
rommelmarkt (de) flea market,
  jumble sale
rompslomp (de) fuss and bother
rond round; surrounding
rondhangen to hang around
ronde (de) round(s), lap, heat
rondje (het) round (of drinks
  or cards)
rondkomen to make ends meet
rondneuzen to nose about, prowl
rondom all round
rondreis (de) tour
rondrit (de) (coach) tour
rondtasten to grope about
rondte: in de – in a circle,
  round about
ronduit outright
rondvaart (de) boat trip
rondvertellen to spread
rondvraag (de) question time
rondwaren to haunt
ronken to snore; to roar
röntgenfoto (de) X-ray
rood red
roodborstje (het) robin

roodgloeiend red-hot
roodharig red-haired, red-headed
Rood'kapje Little Red Riding Hood
roof (de) plunder, robbery, prey
roofdier (het) beast of prey
roofoverval (de) hold-up
rooftocht (de) foray
rooien to dig (up); to manage
rook (de) smoke
rookgordijn (het) smoke screen
rookverbod (het) ban on smoking
rookvlees (het) smoked beef
rookwolk (de) cloud of smoke
room (de) cream
roomboter (de) butter
roomijs (het) ice cream
Rooms(-Katholiek) Roman
  (Catholic)
roomsoes (de) cream puff
roos (de) rose; dandruff; bull's eye
roos'kleurig rosy
rooster (het) grating, grate, grill,
  ventilator; rota, timetable
roost(er)en to roast, to grill, to toast
ros (het) steed
rosbief (het) roast beef
rose pink
rot rotten **zich – lachen** to laugh
  oneself stupid
ro'teren to rotate
rotjong (het) brat, little pest
rots (de) rock, cliff
rotsachtig rocky
rotsblok (het) boulder
rotstreek (de) dirty trick, mean trick
rotsvast firm as a rock
rotten to rot, to decay
rotzak (de) (inf) bastard, jerk
rotzooi (de) ruddy mess (up)
rou'leren to circulate
rouw (de) mourning
rouwdienst (de) memorial service
rouwen to be in mourning
rouwig sorry

roven to pillage, to steal, to kidnap
rover (de) robber
ro'yaal generous, sporting, lavish, ample
rozenbottel (de) rosehip
rozenkrans (de) rosary; garland of roses
ro'zijn (de) raisin
rubber (de, het) rubber
ru'briek (de) heading, rubric, column
rug (de) back, ridge **achter de –** over and done with
ruggegraat (de) backbone
ruggelings backward(s), back to back
rugleuning (de) back of the chair
rugnummer (het) (player's) number
rugpijn (de) backache
rugzak (de) rucksack
ruig shaggy, hairy; rough
ruiken to smell, to scent
ruil (de) exchange
ruilen to (ex)change, to swap
ruim ample, spacious, wide
ruimen to clear (away) **het veld –** to give way to
ruimschoots amply
ruimte (de) room, space
ruimtegebrek (het) lack of space
ruimtevaarder (de) astronaut
ruimtevaartuig (het) spacecraft
ru'ïne (de) ruin(s), wreck
ruï'neren to ruin
ruisen to rustle, to rush, to swish

ruit (de) (glass) pane(l); check; diamond
ruiten diamonds; checked, chequered:
ruitenheer king of diamonds
ruitenwisser (de) windscreen wiper
ruiter (de) horseman, trooper
ruiterpad (het) bridle path
ruk (de) jerk, tug; gust (of wind); time, spell **in één – door** in one stretch
rukken to jerk/tug (at); tear, wrench
rukwind (de) squall, gust (of wind)
rul loose, running
ru'moer (het) clamour
ru'moerig noisy
rund (het) ox
rundergehakt (het) minced beef, mince
rundvee (het) (horned) cattle
rundvlees (het) beef
rups (de) caterpillar
Rus(sisch) Russian
rust (de) rest, quiet, peace; half time **op de plaats –!** stand easy!
rusteloos restless, untiring
rusten to rest **wel te –!** night night!
rustgevend comforting, restful, calming
rustig quiet, tranquil
ruw rough, coarse, raw
ruwweg roughly
ruzie (de) quarrel, row
ruziën to quarrel

S

saai dull, drab
saam'horigheid (de) solidarity
saam'horigheidsgevoel (het) team spirit
sabbat (de) sabbath
sabbelen to suck
sabo'teren to sabotage
sa'disme (het) sadism

saf'fier (de) sapphire
saf'fraan (de) saffron
sage (de) saga, legend
sa'lade (de) salad
sa'laris (het) salary
sa'larisverhoging (de) (salary) increase, (pay) rise
saldo (het) balance **per –** after all

sa'lon (de) drawing room; saloon
salu'eren to salute
sa'luut (het) salute; cheerio!
salvo (het) salvo, volley; round
samen together
samendoen to put together;
to go shares
samengesteld compound(ed),
complex, composite
samenhangen to be connected
samenkomen to come together
samenleven to live together
samenleving (de) society
samenlevingscontract (het)
cohabitation agreement
**samenloop van omstandigheden
(de)** coincidence
samenscholing (de) gathering
samensmelten to fuse,
to amalgamate
samenspel (het) ensemble,
team work
samenstellen to compose
samenstelling (de) composition,
compound
samenvallen to coincide
samenvatten to summarize
samenvloeien to unite; to merge,
to blend
samenvoegen to join
samenzweerder (de) conspirator
samenzwering (de) conspiracy
sanctie (de) sanction
san'daal (de) sandal
sa'neren to put in order; to
reorganize, redevelop
sani'tair (het) sanitary fittings
sani'tair sanitary
sap (het) sap, juice
sappig juicy, luscious
sar'castisch sarcastic
sarren to bait, to provoke
sa'tanisch fiendish
sa'té (de) satay

sa'téstokje (het) skewer
sa'tijn (het) satin
sau'cijzenbroodje (het)
sausage roll
Saudi-A'rabië Saudi Arabia
sauna (de) sauna
saus (de) sauce
saxo'foon (de) saxophone
Scandi'navië Scandinavia
Scandi'navisch Scandinavian
schaaf (de) plane, slicer
schaafwond (de) graze, abrasion
schaakbord (het) chessboard
schaakmat (de) checkmate;
stale mate
schaakspel (het) game of chess;
chess set
schaakstuk (het) chess piece
schaal (de) scale; shell; dish
schaaldier (het) crustacean
schaalverdeling (de) graduation
schaamdelen (de) private parts
schaamhaar (het) pubic hair
schaamrood blush of shame
schaamte(loos) shame(less)
schaap (het) sheep; ninny
zwart – black sheep, scapegoat
schaar (de) (pair of) scissors, shears
schaars scarce, sparse
schaats (de) skate
schaatsen to skate
schaatser (de) skater
schacht (de) shaft
schade (de) damage, harm,
detriment **de – inhalen** to make
up arrears
schadeclaim (de) insurance claim
(for damage)
schadelijk harmful, noxious
schadeloos stellen to indemnify
schaden to harm, to do damage to
schadevergoeding (de)
compensation
schaduw (de) shadow, shade

schaduwzijde (de) shaded side; drawback
schaften to knock off for lunch
schakel (de) link
schakelaar (de) switch
schaken to play chess: to abduct
scha'kering (de) shade
schamel meagre, wretched
schamen: zich – to be ashamed
schan'daal (het) scandal, shame
schan'dalig disgrace, shameful
schande (de) disgrace, shame
schandelijk disgraceful
schappelijk fair, decent
schar'minkel (het) scrag(gy person)
schar'nier (de, het) hinge
scharrelen to rummage; to get along somehow
schat (de) treasure, wealth; darling
schatbewaarder (de) treasurer
schateren to scream (with laughter)
schatkist (de) treasury
schatrijk fabulously rich
schattebout (de) poppet, sweetheart
schatten to value; to estimate
schattig sweet
schatting (de) estimate, valuation; tribute
schaven to plane, to graze; to polish
schedel (de) skull
scheef crooked, lop-sided, raked **scheve voorstelling** misrepresentation **scheve verhouding** wry relationship
scheel cross-eyed
scheelkijken, scheelzien to squint
scheenbeen (het) shin bone
scheepsjournaal (het) log(book)
scheepvaart (de) shipping
scheerapparaat (het) (safety) razor
scheermes (het) razor
scheermesje (het) razor blade
scheerzeep (de) shaving soap

scheidbaar separable
scheiden to separate, to part; to divorce
scheiding (de) separation; parting; divorce **– van tafel en bed** legal separation
scheidslijn (de) dividing line
scheidsrechter (de) umpire, referee; arbitrator
scheikunde (de) chemistry
schei'kundig chemical
schel shrill, glaring
schelden (op) to swear (at)
scheldnaam (de) (rude) name
scheldpartij (de) slanging match
scheldwoord (het) term of abuse
schelen to matter; to make a difference **het kan me niet –** I don't mind **we – maar twee jaar** there are only two years between us
schelp (de) shell, scallop
schelpdier (het) shellfish
schema (het) sketch diagram, rough draft
sche'matisch schematic
schemer(ing) (de) twilight, dusk
schemeren to dawn, to grow dusk; to be dimly visible
schemerlamp (de) floor lamp
schenden to violate; to damage, to disfigure; to desecrate
schenken to pour (out); to present with, to grant
schenking (de) gift
schep (de) shovel, scoop **een – geld** heaps of money
schepje (het) spoonful **er een – (boven) opdoen** to go one better
scheppen to scoop, to shovel, to ladle; to create
schepper (de) creator
schepping (de) creation
schepsel (het) creature
scheren to shave, to shear, to skim

scherf (de) fragment, splinter

scherling en inslag (de) warp and weft; everyday occurrence

scherm (het) screen, curtain **achter de schermen** behind the scenes

schermen to fence

scherp sharp, keen; trenchant **scherpe hoek** acute angle; sharp corner.

scherpschutter (de) marksman

scherp'ziend keen-sighted; penetrating

scherp'zinnig acute, astute

schets (de) sketch

schetsen to sketch

schetteren to blare; to rant

scheur (de) tear, crack

scheuren to tear; to crack

scheutig open-handed

schichtig shy, skittish

schiereiland (het) peninsula

schietbaan (de) rifle range

schieten to shoot, to fire **een plan laten –** to drop a plan **te binnen –** to come back to mind

schietschijf (de) target

schiften to curdle

schijf (de) disk; slice; target, dial

schijn (de) light; appearance, semblance

schijnaanval (de) sham attack

schijnbaar seemingly

schijnbeweging (de) apparent movement

schijnen to shine; to seem

schijn'heilig hypocritical

schijnsel (het) light, glimmer

schijnwerper (de) spotlight, searchlight, floodlight

schijt (de) shit

schijten (inf) to shit, crap

schijter(d) (de) scaredy-cat

schijterig chicken-hearted

schik: in zijn – zijn to be pleased (with life)

schikken to arrange, to settle, to be convenient (to) **zich – in** to resign onself to

schikking (de) arrangement, agreement

schil (de) peel, skin

schild (het) shield **iets in het – voeren** to be up to something

schilder (de) painter; decorator

schilderachtig picturesque

schilderen to paint; to depict

schilde'rij (het) painting, picture

schilderkunst (de) painting, art

schildpad (de) tortoise(shell), turtle

schildwacht (de) sentry

schilferen to peel, to flake off

schillen to peel

schim (de) shadow, ghost

schimmel (de) mould, mildew

schimmelen to go mouldy

schip (het) ship; nave **schoon – maken** to clear out (or up)

schipbreuk lijden to be shipwrecked

schipper (de) skipper

schipperen to give and take

schitteren to glitter, to be brilliant; to be conspicuous

schitterend brilliant, splendid

schlager (de) popular song

schmink (de) stage make-up

schminken to make someone up **zich –** to make oneself up

schoen (de) shoe **de stoute schoenen   aantrekken** to pluck up courage **iemand iets in de schoenen schuiven** to lay something at a person's door

schoener (de) schooner

schoenmaker (de) shoe repairer

schoensmeer (de) shoe polish

schoenenzaak (de) shoe shop

schoft (de) bastard
schok (de) shock, jolt
schokbreker (de) shock absorber
schokken to shake, to jerk, to jolt
schol (de) plaice
scholengemeenschap (de) comprehensive school
scho'lier (de) pupil
schommel (de) swing
schommelen to swing, to rock, to roll; to fluctuate
schooier (de) beggar, tramp
school (de) school; shoal
schoolblijven to be kept in (after school)
schoolbord (het) blackboard
schoolgeld (het) school fees
schooljuffrouw (de) schoolmistress
schoolmeester (de) schoolmaster; pedant
schoolplein (het) playground
schoolreisje (het) school outing
schools school(ish); scholastic
schoolslag (de) breast stroke
schoolverzuim (het) absence(s)
schoon clean; beautiful, fine
schoonfamilie (de) in-laws
schoonheid (de) beauty
schoonheidsmiddel (het) beauty preparation
schoonhouden to keep clean
schoonmaak (de) (spring) cleaning; clear-out
schoonmaken to clean
schoonouders schoonvader en schoonmoeder (de) father- and mother-in-law
schoonrijden figure skating
schoonzoon (de) son-in-law
schoonzuster (de) sister-in-law
schoorsteen (de) chimney (pot); funnel
schoorsteenmantel (de) mantel piece

schoorsteenveger (de) chimneysweep
schoot (de) lap; womb
schop (de) spade; shovel; kick
schoppen to kick (up)
schoppen'heer (de) etc.; king etc. of spades
schor hoarse
schor (de) mud flat
schorem (het) riffraff, scum
schorpi'oen (de) scorpion
schors (de) bark (tree)
schorsen to suspend; to adjourn
schort (de, het) apron, pinafore
schort: wat – eraan? what is the matter?
schot (het) shot; partition, bulkhead
Schot (de) Scot(sman)
schotel (de) dish; saucer
schots (de) (ice)floe
schouder (de) shoulder
schouderblad (het) shoulder blade
schouw (de) fireplace; scow
schouwburg (de) theatre
schouwspel (het) spectacle
schraal meagre, lean, bleak
schram (de) scratch
schransen to gorge
schrapen to scrape; to clear
schrappen to scrap(e), to cross out
schreeuw (de) yell, cry
schreeuwen to shout, yell, scream, screech
schreeuwlelijk (de) bawler
schriel frail; meagre; mingy
schrift (het) (hand)writing; exercise book
schriftelijk written, in writing
schrijden to stride
schrijfster (de) (female) writer
schrijver (de) (male) writer
schrijftaal (de) formal language
schrijven to write
schrik (de) fright, terror

> ## Insight
>
> The word *writer* has a male and a female form in Dutch: **de schrijver** is used for male writers and **de schrijfster** is used for female writers. Many words describing jobs or professions have a male and a female form. Some examples: **de leraar/lerares** *teacher*, **de chauffeur/chauffeuse** *driver*, **de acteur/actrice** *actor/actress*, **de boer/boerin** *farmer* (note that **boerin** can both mean *woman farmer* or *farmer's wife*), **de advocaat/advocate** *lawyer*, **de redacteur/redactrice** *editor*.

schrikaanjagend terrifying
schrik'barend appalling
schrikbeeld (het) nightmarish vision
schrikbewind (het) reign of terror
schrikkeljaar (het) leap year
schrikken to have a (nasty) fright, to be taken aback **wakker –** to wake with a start
schrik'wekkend terrifying
schril shrill, glaring
schrobben to scrub
schroef (de) screw, propeller **op losse schroeven staan** to be uncertain
schroeien to scorch, to singe
schroevendraaier (de) screw driver
schroeven to screw
schrokken to gorge
schroom diffidence
schroot (het) scrap metal
schub (de) scale
schuchter bashful
schudden to shake; to shuffle
schuieren to brush
schuif (de) bolt
schuifdak (het) sun roof
schuifdeur sliding door
schuifelen to shuffle, to slither
schuifladder (de) extending ladder
schuifraam (het) sash window
schuilen to (take) shelter, to lurk

schuilhouden to lie low
schuilkelder (de) air raid shelter
schuilkerk (de) clandestine church
schuilplaats (de) hiding place
schuim (het) foam, froth, lather; scum; meringue
schuimbekken to foam at the mouth
schuimen to foam, to froth, to lather; to skim
schuin slanting, oblique; smutty
schuit (de) boat, barge
schuiven to push **laat hem maar –** he can fend for himself
schuld (de) debt; fault, blame, guilt
schuldbekentenis (de) IOU; confession of guilt
schuldeiser (de) creditor
schuldenaar (de) debtor
schuldgevoel (het) feeling of guilt, guilty conscience
schuldig guilty **– zijn** to be guilty; to owe
schuldige (de) culprit, guilty party
schunnig shabby; filthy (language)
schuren to scour, to sandpaper; to graze
schurft (de) scabies
schurk (de) scoundrel, villain
schutkleur (de) camouflage
schutsluis (de) lock
schutter (de) marksman

schutting (de) fence
schuur (de) barn; shed
schuurmachine (de) sander, sanding machine
schuurmiddel (het) abrasive
schuurpapier (het) sandpaper
schuw timid, shy
schuwen to shun, to fight shy of
scriptie (de) thesis
secon'dair secondary
se'conde(wijzer) (de) second(s) (hand)
secreta'resse (de) (female) secretary
secretari'aat (het) secretariate
secre'taris (de) secretary
sectie (de) section; incision, autopsy
secu'lair secular
se'cuur safe; accurate; certain
sedert since, for
sein (het) signal
seinen to signal, to wire
sei'zoen (het) season
sei'zoenkaart (de) season ticket
sei'zoenopruiming (de) (clearance) sale(s)
seks (de) sex
sekse (de) sex, gender
sek'sisme (het) sexism, male chauvinism
sek'sist (de) sexist, male chauvinist
sek'sistisch sexist; like a sexist
seksuali'teit sexuality
seksu'eel sexual
sekte (de) sect
selderij (de) celery
se'naat (de) senate
se'niel senile
sen'satie (de) sensation
sensatio'neel sensational, spectacular
sensu'eel sensual
sentimen'teel sentimental
septisch septic
serie (de) series, serial

seriemoordenaar (de) serial killer
seri'eus serious
serieux: au – nemen to take seriously
seroposi'tief HIV-positive
ser'pent (het) serpent; shrew
serre (de) conservatory, sun parlour
ser'veren to serve
ser'vet (het) napkin
servicebeurt (de) service
ser'vies (het) dinner service, tea set
sfeer (de) (atmo)sphere
sferisch spherical
shag (de) (rolling) tobacco
sho'arma (de) doner kebab
schoenveter (de) shoelace
sidderen (voor) to quake (at the thought of)
sieraad (het) ornament, (piece of) jewellery
sieren to adorn, to enhance
  dat siert hem that is to his credit
sierlijk elegant
sierplant (de) ornamental plant
si'gaar (de) cigar
si'garenwinkel (de) tobacconist's (shop)
siga'ret (de) cigarette
si'gnaal signal
signale'ment (het) (police) description
signa'leren to see, to signal
sijpelen to seep
sik (de) goatee
sikkel (de) sickle, crescent
simpel simple, silly
simu'leren to simulate
sinaasappel (de) orange
sinaasappelsap (de) orange juice
sinds('dien) (ever) since (then)
singel (de) (street on either side of a) town canal
sint (de) saint
Sinter'klaas (de) Santa Claus

sinterklaas'avond (de) St Nicholas' Eve (Dec. 5)

sip kijken to look glum

Sire your Majesty

si'rene (de) siren

si'roop (de) syrup

sissen to hiss, to sizzle

sisser: met een – aflopen to fizzle out, to blow over

sjaal (de) shawl

sjacheren to run a shady business; to haggle

sjansen to flirt, make eyes at someone

sjekkie (het) (hand-rolled) cigarette, roll-up

sjerp (de) sash

sjoelbak (de) shovelboard

sjofel shabby

sjokken to trudge

sjorren to lash (up); to haul

sjouwen to lug; to drudge

skeeleren to rollerblade

ske'let (het) skeleton

skelterbaan (de) go-kart (race)track

skelteren to go-kart

skiën to ski

skileraar (de) ski instructor

sla (de) salad; lettuce

slaaf (de) slave

slaafs slavish, servile

slaags raken to come to blows

slaan to hit, to strike, to beat, to smack **dat slaat op mij** that applies to me

slaap (de) sleep; temple **– hebben** to feel sleepy

slaapdronken not fully awake

slaapje (het) nap; bedmate

slaapkop (de) sleepyhead

slaapliedje (het) lullaby

slaapver'wekkend sleep-inducing, soporific; tedious

slaapwandelaar (de) sleepwalker

slaapwandelen to walk in one's sleep

slaap'wekkend soporific

slaapzaal (de) dormitory

slaatje (het) salad

slab (de) bib

slachten to slaughter

slachting (de) slaughter

slachtoffer (het) victim

slag (de) blow, stroke, beat, crash; battle; knack; turn; kind **een – om de arm houden** not to commit oneself

slagader (de) artery

slagbal (het) rounders

slagboom (de) boom, barrier

slagen to succeed, to pass

slager('ij) (de) butcher('s) shop

slaghout (het) bat

slagregen (de) downpour

slagroom (de) (whipped) cream

slagtand (de) fang, tusk

slagwerk (het) striking mechanism; percussion (section)

slagzin (de) slogan

slak (de) snail, slug: slag

slaken to utter, to heave

slakkengang (de) snail's pace

slakkenhuis (het) snailshell; cochlea

slang (de) snake, serpent; hose(pipe)

slangenbezweerder (de) snake charmer

slank slim, slender

slaolie (de) salad oil

slap slack, soft, flabby, weak; spineless

slape'loosheid (de) insomnia

slapen to (be a)sleep

slaperig sleepy

slapjanus (de) wimp, weed

slapjes slack, weak

slappeling (de) weakling, wimp

slavenarbeid (de) slavery

slavendrijver (de) slave driver

slaver'nij (de) slavery, servitude
Slavisch Slav(onic)
slecht bad, poor
slechten to level (out); to demolish; to settle
slechts only
sle(d)e (de) sled(ge) **een – van een wagen** a large luxury car
sleep (de) train, trail, tow
sleepboot (de) tug
sleepnet (het) dragnet
sleeptouw (het) towrope
slenteren to saunter
slepen to drag; to tow
slet (de) slut
sleuf (de) groove; slot
sleur (de) rut, humdrum routine
sleuren to drag (on)
sleutel (de) key; clef
sleutelbeen (het) collar bone
sleutelbos (de) bunch of keys
sleutelen to work (on), repair; to fiddle/tinker (with)
sleutelgat (het) keyhole
sleutelhanger (de) keyring
slier(t) (de) stream(er); winding trail
slijk (het) mire, slime
slijm (het) slime, phlegm, mucus
slijmvlies (het) mucous membrane
slijpen to sharpen, to grind; to cut and polish
slij'tage (de) wear (and tear)
slijten to wear out, to wear off; to spend, to retail
slijter (de) wine merchant, liquor dealer
slijte'rij (de) off-licence
slikken to swallow
slim clever, crafty; bad
slinger (de) festoon; pendulum; sling; (crank) handle
slingeren to swing; to lurch; to wind; to lie about; to fling
slingerplant (de) creeper

slinken to shrink (to nothing), to subside
slinks sly, underhand
slipgevaar! beware of skidding!
slip'over (de) pullover
slippen to slip, to skid
slippertje: een – maken to have a bit on the side
slissen to lisp
sloddervos (de) slob
sloep (de) (ship's) boat, (naval) barge
sloerie (de) slut
slof (de) slipper; briquette; carton **het op zijn sloffen doen** to take things easy
sloffen to shuffle
slok (de) gulp, draught
slokdarm (de) gullet
slokje (het) sip, drop
slokken to guzzle
slons (de) slattern, frump
sloom languid
sloop (de) demolition; scrapyard (cars)
sloop (het) pillowcase
sloot (de) ditch
slopen to demolish, to break up
sloppenwijk (de) slums, slum area
slordig untidy, slipshod
slot (het) lock; castle; conclusion **ten slotte** finally **per – van rekening** when all is said and done
slotscène (de) final scene
slotsom (de) conclusion; upshot
sluier (de) veil
sluimeren to slumber
sluipen to steal, to creep
sluis (de) lock; floodgate
sluisdeur lockgate
sluiten to shut (up), to close (down), to lock (up); to conclude; to fit
sluiting (de) closing (down); fastening

slungel (de) beanpole; oaf
slurf (de) trunk, proboscis
slurpen to sip noisily, to gulp
sluw sly, wily
smaad (de) libel
smaak (de) taste, flavour;
relish; palate
  in de – vallen to be popular, to be
  to a person's liking
smaakvol in good taste
smachten to pine (away)
smak (de) thud
smakelijk toothsome – eten! enjoy
your meal!
smakeloos tasteless; in bad taste
smaken (naar) to taste (of)
smakken to fall with a thud; to fling;
to smack (one's lips)
smal narrow
smaragd (de) emerald
smart (de) grief, anguish
smartelijk grievous
smartlap (de) tear jerker
smeden to forge; to plan
smede'rij (de) smithy, forge
smeedijzer (het) wrought iron
smeer (de) grease
smeerkaas (de) cheese spread
smeermiddel (het) lubricant
smeerolie (de) lubricating oil
smeerpoets (de) dirty tyke
smeerworst (de) pâté
smeken to implore, to beseech
smelten to (s)melt, to fuse
smeltkroes (de) crucible
smeren to spread; to grease,
to lubricate 'm – to beat it
smerig filthy, shabby
smeris (de) cop(per)
smetteloos spotless, blameless
smeuïg smooth, creamy; vivid
smeulen to smoulder
smid (de) blacksmith
smidse (de) forge

smiezen: ik heb het in de – I've got
it taped
smijten (met) to chuck; to throw
(about)
smoesje (het) excuse
smoezelig soiled
smoezen to whisper together
smoking (de) dinner jacket
smokkelaar (de) smuggler
smokkelen to smuggle; to cheat
smokkelwaar (de) contraband
smoor: de – hebben to be
utterly fed up
smoor'heet sweltering
smoorver'liefd madly in love,
smitten
smoren to strangle, to stifle
smullen to tuck in
snaar (de) string, chord
snakken naar to yearn for,
to gasp for
snappen to get, to understand
  ik snap 'm I get it hij snapt het
  niet he doesn't get it ik snap er
  niets van I don't get it at all
snateren to quack, to cackle
snauwen to snarl
snavel (de) beak, bill
sne(d)e (de) cut; slice
sneeuw (de) snow
sneeuwbal (de) snowball
sneeuwen to snow
sneeuwklokje (het) snowdrop
sneeuwpop (het) snowman
snel quick, fast
snelheid (de) speed
snellen to hurry
sneltrein (de) express train,
intercity (train)
snelweg (de) motorway, freeway
snerpend biting, piercing
snert (de) pea soup; trash(y)
sneu rotten (luck)
sneuvelen to be killed (in action)

snijboon (de) French bean, string
bean **rare –** strange fellow
snijden to cut (in), to carve;
to intersect
snijtand (de) incisor
snik (de) sob, gasp **niet goed –**
not all there
snik'heet sweltering
snikken to sob
snipperdag (de) day off
snoeien to prune, to lop, to clip
snoek (de) pike
snoep (de) sweets
snoepen to eat sweets, to tuck in
snoepgoed (het) confectionery,
sweets/candy
snoer (het) flex; string; line
snoeren: iemand de mond –
to shut a person up
snoet (de) snout; face
snoezig sweet, dinky
snor (de) moustache
snorren to roar, to drone, to hum
snotaap (de) brat
snotjongen (de) brat
snotneus (de) runny nose; little kid;
brat
snowboarden to go snowboarding
snuffelen to sniff; to ferret (about)
snugger bright, brainy
snuiste'rij (de) trinket
snuit (de) snout, trunk; (little) face
snuiten to blow (one's nose);
to snuff
snuiter (de) chap, fellow
snuiven to (give a) sniff, to snort
snurken to snore
soci'aal social(ly); socially minded
socia'lisme (het) socialism
socië'teit (de) club(-house)
soep (de) soup
soepel supple
soezen to doze
software (de) software

sojasaus (de) soysauce
sok (de) sock
sol'daat (de) soldier
sol'deerbout (de) soldering iron
sol'deren to solder
soli'dair loyal, sympathetic;
to show solidarity
solidari'teit (de) solidarity
so'lide sound, substantial
so'list (de) soloist
sollici'tant (de) applicant
sollici'tatiebrief (de) letter
of application
sollici'tatiegesprek (het)
(job) interview
sollici'tatieprocedure (de)
selection procedure
sollici'teren to apply (for a job)
solocarrière (de) solo career
som (de) sum
somber gloomy, sombre
sommige(n) some
soms sometimes; perhaps
so'nate (de) sonata
soort (de) brand, species
soort (het) sort, type, kind
soortge'lijk similar
soos (de) club
sop (het) broth; (soap) suds
het ruime –, the sea
soppen to sop, to steep
so'praan (de) soprano, treble
sor'teren to (as)sort, to grade
sor'tering (de) assortment
soulmuziek (de) soul music
sou'peren to sup
souter'rain (het) basement
souvereini'teit (de) sovereignty
spaak (de) spoke, rung
– lopen to come to grief
Spaans Spanish
spaarbank (de) savings bank
spaargeld (het) savings
spaarlamp (de) low-energy light bulb

spaarpot (de) money box
spaarvarken (het) piggy bank
spaarzaam sparing, thrifty
spade (de) spade
spalk (de) splint
spalken to put in splints
span (het) span; team, yoke
spandoek (de, het) banner
Spanje Spain
spannen to stretch, to strain **het zal er om –** it will be touch and go
spannend tense, thrilling
spanning (de) tension; span
spanwijdte (de) span
spar (de) spruce (tree)
sparen to save (up); to spare
spartelen to sport, to splash, to kick
spatader (de) varicose vein
spatbord (het) mudguard
spatie (de) space (word processing)
spatiebalk (de) space bar
spatten to splash, to spatter
spece'rij (de) spice
specht (de) woodpecker
speci'aal special
speciali'satie (de) specialization
speciali'seren: zich – (in) to specialize (in)
specia'lisme (het) specialism
specia'list (de) specialist; (hospital) consultant
specie (de) mortar
specifi'ceren to specify
speci'fiek specific
specu'laas (de) a kind of ginger biscuit
specu'leren to speculate
speeksel (het) saliva
speelautomaat (de) slot machine
speelbal (de) cue ball; plaything
speelgoed (het) toy(s)
speelgoedafdeling (de) toy department
speelplaats (de) playground

speels playful
speeltuin playground
speen (de) teat, dummy
speer (de) spear, javelin
spek (het) bacon, fat pork; blubber
spekken: zijn beurs – to line one's purse
spek'takel (het) spectacle
spel (het) game; pack, hand (of cards), play(ing), acting **op het – staan** to be at stake
spelbreker (de) spoilsport
speld (de) pin
spelen to play, to act; to chime
speler (de) player, musician, actor
spelfout (de) spelling mistake
speling (de) (free) play; scope
spellen to spell
spelletje (het) game
spelregel (de) rule (of the game): spelling rule
spen'deren to spend
sperma (het) sperm
spermabank (de) sperm bank
spermadonor (de) sperm donor
sperzieboon (de) French bean
spett(er)en to spatter
speuren to search
speurhond (de) tracker dog
spiegel (de) mirror
spiegelbeeld (het) reflection; phantom
spiegelei (het) fried egg
spiegelen: zich – aan to learn from
spiegel'glad as smooth as glass; icy (roads)
spiegeling (de) reflection
spieken to crib
spier (de) muscle
spierbal (de) muscle
spierkracht (de) muscular strength, muscle (power)
spier'naakt stark naked

spierpijn (de) aching/sore muscles, muscular pain
spier'wit white as a sheet
spies (de) spear, pen
spijbelen to play truant
spijker (de) nail **spijkers met koppen slaan** to get down to business **spijkers op laag water zoeken** to make a song and dance about nothing; to quibble
spijkerbroek (de) (pair of) jeans
spijkerjasje (het) denim jacket
spijkerstof (de) denim
spijl (de) bar, spike
spijskaart (de) menu
spijsvertering (de) digestion
spijt (de) regret **daar krijg je – van** you'll regret that **het – me** I'm sorry
spijtig: het is – it is a pity
spiksplinter'nieuw brand new, gleaming new, spanking new
spil (de) pivot, axis; capstan
spilziek (de) spendthrift
spin (de) spider
spi'nazie (de) spinach
spinnen to spin; to purr
spinnenweb (het) cobweb; spider's web
spinnewiel (het) spinning wheel
spinrag (het) cobweb
spi'on (de) spy
spio'neren to spy
spi'raal (de) spiral; woven bedspring
spiritus (de) methylated spirits
spit (het) spit; lumbago
spits point(ed), sharp: peak **spitse toren (de)** steeple, pinnacle **op de – drijven** to bring to a head
spitsuur (het) rush hour, peak hour
spits'vondig smart, sophisticated
spitten to dig
spleet (de) slit, split
splijten to split, to cleave

splinter (de) splinter
splinter'nieuw brand new
split (de) slit, placket
splitsen to split (up), to fork
splitsing (de) split(ting up), fork, fission
spoed (de) haste
spoedcursus (de) crash course, intensive course
spoedgeval (het) emergency case
spoedig soon, speedy
spoelen to rinse, to wash
spoken to haunt; to be astir
spons (de) sponge
spon'taan spontaneous
spook (het) ghost; freak, bogey
spookhuis (het) haunted house
spoor (het) platform (at railway station)
spoorbaan (de) railway
spoorboekje (het) (railway) timetable
spoorboom (de) level-crossing barrier
spoorlijn (de) railway (line)
spoorloos without a trace
spoorverbinding (de) railway communication; connection
spoorweg (de) railway
spoorwegovergang (de) level crossing
spo'radisch sporadic
sport (de) sport
sportbroekje (het) shorts
sportclub (de) sports club
sporten to do/play sports
sporter (de) sportsman
spor'tief sports, sporty; sports-loving; sportsmanlike, be sporting
sporttas (de) sports bag
spot mockery
spotgoedkoop dirt-cheap
spotprent (de) caricature, cartoon
spotten (met) to mock; to defy

spraak (de) speech
spraakgebrek (het) speech defect
spraakgebruik (het) usage
spraakzaam talkative
sprake (de) talk, question **ter –** up for discussion
sprakeloos speechless
sprankelen to sparkle
spreekbeurt (de) talk, lecturing engagement
spreekbuis (de) mouthpiece
spreekkamer (de) consulting room
spreektaal (de) conversation(al) language
spreekuur (het) office hours, surgery (hours)
spreek'vaardigheid (de) fluency, speaking ability
spreekwoord (het) proverb
spreek'woordelijk proverbial
spreeuw (de) starling
sprei (de) bedspread
spreken to speak (to), to mention **het spreekt vanzelf** it stands to reason
sprekend striking, telling
spreker (de) speaker
sprenkelen to sprinkle
spreuk (de) motto, maxim
spriet (de) blade (of grass); antenna
springen to jump; to snap, to burst, to become insolvent **ik zit erom te –** I just can't wait for it
spring'levend very much alive
springplank (de) springboard
springstof (de) explosive
springtij (het) spring tide
springtouw (het) skipping rope
sprinkhaan (de) locust, grasshopper
sprint (de) sprint
sprinten to sprint
sproeien to sprinkle, to spray
sproet (de) freckle
sprokkelen to gather (wood)

sprong (de) jump, leap, bound
sprookje (het) fairytale
sprookjesachtig make-believe, dream-like
spruit (de) sprout; offspring
spruiten to sprout; to spring
spruitjes (de) Brussel sprouts
spugen to spit
spuien to sluice; to vent(ilate)
spuigaten: dat loopt de – uit that's going too far
spuit (de) syringe; needle; shot
spuiten to gush, to spray, to squirt, to inject
spul (het) stuff; trouble **spullen (de)** bits and pieces; togs
sputteren to sputter
spuug (het) spit
squashbaan (de) squash court
squashen to play squash
staaf (de) bar, rod
staal (het) steel; sample, piece
staal(draad)kabel (de) steel-wire rope
staan to stand, to be; to suit **laat –** leave alone; let alone **erop –** to insist on it **hoe staat hij ervoor?** how is he doing? **zich staande houden** to keep on one's feet; to hold one's own **op staande voet** then and there
staanplaats (de) standing room; terrace (football)
staar (de) cataract
staart (de) tail; pigtail
staat (de) state; rank; list **in – zijn** to be able
staatsgreep (de) *coup d'état*
staatshoofd (het) head of state
staatsman (de) statesman
staatsrecht (het) constitutional law
staatsschuld (de) national debt
staatssecretaris (de) state secretary
sta'biel stable

stad (de) town, city
stad'huis (het) town hall, city hall
stadion (het) stadium
stadium (het) stage, phase
stadslichten sidelights
stadsmens (de) city dweller, townsman
stadsschouwburg (de) municipal theatre
staf (de) staff; mace, crosier
stage (de) work placement; teaching practice
stageplaats (de) trainee post
stagi'air(e) (de) student on work placement, student teacher
stag'neren to stagnate
sta-in-de-weg (de) obstacle
staken to stop, to strike
staking (de) stoppage, suspension, strike
stakker(d) (de) poor devil, poor thing
stal (de) stable, cowshed, stall
stallen to stable, to put away
stalling (de) garage; shelter
stam (de) stem, trunk; tribe, race
stamboom (de) family tree
stamcafé (het) favourite pub/bar; local; hangout
stamelen to stammer
stamgast (de) regular (customer)
stammen to hail, to date
stampen to pound, to mash; to stamp, to drum; to pitch
stamper (de) pestle, (potato) masher; pistil
stamppot (de) mashed potatoes and cabbage, hotchpotch
stampvoeten to stamp (one's foot)
stamp'vol packed
stamvader (de) ancestor
stand (de) position, attitude; score; class, order, state **tot – komen** to come into being
standaard standard; stand

standbeeld statue
standhouden (het) to hold (one's own)
standje (het) position, posture; rebuke **iemand een – geven** to tell someone off
standplaats (de) stand, pitch, (taxi) rank; post, living
standpunt (het) point of view
stand'vastig steadfast
stang (de) bar, rod, stave; crossbar **op – jagen** to bait, to needle
stank (de) stench
stap (de) step, pace; move **op –** on (our) way
stapel (de) pile, heap **hard van – lopen** to go too fast
stapelen to stack, to heap
stapel('gek) mad, crazy
stappen to step, to get
stapvoets at a walking pace
star fixed, rigid
staren to stare, to gaze
startbaan (de) runway
starten to start
Statenbijbel (de) Authorized Version (of the Dutch Bible)
Staten-Gene'raal (de) States General, the Upper and Lower Chambers
sta'tief (het) tripod, stand
statiegeld (het) refundable deposit (on glass bottles)
statig stately, majestic
sta'tion (het) station
stati'onshal (de) station concourse
statis'tiek (de) statistics
sta'tuut (het) statute, regulation
stedelijk urban, municipal
stedeling (de) townsman/woman
steeds ever, still; town(ish)
steeg (de) alley, lane
steek (de) stitch, sting, stab, dig **in de – laten** to leave in the lurch; to abandon

steekproef (de) sample taken
at random
steekvlam (de) (burst of) flame
steel (de) stem, stalk; handle
steelpan (de) saucepan
steen (de) stone
steenbok (de) ibex; Capricorn
steengroeve (de) quarry
steenhouwer (de) stonemason
steenkool (de) coal
steenpuist (de) boil
steentijd (de) stone age
steentje (het) stone, pebble **een –
bijdragen** to do one's (little) bit
steevast regularly
steiger (de) landing stage;
scaffolding
steigeren to rear
steil steep, sheer
stek (de) cutting
stekel (de) prickle, spine
stekelig prickly
stekelvarken (het) porcupine
steken to sting, to stab, to smart;
to stick **van wal –** to push off, start
stekker (de) plug (top)
stel (het) set; couple
stelen to steal
stellen to put; to adjust; to suppose;
to manage
stellig definite
stelling (de) proposition, thesis;
position; scaffolding
stelpen to staunch
stelsel (het) system
stelsel'matig systematic
stelten (de) stilts **op – zetten**
to raise hell
stem (de) voice, part; vote
stembanden vocal chords
stembiljet (het) voting paper
stembureau (het) polling station
stembus (de) ballot box
stemge'rechtigd entitled to vote

stem'hebbend voiced; entitled to vote
stemloos voiceless
stemmen to vote; to tune (up)
stemmig demure, sober
stemming (de) mood, atmosphere:
vote
stempel (de, het) (post)mark; stigma
stempelen to stamp,
to (post-hall-) mark
stemrecht (het) right to vote
stemvork (de) tuning fork
stengel (de) stalk, stem
stenigen to stone (to death)
steno(gra'fie) (de) shorthand
step (de) scooter
ster (de) star
stereo (de) stereo; hi-fi system, music
centre
stero'tiep stereotype(d)
stereotoren (de) hi-fi system,
music centre
stereo'type (de) stereotype
sterfbed (het) deathbed
sterfelijk mortal
sterfgeval (het) death
sterftecijfer (het) mortality rate
ste'riel sterile
sterk strong; extraordinary; greatly
– verhaal tall story
sterken to strengthen; to comfort
sterkte strength; all the best!
sterrenkijker (de) telescope
sterrenbeeld (het) constellation
sterrenwacht (de) observatory
sterretje (het) star, asterisk
sterveling (de) mortal
sterven (aan) to die (from)
steun (de) support
steunen to support, to lean; to groan
steunpilaar (de) pillar, mainstay
steuntrekken to be on the dole
stevig firm, substantial, sturdy
stichten to found, to establish;
to edify

stichting (de) foundation, institution; edification
stief(moeder) (de) step(mother)
stiekem on the quiet
stier (de) bull, Taurus
stierlijk: zich – vervelen to be bored stiff
stift (de) stylo, pin, pencil (lead)
stifttand (de) crowned tooth
stijf stiff, starchy
stijfjes stiff, formal
stijfkop (de) pig-headed person
stijgen to rise; to (dis)mount
stijl (de) style
stijldansen (het) ballroom dancing
stik'donker (het) pitch dark(ness)
stikken to stifle, to suffocate; to stitch
stikstof (de) nitrogen
stil silent, quiet; still
stilhouden to stop; to keep quiet
stilleggen to stop
stillen to quiet(en), to alleviate
stilletjes quietly, stealthily
stilliggen to lie still, to lie idle
stilstaan to stand still; to pull up
– bij to give (some) thought to
stilstaand stationary, stagnant
stilstand (de) standstill
stilte (de) silence **in –** quietly, privately
stilzwijgen (het) silence
stil'zwijgend tacit
stimu'lans (de) stimulant, stimulus
stimu'leren to stimulate
stinkdier (het) skunk
stinken to stink
stip(pel) (de) dot, speck
stippellijn (de) dotted line
stipt punctual, prompt; strict
stiptheidsactie (de) work-to-rule, go-slow, slow-down (strike)
stoeien to romp
stoel (de) chair

stoelendans (de) musical chairs
stoelgang (de) (bowel) movement
stoep (de) front doorstep(s); pavement, kerb
stoer sturdy, tough
stoet (de) procession
stof (de) material, (subject) matter
stof (het) dust **– afnemen** to dust **lang van –** long-winded
stofdoek (de) duster
stoffelijk material, mortal
stoffen to dust
stoffer (de) brush
stof'feren to upholster
stoffig dusty
stofje (het) speck of dust; bit of material
stofwisseling metabolism
stofzuiger (de) vacuum cleaner
stoï'cijns stoical
stok (de) stick; perch, roost; truncheon
stok'doof stone deaf
stoken to burn, to keep a fire going, to distil; to stir up
stokje (het) stick, baton **er een – voor steken** to put a stop to something
stok'oud ancient
stokpaard (het) hobby (horse)
stok'stijf rigid
stollen to congeal
stom dumb, mute, speechless; stupid
stomen to steam, to smoke; to dry clean; to cram
stome'rij (de) dry cleaners
stommelen to clump (about)
stommeling (de) idiot, fool
stommerik (de) idiot, fool
stommi'teit (de) stupidity, blunder
stomp (de) blunt, obtuse: stump: punch, dig
stompen to punch, to jab
stomp'zinnig obtuse

stomverbaasd stupefied
stomvervelend deadly dull
stoom (de) steam
stoomboot (de) steamboat
stoomcursus (de) crash course, intensive course
stoot (de) punch, thrust, stab, blow, gust; (vulg) sexually attractive woman
stoornis (de) disturbance
stop (de) plug, stopper; fuse
stopcontact (het) (wall) socket
stoppel (de) stubble
stoppen to stop (up); to put; to fill; to darn; to constipate
stoptrein (de) slow train
stopverf (de) putty
stopwoord (het) stopgap
stopzetten to stop, to shut down
storen to disturb, to interrupt **zich – aan** to bother about
storing (de) interference, failure, dislocation
storm (de) gale, storm
stormen to storm, to blow a gale
stormlamp (de) hurricane lamp
stormloop (de) rush, stampede
stormvloed (de) gale-swept high water
stortbui (de) heavy shower
storten to plunge, to dump, to shed; to pay in
stortregenen to pour with rain
stortvloed (de) torrent
stoten to bump, to knock, to butt **zich – aan** to take offence at
stotteren to stammer
stout naughty
stoven to stew
straal (de) ray; radius; jet
straalaandrijving (de) jet propulsion
straalvliegtuig (het) jet plane
straat (de) street, road; straits
straat'arm penniless

straatlantaarn (de) street lamp
straatweg (de) high road
straf (de) punishment, penalty
strafbaar punishable
straffen to punish
strafrecht (het) criminal law
strafschop (de) penalty kick
strafwet (de) criminal law
strak tight, hard
strak(je)s in a moment, soon
stralen to shine, to beam
stralend radiant
stram stiff, rigid
strand (het) beach
stranden to (be) strand(ed)
strandjutter (de) beachcomber
stra'teeg (de) strategist
stratenmaker (de) road worker, paviour
streber (de) careerist, (social) climber
streek (de) district, region; trick; stroke **van –** upset
streekroman (de) regional novel
streep (de) stripe, stroke, line **er een – onder zetten** to call it a day
streepje (het) dash, hyphen
streepjescode (de) barcode
strekken to stretch
strekking (de) purport
strelen to stroke; to tickle
streng severe, strict, strand, skein
stress (de) stress, strain
stressen to be under strain, to be stressed
streven naar to strive for
strijd (de) fight, struggle, conflict
strijden met to fight (against), to go against
strijdig contrary
strijdkrachten (de) military forces
strijd'lustig bellicose, pugnacious
strijkbout (de) iron

strijken to iron; to haul down; to stroke, to brush
strijkgoed (het) ironing
strijkijzer (het) iron
strijkinstrument (het) stringed instrument
strijkkwartet (het) string quartet
strijkplank (de) ironing board
strik (de) bow(tie); snare
strikken to tie; to (en)snare
strikt strict
strikvraag (de) trick question
stripboek (het) comic (book)
stripfiguur (de) comic (strip) character
stripheld (de) comic (strip) hero
strippenkaart (de) bus and tram card/ticket
stripverhaal (het) comic (strip)
stro (het) straw
stroef stiff, harsh
stromen to flow
stroming (de) current; trend
strompelen to hobble
strooien to strew, to sprinkle: straw
strook (de) strip; frill; counterfoil
stroom (de) stream, flood, current
stroom'af(waarts) downstream
stroomgebied (het) river basin
stroom'op(waarts) upstream
stroomversnelling (de) rapid(s)
stroop (de) syrup, treacle
strooplikken to curry favour
strooptocht (de) marauding expedition
strop (de) noose; tough luck
stropdas (de) stock, tie
stropen to skin, to strip; to poach, to pillage
stroper (de) poacher
strot (de) throat
strottenhoofd (het) larynx
struc'tuur (de) structure
struik (de) bush, shrub

struikelblok (het) stumbling block
struikelen to stumble, to trip (up)
struisveer (de) ostrich feather
struisvogel (de) ostrich
stu'deerkamer (de) study
stu'dentenflat (de) (block of) student flats; hall of residence, student apartments
stu'dentenhaver (de) almonds and raisins
studenti'koos undergraduate, varsity
stu'deren to study, to read; to practise; to be at university
studie (de) study, studies
studiebeurs (de) grant
studieboek (het) textbook
studiefinanciering (de) student grant(s)
studiepunt (de) credit
studierichting (de) subject, course, discipline, branch of studies
stuff (de) dope, stuff; pot; grass, weed
stug dour, gruff; tough
stuiptrekking (de) convulsion
stuitbeen (het) tailbone, coccyx
stuiten to check; to bounce **– op** to encounter **tegen de borst –** to go against the grain
stuitend offensive
stuiven to blow dust about; to dash
stuiver (de) 5-cent coin (of guilder)
stuk (het) piece; play; document; broken, to pieces **een – of vier** three or four **aan één – door** without a break **op geen stukken na** not by a long chalk **klein van –** small **iemand van zijn – brengen** to upset a person
stuka'door (de) plasterer
stukhakken to chop up
stukslaan to smash (to pieces)
stumper(d) (de) wretch

stuntelig clumsy
stunten to stunt
stuntprijs (de) very low price
sturen to send; to steer
stutten to prop (up)
stuur (het) handlebar(s), (steering) wheel, helm
stuurboord starboard
stuurknuppel (de) control column
stuurman (de) mate; cox(swain)
stuwdam (de) (flood-control) dam, barrage
stuwen to drive; to stow; to dam up
stuwkracht (de) driving force
subjec'tief subjective, personal
su'bliem sublime
sub'sidie (de) subsidy, aid, grant, allowance
subsidi'ëren to subsidize, grant (an amount)
sub'stantie (de) substance
substitu'eren to substitute
sub'tiel subtle
sub'tropisch subtropical
suc'ces (het) success
succes'sievelijk successively
suc'cesvol successful
suf dopey, groggy
suffen to day dream
suffer(d) (de) dope, fathead
sugge'reren to suggest, to prompt
suiker (de) sugar
suikergoed (het) candy
suikerklontje (het) lump of sugar, sugar cube
suikeroom, (de) rich uncle
suikerpot (de) sugar bowl

suikerriet (het) sugar cane
suikerziekte (de) diabetes
suizen to whisper, to murmur
sukkel (de) idiot, dope, twerp
sukkelaar (de) weakling; booby
sukkelen to be in poor health; to plod
sul (de) nincompoop
summum (het) height
supermarkt (de) supermarket
super'sonisch supersonic
supple'ment (het) supplement
sup'poost (de) attendant
sup'porter (de) supporter
surfen to be surfing/surfboarding; to surf (also on the internet)
surfer (de) surfer, windsurfer
surfplank (de) surfboard, sailboard
Suri'name Surinam
Suri'namer (de) Surinamese
surro'gaat (het) substitute
surveil'leren to supervise, to invigilate
sussen to soothe; to salve
s.v.p. (s'il vous plaît) please
sweater (de) sweatshirt
sweatshirt (het) sweatshirt
symbo'liek (de) symbolism
sym'bool (het) symbol
symfo'nie (de) symphony
sympa'thiek congenial, engaging
symp'toom (het) symptom
syno'niem synonymous
syn'thetisch synthetic
sys'teem (het) system
sys'teembeheerder (de) system manager

T

taak (de) task
taal (de) language
taal'kundige (de) linguist
taart (de) tart, *gâteau*

ta'bak (de) tobacco **ergens – van hebben** to be fed up with something
ta'bel (de) table, index

ta'blet (de) tablet
tachtig eighty
tachtiger (de) octogenarian; writer of the movement of 1880
tac'tiek (de) tactic(s)
tactloos tactless
tafel (de) table
tafelblad tabletop, tableleaf
tafeldekken to lay the table
tafelen: lang – to linger over a meal
tafelkleed (het) table cover
tafellaken (het) tablecloth
tafeltennissen to play table tennis
tafeltennisser (de) table-tennis player
tafe'reel (het) scene
taille (de) waist(line)
tak (de) branch
takel (de) tackle, rigging
takelen to rig (out); to hoist
takelwagen (de) breakdown lorry
tal (het) number **een viertal, twaaftal, twintigtal etc.** (about) four, a dozen, a score etc.
talenknobbel (de) gift for languages, linguistic talent
talenpracticum (het) language lab
talkpoeder (het) talcum powder
talloos countless
talrijk numerous
tam tame(d), domestic(ated)
tamboe'rijn (de) tambourine
tamelijk fair(ly), rather
tam'pon (de) tampon
tand (de) tooth, prong **iemand aan de – voelen** to put a person through his paces
tandarts (de) dentist
tandem (de) tandem
tandenborstel (de) toothbrush
tandenstoker (de) toothpick
tandpasta (de) toothpaste
tandplak (de) (dental) plaque
tandsteen (de) tartar

tandvlees (het) gum(s)
tang (de) (pair of) tongs, forceps; witch **dat slaat als een – op een varken** that is neither here nor there
tanken to (re)fuel
tankschip (het) tanker
tante (de) aunt
tantième (het) bonus
tapdansen to tap dance
tapdanser (de), tap dancer
ta'pijt (het) carpet
tapkast (de) bar
tappen to tap; to crack
taps tapering
ta'rief (het) tariff, terms, fare
tarten to defy, to flout
tarwe (de) wheat
tas (de) (hand)bag, briefcase
tast: op de – by feeling
tastbaar tangible
tasten to feel, to grope
tatoe'age (de) tattoo
tatoe'ëren to tattoo **zich laten –** to have oneself tattooed
t.a.v. (ten aanzien van) with regard to
t.a.v. (ter attentie van) (for the) attention (of)
tau'gé (de) beansprouts
taxa'teur (de) valuer
tax'eren to value, to assess
t.b.v. (ten behoeve van) on behalf of
te at, in; too; to
T-biljet (het) tax reclaim form
tech'niek (de) technique; technics
technisch technical
te(d)er tender, delicate
teef (de) bitch, vixen
teelbal (de) testicle
teelt (de) cultivation, culture, breeding
teen (de) toe

teer (de, het) tar (*see* **teder**)
tegel (de) tile
tege'lijk(ertijd) at the same time
tege'moet- to ... to meet
tege'moetkomend accommodating
tegen against; towards; at
  ik kan er niet – I cannot stand it
tegen- counter-
tegen'aan against, into
tegendeel (het) contrary
tegengaan to counter(act)
tegengesteld opposite
tegengif (het) antidote
tegenhanger (de) counterpart
tegenhouden to check, to hold
tegenkandidaat opposing candidate
tegenkomen to come across
tegenligger (de) oncoming vehicle or vessel
tegenlopen: het liep me tegen I had bad luck
tegen'over opposite (to), (as) against, towards
tegen'overgesteld contrary
tegenpartij (de) opponent
tegenpool (de) antipole
tegenprestatie: als – in return
tegenslag (de) setback
tegenspartelen to struggle; to protest
tegenspeler (de) opponent; opposite number
tegenspoed (de) adversity
tegenspreken to contradict
tegenstaan to be repugnant to
tegenstand (de) resistance
tegenstander (de) adversary
tegenstelling (de) contrast
tegenstemmen to vote against
tegenstribbelen to struggle; to protest
tegen'strijdig conflicting

tegenvallen to be disappointing **het viel tegen** it was worse than (or not what) I'd expected
tegenvaller (de) blow
tegenwerken to oppose
tegenwind (de) headwind; opposition
tegen'woordig present(-day), nowadays
tegen'woordigheid (de) presence
tegenzin (de) aversion **met –** reluctantly
tegenzitten: alles zit me tegen I'm up against it
te'goed (het) credit: owing
te'goedbon (de) credit note
te'huis (het) home
teil (de) (zinc, enamel) bowl or bath
te'keergaan to rant (and rave)
teken (het) sign, token **in het – staan van** to be overshadowed by
tekenaar (de) artist; draughtsman
tekenen to draw; to sign
tekenfilm (de) cartoon
tekening (de) drawing, plan; marking(s)
te'kort (het) shortage, deficit, deficiency **te'kort doen** to stint; to wrong
tekst (de) text, script, words
tekstverklaring (de) close reading
tekstverwerker (de) word processor
tel (de) count; second **in – zijn** to be highly thought of
telebankieren (het) computerized banking
telecommunicatie (de) telecommunication
tele'foon (de) telephone
tele'foonaansluiting (de) (telephone) connection
tele'fooncel (de) telephone box/booth
tele'fooncentrale (de) telephone exchange

tele'foongids (de) telephone directory
tele'foonrekening (de) telephone bill
tele'foontje (het) (telephone) call
teleshoppen (het) teleshopping
te'leurstellen to disappoint
te'leurstelling (de) disappointment
telg (de) offspring
telkenmale, telkens (weer) again and again, every time
tellen to count, to total
telwoord (het) numeral
temmen to tame
tempel (de) temple
tempera'mentvol temperamental
tempera'tuur (de) temperature
temperen to temper, to moderate
tempo (het) tempo, pace
ten'dens (de) tendency
teneinde so that, in order to
tenger slight, delicate
tenge'volge van as a result of
te'nietdoen to nullify, to vitiate
ten'minste at least
tennis (het) tennis
tennisbaan (de) tennis court
tennishal (de) indoor tennis court(s)
tennissen to play tennis
tennisser (de) tennis player

tent (de) tent, booth, joint
ten'tamen (het) preliminary examination
ten'toonstelling (de) exhibition, show
te'nue (het): (groot) – (full) dress
ten'zij unless
tepel (de) nipple, teat
ter'dege thoroughly
te'recht rightly
te'rechtbrengen to make a job of
te'rechtkomen to turn out all right; to turn up; to end up
te'rechtstaan to stand trial
teren op to live on
tergen to provoke
tering (de) consumption, TB
ter'loops incidental
term (de) term, expression
ter'mijn (de) term; instalment **op korte –** at short notice; short term
ter'nauwernood scarcely
ter'neergeslagen disheartened
terpen'tijn (de) turpentine
terpen'tine (de) white spirit
ter'ras (het) terrace
ter'rein (het) terrain, ground, field
ter'reur (de) terror
terrori'seren to terrorize

Insight

The English word *tennis* has been adopted into the Dutch language, as it has been by many other languages. However, the Dutch often take words describing sports (or other activities) such as tennis and make them into verbs by adding -en at the end. In other words, **tennissen** (note that the 's' is doubled to keep the right pronunciation) means *to play tennis*. Similarly, **volleybal** becomes **voleyballen** *to play volleyball*, **hockey** becomes **hockeyen** *to play hockey*, **ski** becomes **skiën**, **basketbal** becomes **basketballen**, and **voetbal** (a bastardization of English) becomes **voetballen** *to play football*, the national sport.

terro'risme (het) terrorism
terro'rist (de) terrorist
terro'ristisch terrorist(ic)
ter'stond at once
te'rug back
te'rugblik (de) retrospect(ion)
te'rugdenken aan to recall (to mind)
te'rugfluiten to call back
te'ruggeven to give back, to return
te'rugkeer (de) return
te'rugkeren to return, to turn back
te'rugkomen to come back, to
   return
te'ruglopen to walk back; to decline
te'rugnemen to take back, to
   withdraw
te'rugreis (de) return journey, way
   back
te'rugroepen to call back, to recall
te'rugslaan to hit back, to repulse;
   to backfire
te'rugtraprem (de) back-pedal
   brake
te'rugtrekken to draw back, to
   retract; to retreat **zich –** to retire
te'rugverdienen to recover the
   costs on
ter'wijl while; whereas
testa'ment (het) will, testament
testen to test
teugel (de) rein
teugje (het) sip
teuten to dawdle
te'veel surplus
tevens as well
tever'geefs to no purpose
te'vreden content(ed), satisfied
tex'tiel (de, het) textile
te'zamen together
thans at present
thea'traal theatrical
thee (de) tea
theedoek (de) tea towel
theelepel (de) teaspoon

theelepeltje (het) teaspoon,
   teaspoonful
theeleut (de) inveterate tea drinker
theelichtje (het) (heated)
   tea pot stand
Theems (de) Thames
theemuts (de) teacosy
theeservies (het) tea set
theezeefje (het) tea strainer
thema (het) theme; exercise
theo'loog (de) theologian,
   theological student
theo'retisch theoretical
theo'rie (de) theory
thera'pie (de) therapy, therapeutics
thermosfles (de) thermos (flask)
thermo'pane (de, het) double
   glazing
thuis (at) home
thuisbankieren (het) home banking
thuisbezorgen to deliver (to the
   house/door)
thuisbrengen to take home; to place
thuisfront (het) home front
thuishoren to belong
tien ten
tiend(e) tenth
tien'delig ten-piece, in ten parts;
   decimal
tien'tallig decimal
tientje (het) ten-guilder note
tier(e)lan'tijntje (het) frill,
   furbelow
tieren to thrive; to rage
tij (het) tide
tijd (de) time; tense
tijdelijk temporary; temporal
tijdens during
tijdgenoot (de) contemporary
tijdig timely, in good time
tijdlang: een – for some time
tijdopname (de) time exposure;
   timing
tijdperk (het) period

tijd'rovend protractive
tijdsbestek (het) space of time
tijdschrift (het) periodical, magazine
tijdstip (het) epoch, moment
tijdsverloop (het) lapse of time
tijdvak (het) period
tijdverdrijf (het) pastime
tijdverspilling (de) waste of time
tijger (de) tiger
tijm (de) thyme
tik (de) tap, rap
tikje (het) gentle tap; touch, shade
tikken to tap; to tick; to type
tillen to raise, to lift
timmeren to carpenter, to hammer
timmerman (de) carpenter
tingelen to tinkle
tint (de) tint, shade
tintelen to sparkle, to twinkle;
  to tingle
tip (de) tip, corner
tippelen (prostitution) to be
  on the streets, to solicit
ti'ran (de) tyrant
tiranni'seren to bully
titel (de) title, heading
titelrol (de) title role
tja well
tjilpen to chirp
tjok'vol chock-full
tl-buis (de) strip light, neon light
tl-verlichting (de) neon light(ing)
tobben to brood; to slave; to have a
  tough time
toch still, for all that; surely, after all
  zeg het –! do tell me! **waarom –?**
  whatever for?
tocht (de) draught; trip, drive
tochten to be draughty
tochtig draughty
toe to – **maar!, – nou!** go on! **er**
  slecht aan – zijn to be in a bad
  way **het is tot daar aan –** it is bad
  enough

toebrengen to inflict on;
  to administer
toedekken to cover up; to mulch
toedienen to administer, to serve up
toeëigenen: zich – to appropriate
toegaan: het gaat er raar toe there
  are strange goings-on there
toegang (de) admission, entry
toegangsbewijs (het) ticket
  of admission
toe'gankelijk accessible, open
toe'geeflijk lenient
toegeven to admit; to give way (to)
toegewijd devoted
toegift (de) encore
toehoorders (de) audience,
  observers
toejuichen to applaud; to welcome
toekennen to confer on, to attach to
toekijken to look on
toekomen to come to(wards);
  to make ends meet; to be due to
toe'komend future; due
toekomst (de) future
toelage (de) allowance
toelaten to admit, to permit
toelatingsexamen (het) entrance
  examination
toelichten to elucidate
toeloop (de) concourse, rush
toelopen to run (up) to; to taper
toen then; when
toenaam: met naam en – in detail
toenadering (de) advance, approach
toename (de) increase
toenemen to increase
toenmaals at that time
toen'malig then, of the day
toe'passelijk applicable, appropriate
toepassen to apply
toepassing: van – applicable
toer (de) tour; feat; rev(olution); row
  (of knitting) **een hele –** quite a job
toereiken to hand (to)

toe'reikend sufficient
toe'rekenbaar responsible
toeren: gaan – to go for a drive
toe'risme (het) tourism
toe'rist (de) tourist
toer'nooi (het) tournament
toe'schietelijk responsive, obliging
toeschouwer (de) spectator,
  onlooker
toeschrijven to attribute
toeslaan to hit home, strike
toeslag (de) excess (fare); bonus
toespeling (de) allusion
toespraak (de) address
toespreken to speak to, to address
toestaan to allow, to grant
toestand (de) state of affairs,
  situation, position, condition
toestel (het) apparatus, machine
toestemmen (in) to consent (to)
toestemming (de) permission
toestoppen to slip into (a person's)
  hand; to tuck in
toestromen to pour (in)
toetakelen to doll up; to knock about
toetasten to help oneself
**toeten: hij weet van – noch
  blazen** he doesn't know a thing
  (about it)
toeter (de) horn
toeteren to hoot, to honk
toetje (het) pudding, second course
toetreden tot to join
toets (de) key; test
toetsen to test
toetsenbord (het) keyboard
toeval (het) accident; epileptic fit
toe'vallig (by) chance **wat –!** what a
  coincidence!
toevalstreffer (de) chance hit, stroke
  of luck
toevertrouwen to (en)trust with **dat
  is hem wel toevertrouwd** you can
  leave that to him

toevlucht (de) recourse
toevoegen to add
toevoer (de) supply
toewensen to wish
toewijding (de) devotion
toewijzen to allocate
toezeggen to promise
toezicht (het) supervision
toezien to look on; to take care (of)
tof great, ok
toi'letreiniger (de) toilet cleaner
toi'letrol (de) toilet paper
toi'lettafel (de) dressing table
toi'lettas (de) toilet bag
toi'letverfrisser (de) toilet freshener
tokkelen to pluck, to strum
tol toll; top
tole'reren to tolerate
tolk (de) interpreter; spokesman
tollen to play with a top, to spin
  round
tolweg (de) toll road
to'maat (de) tomato
to'matenketchup (de) tomato
  ketchup
to'matenpuree (de) tomato purée
to'matensap (de) tomato juice
to'matensoep (de) tomato soup
tomeloos unbridled
tom'poes (de) cream slice
ton (de) barrel; buoy;
  ton; 100,000 euros
ton'deuse (de) hair clippers
to'neel (het) stage; scene, theatre
to'neelgezelschap (het) theatre
  company
to'neelschool (de) school of
  dramatic art
to'neelschrijver (de) playwright
to'neelspeler (de) actor
to'neelstuk (het) play
tonen to show
tong (de) tongue; sole
tongval (de) accent

tongzoen (de) French kiss
tooien to adorn
toom (de) bridle **in – houden** to keep in check
toon (de) tone; pitch
toonaan'gevend leading
toonbaar presentable
toonbank (de) counter
toonbeeld (het) model
toonladder (de) scale
toonsoort (de) key
toontje lager zingen to come down (a) peg or two
toorts (de) torch
toost (de) toast
top top, tip, peak
topatleet (de) top-class athlete
topconditie (de) top condition/form
topkwaliteit (de) top quality, (the) highest quality
topo'grafisch topographical, ordnance
topprestatie (de) record/top performance
toppunt (het) summit, height; limit
tor (de) beetle
toren (de) tower
toren'hoog towering
torenspits (de) spire
tornen to unpick; to meddle
torpe'deren to torpedo; to scotch
tor'pedojager (de) destroyer
torsen to labour under (the weight of)
tossen to toss
tot till, (up) to; as **– aan** as far as **– op** to within; up till
to'taal total, utter
totdat until
tou'cheren to touch (up)
tour'nee (de) tour
touw (het) rope, string **op – zetten** to plan, start something **ik kon er geen – aan vastknopen** I couldn't make head or tail of it

touwtje (het) piece of string
touwtjespringen to skip
touwtrekken (het) tug-of-war
tovenaar (de) magician
toverachtig magic, enchanting
toverdrank (de) magic potion
toveren to work charms, to conjure (up)
traag slow, sluggish
traan (de) tear; oil
trachten to attempt, to try
tra'ditie (de) tradition
tra'gedie (de) tragedy
tra'giek (de) tragedy
tragisch tragic
trainen to train, to coach
trainer (de) trainer, coach
training (de) training, practice; workout
trainingspak (het) tracksuit, jogging suit
tra'ject (het) stretch, stage, line
trak'tatie (de) treat
trak'teren (op) to treat (to)
tralies (de) bars, grating
tram(halte) (de) tram (stop)
transfor'mator (de) transformer
tran'sistorradio (de) transistor radio
tran'sito(haven) (de) transit (port)
transpi'reren to perspire
transplan'tatie (de) transplant(ation)
transplan'teren to transplant
transpor'teren to transport; to bring forward
transseksu'eel (de) transsexual
trant (de) style, manner
trap (de) kick; stairs; degree **een hele –** quite a way (by bike)
trapgevel (de) step gable
trapje (het) step, stair
trapleuning (de) banisters
traploper (de) stair carpet
trappelen to stamp **ik sta te –** I'm raring to go

trappen to kick; to tread; to pedal
trappenhuis (het) stairwell
trappers (de) pedals; brogues
trapsge'wijs step by step
traves'tiet (de) transvestite
trechter (de) funnel, hopper
trede (de) step, stair
treden to tread; to go, to come
treffen to hit, to strike; to meet
  het (goed) – to be lucky
treffend striking, touching
treffer (de) good shot, hit
trein (de) train
treinongeval (het) train/
  railway accident
treinramp (de) train/railway disaster
treinreis (de) train journey
treinreiziger (de) rail(way)
  passenger
treintaxi (de) train taxi
treinverkeer (het) train/rail traffic
treiteren to torment
trek (de) pull, draught; stroke;
  feature, trait; inclination, appetite;
  migration **in –** in demand
trekken to pull, to draw, to drag;
  to migrate, to trek
trekker (de) trigger; hiker
trekking (de) (lottery) draw
trekpleister (de) attraction
trektocht (de) hiking tour
treuren to grieve
treurig sad
treurspel (het) tragedy
treurwilg (de) weeping willow
treuzelen to dawdle
triatlon (de) triathlon
tri'bune (de) platform, gallery, stand
trillen to vibrate, to quiver
tri'omf (de) triumph
triom'fantelijk triumphant
triom'feren to triumph
triplex (de, het) three-ply
trippelen to trip

troebel turbid, cloudy
troef (de) trump(s)
troep (de) mess; crowd,
  troop, company
troepenmacht (de) military forces
troetelkind (het) spoiled child
troeven to trump
trom (de) drum
trommel (de) tin, (bread)bin; drum
trommeldroger (de) tumble dryer
trommelen to drum; to strum
trommelvlies (het) eardrum
trom'pet (de) trumpet
tronie (de) mug
troon (de) throne
troonrede (de) queen's/king's
  speech
troost (de) consolation
troosteloos cheerless, dreary
troosten to comfort
tropen (de) tropics
tros (de) cluster, bunch
trots (de) proud: pride
trot'seren to brave, to face
trot'toir (het) pavement
trouw (de) faithfulness, loyalty
trouw- marriage-, wedding-
trouwakte (de) marriage certificate
trouwen (met) to marry, to be
  married (to) **zo zijn we niet
  getrouwd** that's not on
trouwens for that matter
truc (de) trick, stunt
trui (de) jersey, sweater
T-shirt (het) T-shirt
Tsjech (de) Czech
Tsjechië Czech Republic
tsjirpen to chirp
tuimelen to tumble, to topple over
tuin (de) garden
tuinboon (de) broad bean
tuinbouw (de) horticulture
tuinder (de) market gardener
tuinhuisje (het) summerhouse

tui'nieren to garden
tuinkabouter (de) garden gnome
tuinman (de) gardener
tuinstoel (de) garden chair
tuit (de) spout
tuk op keen on
tukje (het) snooze
tulband (de) turban; ring(cake)
tulp (de) tulip
tunnel (de) tunnel, subway
ture'luurs dotty
turen to peer, to pore over
turf (de) peat
Turk (de) Turk
Tur'kije Turkey
Turks Turkish
turnen to do gymnastics
turner (de) (male) gymnast
turnster (de) (female) gymnast
tussen between, among **iemand
  er – nemen** to pull a person's leg
tussen'beide komen to intervene
tussen'door through
tussenhandel (de) middleman's
  trade
tussen'in: er – in between
tussenkomst (de) intervention
tussenmuur (de) partition wall
tussenpersoon (de) middleman;
  go-between
tussenpoos (de) interval
tussenstand (de) score (so far),
  score at halftime
tussentijd (de) interim
tussentijdse verkiezing (de)
  by-election
tussenuur (het) free period
tussenvoegen to insert
tussenwoning (de) terrace(d) house
tutoy'eren to drop the formalities
tv-serie (de) TV series
twaalf twelve
twaalf'uurtje (het) midday meal
twee two

tweebaansweg (de) two-lane road;
  dual carriageway, divided highway
tweede second
tweede'hands second-hand
Tweede-'Kamerlid (het) member
  of the Lower House
tweede'rangs second-rate
tweedracht (de) discord
tweegevecht (het) dual
tweeklank (de) diphthong
twee'ledig twofold, dual
tweeling (de) (pair of) twin(s)
Tweelingen (de) Gemini
tweemaal twice
twee-onder-een-'kapwoning (de)
  semi-detached house, (one side
  of a) duplex
tweepersoons double
twee'slachtig amphibious; ambiguous
tweesprong (de) fork; crossroads
twee'stemmig two-part
tweestrijd (de) inner conflict
twee'talig bilingual
tweeverdieners (de) couple with
  two incomes, double income
  family/couple
tweevoud (het) double, duplicate;
  binary, double
twee'zijdig bilateral
tweezitsbank (de) two-seater sofa,
  settee for two people
twijfel(achtig) (de) doubt(ful)
twijfelen (aan) to doubt
twijg (de) twig
twintig twenty
twist(en) (de) (to) quarrel
twistgesprek (het) dispute
twistpunt (het) vexed question
twistziek quarrelsome
typefout (de) typing error, typo
ty'peren to typify
ty'perend voor typical of
tyfus, typhus (de) typhoid
typisch typical; quaint

U

u you
überhaupt at all; anyway
ufo (de) UFO
ui (de) onion
uier (de) udder
uil (de) owl
uilskuiken (het) numbskull
uit out (of), from; finished **ergens op – zijn** be out for (bent on) something
uitbeelden to depict, to render
uitbesteden to put out to contract; to board out
uitblijven to stay away; to fail to materialize
uitblinken to excel
uitbouw (de) extension
uitbouwen to build out, to add onto (a house); to develop, to expand
uitbraak (de) escape (from prison)
uitbraken to vomit; to belch out
uitbrander (de) dressing-down
uitbreiden to extend
uitbuiten to exploit
uit'bundig exuberant
uitdagen to challenge
uitdelen to distribute

uitdenken to think up
uitdiepen to deepen
uitdijen to expand
uitdokteren to work out, to figure out
uitdoen to take off; to put out
uitdraaien to turn out **zich er –** to wriggle out of it **op (ruzie) –** to end in (a quarrel)
uitdrage'rij (de) junk shop
uit'drukkelijk express
uitdrukken to express; to stub out
uitdrukking (de) expression
uitduiden to point out
uit'eengaan to separate
uit'eenlopend divergent
uit'eenzetten to state, to explain
uiteinde (het) extremity, tip, (far) end; end, close, end of the year
uit'eindelijk ultimate
uiten to utter, to express
uiten'treuren on and on (and on)
uiter'aard naturally
uiterlijk (het) outward appearance
uiterlijk outward(ly), external, from the outside; at the latest, no later than

Insight

U is simply described as the Dutch word for *you* in the dictionary, but don't forget that je and jij mean the same thing. The difference is that they are used in different contexts. U is used in formal situations, when addressing people with whom you are not on a first name basis, whereas je and jij are used in informal situations when talking to people with whom you are on a first name basis. Jij is the stressed form of je, and is generally used in writing and when stressing the pronoun or emphasizing a contrast: **niet ik, maar jij!** *not I, but you!*

uitermate exceedingly
uiterst ut(ter)most, extreme
uiterste (het) extreme
uiterwaarden (de) water meadows
uitfoeteren to blow up, to call names
uitgaan to go out
uitgang (de) exit; ending
uitgangspunt (het) point
　of departure
uitgave (de) expense; publication,
　edition
uitgebreid extensive
uitgehongerd famished
uitgekookt sly, shrewd
uitgelaten elated
uitgemergeld emaciated, exhausted
uitgeslapen wide awake,
　(fully) rested
uitgestreken: met een – gezicht
　without batting an eyelid
uitgeven to spend; to issue;
　to publish **zich – voor** to pose as
uitgever (de) publisher
uitgezonderd except (for)
uitgieren: het – van het lachen
　to scream with laughter
uitgifte (de) issue
uitglijden to slip
uitgommen to rub out
uitgroeien to (out)grow
uithalen to turn out; to unpick;
　to be up to (tricks) **de kosten er –**
　to cover the costs
uithangbord (het) sign(board)
uithangen to hang out; to act
uit'heems foreign; outlandish
uithoek (de) out-of-the-way place
uithollen to hollow out
uithoren to wheedle information
　from
uithouden: het – to stand (it)
uithoudingsvermogen (het)
　stamina, staying power, endurance
uithuw(elijk)en to marry off

uiting (de) expression
uitje (het) jaunt; small onion
uitjouwen to jeer (at)
uitkeren to pay
uitkering (de) pay(ment), benefit
uitkienen to figure (out)
uitkiezen to select
uitkijk (de) view; lookout
uitkijken to look out, to look
　forward; to be careful
uitkleden to undress, to strip
uitknijpen to squeeze out;
　to do a bunk; to peg out
uitkomen to come out, to work out
　ervoor – to state openly
uitkomst (de) result; remedy
uitkramen to spout, to parade
uitlaat (de) exhaust (pipe),
　muffler; funnel
uitlaatgas (het) exhaust fumes/
　gases
uitlaatklep (de) outlet valve, exhaust
　valve, escape valve; outlet
uitlaatpijp (de) exhaust pipe
　(of a car)
uitlachen to laugh at, to have
　a good laugh
uitlaten to let out; to leave off
　(wearing) **zich –** to express
　an opinion
uitleentermijn (de) lending period
uitleg (de) explanation
uitleggen to lay out; to explain;
　to let out
uitlenen to lend (out), loan
uitleven: zich – to live one's (own)
　life (to the full) **uitgeleefd** decrepit
uitleveren to deliver up
uitlezen to finish (reading)
uitloggen to log off/out
uitlokken to invite
uitlopen to run out; to sprout
　– op to lead to
uitloper (de) runner; spur

uitmaken to break off (a relationship), finish, terminate; to matter, to be of importance; determine, establish; call, brand

uitmesten to clear out

uitmonden in to discharge into; to end in

uitmoorden to massacre

uit'munten to excel

uitmuntend excellent

uitnodigen to invite

uitnodiging (de) invitation

uitoefenen to exercise; to carry on, to hold

uitpakken to unpack

uitpluizen to go through with a fine toothcomb

uitpraten to finish talking; to talk over; to hear someone out **zich ergens –** to talk one's way out of something

uitpuilen to bulge

uitputten to exhaust

uitreiken to distribute, to issue

uitrekenen to calculate

uitroeien to root out, to exterminate

uitroep (de) exclamation

uitroepen to call (out), to exclaim; to proclaim

uitroepteken (het) exclamation mark

uitrusten to rest; to equip

uitrusting (de) outfit, equipment

uitschakelen to switch off, disconnect; eliminate

uitscheiden (met) to stop

uitschelden to call names

uitschot (het) scum, dregs

uitslag (de) result; rash

uitslapen to sleep long enough, to lie in; to sleep off

uitsloven: zich – to slave away

uitsluiten to exclude **uitgesloten!** out of the question!

uit'sluitend exclusively

uitsmijter (de) bouncer; fried egg on bread and ham

uitsparen to save

uitspatting (de) extravagance, excess

uitspelen to finish (a game); to play (off)

uitspoken to be up to (mischief)

uitspraak (de) pronunciation; verdict

uitspreiden to spread (out)

uitspreken to pronounce, to express; to finish speaking

uitstaan to stick out, protrude; bear, endure, stand

ik kan hem niet – I can't stand him

uitstallen to display

uitstapje (het) outing

uitstappen to alight, to get out

uitstek: bij – pre-eminently

uitsteken to put out, to stick out

uitstekend protruding

uit'stekend excellent

uitstel (het) postponement

uitstellen to postpone

uitsterven to die (out), to become extinct

uitstippelen to work out (in detail)

uitstorten to pour out

uitstralen to radiate

uitstrekken to stretch (out)

uitstrijkje (het) (cervical) smear, swab

uitstulping (de) bulge

uittocht (de) exodus

uittreden to resign

uittrekken to pull out; to take off; to march out

uittreksel (het) extract; summary

uitvaardigen to issue

uitvaart (de) funeral/burial (service)

uitval (de) explosion; outburst; hair loss

uitvallen to fall out; to turn out; to flare up; to make a sortie
uitvaren to sail (out)
uitverkocht sold out
uitverkoop (de) (clearance) sale
uitverkoren chosen
uitvinden to invent
uitvinding (de) invention
uitvissen to fish out; to ferret out
uitvlucht (de) pretext
uitvoer (de) export(s) **ten – brengen** to put into effect
uit'voerbaar practicable
uitvoeren to export; to carry out, to perform
uit'voerig detailed, fully
uitwaaien to blow out, to be blown out; to get a breath of fresh air
uitwedstrijd (de) away match
uitweg (de) way out, escape, outlet
uitweiden to digress
uit'wendig external
uitwerken to work out, to elaborate; to mature, to wear off
uitwerking (de) effect; elaboration
uitwerpselen (de) excrements
uitwijken to move to one side; to flee the country
uitwijzen to show; to decide; to expel
uitwisselen to exchange
uitwisseling (de) exchange, to swap
uitwissen to wipe out, to erase
uitzendbureau (het) temp(ing) agency, (temporary) employment agency
uitzenden to send out; to broadcast

uitzendkracht (de) temp, temporary worker
uitzet (de) outfit; trousseau
uitzetten to expand; to turn out; to set (out); to lower (boats)
uitzicht (het) view, prospect
uitzieken to get over an illness
uitzien to look out; to look forward to
uitzingen: het – to hold out
uitzitten: zijn straf – to serve one's sentence
uitzoeken to pick out; to sort/ figure out
uitzondering (de) exception
uitzuigen to suck out; to bleed dry; to exploit
uk (de) nipper
una'niem unanimous
unicum (het) unique specimen
unie (de) union
u'niek unique
univer'seel universal; sole
universi'tair university
universi'teit (de) university
un'zippen to unzip, decompress, unpack
urenlang for hours
uur (het) hour; o'clock
uurloon (het) hourly wage, hourly pay
uurtarief (het) hourly rate
uurtje (het) hour **de kleine uurtjes** the small hours
uurwerk (het) timepiece
uw your
uwerzijds for your part

V

vaag vague
vaak often
vaal faded, sallow
vaandel (de) banner, flag
vaardig skilful; ready
vaargeul (de) fairway, channel

vaart (de) speed; waterway **(grote) –** (ocean-going) trade
vaartuig (het) vessel
vaarwater (het) fairway **iemand in het – zitten** to thwart a person
vaar'wel (het) farewell

vaas (de) vase
vaat (de) washing-up, dishes
vaatdoek (de) dishcloth
vaatwasmachine (de) dishwasher
vaatwasser (de) dishwasher
vaca'ture (de) vacancy
vacci'neren to vaccinate
vacht (de) pelt, coat
vader (de) father
vagina (de) vagina
vaderlander (de) patriot
vaderlands'lievend patriotic
vaderlands native, national
vaderschap (het) paternity, fatherhood
vadsig fat, lazy
vagevuur (het) purgatory
vak (het) compartment, panel; subject, trade
va'kantie (de) holiday(s), vacation **op/met – gaan** to go on holiday **prettige –!** have a nice holiday!
va'kantiebestemming (de) holiday destination
va'kantiegeld (het) holiday pay
va'kantiewerk (het) holiday/summer job
vakbeweging (de) trade union
vakblad (het) trade journal
vakbond (de) (trade) union
vakbondsleider (de) (trade) union leader
vakgebied (het) field (of study)
vakje (het) pigeonhole
vakman (de) expert
vakterm (de) technical term
val (de) (down)fall; trap
valbrug (de) drawbridge
Valentijnsdag St Valentine's Day
valhelm (de) (crash) helmet
valk(e'nier) (de) falcon(er)
valkuil (de) pitfall
val'lei (de) valley

vallen to fall **er valt niets aan te doen** nothing can be done about it
valluik (het) trapdoor
valreep: op de – at the last moment
vals false; vicious **– spelen** to cheat; to play out of tune
valsheid in geschrifte (de) forgery
valstrik (de) trap
va'luta (de) currency
van of; from **– de week** this week
van'af (as) from
van'avond this evening
van'daag today
van'daal (de) vandal
van'daan from
van'daar hence **– dat** that is why
vanda'lisme (het) vandalism
van'door: er – (gaan) to be off
vangen to catch
vangnet (het) safety net
vangrail (de) crash barrier
vangst (de) haul, catch
va'nille (de) vanilla
va'nilleijs (het) vanilla ice cream
va'nillevla (de) vanilla custard
van- this (afternoon, morning)
van'nacht last night, tonight
van'ouds (her) of old
van'waar whence
van'wege on account of
vanzelf'sprekend self-evident, quite obvious
varen to sail, to fare **laten –** to give up, to drop
varen (de) fern
varia miscellaneous (items)
vari'ëren to vary
varië'teit (de) variety, diversity
varken (het) pig
varkensvlees (het) pork
vast fixed, permanent, firm, regular, stock; solid; certainly **maar –** in the meantime
vastbe'raden resolute

vastbinden to tie up (tight)
vaste'land (het) continent, mainland
vasten to fast
vastenavond (de) Shrove Tuesday
vastentijd (de) Lent
vastgrijpen to catch hold of
vasthouden to hold (on to), to clutch; to detain
vast'houdend tenacious; conservative
vastklampen: zich – aan to cling to
vastleggen to fix, to tie up; to record
vastlopen to run aground; to jam; to bog down
vastmaken to fasten
vastpakken to seize, grab hold
vastraken to run aground; to get jammed
vastroesten to rust (solid); to get stuck (in one's ways)
vaststaan to stand firm; to be definite
vaststellen to fix, to establish
vastzetten to fix (in position); to corner
vastzitten to be stuck **er aan –** to be entailed, to have to go through with something
vat (het) cask, vat, vessel; hold
vatbaar susceptible
Vati'caan (het) Vatican
Vati'caanstad (de) Vatican City
vatten to catch; to understand; to get
v.Chr (voor Christus) BC
vechten to fight
vecht'lustig pugnacious
vechtpartij (de) fight
vee (het) cattle
veearts (de) veterinary surgeon (cattle)
veeg (de) streak, smudge
veel much, a good deal, many

veelal often
veelbe'lovend promising
veelbe'tekenend significant, suggestive
veelbe'wogen eventful
veel'eisend exacting, demanding
veelom'vattend comprehensive
veel'soortig manifold
veelvoud (het) multiple
veelvraat (de) glutton
veel'vuldig frequent; manifold
veel'zeggend significant
veel'zijdig many-sided, versatile
veen (het) peat(moor)
veer (de) feather; spring; **(het)** ferry(boat)
veerkracht (de) resilience, elasticity
veer'krachtig resilient
veertien fourteen
veertig forty
veertig'plusser (de) over-40
veestapel (de) livestock
veeteelt (de) stock breeding
vegen to sweep, to brush, to wipe
vege'tariër (de) vegetarian
vege'tatie (de) vegetation
veilen to auction
veilig(heid) (de) safe(ty)
veiligheidsagent (de) security officer
veiligheidsdienst (de) security forces
veiligheidsgordel (de) safety belt, seat belt
veiligheidshalve for safety's sake
veiligheidsraad (de) security council
veiling (de) auction
veinzen to feign, to sham
vel (het) skin, hide; sheet **om uit je – te springen** enough to make you wild
veld (het) field **het – ruimen** to make way **uit het – geslagen** taken aback
veldfles (de) water bottle, flask

veldslag (de) battle
velen many (people)
veler'lei all kinds of
ve'nijn (het) venom
ve'nijnig venomous
ven'noot (de) partner
ven'nootschap (de) partnership,
company
venster (het) window
vensterbank (de) window sill
vent (de) chap
ven'tiel (het) valve
venti'latie (de) ventilation
venti'lator (de) fan, ventilator
venti'leren to ventilate
ver far, distant
ver'aangenamen to make
pleasant
ver'achtelijk contemptible,
contemptuous
ver'achten to despise
ver'ademing (de) relief
veraf far (away)
ver'afgoden to idolize
ver'afschuwen to detest
ver'anderen to change, to alter
ver'andering (de) change,
transformation
ver'anderlijk changeable, variable,
inconstant
verant'woordelijk responsible
**verant'woordelijkheid(sgevoel)
(het)** sense of responsibility
ver'antwoorden to answer for;
to justify
ver'antwoording (de) account;
justification
ver'armen to impoverish; to become
poor
ver'band (het) connection; context;
bandage, dressing; bond
ver'bannen to exile
ver'bazen: zich — to be astonished,
to be amazed

ver'beelden to represent **zich —**
to imagine, to fancy
ver'beelding (de) imagination,
(self-)conceit
ver'bergen to hide
ver'beteren to improve; to correct
ver'bieden to forbid, to prohibit
ver'bijsteren to bewilder
verbijten: zich — to clench one's
teeth
ver'binden to join, to connect
zich — tot, to commit oneself to
ver'binding (de) connection,
communication
ver'bindingsstreepje (het) hyphen
ver'bitterd embittered
ver'bleken to grow pale; to fade
ver'blijden to cheer (up)
ver'blijf (het) stay; residence
ver'blijfskosten (de) hotel, living
expenses
ver'blijven to stay, to remain
ver'blinden to blind, to dazzle
ver'bloemen to disguise
ver'bluffend staggering
ver'bod (het) prohibition, ban
ver'bolgen incensed
ver'bond (het) alliance; covenant
ver'bouwen to carry out alterations
(to a building); to grow
verbouwe'reerd flabbergasted
ver'branden to burn (down);
to be burnt (down, out, up), to tan
ver'breden to widen
ver'breiden to spread
ver'breken to break (off), to cut (off)
ver'brijzelen to shatter
ver'brokkelen to crumble
ver'bruien: het bij iemand —
to get into a person's bad books
ver'bruik (het) consumption
ver'bruiken to consume, to use up
ver'buigen to bend, to buckle;
to decline

ver'dacht suspect(ed); suspicious
ver'dampen to evaporate
ver'dedigen to defend
ver'dediger (de) defender, council for the defence
ver'dediging (de) defence
ver'deeld divided
ver'dekt under cover
ver'delen to divide (up)
ver'denken to suspect
verder further(more)
ver'dienen to earn; to deserve
ver'diepen: zich – in to become engrossed in
verdieping (de) floor, storey
ver'doemenis (de) damnation
ver'doen to waste
ver'domd damn(ed)
ver'dommen to flatly refuse
ver'dorie! damn!
ver'dorren to wither, to parch
ver'dorven depraved
ver'doven to deaden, to benumb, to stun, to give an anaesthetic; to deafen
ver'dovingsmiddel (het) anaesthetic, narcotic
ver'draagzaam tolerant
ver'draaien to distort, to twist
ver'drag (het) treaty
ver'dragen to bear
ver'driet (het) grief; regrets
ver'drietig pained, sad, sullen
ver'drijven to drive off; to dispel; to while away
ver'dringen to oust zich – om to crowd round
ver'drinken to be drowned; to drown; to squander on drink; to inundate
ver'drogen to dry up
ver'drukking: in de – komen to suffer
ver'dubbelen to (re)double

ver'duidelijken to elucidate, make clear
ver'duisteren to eclipse, to black out; to embezzle
ver'dunnen to thin, to dilute
ver'duren to put up with
ver'dwaasd vacant
ver'dwijnen to disappear
vereen'voudigen to simplify
vereen'zelvigen to identify
ver'eeuwigen to immortalize
ver'effenen to settle
ver'eisen to require
ver'eiste (de, het) requirement
veren to (be) spring(y)
verend springy, elastic
Verenigd 'Koninkrijk (het) United Kingdom
Verenigde 'Staten (van Amerika) (de) United States of America
ver'eniging (de) association, union
ver'eren to honour
ver'ergeren to deteriorate, to aggravate
verf (de) paint; dye
ver'fijnen to refine
ver'filmen to film
ver'flauwen to flag, to fade
ver'foeien to detest
ver'fomfaaien to dishevel
ver'fraaien to beautify
ver'frissen to refresh; freshen up
verfroller (de) paint roller
ver'frommelen to crumple up
ver'gaan to perish, to decay, to go down **hoe zal het ons –?** what is in store for us?
ver'gaderen to assemble
ver'gadering (de) meeting
ver'gallen to embitter, to spoil
ver'gankelijk transitory
vergapen: zich – aan to gape at (in admiration)
ver'garen to collect

ver'gassen to vaporize; to gas
ver'geeflijk pardonable
ver'geefs (in) vain
ver'geetachtig forgetful
ver'gelden to repay, to pay for
ver'geldingsmaatregel (de) retaliatory measure
ver'gelen to turn yellow
verge'lijken to compare
verge'lijkend comparative, competitive
verge'lijking (de) comparison, simile; equation
verge'makkelijken to make easier
vergen to make demands on, to require
verge'noegd contented
ver'geten to forget
ver'geven to forgive
ver'gevensgezind forgiving
vergevorderd (far) advanced
verge'zellen to accompany
verge'zocht far-fetched
ver'giet (het) colander
ver'gieten to shed
ver'gif(t) (het) poison
ver'giffenis (de) forgiveness
ver'giftig poisonous
ver'giftigen to poison
ver'gissen: zich – to be mistaken, to make a mistake
ver'gissing (de) mistake, slip
ver'goeden to compensate (for), to reimburse
ver'gooien to throw away **zich –** to throw oneself away; to play the wrong card
ver'grijp (het) offence, breach
ver'grijpen: zich – aan to lay hold on
ver'grijzen to age/get old (usually of a population)
ver'grijzing (de) ageing (usually of a population)

ver'grootglas (het) magnifying-glass
ver'groten to enlarge, to increase, to magnify
ver'gruizen to crush
ver'guizen to vilify
ver'guld gilt; delighted
ver'gulden to gild
ver'gunnen to permit
ver'gunning (de) permission, licence
ver'haal (het) story; redress **op zijn – komen** to take it easy (for a bit)
ver'halen to relate; to vent **het – op** to take it out of
ver'handelen to deal in; to discuss
ver'harden to harden
ver'haren to moult
ver'heerlijken to glorify, to elate
ver'heffen to lift (up), to raise, to exhalt
ver'helderen to clarify
ver'helpen to remedy
ver'hemelte (het) palate
ver'heugen to delight **zich –** to rejoice **zich – op** to look forward to
ver'hinderen to prevent, to hinder
ver'hitten to heat
ver'hogen to raise, to heighten
ver'hoging (de) increase; platform; temperature
ver'hongeren to starve (to death)
ver'hoor (het) interrogation, hearing
ver'horen to hear, to grant; to interrogate
ver'houding (de) relation(ship), proportion
ver'huisbedrijf (het) removal firm/company
ver'huisbericht (het) change of address card
ver'huizen to move (house)
ver'huizing (de) move
ver'hullen to conceal
ver'huren to let

ver'huur (de) hire, hiring out
ver'huurder (de) landlord
verifi'ëren to verify
ver'ijdelen to frustrate
vering (de) springiness, springs; suspension (of cars)
ver'jaard out of date
ver'jaardag (de) birthday
ver'jaardagscadeau (het) birthday present
ver'jaardagsfeest (het) birthday party
ver'jaardagskaart (de) birthday card
ver'jaardagskalender (de) birthday calendar
ver'jagen to drive away
ver'kalken to harden, to calcerate
ver'keer (het) traffic; intercourse
ver'keerd wrong, misunderstood, etc.
ver'keersagent (de) traffic policeman
ver'keersbord (het) road sign, traffic sign
ver'keersdrempel (de) speed ramp
ver'keersheuvel (de) traffic island
ver'keerslicht (het) traffic lights
ver'keersongeval (het) traffic accident, road accident
ver'keersovertreding (de) traffic offence
ver'keersregel (de) traffic rule
ver'keerstoren (de) control tower
verkeers'veiligheid (de) road safety, traffic safety
ver'keersweg (de) thoroughfare
ver'kennen to reconnoitre
ver'kenner (de) scout
ver'keren to be, to move
ver'kering (de) courtship **– hebben** to go steady
ver'kiezen to prefer; to elect, to chose
ver'kiezing (de) election; preference

ver'kiezingsprogramma (het) (electoral) platform
ver'kijken: zich – op to make a mistake (with) **je kans is verkeken** you've missed your chance
ver'klappen to let on (about)
ver'klaren to explain; to declare, to certify
ver'klaring (de) explanation; declaration; certificate
ver'kleden: (zich) – to change; dress up
ver'kleinen to reduce, to cut down; to belittle
ver'kleinwoord (het) diminutive
ver'kleumen to get numb with cold
ver'kleuren to fade
ver'klikken to give away, to spill the beans
ver'klikker (de) telltale
ver'kneukelen ver'kneuteren: zich – to gloat
ver'knippen to cut up; to spoil by cutting wrongly
ver'knocht devoted
ver'knoeien to bungle; to waste
ver'kondigen to proclaim
verkoop (de) sale(s)
verkoopdatum (de) date of sale **uiterste –** sell-by date
ver'koopster (de) shop assistant (female)
ver'kopen to sell
ver'korten to shorten; to reduce
ver'kouden: – worden to catch cold **je bent –** you've got a cold
ver'koudheid (de) cold
ver'krachten to violate, to rape
ver'kreuk(el)en to crumple (up)
ver'krijgbaar obtainable
ver'krijgen to obtain
ver'kroppen to swallow
ver'kropt pent-up
ver'kruimelen to crumble (away)

ver'kwisten to waste, to dissipate
ver'lammen to paralyse
ver'lamming (de) paralysis
ver'langen to desire, to long;
  to require
ver'langlijst (de) list of gifts wanted
ver'laten to leave, to desert: lonely,
  deserted **zich — op** to rely on
ver'leden last: **(het)** past
ver'legen shy, embarrassed
ver'legenheid (de) shyness,
  embarrassment
ver'leggen to shift, move
ver'leidelijk tempting
ver'leiden to tempt, to seduce
ver'lenen to grant, to give
ver'lengen to lengthen, to extend
ver'leppen to wilt; to jade
ver'leren to lose the art
ver'licht lit (up); enlightened;
  relieved
ver'lichten to light (up),
  to illuminate; to lighten; to alleviate
ver'liefd in love, amorous
ver'liefdheid (de) being in love
ver'lies (het) loss
verlies'gevend loss-making
ver'liezen to lose
ver'lof (het) leave, permission;
  licence
ver'lokken to entice
ver'loochenen to deny, to belie
verloofde (de) fiancé(e)
ver'loop (het) course, (re)lapse
ver'lopen to elapse; to go down(hill);
  to go (off): expired; down and out
ver'loren gaan to get lost;
  to be wasted
verlos'kundige (de) midwife
ver'loten to raffle
ver'loven to get engaged
ver'loving (de) engagement
ver'lovingsring (de)
  engagement ring

ver'lummelen to laze away
ver'maak (het) pleasure,
  amusement
ver'mageren to reduce
  or lose weight
ver'mageringskuur (de) slimming
  course
ver'makelijk amusing
ver'maken to amuse; to alter;
  to bequeath
ver'meend supposed
ver'meerderen to increase
ver'melden to mention, to record
ver'mengen to mix, to mingle
vermenig'vuldigen to multiply
ver'mijden to avoid, to evade
vermil'joen (het) vermilion
ver'minderen to reduce, to diminish
ver'minken to maim, to mutilate
ver'mist missing
ver'moedelijk presumably, probably
ver'moeden to presume; to suspect:
  (het) conjecture, suspicion
ver'moeid(heid) (de) tired(ness),
  fatigue(d)
ver'moeiend tiring
ver'mogen (het) fortune; ability,
  capacity
ver'mogend wealthy
ver'mogensbelasting (de)
  property tax
ver'mommen to disguise
ver'moorden to murder
ver'morzelen to crush
ver'murwen to mollify
ver'nauwen to take in, to narrow
ver'nederen to humble, to humiliate
ver'nemen to learn, to hear
ver'nielen to destroy, to wreck
ver'nielziek verniel'zuchtig
  destructive
ver'nietigen to destroy; to annul,
  to reverse
ver'nieuwen to renew

ver'noemen naar to name after
ver'nuft (het) ingenuity, wit
veronder'stellen to suppose,
  to assume
ver'ongelijkt hurt, injured
ver'ongelukken to be wrecked,
  to crash, to be killed
veront'reinigen to pollute
veront'rusten to alarm
veront'schuldigen to excuse **zich –**
  to apologize, to excuse oneself
veront'waardigd indignant
veront'waardiging (de) indignation
ver'oordelen to condemn, to convict
ver'oorloofd allowed, permissible
ver'oorloven: zich – to permit oneself,
  to take the liberty of; to afford
ver'oorzaken to cause
ver'ordening (de) regulations,
  by-law
ver'ouderd obsolete, aged
ver'overen to conquer, to capture
ver'pakken to pack, to wrap in paper
ver'pakking (de) packing, wrapping
  paper
ver'pakkingsmateriaal (het)
  packing material
ver'patsen to flog
ver'pesten to contaminate; to wreck
ver'plaatsen to move, to transfer
  zich – to imagine oneself
verpleeg'kundige (de) nurse
ver'pleegster (de) nurse (female)
ver'plegen to nurse
ver'pleger (de) (male) nurse
ver'pletteren to shatter
ver'plicht obliged, indebted;
  compulsory
ver'plichten to oblige; to compel
ver'plichting (de) obligation,
  commitment
ver'pozen: zich – to relax
ver'praten: tijd – to spend time
  talking **zich verpraten** to let on

ver'prutsen to muck up
ver'raad (het) treason
ver'raden to betray
ver'rader (de) traitor
ver'raderlijk treacherous, insidious
ver'rassen to surprise
ver'rassing (de) surprise
ver'regend washed out (by the rain)
ver'reikend far-reaching
ver'rek gosh, get away, get
  out of here
ver'rekenen to settle **zich –**
  to miscalculate
verrekijker (de) binoculars
ver'rekken to sprain, to strain;
  to go to hell
verre'weg by far
ver'richten to carry out, to do
ver'rijken to enrich
ver'rijzen to (a)rise, to spring up
ver'roeren to stir
ver'roest rusty
ver'rotten to rot
ver'ruimen to broaden
ver'rukkelijk delicious; gorgeous
ver'rukt delighted
vers fresh, new-(laid): **(het)** verse,
  poetry, poem
ver'schaffen to provide
ver'scheiden various, several
ver'scheidenheid (de) diversity
ver'schepen to (tran)ship
ver'scherpen to intensify
ver'scheuren to tear (to pieces),
  to rend
ver'schieten to use up; to turn pale,
  to fade
ver'schijnen to appear
ver'schijning (de) appearance;
  figure
verschijnsel (het) phenomenon;
  symptom
verschil (het) difference
ver'schillen to differ

ver'schillend different
ver'schonen to put on clean sheets or clothes; to excuse; to spare
ver'schrikkelijk terrible
ver'schroeien to scorch
ver'schrompelen to shrivel (up)
ver'schuilen to hide, to shelter
ver'schuiven to shift
ver'schuildigd indebted, due
versie (de) version
ver'sieren to decorate; to pick up (someone), to get off (with someone)
ver'siering (de) decoration
ver'siersel (het) ornament
ver'sjouwen to shift
ver'slaafd addicted
ver'slaan to beat, to defeat; to cover
ver'slag (het) report
ver'slagen defeated; put out
ver'slaggever (de) reporter, commentator
ver'slapen: zich – to oversleep
ver'slappen to weaken, to flag
ver'slepen to tow away, to shift
ver'slijten to wear out; to while away **waar verslijt je me voor?** what do you take me for?
ver'slikken: zich – to choke
ver'slinden to devour
ver'slingeren: zich – aan to throw oneself away
ver'sloffen, ver'slonzen to neglect
ver'smachten to pine away
ver'smelten to melt, to blend
ver'snapering (de) titbit, refreshment
ver'snellen to accelerate
ver'snelling (de) acceleration; gear
ver'snellingsbak (de) gearbox
ver'snipperen to cut up; to fritter away
ver'snoepen to spend on sweets
ver'spelen to throw away

ver'sperren to block (up)
ver'spillen to waste
ver'spilling (de) waste, wasting
ver'splinteren to (break into) splinter(s)
ver'spreiden: (zich) – to spread, to scatter
ver'spreken: zich – to make a slip (of the tongue)
verspringen (het) long jump
ver'staan to understand, to hear
ver'staanbaar audible, intelligible
ver'stand (het) sense(s), mind; knowledge **met dien verstande** on the understanding **daar staat mijn – bij stil** it is beyond me
ver'standelijk intellectual, rational
ver'standhouding (de) understanding, terms
ver'standig sensible
ver'standskies (de) wisdom tooth
ver'stard rigid
ver'steend petrified; fossilized
ver'stekeling (de) stowaway
ver'stelbaar adjustable
ver'steld stunned **– staan** to be dumbfounded
ver'stellen to adjust; to mend
ver'sterken to fortify, to reinforce, to intensify; to amplify
ver'sterker (de) amplifier
ver'stevigen to consolidate
ver'stijven to stiffen; to grow numb
ver'stikken to stifle
ver'stoord disturbed; vexed
ver'stoppen to block (up); to hide
ver'stoppertje spelen play hide-and-seek
ver'storen to disturb, to upset
ver'strekken to issue
verstrekkend far-reaching, sweeping
ver'strijken to expire, to elapse
ver'strooid scattered; absent-minded

verstrooien: zich – to disperse;
to find amusement
ver'stuiken to sprain
ver'stuiven to (be) blow(n) about
ver'suft stupefied
ver'takken: zich – to branch
ver'taalbureau (het) translation
agency
ver'taalster (de) (female) translator
ver'talen to translate
ver'taler (de) (male) translator
ver'taling (de) translation
verte (de) distance
ver'tederend tender
ver'teerbaar digestible
vertegen'woordigen to represent
ver'tellen to tell, to say
ver'telling (de), ver'telsel (het)
story
ver'teren to consume, to spend;
to digest; to perish
ver'tikken to jib, to refuse flatly
ver'tillen to lift **zich –** to strain
oneself (lifting something)
ver'timmeren to make alterations to
ver'tolken to interpret
ver'tonen to show, to produce
ver'toon (het) show, presentation
ver'tragen to slow down; to delay
ver'traging (de) delay
ver'trappen to trample under foot
ver'trek (het) room; departure
ver'trekhal (de) departure hall
ver'trekken to leave; to distort
ver'trektijd (de) time of departure
ver'troebelen to confuse
ver'troetelen to pamper
ver'trouwd trusty, safe; conversant
ver'trouwelijk confidential; intimate
ver'trouwen to (en)trust; to rely;
(het) trust, confidence
ver'twijfeld desperate
ver'twijfeling (de) desperation
veruit by far

ver'vaardigen to manufacture
ver'vagen to fade
ver'val (het) decline; disrepair; fall
ver'vallen to lapse, to be cancelled,
to expire, to fall (due); to go to ruin
ver'valsen to fake
ver'vangen to replace
ver'velen: (zich) – to (be) bore(d)
tot vervelens toe *ad nauseam*
ver'velend boring; annoying
ver'veling (de) boredom
ver'vellen to peel
verven to paint; to dye
ver'versen to refresh; to renew
ver'vliegen to evaporate, to vanish
ver'vloeken to curse
ver'voer (het) transport
ver'voeren to transport
ver'voermiddel (het) (means) of
transport
ver'volg (het) sequel, continuation;
future
ver'volgen to continue; to pursue;
to persecute, to prosecute
ver'volgens after that
ver'vreemden to alienate, to grow
estranged
ver'vroegen to put forward
ver'vuilen to get filthy
ver'vullen to fill, to fulfil
ver'waaid dishevelled
ver'waand conceited
ver'waarlozen to neglect
ver'wachten to expect
ver'wachting (de) expectation
ver'want related
ver'wanten (de) relatives
ver'wantschap (de) relationship,
affinity
ver'warmen to heat
ver'warren to confuse, to (en)tangle
ver'warring (de) confusion, disorder
ver'wedden to bet
ver'weerd weather-beaten

ver'wekken to arouse; to beget,
to father
ver'welken to wither, to wilt
ver'welkomen to welcome
ver'wennen to spoil
ver'wensen to curse
ver'weren to weather; to defend
ver'werken to cope with; to work up
ver'werpen to reject
ver'werven to acquire
ver'wezenlijken to realize **zich –**
to materialize
ver'wijderen to remove, to turn out
zich – to withdraw
ver'wijfd effeminate
ver'wijlen to linger
ver'wijt(en) (het) (to) reproach
ver'wijzen to refer
ver'wikkelen to implicate,
to complicate
ver'wikkeling (de) complication, plot
ver'wilderen to run wild,
to degenerate
ver'wisselen to (ex)change
ver'wittigen to notify
ver'woed furious
ver'woesten to devastate
ver'wonden to injure, to wound
ver'wonderen: zich – to be surprised
ver'wonen to pay in rent
ver'zachten to alleviate; to soften
ver'zadigen to saturate; to satisfy
ver'zaken to forsake
ver'zakken to sag, to subside
ver'zamel-cd (de) compilation CD
ver'zamelen to collect, to muster (up)
ver'zameling (de) collection
ver'zamelplaats (de) meeting place,
assembly point
ver'zanden to silt up; to get bogged
down
ver'zegelen to seal (up)
ver'zekeren to assure, to insure;
to secure

ver'zekering (de) assurance,
insurance
ver'zekeringsmaatschappij (de)
insurance company
ver'zekeringspremie (de) insurance
premium
ver'zenden to send (off)
ver'zet (het) resistance
ver'zetje (het) divergence
ver'zetten to move; to get through;
to get over **zich –** to oppose,
to resist
ver'zien: het – hebben op
to be out to get
verziend long-sighted
ver'zilveren to silver (plate);
to convert into cash
ver'zinnen to think (up)
ver'zitten to move to another chair;
to shift one's position
ver'zoek (het) request
ver'zoeken to request; to tempt
ver'zoekschrift (het) petition
ver'zoenen to reconcile
ver'zorgen to take care of
ver'zot op mad on
ver'zuchten to sigh
ver'zuim (het) omission; non-
attendance **zonder –** without fail
ver'zuimen to fail (in); to miss
ver'zuipen to drown
ver'zuren to (turn) sour
ver'zwakken to weaken
ver'zwijgen voor to keep from
ver'zwikken to sprain
vest (het) waistcoat; cardigan
vestigen to establish; to fix **zich –**
to settle
vesting (de) fortress
vet fat; greasy; rich: **(het)** fat **vet
gedrukt** in heavy type
vetarm low-fat
vete (de) feud
veter (de) (shoe)lace

> ## Insight
> Vet *fat, greasy* is a good example of how languages keep
> evolving and changing. In the last couple of years, the word
> has been adopted by younger (often teenage) speakers of
> Dutch (particularly in the Netherlands) as a hip, modish
> word indicating that something is really wonderful, although
> it can also simply intensify what is being said. Some
> examples: **dat was een vet concert** *that was a cool concert;*
> **vet, man!** *awesome, man!;* **die jongen is vet gestoord** *that guy*
> *is completely crazy.*

vete'raan (de) veteran
vetgehalte (het) fat content
vetmesten to fatten (up)
vetplant (de) succulent plant
vettigheid (de) richness, greasiness
vet'vrij greaseproof
vetzak (de) fatty
vetzucht (de) obesity
veulen (het) foal
vezel (de) fibre
vgl. (vergelijk) cf.
V-hals (de) V-neck
via'duct (het) (railway) bridge,
  viaduct
vi'breren to vibrate
video (de) video (tape, recorder)
videocamera (de) video camera
videocassette (de) video cassette
video-opname (de) video recording
videorecorder (de) video (recorder),
  VCR, video cassette recorder
video'theek (de) video shop
vief lively
vier four **onder – ogen** in private
vierbaansweg (de) four-lane
  motorway, dual carriageway,
  divided highway
vierdelig four-part, four-piece
vieren to celebrate: to ease off
vierkant (het) square
vierkantswortel (de) square root

viervoud (het) quadruple
viervoudig fourfold, quadruple
vies dirty, filthy; wry **ik ben er – van**
  it turns my stomach
viezerik (de) pig, slob
vijand (de) enemy
vij'andelijk enemy('s)
vij'andig hostile
vijf five
vijftien fifteen
vijftig fifty
vijftiger (de) someone in his/
  her fifties
vijg (de) fig
vijl(en) (de) (to) file
vijver (de) pond
vijzel (de) mortar
villa (de) villa
villawijk (de) (exclusive)
  residential area
villen to skin, to fleece
vin (de) fin
vinden to find; to think; to get on
vindingrijk inventive
vinger (de) finger **door de vingers**
  zien to overlook
vingerafdruk (de) fingerprint
vingerhoed (de) thimble
vink (de) finch
vinnig cutting, sharp
vio'list (de) violinist

vi'ool (de) violin; violet, pansy
virtu'oos (de) virtuoso
vis (de) fish
visboer (de) fishmonger
visgraat (de) fishbone
vishandelaar (de) fishmonger, fish dealer
visie (de) vision
visi'oen (het) vision
vismarkt (de) fish market
Vissen Pisces
vissen to fish, to angle; drag, dredge
vi'site (de) visit(or)(s)
visser (de) fisherman
vissersboot (de) fishing boat
visse'rij (de) fishing (industry)
visvangst (de) fishing
vi'taal vital
vi'trage (de, het) (curtain) net
vi'trine (de) showcase
vitten op to find fault with
vla (de) custard
vlaag (de) gust; fit
Vlaams Flemish
Vlaamse (de) Flemish woman
Vlaanderen Flanders
vlag (de) flag
vlaggen to put out the flag(s)
vlak flat, smooth; right, close; **(het)** (sur)face
vlakte (de) plain, stretch
vlam (de) flame
vlammen to blaze, to be ardent
Vlaming (de) Flemish man
vlecht (de) plait
vlechten to plait, to weave
vleermuis (de) bat
vlees (het) meat, flesh
vleesmes (het) carving knife
vleeswaren meat products, meats
vleet: geld bij de – pots of money
vleien to flatter, to coax
vlek (de) blot, spot, stain

vlekkeloos spotless
vleugel (de) wing; grand piano
vleugje (het) breath, touch
vlezig fleshy, plump
vlieg (de) fly
vliegdekschip (het) aircraft carrier
vliegen to fly **in brand –** to burst into flames
vliegenmepper (de) (fly) swat
vliegensvlug as quick as lightning
vlieger (de) kite; airman
vlieghaven (de) airport
vliegramp (de) plane crash
vliegticket (het, de) airline ticket
vliegtuig (het) aircraft, plane
vliegveld (het) airport
vliegwiel (het) flywheel
vliering (de) loft
vlies (het) fleece; film, membrane
vlijmscherp sharp as a razor
vlijtig industrious
vlinder (de) butterfly
vlo (de) flea
vloed (de) flood (tide), flow
vloedgolf (de) tidal wave
vloeibaar liquid
vloeien to flow; to blot
vloeiend flowing; fluent
vloeistof (de) liquid
vloeitje (het) cigarette paper
vloek (de) curse, oath
vloeken to swear, to curse; to clash
vloer (de) floor(ing)
vloerbedekking (de) floor covering, carpet
vloeren to floor
vloerkleed (het) carpet
vlonder (de) plank (thrown across a ditch); wooden platform
vloot (de) fleet

vlot fluent, smooth, slick, sprightly; afloat: **(het)** raft
vlotten to float; to proceed smoothly
vlucht (de) flight
vluchteling (de) fugitive, refugee
vluchten to fly, to flee
vluchtheuvel (de) traffic island; mound
vluchtig cursory, fleeting, volatile
vlug quick
VN (Verenigde Naties) (de) UN
VN-'vredesmacht (de) UN peacekeeping force
vocabu'laire (de, het) vocabulary
vocht (het) fluid, moisture
vochtig damp, moist
voeden to feed, to nourish
voeding (de) feeding, nutrition; food; power supply
voedingsbodem (de) breeding ground
voedsel (het) food
voedselhulp (de) food aid
voedselpakket (het) food parcel
voedselvergiftiging (de) food poisoning
voedzaam nourishing
voeg (de) joint
voegen to join, to add; to point
  zich – to join; to comply
voegwoord (het) conjuction
voelbaar perceptible
voelen to feel
voer (het) fodder; load
voeren to take, to carry (on), to wield, to conduct, to feed: to line
voering (de) lining
voertaal (de) official language
voertuig (het) vehicle
voet (de) foot; footing **– bij stuk houden** to stick to one's guns
voetbal (het) football
voetbalclub (de) football club

voetbalcompetitie (de) football competition
voetbalelftal (het) football team
voetbalfan (de) football fan
voetbalknie (de) cartilage trouble
voetballen to play football
voetballer (de) football player
voetbalschoen (de) football boot
voetbalvandaal (de) football hooligan
voetbalveld (het) football pitch
voetbalwedstrijd (de) football match
voet(en)bank (de) footstool
voet(en)einde (het) foot (of the bed)
voetganger (de) pedestrian
voetgangersbrug (de) footbridge, pedestrian crossing, zebra crossing
voetnoot (de) footnote; note in margin, critical remark/comment
voetspoor (het) footmark; track
voetstuk (het) pedestal
voetzoeker (de) (jumping) cracker
vogel (de) bird
vogelnest (het) bird's nest
vogelverschrikker (de) scarecrow
vogelvlucht (de) bird's-eye view
vogel'vrij outlawed
vol full
volautomatisch fully automatic
volbloed (de) thorough(bred)
vol'brengen to accomplish
vol'daan satisfied; paid
vol'doen to satisfy, to give satisfaction to pay **– aan** to fulfil
vol'doend satisfactory; sufficient
vol'doende (de) pass (mark)
vol'doening (de) satisfaction; settlement
volgauto (de) car in procession
volgeboekt booked up
volgeling (de) follower
volgen to follow

volgend following, next
volgens according to
volgieten to fill
volgnummer (het) serial number
volgorde (de) order, sequence
volgzaam docile
vol'harden to persevere
volhouden to keep up, to maintain, to insist
voli'ère (de) aviary
volk (het) nation, people
volkenkunde (de) ethnology
vol'komen complete
vol'korenbrood (het) wholemeal bread
volksaard (de) national character
volksbuurt (de) working-class quarter
volksdans (de) folk dance
volksdansen (de) folk dancing
volksdracht (de) national costume
volksge'zondheid (de) public health, national health
volkslied (het) national anthem; folksong
volksmond: in de – heten to be popularly called
volkstelling (de) census
volkstuin (de) allotment
volksverhuizing (de) mass migration
vol'ledig complete, full
vollopen to fill up
vol'maakt perfect
volmacht (de) power of attorney, proxy
vol'mondig whole-hearted
volop plenty (of)
volproppen to stuff, to clutter up
vol'slagen utter, total
vol'staan: laat ik – met te zeggen suffice it to say
vol'strekt absolute, at all
vol'tallig complete, plenary
vol'tooien to complete

voltreffer (de) direct hit
vol'trekken to execute
vol'uit in full
vol'waardig sound (in body and mind), able
vol'wassen(e) (de) grown-up, full-grown, adult
vondst (de) find
vonk(en) (de) (to) spark
vonnis (het) sentence, verdict
voogd('es) (de) guardian
voog'dij (de) guardianship
voor for; before; in front of: furrow
– … uit ahead of
voor'aan in front, at this end
voor'aanstaand prominent
vooraanzicht (het) front view
voor'af beforehand
voor'afgaand foregoing, preliminary
voor'al especially, by all means, on any account
voorals'nog as yet
vooravond (de) early evening; eve
voorbaat: bij – in anticipation
voor'barig premature
voorbedachte: met – rade with malice aforethought
voorbeeld (het) example, model
voor'beeldig exemplary
voorbehoedmiddel (het) contraceptive
voorbereiden to prepare
voorbereiding (de) preparation
voor'bij past
voor'bijgaan to pass (by)
voor'bijganger (de) passer-by
voor'bijstreven to outstrip, to overshoot
voordat before
voordeel (het) advantage, profit
voor'delig economical, advantageous
voordeur (de) front door
voor'dien until then

voordoen to give a demonstration; to put on **zich –** to arise; to (re)present oneself

voordracht (de) recitation, lecture; delivery, rendering; nomination

voordragen to recite; to propose

voorgaan to lead (the way); to come first

voorgaand preceding

voorganger (de) predecessor; minister

voorgerecht (het) entrée

voorgeslacht (het) ancestors

voorgevel (de) façade

voorgevoel (het) presentiment

voor'goed for good

voorgrond (de) foreground, fore(front)

voor'handen available

voorhebben to intend; to have the advantage

voor'heen formerly

voorhoofd (het) forehead

voorhoofdsholteontsteking (de) sinusitis

voorhuid (de) foreskin

voor'in in (the) front

voor'ingenomen prejudiced

voorjaar (het) spring

voorkamer (de) front room

voorkauwen to repeat over and over again

voorkennis (de) (fore)knowledge

voorkeur (de) preference

voorkomen to occur; to seem; to drive up; to get ahead; to appear: **(het)** appearance; incidence

voor'komen to prevent, to anticipate

voor'komend charming, considerate

voorlaatst penultimate, last but one

voorleggen to submit to

voorletter (de) initial

voorlezen to read (out) to

voorlichten to light the way; to enlighten

voorlichting (de) information

voorliefde (de) preference

voorlopen to go in front; to gain, to be fast

voor'lopig interim, provisional, for the time being

voor'malig one-time

voornaam (de) Christian name

voor'naam distinguished, prominent **het voornaamste is** the main point is

voornaamwoord (het) pronoun

voor'namelijk principally

voornemen: zich – to resolve, to propose

voornemen (het) intention

vooroordeel (het) prejudice

voor'oorlogs pre-war

voor'op in front

voor'opgezet preconceived

voor'opstellen to take for granted; to put first and foremost

voorouders (de) ancestors

voor'over forward

voorpagina (de) front page

voorproefje (het) foretaste

voorraad (de) stock, store

voor'radig in stock

voorrang (de) precedence; right of way

voorrangsweg (de) major road

voorrecht (het) privilege

voorruit (de) windscreen

voorschieten to advance

voorschijn: te – brengen to produce **te – halen** to take out **te – komen** to appear **te – roepen** to evoke

voorschot (het) advance

voorschrift (het) regulation, order

voorschrijven to prescribe, to lay down

voor'spellen to predict; to presage

voor'spiegelen to hold out prospects of
voorspoed (de) prosperity
voor'spoedig prosperous, successful
voorsprong (de) start, lead
voorstad (de) suburb
voorstander (de) advocate
voorste foremost, front
voorstel (het) proposal, suggestion
voorstellen to (re)present, to introduce; to propose **zich —** to introduce oneself; to imagine; to intend
voorstelling (de) performance; representation **zich een — maken van** to visualize
voortaan in future, from now on
voortbestaan (het) future life; survival
voortbrengen to produce, to beget
voort'durend continual, continuous
voortgang (de) progress
voortkomen uit to emanate from
voortmaken to make haste
voortplanten to propagate
voor'treffelijk excellent
voortrekken to favour
voortrekker (de) pioneer
voorts further(more)
voortslepen to drag along
voortspruiten uit to arise from
voortuin (de) front garden
voor'uitbetalen to pay in advance
voort'varend go-ahead
voort'varendheid (de) enterprise, drive
voorverkoop (de) advance booking
voortvloeien uit to result from
voort'vluchtig at large, fugitive
voortwoekeren to spread
voortzetten to continue
voor'uit forward, ahead; before(hand); come on!
voor'uitbetalen to pay in advance

voor'uitgaan to go on ahead; to make progress
voor'uitgang (de) progress, improvement
voor'uitkomen to get on
voor'uitlopen op to anticipate
vooruit'strevend progressive
voor'uitzicht (het) prospect
voorvader (de) ancestor
voorval (het) incident
voorvoegsel (het) prefix
voorwaarde (de) condition
voorwaarts forward(s)
voorwendsel (het) pretext, pretence
voorwerp (het) object
voorwoord (het) foreword
voorzeggen to prompt
voorzetsel (het) preposition
voor'zichtig careful, cautious
voor'zien to foresee; to provide (for)
voorzitter (de) chairman
voorzorg(smaatregel) (de) precaution(ary measure)
vorderen to (make) progress; to requisition, to demand
voren: naar — to the front **te —** before(hand) **van —** (from) in front **van — af aan** from the beginning
vorig last, previous
vork (de) fork
vorm (de) form, shape, mould
vormen to form, to constitute
vorming (de) formation; education
vorm(e)loos shapeless
vorst (de) frost; prince, monarch
vorstelijk royal, regal
vorstendom (het) principality
vorstin (de) queen
vos (de) fox
vouw (de) fold, crease
vouwen to fold
vouwfiets (de) folding bike, collapsible bike
vraag (de) question, request, demand

vraaggesprek (het) interview
vraagstuk (het) problem
vraagteken (het) question mark
vracht (de) freight, load, cargo
vrachtauto (de) lorry
vrachtgoed (het) goods, cargo
vrachtverkeer (het) cargo trade, goods transport(ation), lorry traffic
vrachtwagen (de) lorry
vragen to ask; to charge; to require
vrede (de) peace
vredesmacht (de) peacekeeping force
vredesnaam: in – for goodness' sake
vredestichter (de) peacemaker
vredig peaceful
vreedzaam peaceable
vreemd strange; foreign, alien
vreemde: in den – abroad
vreemdeling (de) stranger; foreigner
vreemdelingenverkeer (het) tourist traffic
vreemd'soortig unusual
vrees (de) fear
vreetzak (de) greedy-guts
vrek(kig) (de) miser(ly)
vreselijk frightful
vreten to devour, to eat, to stuff
vreugde (de) joy
vreugdevol joyful
vrezen to fear
vriend (de) (boy)friend
vriendelijk kind, friendly
vriendendienst (de) kind turn
vriendjespolitiek (de) favouritism, nepotism
vrien'din (de) (girl)friend
vriendschap (de) friendship
vriend'schappelijk friendly, amicably
vriespunt (het) freezing point
vriezen to freeze
vrij free: rather, quite
vrij'af time off

vrij'blijvend subject to alteration in price; without obligation
vrijdag Friday
vrijen to make love, to go to bed with someone; to neck, to pet
vrije'tijdsbesteding (de) leisure activities, recreation
vrije'tijdskleding (de) casual clothes
vrijgeven to decontrol; to give (time) off
vrij'gevig liberal
vrijgevochten undisciplined
vrijge'zel (de) bachelor
vrijge'zellenavond (de) stag-night, hen-party; singles night
vrijheid (de) liberty, freedom
vrijheidsbeeld (het) Statue of Liberty
vrijkomen to get off; to fall vacant; to be decontrolled; to be liberated
vrijlaten to release, to emancipate; to leave free
vrijmarkt (de) unregulated street market
vrij'metselaar (de) freemason
vrij'moedig frank, outspoken
vrijpleiten to exonerate
vrij'postig forward, impertinent
vrijspreken to acquit
vrijstaand detached **een – huis** a detached house
vrijstellen to exempt, to excuse
vrij'uit freely
vrijwel practically
vrij'willig voluntary
vrij'williger (de) volunteer
vrij'zinnig liberal
vroedvrouw (de) midwife
vroeg early **– of laat** sooner or later
vroeger earlier, former, previous **ik woonde daar –** I used to live there
vroeg'tijdig early
vrolijk cheerful
vroom pious

vrouw (de) woman; wife
vrouwelijk female, feminine
vrouwenarts (de) gynaecologist
vrouwenbeweging (de) feminist movement, women's (rights) movement
vrouwtje (het) woman; mistress; female
vrucht (de) fruit; foetus
vruchtbaar fertile; fruitful, prolific
vruchteloos fruitless, in vain
vruchtvlees (het) pulp
vuil dirty: **(het)** dirt, muck
vuilak (de) dirty/filthy person, pig
vuilbek (de) foul-mouthed fellow
vuil(ig)heid (de) filth; obscenity
vuilmaken to (make) dirty; to waste
vuilnis (het) refuse, rubbish, garbage
vuilnisbak (de) dustbin
vuilnisbelt (de) rubbish dump
vuilnisman (de) dustman
vuilverbranding (de) (waste, garbage) incinerator
vuist (de) fist **voor de – (weg)** *ad lib*
vul'gair vulgar
vul'kaan (de) volcano
vul'kaanuitbarsting (de) volcanic eruption
vullen to fill, to stuff
vulpen (de) fountain pen

vuns, vunzig musty, fusty; dirty; obscene
vuren to fire
vurig fiery; fervent, ardent
VUT (vervroegde uittreding) (de) early retirement
vuur (het) fire **– geven** to fire; to give (a person) a light
vuurpeloton (het) firing squad
vuurpijl (de) rocket **de klap op de –** the crowning sensation
vuurproef (de) ordeal by fire; crucial test
vuur'rood flaming red
vuurtje (het) (small) fire; light **een – geven** give a light **het nieuws ging als een lopend – door de school** the news spread through the school like wildfire
vuurtoren (de) lighthouse
vuurvast fire-proof
vuurwapen (het) firearm
vuurwerk (het) firework(s) (display)
VVV (Vereniging voor Vreemdelingenverkeer) (de) tourist information
VVV-kantoor (het) tourist information office
vwo (voorbereidend wetenschappelijk onderwijs) (het) pre-university education

W

waag (de) weighhouse
waaghals (de) daredevil
waagstuk (het) risky enterprise
waaien to blow, to fan
waaier (de) fan
waakhond (de) watchdog
waaks, waakzaam watchful
waakzaamheid (de) vigilance
Waals Walloon
waanzin (de) madness

waan'zinnig mad, crazy
waar where; true; **(de)** ware(s), commodity, stuff **niet –?** isn't that so?
waar-(aan etc.) (to etc.) what, which, whom
waarborg (de) guarantee, security
waarborgen to guarantee
waarborgsom (de) deposit, bail
waard (de) landlord; worth

waarde (de) value
waardebon (de) (gift) voucher/ coupon
waardeloos worthless
waar'deren to appreciate, to value
waardevol valuable
waarheen, waar ... heen where (... to)
waarheid (de) truth
waarmaken to verify
waarmerk (het) hallmark
waar'neembaar perceptible
waarnemen to observe; to deputize; to discharge
waar'om why
waar'schijnlijk probable
waarschuwen to warn
waarschuwing (de) warning; demand note, reminder
waarzegster (de) fortune teller
waas (de) film, haze; air
wacht (de) watch(man), guardduty
in de − slepen to scrounge, to rake in
wachten (op) to wait (for)
wachter (de) watchman
wachtgeld (het) reduced salary, retainer
wachtkamer (de) waiting room
wachtlijst (de) waiting list
wachtwoord (het) password
wad (het) mudflat
waden to wade
wafel (de) waffle, wafer
wagen (de) car, cart; to risk, to venture
wagenziek trainsick, carsick
waggelen to totter, to waddle
wa'gon (de) (railway) carriage, van, truck(load)
wak (het) hole (in the ice)
waken to (keep) watch; to wake
wakker awake **− schrikken** to wake with a start

wal (de) quay(side); bank **aan −** ashore **van − steken** to push off; to fire away **van twee wallen eten** to have it both ways
walg(e)lijk disgusting
walgen to be nauseated
walkman (de) walkman
Wal'lonië the Walloon provinces (Belgium)
walm(en) (de) (to) smoke
walnoot (de) walnut
wals (de) waltz; *(motor) roller*
walvis (de) whale
wanbetaling (de) non-payment
wand (de) wall
wandelaar (de) walker, stroller
wandelen to walk, to wander **gaan −** to go for a walk
wandeling (de) walk, stroll
wandelkaart (de) large-scale map
wandelpad (het) footpath
wandelstok (de) walking stick
wandmeubel (het) wall unit
wandschildering (de) mural
wandtapijt (het) hanging carpet, tapestry
wang (de) cheek
wangedrag (het) misconduct
wanhoop (de) despair
wanhopen to despair
wan'hopig desperate, despairing, hopeless
wankel unsteady, rickety
wankelbaar unstable
wankelen to stagger, to sway from side to side; to waver
wanneer when(ever)
wanorde (de) disorder
wan'staltig deformed
want for, because: **(de)** mitten
wantoestand (de) chaotic situation
wantrouwen (het) (to) distrust
wan'trouwend, wan'trouwig suspicious

WAO (Wet op de Arbeidsongeschiktheids- verzekering) (de) disability insurance act

WAO'er (de) recipient of disablement insurance benefit

wapen (het) weapon, arm; coat of arms

wapenen to arm, to reinforce

wapenspreuk (de) heraldic device

wapenstilstand (de) armistice, truce

wapenwedloop (de) arms race

wapperen to flutter

war: in de – in a muddle, upset

warboel (de) muddle, clutter

ware (de) right person (or thing) (for the job); true one

wa'rempel truly, actually

warenhuis (het) department store

warm warm, hot

warmen to warm

warmpjes warmly

warmte (de) warmth, heat, temperature

warrelen to whirl

wars van averse to

Warschau Warsaw

was (de) wax: wash(ing) **goed in de slappe – zitten** to have plenty of dough

wasautomaat (de) washing machine

wasbaar washable

wasbak (de) wash basin

wasgoed (het) washing, laundry

washandje (het) flannel, face cloth

wasknijper (de) clothes peg

wasmachine (de) washing machine

wasmiddel (het) detergent

waspoeder (het) washing powder, soap powder

wassen to wash; to shuffle; to swell, to wax

wassenbeeld (het) waxwork (model)

wasse'rij (de) laundry

wastafel (de) wash basin, wash stand

wat what, which; how; some(thing), any(thing); somewhat **– voor** what (sort of) **– (dan) ook, – maar** whatever **– blij** only too pleased

water (het) water

waterbouwkunde (de) hydraulic engineering

waterdamp (de) vapour

water'dicht waterproof, watertight

waterfiets (de) pedal boat, pedalo

waterhoen (het) moorhen

waterig watery

waterijsje (het) ice lolly, popsicle

waterkant (de) water's edge, waterfront

waterkering (de) weir

waterlanders (de) tears

waterlinie (de) flooding defence line

watermeloen (de) watermelon

waterpas (de) spirit level

waterpokken (de) chicken pox

waterschade (de) water damage

waterschap (het) district controlled by polder board

watersnood (de) floods

waterspiegel (de) water level

waterstand (de) water (level)

waterstof (de) hydrogen

watertanden: doen – to make the mouth water

waterverf (de) watercolour

watervliegtuig (het) seaplane

watje (het) wad of cotton wool; wally

watten (de) cotton wool, wadding

wattenstaafje (het) cotton bud

wat'teren to pad, to quilt

wauwelen to blather

WA-verzekering (de) third-party insurance

wa'xinelichtje (het) tealight

wazig hazy, filmy
wc (de) WC, toilet, lavatory
wc-bril (de) toilet seat
web (het) web
website (de) website
wedden to bet
weddenschap (de) wager
weer again, re-
weer (het) weather **in de – zijn**
  to be on the move; to be busy
weder'kerend reflexive
weder'kerig mutual
weder'om (once) again
weder'opbouw (de) rebuilding,
  reconstruction
wederzijds mutual
wedijveren to compete
wedloop (de) (running) race
wedstrijd (de) match, competition
weduwe (de) widow
weduwnaar (de) widower
wee sickly, faint: **(de), woe**
  labour pain
weefsel (het) tissue, fabric, texture
weegschaal (de) (pair of) scales,
  weighing machine
week soft
week (de) week
weekblad (het) weekly (paper)
weekdier (het) mollusc
weeklagen to (be)wail
weelde (de) luxury, profusion
weelderig luxurious, luxuriant
weemoed (de) melancholy
Weens Viennese
weerbaar defensible; able-bodied
weer'barstig unruly
weerbericht (het) weather forecast
weer'galmen to reverberate
weergeven to render, to reflect
weerhaak (de) barb(ed hook)
weerhaan (de) weathercock
weer'houden to restrain, to suppress
weer'kaatsen to reflect, to (re)echo

weerklank (de) echo
weer'klinken to resound
weer'leggen to refute
weerlicht (het) lightning
weerloos defenceless
weermacht (de) (fighting) services
weersgesteldheid (de) weather
  conditions
weerskanten both sides
weer'spiegelen to reflect
weer'staan to resist
weerstand (de) resistance
weersverwachting (de) weather-
  forecast
weerzien (het) meeting, reunion
weerzin (de) aversion
weerzin'wekkend repugnant
wees (de) orphan
weeshuis (het) orphanage
weetal (de) knowall
weg (de) way, road: away, gone
  veel van iemand – hebben
  to be very like a person
wegbergen to put away
wegbrengen to take away;
  to see off
wegdek (het) road surface
wegen to weigh
wegennet (het) road system
wegens on account of
wegenwacht (de) AA patrol,
  RAC patrol, AAA road service
weggaan to leave, to go away
weggooien to throw away/
  out, discard
weggooiverpakking (de) disposable
  packaging/package
wegkomen to get away
weglaten to omit, to leave out
wegleggen to put aside
  weggelegd zijn voor to be in store
  for; to be meant for
wegmaken to get rid of, to lose;
  to put under an anaesthetic

wegnemen to take away, to allay
  dat neemt niet weg dat that does not alter the fact that
wegomlegging (de) diversion, detour
wegpraten to explain away
wegraken to get lost
wegrestaurant (het) transport café, wayside restaurant
wegtrekken to pull away; to march away
wegvallen tegen to cancel (out)
wegwerken to get rid of

wel well; very much; certainly, probably, quite **ik geloof van –** I think so **ik zie het –!** I do see it!
wel'dadig beneficial, pleasant
weldoener (de) benefactor
weldoordacht well thought-out
weldra soon
wel'eer of old
welge'steld well-to-do
welgezind kindly disposed
welig lush
weliswaar it is true
wel'ja yes
welk(e) which, what

Insight

Welk, Dutch for *which* or *what*, is inflected in front of de-words, i.e. when it precedes a de-word, welk gets an extra -e and becomes welke. In front of het-words the extra -e is not added: welk boek wil je kopen? *which book do you want to buy?*; welke film heb je gezien? *which film have you seen?*

wegwerpartikel (het) disposable article
wegwezen to clear off/out, push off, buzz off **wegwezen jij!** buzz off, you!
wegwijs maken to show the ropes
wegwijzer (de) signpost
wei (de) meadow; whey
weide meadow, pasture
weids grandiose
weifelen to waver
weigeren to refuse
weiland (het) pasture
weinig little, few
wekelijks weekly
weken to soak, to soften
wekken to wake, to arouse
wekker (de) alarm clock
wekkerradio (de) radio alarm (clock), clock radio

welkom (het) welcome
welkomstgroet (de) (word of) welcome
wellen to weld
welletjes enough
wellicht perhaps
wel'luidend melodious
wel'nee no
wel'nu well (now)
weloverwogen (well-) considered
welp (de) cub
wel'sprekend eloquent
welte'rusten goodnight, sleep tight
welvaartsmaatschappij (de) affluent society
welvaart (de) prosperity
welvaartsstaat (de) welfare state
wel'willend obliging, sympathetic
welzijn (het) welfare, health
wemelen van to swarm with

wenden: (zich) – to turn; to apply
wending (de) turn
Wenen Vienna
wenen to weep
wenkbrauw (de) eyebrow
wenken to beckon
wennen to get used to
wens (de) wish
wenselijk desirable
wensen to wish, to desire
wentelen to roll (over)
wenteling (de) revolution
wenteltrap (de) winding staircase
wereld (de) world **uit de – helpen**
  to dispose of
wereldberoemd world-famous
wereldbevolking (de) world
  population
werelddeel (het) continent
wereldkampioen (de) world
  champion
wereldkampioenschap (het)
  world championship(s)
Wereldna'tuurfonds (het)
  World Wildlife Fund
wereldoorlog (de) world war **de
  Tweede Wereldoorlog** the Second
  World War
wereldrecord (het) world record
wereldrecordhouder (de) world
  record holder
wereldreiziger (de) globetrotter
werelds worldly (minded)
wereldstad (de) metropolis
wereldtaal (de) universal language
wereldtentoonstelling (de) world fair
weren to avert, to present, to keep out
werf (de) shipyard, dockyard; wharf
werk (het) work, job **er – van maken**
  to do something about it
werkdruk (de) pressure of work
werkelijk real
werkelijkheid (de) reality
werkeloos unemployed, idle

werke'loosheid (de) unemployment
werken to work, to be active **naar
  binnen –** to get down (one's throat)
werkervaring (de) work experience
werkgever (de) employer
werking (de) action, operation
werkkamer (de) workroom, study
werkkracht (de) worker, employee
werkloos unemployed, idle
werkloze (de) unemployed person
werkman (de) workman, working man
werknemer (de) employee
werkplaats (de) workshop
werkster (de) cleaner
werktuig (het) tool
werktuigkunde (de) mechanics
werk'tuiglijk mechanical
werkwoord (het) verb
werkzaam active, employed (in)
werkzaamheden (de) activities,
  duties, tasks
werk'zoekende (de) job seeker,
  person looking for work
werpen to throw
wervelkolom (de) spinal column
wervelwind (de) whirlwind, tornado
werven to rope in, to enlist
wesp (de) wasp
wespennest (het) wasps' nest
westelijk westerly, western
westen (het) west **buiten –**
  unconscious
westerling (de) westerner
westers western
wet (de) law, act **de – voorschrijven**
  to lay down the law
wetboek (het) code
weten to know; to manage **er iets
  op –** to know the answer/solution
weten (het) knowledge
wetenschap (de) science;
  learning, knowledge
wetenschappelijk scientific
wetgevend legislative

wethouder (de) councillor
wetsontwerp (het) bill
wettelijk wettig legal, lawful
weven to weave
wezen (het) being, essence
wezenloos vacant
wichelroede (de) divining rod
wicht (het) creature
  (usu. young woman)
wie who(m), anyone who
  – (dan) ook whoever
wiebelen to wobble
wieden to weed
wieg (de) cradle **in de – gelegd**
  voor cut out for
wiegen to rock
wiek (de) wing, sail
wiel (het) wheel
wielklem (de) wheel clamp
wielrennen (het) cycle racing
wielrenner (de) (racing) cyclist,
  bicyclist, cycler
wielrijder (de) cyclist
wier (het) seaweed
wierook (de) incense
wij we
wijd wide, spacious
wijd en zijd far and wide
wijdbeens with legs apart
wijdte (de) width
wijdvertakt widespread
wijf (het) bitch, woman, wife
wijfje (het) female (animal)
wijk (de) district
wijken to yield; to pass (off)
wijkverpleegster, wijkzuster, (de)
  district nurse
wijlen (the) late
wijn (de) wine
wijnfles (de) wine bottle
wijngaard (de) vineyard
wijnhandelaar (de) wine merchant
wijnkaart (de) wine list
wijnkenner (de) connoisseur of wine

wijs wise: **(de)** manner, way; tune;
  mood **van de –** at sea, in a muddle
  – maken to convince; to dupe
wijsbegeerte (de) philosophy
wijselijk wisely
wijsheid (de) wisdom
wijsje (het) tune, air
wijsneus (de) knowall
wijsvinger (de) forefinger
wijten to impute **het is aan het**
  weer te – it is due to the weather
wijze (de) manner, way
wijzen to point (out), show
wijzer pointer, hand
wijzerplaat (de) (clock) face
wijzigen to modify
wikkelen to wrap (up)
wikken en wegen to weigh (up)
wil (de) will, wish **tegen – en dank**
  against one's will **ter wille van**
  for the sake of
wild (het) game; wild **in het**
  wild(e weg) wildly, at random
wilde (de) savage
wildernis (de) wilderness
wildvreemd utterly strange
wilg (de) willow
Wil'helmus (het) Wilhelmus
  (the Dutch national anthem)
willekeur: naar – handelen
  to do as one pleases
wille'keurig arbitrary
willen to want, to like, to be willing
  dat wil zeggen that is to say
willens on purpose
willig willing
wilsbeschikking (de) will
wilskracht (de) will power
wimper (de) eyelash
winden to wind
winderig windy
windhond (de) greyhound
windhoos (de) whirlwind
windmolenpark (het) wind park/farm

windstil(te) (de) calm
windstoot (de) gust of wind
windstreek (de) point of the compass
windvaan, windwijzer (de)
  weather vane
winkel (de) shop
winkelbediende (de) shop assistant
winkelcentrum (het) shopping
  centre, mall
winkeldief (de) shoplifter
winkelen to shop, to go shopping
winke'lier (de) shopkeeper, retailer
winnaar (de) winner
winnen to win, to gain
winst (de) profit, gain
winst'gevend profitable
winstmarge (de) profit margin
winter (de) winter
winters wintry
winterslaap (de) hibernation
winterspelen (de) winter Olympics
wintersport (de) winter sports
wip (de) seesaw
wipneus (de) snub nose
wippen to rock (to and fro),
  to nip; to unseat
wirwar (de) tangle
wiskunde (de) mathematics
wispel'turig fickle
wissel (de) points; bill of exchange
wisselbeker (de) challenge cup
wisselen to (ex)change;
  to shed milk teeth
wisselgeld (het) small change
wisselkoers (de) exchange rate
wisselstroom (de) alternating current
wissel'vallig changeable; precarious
wisselwerking (de) interaction
wissen to wipe
wissewasje (het) slightest
  little thing, trifle
wit white
witlof (de, het) chicory
wittebroodsweken (de) honeymoon

witten to whitewash
**WK (wereldkampioenschap) (de,
  het)** world championship(s)
wodka (de) vodka
woede (de) rage
woedeaanval (de) tantrum, fit
  (of anger)
woedend furious
woekeren to be rife
woelen to toss and turn
woelig turbulent, restless
woensdag Wednesday
woest wild, waste, desolate
woesteling (de) ruffian
woeste'nij (de) wilderness
woes'tijn (de) desert
wol (de) wool
wolf (de) wolf
wolk (de) cloud
wolkenkrabber (de) skyscraper
wolkje (het) little cloud; puff, drop
wollen woolen
wollig woolly
wond (de) wound
wonder (het) wonder, miracle
wonder'baarlijk miraculous,
  stupendous
wonderkind (het) infant prodigy
wonderlijk strange, surprising
wondermiddel (het) panacea
wonen to live
woning (de) house, flat
woningbouwvereniging (de)
  housing association/corporation
woningnood (de) housing shortage
woon'achtig resident
woongroep (de) commune
woonhuis (het) private house
woonkamer (de) living room
woonkeuken (de) open kitchen,
  kitchen–dining room
woonplaats (de) (place of) residence
woonschip (het), woonschuit (de)
  houseboat

woonwagen (de) caravan, trailer
woonwagenbewoner (de) caravan dweller, trailer park resident
woonwagenkamp (het) caravan camp, trailer camp
woon-'werkverkeer (het) commuter traffic
woonwijk (de) residential district
woord (het) word **het hoogste – hebben** to monopolize the conversation **het – voeren** to speak, to be spokesman **onder woorden brengen** to put into words **iemand te – staan** to speak to a person
woordenboek (het) dictionary
woordenschat (de) vocabulary
woordspeling (de) play on words, pun
woordvoerder (de) spokesman
woordvolgorde (de) word order
worden to be(come)
worm (de) worm, grub
worp (de) throw; litter
worst (de) sausage
worstelen to struggle, to wrestle
wortel (de) root; carrot
wortelen to be rooted
woud (het) forest
wraak (de) revenge
wraak'gierig, wraak'zuchtig vindictive

wrak rickety, dilapidated: **(het)** wreck
wrakhout (het) wreckage
wrang sour, tart; bitter
wrat (de) wart
wreed cruel
wreef (de) instep
wreken to revenge, to avenge
wrevel (de) resentment
wrevelig resentful
wriemelen to crawl, to tickle
wrijfwas (de) furniture polish
wrijven to rub; to polish
wrijving (de) friction
wrikken to jerk
wringen to wring, to wrench
zich – to wriggle
wroeging (de) remorse
wroeten to root, to rummage
wrok (de) rancour
wuiven to wave
wurgen to strangle
wurmen to wriggle
WVC (Welzijn, Volksgezondheid en Cultuur) (the Ministry of) Welfare, Health and Cultural Affairs
WW (Werkloosheidswet) (de) unemployment insurance act **in de – lopen/zitten** to be on the dole/ unemployment benefit
WW-uitkering (de) unemploy ment benefit

Y

yoga (de) yoga

yoghurt (de) yogurt

Z

zaad (het) seed; semen, sperm
zaag (de) saw
zaagmeel (het), zaagsel (het) sawdust
zaaien to sow
zaak (de) thing, object; matter, business, affair; deal; shop, business;

case; issue; lawsuit **bemoei je met je eigen zaken** mind your own business **op kosten van de –** on the house **een auto van de –** a company car
zaakgelastigde (de) agent
zaal (de) hall, ward, auditorium

zaalvoetbal (het) indoor football
zacht soft, mild, gentle
zacht'aardig gentle
zachtjes gently, quietly
zachtjes aan gradually
zacht'moedig gentle
zacht'zinnig good-natured
zadel (het) saddle
zadelen to saddle
zagen to saw; to harp (on a subject)
zak (de) pocket; sack, bag
zakdoek (de) handkerchief
zakelijk business-like, to the point
zakenbrief (de) business letter
zakenleven (het) business (life), commerce
zakenman (de) businessman
zakenreis (de) business trip
zakenvrouw (de) businesswoman
zakformaat (het) pocket size
zakken to sink, to fall; to fail (an exam)
zakkenroller (de) pickpocket
zaklantaarn (de) torch
zaklopen (het) sack race
zalf (de) ointment
zalig blessed; heavenly
zalm (de) salmon
zand (het) sand
zandbak (de) sandbox, sandpit
zanderig sandy
zandloper (de) hourglass
zandplaat (de) sandbank
zandweg (de) sandy lane
zang (de) song, canto
zanger('es) (de) singer
zangerig melodious, sing-song
zangles (de) singing lesson
zangstem (de) singing voice; voice part
zaniken to nag, to moan
zat drunken; fed up; plenty
zaterdag Saturday
zatlap (de) drunk
ze they, them; she

zede (de) custom **zeden** morals; manners
zedelijk moral
zedeloos immoral
zedig modest, demure
zee (de) sea
zeebanket (het) seafood
zeef (de) sieve, strainer
zeegat (het) entrance to channel
zeegezicht (het) seascape
zeehond (de) seal
zeem (de) wash leather
zeemacht (de) naval forces
zeeman (de) seaman
zeemeermin (de) mermaid
zeemeeuw (de) seagull
zeemleer (het) chamois leather
zeep (de) soap
zeepaard(je) (het) seahorse
zeepbel (de) soap bubble
zeepsop (het) soapsuds
zeer very (much): sore **– doen** to hurt
zeerob (de) seal
zeerste: ten – highly, greatly
zeespiegel (de) sea level
zeester (de) starfish
Zeeuw(se) (de) inhabitant of Zeeland
zeevaart (de) shipping
zeevarend seafaring
zee'waardig seaworthy
zeewering (de) seawall
zeewier (het) seaweed
zeeziek seasick
zege (de) victory, triumph
zegel (de) seal; stamp
zegelen to seal
zegelring (de) signet ring
zegen(ing) (de) blessing
zegenen to bless
zegevieren to triumph
zeggen to say, to tell **liever gezegd** rather **er valt niets op te –** there is nothing to be said against it **dat zegt niets** that doesn't mean a thing

zeil (het) sail; tarpaulin; lino(leum)
zeildoek (het) canvas, oilcloth
zeilen to sail
zeilplank (de) sailboard
zeis (de) scythe
zeker certain, (for) sure
zekerheid (de) certainty; security
  voor alle – to be on the safe side
zekerheidshalve for safety('s sake)
zekering (de) fuse
zelden seldom, rarely
zeldzaam rare, scarce;
  exceptionally
zelf (one)self **ik (etc.) zelve**
  I (etc.) myself **de eenvoud zelve**
  simplicity itself
zelfbediening (de) self-service
zelfbedieningsrestaurant (het) self-
  service restaurant
zelfbeheersing (de) self-control
zelfbehoud (het) self-preservation
zelfbe'wust self-assured
zelfge'noegzaam self-sufficient
zelfmoord (de) suicide
zelfs even
zelfstandig independent
  – naamwoord (het) noun
zelfvertrouwen (het) self-confidence
zelfvol'daan self-satisfied
zelfver'zekerd self-confident
zendeling (de) missionary
zenden to send
zender (de) sender; transmitter
zending (de) mission; consignment
zendmast (de) (radio, TV) mast,
  radio tower, TV tower
zendstation (het)
  broadcasting station
zenuw (de) nerve; tendon
zenuwachtig nervous,
  nervy; flustered
zenuwgestel (het) nervous
  system
zenuwpees (de) bundle of nerves

zenuw'slopend nerve-racking
zes(de) six(th)
zeshoek (de) hexagon
zestien(de) sixteen(th)
zestig sixty
zestig'plusser (de) over-60,
  senior citizen
zet (de) move, coup; push
zetel (de) seat
zetmeel (de) starch
zetten to set, to put; to make;
  to stake
zeug (de) sow
zeulen to lug
zeuren to whine, to nag
zeurkous (de), zeurpiet (de)
  grouser
zeven seven: to sieve, to strain
zeventien(de) seventeen(th)
zeventig seventy
zgn. (zoge'naamd) so-called
zich one (him, her, it, your)self,
  themselves
zicht (het) sight; visibility **op –** on
  approval; at sight
zichtbaar visible
zich'zelf one (him, her, it)self,
  themselves **uit –** of his own accord
zieden to seethe
ziek ill, sick; diseased
zieke (de) patient
ziekelijk sickly, in bad health
ziekenauto (de) ambulance
ziekenbezoek (het) visit to a patient
ziekenfonds (het) national health
  insurance
ziekenhuis (het) hospital
ziekenhuisopname (de)
  hospitalization
ziekte (de) illness, disease
ziektekosten (de) medical expenses
ziektewet (de) health law **in de**
  – zitten/lopen be on sickness
  benefit/sick pay

ziel (de) soul; heart, lifeblood
zielig pitiful, pathetic
zien to see, to look **er uit –**
  to look (like) **laten –** to show
zienderogen visibly
ziens: tot – goodbye
ziezo there we are
ziften to sift
zi'geuner('in) (de) Gypsy
zij she; they
zijbeuk (de) aisle (in church)
zij(de) side; silk **op zij, ter zijde**
  aside **ter zijde staan** to help
zijdelings sidelong, indirect, oblique
zijden silk(en)
zijderups (de) silkworm
zijkant (de) side
zijn to be: his, its, one's **dat mag**
  er – that takes a lot of beating
zijrivier (de) tributary
zijspiegel (de) wing mirror
zijspoor (het) siding
zijtak (de) side branch, branch
zijwaarts sideways, sideward
zijwind (de) sidewind, crosswind
zilver(en) (het) silver
zin (de) sense; mind, way; sentence
  er – in hebben to feel like it
  naar mijn – to my liking
zindelijk clean; toilet-trained
zingen to sing
zink (het) zinc
zinken to sink: **(de)** zinc
zinloos senseless
zinnelijk sensual, sensory
zinspelen op to hint at
zinsverband (het) context
zintuig (het) sense
zin'tuiglijk sensory
zinvol significant, advisable,
  a good idea
zit: een hele – a long time
  sitting down
zitbad (het) hipbath

zitbank (de) settee
zitje (het) seat (of bicycle);
  seating area
zitkamer (de) sitting room
zitplaats (de) seat
zitten to sit; to be; to fit **gaan –** to sit
  down **iemand laten –** to walk out
  on a person **er zit niets anders op**
  there's no alternative **ik zit met de**
  gebakken peren I'm left holding
  the baby
zittend sitting, sedentary
zitting (de) session; seat
zitvlak (het) bottom
zo so, like that; in a minute; just now:
  if **de zaak zit –** it's like this
  – gaat het niet that won't do
  – iets such a thing
zoals (such) as, like
zo'danig such, in such a way
zodat so that
zo'doende in that way
zo'dra as soon as
zoek missing **op – naar** in search of
zoeken to look (for), to seek
zoeklicht (het) searchlight
zoekmaken to mislay
zoekraken to get lost
zoektocht (de) search (for)
zoemen to buzz, to drone
zoen (de) kiss
zoet sweet
zoetekauw: een – zijn
  to have a sweet tooth
zoethout (het) liquorice (root)
zoetig slightly sweet
zoetigheid (de) sweet things
zoetjes aan gradually
zoet'sappig mealy-mouthed;
  saccharine
zoetwater (het) fresh water
zoëven just now
zogen to suckle
zoge'naamd so-called; ostensibly

zolang as long as; meanwhile
zolder (de) loft, attic
zolderkamer (de) garret, attic room
zomaar just like that; for no reason in particular
zomen to hem
zomer (de) summer
zomers summery
zomerspelen (de) summer games, summer Olympics
zomersproeten (de) freckles
zomertijd (de) summer; summer time
zomervakantie (de) summer holiday
zo'n such (a), a sort of

zonneschijn (de) sunshine
zonnesteek (de) sunstroke
zonnestelsel (het) solar system
zonnestraal (de) sunbeam; ray of sunshine
zonnewijzer (de) sundial
zonnig sunny
zons'ondergang (de) sunset
zons'opgang (de) sunrise
zonsverduistering (de) eclipse of the sun
zonwering (de) awning, sunblind
zoogdier (het) mammal
zooi (de) mess, heap, load
zool (de) sole

Insight

Note that the apostrophe in **zo'n** does not indicate stress – it is actually part of the word, since **zo'n** is a contraction of **zo + een** (*such a*). Also note that a **z** can be pronounced as either a **z** or an **s**. The different pronunciations depend on regional dialect and social background. In southern regions of the Netherlands, and in Flanders in particular, the **z** is more usually pronounced as a z-sound and not as an s-sound.

zon (de) sun
zondag Sunday
zonde (de) sin; shame; waste
zondebok (de) scapegoat
zonder without
zondigen to sin, to offend
zondvloed (de) Flood
zon-en-feestdagen (de) Sundays and bank holidays
zonlicht (het) sunlight
zonnebank (de) sunbed, solarium
zonnebril (de) sunglasses
zonne-energie (de) solar energy
zonnehemel (de) sunbed
zonneklaar clear as daylight
zonnen to bask (in the sun)
zonnescherm (het) sunshade, sunblind

zoom (de) seam, hem; edge; outskirts
zoon (de) son
zootje (het) mess; lot
zorg (de) care, concern, worry **het zal mij een – zijn!** fat lot I care! **– baren** to cause anxiety
zorgeloos carefree
zorgen voor to look after; to provide (for) **zorg dat je op tijd bent** mind you're not late
zorg'vuldig careful
zorg'wekkend worrying, alarming
zorgzaam careful, conscientious
zot (de) fool
zout (het) salt
zoutje (het) nibbles; salt(y) biscuit

zoutloos salt-free
zoutvaatje (het) saltcellar
zoutzak (de) sack of potatoes
zoutzuur (het) hydrochloric acid
zoveel so much, so many
zover so far, thus far **in zover(re)**
 to the extent, in so far as
 voor – as far as
zo'waar believe it or not
zo'wel as well
z.o.z. (zie ommezijde)
 p.t.o., please turn over
zo'zeer so much
z.s.m. (zo spoedig mogelijk)
 a.s.a.p., as soon as possible
zucht (de) sigh
zuchten to sigh
zuid south
Zuid-'Afrika South Africa
Zuid-Afri'kaan (de) South African
Zuid-A'merika South America
Zuid-Ameri'kaans South American
zuidelijk southern, south(erly),
 southward(s)
zuiden (het) south
Zuidoost-'Azië South-East Asia
zuid'wester (de) sou(th)wester
zuigeling (de) infant (in arms)
zuigen to suck
zuiger (de) piston
zuigfles (de) feeding bottle
zuil (de) pillar, column
zuinig economical
zuipen to booze, to swill
zuiplap (de) boozer
zuivel (de) dairy produce
zuivelproduct (het) dairy product
zuiver pure, sheer; clear
zuiveren to purify, to clean(se),
 to refine; to clear
zuivering (de) purge
zulk such
zullen shall, will **dat zal wel** I quite
 believe it **wat zou dat?** so what!

zu
zuurp
zuursto
zuurtje (he
zwaai (de) sw
zwaailicht (het)
zwaaien to wave, to
zwaan (de) swan
zwaar heavy; hard; severe,
 bodied, podgy
zwaard (het) sword
zwaardvechter (de) gladiator
zwaargewapend heavily armed
zwaar'lijvig corpulent
zwaartekracht (de) gravitation
zwaartepunt (het) centre of gravity;
 crux
zwabber (de) swab, mop **aan de
 zwabber** on the razzle
zwabberen to swab, to mop
zwachtel (de) bandage
zwachtelen to swathe
zwager (de) brother-in-law
zwak weak, delicate, feeble
zwakkeling (de) weakling
zwakte (de) weakness
zwak'zinnig mentally disabled
zwalken to drift about
zwaluw (de) swallow
zwaluwstaart (de) swallowtail; dovetail
zwam (de) fungus
zwanger pregnant
zwangerschap (de) pregnancy
zwart black **zwart maken** to blacken
 (someone's name)
zwartkijker (de) pessimist; TV
 licence dodger
zwartrijden (het) evade paying
 road/highway tax; dodge paying
 the fare (bus/train)

ndle, crank
nd, to swerve
ster
le, trek

vander
er;

brag
ide, to hover
d to
to keep quiet
ence

zus en zo so-and-so, this and that
zus (de) sister
zuster (de) sister; nurse
zuur sour; **(het)** acid; pickles
...rkool (de) sauerkraut
...ruim (de) grouch
...f (de) oxygen
...t) acid drop
...ing, sweep
**...lashing light
...wield, to swing
**...full-

zwellen to swell
zwembad (het) swimming pool
zwembroek (de) swimming trunks
zwemmen to swim
zwemvest (het) lifejacket
zwemvlies (de) web, flipper
zwendel (de) swindle, racket

zwijn (het) hog, swine
zwikken to sprain
Zwitserland Switzerland
Zwitser(s) Swiss
zwoegen to toil
zwoel sultry as regards, as far as … goes

A

a(n) een
abandon opgeven, ver'laten; overgave
abashed ver'legen
abate ver'minderen, afnemen
abbey ab'dij
abbot abt
abbreviate afkorten, ver'korten
abbreviation afkorting
abdicate afstand doen van
abdomen buik
abduct ont'voeren
aberration afwijking
abhor ver'afschuwen
abhorrent weerzin'wekkend
abide toeven; uitstaan **to abide by** zich houden aan
ability ver'mogen, be'kwaamheid
abject ver'slagen
abjure afzweren
ablaze in lichterlaaie
able in staat; be'kwaam **to be — to** kunnen
abnegation ver'loochening
abnormal abnor'maal
aboard aan boord
abolish afschaffen
abolition afschaffing
abominable af'schuwelijk
abomination afschuw, gruwel
abortion a'bortus
abound in overvloed zijn
abounding in rijk aan
about om(streeks), onge'veer; over; in de buurt **— to go** op het punt te gaan
above boven **the —** het bovenstaande
abrasion schaafwond
abrasive schuurmiddel; afschurend
abreast naast el'kaar; ter (*or* op de) hoogte (van)

acceptable be'vredigend; welko
acceptance gunstige ont'va
access toegang
accessible (gemakkeli be'reikbaar; ge'na
accession (troon toetreding, a
accessorie
accesso
accid
ac

absolution abso'lutie
absolve ver'geven, vrijspreken
absorb (in zich) opnemen
absorbed ver'diept
absorbent absor'berend
absorbing boeiend
abstain zich ont'houden
abstinence ont'houding
abstract ab'stract; uittreksel
absurd onge'rijmd; be'lachelijk, gek
abundance overvloed
abundant meer dan vol'doende
abundantly in overvloed, rijkelijk
abuse misbruik, scheldwoorden; mis'bruiken; uitschelden
abusive be'ledigend
abut on grenzen aan
abysmal bodemloos, grenzeloos
abyss afgrond
academic(al) aca'demisch
academy aca'demie
accede to be'stijgen, aan'vaarden; toestemmen in
accelerate ver'snellen, gas geven; in snelheid toenemen
acceleration ver'snelling
accelerator gaspedaal
accent ac'cent, klemtoon
accent(uate) accentu'eren
accept aannemen

...m
...ngst
...k)
...kbaar
...)bestijging;
...anwinst
...s toebehoren
...y mede'plichtige
...ent ongeluk; toeval
...cidental toe'vallig; per ongeluk
acclaim toejuiching; toejuichen
acclimatize acclimati'seren
accolade ridderslag; acco'lade
accommodate onderdak ver'lenen,
  (her)bergen; aanpassen
accommodating in'schikkelijk
accommodation accommo'datie
accompaniment bege'leiding
accompany verge'zellen, ge'paard
  gaan met; bege'leiden
accomplice mede'plichtige
accomplish vol'brengen
accomplished ta'lentvol;
  vol'dongen (fact)
accomplishment gave, pres'tatie
accord over'eenstemming; ver'lenen;
  over'eenstemmen **of my own –** uit
  eigen be'weging
according to volgens
accordingly dienovereen'komstig
accost aanklampen
account ver'slag; rekening;
  rekenschap; be'lang **to – for**
  ver'klaren **to take into –** in
  aanmerking nemen **on – of**
  van'wege **on no –** in geen ge'val
accountancy boekhouding
accountant (hoofd)boekhouder
accredit toeschrijven aan
accredited er'kend
accrue toenemen
accumulate (zich) ophopen
accumulator accu(mu'lator)

accuracy nauw'keurigheid
accurate nauw'keurig; pre'cies
accursed ver'vloekt
accusation be'schuldiging
accuse be'schuldigen
accused ver'dachte
accustom wennen aan
accustomed ge'wend; ge'woon
ace aas
acerbity scherpheid
ache pijn (doen); hunkeren (naar)
achieve be'reiken
achievement pres'tatie; bereiken
acid zuur
acknowledge er'kennen;
  be'antwoorden
acknowledgement er'kenning;
  be'antwoording; be'richt van
  ont'vangst
acolyte volgeling, aanhanger
acorn eikel
acoustic akoestiek
acquaint in kennis stellen
acquaintance kennis
acquainted be'kend, op de hoogte
acquiesce in instemmen met;
  be'rusten in
acquire ver'werven, aanschaffen
acquisition aanwinst
acquisitive heb'zuchtig
acquit vrijspreken; kwijten
acquittal vrijspraak
acre acre, 4047 vierkante meter (m^2)
acrid scherp
acrimonious ve'nijnig, boo'saardig
acrobat acro'baat
across aan (*or* naar) de overkant
  (van); (dwars) over *or* door
act daad; be'drijf, nummer;
  handelen, werken; (to'neel)spelen
acting waar'nemend; to'neelspel
action handeling, werking; actie
activate aanzetten (tot)
active ac'tief

activity be'drijvigheid
actor, actress ac'teur, ac'trice
actual werkelijk
actually eigenlijk, feitelijk
acumen scherp'zinnigheid
acute scherp; a'cuut
adamant onver'murwbaar
adapt aanpassen, be'werken
adaptability aanpassingsvermogen
adaptable aan te passen; plooibaar
adaptation be'werking; aanpassing
add (to) toevoegen aan, voegen bij
  – to ver'meerderen **– up**
  optellen; oplopen
addict ver'slaafde
addicted ver'slaafd
addition optelling; toevoeging
  in – boven'dien
additional extra
addled be'dorven; ver'dwaasd
address a'dres; toespraak;
  adres'seren; aanspreken, toespreken
adenoids neusamandelen
adept be'dreven(e) (in)
adequate vol'doende, ge'schikt
adhere (aan)kleven; aanhangen,
  blijven bij
adhesion ad'hesie
adhesive plak-; plakmiddel
adjacent aan'grenzend
adjective bij'voeglijk naamwoord
adjoin grenzen aan
adjourn ver'dagen; (uit'een)gaan
adjudicate uitspraak doen
adjunct aanhangsel; be'paling
adjust bijstellen, reguleren
adjustable ver'stelbaar
ad lib on'voorbereid,
  geïmprovi'seerd
administer be'heren; toedienen
administration be'heer, re'gering
administrative administra'tief
admirable bewonderingswaardig;
  voor'treffelijk

admiral admi'raal
admiration be'wondering
admire be'wonderen
admissible ver'oorloofd;
  aan'nemelijk
admission toegang(sprijs),
  toelating; er'kenning
admit toelaten tot,
  opnemen in; toegeven
admittance toegang
admittedly weliswaar
admonish ver'manen
ad nauseam tot ver'velens toe
ado drukte
adolescence puber'teit
adolescent puber
adopt aannemen
adorable aller'liefst
adoration aan'bidding
adore aan'bidden; dol zijn op
adorn (ver')sieren
adornment ver'siering, sieraad
adrift drijvend, los
adroit(ness) handig(heid)
adulation ophemeling
adult vol'wassen(e)
adultery overspel
advance voor'uitgang; opmars;
  voorschot; naar voren komen,
  oprukken; voorschieten
  in – van te voren
advanced (ver)ge'vorderd
advancement voor'uitgang,
  be'vordering
advantage voordeel **to take**
  advantage of ge'bruik maken van
advantageous gunstig
advent (aan)komst; Ad'vent
adventure avon'tuur, onder'neming
adventurer avontu'rier
adventurous avon'tuurlijk; ge'waagd
adverb bijwoord
adversary tegenstander
adverse on'gunstig; na'delig

adversity tegenspoed
advertise adver'teren, re'clame maken (voor); be'kend maken
advertisement adver'tentie, re'clame
advice raad
advisable raadzaam
advise aanraden
advisedly met over'leg
advisor raadsman, consulent
advisory raadgevend
advocate voorspraak; voorstander; be'pleiten
aerial an'tenne
afar verre
affable minzaam
affair zaak; ver'houding
affect (be')treffen; voorwenden
affectation ge'maaktheid; voorwendsel
affected ge'maakt
affection ge'negenheid
affectionate aan'hankelijk, hartelijk; toegenegen
affidavit be'ëdigde ver'klaring
affiliated to aangesloten bij
affinity ver'wantschap
affirm plechtig ver'klaren
affirmation be'vestiging
affirmative be'vestigend
afflict kwellen, teisteren
affliction kwelling, ramp
affluent (schat)rijk
afford zich ver'oorloven; ver'schaffen
affront be'lediging
afield: far – ver weg
afloat drijvend
afoot aan de gang
aforementioned, aforesaid voor'noemd
afraid bang
afresh op'nieuw
after (daar')na; na'dat

after-effect(s) nawerking
aftermath nasleep
afternoon (na)middag
afterthought latere over'weging
afterwards later, nader'hand
again weer (eens); te'rug **again and again** telkens weer
against tegen
age leeftijd, ouderdom; eeuw; ouder worden **of –** meerder'jarig
aged be'jaard; oud
agency a'gentschap
agenda a'genda
agent tussenpersoon, a'gent
agglomeration op'eenhoping
aggrandize ver'heffen
aggravate (ver')ergeren
aggravating ver'velend; ver'zwarend
aggregate (ge'zamenlijk) to'taal
aggression ag'gressie
aggressive aggres'sief
aggressor aanvaller
aghast at ont'zet over
agile be'hendig
agitate a'geren; schudden
agitation actie; be'roering; ge'jaagdheid
aglow gloeiend
agnostic ag'nosticus
ago ge'leden
agog: to be – zitten te springen
agonizing (vreselijk) pijnlijk
agony vreselijke pijn
agree het eens zijn; over'eenkomen; toestemmen **fish doesn't – with me** ik kan niet tegen vis
agreeable aangenaam; be'reid
agreement over'eenkomst
agricultural landbouw- ('kundig)
agriculture landbouw
aground aan de grond
ahead voor'op, voor'uit; in het voor'uitzicht

aid hulp
ail man'keren; sukkelen
ailment kwaal
aim doel(einde); mikken op; munten op; streven naar
aimless doelloos

alarm a'larm; ont'steltenis; ont'stellen
alarm clock wekker
alarmist alar'mist(isch)
alas he'laas
albeit (al)hoe'wel

Insight

The different Dutch equivalents of *all* cannot all be used in the same contexts. The adjective **al(le)** can be used for both inanimate objects and animate beings (**alle huizen in deze wijk** *all (the) houses in this area*; **alle dansers waren goed** *all (the) dancers were good*) as can **allemaal** *all* or *every one* (**ik heb de boeken allemaal gelezen** *I've read all the books*; **de gasten zijn allemaal vertrokken** *the guests have all left*). **Alles** *all* or *everything*, on the other hand, can only refer to inanimate objects (**ik heb alles opgeruimd** *I've cleared away everything*), while **allen** *all* or *everyone* generally only refers to people (**één voor allen, allen voor één** *one for all, all for one*).

---

air lucht; schijn; wijs; luchten **airs (and graces)** airs
aircraft vliegtuig
aircraft carrier vliegdekschip
airfield vliegveld
airforce luchtmacht
airgun windbuks
air hostess stewardess
airily lucht'hartig
airlift luchtbrug
airline luchtvaartmaatschappij
airliner lijnvliegtuig
airplane vliegtuig
airport luchthaven, vliegveld
air raid luchtaanval
airtight luchtdicht
airy luchtig
aisle zijbeuk, gangpad
ajar op een kier
akin ver'want

alcohol alcohol
alcoholic alco'holisch; alcoho'list
alcove nis; al'koof
alderman wethouder
ale bier
alert waakzaam
algebra algebra
alien vreemd(eling), buitenlander; buitenaardswezen
alienate ver'vreemden
alight aan(gestoken); af(*or* uit) stappen; neerstrijken
align op één lijn plaatsen
alike evenzeer **to be alike** op el'kaar lijken
alive levend, in leven; zich be'wust van
alkali(ne) al'kali(sch)
all al(le); alles, allen; alle'maal – **along** steeds – **but** bijna – **in**

alles inbegrepen – **right** in orde –
the more des te meer **after** –
ten'slotte – **in** – al met al **at** –
über'haupt **not at** – hele'maal
niet **for – that** desondanks **for – I
know** voor zo'ver ik weet
allay stillen
allegation be'wering
allege be'weren
alleged(ly) zoge'naamd
allegiance trouw
allegory allego'rie
allergic al'lergisch
alleviate ver'lichten
alley(way) steeg
alliance ver'bond
allied ver'bonden; ver'want
alliteration allite'ratie
allocate toewijzen
allot toebedelen
allotment volkstuintje
allow toestaan; rekenen
allowance toelage **to (make)
allow(ance) for** rekening
houden met
alloy le'gering
all-round veel'zijdig
allude to zinspelen op
alluring aan'lokkelijk
allusion toespeling
ally bondgenoot; ver'binden
almighty al'machtig
almond a'mandel
almost bijna
alms aalmoes
alone al'leen **let alone**
laat staan
along langs; mee; voort **– with** met
… mee, samen met
alongside langs'zij
aloof op een afstand
aloud hardop
alphabet alfabet
alphabetical alfa'betisch

already al, reeds
also ook; boven'dien
altar altaar
alter ver'anderen, (zich) wijzigen
alteration ver'andering
altercation twistgesprek
alternate afwisselen **on – days**
om de andere dag
alternately om de beurt
alternative alterna'tief
alternatively aan de andere kant
although hoe'wel
altitude hoogte
alto alt
altogether hele'maal; alles bij
el'kaar
altruism altru'ïsme
aluminium alu'minium
always al'tijd
amalgamate samensmelten
amass op'eenhopen
amateur ama'teur
amaze ver'bazen
amazement ver'bazing
ambassador (af)gezant
ambiguity dubbel'zinnigheid
ambiguous dubbel'zinnig
ambition ambi'tie;
aspi'ratie, ide'aal
ambitious ambi'tieus;
groots opgezet
amble kuieren
ambulance ziekenauto,
ambulance
ambush hinderlaag
amenable ont'vankelijk (voor)
amend ver'beteren, wijzigen
amendment amende'ment
amends: to make – het weer
goedmaken
amenity ge'mak
amiable be'minnelijk
amicable vriend'schappelijk
amid(st) te midden van

amiss ver'keerd
ammonia ammoni'ak
ammunition (am)mu'nitie
amnesty amnes'tie
among(st) onder, tussen
amorous ver'liefd; liefdes-
amount be'drag, hoe'veelheid
  to – to be'dragen; be'tekenen
amphibian amfi'bie
ample ruim (vol'doende)
amplify aanvullen; ver'sterken
amply ruimschoots
amputate ampu'teren
amuse ver'maken; pret hebben
amused: to be – grappig vinden
amusement ver'maak, tijdsverdrijf
amusing amu'sant, onder'houdend
anaemia bloedarmoede
anaesthetic ver'dovend;
  ver'dovingsmiddel
analogous ana'loog
analogy analo'gie
analyse anali'seren
analysis ana'lyse
anarchy anar'chie
anatomy anato'mie
ancestor voorvader
ancestral voorvaderlijk
ancestry voorgeslacht; afstamming
anchor anker; (ver')ankeren
anchorage ankergrond; steun
anchovy an'sjovis
ancient (zeer) oud
and en
anecdote anek'dote
anew op'nieuw
angel engel
angelic(al) engelachtig, engelen-
anger boosheid
angle hoek; ge'zichtspunt;
  hengelen
Anglican angli'caan(s)
angry boos
anguish leed, pijn

angular hoekig
animal dier; dierlijk, dieren-
animate levend; be'zielen
animated geani'meerd, levendig
  – cartoon tekenfilm
animation tekenfilm, poppenfilm;
  levend(ig) maken
animosity vij'andigheid
ankle enkel
annals an'nalen
annex anne'xeren; toevoegen
annexe uitbouw, depen'dance;
  bijlage
annihilate ver'nietigen
anniversary jaarfeest, ge'denkdag
announce aankondigen
announcement aankondiging
announcer omroeper
annoy ergeren
annoyance ergenis
annoying ver'velend
annual jaar'lijks; éénjarige plant
annuity jaargeld, lijfrente
annul te'nietdoen
anoint zalven
anomaly afwijking
anonymous ano'niem
another een ander(e), nog een
answer antwoord, oplossing;
  (be')antwoorden
answerable aan'sprakelijk;
  te be'antwoorden
ant mier
antagonism vijandschap
antagonist tegenstander
antagonize ophitsen
antarctic zuidpool
antecedent voor'afgaand;
  antece'dent
anthem: national – volkslied
anthill mierenhoop
anthology bloemlezing
anthracite antra'ciet
anti-aircraft luchtafweer-

antics streken
anticipate ver'wachten;
voor'uitlopen op, vóór zijn
anticipation ver'wachting
anticlimax anti'climax
antidote tegengif
antipathy antipa'thie
antiquarian oudheid'kundig(e),
anti'quair
antiquated ouder'wets
antique an'tiek; antiqui'teit
antiquity oudheid; ouderdom
antiseptic anti'septisch (middel)
antithesis tegenstelling,
tegenge'stelde
antlers ge'wei
anvil aanbeeld
anxiety be'zorgdheid
anxious be'zorgd **to be – to**
heel graag willen
any ieder, iemand; wat (ook),
enig **not –** geen; niets
anybody anyone iemand, iedereen;
wie ook
anyhow hoe dan ook; zo maar
anything iets; alles
anyway in ieder ge'val
anywhere ergens; over'al
apace vlug
apart uit el'kaar; afgezien;
afgezonderd
apartment etage, flat
apathetic a'patisch
apathy onver'schilligheid
ape aap; na-apen
aperture opening
apex top(punt)
apiece per stuk, elk
apologetic veront'schuldigend
apologize zich veront'schuldigen
apology veront'schuldiging
apoplectic fit be'roerte
apostle a'postel
apostrophe apos'trof

appal ont'zetten
appalling schrik'barend
apparatus appa'raten, appa'raat,
toestel(len)
apparel kle'dij
apparent duidelijk; ogen'schijnlijk
apparently blijkbaar
apparition (geest)ver'schijning
appeal be'roep, smeekbede;
aantrekkingskracht; een be'roep
doen (op), smeken; in be'roep gaan
(bij); aantrekken
appear (ver')schijnen, blijken
appearance ver'schijning, optreden;
voorkomen
appease sussen, stillen
appeasement ver'zoening
append (bij)voegen
appendage aanhangsel
appendicitis blinde'darmontsteking
appendix ap'pendix; aanhangsel
appertain to be'trekking hebben
op; be'horen aan
appetite (eet)lust
appetizing smakelijk
applaud toejuichen, applaudis'seren
applause ap'plaus, toejuiching(en)
apple appel
appliance appa'raat; toepassing
applicable toe'passelijk
applicant sollici'tant
application aanbrengen; (ma'nier
van) toepassing, ge'bruik;
sollici'tatie; ijver
applied toegepast
apply aanbrengen; toepassen,
van toepassing zijn; zich wenden;
sollici'teren; toeleggen (op)
appoint be'noemen, aanwijzen
appointed time vastgesteld uur
appointment afspraak; be'noeming,
ambt
apportion ver'delen
apposite toe'passelijk

appraisal schatting
appreciable aan'merkelijk
appreciate waar'deren, ge'voelig
  zijn voor; stijgen
appreciation waar'dering, ge'voel;
  stijging
appreciative dankbaar
apprehend ge'vangen nemen;
  vatten; vrezen
apprehension in'hechtenisneming;
  be'grip; angst
apprehensive angstig
apprentice leerling: in de leer doen
approach nader'bij komen;
  toegang(sweg); aanpak; naderen;
  zich wenden tot
approachable toe'gankelijk
approbation goedkeuring, bijval
appropriate ge'schikt; zich
  toeëigenen, be'stemmen
approval goedkeuring, bijval
approve goedkeuren, er'kennen
approximate be'naderen **the
  (approximate) length is
  (approximately)** de lengte
  is onge'veer
approximation schatting
apricot abri'koos
April a'pril
apron schort
apt ge'neigd; passend; vlug
aptitude aanleg
aquarium a'quarium
aquatic water
aqueduct waterleiding
aquiline arends-
Arab Ara'bier
Arabian, Arabic A'rabisch
arbitrary wille'keurig
arbitration arbi'trage
arc boog
arcade gale'rij
arch boog, ge'welf; aarts
archaeology oudheidkunde

archaic ver'ouderd
arched ge'bogen
archer boogschutter
archery boogschieten
architect archi'tect
architectural bouw'kundig
architecture bouwkunde,
  bouwstijl
archives ar'chief, ar'chieven
archway poort
arctic noordpool
ardent vurig
arduous zwaar
area oppervlak, ge'bied
arena a'rena
argue debat'teren; tegenspreken;
  be'togen
argument ruzie; argument,
  rede'nering; discussie
argumentative twistziek
arid dor, droog
arise ont'staan, zich voordoen;
  ver'rijzen
aristocracy aristocra'tie
aristocrat aristo'craat
arithmetic rekenkunde
ark ark
arm arm, leuning; wapen;
  be'wapenen **– in –** ge'armd
armament be'wapening
armchair leunstoel
armful vracht
armistice wapenstilstand
armour harnas; wapenrusting
armoured pantser-
armoury wapenzaal
armpit oksel
army leger
aroma a'roma
aromatic geurig
around rond('om); over'al;
  in de buurt (van)
arouse opwekken; wakker maken
arraign aanklagen; be'schuldigen

arrange (rang)schikken; regelen, afspreken; arran'geren

arrangement schikking; afspraak; arrange'ment

array (slag)orde; uitstalling; opstellen; uitdossen

arrears achterstand

arrest ar'rest, arres'tatie; arres'teren; tegenhouden

arrival (aan)komst; aangekomene

arrive (aan)komen

arrogance arro'gantie

arrogant arro'gant

arrow pijl

arsenal arse'naal

arsenic ar'senicum

arson brandstichting

art kunst

artery (slag)ader

artful ge'slepen

arthritis ar'tritis, jicht

artichoke arti'sjok

article ar'tikel; voorwerp; lidwoord
 – of clothing kledingstuk

articulate duidelijk; articu'leren; koppelen

artifice kunst(greep)

artificer handwerksman

artificial kunst'matig, ge'kunsteld, kunst-

artillery artille'rie

artisan vakman, ambachtsman

artist kunstenaar, schilder

artistic kunst'zinnig, artis'tiek

artistry kunstenaarstalent

artless argeloos; ruw

as (zo)als; ter'wijl; daar **(just) – ...**
 (–) even ... (als) **– to** wat betreft

asbestos as'best

ascend (be')stijgen

ascendancy overwicht

Ascension hemelvaart

ascent stijgen, be'stijging; helling

ascertain te weten komen

ascetic as'ceet; as'cetisch

ascribe toeschrijven

ash as; es

ashamed be'schaamd **to be –**
 zich schamen

ashen lijkbleek

ashore aan wal, aan land

ashtray asbak

aside op'zij, ter'zijde

ask vragen **– a question** een vraag
 stellen

askance wan'trouwend

askew scheef

aslant schuin

asleep in slaap **to be –** slapen

asparagus as'perge

aspect as'pect, kant; aanblik; ligging

asphalt asfalt

asphyxiate (ver')stikken

aspirant aspi'rant

aspiration aspi'ratie

aspire streven (naar)

ass ezel

assail be'stormen, aanvallen

assailant aanvaller

assassin sluipmoordenaar

assassinate ver'moorden

assault be'storming, aanval(len), be'stormen

assemble (zich) ver'zamelen, mon'teren

assembly bij'eenkomst; mon'tering

assent instemming; instemmen

assert be'weren; doen gelden, opkomen voor

assertion be'wering

assess ta'xeren; aanslaan

asset creditpost; goed, bezit, kwaliteit

assiduous naarstig

assign toewijzen; vaststellen

assignment opdracht

assimilate ver'werken, opnemen

assimilation assimi'latie

assist helpen
assistance hulp
assistant assis'tent, be'diende
associate partner; ver'want;
 ver'binden, 'associ'ëren, omgaan
association associ'atie;
 ge'nootschap
assorted ge'mengd
assortment sor'tering; ver'zameling
assuage stillen, lessen
assume aannemen; voorwenden;
 op zich nemen
assumption veronder'stelling;
 aanvaarding
assurance ver'zekering
assure ver'zekeren
assuredly stellig; zelfbe'wust
astonish ver'bazen
astonishment ver'bazing
astound (ten hoogste) ver'bazen
astray op een dwaalspoor
astride schrijlings (op)
astronaut astronaut, ruimtevaarder
astronomical astro'nomisch
astronomy sterrenkunde
astute slim
asunder uit el'kaar
asylum ge'sticht; a'siel
asymmetric(al) asym'metrisch
at aan (position); in, op, te (place);
 om (time); naar (direction); voor
 (price) – (my) leisure op mijn
 ge'mak – that moment op dat
 ogenblik – the time toen
atheism athe'ïsme
athlete at'leet
athletic at'letisch
athletics atle'tiek
Atlantic At'lantische Oce'aan
atlas atlas
atmosphere dampkring; (atmo')
 sfeer
atmospheric atmos'ferisch
atom a'toom

atomic a'tomisch, a'toom-
atone boeten
atonement boete(doening),
 ver'zoening
atrocious af'schuwelijk
atrocity gruwel(daad)
attach vastmaken, ver'binden;
 hechten
attachment onderdeel, ver'binding;
 ge'hechtheid
attack aanval(len)
attain be'reiken, be'halen
attainable be'reikbaar
attainment be'reiken; ta'lent
attempt poging, aanslag; trachten
attend bijwonen; verge'zellen
 attend to opletten; ver'zorgen
attendance opkomst; aan'wezigheid
 in attendance aan'wezig; in het
 ge'volg
attendant be'diende; be'zoeker:
 bege'leidend; dienstdoend
attention aandacht; at'tentie;
 houding
attentive op'lettend; at'tent
attenuate ver'dunnen; ver'zachten
attest ge'tuigen van, attes'teren
attic zolder(kamer)
attire tooi(en)
attitude houding
attorney gevol'machtigde,
 procu'reur
attract (aan)trekken
attraction aantrekking(skracht)
attractive aan'trekkelijk
attribute eigenschap, kenmerk;
 attri'buut; toeschrijven
attune (over'een)stemmen met
auburn kas'tanjebruin
auction veiling; veilen
auctioneer afslager
audacious dapper; roekeloos
audacity dapperheid, brutali'teit
audible hoorbaar

audience ge'hoor, toehoorders
audit ac'countantsverslag; verifi'ëren
audition auditie
auditor ac'countant; toehoorder
auditorium zaal
augment ver'meerderen, uitbreiden
August au'gustus
aunt tante
aura aura
auspices auspiciën
auspicious gunstig
austere streng, sober
austerity ver'sobering
Austria Oostenrijk
authentic authen'tiek
authenticate verifi'ëren
authenticity echtheid
author schrijver; schepper
authoritarian autori'tair (per'soon)
authoritative autori'tair, ge'zaghebbend
authority autori'teit; bron; machtiging
authorize machtigen; be'krachtigen
autobiography autobiogra'fie
autocracy onbeperkte heerschap'pij
autograph handtekening
automatic auto'matisch
autonomous auto'noom
autopsy lijkschouwing
autumn(al) herfst(-)
auxiliary hulp; hulpwerkwoord
avail baten **of no —** vruchteloos **to — oneself of** be'nutten
available be'schikbaar
avalanche la'wine
avarice gierigheid

avaricious gierig; be'gerig
avenge wreken
avenue laan; weg
average ge'middeld (doen); ge'middelde
averse to af'kerig van
aversion afkeer, tegenzin
avert afwenden
aviary voli'ère
aviation luchtvaart
avid gretig, be'gerig
avoid (ver')mijden
avoidance ver'mijding
avow be'lijden, be'kennen
avowal be'kentenis, be'lijdenis
await afwachten; wachten op
awake wakker; zich be'wust (worden) van; ont'waken; wekken
awaken wekken
awakening: rude — ont'nuchtering
award be'kroning, prijs; toekennen, toewijzen
aware be'wust
awareness be'sef
awash over'spoeld
away weg; er op los **do — with** opruimen
awe ont'zag
awe-inspiring ontzag'wekkend
awful ver'schrikkelijk, vreselijk
awfully (heel) erg
awhile een tijdje
awkward on'handig; lastig
awning dekzeil, zonnescherm
awry scheef
axe bijl; drastisch be'perken
axis as(lijn); spil
azure hemelsblauw

B

babble babbelen, kabbelen
baboon bavi'aan
baby kindje, baby; jong, klein

babyish kinderachtig
bachelor vrijge'zel
bacillus ba'cil

back rug, achterkant, rugleuning;
te'rug, achter-; achter'uitgaan;
wedden op; bijvallen **– to front**
achterstevoren **at the –** achter'aan
(*or* 'in) **on the –** achter'op **to –**
down zich te'rugtrekken **to –**
out te'rugkrabbelen **to – up**
steunen
backbiting kwaadspreke'rij
backbone ruggegraat
backfire te'rugslaan
background achtergrond
backing steun; achterkant
(bekleding)
backstage achter de schermen
backward(s) achter'uit, te'rug-;
achterlijk, traag **– and forwards**
heen en weer
backwater kreek, uithoek
bacon spek, bacon
bacteria bac'teriën
bad slecht, naar; vals; be'dorven
to go – be'derven **– luck** pech
badge in'signe
badger das; lastig vallen
badly erg; dolgraag
bad-tempered slecht-gehu'meurd
baffle ver'bijsteren
bag zak, tas; vangst; gappen
baggage ba'gage
baggy uitgezakt, hang-
bagpipe doedelzaak
bail borg(tocht); borgstaan; hozen
bailiff rentmeester; deurwaarder
bait lokaas; van aas voor'zien
bake bakken
baker bakker
bakery bakke'rij
balaclava bivakmuts
balance evenwicht; saldo, res't(ant);
weegschaal; in evenwicht brengen,
opwegen tegen; sluitend maken
(*or* zijn)
balanced even'wichtig

balance sheet ba'lans
balcony bal'kon
bald kaal; naakt
bale baal; in balen ver'pakken
baleful onheil'spellend, ge'pijnigd
balk balk; ver'ijdelen, tegenstribbelen
ball bal(len); bal (*dance*)
ballad bal'lade
ballast ballast
ball bearing kogellager
ballet bal'let
balloon bal'lon; bol staan
ballot (ge'heime) stemming; lot
balm balsem, geur
balmy zacht, geurig; ge'tikt
balsam balsem
balustrade balu'strade
bamboo bamboe
bamboozle bedriegen
ban ver'bod, ban(vloek); ver'bieden;
ver'bannen
banal ba'naal
banana ba'naan
band band, rand; troep; ka'pel;
ver'enigen
bandage ver'band
bandit ban'diet
bandstand mu'ziektent
bandy-legged met o-benen
bane vloek
bang klap, knal; (dicht)slaan
banish ver'bannen
banishment ver'banning
banisters trapleuning
banjo banjo
bank oever, berm; bank; ophopen;
depo'neren; overhellen; afdekken
to – on specu'leren op
banker ban'kier
bank holiday offici'ële
va'kantiedag
banknote bankbiljet
bankrupt fai'lliet
bankruptcy faillisse'ment

banner ba'nier, vaandel
banquet gastmaal
banter gekscheren
baptism doop
Baptist doopsge'zinde
baptize dopen
bar stang, reep, staaf; barri'ère; bar; balie; maat; uitgezonderd; afsluiten, ver'sperren; uitsluiten
barbarian bar'baar(s)
barbarity bar'baarsheid
barbarous bar'baars

barely nauwelijks
bargain over'eenkomst; koopje; dingen **into the –** op de koop toe **to – for** rekenen op
barge schuit, sloep; botsen, zich werken
baritone bariton
bark schors; ge'blaf; bark; schaven; blaffen
barley gerst
barn schuur
barometer barometer

Insight

The Dutch equivalent of the verb *to be* is **zijn**. However, in practice the verb **zijn** is felt to be too generalized, and when speakers of Dutch describe objects, they usually refer to their position, as they see it, using the verbs **liggen** *to lie*, **staan** *to stand*, **hangen** *to hang* or a number of similar verbs. *There are 110 books in my book case* is **er staan 110 boeken in mijn boekenkast**, using the verb **staan** because the books are seen to be standing upright. When a book is lying flat on a table, you say: **er ligt een boek op tafel**. The position of other objects may not always seem logical (**er staat een bord op tafel** *there is a plate on the table*), but on the whole it is obvious what description should be used: **er ligt bestek in de linkerla** *there's cutlery in the left hand drawer*; **er staat een lamp achter de bank** *there's a lamp behind the sofa*; **er hangt een mooie poster aan de muur** *there's a nice poster on the wall*. The verb **zitten** *to sit* is used for objects in enclosed spaces: **er zit een sleutel in m'n tas** *there's a key in my bag*.

---

barbed hekelend **– wire** prikkeldraad
barber kapper
barcode streepjescode
bard zanger-dichter
bare (ont')bloot, kaal; mini'maal; ont'bloten
barefaced onbe'schaamd
barefoot(ed) bloots'voets
bareheaded bloots'hoofds

baron ba'ron; mag'naat
baroque ba'rok(stijl)
barracks ka'zerne(woning)
barrel vat, ton; loop
barren on'vruchtbaar, dor
barricade barri'cade; barrica'deren
barrier barri'ère, con'trole
barrister advo'kaat
barrow handkar; grafheuvel

barter ruilhandel drijven; ver'kwanselen
base basis, voetstuk; ge'meen
baseball honkbal
basement kelder, souter'rain
bash dreun; stoot; slaan
bashful schuchter, verlegen
basic fundamen'teel, grond-
basin kom, bak; dok
basis basis
bask zich koesteren
basket mand
basketball basketbal
bass bas; baars
bassoon fa'got
bastard bastaard; on'echt
baste met vet over'gieten
bastion basti'on
bat slaghout; vleermuis; batten
 off one's own — op eigen houtje
batch par'tij, baksel; groep
bath bad; in bad doen (or gaan)
bathe (zich) baden **bathed**
 (in light) baden (in licht)
bathrobe badjas
bathroom badkamer
baton stok(je)
battalion batal'jon
batten lat
batter be'slag
battery batte'rij, accu
battle (veld)slag; strijd(en)
battleaxe strijdbijl
battlefield slagveld
battlement kan'teel
battleship slagschip
bawl schreeuwen, brullen
bay baai; erker, hoek; blaffen
 at bay in het nauw
bayonet bajo'net
bazaar ba'zaar
be zijn; zitten, worden **to — hungry,**
 sleepy, thirsty, cold honger,
 slaap, dorst, het koud hebben

how are you? hoe maakt u het?
how is it that? hoe komt het dat?
beach strand
beacon baken
bead kraal
beak snavel
beaker beker(glas)
beam balk; stralenbundel; stralen (van)
bean boon
bear beer; (ver)'dragen; baren
 to — down neerdrukken; afkomen op **to — out** staven **to — witness** ge'tuigen
beard baard; trot'seren
bearer drager, brenger; toonder
bearing houding; be'trekking; richting; kogellager
beast beest
beastly beestachtig; akelig
beat (maat)slag; ronde; (ver)' slaan, kloppen; la'veren
beating afranseling; klappen
beautiful mooi
beautify ver'fraaien
beauty schoonheid; prachtexemplaar
beaver bever
because omdat **— of** van'wege
beckon wenken
become worden **to — of** ge'beuren met
becoming be'tamelijk, flat'teus
bed bed
bedding beddengoed; onderlaag
bedlam gekkenhuis
bedraggled nat en ver'wilderd
bedridden bed'legerig
bedroom slaapkamer
bedspread sprei
bedstead ledi'kant
bee bij
beech beuk

beef rundvlees
beefsteak runderlap
beehive bijenkorf
beer bier
beetle kever
beetroot rode biet
befall over'komen
befit be'tamen
befog be'nevelen
before voor('af, 'op *or* 'uit), te'voren;
  voordat **– long** weldra
beforehand voor'af, van te'voren
befriend vriendschap be'wijzen
befuddle be'nevelen
beg bedelen; smeken, ver'zoeken;
  zo vrij zijn
beget voortbrengen
beggar bedelaar; stakker
begin be'ginnen
beginning be'gin
begrudge mis'gunnen
beguile be'driegen; ver'drijven
behalf: on – of ten be'hoeve van,
  uit naam van
behave (oneself) zich (netjes)
  ge'dragen
behaviour ge'drag
behead ont'hoofden
behind achter(ste)
behold aan'schouwen
beige beige
being wezen **to come into –**
  ont'staan **for the time –** voor'lopig
belated (ver')laat
belch boeren; uitbraken
belfry klokkentoren
Belgium België
belie logenstraffen
belief ge'loof
believe ge'loven
believer ge'lovige; voorstander (van)
belittle klei'neren
bell bel, klok
bellicose oorlogs'zuchtig

belligerent strijd'lustig
bellow ge'brul; brullen
bellows blaasbalg
belly buik
belong (be')horen **to – to** (toebe)
  horen aan
belongings spullen
beloved ge'liefd(e)
below onder, be'neden
belt gordel, riem; zone; afranselen
bemoan be'jammeren
bench (recht)bank
bend bocht; (zich) buigen; ver'buigen
beneath be'neden, onder
benediction zegen
benefactor weldoener
beneficial heilzaam
benefit voordeel; uitkering; goed
  doen, voordeel trekken
benevolent wel'willend
benign goed('aard)ig, wel'dadig
bent ge'bogen; be'sloten, uit op;
  aanleg
benumb ver'kleumen
bequeath ver'maken
bequest le'gaat
bereave be'roven
bereaved diep be'droefd
bereavement zwaar ver'lies
beret ba'ret
berry bes
berth ligplaats; kooi
beseech smeken
beside naast **– oneself with** buiten
  zichzelf van
besides boven'dien; be'halve
besiege be'legeren; be'stormen
besmirch be'vuilen; be'zoedelen
best (het) best **– man** getuige (at a
  wedding) **– part of** bijna **at –** in het
  gunstigste ge'val **to make the – of**
  zich schikken in
bestial beestachtig
bestow ver'lenen, schenken

bet wedden(schap)
betray ver'raden
betrayal ver'raad
better beter; ver'beteren **better off** er beter aan toe **had better** moet(en) maar
between tussen
beverage drank
bewail be'jammeren
beware of oppassen voor
bewilder ver'bijsteren
bewitch be'heksen
beyond voor'bij; boven; meer dan **it is – me** het gaat mijn verstand te boven
bias neiging; bevoor'oordelen
bib slabbetje
Bible bijbel
bibliography bibliogra'fie
bicker kibbelen
bicycle fiets
bid bod; beiden; ge'lasten
big groot
bigamy biga'mie
big-headed verwaand
bigot(ed) kwezel(achtig)
bill rekening; wetsontwerp; aanplakbiljet; snavel
billiards bil'jart
billion bil'joen
billow bollen; in wolken opstijgen
bin bak
bind (in-, vast- *or* ver')binden; ver'plichten
binder (boek)binder; omslag
binding band; bindend
binoculars verrekijker
biography levensbeschrijving, biografie
biology biolo'gie
birch berk
bird vogel
birth ge'boorte **to give – to** het leven schenken aan

birthday ver'jaardag
birth rate ge'boortecijfer
biscuit koekje, biskwietje
bishop bisschop
bit beetje, stukje; bit **wait a –** even wachten
bitch (term of abuse) teef, kreng; teef (female dog)
bite beet, hap; bijten
bitter bitter
blab ver'klikken
black zwart, blauw (eye)
blackberry braam
blackbird merel
blackboard schoolbord
blackmail chan'tage; geld afpersen
blackout ver'duistering; tijdelijke bewuste'loosheid
blacksmith smid
bladder blaas
blade kling, lemmet, mesje; spriet
blame (de) schuld (geven)
blameless onbe'rispelijk
blanch (ver')bleken, pellen
bland nietszeggend; flauw
blank blanco; wezenloos; los (cartridge) **to draw a –** botvangen
blanket deken
blare schallen
blasphemy godslastering
blast rukwind, luchtdruk; laten springen
blast furnace hoogoven
blatant over'duidelijk
blaze laaiend vuur, (vlammen)zee; opvlammen, in lichterlaaie staan
bleach (doen ver')bleken
bleak troosteloos
bleat blaten
bleed bloeden; uitzuigen
blemish smet, ont'siering; be'kladden
blend mengsel; (zich) ver'mengen, harmoni'ëren

bless zegenen
blessing zegen(ing)
blight plantenziekte; be'derf
blind blind; doodlopend; rolgordijn;
  foefje; ver'blinden
blindfold ge'blinddoekt; blinddoeken
blindness blindheid
blink knipperen
bliss geluk'zaligheid
blister blaar
blizzard sneeuwjacht
block blok; (ver')stoppen
blockade blok'kade; blok'keren
blockhead domkop
blond(e) blon'd(ine)
blood bloed
bloodshed bloedvergieten
bloodshot met bloed be'lopen
bloody bloed(er)ig; ver'domd
bloom bloem; waas; bloei(en)
blossom bloesem; bloeien
blot vlek, smet; afvloeien; be'kladden
  to – out ver'nietigen
blotting paper vloeipapier
blouse bloes
blow slag; waaien, blazen; snuiten
  to – up opblazen; opvliegen,
  uitschelden; opsteken
blowlamp brander
blue blauw
blueprint blauwdruk; plan
bluff bluf(fen); steil(e oever)
bluish blauwachtig
blunder blunder; struikelen
blunt stomp, bot (maken); ab'rupt
blur ver'vagen
blurt out er'uit flappen
blush blos; blozen, zich schamen
bluster bulderen
boar zwijn
board plank, bord; kost(geld);
  be'stuur **to (go on) –** aan boord
  gaan **above –** bona fide
boarding school kostschool

boast pochen; bogen (op)
boat boot
bob dobberen
bode ill (well) wat slechts (goeds)
  be'loven
bodily li'chamelijk; in zijn ge'heel
body lichaam, lijf; sub'stantie;
  carrosse'rie; groep
bodyguard lijfwacht
bog moe'ras **to be bogged (down)**
  vastzitten
bogey boeman, schrikbeeld
bogus vals
boil kook; steenpuist; koken **to –
  down** inkoken; neer komen (op)
boiler ketel, boiler
boisterous on'stuimig
bold stout('moedig)
bolt bout; grendel(en); ervan
  doorgaan **bolt upright** kaarsrecht
bomb(ard) bom(bar'deren)
bombastic bom'bastisch
bomber bommenwerper
bomb scare bommelding
bond band; obli'gatie; entre'pot;
  ver'binden
bondage slaver'nij;
  onderworpenheid; bondage
bone been, graat
bone-dry kurkdroog
bonfire (vreugde)vuur
bonnet kap
bonny leuk, fris, knap
bonus premie
bony knokig, vol benen (*or* graten)
boob flater, blunder; borst, (inf) tiet
book boek(je); reser'veren, boeken
bookcase boekenkast
bookish leesgraag; boekachtig,
  stijf, saai
bookkeeping boekhouden
bookseller boekhandelaar
boom ge'dreun; dreunen
boon weldaad

boost aanjagen, opdrijven; een zetje geven

boot laars; bak; trappen **to boot** op de koop toe

booth kraam

booty buit

booze (sterke) drank

border grens; rand; bloembed; om'zomen; **to – on** grenzen aan

bore boren; ver'velen **to be bored** zich ver'velen

boredom ver'veling

born ge'boren

borough (stads)ge'meente

borrow lenen (van), ont'lenen (aan)

bosom boezem; schoot

boss baas; comman'deren

botany plantkunde

both beide, allebei **– ... and** zo'wel ... als

bother last, drukte; bah!; lastig vallen

bottle fles; inmaken, botelen **to – up** opkroppen

bottom achterste; bodem; onderste; basis

bough (grote) tak

boulder grote kei

bounce stuiten; springen

bound ver'bonden; ver'plicht; sprong; springen; be'grenzen **to be –** moeten; op weg zijn

boundary grens(lijn)

boundless onbe'grensd

bountiful vrijgevig, gul; overvloedig

bout par'tij; peri'ode, vlaag

bow buiging; boeg; boog; strik; strijkstok; buigen

bowels ingewanden

bower pri'eel

bowl schaal, bak; bowlen **to – over** om'vergooien; van (zijn) stuk brengen

bow-legged: he is – hij heeft o-benen

box doos(je); kist(je); loge; oorvijg; boksen

Boxing Day tweede kerstdag

box office lo'ket, kassa

boy jongen

boycott boycot(ten)

boyish jongens(achtig)

bra be'ha

brace klamp; (zich) scherp zetten

bracelet armband

braces bre'tels

bracing op'wekkend

bracket steun; haakje **in –s** tussen haakjes

brag opscheppen

braggart opschepper

braid vlecht(en)

braille braille

brain hersenen

brains hersens, ver'stand

brainwave lumi'neus idee

brainy knap, slim

braise smoren

brake rem(men)

bramble braam(struik)

bran zemelen

branch tak; bijkantoor; fili'aal; afdeling; zich ver'takken

brand merk; brandmerk(en)

brandish (dreigend) zwaaien

brand-new splinternieuw

brandy co'gnac

brass (geel)koper(en) **– band** fan'farekorps

brat snotaap, rotkind

bravado bra'voure

brave moedig; trot'seren

bravery moed

brawl vechtpartij

brawn spieren

bray balken

brazen bru'taal

breach (in)breuk, schending; bres; door'breken

bread brood **slice of – and butter** boterham
breadth breedte; ruimte
break breuk, onder'breking, pauze; (ver)breken **to – down** afbreken; weigeren; vastlopen; over'stuur raken **to – up** stukbreken; zich (or doen) ver'spreiden; eindigen
breakdown de'fect; mis'lukking; instorting
breakers branding
breakfast ont'bijt(en)
breakwater golfbreker
breast borst
breath adem; zuchtje **out of –** buiten adem
breathalyser blaaspijpje
breathe ademen, ademhalen
breathless ademloos, buiten adem
breed ras; voortbrengen, fokken
breeding fokken; goede manieren
breeze bries
breezy winderig; vrolijk
brevity kortheid
brew brouwsel; brouwen; broeien
brewery brouwe'rij
bribe omkoopgeld; omkopen
bribery omkope'rij
brick baksteen, blok **to drop a –** een flater be'gaan
bricklayer metselaar
brickwork metselwerk
bridal bruids-
bride(groom) bruid(egom)
bridesmaid bruidsmeisje
bridge brug; bridge; over'bruggen
bridle teugel, toom; tomen
brief kort; instru'eren
briefcase aktentas
brigade bri'gade
brigand ban'diet
bright hel(der); pienter; hoopvol
brighten oplichten; opvrolijken
brilliance schittering; geniali'teit

brilliant schitterend; bril'jant
brim rand
brimful boordevol
brine pekel; zout water
bring (mee)brengen **to – about** te'weegbrengen **to – back** te'rugbrengen; oproepen **to – on** ver'oorzaken **to – out** doen uitkomen **to – round** bijbrengen; overhalen **to – up** bovenbrengen; grootbrengen; te berde brengen
brink rand
brisk kwiek
bristle borstel(haar); gaan over' eind staan
Britain Groot Brit'tannië, VK, Verenigd Koninkrijk
British Brits
Briton Brit(se)
brittle broos, bros
broach aansteken; ter sprake brengen
broad breed; ruim
broadcast uitzending; uitzenden; ver'spreiden
broaden (zich) ver'breden; ver'ruimen
broad-minded ruimdenkend, tolerant
brocade bro'kaat
broil roosteren
broke blut
broken-hearted diep onge'lukkig
broker makelaar
bronchitis bron'chitis
bronze brons; bronzen
brooch broche
brood kroost, gebroed; tobben, piekeren; broeden
brook beek
broom bezem; brem
broth boui'llon
brothel bor'deel
brother broer, broeder

brotherhood broederschap
brother-in-law zwager
brow voorhoofd; rand
browbeat intimi'deren
brown bruin **– paper** pakpapier
browse grasduinen
bruise (blauwe) plek; kneuzen
bruiser rouwdouwer
brunette bru'nette
brunt volle kracht
brush borstel, kwast, pen'seel; staart; (af)borstelen, (af)vegen **to – past** rakelings gaan langs
brush(wood) kreupelhout
brusque bruusk
Brussels sprouts spruitjes
brutal beestachtig
brutality wreedheid
brute bruut
BSE gekkekoeienziekte (mad cow disease)
bubble (lucht)bel
bucket emmer
buckle gesp; vastgespen; krommen
bud knop; uitbotten
Buddhism boed'dhisme
budding in de dop
budge (zich) ver'roeren
budget be'groting
buff okergeel; po'lijsten
buffalo buffel
buffet buf'fet; stomp(en)
buffoon pi'as
bug beestje
bugle si'gnaalhoorn
build bouw(en) **to – up** opbouwen; be'bouwen
builder aannemer
building ge'bouw
bulb (bloem)bol; gloeilamp
bulge uitpuiling; uitpuilen
bulk massa; grootste deel
bulky lijvig, groot
bull stier; bul

bullet kogel
bulletin bulle'tin
bullion (goud)staven
bullock os
bull's eye roos; schot in de roos; rake opmerking
bully beul, pestkop; intimi'deren
bulwark bolwerk
bumble-bee hommel
bump stoten, botsen (tegen), schokken; buil, bult, hobbel; **to – into** tegen het lijf lopen
bumpy hobbelig
bun luxe broodje
bunch bos(je), tros; op'eenhopen
bundle pak, bos; samenbinden
bungalow bungalow
bungle (ver')knoeien
bunk kooi; kletspraat; er vandoor gaan
bunkbed stapelbed
bunting vlaggen
buoy boei
buoyant: to be – drijven; veerkracht hebben
burden last; laden; drukken
bureau bu'reau
burglar inbreker
burglary inbraak
burial be'grafenis
burly stoer
burn brandwond; (ver')branden; aanbranden
burnish po'lijsten
burrow hol; wroeten
burst barst(en); vlaag; springen
bury be'graven; ver'bergen
bus bus
bush struik; rimboe
business zaak, zaken
businesslike zakelijk
busker straatmuzikant
bust borstbeeld, buste
bustle drukte; druk in de weer zijn

busy (druk) bezig **to be –** het druk hebben
busybody be'moeial
but maar; be'halve
butch (vulg) pot (lesbian); macho, stoer
butcher slager; beul; afslachten
butler hoofdbediende
butt ton; kolf; peukje; schietbaan; stoten
butter boter; smeren
buttercup boterbloem
butterfly vlinder
buttocks billen
button knoop; knopen

buttonhole knoopsgat; aanklampen
buttress beer; steunen
buxom mollig
buy koop; kopen
buyer (in)koper
buzz ge'gons; gonzen
by door; bij; langs; per; volgens
– train met de trein **– night and**
by day 's nachts en over'dag **– and**
large over het alge'meen
by-election tussentijdse ver'kiezing
by-law plaatselijke ver'ordening
bypass ringweg; omloopleiding
by-product nevenprodukt
bystander toeschouwer

C

cab taxi; ca'bine
cabbage kool
cabin hut; ca'bine
cabinet kabi'net, kastje; mi'nisterraad
cable kabel; telegra'feren
caboodle rataplan
cackle kakelen
cacophony tegen'strijdig ge'schetter
cactus cactus
cad ploert
caddie golfjongen
caddy (thee)busje
cadence ca'dans
cadet ca'det
cadge schooieren
café ca'fé(-restaurant)
cage kooi; opsluiten
cajole aftroggelen
cake cake, ge'bak(je); taart koek(en)
calamity ramp
calculate (be')rekenen
calendar ka'lender
calf kalf; kuit
calibre ka'liber
call tele'foontje; roepen; noemen
  to give a – roepen **to pay a –** een

be'zoek afleggen **to be called**
heten **to – off** aflasten **to – on**
be'zoeken; een be'roep doen op
calling roeping
callous onge'voelig
calm kalm(te); be'daren
calumny laster
camel ka'meel
camera fototoestel
camouflage camou'flage; camou'fleren
camp kamp('eren)
campaign veldtocht; cam'pagne
can kan, blik; kunnen
canal ka'naal, gracht
canary ka'narie
cancel schrappen, afzeggen
cancer kanker
candid open('hartig)
candidate kandi'daat
candle kaars
candlestick kaarsenstandaard
candour op'rechtheid
candy kan'dij; kon'fijten **candied**
peel su'kade
cane rotting; riet(en); afranselen

cannibal kanni'baal
cannon ka'non; ge'schut
canny slim
canoe kano
canoodle knuffelen, scharrelen
canopy balda'kijn
cantankerous cha'grijnig
canteen kan'tine
canter (in) korte ga'lop (draven)
canvas (zeil)doek
canvass stemmen werven
canyon diep ra'vijn
cap pet; dop; over'treffen **capped** ge'huld (in)
capable be'kwaam, flink **capable of** in staat tot; vatbaar voor
capacious ruim
capacity inhoud; ver'mogen; hoe'danigheid
cape kaap; cape
caper capri'olen maken
capital hoofdstad; kapi'taal; hoofdletter; kapi'teel; prima
capitalist kapita'list
capitulate capitu'leren
caprice gril
capsize omslaan
captain kapi'tein, ge'zagvoerder, aanvoerder
caption onderschrift
captivate be'toveren
captive ge'vangen(e)
captivity ge'vangenschap
capture ver'overing; ver'overen, ge'vangennemen
car auto
caravan woonwagen, kam'peerwagen; kara'vaan
carbon koolstof; doorslag(papier)
card kaart(je)
cardboard kar'ton
cardigan vest
cardinal kardi'naal; hoofd-
cards kaartspel **to play –** kaarten

care zorg; lust hebben **to take – of** zorgen voor; passen op **I don't – het** kan me niets schelen **to – about** geven om **to – for** (iets) voelen voor
career loopbaan, carri'ère
carefree onbe'zorgd
careful voor'zichtig; zorg'vuldig
careless slordig
caress liefkozing; liefkozen
caretaker conci'ërge
cargo lading, vracht
cargo boat vrachtschip
caricature karika'tuur
carillon klokkenspel
carnage slachting
carnal vleselijk
carnation anjer
carnival carnaval
carol (kerst)lied
carp karper; vitten
carpenter timmerman; timmeren
carriage rijtuig, wa'gon; ver'voer; houding
carrion kadaver
carrot wortel
carry dragen, houden **to – away** meeslepen **to – off** in de wacht slepen; klaarspelen **to – on** doorgaan; uitoefenen **to – out** uitvoeren
cart kar; ver'voeren
cartilage kraakbeen
carton kar'ton
cartoon (spot)prent; tekenfilm
cartridge pa'troon
cartwheel karrenwiel; radslag
carve snijden; beeldhouwen
carving snijwerk
cascade kleine waterval; stortvloed; neerstorten
case koker, koffer, kist; ge'val; zaak **in – voor** het ge'val dat
cash contant geld; (om)wisselen

cash dispenser geldautomaat
cashier kas'sier; cas'seren
cask vat
cast worp; afgietsel; rolverdeling;
  werpen; gieten
cast iron ge'goten ijzer
castle kas'teel
castor rolletje
casual noncha'lant; toe'vallig;
  vluchtig
casualty ongeval **casualties**
  doden en ge'wonden
cat kat
catalogue ca'talogus
catapult katapult
cataract waterval; staar
catastrophe cata'strofe, ramp
catch vangst; valstrik; haak; (op)
  vangen; halen; be'trappen; vatten;
  (blijven) haken; treffen **to – on**
  ingang vinden **to – up** inhalen
categorical cate'gorisch
category catego'rie
cater maaltijden ver'zorgen;
  rekening houden (met)
caterpillar rups
cathedral kathe'draal
catholic katho'liek
cattle vee
cauliflower bloemkool
cause oorzaak, (be'weeg)reden;
  zaak; ver'oorzaken
causeway dam
caustic brandend; bijtend
caution voor'zichtigheid;
  waarschuwen
cautious voor'zichtig
cavalry cavale'rie
cave(rn) grot **to cave in** inzakken
cavity holte
cease ophouden (met)
ceaseless voort'durend
cedar ceder(hout)
cede afstaan

ceiling pla'fond; maximum
celebrate vieren
celebration viering, feest
celebrity be'roemdheid
celery selderij
celestial hemels, hemel-
celibacy celi'baat
cell cello
cellar kelder
cello cel
cellophane cello'faan
cellulose cellu'lose
cement ce'ment
cemetery be'graafplaats
censor censor; censu'reren
censure be'risping; bekriti'seren
census volkstelling
centenary eeuwfeest
centigrade Celsius
central cen'traal, midden-, hoofd-
centralize centrali'seren
centre middelpunt, centrum
  in the – of midden in
century eeuw
cereal graan(pro'duct)
ceremonial ceremoni'eel
ceremony cere'monie,
  formali'teit(en)
certain(ty) zeker(heid)
certificate di'ploma, akte, at'test
certify (plechtig) ver'klaren
chafe schuren
chaff kaf
chagrin ergernis
chain ketting; keten(en); reeks
chair stoel
chairman(ship) voorzitter(schap)
chalice kelk
chalk krijt
challenge uitdaging; uitdagen,
  aanroepen, be'twisten
chamber kamer
champion kampi'oen, voorstander;
  voorstaan

chance kans; toeval; toe'vallig; wagen
chancellor kanse'lier
chandelier kroon(luchter)
change ver'andering, overgang; kleingeld; ver'anderen; (ver) wisselen, ver')ruilen; (zich) ver'kleden; overstappen **to – one's mind** zich be'denken
changeable ver'anderlijk
channel ka'naal; vaargeul, goot; weg
chant (be')zingen; dreunen
chaos chaos
chap kerel; barsten
chapel ka'pel
chaplain (to the forces), (leger)- predi'kant
chapter hoofdstuk; epi'sode
char schroeien, ver'kolen
character ka'rakter; type
characteristic kenmerk(end) (voor)
characterize kenmerken
charcoal houtskool
charge aanval(len); (be')last(en); lading; be'schuldiging; laden; be'schuldigen **to be in – of** de leiding hebben van; be'last zijn met **to (make a) –** rekenen
charitable mens'lievend
charity lief'dadigheid(s-), naastenliefde
charm charme; tovermiddel; be'koren; be'toveren
charming char'mant; aller'aardigst
chart kaart; grafische voorstelling; in kaart brengen
charter recht; handvest; charteren, huren
chase jacht; (na)jagen; drijven
chasm kloof
chassis chassis
chaste kuis
chasten, chastize kas'tijden
chat babbeltje; babbelen

chatline babbellijn
chatter kletsen, ratelen
chatterbox kletskous
cheap goed'koop, waardeloos
cheat valsspeler; be'driegen, valsspelen
check rem; ruit; stuiten; contro'leren **– (mate)** schaak(mat) (zetten) **in –** in toom **to – up** nagaan
cheek wang; brutali'teit
cheekbone jukbeen
cheer juichkreet; (toe)juichen; opmonteren **three cheers** een hoe'raatje; lang leve …
cheerful vrolijk
cheerless troosteloos
cheese kaas
chemical chemisch(e stof); schei'kundig
chemist schei'kundige; dro'gist
chemistry scheikunde
cheque cheque
chequered af'wisselend
cherish koesteren
cherry kers
cherub cheru'bijn
chess: to play – schaken
chess (set) schaakspel
chest borst(kas); kist
chestnut kas'tanje(boom)
chew kauwen
chick kuiken; meisje, grietje
chicken kip
chicken pox waterpokken
chicory witlof
chide be'rispen
chief hoofd(-); voor'naamste
chiefly voor'namelijk
chieftain opperhoofd
child(ren) kind(eren)
childbirth be'valling
childhood kinderjaren
childish kinderachtig, kinderlijk
childlike kinderlijk

chill kou; afkoelen
chill(y) kil; koel
chime klokkenspel, klokslag; luiden
chimney schoorsteen
chin kin
china porse'lein(en)
chink spleet; rinkelen
chip scherf; fiche; stoten, bikken
chiropodist pedi'cure
chirp tjilpen
chisel beitel(en)
chivalrous ridderlijk
chivalry ridderlijkheid
chlorine chloor
chocolate choco'la(de), choco'laatje
choice keus; prima
choir koor
choke (doen) stikken, zich ver'
slikken; ver'stoppen
choose (uit)kiezen, ver'kiezen
chop karbo'nade; (fijn)hakken
choppy woelig
chord ak'koord; snaar
chortle hardop grinniken van pret
chorus koor; re'frein
christen dopen
christening doop(dienst)
Christian christelijk; christen
  Christian name voornaam
Christianity christendom;
  christelijkheid
Christmas kerst
Christmas Day eerste kerstdag
chromium(-plated) (ver')chroom(d)
chronic chronisch
chronical kro'niek; boekstaven
chronological chrono'logisch
chubby mollig
chuck smijten
chuckle ge'grinnik; grinniken (om)
chug puffen
chum maat
chunk klomp, homp
church kerk

Church of England angli'caanse kerk
churchyard kerkhof
churlish lomp
churn karn, melkbus; karnen; woelen
chute glijbaan, glijkoker
cider cider
cigar si'gaar
cigarette siga'ret
cinder sintel
cinema bios'coop
cinnamon ka'neel
cipher cijferschrift; nul
circle cirkel(en); kring; groep;
  om cirkelen
circuit kring(loop); (stroom)-baan
circuitous om'slachtig
circular cirkel'vormig, rond(gaand);
  circu'laire
circulate (laten) circu'leren
circulation circu'latie; bloedsomloop;
  oplaag
circumference omtrek
circumscribe om'schrijven
circumspect om'zichtig
circumstance om'standigheid,
  bij'zonderheid
circus circus
cistern waterreservoir
cite ci'teren; noemen
citizen (staats)burger
city stad(s-)
civic burger-, stads-
civil burgerlijk, burger-; be'leefd
civilian burger
civilization be'schaving
civilize be'schaven
civil servant ambtenaar
clad ge'kleed
claim aanspraak (maken op);
  vordering; (op)eisen; be'weren
clamber klauteren
clammy klam
clamorous luid('ruchtig)
clamour ge'tier; schreeuwen

clamp klamp(en)
clan stam
clang galm; kletteren
clap slag; klap(pen (met)),
  applaudis'seren; slaan
clarify klaren; ophelderen
clarity duidelijkheid
clash botsing; botsen; vloeken
clasp gesp(en); (vast)grijpen
class klas(se); stand; lesuur; plaatsen
classic klas'siek (werk)
classical klas'siek
classify klassifi'ceren
classroom klaslokaal
clatter ge'kletter; kletteren
clause clau'sule, bijzin
claw klauw(en), poot
clay klei
clean schoon(maken), rein(igen);
  zindelijk
cleaner schoonmaker/
  schoonmaakster, werkster
cleanliness zindelijkheid
cleanse zuiveren
clear helder, duidelijk; vrij(maken);
  ophelderen; vrijspreken; ont'ruimen
  to – off maken dat men wegkomt
  to – up ver'duidelijken; opruimen;
  ophelderen
clear-cut scherp om'lijnd
clearing open plek
cleavage scheiding; gleuf (between
  breasts), decolleté
cleave kloven; kleven
cleft kloof; ge'spleten
clemency mildheid
clench ballen; vastklemmen
  clenched teeth tanden op el'kaar
clergy geestelijkheid
clergyman dominee
clerical administra'tief; geestelijk
clerk klerk, grif'fier
clever knap
click klik(ken)

client klant, cliënt
cliff klif
climate kli'maat
climax climax
climb (be')klim(men) **to climb down**
  afklimmen; inbinden
clinch vastklinken; be'klinken,
  be'slechten
cling zich vastklemmen, plakken
clinic kli'niek
clink klink(en)
clip klem(metje); mep; klemmen;
  knippen
clippers schaar, ton'deuse; klippers
clipping (uit)knipsel
cloak (dek)mantel; hullen
cloakroom garde'robe
clock klok
clockwise met de klok mee
clockwork (met) mecha'niek
clod (aard)kluit
clog klomp; ver'stoppen
cloister klooster(gang)
close dicht'bij; scherp; nauw; in'tiem;
  ingesloten ruimte; einde; (af)sluiten
  to – down (*or* up) sluiten
closed-circuit: – television
  videobewaking
close-fisted gierig
closet kabi'net; opsluiten
clot kluit; klonteren, stollen
cloth stof; kleed, doek
clothe kleden
clothes kleren
clothesline drooglijn
clothes-peg knijper
clothing kleding
cloud wolk; ver'troebelen
  to – over be'trekken
cloudy be'wolkt; troebel
clout invloed, macht; mep, klap
clove kruidnagel
clover klaver
clown clown

club knots; club, socië'tiet; klaver; knuppelen
cluck klokken
clue aanwijzing, sleutel
clump groep, brok; klossen
clumsy on'handig
cluster tros, bos, groep; zich scharen
clutch klauw; koppeling; (vast)pakken
clutter warboel; volproppen
coach koets; spoorwagon; (reis)bus; trainer, coach; trainen, coachen
coagulate stremmen, stollen
coal kolen(-); steenkool

cocoa ca'cao
coconut kokosnoot
cod kabel'jauw
code code(stelsel); wet
coercion dwang
coffee koffie
coffin doodkist
cog tandrad
cogent over'tuigend
cogitate nadenken
coherent samenhangend, logisch
coil tros, spi'raal; oprollen
coin munt(stuk); smeden
coincide samenvallen

Insight

Coffee or **koffie** is extremely popular in the Netherlands. The Dutch drink an average of well over **drie kopjes koffie per dag** *three cups of coffee a day*. However, when you come across **een coffeeshop** in the Netherlands, don't expect to find just coffee on the menu: a Dutch **coffeeshop** is a café where customers are tolerated by the authorities to buy and smoke marijuana (**marihuana, hasj, weed, wiet**) in small quantities.

coalesce samensmelten
coalition coa'litie
coarse grof
coast kust; glijden, freewheelen
coat jas, mantel; vel; (verf)laag; bedekken **– of arms** wapen **– hanger** kleerhanger
co-author medeauteur
coax vleiend be'praten
cobble(-stone) keisteen
cobbler schoenlapper
cobweb spinnenweb
cock haan; de haan spannen van; scheefhouden
cock-eyed scheef
cockpit cockpit
cocktail cocktail
cocky bru'taal

coincidence samenloop van om'standigheden
coke cokes, coke
colander ver'giet
cold koud; koel; ver'koudheid **to have a –** ver'kouden zijn
collaborate samenwerken
collapse in'storting; in el'kaar zakken
collapsible op'vouwbaar
collar kraag, boord, halsband
colleague col'lega
collect (zich) ver'zamelen
collection ver'zameling, col'lecte; buslichting
collector ver'zamelaar
college college, (hoge')school
collide botsen
colliery kolenmijn

collision botsing, aanvaring
colon dubbele punt
colonel kolo'nel
colonial koloni'aal
colonize koloni'seren
colonnade zuilengang
colony ko'lonie
colossal reus'achtig
colour kleur(en), verf
colourful kleurrijk
colt (hengst)veulen
column zuil; ko'lom
coma coma
comb kam(men); afzoeken
combat strijd; be'strijden
combination combi'natie
combine syndi'caat; com'bine;
  combi'neren
combustion ver'branding
come komen, meegaan **to – about**
  ge'beuren **to – across** overkomen;
  tegenkomen **to – round** aanlopen;
  (bij)draaien; bijkomen **to – in**
  binnenkomen; mode worden **to –**
  off afkomen; doorgaan, lukken
comedian ko'miek, komedi'ant
comedy blijspel
comely be'vallig
comet ko'meet
comfort troost(en); ge'mak, welstand
comfortable be'hagelijk **to be –**
  ge'makkelijk zitten (*or* liggen)
comfortably off in goede doen
comic komisch; (kinder)krantje
coming (op)komend; komst
comma komma
command be'vel(en); com'mando
  (voeren); be'schikking; be'schikken
  over; be'strijken **commanding**
  officer comman'dant
commandeer (op)vorderen
commander be'velhebber; kapi'
  tein-luitenant
commandment ge'bod

commemorate her'denken
commence be'ginnen
commend prijzen; aanbevelen
commendable prijzens'waardig
comment kritiek, aantekening;
  becommentariëren
commentary commen'taar
commentator ver'slaggever
commerce handel(sverkeer)
commercial commer'cieel, handels-
commiserate sympathi'seren
commission opdracht (geven);
  (offi'ciers) aanstelling; pro'visie;
  machtigen; aanstellen; in dienst
  stellen
commissioner ge'volmachtigde,
  (hoofd)commis'saris
commit plegen, be'gaan;
  toevertrouwen **to – oneself**
  zich ver'binden
commitment ver'plichting
committee comi'té, be'stuur
  com'missie
commodious ruim
commodity ge'bruiksartikel
common ge'meen('schappelijk),
  ge'woon, algemeen **– sense**
  ge'zond ver'stand **in –** ge'meen
commonplace alle'daags;
  ge'meenplaats
commonwealth gemene'best
commotion opschudding
communal gemeen'schappelijk
communicate ver'binding hebben,
  zich in ver'binding stellen;
  mededelen
communication mededeling;
  communicatie
communicative mede'deelzaam
communion gemeenschap;
  communie, Avondmaal
communism commu'nisme
community ge'meenschap;
  broederschap

compact com'pact; over'eenkomst
companion metgezel
companionable ge'zellig
companionship ge'zelschap,
  vriendschap
company gezelschap; bezoek;
  onder'neming, firma, be'drijf
comparable te verge'lijken
comparative be'trekkelijk,
  verge'lijkend
compare (te) verge'lijken (zijn)
comparison verge'lijking
compartment afdeling; cou'pé
compass kom'pas; passer; vatten
compassion medelijden
compassionate mee'warig
compatriot landgenoot
compel (af)dwingen
compensate for schadeloos stellen
  voor, ver'goeden; opwegen tegen
compensation ver'goeding,
  compen'satie
compete wedijveren, me(d)
  edingen (naar)
competence be'voegdheid,
  be'kwaamheid
competent be'kwaam, be'voegd
competition wedstrijd; concur'rentie
competitive verge'lijkend
competitor deelnemer, concur'rent
compile samenstellen
complacent gauw te'vreden
complain klagen
complaint (aan)klacht; kwaal
complement aanvulling;
  be'manning
complete vol'ledig, vol'tallig,
  vol'slagen; vol'tooien;
  be'sluiten, aanvullen
complex com'plex
complexion gelaatskleur, teint
compliance mee'gaandheid;
  inwilliging
complicate compli'ceren

complicated inge'wikkeld
complication compli'catie
complicity mede'plichtigheid
compliment compli'ment('eren)
complimentary complimen'teus;
  pre'sent-, vrij-
comply with vol'doen aan
component be'standdeel;
  samenstellend
compose samenstellen,
  compo'neren **to be composed of**
  be'staan uit **to – oneself** be'daren
composer compo'nist
composite samengesteld
composition samenstelling;
  compo'sitie; opstel
composure zelfbeheersing
compound samengesteld;
  samenstelling, ver'binding; erf;
  (ver')mengen
comprehend (om')vatten
comprehension be'grip
comprehensive veelom'vattend
compress kom'pres: samenpersen,
  compri'meren
comprise be'vatten
compromise compro'mis; tot een
  schikking komen; compromit'teren
compulsion dwang
compulsory ver'plicht
compunction scru'pules
compute be'rekenen
computer com'puter
comrade kame'raad
concave hol
conceal ver'bergen
concede toegeven, toestaan
conceit ver'waandheid;
  spits'vondigheid
conceited ver'waand
conceivable denkbaar
conceive zich een voorstelling
  maken van; be'vrucht worden
concentrate (zich) concen'treren

concentric con'centrisch
concept be'grip
conception voorstelling, opvatting;
  be'vruchting
concern zaak, be'lang; be'zorgdheid;
  onder'neming; aangaan **to be**
  concerned be'lang hebben bij;
  be'trokken zijn bij; zich bezighouden
  met; be'zorgd zijn over **as far as**
  I'm concerned wat mij be'treft
concerning be'treffende
concert(o) con'cert
concerted ge'zamenlijk
concession con'cessie
conciliate gunstig stemmen
concise be'knopt
conclude (be')sluiten; opmaken
conclusion be'sluit, slot;
  ge'volgtrekking
conclusive af'doend, beslissend
concoct brouwen; ver'zinnen
concord eendracht
concrete be'ton(nen); con'creet
concubine concubine
concur het eens zijn; bijdragen
concurrence instemming;
  samenwerking
concurrent gelijk'tijdig
concussion (hersen)schudding
condemn ver'oordelen, afkeuren
condensation conden'satie
condense conden'seren;
  samenvatten
condescend zich ver'waardigen
condescending neer'buigend
condition voorwaarde;
  con'ditie, staat, toestand
  (weather) conditions (weers)-
  om'standigheden
condolence deelneming
condone ver'goelijken
conducive be'vorderlijk
conduct ge'drag(en); be'handeling;
  (ge')leiden; diri'geren

conductor (ge')leider; diri'gent;
  conduc'teur
cone kegel; (denne)appel
confectionery suikergoed
confederate mede'plichtige;
  ver'bonden
confederation ver'bond
confer ver'lenen (aan);
  be'raadslagen
conference confe'rentie
confess be'kennen; be'lijden;
  biechten
confession be'kentenis; biecht
confidant(e) ver'trouweling(e)
confide (in) in ver'trouwen nemen
confide (to) toevertrouwen
confidence ver'trouwen
confident vol ('zelf)ver'trouwen;
  over'tuigd
confidential ver'trouwelijk
confine grens; be'perken
confinement be'valling;
  ge'vangenschap
confirm be'vestigen; be'krachtigen;
  vormen
confirmed vaststaand; chronisch,
  ver'stokt
confiscate ver'beurd ver'klaren
conflagration vlammenzee
conflict con'flict; in strijd zijn
conflicting (tegen')strijdig
conform zich schikken (naar);
  over'eenkomen
confound in de war brengen;
  ver'vloeken
confront confron'teren **to be**
  confronted by komen te staan
  tegen'over; zich ge'plaatst zien in
confuse ver'warren
confusion ver'warring
confute weer'leggen
congeal stollen
congenial prettig, sympa'thiek
congenital (aan)ge'boren

congest (zich) ophopen
conglomeration conglome'raat
congratulate ge'lukwensen
congratulation ge'lukwens
congregate (zich) ver'zamelen
congregation ge'meente;
  verzameling
congress con'gres
conical kegelvormig
coniferous kegeldragend
conjecture gissing
conjugate ver'voegen
conjunction voegwoord **in – with**
  samen met
conjure goochelen; be'zweren
  to – up oproepen
conjurer goochelaar
connect (aan el'kaar) ver'binden; in
  ver'band brengen; aansluiten (op)
connection ver'binding; ver'band;
  re'latie
connive at door de vingers
  zien; **– (with)** in ge'heime
  ver'standhouding staan (met)
connoisseur fijnproever, kenner
connote (tege'lijk) be'tekenen
conquer ver'overen, over'winnen;
  meester worden
conscience ge'weten
conscientious plichtsgetrouw
conscious (zich) be'wust (zijn);
  bij kennis
consciousness be'wustzijn
conscript dienst'plichtig(e);
  oproepen, vorderen
conscription con'scriptie
consecrate (in)wijden
consecutive op'eenvolgend,
  samenhangend
consent toestemming, instemming;
  toe(or in)stemmen
consequence ge'volg **in –**
  dientenge'volge **of –** be'langrijk
consequent daaruit voortvloeiend

conservation in'standhouding,
  be'houd
conservative conserva'tief
conservatory serre
conserve op peil houden;
  conser'veren
consider over'wegen; beschouwen
  als, in aanmerking nemen, rekening
  houden met; menen **all things**
  considered alles welbe'schouwd
considerable aan'zienlijk
considerate at'tent
consideration over'weging; factor;
  conside'ratie; ver'goeding
considered welover'wogen; ge'acht
considering ge'zien; (alles)
  welbe'schouwd
consign depo'neren; overleveren,
  toevertrouwen
consignment zending
consist (of) be'staan (uit)
consistency consis'tentie
consistent conse'quent;
  op één lijn met
consolation troost
consolidate ver'sterken;
  consoli'deren
consonant medeklinker
consort metgezel, partner **to – with**
  omgaan met
conspicuous in het oog lopend;
  treffend
conspiracy samenzwering
conspirator samenzweerder
conspire samenzweren
constable po'litieagent
constancy stand'vastigheid; trouw
constant vast; voort'durend; trouw;
  con'stante
constellation sterrenbeeld
consternation ont'steltenis
constipation consti'patie
constituency kiesdistrict
constituent be'standdeel; kiezer

constitute vormen; aanstellen
constitution ge'stel; samenstelling; grondwet
constitutional aangeboren, voor het ge'stel; constitutio'neel
constrain be'dwingen
constraint (be')dwang; ge'dwongenheid
constrict be'klemmen; binden; samentrekken
construct (op)bouwen
construction (aan)bouw, con'structie; uitleg
constructive opbouwend
construe ver'klaren, constru'eren
consul(ate) consul('aat)
consult raadplegen
consultation raadpleging, con'sult; be'raadslaging
consume ver'bruiken, ver'orberen; ver'teren, ver'nietigen
consummate vol'maakt: in ver'vulling doen gaan
consumption ver'bruik, con'sumptie; (ver)tering
contact con'tact; zich in ver'binding stellen met
contagious be'smettelijk; aan'stekelijk
contain be'vatten; inhouden
container blik, doos
contaminate veront'reinigen
contemplate (over')peinzen; be'schouwen; van plan zijn
contemplation ge'peins, over'weging; be'spiegeling
contemporary van de'zelfde tijd, hedendaags; tijdgenoot
contempt ver'achting
contemptible ver'achtelijk
contemptuous minachtend
contend be'togen **to contend with** kampen met, aankunnen
content(s) inhoud; ge'halte

content(ed) te'vreden
contention twist; be'wering
contentment te'vredenheid
contest (wed)strijd; be'twisten
contestant mededinger, deelnemer
context ver'band
continent vaste'land, werelddeel
continental continen'taal
contingency eventuali'teit
contingent af'hankelijk, eventu'eel; contin'gent; situ'atie
continual(ly) voort'durend, her'haald(elijk)
continuance voortzetting
continuation voortzetting, ver'volg
continue voortgaan (met); voortzetten
continuity samenhang; continuï'teit
continuous on'afgebroken, door'lopend
contort (ver')draaien
contour con'tour
contraband contrabande
contract con'tract (aangaan); (zich) samentrekken; aannemen, oplopen
contraction inkrimping, samentrekking
contractor aannemer
contradict tegenspreken, ont'kennen
contradiction tegenspraak, tegen'strijdigheid
contradictory (tegen')strijdig, weer'spannig
contraption geval, ding, apparaat
contrary tegengesteld(e), tegen-; ba'lorig **– to** tegen … in **on the –** in'tegendeel
contrast tegenstelling; tegenover el'kaar stellen, een con'trast vormen
contravene in strijd zijn met
contribute bijdragen
contribution bijdrage
contributory secun'dair, zij-
contrition diep be'rouw

contrivance apparaat; handigheid
contrive be'ramen; ervoor zorgen
contrived ge'maakt, gefor'ceerd
control be'heer(sing); con'trole; stuurinrichting; in be'dwang houden, be'heersen, be'heren, regelen
controversial controver'sieel, om'streden
controversy ge'schil; on'enigheid
convalescence her'stel
convene bij'eenroepen, bij'eenkomen
convenience ge'rief(elijkheid), ge'mak
convenient ge'schikt, ge'riefelijk
convent nonnenklooster; zusterschool
convention con'ventie; samenkomst; over'eenkomst
conventional conventio'neel
converge conver'geren; zich concen'treren
conversant ver'trouwd
conversation ge'sprek
converse omgekeerd(e); conver'seren
conversion omzetting; be'kering
convert be'keerling; omzetten, ver'anderen; be'keren
convex bol
convey ver'voeren, overdragen; betekenen, overbrengen
conveyance ver'voer(middel); overdracht; overbrengen
convict dwangarbeider; schuldig ver'klaren
conviction over'tuiging; schuldigverklaring
convince over'tuigen
convivial feestelijk
convoy kon'vooi
convulse (doen) schudden; samentrekken; stuiptrekken

coo kirren
cook kok('kin); koken; knoeien met
cooker for'nuis
cookery koken; kook-
cooking koken, keuken
cool koel(te); kalm, bru'taal; ver'koelen, afkoelen
coop hok; opsluiten
cooperate samenwerken
cooperative be'hulpzaam; coöpera'tief
coordinate coördi'neren
cope klaarspelen **to — (with it)** het aankunnen
copious ruim
copper (rood)koper(en); kopergeld; smeris
copse kreupelbosje
copy ko'pie; exem'plaar; namaken, nadoen **to — out** overschrijven
copyright auteursrecht
coquetry kokette'rie
coral ko'raal; ko'ralen
cord koord
cordial hartelijk; limo'nadesiroop
corduroy ribfluweel
core klokhuis; kern
cork kurk(en)
corkscrew kurkentrekker
corn koren; likdoorn
corner hoek; in het nauw drijven
cornflour mai'zena
coronation kroning
coroner magi'straat bij een lijkschouwing
coronet kroontje
corporal korpo'raal; lijf-
corporate collectief; bedrijfs-, ondernemings- **— identity** bedrijfsidentiteit
corporation corpo'ratie, lichaam (legal body); onder'neming; ge'meenteraad
corps korps

corpse lijk
corpulent zwaar'lijvig
correct juist, goed, cor'rect;
corri'geren
correction cor'rectie
corrective ver'beterend; correc'tief
correspond over'eenkomen;
correspon'deren
correspondence correspon'dentie;
over'eenkomst
correspondent correspon'dent
corresponding overeen'komstig
corridor gang
corroborate be'vestigen
corrode aantasten, ver'roesten
corrosion cor'rosie, roest
corrugated golf-
corrupt cor'rupt, ver'dorven;
be'derven
corruption cor'ruptie, ver'derf
corset(s) kor'set
cosmetic kos'metisch;
schoonheidsmiddel
cosmonaut kosmo'naut
cosmopolitan kosmopo'litisch
cost prijs, kosten
costly duur, kostbaar
costume kos'tuum, klederdracht
cosy knus; muts
cot kinderbedje
cottage huisje
cottage cheese hüttenkäse
cotton ka'toen(en), garen; snappen
cotton wool watten
couch (rust)bank; stellen
cough hoest(en)
council raad
counsel raad(geven), be'raadslaging;
advo'caat
count tel(ling); graaf; (mee)
tellen; rekenen **to – out** uittellen;
uitschakelen
countenance ge'laat(suitdrukking);
sanctio'neren

counter toonbank; balie, lo'ket; fiche,
teller; tegen ... in; be'antwoorden
counter- tegen-
counteract neutrali'seren,
tegenwerken
counterbalance tegenwicht;
opwegen tegen
counterfeit nagemaakt; namaken
counterfoil strook
counterpart tegenhanger
countersign medeondertekenen
countess gra'vin
countless talloos
country (platte')land, streek;
landelijk **in the –** buiten
countryman landgenoot; buitenman
countryside landschap
county graafschap
couple paar, stel; koppelen;
combi'neren
coupon bon, cou'pon
courage(ous) moed(ig)
courier koe'rier
course (be')loop, koers, richting;
gang; renbaan; cursus; ge'dragslijn
in due – te zijner tijd **in the – of**
in de loop van **of – na'tuurlijk
court hof(houding), (binnen)plaats;
rechtbank, rechtszaal; baan;
het hof maken; zoeken
courteous hoffelijk
courtesy hoffelijkheid; gunst
courtier hoveling
court martial (voor de) krijgsraad
(brengen)
courtyard binnenplaats
cousin neef, nicht
cove inham
covenant ver'bond; con'tract
cover deksel; (buiten)band; dekking;
(be')dekken; ver'bergen; afleggen;
onder vuur hebben; ver'slaan
covert heimelijk; schuilplaats
covet be'geren

cow koe; intimi'deren
coward lafaard
cowardice lafheid
cower in'eenkrimpen
cowhide rundleer
coxswain stuurman
coy schuchter, koket
crab krab
crack barst(en), kier; klap(pen); krieken; prima; kraken; tappen (jokes); overslaan **to – up** be'zwijken; ophemelen
cracker knalbonbon voetzoeker; cracker
crackle knappen, kraken
cradle wieg; bakermat
craft ambacht, kunst'vaardigheid; sluwheid; vaartuig(en)
craftsman(ship) vakman(schap)
crafty listig, sluw
crag steile rots(punt)
cram (vol)proppen, schrokken; (in)pompen
cramp kram(p); opsluiten, be'krimpen; be'lemmeren
crane kraan(vogel); uitrekken
crank slinger; zonderling; aanslingeren
crash klap, slag; botsing, neerstorting; in('een)storten, neerstorten; over de kop gaan
crass grof
crate krat
crater krater
crave hunkeren; smeken
craving be'geerte
crawl slakkengang; kruipen; wemelen
crayon kleurpotlood; kleuren
craze rage
crazy gek; fanta'sie-
creak kraken
cream (slag)room, crème; puik; afromen
creamy romig

crease vouw(en); kreuken
create scheppen; te'weegbrengen
creation schepping; cre'atie
creative scheppend
creature schepsel
credentials ge'loofs (or intro'ductie) brieven
credible geloof'waardig
credit kre'diet, te'goed, batig saldo; ge'loof, eer; credi'teren; ge'loven; toeschrijven
creditor schuldeiser
credulous lichtge'lovig
creed ge'loofsbelijdenis
creek kreek
creep kruipen, sluipen
creeper klimplant
cremate cre'meren
crepe crêpe
crescent wassende maan; ge'bogen straat
cress sterrekers
crest kuif, pluim; hemelteken; top
crestfallen ter'neergeslagen
crevice scheur
crew be'manning, ploeg; troep
crib kribbe; spiekbriefje; spieken
crick kramp
cricket cricket; krekel
crime misdaad, misdrijf
criminal mis'dadig, straf-; misdadiger
crimson karmo'zijn(rood)
cringe in'eenkrimpen, kruipen
crinkle kronkel(en)
cripple ge'brekkige; ver'minken; ont'wrichten, ver'lammen
crisis crisis
crisp bros; scherp
criss-cross kriskras
criterion criterium
critic criticus, recensent
critical kritisch; kri'tiek
criticism kri'tiek

criticize (be)kriti'seren
croak ge'kwaak; kwaken, krassen
crochet haken
crock aarden pot; wrak
crockery ser'viesgoed
crocodile kroko'dil
crocus krokus
crony makker, gabber
crook staf; oplichter; krommen
crooked scheef, krom; vals
crop oogst, ge'was; krop; zweep;
  afvreten; kortknippen
croquet croquet
croquette kroket
cross kruis(ing); dwars-; boos;
  (el'kaar) kruisen; tegenwerken
  to – oneself een kruis slaan
  to – out doorhalen **to – (over)**
  oversteken **it crossed my mind** het
  schoot me door het hoofd
cross-country dwars door het land
cross-examination kruisverhoor
cross-eyed scheel
crossing kruispunt; overtocht;
  oversteekplaats
cross purposes: at – langs
  el'kaar heen
crossroads kruispunt; tweesprong
cross-section (dwars)doorsnee
crosswise kruiselings
crotchet kwartnoot
crouch in el'kaar duiken
croup kroep
crow kraai(en)
crowbar koevoet
crowd menigte; (zich) (ver')dringen
crowded vol, druk
crown kroon, krans; kruin, bol; kronen
  (tot); be'kronen
crucial cruciaal
crucible smeltkroes
crucifix kruisbeeld
crucifixion kruisiging
crucify kruisigen

crude ruw; grof
cruel(ty) wreed(heid)
cruise cruise, (zee)reis; kruisen
cruise missile kruisraket
cruiser kruiser
crumb kruimel(en)
crumble (ver')kruimelen; afbrokkelen
crumple ver'frommelen
crunch (fijn)kauwen, knarsen
crusade kruistocht; cam'pagne
crush ge'drang; (samen)persen,
  ver'brijzelen; ver'pletteren
crust (met een) korst (be'dekken)
crutch kruk; kruis; vork
crux kern
cry kreet; leus; huilen; schreeuwen,
  roepen
crying ge'huil; schreeuwend
crypt crypt
cryptic ge'heim ('zinnig)
crystal kris'tal(len)
crystallize kristalli'seren
cub welp, jong
cube kubus, blokje; derde'macht
cubic kubusvormig; ku'biek, inhouds-;
  derde'machts-
cuckoo koekoek; sul
cucumber kom'kommer
cuddle pakkerd; knuffelen
cudgel knuppel(en)
cue signaal, wachtwoord; keu
cuff man'chet; oorveeg (geven)
cufflink man'chetknoop
culinary keuken-, kook-
cull plukken; uitzoeken
culminate culmi'neren
culpable be'rispelijk
culprit schuldige
cult cultus
cultivate be(or ver)'bouwen;
  aankweken, ont'wikkelen
cultural cultu'reel
culture cul'tuur, be'schaving;
  aankweking; teelt

cultured be'schaafd; ge'kweekt
cumbersome on'handelbaar
cumulative cumula'tief
cunning listig(heid)
cup kopje; kelk; hol maken
cupboard kast
cupid cupido(otje)
curb be'teugelen
curdle schiften
cure ge'nezing, ge'neesmiddel,
 kuur; ge'nezen; zouten en roken
curfew avondklok; spertijd
curio curiosi'teit
curiosity nieuws'gierigheid;
 curiosi'teit
curious nieuws'gierig; vreemd,
 curi'eus
curl krul(len)
currant krent, bes
currency be'taalmiddel;
 ruchtbaarheid
current stroom; stroming; cou'rant,
 actu'eel; in omloop, heersend
curriculum leerplan
curry kerrie(schotel); met kerrie
 kruiden
curse ver'vloeking, vloek(en),
 ver'vloeken
cursory vluchtig
curt bruusk, kort'af
curtail ver'korten; be'knotten
curtain gor'dijn, doek
curtsy révé'rence (maken)
curve bocht, kromming, ronding;
 (zich) buigen

cushion kussen; bil'jartband
custard custard, vla
custody zorg, be'waring; hechtenis
custom ge'woonte, (oud)
 ge'bruik; klan'dizie **customs**
 dou'ane(rechten)
customary ge'bruikelijk
customer klant
cut snee, knip; ver'mindering;
 snit; (door)snijden, (af)knippen;
 slijpen; graven; banen; (door')
 klieven; ver'minderen; ne'geren;
 ver'zuimen; maaien **to – across**
 oversteken **to – down** vellen;
 ver'minderen **to – in** snijden; in
 de rede vallen **to – off** afsnijden;
 afsluiten, iso'leren; ver'breken **to –
 out** (uit)knippen, ver'wijderen;
 afslaan; schrappen, uitscheiden met
 to – up kleinsnijden, ver'snipperen;
 erg aangrijpen; opspelen
cuticle nagelriem
cutlery be'stek
cutting scherp; holle weg;
 uitknipsel; stek
cycle kringloop, cyclus; fietsen
cyclist fietser
cyclone cy'cloon
cygnet jonge zwaan
cylinder ci'linder
cymbal cim'baal
cynic cynicus
cynical cynisch
cyst cyste
Czech Tsjech(isch)

D

dab tik, likje; deppen, aantippen
dabble: to ~ in (wat) rommelen in
dachshund tekel
dad(dy) papa, vader
daffodil (gele) nar'cis

daft dwaas
dagger dolk
daily dagelijks, dag-
dainty sierlijk, fijn, tenger;
 kies'keurig; lekker'nij

dairy melkinrichting, melker'ij:
  melk-, zuivel-
daisy made'liefje, mar'griet
dale dal
dally talmen; spelen
dam dam; afdammen
damage schade(n); be'schadigen
damages schadevergoeding
damask da'mast(en)
dame vrouwe

daring durf; ge'durfd
dark donker; duister
darken donker maken (*or* worden)
darkness donker
darling lieveling; liefste
darn stop(pen); ver'dikkeme!
dart pijl(tje); schieten
dash streepje; scheutje, snuifje; run;
  zwier; slaan; hollen; ver'nietigen
dastardly laf'hartig

Insight

The way dates are written in Dutch differs somewhat from English. The names of the days of the week and the months of the year are not written with a capital letter: **maandag, donderdag, januari, september,** etc. When writing out a date in full, such as *10th January 2010*, the day of the month is simply indicated with a cardinal number 10, and the month and year follow without commas: **10 januari 2010.** When speaking the ordinal number **tiende** *tenth* can be used, but this has to be preceded by the definite article **de: de tiende januari 2010.**

damn donder; ver'domme!; (ver')
  doemen
damnable ver'vloekt
damp vochtig(heid); be'vochtigen;
  doen dempen be'koelen
damson pruim
dance dans(partij), bal; dansen
dandelion paardenbloem
dandruff roos
dandy fat; reuze
danger(ous) ge'vaar(lijk)
dangle bengelen
Danish Deens
dank muf en vochtig
dapper kwiek
dappled be'vlekt
dare (aan)durven; tarten
daredevil waaghals

data ge'gevens
date datum, jaartal; afspraak;
  dadel(palm); da'teren, ver'ouderen
  out of – uit de tijd; ver'lopen **to** –
  tot op heden **up to** – tot dusver;
  op de hoogte; mo'dern
daub (be')smeren; kladschilderen
daughter dochter
daughter-in-law schoondochter
daunt afschrikken
dauntless onver'vaard
dawdle treuzelen
dawn dageraad; aanbreken;
  doordringen tot
day dag; tijd **all** – de hele dag
daybreak het aanbreken van
  de dag
daycare dagopvang

daydream mijmeren, dromen
daylight daglicht
daytime: in the – over'dag
daze ver'bijstering; ver'doven, ver'bijsteren
dazzle ver'blinden
dead dood(s), levenloos, ge'voelloos, abso'luut; pal; dode(n); holst (of the night) **– beat** doodop
deaden dempen, ver'doven
deadlock im'passe
deadly dodelijk; dood(s)-, ver'schrik'elijk
deaf doof
deafen ver'doven
deafening oorver'dovend
deal trans'actie, be'handeling; handelen; geven; toebrengen
a good (or great deal) nogal (or heel) veel **to – out** uitdelen
to – with te doen hebben met, be'handelen, helpen; afrekenen met
dealer handelaar; gever
dealings zaken, omgang
dean deken
dear lief, dierbaar; duur; ach!
dearly dolgraag, innig; duur
dearth schaarste, ge'brek
death dood; sterfgeval **to (bleed) to –** dood(bloeden)
death duties suc'cessierechten
debar uitsluiten, be'letten
debase ver'lagen; ver'nederen
debatable be'twistbaar
debate de'bat('teren (over)); be'twisten
debauched liederlijk
debauchery los'bandigheid
debility ge'brek
debit debet(saldo); debi'teren
debris puin, rommel
debt(or) schuld(enaar)
to be in – schuld(en) hebben
début de'buut

decade de'cennium
decadence deca'dentie
decamp opbreken; zijn biezen pakken
decant overgieten
decanter ka'raf
decapitate ont'hoofden
decay ver'rotting; (in) ver'val (raken); (doen) ver'rotten
decease over'lijden
deceased over'leden(e)
deceit be'drog
deceitful vals
deceive be'driegen
decency fat'soen
decennial tienjaarlijks
decent net(jes), aardig; be'hoorlijk
deception be'drog
deceptive be'drieglijk
decide (doen) be'sluiten; be'slissen
decided be'slist; vastbesloten
deciduous tree loofboom
decimal decimaal
decipher ont'cijferen
decision be'slissing, be'sluit; be'slistheid
decisive be'slissend; be'slist
deck dek; tooien
deckchair ligstoel
declaim decla'meren
declaration ver'klaring; aangifte
declare ver'klaren, be'kendmaken; aangeven
decline daling, achter'uitgang; be'danken (voor); afdalen, achter'uitgaan; ver'buigen
decompose ont'binden
decorate ver'sieren; schilderen (en be'hangen); deco'reren
decoration ver'siering; deco'ratie
decorative decora'tief
decorous correct, fatsoenlijk
decorum de'corum
decoy lok(aas); in de val lokken

decrease afname; ver'minderen
decree de'creet; decre'teren
decrepit af'tands
decry afkeuren,
  in diskrediet brengen
dedicate wijden; opdragen
dedication (toe)wijding; opdracht
deduce afleiden
deduct aftrekken
deduction aftrek, korting;
  ge'volgtrekking
deed daad, akte
deem achten
deep diep
deepen dieper worden (*or* maken)
deer hert(en)
deface ont'sieren
defamatory lasterlijk
defame be'lasteren
default ver'zuim; in ge'breke blijven
defeat nederlaag; ver'slaan;
  ver'ijdelen
defect ge'brek
defection af'valligheid
defective ge'brekkig, de'fect
defence ver'dediging
defenceless weerloos
defend ver'dedigen
defendant ge'daagde
defensive ver'dedigend
defer uitstellen; zich onder'
  werpen aan
deference eerbied
defiance tarting **in** – **of** … …
  ten spijt
defiant uit'dagend
deficiency te'kort
deficient ontoe'reikend
deficit te'kort
defile bergengte; defi'leren;
  be'vuilen, be'zoedelen
define defini'ëren
definite be'paald, defini'tief, vast
definition om'schrijving; scherpte

deflate laten leeglopen; de'flatie
  tot stand brengen van
deflect ombuigen
deform mis'vormen
deformed mis'maakt
defraud bedriegen
defray be'strijden
deft vaardig
defunct over'leden; ver'ouderd
defy trot'seren
degenerate ont'aard(en)
degradation degra'datie
degrade degra'deren; ver'nederen
degree graad, mate, rang
dehydrate (uit-, ver-)drogen
deify ver'goddelijken
deign zich ver'waardigen
deity godheid
dejected neer'slachtig
delay ver'traging, uitstel(len);
  ver'tragen
delectable ge'notvol
delegate afgevaardigde;
  afvaardigen, overdragen
delegation dele'gatie
delete doorhalen, de'leten
deli delica'tessenwinkel
deliberate op'zettelijk,
  weloverwogen, be'dachtzaam;
  over'wegen, be'raadslagen
delicacy fijnheid; hachelijkheid;
  zwak ge'stel; delica'tesse
delicate fijn(ge'voelig); teer
delicious heerlijk
delight ge'not, ver'rukking;
  ver'rukken, ge'noegen be'zorgen
delightful ver'rukkelijk, enig
delineation tekening, omtrek
delinquent schuldig(e)
delirious aan het ijlen; waan'zinnig
deliver be'zorgen, overleveren;
  geven; ver'lossen
delivery be'zorging, over'handiging;
  voordracht; ver'lossing

delude mis'leiden, be'goochelen
deluge wolkbreuk, (stort)vloed; over'stromen, over'stelpen
delusion be'drog, waan
de luxe luxe
delve delven; vorsen
demagogue dema'goog
demand vraag, aanspraak; eisen, vragen
demarcation afbakening
demeanour optreden
demented gek, gestoord; dement
demigod halfgod
demise over'lijden; overdracht
demobilize demobili'seren
democracy democra'tie
democratic demo'cratisch
demolish afbreken
demolition afbraak
demon boze geest, duivel
demonic de'monisch
demonstrate demon'streren, aantonen
demonstration demon'stratie, be'wijs, ver'toon
demonstrative demonstra'tief; aan'wijzend
demoralize demorali'seren
demur pro'test('eren)
demure zedig; preuts
den hol; hok
denial ont'kenning, ver'loochening
Denmark Denemarken
denomination be'naming; ge'loofsrichting
denote duiden op, aanduiden
denouement ont'knoping
denounce openlijk ver'oordelen, aanbrengen
dense dicht; dom
density dichtheid; domheid
dent (in)deuk(en)
dental tand-
dentist tandarts

dentures kunstgebit
deny ont'kennen, ver'loochenen; ont'houden
depart ver'trekken
departed over'ledene
department afdeling
departure ver'trek; afwijking
depend (on) af'hankelijk zijn (van), ver'trouwen (op), afhangen (van)
dependable be'trouwbaar
dependant af'hankelijk persoon
dependent af'hankelijk
depict afbeelden
deplete ver'minderen, uitputten
deplorable betreurens'waardig
deplore be'treuren
deploy ont'plooien
depopulate ont'volken
deport depor'teren; ge'dragen
depose afzetten
deposit be'zinksel, laag; storting, waarborgsom; achterlaten; depo'neren
depot de'pot
depraved ont'aard
depravity ver'dorvenheid
deprecate (ernstig) afkeuren
depreciate in waarde (doen) dalen; onder'schatten
depreciation waardevermindering; ge'ringschatting
depress neerdrukken; depri'meren
depression daling, uitholling; ma'laise; neer'slachtigheid
deprive of ont'nemen
depth diepte, hoogte
deputation afvaardiging
deputize waarnemen
deputy afgevaardigde; plaatsvervanger; plaatsvervangend
derail (doen) ontsporen
derange in de war brengen
derelict ver'laten; ver'vallen
deride honend uitlachen

derision be'spotting
derisive spottend
derive afleiden; ont'lenen,
ver'krijgen
derogatory ge'ringschattend
descend afdalen
descendant afstammeling
descent (af)daling; afstamming
describe be'schrijven
description be'schrijving,
signale'ment; soort
descriptive be'schrijvend
desecrate ont'wijden
desert woes'tijn; ver'diende loon;
ver'laten; deser'teren
deserter deser'teur, af'vallige
deserve ver'dienen
deservedly te'recht
deserving waardevol, ver'dienstelijk
design ont'werp(en), des'sin;
oogmerk, opzet
designate be'noemd; aanduiden;
(be')noemen
designer ont'werper
desirable wenselijk
desire ver'langen, be'geerte;
be'geren
desist ophouden (met)
desk bu'reau, lessenaar; kas
desolate ver'laten, triest;
ver'woesten
desolation woeste'nij;
troosteloosheid; ver'woesting
despair wanhoop; wanhopen
desperado woesteling
desperate tot het uiterste ge'dreven,
wanhopig, schreeuwend
desperation wanhoop, ver'twijfeling
despicable ver'achtelijk
despise ver'achten, ver'smaden
despite on'danks
despondent moedeloos
despot des'poot
despotism despo'tisme

dessert des'sert
destination (plaats van)
be'stemming
destine be'stemmen **he was**
destined for hij was bestemd voor
destiny (nood)lot; be'stemming
destitute be'hoeftig, be'rooid
destroy ver'nietigen, ver'nielen
destroyer tor'pedojager
destruction ver'nietiging,
ver'woesting; ver'derf
destructive ver'nielziek,
schadelijk; afbrekend
detach scheiden, losmaken;
deta'cheren
detached los(geraakt),
vrijstaand; onbe'vangen
detachment detachering;
scheiding; gereser'veerdheid
detail de'tail
detailed uit'voerig
detain ophouden, vasthouden
detect be'speuren, be'trappen
detective detec'tive, recher'cheur
detention oponthoud;
ge'vangenhouden,
schoolblijven, nablijven
deter afschrikken
detergent wasmiddel
deteriorate achter'uitgaan
deterioration achter'uitgang
determination vastbe'radenheid;
vaststellen; be'slissing
determine be'sluiten;
vaststellen, be'palen
determined vastbe'sloten,
vastbe'raden
deterrent afschrikkend (middel)
detest ver'afschuwen
detestable ver'foeilijk
dethrone ont'tronen
detonate (doen) ont'ploffen
detour omweg
detract from afbreuk doen aan

detriment(al) schade(lijk)
devastate ver'woesten
develop (zich) ont'wikkelen, uitwerken
development ont'wikkeling
deviate afwijken
device toestel; list; sym'bool, de'vies
devil duivel
devilish duivels; ver'duiveld
devious om'slachtig
devise ver'zinnen
devoid of zonder
devolve overdragen (aan), overgaan (op)
devote (toe)wijden
devoted (toe)gewijd, ver'knocht
devotee enthousi'ast
devotion toewijding, ver' knochtheid; de'votie; ge'bed
devour ver'slinden
devout vroom
dew dauw
dexterous be'hendig
diabetes suikerziekte
diabolic(al) duivels
diagnose diag'nose opmaken
diagnosis diag'nose
diagonal diago'naal
diagram dia'gram
dial wijzer(plaat), schijf; facie; draaien
dialect dia'lect
dialogue dia'loog
diameter middellijn
diametrically diame'traal; lijnrecht
diamond dia'mant(en); ruit (-'vormig)
diaphragm middenrif; dia'fragma
diarrhoea dia'rree
diary dagboek, a'genda
dice dobbelstenen; dobbelen
dictate voorschrift; stem; dic'teren; voorschrijven
dictation dic'teren; dic'tee; voorschrift

dictator dic'tator
dictatorial dictatori'aal
dictatorship dicta'tuur
dictionary woordenboek
didactic di'dactisch
die sterven, doodgaan; snakken naar
  to – out uitsterven
die-hard onver'zettelijk
diesel diesel
diet di'eet (houden)
dietician diëtiste
differ ver'schillen; het niet eens zijn
difference ver'schil
different ver'schillend, anders
differentiate onder'scheiden; onderscheid maken
difficult moeilijk
difficulty moeilijkheid be'zwaar
diffident terughoudend
diffuse dif'fuus; (zich) ver'spreiden
dig por; steek; graven, omspitten, porren
digest ver'teren; ver'werken
digestion (spijs)ver'tering
digit vinger; cijfer
dignified waardig
dignify opluisteren
dignitary waardigheidsbekleder
dignity waardigheid
digress afdwalen, uitweiden
dilapidated bouw'vallig
dilate (zich) uitzetten
dilemma di'lemma
diligence vlijt; dili'gence
diligent vlijtig
dilute ver'dund; ver'dunnen
dim flauw, vaag, schemerig; dom; dof worden, ver'flauwen, ver'zwakken
dimension afmeting, di'mensie
diminish ver'minderen
diminutive klein; ver'kleinwoord
dimple kuiltje
din la'waai

dine di'neren
diner eter
dinghy kleine boot;
  opblaasbare boot
dingy vuil, goor
dinner warme maaltijd, di'ner
dip duik(en); inzinking; dompelen;
  dalen
diploma di'ploma
diplomacy diploma'tie
diplomat diplo'maat
diplomatic diploma'tiek
dire ver'schrikkelijk
direct rechtstreeks, di'rect;
  on'middellijk; open'hartig; leiden;
  ge'lasten; de weg wijzen; richten;
  adres'seren
direction richting; aanwijzing; leiding
directly on'middellijk; pre'cies
director direc'teur; raadsman
directory a'dresboek, gids
dirge klaagzang
dirt vuil; aarde
dirt cheap spotgoedkoop
dirty vuil(maken); ge'meen
disability onvermogen
disabled inva'lide
disablement invalidi'teit
disadvantage nadeel **at a –**
  in een na'delige po'sitie
disadvantageous na'delig
disagree (with) het on'eens
  zijn (met)
disagreeable on'aangenaam
disagreement (menings)verschil
disallow niet toestaan, ongeldig
  verklaren
disappear(ance) ver'dwijnen
disappoint te'leurstellen **to be**
  disappointing tegenvallen
disappointment te'leurstelling,
  tegenvaller
disapproval afkeuring
disapprove afkeuren; erop tegen zijn

disarm ont'wapenen
disarmament ont'wapening
disaster ramp
disastrous ramp'spoedig
disband ont'binden
disbelief ongeloof
disbelieve onge'lovig zijn, in
  twijfel trekken
disc schijf
discard ver'werpen, afdanken;
  uittrekken; wegleggen
discern onder'scheiden
discernible waar'neembaar
discernment
  onder'scheidingsvermogen, inzicht
discharge ont'lading; ont'ploffing;
  ont'slag; afvoer; etteren; zich kwijten
  van; lossen; afschieten; ont'laden;
  ont'slaan; uitmonden; afdoen
disciple dis'cipel
disciplinary discipli'nair, tucht-
discipline disci'pline; discipli'neren
disclaim van de hand wijzen,
  ont'kennen
disclose ont'hullen, blootleggen;
  loslaten
discolour (doen) ver'kleuren
discomfort onbe'haaglijkheid
disconcert van de wijs brengen
disconcerting storend
disconnect uitschakelen, afkoppelen
disconnected on'samenhangend
disconsolate troosteloos
discontent(ment) onte'vredenheid
discontented onte'vreden
discontinue opheffen, ophouden
  met, staken; opzeggen
discord tweedracht; disso'nant
discordance wangeluid
discordant dishar'monisch;
  tegen'strijdig
discotheque discotheek
discount korting; discon'teren;
  buiten be'schouwing laten

discourage ont'moedigen; afraden; weer'houden

discouragement ont'moediging; tegenwerping; afschrikking

discourse ver'handeling (houden)

discourteous onbeleefd

discover ont'dekken

discovery ont'dekking

discredit schande; in diskrediet brengen; geen ge'loof hechten aan

discreet dis'creet

discrepancy onregel'matigheid, ver'schil

discretion goedvinden; tact; onderscheid

discriminate discrimineren; onderscheid maken

discrimination discrimi'natie; onderscheid

discursive discursief

discuss be'spreken

discussion be'spreking, dis'cussie

disdain ver'achting; ver'smaden

disdainful minachtend

disease ziekte; kwaal

diseased ziek, be'smet

disembark (zich) ont'schepen

disengage losmaken

disengaged onbe'zet

disentangle ont'warren

disfigure ont'sieren, mis'vormen

disgorge uitbraken; uitstorten

disgrace schande; ongenade; te schande maken

disgraceful schandelijk

disgruntled ver'zuurd

disguise (ver')mom(ming); ver'mommen, ver'bloemen

disgust afkeer, walging; doen walgen

  to be disgusted at walgen van

  to be disgusted with meer dan ge'noeg hebben van

disgusting walgelijk, af'schuwelijk

dish schaal; ge'recht **to – up** opdienen, serveren

disharmony disharmo'nie

dishcloth vaatdoek

dishearten ont'moedigen

dishevelled ver'fomfaaid

dishonest(y) on'eerlijk(heid)

dishonour oneer, schande; ont'eren

dishonourable ont'erend; on'eervol

disillusion ont'goochelen

disillusionment ont'goocheling

disinclination tegenzin

disinclined onge'negen

disinfect ont'smetten

disinfectant ont'smettingsmiddel

disinherit ont'erven

disintegrate uitel'kaar vallen, (zich) ont'binden

disinterested be'langeloos

disjointed onsamen'hangend

dislike afkeer; on'prettig vinden

dislocate ont'wrichten

dislodge losmaken ver'drijven

disloyal(ty) ontrouw

dismal triest

dismantle ont'mantelen

dismay ont'zetting; ont'stellen

dismiss ont'slaan, wegsturen; afwijzen

dismissal ont'slag

dismount afstijgen; demon'teren

disobedience onge'hoorzaamheid

disobedient onge'hoorzaam

disobey geen ge'hoor geven (aan), onge'hoorzaam zijn

disorder wanorde; onge'regeldheid; onge'steldheid

disorderly wan'orderlijk; op'roerig

disorganize in de war sturen

disown ver'loochenen

disparage klei'neren

disparity onge'lijkheid

dispassionate onpar'tijdig, objec'tief

dispatch ver'zending; (offici'eel) be'richt; spoed; ver'zenden; afmaken; ver'orberen
dispel ver'drijven
dispensary apo'theek
dispensation uitdeling; dispen'satie; be'schikking
dispense uitdelen; klaarmaken
  to dispense with het stellen zonder
dispersal ver'spreiding
disperse ver'strooien
dispirit ont'moedigen
displace ver'plaatsen, ver'vangen
displacement ver'plaatsing
display ver'toon, demon'stratie; (ver')tonen, ten'toonspreiden; ont'plooien
displease mis'hagen
displeased ont'stemd
displeasing on'aangenaam
displeasure mis'noegen
disposal opruimen; (be')-schikking
dispose (rang)schikken; be'wegen
  to – of van de hand doen
disposed ge'neigd, ge'stemd
disposition rangschikking; aard, neiging
dispossess uit het be'zit stoten
disproportionate oneven'redig
disprove weer'leggen
dispute woordentwist dis'puut; (be') twisten, dispu'teren; be'strijden
disqualification diskwalifi'catie; be'lemmering
disqualify diskwalifi'ceren; onge'schikt maken
disquiet onrust; veront'rusten
disregard veron'achtzaming; veron'achtzamen
disrepair ver'val
disreputable be'rucht; haveloos
disrespect oneer'biedigheid
disrupt ver'storen, ont'wrichten
dissatisfaction onte'vredenheid

dissatisfied onte'vreden
dissect ont'leden
disseminate ver'spreiden
dissent van mening ver'schillen
dissertation ver'handeling
dissident dissident, andersdenkend(e)
dissimilar(ity) onge'lijk(heid)
dissipate ver'strooien; ver'doen
dissipated ver'lopen, los'bandig
dissociate (af)scheiden, niet stellen achter
dissolute liederlijk
dissolution opheffing
dissolve (zich) oplossen; ont'binden; wegsmelten
dissonant wan'luidend
dissuade afraden, afbrengen (van)
distance afstand; verte
distant ver; weg; koel
distaste afkeer
distasteful on'smakelijk
distil distil'leren
distillery distilleerde'rij
distinct duidelijk; ver'schillend; be'slist
distinction onderscheid, onder'scheiding; aanzien
distinctive kenmerkend
distinguish onder'scheiden, onderscheid maken
distinguished aan'zienlijk
distort ver'wringen; ver'draaien
distract afleiden; krank'zinnig maken
distraction afleiding; rade'loosheid
distraught radeloos
distress ellende, smart; be'droeven
distribute uitdelen, ver'spreiden
distribution uitreiking, ver'deling
district streek, wijk
distrust wantrouwen
disturb storen; komen aan; veront'rusten
disturbance storing; ver'warring; stoornis

disuse onbruik
disused oud, in onbruik ge'raakt
ditch sloot; lozen
dive duik(en); tent; tasten
diver duiker; duikvogel
diverge uit'eenlopen
divergence ver'schil
diverse ver'scheiden
diversion ver'legging
  wegomlegging; ont'spanning
diversity ver'scheidenheid
divert ver'leggen; afleiden
divest ont'doen
divide (zich) ver'delen; stemmen
dividend divi'dend; deeltal
divider (steek)passer
divine goddelijk, gods-; aanbiddelijk;
  godgeleerde; peilen, gissen
divinity god(delijk)heid;
  godgeleerdheid
divisible deelbaar
division (ver')deling, afdeling;
  di'visie; ver'deeldheid; stemming
divorce (echt)scheiding;
  (zich laten) scheiden (van)
divulge be'kend maken
dizzy duizelig, duizeling'wekkend
do doen **to – away with** afschaffen
  to – up vastmaken, inpakken;
  opknappen **to – with** ge'bruiken;
  te maken met **to do without** het
  stellen zonder
docile volgzaam
dock dok(ken); be'klaagdenbank;
  korten
dockyard scheepswerf
doctor dokter; doctor; be'handelen
doctrine leer(stuk)
document docu'ment('eren)
documentary documen'tair(e film)
dodge foefje; op'zijspringen;
  ont'wijken
dog hond; (achter)volgen
dogged hard'nekkig

dogma dogma
dogmatic dog'matisch
doings ge'doe; spul(len)
dole werk'loosheidsuitkering
  to – out uitdelen
doleful somber
doll pop
dollar dollar
dolphin dol'fijn
domain do'mein, landgoed; ge'bied
dome koepel
domestic huis('houd)elijk,
  huis(houd)-; binnenlands
domesticated huiselijk; ge'temd
domicile domi'cilie
dominant (over')heersend;
  domi'nerend; domi'nant
dominate (over')heersen,
  be'heersen; be'strijken
domination over'heersing
domineer de baas spelen over
domineering bazig
dominion heerschap'pij;
  ge'bied (met zelfbestuur)
dominoes dominospel
don ge'leerde; aandoen
donate schenken
donation do'natie
done klaar, af; gaar **done for**
  er ge'weest
donkey ezel
donor schenker, donor
doom noodlot, ondergang; laatste
  oordeel; doemen
door deur, ingang **out of doors**
  buiten
doorstep stoep
doorway deuropening
dope drugs; doping; sufferd (person)
dormant slapend
dormer window dakkapel
dormitory slaapzaal
dose dosis; do'seren
dot stip(pelen), punt

dote kinds zijn; ver'zot zijn op
dotty niet goed snik
double dubbel, tweepersoons-;
  dubbele, dubbelganger; (zich)
  ver'dubbelen, dubbelvouwen;
  zich omwenden
doubt twijfel(en), be'twijfelen
doubtful twijfelachtig
doubtless onge'twijfeld
douche douche
dough deeg; geld
doughnut donut
dour stug
douse drijfnat maken
dove duif(je)
dovecote duiventil
dowdy truttig
down naar be'neden, neder;
  af; down; dons **– and out** door
  en door; aan lager wal **– payment**
  bedrag in'eens **– with** weg met
downcast (ter')neergeslagen
downfall val; zware bui
down-hearted neer'slachtig
downhill de heuvel af;
  berg'afwaarts
downpour stortbui
downright uitgesproken
downstairs (naar) be'neden
downstream stroom'afwaarts
downtrodden plategetrapt; ver'trapt
downward(s) naar be'neden
downy donzig
dowry bruidschat
doze dutje; dutten
dozen do'zijn
drab saai; vaal(bruin)
draft schets, klad; inlijven,
  deta'cheren
draftsman ont'werper
drag (mee)slepen, (voort)zeulen;
  kruipen (time); rem; saai gedoe
  in – als vrouw verkleed
dragon draak

drain afvoer(buis), ri'ool; afvoeren,
  lopen; droogleggen; ont'trekken **to
  be a – on** veel vergen van
drainage afwatering; afvoer
draining board aanrecht
drainpipe afvoerbuis
drama drama('tiek)
dramatic dra'matisch
dramatics to'neelkunst
dramatize (zich laten) dramati'seren
drape drape'rie; dra'peren
drastic drastisch
draught tocht, trek; vangst;
  diepgang; teug; trek-; ge'tapt
draughts damspel
draughty tochtig
draw ge'lijkspel(en); at'tractie;
  ver'loting; trekken; tekenen **to –
  near** naderen **to – up** stilhouden;
  opstellen; bijschuiven
drawback be'zwaar, nadeel
drawbridge ophaalbrug
drawer la(de); tekenaar
drawing tekening, tekenen
drawing pin pu'naise
drawing room sa'lon
drawl lijzige manier van praten
drawn afgetobd; onbe'slist
dread (met) angst (en beven
  tege'moetzien)
dreadful vreselijk
dream droom; dromen
dreamy dromerig; vaag
dreary somber
dredge baggermolen; (uit)baggeren
dregs be'zinksel
drench door'weken
dress ja'pon; kleding, te'nue;
  gala-; (zich) (aan)kleden; tooien;
  ver'binden **to – up** (zich) opdirken
dresser (keuken)buf'fet
dressing verband; slasaus
dressing gown kamerjas
dressmaker naaister

dressmaking naaien
dress rehearsal gene'rale repe'titie
dribble druppelen, kwijlen; dribbelen
drift drijven; jachtsneeuw; neiging, strekking; zich laten meeslepen, dwalen
driftwood drijfhout
drill dril(boor); oefening, exer'citie; (door)boren; drillen
drink (iets te) drinken, borreltje to – to drinken op
drip druppel(en), druipen
dripping braadvet
drive rit; oprijlaan; drijfkracht; cam'pagne; slag; (voort)drijven; rijden; slaan to – at doelen op
drivel ge'wauwel; wauwelen
driver be'stuurder
driving licence rijbewijs
drizzle motregen(en)
droll grappig, zot
drone ge'gons; gonzen, dreunen
droop hangen; omvallen
drop drupel; glaasje; daling; hoogte: (laten) vallen; (laten) dalen; weglaten; afzetten to – in (even) langskomen to – off in slaap vallen
dross afval
drought droogte
drown ver'drinken; over'stemmen to be drowned ver'dronken
drowse dommelen
drowsy slaperig; slaap'wekkend
drudge werkezel; sloven
drudgery ge'zwoeg
drug be'dwelmend middel; be'dwelmen
drum trom(mel), ton; trommelen
drunk dronken
drunkard dronkaard
dry droog; (af)drogen
dry clean(ing) chemisch reinigen
dual twee'ledig, dubbel

dub tot ridder slaan; dubben
dubious twijfelachtig, dubi'eus
duchess herto'gin
duchy hertogdom
duck eend; duik; (onder)duiken
duct ka'naal, buis
dud prul; blindganger (bomb)
due ver'schuldigd, ver'diend, ge'past; ver'wacht; wat iemand toekomt – to dankzij, ten ge'volge van
duel du'el; duel'leren
dug-out uitgegraven schuilplaats
duke hertog
dull dof; saai; traag; somber afstompen
duly dan ook; dus, naar be'horen
dumb stom, sprakeloos
dumbfound ver'stomd doen staan
dummy pop; blinde; namaak-
dump belt, stortplaats; opslagplaats storten, neerzetten
dunce domkop
dune duin
dung (be')mest(en)
dungarees over'all
dungeon kerker
dupe dupe; be'driegen
duplicate dupli'caat; ver'dubbelen in – in duplo
duplicity dubbel'hartigheid
durable duurzaam
duration duur
duress dwang
during tijdens
dusk schemering
dusky donker, schemerig
dust stof; afstoffen; be'stuiven
dustbin vuilnisbak
dustman vuilnisman
dustpan (and brush) (veger en) blik
dusty stoffig; poeierig
Dutch Nederlands; Nederlanders

dutiful plichtsgetrouw
duty plicht; functie; (invoer)-rechten
dwarf dwerg; minia'tuur;
  over'schaduwen
dwell wonen **to – on** lang stilstaan bij
dweller be'woner
dwelling woning
dwelling place woonplaats

dwindle (away) wegteren;
  uitsterven, ver'dwijnen
dye verf(stof); verven, kleuren
dynamic dy'namisch
dynamite dyna'miet
dynamo dy'namo
dynasty dynas'tie
dysentery dysente'rie

E

each elk, ieder; per stuk
  – other el'kaar
eager enthousi'ast, gretig,
  ver'langend **to be –** dolgraag
  (zouden) willen
eagerness enthousi'asme,
  ver'langen
eagle arend
ear oor; ge'hoor; aar
eardrum trommelvlies
earl graaf
early (te) vroeg, vroeger, vroeg'tijdig
earmark be'stemmen
earn ver'dienen; ver'werven,
  be'zorgen
earnest ernstig, vurig **in –** in (alle)
  ernst
earnings verdiensten
earring oorbel
ear-splitting oorver'dovend
earth aarde, grond; hol;
  aardverbinding **what (or how) on –**
  ... wat (or hoe) in vredesnaam ...
earthenware aardewerk
earthly aards, stoffelijk
earthquake aardbeving
earthworm aardworm
earthy grond-; laag bij de gronds
ease ge'mak; ver'lichten; losser
  maken; voor'zichtig schuiven;
  ver'minderen
easel ezel
easily (ge')makkelijk; verreweg

east oosten; oost(waarts)
Easter pasen **– Day** eerste paasdag
easterly oostelijk, ooster-
eastern oosters, oostelijk
easy (ge')makkelijk; kalm
easy-going gemak'zuchtig;
  flegma'tiek
eat (op)eten; vreten
eaves overhangende dakrand
eavesdrop afluisteren
ebb eb(ben); ver'val; afnemen
ebony ebbenhout(en)
eccentric ex'centrisch;
  excen'triek; zonderling
ecclesiastical geestelijk, kerkelijk
echo echo; weerklank; weer'klinken;
  weergeven, her'halen
eclipse ver'duistering; ver'duisteren;
  in de schaduw stellen
economic eco'nomisch
economical zuinig, voor'delig;
  eco'nomisch
economics econo'mie
economist eco'noom
economize be'zuinigen
economy zuinigheid; be'heer
ecstasy ex'tase
ecstatic geest'driftig
eddy draaikolk; dwarrelen
edge rand; scherpe kant
  on edge zenuwachtig
edible eetbaar
edict e'dict

edifice ge'bouw
edify stichten
edit uitgeven; redi'geren
edition uitgave, e'ditie
editor redac'teur, be'werker
editorial hoofdartikel **editorial board (staff)** re'dactie
educate onder'wijzen, opvoeden
education onderwijs, ont'wikkeling
educational opvoedings-, onderwijs-
eel paling
eerie griezelig
efface uitwissen; wegcijferen
effect ge'volg, uitwerking, resul'taat; ef'fect; be'werkstelligen **in –** in feite; van kracht
effective ge'slaagd, treffend; af'doend; van kracht
effeminate ver'wijfd
effervesce mous'seren; bruisen
efficacy doel'treffendheid
efficiency vaardigheid; nuttig ef'fect
effigy beeltenis, beeldenaar
effort krachtsinspanning, poging; pres'tatie
effrontery brutali'teit
effusive uit'bundig
egg ei **to – on** aanzetten
egoist ego'ïst
egotism egotisme, egoïsme
eiderdown donzen dekbed
eight(h) acht(ste)
eighteen(th) achttien(de)
eighty tachtig
Eire Ierland
either één (van beide); beide; elk; ook **– ... or** of ... of
ejaculation zaadlozing; uitroep
eject uitwerpen, uitzetten
eke out rekken
elaborate inge'wikkeld, door'wrocht, uitgebreid; be'werken, bijwerken; uitweiden
elapse ver'strijken, ver'lopen

elastic e'lastisch; rekbaar; elas'tiek
elasticity elastici'teit; rekbaarheid
elated opgetogen
elbow elleboog; door'heenwerken **– grease** zwaar werk; schoonmaakwerk
elder ouder(e), oudst(e); ouderling
elderly op leeftijd
elect ge'kozen(e), uitverkoren(e); (ver')kiezen (als), uitkiezen
election (uit)ver'kiezing
elector(ate) kiezer(s)
electric(al) e'lektrisch
electrician elektri'cien
electricity elektrici'teit
electrify elektrifi'ceren; elektri'seren
elegant ele'gant
elegy ele'gie
element ele'ment; be'standdeel
elemental na'tuur-, essen'tieel
elementary elemen'tair; een'voudig **– school** basisschool
elephant olifant
elevate ver'heffen
elevation ver'hoging, hoogte; ver'heffing; opstand
eleven elf(tal)
elf elf, ka'bouter
elicit ont'lokken
eligible ver'kiesbaar; be'voegd; ge'schikt
eliminate uitschakelen
ellipse el'lips
elm iep(enhout)
elongate (zich) ver'lengen, uitrekken
elope weglopen
eloquence wel'sprekendheid
else anders; verder
elsewhere ergens anders
elucidate toelichten
elude ont'wijken, ont'duiken, ont'gaan
elusive moeilijk te vinden (*or* vatten)
emaciate uitmergelen

e-mail e-mail, email
emanate from voortkomen
uit, uitstralen van
emancipation emanci'patie
embalm balsemen
embankment kade
embargo be'slag, ver'bod,
embargo
embark (zich) inschepen **to embark
on** aanvangen
embarrass ver'legen maken,
in ver'legenheid brengen;
be'moeilijken
embarrassing pijnlijk
embarrassment ver'legenheid
embassy ambas'sade, ge'zantschap
embedded ge'nesteld, vastge'raakt
embellish ver'fraaien
ember gloeiend kooltje (*or* stuk hout)
embezzle ver'duisteren
embitter ver'bitteren, ver'gallen
embody be'lichamen; be'vatten
embossed in re'liëf
embrace om'helzing; (el'kaar)
om'helzen; om'sluiten; zich
eigen maken
embroider bor'duren
embroidery bor'duurwerk
embroil ver'wikkelen
embryo embryo
emerald sma'ragd(en)
emerge te voorschijn komen
emergency nood(geval),
noodtoestand
emigrant emi'grant; emi'grerend
emigrate emi'greren
eminence emi'nentie,
ver'maardheid
eminent uit'zonderlijk (ver'maard)
emissary ge'zant
emit uitstralen, afgeven; uiten
emotion (ge'moeds)aandoening,
e'motie
emotional emotio'neel, ge'voels-

emperor keizer
emphasis nadruk
emphasize de nadruk leggen
op, duidelijk doen uitkomen
emphatic na'drukkelijk
empire (keizer)rijk
employ (in)dienst(hebben);
ge'bruiken, bezighouden
employee werknemer
employer werkgever
employment werk; ge'bruik
empower machtigen
empty leeg (maken *or* worden);
niets'zeggend; lozen
emulate nastreven
emulsion e'mulsie
enable in staat stellen
enact tot wet ver'heffen; opvoeren
enamel e'mail('leren), brandverf,
gla'zuur; lakken
enamour be'koren; ver'zotten
encamp een kamp opslaan; legeren
encase om'sluiten, opsluiten
enchant be'toveren; ver'rukken
enchanting sprookjesachtig,
char'mant; be'toverend
encircle om'ringen, om'singelen
enclose insluiten
enclosure om'sloten ruimte; bijlage
encompass om'sluiten; be'vatten
encounter ont'moeting; treffen;
tegenkomen; onder'vinden
encourage aanmoedigen
encouragement aanmoediging
encroach on doordringen tot;
inbreuk maken op
encrust be'slaan; be'zetten
encumber be'lasten
encyclopaedia encyclope'die
end eind(igen); doel **no – of** vreselijk
veel **in the –** ten'slotte **make both
ends meet** rondkomen
endanger in ge'vaar brengen
endear ge'liefd maken, innemen

endeavour poging; trachten
ending eind; uitgang
endless eindeloos, zonder einde
endorse endos'seren;
   onder'schrijven
endow be'giftigen
endowment gave, gift
endurance uithoudingsvermogen;
   ver'dragen
endure ver'dragen; ver'duren

engaging in'nemend
engender ver'wekken; ver'oorzaken
engine ma'chine, motor,
   locomo'tief
engineer inge'nieur, technicus,
   machi'nist, lid van de
   ge'nietroepen; klaarspelen
engineering tech'niek
England Engeland
English(man) Engels(man)

Insight

The Dutch translation of *English* is **Engels**. However, Dutch speakers often use **Engels** to refer to more than objects, ideas and people from *England* (spelt **Engeland** in Dutch). From across the English Channel or **het Kanaal**, the difference between England and the *United Kingdom* **het Verenigd Koninkrijk** in Dutch, is not always fully understood, and therefore **Engels** (and **Engeland**) is often used to refer to everything and everyone from the United Kingdom (and the United Kingdom itself), thereby frequently unwittingly upsetting the people from *Scotland* **Schotland**, *Wales* **Wales** and *Northern Ireland* **Noord-Ierland**.

---

enemy vijand(elijk)
energetic ener'giek; krachtig
energy ener'gie
enfold om'wikkelen; om'helzen,
   om'strengelen
enforce (krachtig) uitvoeren;
   dwingen tot
enforcement handhaving
enfranchise vrijmaken; kiesrecht
   ver'lenen
engage in dienst nemen; in be'slag
   nemen; slaags raken met; in el'kaar
   grijpen
engaged ver'loofd; in ge'sprek,
   be'zet, bezig **to get engaged** zich
   ver'loven met
engagement afspraak; ver'loving;
   in'dienstneming; ge'vecht

engraving gra'vure, gra'veren
engross ver'diepen; fasci'neren
engulf ver'zwelgen
enhance ver'hogen
enigma(tic)(al) raadsel(achtig)
enjoy ge'nieten (van)
enjoyable prettig
enjoyment ple'zier, ge'nieten
enlarge (zich) ver'groten
   to – on uitweiden over
enlighten opheldering geven aan;
   ver'lichten
enlist (in) dienst nemen; een
   be'roep doen op
enliven opvrolijken
enmity vijandschap
enormous e'norm
enormously e'norm

enough ge'noeg; heel **kind —**
zo vriendelijk
enrage woedend maken
enrapture in ver'voering brengen
enrich ver'rijken
enrol (zich laten) inschrijven; lid
worden
ensue het ge'volg zijn, volgen
ensure veiligstellen; garanderen
entail met zich meebrengen
entangle vastraken; ver'strikken
enter binnengaan, binnenkomen;
gaan in; opgeven; boeken
enterprise onder'neming(sgeest)
enterprising onder'nemend
entertain ver'maken onder'houden;
ont'halen, ont'vangen; over'wegen;
koesteren
entertaining amu'sant; so'ciale
plichten
entertainment amuse'ment
enthrall boeien
enthrone op de troon plaatsen,
wijden
enthusiasm enthousi'asme
enthusiast(ic) enthousi'ast
entice (ver')lokken
entire (ge')heel
entirely helemaal
entirety ge'heel
entitle (be')titelen; het recht geven
entity eenheid, entiteit, bestaan
entomb be'graven
entrails ingewanden
entrance ingang; opkomen;
in ver'voering brengen
entreat smeken
entreaty smeekbede
entrust toevertrouwen
entry intocht, ingang; boeking;
inschrijving
enumerate opnoemen
envelop hullen
envelope enve'loppe

enviable benijdens'waardig
envious af'gunstig
environment om'geving
envisage voor'zien
envoy (af)ge'zant
envy afgunst; be'nijden
ephemeral kort'stondig
epic epos, heldendaden; episch
epicure gastro'noom
epidemic epide'mie; rage
epilepsy epilep'sie
epilogue epi'loog
episode af'levering, epi'sode
epitaph grafschrift
epoch tijdperk
equal ge'lijk (zijn aan); eve'naren
— to opgewassen tegen
equality ge'lijkheid
equalize ge'lijk maken
equally even('zeer)
equation verge'lijking
equator evenaar
equilateral gelijk'zijdig
equilibrium evenwicht
equip uitrusten, toerusten
equitable billijk
equity billijkheid, aandelenvermogen
equivalent equivalent
equivocal dubbel'zinnig,
twijfelachtig
era tijdperk, jaartelling
eradicate uitroeien
erase schrappen; uitwissen
erect over'eind (zetten); oprichten
erection erectie; gebouw; het
oprichten, het opbouwen
erode uitschuren
erosion e'rosie
erotic e'rotisch
err dwalen
errand boodschap
erratic inconse'quent, onregel'matig
erroneous on'juist
error fout, a'buis

erudite ge'leerd
erupt uitbarsten, uitspuwen
escalator roltrap
escapade esca'pade
escape ont'vluchting; ont'snappen,
  ont'komen aan; ont'gaan
escarpment steile wand
escort ge'leide, es'corte;
  bege'leiden, escor'teren
especial bij'zonder
especially bijzonder, voor'al
espionage spion'nage
essay opstel
essence wezen, es'sentie; es'sence
essential essen'tieel; hoofdzaak
essentially in wezen
establish oprichten; (vast)stellen;
  vestigen; instellen
establishment (handels)huis,
  instelling; oprichten; gevestigde
  orde
estate landgoed, vastgoed **– agent**
  makelaar
esteem achting; achten
estimable achtens'waardig; te
  be'rekenen
estimate schatting; schatten
estimation mening; schatting,
  achting
estrange ver'vreemden
estuary ri'viermond
etc(etera) enz(ovoorts)
etch etsen
etching ets
eternal eeuwig
eternity eeuwigheid
ether ether
ethereal e'therisch
ethical ethisch
ethics ethica
euro euro (pl: euro's)
Europe Eu'ropa
European Euro'pees; Europe'aan
evacuate evacu'eren

evacuation evacu'atie
evade ont'wijken
evaluate ta'xeren, schatten
evangelic(al) evan'gelisch
evangelist evange'list
evaporate ver'dampen; ver'dwijnen
evasion ont'wijking, ont'duiking
evasive ont'wijkend
eve (voor)avond, dag voor
even ge'lijk('matig); effen; even;
  quitte; gelijk'moedig; zelfs; pre'cies;
  nog; ge'lijkmaken **– so** maar toch
evening avond
event ge'beurtenis, ge'val; nummer
  at all events in ieder ge'val
eventful veelbe'wogen
eventual uit'eindelijk; eventu'eel
eventually ten'slotte
ever ooit, te allen tijde
evergreen altijd groen(e plant)
everlasting eeuwig('durend)
evermore altijd
every ieder; alle **– other week**
  om de twee weken
  – now and then af en toe
everybody, everyone ieder'een
everyday alle'daags, dagelijks
everything alles
everywhere overal (waar)
evict uitzetten
evidence be'wijs(materi'aal),
  ge'tuigenis; blijk **to give –**
  ge'tuigenis afleggen
evident duidelijk klaar'blijkelijk
evil kwaad; onheil, euvel
evildoer boosdoener
evince (aan)tonen
evoke oproepen
evolution evo'lutie
evolve (zich) ont'plooien
exact pre'cies; eisen
exacting veel'eisend
exactitude nauw'keurigheid
exaggerate over'drijven

exaltation ver'heerlijking; (geest) ver'voering
examination e'xamen; onderzoek; ver'hoor
examine exami'neren; onder'zoeken, onder'vragen; goed be'kijken
example voorbeeld, mo'del **to set an –** een voorbeeld geven
exasperate ergeren, irriteren
excavate uitgraven, opgraven
excavation opgraving
exceed te boven gaan, over'schrijden
exceedingly bij'zonder
excel uitmunten; over'treffen
excellence voor'treffelijkheid
excellent uit'stekend
except be'halve; uitzonderen
exception uitzondering **to take – to** bezwaar maken tegen
exceptional onge'woon, exceptio'neel
excerpt (aangehaalde) passage
excess overmaat; surplus; uitspatting; extra
excessive over'dadig, buiten'sporig
exchange ruil(en); beurs; cen'trale; (uit)wisseling; (in)wisselen
exchequer schatkist
excise ac'cijns; uitsnijden
excitable gauw opgewonden
excite opwinden, prikkelen; opwekken
excitement opwinding
exclaim uitroepen
exclamation uitroep
exclude uitsluiten, buitensluiten
exclusive uit'sluitend; exclu'sief
excommunicate in de ban doen
excrements uitwerpselen
excretion afscheiding
excruciating folterend, pijnlijk
excursion ex'cursie, uitstapje; uitweiding
excusable be'grijpelijk

excuse ex'cuus; excu'seren, niet kwalijk nemen; veront'schuldigen; vrijstellen **– me** par'don; neem me niet kwalijk
execute uitvoeren; ter dood brengen
execution uitvoering; te'rechtstelling
executioner beul
executive uitvoerend(e macht); be'drijfsleider
executor execu'teur
exemplary voor'beeldig
exemplify als voorbeeld dienen van, be'lichamen
exempt vrij(gesteld); vrijstellen
exercise oefening; (uit)oefenen; in acht nemen
exert aanwenden, inspannen
exertion inspanning; ge'bruik
exhale uitademen
exhaust uitlaat; uitputten
exhaustion uitputting
exhibit inzending, be'wijsstuk; ten'toonstellen; (ver')tonen
exhibition ten'toonstelling; ver'toon, ver'toning
exhibitor expo'sant
exhilarate stimu'leren, opvrolijken
exhort aansporen, ver'manen
exhume opgraven
exile balling(schap)
exist be'staan
existence be'staan
exit uitgang; aftreden
exonerate zuiveren
exorbitant buiten'sporig
exorcize be'vrijden; uitdrijven
exotic uit'heems
expand (doen) uitzetten, (zich) uitbreiden, (zich) uitspreiden; uitwerken
expanse uitge'strektheid
expansion expansie, uitbreiding
expatriate ver'bannen
expect ver'wachten; denken

expectant vol verwachting – **mother** aanstaande moeder
expectation ver'wachting
expedient be'vorderlijk, raadzaam, redmiddel
expedite be'spoedigen
expedition expe'ditie
expel uitdrijven; wegsturen
expend uitgeven; be'steden
expenditure uitgeven, be'steden; uitgaven
expense (on)kosten, uitgave
expensive duur
experience er'varing; onder'vinden
experienced er'varen
experiment proef; experimen'teren
experimental proef(onder'vindelijk)
expert des'kundig(e); be'dreven
expiate boeten voor
expire aflopen; de laatste adem uitblazen; uitademen
expiry afloop
explain uitleggen
explanation ver'klaring
explanatory ver'klarend
explicit uit'drukkelijk
explode (doen) ont'ploffen; losbarsten; ont'zenuwen
exploit (helden)daad; exploi'teren
exploration onder'zoeking(stocht)
explore ver'kennen, onder'zoeken
explorer ont'dekkingsreiziger
explosion ont'ploffing; uitbarsting
explosive springstof; ont'plofbaar; op'vliegend
exponent expo'nent
export export(eren); uitvoer(artikel); uitvoeren
expose blootstellen; uitstallen; ont'hullen, aan de dag brengen; be'lichten
exposed onbe'schut
exposition uit'eenzetting; ten'toonstelling

exposure ont'maskering; blootstellen; be'lichting
expound uit'eenzetten
express uit'drukkelijk, speci'aal, op'zettelijk; ex'pres(trein); uitdrukken; uitpersen
expression uitdrukking
expressive expres'sief; veel'zeggend
expulsion uitdrijving; wegsturen
expunge uitwissen
exquisite buitengewoon fijn; zeer ver'fijnd
extend (zich) uitstrekken, ver'lengen; uitbreiden; ver'lenen
extension bijgebouw; ver'lenging; lijn
extensive uitgebreid, uitgestrekt
extent uitge'strektheid; omvang
to what (*or* **this**) – in hoe-(*or* zo)'verre
extenuate ver'zachten, ver'goelijken
exterior buiten(kant), uit'wendig
exterminate uitroeien
external uit'wendig, buiten(lands); uiterlijk(heid)
extinct uitgestorven
extinguish blussen, doven; een eind maken aan
extort afpersen
extortionate buiten'sporig
extra extra
extract passage; ex'tract; (uit)trekken, uithalen; afpersen
extraction ex'tractie; afkomst
extraneous vreemd, niet ter zake dienend
extraordinary buitenge'woon, extra
extravagance buiten'sporigheid, ver'kwisting; uitspatting
extravagant ver'kwistend; extravagant, over'dreven
extreme uiterst(e)

extremely uitermate
extremist extre'mist(isch)
extremity uiterste (nood), uiteinde
extricate loswerken losmaken,
 ont'warren
exuberant uit'bundig
exude afscheiden; ver'spreiden
exult jubelen
exultant triom'fantelijk, opgetogen
exultation tri'omf, opge'togenheid

F

fable fabel
fabric stof, weefsel; struc'tuur
fabricate fabri'ceren; ver'zinnen
fabulous legen'darisch; fabelachtig
façade gevel; voorwendsel
face ge'zicht; wijzerplaat;
 oppervlakte; pres'tige; nominaal;
 liggen op; het ge'zicht keren naar;
 onder de ogen zien; be'dekken
 – to – tegenover elkaar **in the –**
 of ondanks, tegenover **on the –**
 of it ogen'schijnlijk **faced with**
 ge'plaatst voor (or in)
facecloth washandje
facet fa'cet
facetious gek(scherend), schertsend
facial ge'zichts-
facile (licht')vaardig, opper'vlakkig
facilitate verge'makkelijken
facility voor'ziening, facili'teit;
 ta'lent
facing tegen'over, met het
 ge'zicht naar (or op)
fact feit **in (point of) –**
 in feite, eigenlijk, zelfs, immers
faction par'tij(strijd)
factor factor
factory fa'briek
factual feitelijk
faculty ver'mogen, aanleg;
 facul'teit; ver'gunning

eye oog; aankijken **to catch a**
 person's eye de aandacht van
 iemand trekken **to see eye to eye**
 het ge'heel eens zijn
eyebrow wenkbrauw
eyelash wimper
eyelid ooglid
eye-opener open'baring
eyesight ge'zicht (svermogen)
eyesore gruwel (voor het oog)

fad be'vlieging
fade (doen) ver'schieten;
 ver'weken; wegsterven
faggot bundel houtjes; bal gehakt;
 flikker (gay man)
fail mis'lukken, (laten) zakken;
 nalaten; in de steek laten; opraken
 without – zonder man'keren
failing ge'brek; bij ge'brek aan
failure mis'lukk(el)ing
faint flauw(te), vaag, zwak;
 flauwvallen
fair billijk, eerlijk; be'hoorlijk;
 blond; mooi, net; kermis, markt
fairly tamelijk; eerlijk
fairy fee
fairytale sprookje
faith ge'loof; ver'trouwen; trouw
faithful trouw; ge'lovig(en)
faithless onge'lovig; trouweloos
fake be'drog; namaak;
 knoeien met; namaken; fin'geren
falcon valk
fall val(len), daling; overgave,
 ondergang; ver'val; be'zwijken;
 dalen **to – back on** zijn toevlucht
 nemen tot; te'rugtrekken op
 to – out ruzie krijgen **to – short**
 te'kortschieten **to – to**
 aanpakken, toetasten; dichtvallen;
 ten deel vallen

fallow braak; geelbruin
false on'juist; vals; on'trouw; scheef; loos **– teeth** kunstgebit
falsehood on'waarheid
falsify ver'valsen
falter wankelen, weifelen; stamelen
fame roem, ver'maardheid
famed be'roemd
familiar be'kend, ver'trouwd; famili'aar
familiarity familiari'teit
family ge'zin, fa'milie; ge'slacht; kinderen
famine hongersnood; schaarste
famish uithongeren, ver'hongeren
famous be'roemd; prachtig
fan waaier, venti'lator; enthousi'ast; waaieren; aanwakkeren
fanatic dweper, fana'tiek(eling)
fanaticism fana'tisme
fanciful fan'tastisch; grillig
fancy ver'beelding(skracht); be'vlieging; fanta'sie-, luxe; zich in (*or* ver')beelden; een i'dee hebben; zin hebben in
fancy dress gecostu'meerd
fanfare fan'fare
fantastic fan'tastisch, grillig
fantasy fanta'sie
far ver; veel **– off** ver weg **the – side** de overkant **as – as** voor zo'ver; tot aan **by –, – and away** verreweg **– and wide** heinde en ver
farce klucht; farce, schijnvertoning
farcical be'spottelijk
fare ta'rief, vracht(je); ver'voerskosten; kost; gaan
farewell afscheid(s-)
far-fetched verge'zocht
farm boerde'rij, fokke'rij, kweke'rij; een boerde'rij hebben (van)
farmer boer
farmhouse boerde'rij

farmyard (boeren')erf
far-off ver
far-reaching verstrekkend
far-sighted verziend; voor'uitziend
farther verder
farthest verst
fascinate boeien, fasci'neren
fascination iets boeiends, be'koring; ge'boeide be'langstelling
fashion mode; ma'nier; scheppen, vormen
fashionable modi'eus, deftig, (in de) mode
fast snel, hard; vóór; ge'raffi'neerd; vast; wasecht; trouw; vasten **to be – asleep;** als een roos slapen
fasten vastmaken; gooien
fastening sluiting, knip
fastidious kies'keurig
fat dik, vet
fatal dodelijk; nood'lottig; be'slissend
fatalist(ic) fata'list(isch)
fate lot; dood
fateful nood'lottig
father vader
fathom vadem; peilen
fathomless peilloos
fatigue ver'moeidheid ver'moeienis; afmatten
fatten aanzetten; vetmesten
fatty vet(tig); dikkerd
fatuous stom, dwars
fault fout, de'fect; schuld **to find – with** vitten op; aanmerkingen maken op
faultless onbe'rispelijk, feilloos
faulty ge'brekkig, de'fect
favour (be')gunst(igen); ingang; voorliefde; in'signe; de voorkeur geven aan **in – of** vóór; ten gunste van **to do someone a –** iemand een ge'noegen doen
favourable gunstig

favourite gunsteling, favo'riet;
lievelings-
favouritism be'voorrechting
fax fax; faxen
fear angst, vrees; vrezen, bang zijn
fearful vreselijk
fearless onbe'vreesd
feasible uit'voerbaar; aan'nemelijk
feast feest(maal); zich ver'gasten
aan, ont'halen
feat pres'tatie
feather veer, pluim; veren
feature (ge'laats)trek; onderdeel,
(op'vallende) eigenschap;
gaan over
feature film speelfilm
February febru'ari
fecund(ity) vruchtbaar(heid)
federal fede'raal
federation fede'ratie
fed up: to be – er meer dan genoeg
van hebben
fee hono'rarium, be'drag,
(school)geld
feeble zwak, flauw
feed voer(en); voeding; eten
feel ge'voel; (zich) voelen;
(be')tasten; aanvoelen; ge'loven;
(meelij) hebben **to – like**
aanvoelen als; zich voelen (als);
zin hebben in

felicitous ge'lukkig
felicity ge'luk('zaligheid)
feline katachtig
fell hevig; (neer)vellen
fellow kerel; mede-
fellowship ge'meenschap
felony zware misdaad
felt vilt(en)
female vrouwelijk; vrouw
feminine vrouwelijk
fen moe'rasland, polder
fence om'heining, schutting;
om'heinen; schermen
fend for oneself voor zich'zelf
zorgen **to – off** afweren
ferment gist(ing); be'roering;
(doen) gisten
fern varen
ferocious woest
ferret fret; opsporen; snuffelen
ferry veer(pont); overzetten
fertile vruchtbaar; rijk
fertilize vruchtbaar maken;
be'vruchten
fertilizer (kunst)mest
fervent vurig, innig
fervid heftig
fervour vuur
fester zweren; woekeren
festival feest
festive feestelijk, feest-

Insight

The verb *to feel* is **zich voelen** in Dutch, in other words, it is
reflexive. This may seem odd (*I feel great* is **ik voel me goed**,
literally, *I feel me good* in Dutch), but quite a few reflexive
Dutch verbs are not reflexive in English: **zich vervelen** *to be
bored*, **zich schamen** *to be embarrassed*, **zich vergissen** *to be
mistaken*, **zich bemoeien met** *to interfere with*.

feeling ge'voel, voelen
feign veinzen

festivity festivi'teit
festoon slinger; met slingers tooien

fetch (af)halen; opbrengen
fetish fetisj
fetter keten(en)
feud vete
feudal feo'daal
fever koorts(achtige opwinding)
feverish koorts(achtig)
few weinig(en) **a –** een paar, enkele
fiancé(e) ver'loofde
fiasco fi'asco
fib leugentje; jokken
fibre vezel; stoerheid, aard
fibreglass glasvezel
fickle wispel'turig
fiction ro'mans en korte ver'halen; fictie, ver'dichtsel
fictitious fic'tief, gefin'geerd
fiddle vi'ool (spelen); scharrelen
fidelity trouw, ge'trouwheid
fidget draaitol; wiebelen
field veld, akker; ge'bied
fiend duivel; mani'ak
fiendish duivels
fierce woest, fel
fiery vuur(rood); vurig
fifteen(th) vijftien(de)
fifty vijftig
fig vijg
fight ge'vecht, strijd; vechtlust; (be')vechten
figment ver'zinsel
figurative fi'guurlijk
figure cijfer; prijs; ge'daante, fi'guur; voorkomen **– of speech** zegswijze
to – out uitkienen
figurehead boegbeeld; leider in naam
filament (gloei)draad
filch kapen
file dos'sier, map; file; vijl(en); opbergen; (een voor een) trekken
fill (op)vullen; stoppen
fillet fi'let; fi'leren

filling vulling
film film; vlies(je), waas; (ver')filmen
filmy dun, wazig
filter filter; fil'treren; sijpelen
– through uitlekken
filth vuiligheid; vuile taal
filthy vuil, vies
fin vin
final laatste, eind-, slot-; defini'tief; eindwedstrijd
finally ten'slotte
finance fi'nanciën; finan'cieren
financial finan'cieel
financier finan'cier
find vondst; (be')vinden; ont'dekken; merken; (op)zoeken
finding be'vinding
fine mooi; (haar)fijn; best; geldboete
finery opschik
finesse fi'nesse
finger vinger; be'tasten
fingernail nagel
fingerprint vingerafdruk
finicky kies'keurig piete'peuterig
finish eind(igen); afwerking: af (or op)maken; afwerken
finite eindig
Finn(ish) Fin(s)
fiord fjord
fir den(nenboom)
fire vuur, brand; haard; (af)vuren, (af)schieten, lossen; bakken; aanwakkeren; op straat zetten
to catch – vlam vatten **on –** in brand; brandend (van ver'langen)
to set – to, to set on – in brand steken
firearm vuurwapen
fire escape brandtrap
fire extinguisher blusapparaat
firefighter brandweerman
fireside (open) haard
fireworks vuurwerk

firm vast(be'raden), stevig, hecht; stand'vastig; firma

first (voor het) eerst; ten eerste **at –** in het be'gin **– of all** eerst, om te be'ginnen

first aid eerste hulp

first-rate eersteklas, prima

fiscal fis'caal, be'lasting-

fish vis(sen); opdiepen

fisher(man) visser, hengelaar

fishery visse'rij

fishing vissen; visge'legenheid

fishing rod hengel

fishmonger visboer, viswinkel

fishy visachtig, vis-; ver'dacht

fissure kloof, spleet

fist vuist

fit ge'zond, fit; ge'schikt; klaar; aanval; bui, toeval; passen; kloppen met; voor'zien, uitrusten **to – in** plaats (*or* tijd) vinden voor; zich aanpassen, passen bij

fitful on'rustig, grillig

fitting ge'past; pas; fitting

fittings toebehoren, be'nodigdheden

five vijf

fix knel; vastmaken; vaststellen; vestigen; opknappen; fi'xeren

fixed vast

fixture vaste fitting; wedstrijd, vaste datum

fizz sissen

fizzle sissen, sputteren **to – out** met een sisser aflopen

flabbergast stomverbaasd doen staan

flabby pafferig

flag vlag; pla'vuis; ver'slappen

flagpole vlaggenstok

flagrant schandelijk

flagship vlaggenschip

flake volk; (af)schilferen

flamboyant zwierig, op'zichtig

flame vlam(men); vuurrood zijn

flank flank('eren)

flannel fla'nel(len); waslapje

flap klep, (tafel)blad, pand; klapperen; (op en neer) slaan met

flare opflikkering; fakkel, si'gnaalvlam **to – up** opvlammen; opstuiven

flash flits(en); flikkeren; schieten

flashlight zaklantaren

flashy op'zichtig

flask fla'con

flat plat, vlak; vierkant (refusal); standaard (rate); ver'schaald; mat; te laag; flat, é'tage

flatten plat maken

flatter vleien, flat'teren

flattery vleie'rij

flatulence opgeblazen ge'voel

flaunt geuren met

flavour smaak; tintje; kruiden, toebereiden

flavouring a'roma

flaw fout; leemte

flawless gaaf; onbe'rispelijk

flax(en) vlass(ig)

flay villen

flea vlo

fleck (be')spikkel(en)

flee vluchten

fleece vacht; villen

fleecy wollig; schapen-

fleet vloot; leger; snel

fleeting bliksemsnel, voor'bijflitsend

Flemish Vlaams

flesh vlees

fleshy vlezig

flex snoer; buigen

flexible buigzaam; soepel

flexitime variabele werktijden

flick tik(ken), knip(pen)

flicker flikkeren

flight vlucht; groep, zwerm; trap
flighty wuft
flimsy broos, fragiel
flinch te'rugdeinzen; (in'een)krimpen
fling korte affaire; gooien
flip (weg)slaan
flippant onge'past spottend
flirt flirt(en)
flit fladderen, dartelen
float dobber, drijver; (laten) drijven, vlot maken
floating vlottend
flock kudde, schare; (samen)stromen
flog (af)ranselen **to – sth** iets ver'patsen/aansmeren
flood over'stroming; (zond)vloed, zee; (doen) over'stromen; stromen
floodlight floodlight; ver'lichten
floor vloer, ver'dieping; over'donderen
flop fi'asco; (in el'kaar) ploffen
floral bloemen-
florid bloemrijk
florist bloe'mist
flounder ploeteren, spartelen; worstelen
flour bloem, meel
flourish zwierig ge'baar, krul; ge'dijen; zwaaien; geuren met
flout in de wind slaan
flow stroom; vloed; stromen
flower bloem, bloei(en)
fluctuate schommelen, op en neer gaan
flue rookkanaal
fluent vloeiend
fluff pluisjes; pluizen
fluffy donzig
fluid vloeibaar; on'vast; vloeistof
fluke meevaller, mazzel, stom geluk
fluorescent fluore'scerend

flurry vlaag; trilling; zenuwachtig maken
flush blos; opwelling, ge'lijk; blozen; (schoon)spoelen
fluster ner'veus maken
flute fluit; groef; groeven
flutter ge'klapwiek; fladderen, klapwieken; flikkeren
flux voort'durende ver'andering
fly vlieg(en); gulp; vluchten (uit); oplaten; voeren
foal veulen
foam schuim(en)
foamy schuimend
focus brandpunt scherpte; scherp stellen; zich concentreren
fodder (vee)voer
foe vijand
fog mist; be'nevelen
foggy mistig; vaag
foible zwak(ke punt)
foil folie; verhinderen
foist off on aansmeren
fold vouw(en), plooi; kooi, kudde; slaan
folder map; folder
folding op'vouwbaar, vouw-
foliage ge'bladerte
folio folio
folk mensen; volks-
follow volgen (op), opvolgen; be'grijpen
follower volgeling
following aanhang
folly dwaasheid
fond innig **to be – of** houden van
fondle liefkozen
font lettertype; doopvont
food voedsel, eten; stof
foodstuffs voedingsmiddelen
fool dwaas; voor de gek houden
foolhardy roekeloos
foolish dwaas

foot voet, poot; voeteneinde;
  voetvolk; lopen; be'talen **on –**
  te voet; aan de gang **to put one's**
  – in it een blunder begaan
football(er) voetbal(ler)
foothold vaste voet
footing houvast; (vaste) voet
footlights voetlicht
footpath voetpad
footprint voetafdruk
footstep voetstap
footwear schoeisel
for voor; naar; ge'durende; wegens;
  ondanks; want; (om)dat
foray rooftocht; plunderen
forbear nalaten
forbid ver'bieden; ver'hoeden
forbidding afschrik'wekkend
force (strijd) kracht, ge'weld;
  dwingen, for'ceren **in –** van kracht
forceful krachtig
forceps tang
forcible geweld'dadig; krachtig
ford door'waden
fore voor('aan); voorgrond
forearm onderarm
forebear voorzaat
forebode voor'spellen
foreboding voorgevoel; voor'spelling
forecast voor'spelling; voor'spellen
forefather voorvader
forefinger wijsvinger
foregoing voor'afgaand(e)
foregone conclusion
  uitgemaakte zaak
foreground voorgrond
forehead voorhoofd
foreign buitenlands; vreemd
foreigner vreemdeling, buitenlander
foreman (ploeg)baas
foremost voorste, eerste
foresee voor'zien
foreshadow de voorbode zijn van

foreshorten ver'korten
foresight voorzorg
forest woud, bos
forestall voor'komen, voorzijn
forestry bosbouw
foretaste voorsmaak
foretell voor'spellen
forethought voorzorg
forever (voor) altijd
forfeit boete, pand; ver'spelen
forge smidsvuur, smidse;
  smeden; ver'valsen
forgery ver'valsing
forget ver'geten
forgetful ver'geetachtig
forgive ver'geven
forgiveness ver'giffenis
forgiving vergevensge'zind
forgo opgeven
fork vork; tweesprong, ver'takking;
  zich splitsen **to – out** dokken
forked ge'vorkt; zigzag
forlorn troosteloos, zielig
form vorm, ge'daante, lichaam;
  klas; bank; formu'lier; stijl;
  formali'teit; con'ditie; (zich)
  vormen, (zich) opstellen
formal for'meel
formality formali'teit
formation vorming, for'matie
former eerst(genoemd); vroeger
formidable ge'ducht
  ontzag'wekkend
formula for'mule; vorm
formulate formu'leren
fornication ontucht
forsake ver'laten
fort fort
forth voort; uit; te voorschijn
  and so – enzovoorts
forthcoming (tege'moet)komend
forthright open'hartig
forthwith ter'stond

fortification ver'sterking
fortify ver'sterken
fortitude stand'vastigheid
fortnight veertien dagen
fortress vesting
fortuitous toe'vallig
fortunate ge'lukkig
fortune for'tuin **good fortune**
  ge'luk
forty veertig
forward voor'uit, voorwaarts;
  naar voren; voorst; voorlijk;
  vrij'postig; voor(speler); doorsturen,
  ver'zenden; voor'uithelpen
fossil fos'siel
fossilize ver'stenen
foster kweken; koesteren
foster(-mother) pleeg(moeder)
foul vies; laag; vals, ge'meen;
  be'vuilen; onklaar raken (*or*
  maken)
found stichten, oprichten; ba'seren
foundation funda'ment; oprichting;
  stichting; grond(slag)
founder stichter, oprichter;
  grondlegger; ver'gaan; mis'lukken
foundling vondeling
foundry (me'taal)gieter'ij
fount bron; lettertype
fountain fon'tein; bron
fountain pen vulpen
four vier(tal) **on all fours**
  op handen en voeten
fourteen(th) veertien(de)
fourth vierde (man); kwart
fowl ge'vogelte; hoender
fox vos; be'driegen
foxglove vingerhoedskruid
fraction breuk; mi'niem
  ge'deelte, onderdeel
fractious humeurig, prikkelbaar
fracture breuk; breken
fragile broos, breekbaar
fragment frag'ment, brokstuk

fragrance geur
fragrant geurig
frail teer
frailty zwakheid
frame lijst, mon'tuur, ko'zijn;
  lichaamsbouw; inlijsten; (op)stellen
  – of mind ge'moedstoestand
framework schema, kader; frame
France Frankrijk
franchise recht; con'cessie
frank open'hartig
frantic dol, razend, wild, radeloos
fraternal broederlijk
fraud be'drog, fraude; oplichter
fraudulent fraudu'leus
fraught with vol (van)
fray strijd; (uit)rafelen, ver'slijten
freak gril, ge'drocht
freckle(d) (vol) sproet(en)
free vrij; gratis; los(lippig); open(lijk);
  over'vloedig; be'vrijden, vrijlaten
  – from (*or* **of)** zonder, be'vrijd van
  to set – be'vrijden
freebie weggevertje
freedom vrijheid
freehand met de hand
freehold vrij (grondbezit)
freeze (doen) (be')vriezen
freighter vrachtboot, vrachtschip
French Frans(en) **– bean**
  sperzieboon **– polish** poli'toeren
  – windows openslaande deuren
Frenchman Fransman
frenzied razend
frenzy razer'nij
frequency veel-vuldigheid,
  fre'quentie
frequent veel'voorkomend
  ge'regeld; dikwijls be'zoeken
frequently her'haaldelijk
fresco fresco
fresh vers, fris; nieuw; zoet
freshman eerste'jaars (stu'dent)
fret kniezen, pruilen; wegvreten

fretwork uitgezaagd werk
friar monnik
friction wrijving
Friday vrijdag
friend vriend('in), kennis **to make friends with** be'vriend raken met
friendly vriend('schapp)elijk
friendship vriendschap
frieze rand, fries
fright schrik
frighten doen schrikken
frightful ver'schrikkelijk
frigid ijzig; kil
frill ge'rimpelde strook; tierelan'tijntje
fringe franje; pony; buitenkant; om'zomen; grenzen (aan)
frisky vrolijk, speels
fritter bei'gnet; ver'snipperen
frivolous licht'zinnig; onbelangrijk
frizzle sissen; bakken
fro: to and – heen en weer, op en neer
frock jurk(je)
frog kikvors
frolic pret, lol; stoeien
from van('daan), van'af; uit; wegens
front voorkant, voorste deel; voor-, voorste **at the – (of)** voor'aan (in) **in – of** voor **in the – (of)** voor'in (in)
frontier grens
frost vorst; rijp
frostbite be'vriezing
froth schuim
frown frons; het voorhoofd fronsen **to – upon** niet graag zien
frugal sober, karig
fruit vrucht(en), fruit
fruitful vruchtbaar
fruition ver'vulling
fruitless vruchteloos

frustrate ver'ijdelen; tegenwerken
frustrated te'leurgesteld en onbe'vredigd
frustration frustratie
fry bakken, braden
fuck (vulg) neuken, naaien, wippen
fuddle be'nevelen
fuel brand(stof); tanken
fugitive vluchteling: (voort')-vluchtig
fulfil ver'vullen; waarmaken; be'antwoorden aan
full vol('ledig) **– of** vol **in –** ten volle; vol'uit
fully vol'komen, ten volle
fumble tasten; frommelen
fume damp(en); koken
fumigate uitroken
fun pret **for (or in) –** voor de grap **to make – of** de gek steken met
function functie; functio'neren
functional functio'neel; praktisch
fund fonds; voorraad
funds geld
fundamental fundamen'teel; grond(beginsel)
funeral be'grafenis(-); lijk-, graf-
fungus zwam
funky funky, lekker, gevoelsmatig (music)
funnel trechter; pijp
funny grappig; raar
fur bont; be'slag, ketelsteen
furious woedend
furl oprollen
furnace (smelt)oven, kachel
furnish meubi'leren; voor'zien van, ver'schaffen
furnishings stof'fering (en meubi'lering)
furniture meubelen
furrow voor; groef

further verder, nader; be'vorderen
furtive steels, heimelijk
fury woede, razer'nij
fuse (doorgeslagen) stop; lont; samensmelten
fuselage romp
fusion samensmelting; fusie

fuss drukte; zich druk maken; zenuwachtig maken
fussy lastig; druk
fusty muf
futile ver'geefs, zinloos, onbe'nullig
future toekomst; toe'komstig
   in future voortaan

G

gabble kakelen **– away** erop los kletsen
gable gevelspits
gadget snufje, ge'val
gag prop; mop; knevelen
gaiety vrolijkheid
gain winst; be'halen; toenemen; ver'werven; be'reiken; voorlopen
gait gang
gala feest; gala-
galaxy melkweg
gale storm
gall gal; gruwelijk ergeren
gallantry dapperheid; hoffelijkheid
gallery gale'rij; mu'seum
galley ga'lei; kom'buis
gallon gallon, 4½ liter
gallop ga'lop('peren)
gallows galg
galore in overvloed
galvanize galvani'seren
gamble gokje; gokken
gambler gokker
game spel(letje); par'tij(tje); wild; flink; be'reid; lam; gokken
gamekeeper jachtopziener
gang troep, bende
gangster gangster
gangway pad; loopplank
gap gat, opening, hi'aat
gape gapen
garage ga'rage

garb kle'dij
garbage vuilnis
garden tuin('ieren)
gardener tuinman, tui'nier
gargle gorgelen
garish schel, op'zichtig
garlic knoflook
garment kledingstuk, ge'waad
garnish gar'neren
garrison garni'zoen; legeren
garrulous praatziek
garter kouseband
gas gas; ver'gassen
gash snee; snijden, scheuren
gasp snak(ken)
gastric maag-
gate hek, poort; ingang
gatecrash binnenvallen
gateway poort, hek
gather (zich) ver'zamelen; binnenhalen; krijgen (speed); samentrekken; opmaken (uit)
gathering bij'eenkomst
gauche links
gaudy op'zichtig
gauge (standard)maat; meetinstrument; meten, ijken; schatten
gaunt (brood)mager
gauntlet (kap)handschoen; spitsroede
gauze gaas

gawky slungelig
gay homo; vrolijk
gaze starre blik; staren
gear ver'snelling; inrichting; tuig;
  instellen **to change –** overschakelen
  out of – uitgeschakeld; in de war
gelatine gela'tine
gem edelsteen; ju'weel
gender ge'slacht
gene gen
general algemeen; gene'raal
  in – over het algemeen
generalize generali'seren
generally ge'woonlijk; (over het)
  algemeen
generate opwekken
generation gene'ratie; opwekking
generator gene'rator
generosity edel'moedigheid
generous edel'moedig; ro'yaal
genetic ge'netisch
genial vriendelijk; groeizaam
genitalia geslachtsorganen
genitive genitief
genius ge'nie; ta'lent
gentle licht, zacht('aardig); matig
gentleman gentleman, heer
genuine echt, op'recht
geographic(al) aardrijks'kundig
geography aardrijkskunde
geology geolo'gie
geometry meetkunde
geranium ge'ranium
germ kiem, ba'cil
German Duits(er) **– measles** rode
  hond
Germany Duitsland
gesticulate gesticu'leren
gesture ge'baar
get krijgen; komen; worden **I have
  got** ik heb **I have got to** ik moet
  to – something done iets (laten)

doen; iets ge'daan krijgen **to –
about** buitenkomen, rondlopen **to
– along** (weg)gaan; opschieten; het
maken **to – around** overal komen;
be'kend worden; om'zeilen **to – at**
be'reiken; achter komen; be'doelen
to – away wegkomen; ont'snappen
to – back te'rugkomen;
te'rugkrijgen **to – in** binnenkomen,
instappen **to – off** (er) afkomen
(van), afstappen van; afkrijgen
to – on opstappen; aankrijgen;
opschieten; het stellen; het maken
to – out (onder')uitkomen,
uitstappen; voor de dag halen **to –
over** te boven komen **to – through**
doorkomen; antwoord krijgen **to –
to** komen in (or aan) **to – up**
opstaan; opsteken; op touw zetten
geyser geiser
ghastly af'grijselijk, doodsbleek
ghost spook; zweem
giant reus('achtig)
gibber brabbelen
gibberish koeter'waals
giblets inwendige organen
  van ge'vogelte
giddy duizelig; duizeling'wekkend; mal
gift ge'schenk; gave
gifted be'gaafd
gig optreden, concert
gigantic gigantisch, enorm
giggle giechelen
gild ver'gulden
gill kieuw
gilt ver'guld(sel)
gin jonge jenever
ginger gember
gingerly be'hoedzaam
giraffe gi'raffe
girder (stalen) balk
girdle gordel

Insight

In English *boyfriend* and *girlfriend* usually refer to the person you are having a relationship with. In Dutch **vriend** and **vriendin** (or their diminutive forms **vriendje/vriendinnetje**) can mean the same, but, sometimes confusingly, they can also refer to an ordinary friend who happens to be male or female. To indicate what you mean, someone you are having a relationship with is usually called **mijn vriend(in)** *my boy/girlfriend* (or **jouw/zijn/haar vriend(in)** *your/his/her boy/girlfriend*), as opposed to **een vriend(in)** *a boy/girlfriend*. The plural forms of **vriend** and **vriendin** are **vrienden** and **vriendinnen**. When speaking, note that in **vriendin** *girlfriend* the stress is on the last syllable, while the stress in **vrienden** *friends* is on the first.

girl meisje
girlfriend vriendin(netje)
girlish meisjesachtig
giro giro(dienst), giro(cheque)
girth omvang; buikriem
gist kern
give geven; doorzakken, buigen **to**
 – away weggeven; ver'klappen **to**
 – in zich ge'wonnen geven **to – out**
 uitdelen; aankondigen; be'zwijken
 to – up overgeven; (het) opgeven
given be'paald; ge'neigd (tot)
glacier gletsjer
glad blij(de)
gladden ver'blijden
glade open plek, moerassig gebied
gladly graag
glamorous aantrekkelijk,
 be'toverend
glamour be'tovering
glance (vluchtige) blik;
 een blik werpen; afschampen
gland klier
glare ver'blindend licht;
 woeste blik; woest kijken
glaring schel; vlammend;
 in het oog springend

glass glas(werk); glazen **glasses** bril
glaze gla'zuur; van glas voor'zien;
 gla'zuren
gleam schijnsel, straaltje,
 glans; glimmen
glean lezen; ver'garen
glee vreugde, leedvermaak
glen bergdal
glib glad, rad van tong
glide zweven, glijden
glider zweefvliegtuig
glimmer flikkering; glimp; flikkeren
glimpse glimp
glint glinstering
glisten glinsteren
glitter ge'schitter; schitteren
gloat zich ver'lustigen, leedvermaak
 hebben
globe (aard)bol
gloom duister; droef'geestigheid
gloomy duister, somber;
 droef'geestig
glorify ver'heerlijken
glorious roemrijk; heerlijk
glory glorie, heerlijkheid
gloss glans **to – over** ver'doezelen
glossy glanzend

glove handschoen
glow gloed; blos; gloeien; stralen
glower dreigend kijken
glue (hout)lijm; lijmen
glum mistroostig
glut (over)ver'zadiging; over'voeren
glutton gulzigaard
gnarled knoestig, knokig
gnash one's teeth knarsetanden
gnat mug
gnaw (af)knagen
gnome aardmannetje
go (weg)gaan; lopen; worden;
horen as things – verge'leken
bij anderen to – by gaan per
(or over); voor'bijgaan; zich laten
leiden door; be'kend staan onder
to – down afgaan; naar be'neden
gaan, ondergaan, zinken, er'in gaan
to – into binnengaan; ingaan (op);
treden in (details); zich ver'diepen
in to – off af (or weg)gaan; aflopen
to – on gaan op; voor'uitgaan,
voortgaan to – up stijgen to – with
meegaan met; passen bij, horen bij
to – without het stellen zonder to
let – loslaten
goad prikkel(en); aanzetten
go-ahead toestemming
goal doel(punt)
goat geit
gobble schrokken; klokken
goblet bo'kaal
goblin ka'bouter
god god
goddess go'din
godmother peettante
godsend zegen
gobble schrokken
going: to get (or to keep) – aan de
gang brengen, (or houden); lopen
gold goud(en)
golden gouden; gulden
goldfish goudvis

golf golf
gondola gondel
gone weg; op; zoek; dood
gong gong
good goed; zoet; bestwil a – deal
vrij veel for – voor'goed; ten goede
goodbye dag
goodies iets lekkers
good-looking knap
good-natured ge'moedelijk,
goed'aardig
goodness goedheid; voeding
good night welterusten
goods goederen, spullen
goodwill wel'willendheid; klan'dizie
goody-goody schijnheilige
goose gans
gooseberry kruisbes(sen)
gore ge'ronnen bloed; spietsen
gorge bergengte: (zich) volstoppen
gorgeous magni'fiek
gospel evan'gelie
gossip ge'roddel; roddelaar(ster);
roddelen, kletsen
gothic gotisch
govern re'geren; leiden
government re'gering; be'leid
governor gouver'neur; cu'rator
gown ja'pon; toga
grab greep; grijpen naar
grace gratie; ge'nade; tafelgebed;
res'pijt; ver'eren
graceful graci'eus
gracious minzaam, hoffelijk
grade graad, kwali'teit; sor'teren
gradient helling(shoek)
gradual ge'leidelijk
graft (poli'tieke) knoeie'rij;
enten, transplan'teren
grain graan, korrel; greintje; nerf
grammar gram'matica
grammar school gym'nasium
granary graanschuur
grand groot(s), prachtig

grandchild kleinkind
grandeur grootsheid
grandiose grandi'oos
grandmother grootmoeder
granite gra'niet(en)
grant toelage; (toe)geven; ver'lenen; inwilligen
grape druif
grapefruit grapefruit
graph gra'fiek
graphic grafisch; aan'schouwelijk
graphite gra'fiet
grapple worstelen
grasp greep; begrip; be'reik; vastpakken
grass gras
grasshopper sprinkhaan
grassy gras(rijk)
grate rooster; raspen; knarsen; tegen de borst stuiten
grateful dankbaar
gratification vol'doening
gratify strelen; be'vredigen
gratifying be'vredigend, dankbaar
grating traliewerk; knarsen
gratitude dankbaarheid
gratuitous gratis; ongegrond
gratuity fooi
grave graf; ernstig
gravel grint(-)
graveyard kerkhof
gravitation aantrekking(skracht)
gravity zwaartekracht; ernst
 centre of **–** zwaartepunt
gravy jus
graze schaafwond; even aanraken; schaven; grazen, weiden
grease smeer, vet; (in)smeren, invetten
greasy vet(tig), vuil
great groot; voor'naamste; nobel; enthousi'aste **a – deal (of)** heel veel
great-grandchild achterkleinkind

great-grandmother overgrootmoeder
greatly zeer
greed gulzigheid, hebzucht
greedy gulzig, hebberig
Greek Griek(s)
green groen; brink
greens bladgroenten
greengrocer groenteboer
greenhouse broeikas
greet (be')groeten
greeting groet
grey grijs (worden), grauw
greyhound haze'wind; windhonden-
grid (braad)rooster; hoogspanningsnet
grief ver'driet
grievance grief, klacht
grieve treuren; be'droeven
grievous erg; verschrikkelijk
grill rooster(en)
grim onver'biddelijk; onaan'lokkelijk; akelig
grimace gri'mas
grime vuil; be'vuilen
grin grijns; grijnzen
grind ge'zwoeg; malen; slijpen; knarsen (op)
grindstone slijpsteen
grip (hand)greep, vat, houvast; tas; be'grip; (vast)pakken
gristle kraakbeen
grit gruis; durf
grizzly grijs(achtig)
groan ge'kreun; kreunen
grocer kruide'nier
groceries levensmiddelen
groggy suf, wankel op de benen
groin lies
groom ver'zorgen
groove groef; sleur; groeven
grope (rond)tasten
gross bruto; grof; gros
grotesque gro'tesk

grotto grot
ground grond(-); ter'rein; aan de grond lopen; grondig onder'leggen
  to cover – ter'rein be'strijken
  to give – wijken **to stand one's –** standhouden; voet bij stuk houden
ground floor be'nedenver'dieping
groundless onge'grond
grounds ter'rein, park; reden(en)
group groep('eren)
grouse korhoen(ders); kankeren
grove bos(je)
grovel kruipen
grow (aan)groeien; ver'bouwen, kweken; worden **to – up** opgroeien, ouder worden; ont'staan
growing toenemend
growl grom(men)
grown-up vol'wassene
growth groei; aanwas; gezwel
grub larve; kost; wroeten
grudge wrok; mis'gunnen
grudgingly met tegenzin
gruel gruwel
gruelling af'mattend
gruesome gruwelijk
gruff bars
grumble mopperen
grunt ge'knor; ge'brom; knorren; brommen
guarantee (waar)borg, ga'rantie; waarborgen, garan'deren
guard wacht; scherm, be'scherming; hoede; conduc'teur; (be')waken; be'schermen
guarded voor'zichtig

guardian voogd, be'waarder; be'scherm-
guess gis(sing); raden
guest gast, lo'gé(e)
guidance leiding, ad'vies
guide gids; padvindster; leiden
guild gilde
guilder gulden
guile list
guileless argeloos
guillotine guillo'tine
guilt schuld
guiltless on'schuldig
guilty schuldig, schuldbe'wust
guitar gi'taar
gulf golf; kloof
gull meeuw; beetnemen
gullet slokdarm, keel
gullible lichtge'lovig
gully geul
gulp slok, teug; opslokken; inslikken
gum gom(men); tandvlees
gun ka'non, ge'weer, pis'tool
gurgle kabbelen, klokken, kirren
gush stroom; gutsen, stromen
gushing dwepend
gust vlaag
gusto animo
gusty stormachtig
gut darm; schoonmaken; uitbranden
gutter goot
guttersnipe straatkind
guy vent, man; **–s** jongens, mensen
guzzle opschrokken
gymnasium gymnas'tiekzaal
gymnastics gymnas'tiek
gypsy zi'geuner('in)

H

haberdashery fourni'turen(winkel)
habit ge'woonte; pij
habitable be'woonbaar
habitation woonplaats

habitual ge'woon(lijk), ge'woonte-, regel'matig
hack hakken
hackneyed afgezaagd

haddock schelvis
haemorrhage bloeding
haggard uitgeteerd
haggle knibbelen
hail hagel(en); toejuichen, (luidkeels) be'groeten; aanroepen; af'komstig zijn
hair haar; haren **to split hairs** muggenziften
hairdresser kapper
hairy harig, be'haard
half half; (de) helft **half past one** half twee
halfway halver'wege
hall hal, zaal
hallmark keur; stempel(en)
hallow heiligen
hallucination halluci'natie
halo aure'ool, halo
halt halt (houden); stoppen, pauzeren
halter halster
halve hal'veren
ham ham
hamlet ge'hucht
hammer hamer(en)
hammock hangmat
hamper mand; be'lemmeren
hand hand; wijzer; arbeider; spel; over'handigen, aangeven
 at – bij de hand; op handen **in –** in be'dwang; onder handen; over **on the other –** aan de andere kant **to – down** overleveren **to – in** inleveren **to – out** uitdelen **to – over** overdragen, over'handigen **to – round** ronddienen, ronddelen
handbag handtas
handcuff handboei
handful hand(je)vol
handicap handicap(pen)
handicraft handwerk handenarbeid
handiwork (hand)werk
handkerchief zakdoek

handle handvat, knop, oor; be'dienen, han'teren; aanpakken; be'handelen; handelen in
handle bars stuur
handmade handgemaakt
handshake handdruk
handsome knap; flink, ro'yaal
handwriting (hand)schrift
handy handig; bij de hand; van pas
hang slag; (op)hangen; laten hangen; be'hangen **to – about** rondlummelen **to – on** (zich) vasthouden; wachten
hangar han'gar
hangover kater
haphazard luk'raak
happen (toe'vallig) ge'beuren **I – to** ... ik ... toe'vallig; ik ... nu eenmaal
happenings ge'beurtenissen
happiness ge'luk
happy ge'lukkig
harass be'stoken; kwellen
harbour haven; (ver')bergen, koesteren
hard hard('vochtig); moeilijk; vast **to try –** zijn best doen
harden harder worden (*or* maken)
hard-hearted hard'vochtig
hardly nauwelijks; hard
hardship ont'bering, last
hardware ijzerwaren
hardwood hardhout(en)
hardy ge'hard, sterk
hare haas
harlequin harle'kijn
harm schade, letsel; kwaad doen
harmful na'delig, schadelijk
harmless on'schadelijk; argeloos
harmonic har'monisch
harmonica mondharmonika
harmonious har'monisch harmoni'eus

harmonize (doen) harmoni'ëren;
harmoni'seren
harmony harmo'nie
harness (paarden)tuig; ga'reel;
optuigen
harp harp; hameren
harpoon har'poen('eren)
harpsichord klave'cimbel
harsh ruw, wrang; hard
harvest oogst(tijd); oogsten
hash mengelmoes; hasj(iesj)
haste haast
hasten zich haasten, ver'haasten
hasty haastig; driftig
hat hoed
hatch luik; uitbroeden, uitkomen
hatchet bijl
hate haat; haten, een hekel
hebben aan
hateful akelig
hatred haat
haughty hoog'hartig
haul vangst; slepen, halen
haunch lende, hurk
haunt oord, speelplaats;
hol; veel'vuldig be'zoeken;
achter'volgen
haunted spook-, door geesten
be'zocht
have hebben; laten; moeten;
nemen; krijgen
haven (veilige) haven
havoc ver'woesting
hawk havik; venten
hawthorn haagdoorn
hay hooi
haystack hooiberg
hazard risico; wagen
hazardous ris'kant
haze waas, nevel
hazel hazelaar; lichtbruin
hazy wazig; vaag
he hij

head hoofd(-), kop; spits; tegen-;
leiden; sturen **to keep one's –**
zijn ver'stand bij el'kaar houden
to lose one's – in de war raken
headache hoofdpijn
headgear hoofdtooi
heading ru'briek, opschrift
headlight koplamp
headline kop
headlong hals over kop
headmaster direc'teur, (school)hoofd
headquarters hoofdkantoor
headstrong koppig
headway voortgang
heal ge'nezen
health ge'zondheid
healthy ge'zond
heap hoop, massa; ophopen
hear horen; luisteren
hearing ge'hoor; ver'hoor
hearsay praatjes
hearse lijkwagen
heart hart; moed; kern, binnenste
by – uit het hoofd **to take –**
moed scheppen
heart-breaking hartver'scheurend
heartbroken ge'broken
hearten opbeuren
heartfelt innig
hearth haard
heartless harteloos
hearty hartelijk; ge'zond;
stevig; hart'grondig
heat hitte; vuur; loop; ver'
warmen; opwinden
heater ver'warmingsapparaat
heath heide
heathen heiden(s)
heather heide
heave hijsen, lichten; trekken;
slaken; deinen
heaven hemel
heavenly hemels, hemel-

heavy zwaar, klef
Hebrew Hebreeuws; Ivriet
heckle jouwen, scherp onder'vragen
hectic koortsachtig
hedge heg; om'heinen;
  er omheen draaien
hedgehog egel
hedgerow haag
heed aandacht; letten op
heedless achteloos
heel hiel, hak; overhellen
hefty stoer
height hoogte; top(punt)
heighten ver'hogen; ver'sterken
heinous gruwelijk
heir erfgenaam
heiress erfgename
heirloom erfstuk
helicopter heli'kopter
hell hel
hello hal'lo

hemp hennep
hen kip
hence van'daar (dat); hier van'daan,
  van nu af aan
henceforth van nu af aan
henchman handlanger
henpeck op de kop zitten
her haar
herald her'aut, voorbode;
  aankondigen
heraldry heral'diek
herb kruid
herd kudde; (samen-)drijven
here hier
hereabout(s) hier in de buurt
hereafter hier'na(maals)
hereby hierbij, hierdoor
hereditary erfelijk, erf-
heredity erfelijkheid, over'erving
heretic(al) ketter(s), her'metisch
hermit kluizenaar

Insight

Hello is easily translated into Dutch as **hallo**. **Hallo** is a
neutral way of greeting people, as is **dag**. Some more informal
greetings are **hoi, hi** and **hé**. More formal ways of greeting
people are **goedendag** (literally *good day*), or depending on
the time of day **goedemorgen** *good morning*, **goedemiddag**
good afternoon and **goedenavond** *good evening*. Note that in
many regions **goede-** is pronounced as **goeie-**, where the **d** is
replaced by an English 'y' sound.

helm roer
helmet helm
help hulp; steun, helper(s); helpen;
  nalaten **I can't – it** ik kan er niets
  aan doen
helpful hulp'vaardig; be'vorderlijk,
  ge'makkelijk
helping portie
helpless hulpeloos
hem zoom; zomen
hemisphere halfrond

hero held
heroic held'haftig, helden-
heroics bombast
heroine hel'din
heron reiger
herring haring
hesitant aarzelend
hesitate aarzelen
hesitation aarzeling
heterogeneous hetero'geen
heyday bloeitijd

hiatus hi'aat
hibernate winterslaap doen
hiccup(s) hik(ken) **to have –**
de hik hebben
hide huid; afrossen; (zich)
ver'bergen
hide-and-seek ver'stoppertje
hideous af'zichtelijk, af'schuwelijk
hierarchy hiërar'chie
high hoog; adellijk
highland hoogland(s)
highly hoog-, zeer
high-pitched hoog, schel
highway grote weg
hike trektocht; trekken
hilarious uitgelaten
hill heuvel, berg
hilly heuvelachtig
him hem
hind achter(ste); hinde
hinder (ver)hinderen
hindrance belemmering
hinge schar'nier; spil; draaien
hint wenk; zweem; laten
doorschemeren **to – at** zinspelen op
hip heup; rozebottel; hip
hippopotamus nijlpaard
hire huur; (ver')huren
hire purchase huurkoop; op
afbetaling kopen
his zijn, van hem
hiss sissen; (uit)fluiten
historian ge'schiedschrijver
historic his'torisch; ge'wichtig
historical his'torisch
history ge'schiedenis
hit slag, treffer; suc'ces; slaan; raken,
treffen **to – upon** treffen, vinden
hitch ruk; kink in de kabel;
(op)trekken; vastmaken
hitchhike liften
hither hier(heen)
hitherto tot nu toe
hive korf

hoard voorraad; opsparen,
hamsteren
hoarding re'clamebord
hoar frost rijp
hoarse hees, schor
hoax bedrog; om de tuin leiden
hobble strompelen
hobby liefhebbe'rij
hockey hockey
hog varken; zwijn
hoist hijstoestel; (op)hijsen
hold houvast, vat; invloed; ruim;
(vast)houden; be'vatten;
(in zijn be'zit) hebben; opgaan
to – out geven; volhouden; in
leven blijven **to – up** ophouden;
aanhouden **to – with** goedkeuren,
het eens zijn met **to get – of** te
pakken krijgen; vastpakken
hole gat, hol
holiday vakantie(dag); feestdag
Holland Nederland
hollow hol(te); leeg
to – out uithollen
holly hulst
holocaust holocaust, vernietiging
holster holster
holy heilig
homage hulde(betuiging)
home (t)huis, tehuis; binnenlands;
naar huis; raak **at –** thuis
homeland ge'boorteland
homeless dakloos
homely huiselijk; ge'moedelijk
homemade eigengemaakt
homesick: to be – heimwee
hebben
homicide doodslag
homogeneous homo'geen
homosexual homoseksueel
honest(y) eerlijk(heid)
honey honing
honeycomb honingraat
honeymoon huwelijksreis

honeysuckle kamper'foelie
honk toeteren; snateren
honorary ere-
honour eer(gevoel); eerbewijs; (ver')eren
honourable eervol
hood kap
hoodwink zand in de ogen strooien
hoof hoef
hook haak; aan de haak slaan
hooligan hooligan, van'daal, herrieschopper
hoop hoepel
hoot krassen; toeteren; uitjouwen
hop sprong; hop(plant); hinken, springen
hope hoop(volle ver'wachting); hopen
hopeful hoopvol
hopeless hopeloos, wan'hopig
horde horde
horizon horizon
horizontal horizon'taal
horn horen
horoscope horos'coop
horrible, horrid af'grijselijk, af'schuwelijk
horrify ont'zetten
horror afgrijzen; gruwel(daad)
horse paard
horseback: on – te paard
horseshoe hoefijzer
horticulture tuinbouw
hose (tuin)slang
hospitable gastvrij
hospital ziekenhuis
hospitality gast'vrijheid
host gastheer/gastvrouw; massa, horde(n); optreden als gastheer/vrouw
hostage gijzelaar
hostel te'huis
hostess gastvrouw

hostile vij'andelijk, vij'andig
hostility vij'andelijkheid, vij'andigheid
hot heet, warm
hotel ho'tel
hothouse broeikas
hound (jacht)hond
hour uur
house huis: huisvesten **to keep –** de huishouding doen
household huisgezin; huis ('houd)elijk
householder ge'zinshoofd
housekeeper huishoudster
housekeeping huishouden; huishoud(geld)
housewife huisvrouw
housework huishoudelijk werk
housing woning-, woon-; huisvesting
hovel krot
hover zweven, hangen
how hoe
however hoe dan ook; echter
howl huilen, janken; gillen, joelen
howler flater; giller
hub naaf; middelpunt
hubbub herrie
huddle (bij *or* in el'kaar) kruipen
hue tint
hug pakken; tegen zich aandrukken; koesteren
huge reus'achtig
hulk romp
hulking log
hull romp
hum ge'gons; gonzen, snorren; neuriën
human menselijk, mens(en-) **– being** menselijk wezen
humane mens'lievend
humanitarian humani'tair
humanity het mensdom

humanly menselijkerwijs
humble nederig; ver'nederen
humbug bedrieger('ij)
humdrum saai(e sleur)
humid(ity) vochtig(heid)
humiliate ver'nederen
humility nederigheid
humorist humo'rist
humorous grappig, humo'ristisch
humour humor; hu'meur; luim;
toegeven aan
hump bult
hunch samentrekken, krommen
hunchback ge'bochelde
hundred(th) honderd(ste)
hunger honger
hungry hongerig **to be –** trek
(*or* honger) hebben
hunk homp
hunt jacht(stoet); jagen (op); (af)
zoeken **to – down** in het nauw
drijven; opsporen
hunter jager
hurdle horde; hindernis
hurl slingeren
hurricane or'kaan

hurried haastig, ge'haast
hurry (zich) haasten
to be in a – haast hebben
hurt pijn doen; deren, kwetsen
hurtle ratelen, schieten
husband man, echtgenoot
hush stilte; stil!; tot zwijgen
brengen
husky schor
hustle ge'jacht; jachten, drijven;
dringen
hut hut, ba'rak
hybrid hy'bride; bastaard-
hydraulic hy'draulisch
hydrogen waterstof
hygiene hygiëne
hygienic hygi'ënisch
hymn hymne
hyphen(ate) (door een) streepje
(ver'binden)
hypnotize hypnoti'seren
hypocrite huichelaar
hypocritical huichelachtig
hypothesis hypo'these
hysterical hys'terisch
hysterics zenuwaanval

I

I ik
ice ijs(je); (doen) be'vriezen;
gla'ceren
iceberg ijsberg
ice cream roomijs; ijsje
iced ijskoud; gegla'ceerd
icicle ijskegel
icing sugar poedersuiker
icy ijskoud, glad; ijs-, ijzig
idea i'dee
ideal ide'aal
idealism idea'lisme
idealist(ic) idea'list(isch)
idealize ideali'seren

identical iden'tiek
identification identifi'catie
identify identifi'ceren,
vereen'zelvigen
identity identi'teit
idiom idi'oom
idiosyncracy eigen'aardigheid
idiot(ic) idi'oot
idle nietsdoend; lui; leeg; niets doen
to be – niets doen; stilliggen
idler leegloper
idol afgod (sbeeld)
idolize ver'afgoden
idyll i'dylle

Insight

The English word *if* has two meanings in Dutch: **als,** meaning *if* in the sense of *when*; and **of,** meaning *if* in the sense of *whether.* Just have a look at the following examples: **ik ga niet joggen als het regent** *I'm not going jogging if it rains;* **Klaus weet niet of hij mee wil** *Klaus doesn't know if he wants to come along.* Beware that 'of' also means 'or': **wil je een pannekoek of een patatje?** *do you want a pancake or chips?*

---

if als, in'dien, of
iffy on'zeker, dubi'eus
ignite in brand steken (*or* raken)
ignoble laag
ignominious smadelijk
ignorance on'wetendheid
ignorant on'wetend, on'kundig
ignore ne'geren
ill ziek; slecht, kwaad; kwalijk **to cause – feeling** kwaad bloed zetten
ill-advised onver'standig
illegal on'wettig, onrecht'matig
illegible on'leesbaar
illegitimate on'wettig; onge'oorloofd
ill-fated ramp'spoedig
illicit on'wettig
illiterate onge'letterd; analfa'beet
illness ziekte
illogical on'logisch
ill-tempered slecht gehu'meurd
ill-treat slecht be'handelen
illuminate ver (*or* be)'lichten, toelichten; ver'luchten
illumination ver'lichting; ver'luchting
illusion il'lusie
illustrate illu'streren; toelichten
illustration ilu'stratie, toelichting
illustrious gerenommeerd
image beeld; imago, repu'tatie
imaginable denkbaar
imaginary denk'beeldig

imagination ver'beelding-(skracht)
imaginative vindingrijk, rijk aan ver'beelding; fan'tastisch
imagine zich voorstellen
imam imam
imbecile imbe'ciel
imbibe drinken; (in zich) opnemen
imbue door'drenken
imitate nabootsen
imitation nabootsing; namaak-
immaculate onbe'rispelijk
immaterial on'stoffelijk; onver'schillig; onbe'langrijk
immature on'rijp
immeasurable on'meetbaar; niet te over'zien, on'noemelijk
immediate on'middellijk, naast
immense on'metelijk
immerse onderdompelen, indompelen
immersed onder'water; ver'diept
immigrant immi'grant; immi'grerend
immigration immi'gratie
imminent op handen, dreigend
immobile onbe'weeglijk
immoderate on'matig
immodest onbe'scheiden, on'zedig
immoral immo'reel
immortal(ity) on'sterfelijk(heid)
immovable on'beweeglijk
immune im'muun (voor); vrijgesteld
immutable onver'anderlijk

impact botsing, samentreffen;
  ef'fect
impair na'delig be "invloeden,
  schaden
impart ver'lenen; mededelen
impartial(ity) onpar'tijdig(heid)
impassable onbe'gaanbaar
impassioned harts'tochtelijk
impassive onver'stoorbaar;
  ge'voelloos
impatient onge'duldig
impeach in twijfel trekken; aanklagen
impeccable onbe'rispelijk, feilloos
impede be'lemmeren
impediment be'letsel, ge'brek
impel voortdrijven, aanzetten
impend dreigen
impenetrable ondoor'dringbaar
imperative hoogstnood'zakelijk;
  ge'biedend
imperceptible on'merkbaar
imperfect imper'fect(um);
  afwijkend, on'gaaf
imperial keizerlijk, keizer(s)-, rijks-
imperialism imperia'lisme
imperious aan'matigend
impermeable ondoor'dringbaar
impersonal onper'soonlijk
impersonate voorstellen
impertinent onbe'schaamd
imperturbable onver'stoorbaar
impervious ondoor'dringbaar;
  doof (voor)
impetuous on'stuimig
impetus drijfkracht; stuwkracht
impinge on raken
implacable onver'zoenlijk
implant inplanten
implement werktuig; uitvoeren
implicate ver'wikkelen,
  be'trekken (bij)
implication bijgedachte, implicatie
implicit impli'ciet, onvoor'waardelijk
implore (af)smeken

imply impli'ceren, inhouden,
  te ver'staan geven
impolite onbe'leefd
import invoer(en)
importance be'tekenis, be'lang
important be'langrijk,
  gewichtig(doend)
importunity op'dringerigheid
impose on opleggen;
  misbruik maken van
imposing indruk'wekkend
impossible on'mogelijk
impostor be'drieger
impotent impo'tent, machteloos
impoverish ver'armen, uitputten
impracticable onuit'voerbaar
impregnable on'neembaar;
  onaan'tastbaar
impregnate impreg'neren;
  be'vruchten
impress stempel(en); indruk
  maken op, op het hart drukken
impression indruk, i'dee;
  afdruk; oplage
impressionable ont'vankelijk
impressive indruk'wekkend
imprint afdruk; stempel(en);
  inprenten
imprison ge'vangen zetten
  (*or* houden)
imprisonment ge'vangenschap
improbable onwaar'schijnlijk
impromptu voor de vuist
improper incor'rect, onfat'soenlijk
improve ver'beteren; voor'uitgaan
improvement ver'betering;
  voor'uitgang
improvise improvi'seren
imprudent onvoor'zichtig
impudence brutali'teit
impudent bru'taal
impulse im'puls; opwelling, aandrift
impulsive stuw-; impul'sief
impunity: with — onge'straft

impure on'zuiver; on'kuis
impute toeschrijven
in in, (naar) binnen
inability onvermogen
inaccessible onbe'reikbaar;
onge'naakbaar
inaccurate onnauw'keurig
inactive nietsdoend
inactivity nietsdoen
inadequate ontoe'reikend
inadvertent onop'zettelijk
inadvisable onver'standig
inalienable onver'vreemdbaar
inane zinloos
inanimate levenloos
inappropriate onge'schikt
inarticulate ongearticu'leerd;
sprakeloos
inasmuch as voorzo'ver; aange'zien
inattentive onop'lettend; onat'tent
inaudible on'hoorbaar
inaugural inaugu'reel
inaugurate inhuldigen; inluiden
inbreeding inteelt
incalculable onbe'rekenbaar
incandescent gloei-
incantation toverformule
incapable onbe'kwaam; niet in
staat
incapacitate onge'schikt maken;
ver'hinderen
incense wierook; boos maken
incensed woedend zijn
incentive prikkel
inception ont'staan
incessant onop'houdelijk
incest incest
inch inch, duim(breed); beetje
inch forward zich een weg banen
incident voorval; epi'sode
incidental toe'vallig; bij'komstig
incidentally ter'loops,
tussen twee haakjes

incision insnijding
incite aanzetten
inclination buiging, helling; neiging
incline helling; overhellen (tot)
to be inclined ge'neigd zijn,
de neiging hebben
include be (*or* om)'vatten;
meerekenen **to be included**
(er'bij) inbegrepen zijn
including met inbegrip van,
waar'onder
inclusive allesom'vattend, inclu'sief;
tot en met
incoherent onsamen'hangend
income inkomen, inkomsten
income tax inkomstenbelasting
incomparable niet te verge'lijken;
weergaloos
incompatible onver'enigbaar
incompetent onbe'voegd;
ineffici'ënt
incomplete onvol'ledig
incomprehensible onbe'grijpelijk
inconceivable on'denkbaar
inconclusive niet be'slissend,
niet over'tuigend
incongruous niet passend,
onge'rijmd
inconsiderate onat'tent
inconsistent inconse'quent,
tegen'strijdig
inconspicuous onop'vallend
incontestable onbe'twistbaar
inconvenience ongemak; ongerief
bezorgen
inconvenient lastig, onge'legen;
onge'riefelijk
incorporate opnemen; ver'enigen
incorrect on'juist
incorrigible onver'beterlijk
increase toename, ver'hoging;
toenemen, ver'hogen
increasingly steeds meer

incredible onge'lofelijk
incredulous onge'lovig
incriminate be'schuldigen
incubator broedmachine
inculcate inprenten
incur zich op de hals halen; oplopen
incurable onge'neeslijk(e zieke)
indebted schuldig, ver'plicht
indecent on'zedelijk; onwel'voeglijk
indecision be'sluiteloosheid
indecisive onbe'slist; be'sluiteloos
indeed inder'daad; werkelijk,
   (ja) zelfs
indefatigable onver'moeibaar,
   onver'moeid
indefinite onbe'paald
indelible onuit'wisbaar; inkt-
indemnity schadeloosstelling
independence onaf'hankelijkheid
independent onaf'hankelijk
indescribable onbe'schrijfelijk
index re'gister; aanwijzing
indicate aanwijzen; wijzen op
indication aanwijzing
indicator wijzer
indictment aanklacht
indifferent onver'schillig;
   (middel')matig
indigenous in'heems
indigestible onver'teerbaar
indigestion indi'gestie
indignant veront'waardigd
indignation veront'waardiging
indignity smaad
indirect indi'rect
indiscreet indis'creet
indiscretion indiscretie
indiscriminate luk'raak, zonder
   onderscheid; ver'ward
indispensable on'misbaar
indisposed onwel; onge'negen
indisputable onbe'twistbaar
indistinct on'duidelijk

individual individu'eel; indivi'du
individuality individuali'teit
indolence traagheid
indomitable onover'winnelijk,
   on'tembaar
indoor(s) binnen(s'huis)
induce brengen tot; veroorzaken,
   opwekken **(of birth)**
inducement stimu'lans, lokmiddel
induction in'ductie; aanvoering;
   instal'latie
indulge toegeven aan **to – in**
   zich permit'teren
indulgence toe'geeflijkheid;
   uitspatting; aflaat
industrial industri'eel, be'drijfs
industrialist industri'eel
industrious vlijtig
industry indust'rie, be'drijf-
   (sleven); vlijt
inebriated dronken
inedible on'eetbaar
ineffective, ineffectual
   ondoel'treffend, vruchteloos
inefficient ondoel'matig,
   onbe'kwaam
inept onge'rijmd, dwaas
inequality onge'lijkheid
inert(ia) in'ert(ie); stil(stand)
inestimable on'schatbaar
inevitable onver'mijdelijk
inexcusable onver'geeflijk
inexhaustible onuit'puttelijk
inexorable onver'biddelijk
inexpensive voor'delig
inexperienced oner'varen
inexplicable onver'klaarbaar
inexpressible onuit'sprekelijk
infallible on'feilbaar
infamous schandelijk, be'rucht
infancy kindsheid
infant zuigeling, kind(er-)
infantry infante'rie

infatuated verliefd/gek (zijn) (op)
infect be'smetten; aansteken
infection in'fectie
infectious be'smettelijk; aan'stekelijk
infer afleiden; laten doorschemeren
inference ge'volgtrekking
inferior inferi'eur; onderge'schikt(e)
  to be – to lager zijn dan;
  onderdoen voor
inferiority minder'waardigheid(s-)
inferno hel
infest teisteren
infidel onge'lovig(e)
infidelity ontrouw
infinite on'eindig (veel)
infinitesimal on'eindig klein
infinity on'eindigheid
infirmary ziekenafdeling, ziekenhuis
infirmity ge'brek
inflammable ont'vlambaar
inflammation ont'steking
inflate opblazen, oppompen;
  opdrijven
inflation in'flatie
inflexible onver'zettelijk, rotsvast, star
inflict toebrengen, opleggen,
  ver'oorzaken; lastig vallen met
influence invloed; be'ïnvloeden
influential invloedrijk
influenza griep ·
influx toevloed, instroming
inform informeren, be'richten;
  aanbrengen
informal infor'meel
information informatie,
  inlichting(en), be'richt(en)
infrequent zeldzaam
infringe inbreuk maken; over'treden
infuriate woedend maken
infuse laten trekken; be'zielen
ingenious ver'nuftig
ingenuity ver'nuft
ingenuous onge'kunsteld
ingrained inge'worteld

ingratiate zich in de gunst dringen
ingratitude on'dankbaarheid
ingredient be'standdeel
inhabit wonen in
inhabitant in(or be')woner
inhale inha'leren
inherent inhe'rent
inherit erven
inheritance erfenis
inhibition remming
inhospitable ongast'vrij,
  onher'bergzaam
inhuman on'menselijk
inimitable onna'volgbaar
iniquity onrecht'vaardigheid, ver'derf
initial be'gin-, eerst;
  voorletter; para'feren
initially in het be'gin
initiate inwijden
initiative initia'tief
inject inspuiten
injudicious onverstandig
injunction be'vel
injure (ver)wonden; schade
  doen; kwetsen
injurious schadelijk
injury ver'wonding; schade;
  be'lediging
injustice onrecht('vaardigheid)
ink inkt
inkling flauw vermoeden
inlaid ingelegd
inland binnen(land)(s); het land in
in-laws schoonfamilie **father-**
  (mother- or **sister-) in-law**
  schoonvader(moeder or zuster)
inlet inham, zeegat
inmate (tijdelijk)
  ('mede)be'woner
inn herberg
innate aangeboren
inner binnen-; innerlijk
innermost binnenste
innkeeper waard

innocence onschuld
innocent on'schuldig
innocuous on'schadelijk
innovation nieuwigheid
innuendo (hatelijke) toespeling
innumerable on'telbaar
inoculate inenten
inoffensive geen ergernis wekkend
inopportune onge'legen
inordinate buiten'sporig
inquest ge'rechtelijk onderzoek naar de doodsoorzaak
inquire infor'meren (naar), vragen (naar)
inquiry vraag, poging (om inlichtingen in te winnen); onderzoek
inquisitive nieuws'gierig
inroad inval, ver'overing; gat
insane krank'zinnig
insatiable onver'zadelijk
inscribe schrijven op, gra'veren; inschrijven
inscription opschrift; opdracht
inscrutable ondoor'grondelijk
insect in'sekt
insemination be'vruchting **artificial** – kunst'matige insemi'natie
insensible onge'voelig (voor); onbe'wust
inseparable onaf'scheidelijk
insert inlas(sen), insteken, plaatsen
inside binnen(kant); naar binnen; in
insidious ge'niepig
insight inzicht
insignia onder'scheidingstekens
insignificant zonder be'tekenis, onbe'tekenend, onbe'duidend
insincere onop'recht
insinuate indringen; insinu'eren
insipid flauw
insist er op staan; (blijven) volhouden; (er op) aandringen
insistent vol'hardend; dringend

insolent onbe'schoft
insoluble onop'losbaar
insomnia slape'loosheid
inspect onder'zoeken; inspec'teren
inspection in'spectie; onderzoek
inspector inspec'teur
inspiration inspi'ratie; bezielend voorbeeld; ingeving
inspire inspi'reren; inblazen; inboezemen
install instal'leren
instalment ter'mijn; ge'deelte, aflevering
instance voorbeeld; ver'zoek; aanhalen
instant ogenblik; ogen'blikkelijk
instantaneous on'middellijk
instead of in plaats van
instep wreef
instigate aanstichten
instil bijbrengen
instinct(ive) in'stinct('ief)
institute insti'tuut; instellen
institution instelling; tra'ditie
instruct onder'richten; ge' lasten; mededelen
instruction onderricht; in'structie
instructive leerzaam
instrument instru'ment
instrumental instrumen'taal; be'vorderlijk (voor)
insubordinate weer'spannig
insufferable onuit'staanbaar
insufficient onvol'doende
insular eiland-; geïso'leerd, be'krompen
insulate iso'leren
insult be'lediging; be'ledigen
insuperable onover'komelijk
insurance ver'zekering
insure ver'zekeren
insurrection opstand
intact in'tact, gaaf
intake inlaat; aanvoer

intangible on'tastbaar
integral inte'grerend; inte'graal
integrate inte'greren
integrity on'kreukbaarheid
intellect(ual) intel'lect(u'eel)
intelligence intelli'gentie; inlichtingen
intelligent intelli'gent, be'vattelijk
intelligible be'grijpelijk
intemperate on'matig
intend van plan zijn; be'doelen
intense in'tens
intensify ver'hogen, ver'scherpen
intensity intensi'teit
intensive inten'sief
intent ('in)ge'spannen; be'doeling
intention be'doeling
intentional op'zettelijk
inter ter aarde be'stellen
interaction wisselwerking
intercept onder'scheppen, de pas afsnijden
interchange ver'wisselen, afwisselen
interchangeable ver'wisselbaar
intercom intercom
intercourse omgang, sociaal verkeer; ge'slachtsgemeenschap
interest be'lang(stelling); aandeel; rente; interes'seren **to be interested in** be'lang stellen in (*or* hebben bij)
interfere tussen'beide komen; zich mengen in
interference be'moeienis; stoornis; storing
interim interim; tijdelijk; tussentijd(s)
interior inwendig, binnen(s)huis, binnenland(s)
interlock interlock; in el'kaar grijpen
interlude pauze, tussenperiode; tussenspel

intermediary be'middelaar; be'middeling
intermediate tussen-
interminable eindeloos
intermingle (zich) ver'mengen
intermittent met tussenpozen
intern in'tern; inter'neren
internal in'wendig; binnenlands
international internatio'naal
interplay wisselwerking
interpose tussenbeide komen
interpret (ver)'tolken, uitleggen
interpreter tolk
interrogate onder'vragen
interrupt onder'breken, in de rede vallen; be'lemmeren
intersect door'snijden; el'kaar snijden
intersperse door'spekken; ver'spreiden
interval pause, tussentijd(*or* ruimte)
intervene tussen'beide komen; liggen (tussen)
intervention tussenkomst
interview inter'view(en)
intestine darm **intestines** ingewanden
intimate in'tiem, ver'trouwd; laten merken
intimation aanduiding
intimidate intimi'deren
into in, tot (in)
intolerable onver'draaglijk
intolerant onver'draagzaam
intonation into'natie
intoxicant be'dwelmend (middel)
intoxicate dronken maken
intoxication dronkenschap; roes
intractable on'handelbaar; hard'nekkig
intrepid onver'saagd
intricate inge'wikkeld
intrigue in'trige, ge'konkel; intri'geren

intrinsic intrin'siek
introduce introdu'ceren;
  brengen in; indienen
introduction invoeren; inleiding
intrude (zich) in(or op)dringen;
  storen
intuition intu'ïtie; ingeving
intuitive intuï'tief
inundate overstelpen
invade binnenvallen
invalid zieke, inva'lide; on'geldig
invaluable on'schatbaar
invariable con'stant
invariably zonder uitzondering
invasion in'vasie, inval; inbreuk
invent uitvinden, ver'zinnen
invention uitvinding, ver'zinsel
inventive vindingrijk
inventor uitvinder
inventory inven'taris
inverse omgekeerd
invert omkeren, omzetten
invest be'leggen; ver'lenen
investigate onderzoeken
investigation onderzoek
investment (geld)be'legging
inveterate ver'stokt
invigorate kracht geven
invincible onover'winnelijk
invisible on'zichtbaar
invitation uitnodiging
invite uitnodigen; vragen om
inviting aan'lokkelijk
invoice fac'tuur
invoke aan(or op)roepen; een
  be'roep doen op
involuntary onwille'keurig
involve met zich meebrengen,
  be'trekken **involved**
  (in)ge'wikkeld
invulnerable on'kwetsbaar
inward naar binnen; innerlijk
irate woedend

Ireland Ierland
Irish Iers
iron (strijk)ijzer; ijzeren; strijken
ironic(al) i'ronisch
ironmongery ijzerwaren
irony iro'nie
irreconcilable onver'zoenlijk
irrefutable onweer'legbaar
irregular onregel'matig;
  tegen de regel
irrelevant niet ter zake dienend
irreparable onher'stelbaar
irrepressible onbe'dwingbaar
irreproachable onbe'rispelijk
irresistible onweer'staanbaar
irresolute be'sluiteloos
irrespective of afgezien
  van, ongeacht
irresponsible onverant'woordelijk
irretrievable onher'stelbaar;
  reddeloos
irreverent oneer'biedig
irrevocable onher'roepelijk
irrigate be'vloeien
irrigation irri'gatie
irritable prikkelbaar
irritate prikkelen; irri'teren
irritation irritatie, ge'prikkeldheid;
  branderigheid
Islam islam
Islamic islamitisch
island eiland; vluchtheuvel
isle eiland
isolate iso'leren
issue uitgifte, nummer; uitkomst;
  kwestie; ver'strekken; uitgeven;
  (voort)komen uit
it het
Italian Itali'aan(s)
italic cur'sief
Italy I'talië
itch jeuk(en), verlangen
item stuk, punt; be'richt

itinerant rondtrekkend
itinerary reisplan
its zijn

itself (zich')zelf
ivory i'voor; i'voren
ivy klimop

J

jab steek; steken
jack (op)krik(ken); boer
jacket jasje; omslag
jagged ruw, ge'tand, puntig
jam jam; opstopping; (samen) duwen, klemmen; storen
January janu'ari
Japanese Ja'pans; Ja'panner
jar pot; schok; krassen; een schok geven
jargon jargon, vaktaal
jaundice geelzucht
jaunt uitstapje
jaunty zwierig

jest scherts(en)
jettison over'boord werpen
jetty pier
Jew jood
jewel (edel)steen, ju'weel
jewellery ju'welen
Jewish joods
jigsaw puzzle legpuzzel
jihad jihad
jilt de bons geven
jingle (laten) rinkelen
job kar'wei, werk(je), baan(tje)
jockey jockey; manoeu'vreren
jocular schertsend

Insight

A *job* is usually **werk** or **een baan** in Dutch. If the job is not particularly important, for instance because it is temporary, then the diminutive is also frequently used: **een baantje**. In Flanders **de job** is also commonly used. When talking about your job, you usually talk about **mijn werk**, literally *my work* (or **jouw/zijn/haar** etc. **werk**). For instance: **ik ga vroeg naar mijn werk** *I'm going to work early*; **hoe is het op je werk?** *how are things at work?*

jaw kaak
jazz jazz
jealous ja'loers; angst'vallig be'zorgd
jeer schimpen
jelly ge'lei, gela'tinepudding
jellyfish kwal
jeopardize in ge'vaar brengen
jerk ruk, schok; (vulg) lul, zak; schokken, rukken
jersey trui(tje)

jog stoten; wippen; sukkelen; opfrissen
join ver'binding, naad; ver'binden, ver'enigen, samenkomen, in elkaar slaan; zich voegen bij, meedoen, komen bij
joint ge'wricht; ver'binding, naad; groot stuk vlees; ge'zamenlijk
joke grap(pen maken)
joker grappenmaker; joker
jolly jolig; reuze
jolt schok; hotsen

jostle (ver')dringen
jot jota; vlug no'teren
journal dagboek; tijdschrift
journalism journalis'tiek
journalist journa'list
journey reis (maken)
jovial jovi'aal
joy(ful) vreugde(vol)
jubilant jubelend, in de wolken
jubilee jubi'leum
judge rechter, jurylid, kenner; (be')
  oordelen
judgement uitspraak, oordeel, vonnis
judicial ge'rechtelijk
judicious oordeel'kundig
jug kan
juggle goochelen
juice sap
juicy sappig
July juli
jumble warboel; door el'kaar gooien
jump sprong; springen; opschrikken

jumper jumper; springer
junction knooppunt, kruispunt
June juni
jungle jungle, oerwoud; warboel
junior junior, jonger(e)
junk (oude) rommel
jurisdiction juris'dictie
jury jury
just recht'vaardig; welverdiend;
  ge'grond; pre'cies; net; maar;
  even; een'voudig
justice recht('vaardigheid),
  ge'rechtigheid; jus'titie; rechter
  to do – billijk be'handelen; eer
  aandoen, goed doen uitkomen
justifiable gerecht'vaardigd;
  ver'dedigbaar
justification grond, recht'vaardiging
justify recht'vaardigen
jut out uitsteken
jute jute
juvenile jeugd(ig), jong(eling)

K

kangaroo kangoeroe
karaoke kara'oke
keel kiel
keen scherp('zinnig); enthousi'ast
keep kost; slottoren; (onder')houden),
  be'waren; weer'houden; (goed)
  blijven **to – away** wegblijven **to –
  on** blijven, door-; aan (or op)houden
  to – up volhouden; onder'houden
  to – up with; bijhouden
keeper oppasser, opzichter
keeping hoede; over'eenstemming
kennel hondenhok, kennel
kerb stoeprand
kernel kern
kettle ketel
key sleutel(-); toets; toonaard
keyboard toetsenbord;
  toetsinstrument

keynote grondtoon
keypad toetsenpaneel
khaki kaki
kick schop(pen); te'rugstoot;
  trappen; stoten
kid geitje; kind; voor de gek houden
kidnap ont'voeren
kidney nier
kill doden **to be killed** sneuvelen,
  omkomen
kiln oven
kilt kilt
kin fa'milie
kind soort; vriendelijk
kind-hearted goed'hartig
kindle aansteken
kindly goed'aardig, vriendelijk
kindness vriendelijkheid
kindred ver'want(en)

king koning
kingdom koninkrijk

knickknack snuisterij
knife mes; door'steken

Insight

Kingdom: The Dutch language is spoken in two kingdoms, i.e. **het Koninkrijk België** *the kingdom (of) Belgium* and **het Koninkrijk der Nederlanden** *the kingdom of the Netherlands* (note the plural form 'Nederlanden'). In **het Koninkrijk België** Dutch is spoken in **het Vlaams Gewest** *Flemish region*, or **Vlaanderen** *Flanders*, and in the bilingual **Brussels Hoofdstedelijk Gewest** *the region of the capital Brussels* (note that in Dutch **Brussels** is an adjective derived from the place name **Brussel**). In **het Koninkrijk der Nederlanden** Dutch is spoken in **Nederland** *the Netherlands* and in the islands of **de Nederlandse Antillen** *the Dutch Antilles* and **Aruba** in the Caribbean, where English and Papiamento are also official languages.

---

kink slag, kink; kronkel
kinky perverse; sexy, op'windend
kinship ver'wantschap
kiosk ki'osk
kiss kus(sen)
kit uitrusting; ba'gage; ge'reedschap
kitchen keuken
kite vlieger
kitten katje
kiwi kiwi(vrucht)
knack slag, kneep
knackered bekaf, doodop
knave schurk; boer
knead kneden
knee knie
kneel knielen, ge'knield liggen
knell doodsklok
knickers slipje, broekje

knight (tot) ridder (slaan)
knighthood ridderorde, ridderschap
knit breien; samengroeien
knitting breiwerk
knob knop; knobbel
knock slag, klop(pen), slaan
 stoten **to – down** om'vergooien,
 aanrijden; toeslaan **to – off**
 afslaan; ophouden, schaften
 to – out uitkloppen; be'wusteloos
 slaan **to – over** om'vergooien
knocker klopper
knot knoop; kwast; knopen
knotty vol knopen; vol kwasten; lastig
know (het) weten; (her')kennen
knowing schrander; veelbe'tekenend
knowledge (voor)kennis; wetenschap
knuckle knokkel

L

label eti'ket, label; van (een)
 eti'ket(ten) voor'zien
laboratory labora'torium

laborious afmattend; zwaar
labour arbeid(en); werkkrachten;
 weeën; doorzagen over

labourer arbeider
labyrinth doolhof
lace kant; veter; vastrijgen
lacerate (ver')scheuren
lack ge'brek (hebben aan) **to be lacking** ont'breken
laconic laco'niek
lacquer lak(werk)
lad knaap
ladder ladder
laden be'laden
ladle scheplepel; opscheppen
lady dame
lag achterblijven; be'kleden
lagoon la'gune
laid-back ont'spannen, re'laxed
lair hol
lake meer
lamb lam(svlees); lammeren
lame kreupel; zwak
lament weeklacht; be'treuren
lamentable jammerlijk
lamentation weeklacht
lamp lamp, lan'taren
lamp post lan'tarenpaal
lance lans; lan'ceren
land land(e'rij); neerkomen; (doen) be'landen; aan land zetten
landed land-, grond-
landing landing; overloop **landing stage** steiger
landlady hospita
landlord huisbaas, landheer; hospes, waard
landmark baken, be'kend punt; mijlpaal
land owner grondbezitter
landscape landschap
landslide (aard)ver'schuiving
lane landweg(getje); rijbaan; vaargeul
language taal
languid loom, flauw
languish ver'slappen; wegkwijnen; smachten (naar)

lank schraal; sluik
lanky slungelachtig
lantern lan'taren
lap schoot; ronde; (op)leppen; kabbelen
lapse foutje; periode, tijdje; afnemen, ver'vallen
lard reuzel
larder pro'visiekamer (*or* -kast)
large groot
largely grotendeels
lark leeuwerik; pretje; lol maken
larva larve
lash zweepkoord; zweepslag; geselen; (doen) zwiepen; vastsjorren
lass meisje
lassitude matheid
last (het) laatst; ver'leden; leest; duren, het uithouden **– straw** laatste druppel **at –** ten'slotte; eindelijk
lasting blijvend; duurzaam
lastly ten'slotte
latch klink, slot
late (te) laat; re'cent; wijlen, ge'wezen
lately (in de) laatst(e tijd)
latent la'tent
lateral zij(delings)
lathe draaibank
lather schuim(en)
Latin La'tijn(s)
latitude breedte; speling
latter laatst(genoemd)(e)
latterly tegen het eind; in de laatste tijd
lattice traliewerk
laudable lof'waardig
laugh lach(en) **to – at** lachen om; uitlachen
laughable lach'wekkend
laughter ge'lach
launch (zware) sloep; te water laten; insturen; afschieten; op touw zetten, ont'ketenen

laundry wasse'rij; was(goed)
laurel lau'rier; lauwer- **laurels** lauweren
lava lava
lavatory WC, toilet
lavender la'vendel
lavish kwistig; over'laden
law recht(en); wet
law-abiding orde'lievend
law court rechtbank
lawful wettig, recht'matig
lawless los'bandig
lawn ga'zon
lawsuit pro'ces
lawyer advo'caat
lax(ity) laks(heid)
laxative la'xeermiddel
lay lied; leke(n)-; leggen; dekken **to – down** voorschrijven; geven; neerleggen **to – in** inslaan
layer laag
layman leek
layout plan, aanleg
laze luieren
lazy lui
lead leiding; eerste plaats, voorsprong; riem; voorbeeld; lood; leiden, ertoe brengen; voor('op) gaan; aanvoeren
leaden loodzwaar
leader leider; hoofdartikel
leadership leiding; leiderschap
leading voor'aanstaand, hoofd-
leaf blad
leaflet blaadje, folder
leafy be'bladerd
league (ver')bond
leak lek(ken)
leakage lek; uitlekking
lean mager; schraal; overhellen; leunen; zetten
leaning neiging
lean-to afdak

leap sprong; springen
leap year schrikkeljaar
learn leren; ver'nemen
learned ge'leerd
learner leerling
learning ge'leerdheid, wetenschap
lease huurcontract, pacht; huurtijd; (ver')huren
leasehold pacht(goed)
leash riem
least minst **at –** ten'minste, minstens
leather leer; leren
leave ver'lof; afscheid; ver'trekken (uit), weggaan; (ver')laten; achter (*or* na)laten; overlaten **to – alone** afblijven van; met rust laten **to – off** ophouden (met) **to – out** weglaten; er buiten laten
lecture lezing (houden), col'lege (geven); de les lezen
lecturer universitair docent
ledge richel, rand
leek prei
leer gluren
left linker(hand); links(handig)
left-handed links
leg been, poot; (broeks)pijp; e'tappe
legacy le'gaat; erfenis
legal rechts'kundig, rechterlijk; wettig; wettelijk; rechts'geldig
legend le'gende; onderschrift
legendary legen'darisch
legible leesbaar
legion legi'oen; legio
legislation wetgeving
legitimate wettig; gerecht'vaardigd; recht'matig
leisure vrije tijd
leisurely be'daard
lemon(ade) ci'troen(limo'nade)
lend (uit)lenen; ver'lenen

Insight

Dutch only has one word for the verbs *to lend* and *to borrow*, i.e. **lenen**. This is the reason many Dutch speakers make mistakes in English such as asking '*can you borrow me your pen?*' So, in English, *can you lend my your pen?* is translated as **kun je me je pen lenen?** and *do you want to borrow my pen?* is **wil je mijn pen lenen?** Confusingly therefore, **geld lenen** means both *to borrow* and *to lend* money, although the context usually makes it clear which is meant in a particular situation; to emphasize that you're talking about 'to lend', you can add **aan iemand**, literally *to someone*: **Harry leent geld aan zijn broer** *Harry is lending his brother (some) money.*

length lengte, duur; eind(je) **at length** eindelijk; uit'voerig
lengthen ver'lengen; langer worden
lengthwise in de lengte
lengthy lang('durig)
lenient cle'ment
lens lens
lentil linze
leopard luipaard
leotard tricot, balletpakje
leprosy me'laatsheid
lesbian lesbisch; lesbienne
less min(der)
lessen ver'minderen, (doen) afnemen
lesser minder
lesson les; schriftlezing
lest voor het ge'val dat; opdat niet; dat
let laten, toestaan; ver'huren **to – down** neerlaten; uitleggen; du'peren, in de steek laten **to – go** loslaten; laten gaan **to – in** binnen laten **to – off** laten gaan
lethargic slaperig, loom
letter brief; letter
lettuce (krop)sla

level vlak, ge'lijk (met); hoogte; ni'veau; ge'lijk maken
level-headed ver'standig, nuchter
lever hefboom
levy heffing, lichting; heffen, werven
lewd on'tuchtig, ob'sceen
liability aan'sprakelijkheid, ver'antwoording; blok aan het been
liable verplicht; vatbaar; aan'sprakelijk; de neiging hebben **– to** strafbaar, last hebben v an
liaison ver'binding(s-); liai'son
liar leugenaar
libel smaadschrift; op schrift be'lasteren
liberal roy'aal, ruim'denkend; liberaal
liberate be'vrijden
liberty vrijheid
librarian bibliothe'caris
library biblio'theek
licence ver'gunning; vrijheid
licentious los'bandig
lick (af)likken
lid deksel
lie leugen; liegen; (gaan) liggen **to – down** gaan liggen; liggen te rusten

lieutenant luitenant
life leven(sbeschrijving)
lifebelt reddingsgordel
lifeboat reddingsboot
lifeless levenloos
lifelike na'tuurgetrouw
lifelong levenslang
lifetime leven(sduur)
lift lift; (op)tillen; optrekken; pikken
ligament band, pees
light licht; vuurtje; aansteken;
ver'lichten; ver'helderen
lighten lichter worden; ophelderen;
weerlichten; ver'lichten
lighter aansteker; lichter
light-hearted luchtig
lighthouse vuurtoren
lighting ver'lichting
lightly zachtjes; licht('vaardig);
luchtig
lightning bliksem(snel)
lightweight licht ge'wicht
like (zo)als; houden van, aardig
vinden; graag willen **it is just – him**
het is echt iets voor hem; het lijkt
sprekend op hem **nothing –** lang
niet **something –** onge'veer,
zo(iets) als
likeable prettig
likelihood kans
likely waar'schijnlijk **he is – to**
het is aan'nemelijk dat hij
likeness ge'lijkenis
likewise even'eens; insge'lijks
liking voorliefde, zin
lilac se'ring; lila
lily lelie
limb lid; tak
limbs ledematen
lime kalk; li'moen; linde
limelight voorgrond
limit grens; be'perken
limitation be'perking; grens,
te'kortkoming

limited company naamloze
vennootschap
limp slap; mank lopen
limpid helder
line lijn; linie; rij; regel; spoor;
lini'ëren; voeren, be'kleden
linen linnen(goed)
linger dralen
linguistic taal('kundig)-
lining voering, be'kleding
link schakel(en); inhaken;
ver'binden; met elkaar
in ver'band brengen
lion(ess) leeuw('in)
lip lip; rand
lipstick lippenstift
liqueur li'keur
liquid vloeibaar; vloeistof
liquidate liqui'deren
liquor (sterke) drank
liquorice drop
lisp ge'lispel; lispelen
list lijst; slagzij; overhellen
listen luisteren
listless lusteloos
literal letterlijk
literary lite'rair
literature litera'tuur
lithe soepel
litre liter
litter afval, rommel; nest, worp;
(met rommel) be'zaaien
little klein; weinig; beetje **a little
late** wat laat
liturgy litur'gie
live levend(ig); ge'laden, scherp;
(blijven) leven; wonen
liveable be'woonbaar; leefbaar
livelihood kost, be'staan
lively levendig, be'drijvig, druk
liver lever
livery li'vrei
livestock vee
livid razend; lijkbleek

living levend, levens-; kost; leven
living room huiskamer
lizard hage'dis
load vracht, lading; (in)laden,
  be'laden; over'laden
loaf brood; lummelen
loan lening; (uit)lenen
loath onge'negen
loathe walgen van
loathsome walgelijk
lobby hal, fo'yer
lobe lel
lobster kreeft
local plaatselijk; lo'kaal
locality om'geving
localize lokali'seren
locate opsporen, thuisbrengen;
  vestigen
location ligging; plaatslokatie
lock slot; sluis; lok; op slot doen
  (*or* gaan), (op)sluiten; vastraken
locker kastje
locket medail'lon
locomotive locomo'tief; be'wegings-
locust sprinkhaan
lodge (por'tiers)woning; lo'geren,
  in de kost zijn, onderbrengen;
  blijven steken; indienen
lodger kostganger
lodgings (ge'huurde) kamers
loft zolder; gale'rij
lofty hoog; ver'heven
log blok hout; log(boek); blok-;
  no'teren; afleggen
loggerheads, to be at –
  over'hoop liggen
logic logica
logical logisch
loin lende(stuk)
loiter omhangen
loll hangen
London Londen(s)
lone(ly) eenzaam, ver'laten
long lang; door; ver'langen

longing ver'langen
longitude lengte
long-winded lang'dradig
look (aan)blik; voorkomen; kijken; er
  uitzien **to – after** zorgen voor **to –
  at** be'kijken, kijken naar **to – back**
  omzien; te'rugzien **to – for** zoeken
  (naar); ver'wachten **to – forward
  to** zich ver'heugen op **to – into**
  onder'zoeken **to – like** lijken op,
  er uitzien als **to – on** toekijken **to
  – out** uitkijken **to – up** opkijken;
  opzoeken; opknappen
look-alike evenbeeld, dubbelganger
lookout uitkijk **keep a – for**
  uitkijken naar
looks uiterlijk
loom weefgetouw; opdoemen
loony gek, getikt; gek, dwaas
  (person)
loop lus
loophole uitvlucht
legal –s mazen in de wet
loose los, vrij
loosen los(ser) maken
loot buit; plunderen
lop (af)snoeien
lop-sided scheef
lord heer, lord
lorry vrachtauto
lose (doen) ver'liezen, kwijtraken;
  missen; voor'bij laten gaan
loss ver'lies
lost ver'loren; ver'dwaald;
  ver'ongelukt **to get –** ver'dwalen
lot lot; perceel; stel; heel wat
lotion lotion
lottery lote'rij
loud luid('ruchtig)
loudspeaker luidspreker; box
lounge sa'lon, conver'satiezaal;
  leunen, liggen
louse luis
lout lummel, hufter

lovable lief
love liefde; liefje; houden van;
  dolgraag (willen) **(to fall) in – with**
  ver'liefd (worden) op
  to make – vrijen
lovely prachtig, mooi; heerlijk
lover minnaar
loving aan'hankelijk; liefhebbend
low laag; bijna op (or leeg); loeien
lower laten zakken; strijken;
  dreigend kijken
lowland laagland
lowly nederig
loyal(ty) trouw
lubricant smeermiddel
lubricate smeren
lucid(ity) helder(heid)
luck ge'luk **bad –** pech **good –**
  ge'luk; suc'ces!
lucky: to be – boffen; ge'luk hebben
lucrative winstgevend
ludicrous be'lachelijk
lug slepen
luggage ba'gage
lugubrious lu'guber
lukewarm lauw
lull stilte; sussen
lullaby wiegeliedje

lumber ge'kapt hout; rommel;
  dreunen
luminous lichtgevend
lump klomp, brok, klontje,
  knobbel; rond
lunacy krank'zinnigheid
lunar maan-
lunatic krank'zinnig(e)
lunch lunch(en)
lung long
lunge uitval (doen); dres'seren
lurch stoot; steek; voor'uit
  (or op'zij)schieten, slingeren
lure lokstem; (ver')lokken
lurid gloeiend; gruwelijk
lurk zich schuil houden,
  ver'borgen zijn, loeren
luscious heerlijk sappig
lush mals
lust (wel)lust, zucht; be'geren
lustre glans; luister
lusty wellustig; flink
luxurious weelderig
luxury weelde, luxe
lying leugenachtig
lynch lynchen
lyric lyrisch (ge'dicht)
lyrical lyrisch

M

machine ma'chine; organi'satie
machinery machine'rieën;
  mecha'nisme; organi'satie(s)
mackerel ma'kreel
mad gek; dol
madam me'vrouw, juf'frouw
madden gek maken; gruwelijk
  ergeren
madman gek
madness krank'zinnig(heid);
  gekkigheid
madrigal madri'gaal
magazine tijdschrift

maggot made
magic toverkunst, tove'rij;
  tover(achtig)
magician tovenaar
magistrate magis'traat
magnanimous groot'moedig
magnate mag'naat
magnet mag'neet
magnetic mag'netisch
magnificence luister, pracht
magnificent luisterrijk, groots
magnify ver'groten
magnitude grootte

magpie ekster
mahogany ma'honie(hout)
maiden maagd(elijk);
  onge'trouwd, meisjes-; eerste
mail post
maim ver'minken
main hoofd-, voor'naamste
mains hoofdleiding, net
mainland vaste'land
mainly hoofd'zakelijk
mainsail grootzeil
maintain handhaven; onder'houden;
  be'weren
maintenance onderhoud
maize maïs
majestic majestu'eus
majesty majesteit
major groot(ste), hoofd-;
  ma'joor; majeur
majority meerder('jarig)heid
make merk; maken; dwingen, laten;
  ver'dienen; schatten, denken; halen;
  opmaken (a bed); zetten (tea); doen
  (a promise) **to – out** opstellen;
  be'weren; snappen; ont'cijferen;
  onder'scheiden urÿen **to – up**
  maken; ver'zinnen; ver'goeden,
  aanvullen; het weer goedmaken;
  (zich) opmaken **to – up for**
  goedmaken; inhalen
make-believe een spelletje;
  ver'zonnen
maker schepper, fabri'kant
makeshift geïmprovi'seerd
  (lapmiddel)
make-up schmink; make-up
malady kwaal
malaria ma'laria
male mannelijk (per'soon *or* dier),
  mannen-
malevolent boos'aardig
malice boos opzet, haat
malicious boos'aardig
malign be'lasteren

malignant kwaad'aardig
malleable kneedbaar
malnutrition onder'voeding
malt mout(en)
mammal zoogdier
mammoth mammoet; reuzen-
man man; (de) mens; be'mannen,
  be'zetten
manage aankunnen; managen;
  leiden; klaarspelen
management be'heer; di'rectie,
  be'stuur, management
manager direc'teur, chef, manager
mandate opdracht;
  man'daat(gebied)
mane manen
manger voerbak, kribbe
mangle mangel(en); ver'scheuren
manhandle ver'sjouwen, toetakelen
manhood mannelijkheid,
  vol'wassenheid
mania waanzin; manie
maniac waan'zinnige
manicure mani'cure
manifest duidelijk; mani'fest; tonen
manifestation uiting
manifesto mani'fest
manifold veel'vuldig
manipulate manipu'leren,
  han'teren; be'werken; knoeien met
manipulation han'tering;
  manipu'latie
mankind mensdom, mensheid
manly man'haftig, mannelijk
manner ma'nier (van doen); soort
mannerism hebbelijkheid
manoeuvre ma'noeuvre;
  manoeu'vreren
manor manor, groot (heren)
  huis met grondgebied
mansion herenhuis
manslaughter doodslag
mantelpiece schoorsteenmantel
mantle mantel; gloeikousje

manual hand(en)-; manu'aal; handboek, handleiding

manufacture fabri'cage, fabri'kaat; fabri'ceren

manure mest; be'mesten

manuscript handschrift; manuscript

many veel; velen **a good — heel wat a great —** heel veel, heel wat

map (land)kaart, platte'grond

maple esdoorn

mar ont'sieren; be'derven

maraud plunderen

marble marmer(en); knikker

march mars; (doen) mar'cheren; oprukken

March maart

mare merrie

margarine marga'rine

margin kant(lijn); speling

marginal kant-; onbeduidend

marijuana marihu'ana

marigold goudsbloem

marine zee-, scheeps-; mari'nier

mariner zeeman

marital echtelijk

maritime zee(vaart)-

mark plek, streep, vlek, spoor; moet, put; merk; stempel, (ken)teken; doel; peil; een vlek (etc) achterlaten; aanduiden; (ken)merken; prijzen; corri'geren; letten op

marked duidelijk; ver'dacht

market markt; afzetgebied; op de markt brengen

market place markt(plein)

marksman scherpschutter

marmalade marme'lade

maroon paars'rood **to be marooned** stranden

marquis mar'kies

marriage huwelijk

marrow merg; pom'poen

marry trouwen (met); uithuwelijken

marsh(y) moe'ras(sig)

marshal maarschalk; ordenen; ge'leiden

martial krijgs('haftig)

martyr martelaar; de marteldood doen sterven

martyrdom martelaarschap; marteling

marvel wonder; zich ver'wonderen

marvellous wonder'baarlijk, fan'tastisch; heerlijk

masculine mannelijk

mash pap; (fijn)stampen

mask masker(en); mas'keren

mason steenhouwer, metselaar

masquerade maske'rade; zich ver'mommen

mass massa; mis

massacre massamoord; slachting

massage mas'sage; mas'seren

massive mas'saal

mast mast

master (jonge) heer; ge'zagvoerder; leraar; meester(-); hoofd-; meester worden

masterful bazig

masterly meesterlijk

masterpiece meesterstuk

mastery overhand; meesterschap

masturbate mastur'beren

mat mat(je), kleed(je); mat, dof

match lucifer; par'tij, combi'natie; wedstrijd; eve'naren; bij el'kaar passen

matchless onverge'lijkelijk

mate maat; levensgezel('in); stuurman; (zich) paren

material stof(felijk), materi'aal, materi'eel; essenti'eel

materialist(ic) materia'list(isch)

materialize ver'wezenlijkt worden; ver'wezenlijken; ver'schijnen

maternal moederlijk, moeder-

maternity moederschap; kraam-

mathematical wis'kundig

mathematician wis'kundige
mathematics wiskunde
matrimonial huwelijks-
matrimony huwelijk(se staat)
matron ma'trone; moeder; direc'trice
matter stof; kwestie; pus; van be'lang zijn **as a – of fact** eigenlijk; overigens **as a – of course** als vanzelf'sprekend **for that –** wat dat be'treft, trouwens **it does not –** het geeft niets, het doet er niet toe **what is the –?** wat scheelt er aan?
matter-of-fact zakelijk
mattress ma'tras
mature rijp(en); ver'vallen
maturity rijpheid; ver'valtijd
maul toetakelen
mauve lichtpaars
maxim stelregel
may mogen, mis'schien kunnen
May mei
maybe mis'schien
mayonnaise mayon'naise
mayor burge'meester
maze doolhof
me mij, me
meadow wei(de)
meagre schraal
meal maal(tijd); meel
mean ge'meen, krenterig; ge'ring, schriel; middenweg, ge'middelde; be'doelen, menen; be'tekenen
meander kronkelen; dolen
meaning be'tekenis; be'doeling; veelbe'tekenend
meaningless niets'zeggend
means middel(en) **by all –** ge'rust **by no –** geenszins
meantime: in the – in'tussen
meanwhile onder'tussen
measles mazelen
measure maat(regel); (op)meten; zijn

measurement maat
meat vlees
mechanic mecani'cien
mechanical me'chanisch, machi'naal, werktuig'kundig; werk'tuiglijk
mechanics werktuigkunde
mechanism mecha'nisme, mecha'niek
mechanize mechani'seren
medal me'daille
meddle (with) zich be'moeien (met); komen aan
meddlesome be'moeiziek
mediaeval middeleeuws
mediate als be'middelaar optreden
medical medisch; keuring
medicinal genees'krachtig
medicine ge'neesmiddel; ge'neeskunde, medi'cijnen
mediocre middel'matig
mediocrity middel'matigheid
meditate be'peinzen, over'peinzen
meditation over'peinzing; medi'tatie
Mediterranean Middellandse Zee
medium middel('matig); medium
medley mengelmoes; potpour'ri
meek zacht'moedig
meet (el'kaar) ont'moeten; (aan)treffen; samenkomen; afhalen; vol'doen aan
meeting ver'gadering, samenkomst; ont'moeting
megaphone mega'foon
melancholy zwaar'moedig(heid)
mellow zacht (en sappig); rijp
melodious wel'luidend
melodrama melo'drama
melody melo'die
melon me'loen
melt (doen) smelten
member lid(maat)
membership lidmaatschap; ledental
membrane vlies

memento aandenken
memoirs me'moires
memorable gedenk'waardig
memorandum memo'randum; nota
memorial ge'denkteken; monument
memorize uit het hoofd leren
memory ge'heugen; her'innering;
nagedachtenis
menace be'dreiging; gevaar
menagerie menage'rie
mend repa'reren
menial nederig, onderge'schikt
mental geestelijk, men'taal,
psychisch; met het hoofd;
psychi'atrisch – **hospital**
psychiatrische inrichting
mentality mentali'teit
mention (ver')melding; ver'melden
mentor mentor
menu me'nu
mercantile handels-
mercenary geld'zuchtig; huurling
merchandise koopwaar
merchant koopman; koopvaar'dij-
merciful ge'nadig; ge'zegend
merciless mee'dogenloos
mercury kwik(zilver)
mercy ge'nade; zegen
merely alleen maar
merge opgaan (in), samengaan
(met), fu'seren (met); (ge'leidelijk)
overgaan (in el'kaar)
merger samensmelting; fusie
meridian meridi'aan
meringue schuim(gebak)
merit ver'dienste; ver'dienen
mermaid zeemeermin
merriment vrolijkheid
merry vrolijk
merry-go-round draaimolen
mesh maas
mess rommel, bende; lelijke
toestand; (offi'ciers)tafel; vuil
maken – **about** prutsen, (lui)

rondhangen; rotzooien met,
be'lazeren **to – up** ver'knoeien
message boodschap, be'richt
messenger (voor)bode
Messiah Mes'sias
messy slordig, vuil
metal me'taal; me'talen
metabolism metabo'lisme,
stofwisseling
metallic me'talen, me'taalachtig
metamorphosis
ge'daanteverwisseling
metaphor beeldspraak
metaphorical fi'guurlijk
meteor mete'oor
meteorological meteoro'logisch
meter meter
method me'thode; sys'teem
methodical syste'matisch
meticulous (al te) zeer; nauwge'zet
metre meter; metrum
metropolis wereldstad
metropolitan hoofd'stedelijk
mew mi'auwen
mews stal(woning)
microbe mi'crobe
microphone micro'foon
microprocessor microprocessor
microscope micro'scoop
microwave magne'tron, microgolf
mid midden
midday twaalf uur; middag-
middle middel(ste), midden
– **classes** middenstand
middle-aged van middelbare leeftijd
Middle Ages middeleeuwen
middleman tussenpersoon
midge mug
midget dwerg; minia'tuur
midnight midder'nacht(elijk)
midriff middenrif
midst midden
midsummer mid'zomer
midway halver'wege

midwife verlos'kundige
might(y) macht(ig)
migrate mi'greren, trekken
migration mi'gratie, trek
mild zacht('aardig); licht
mildew (be')schimmel(en)
mile mijl
mileage afstand in mijlen
milestone mijlpaal
militant strijdend; strijd'lustig
militarism milita'risme
military mili'tair, krijgs-
militate (tegen)werken
militia mi'litie
milk melk(en)
milkman melkboer
Milky Way melkweg
mill molen; fa'briek; malen; kri'oelen
miller molenaar
million mil'joen
millionaire miljo'nair
mime ge'barenspel; met
  ge'baren uitbeelden
mimic mimicus; nabootsen
mince ge'hakt; fijnhakken
mind geest, ver'stand, ge'dachte;
  zin; er iets op tegen hebben;
  letten op; oppassen **to make up
  one's –** be'sluiten
mind-blowing fan'tastisch,
  duizeling'wekkend
mindful ge'dachtig (aan)
mine van mij, het (*or* de) mijne;
  mijn; bron; delven
miner mijnwerker
mineral delfstof; mine'raal
mingle (zich) mengen; omgaan
miniature minia'tuur
minimize zo klein mogelijk
  maken; ge'ringschatten
minimum minimum
mining mijn(bouw)
minister predi'kant; mi'nister;
  ge'zant; ver'zorgen

ministry mini'sterie; dienst;
  geestelijk ambt
mink nerts
minor klein, minder (be'langrijk);
  mineur; minder'jarige
minority minder('jarig)heid
minstrel min'streel
mint munt(en)
minus min; zonder
minute mi'nuut; ogenblik; notule;
  mi'niem; minuti'eus
miracle wonder
miraculous wonder'baarlijk
mirage fata mor'gana;
  zinsbegoocheling
mirror spiegel; weer'kaatsen
mirth vrolijkheid
misadventure ongeluk; onge'
  lukkig voorval
misapprehension misvatting
misbehave zich mis'dragen
misbehaviour wangedrag
miscalculate zich ver'rekenen;
  misrekenen
miscarriage mis'lukking; miskraam
miscarry mis'lukken; ver'loren gaan
miscellaneous ge'mengd; veelzijdig
miscellany ge'mengde ver'zameling
mischief (katte)kwaad;
  on'deugendheid
mischievous on'deugend;
  kwaa'daardig
misconception ve'rkeerde
  opvatting, mis'vatting
misconduct wangedrag;
  wanbeheer; slecht be'heren
misconstrue ver'keerd opvatten
misdeed misdaad
misdemeanour wangedrag
miser vrek
miserable diep onge'lukkig;
  naar'geestig; el'lendig
misery el'lende
misfire ketsen; overslaan

misfit: to be a – niet passen; uit de toon vallen
misfortune ongeluk
misgiving bang ver'moeden
misguided onver'standig
mishap ongeluk(je)
misinform ver'keerd inlichten
misinterpret ver'keerd uitleggen
misjudge ver'keerd (be')oordelen
mislay kwijtraken
mislead mis'leiden
mismanagement wanbeheer
misnomer ver'keerde be'naming
misplace ver'keerd plaatsen
misplaced mis'plaatst
misprint drukfout; ver' keerd drukken
misrepresent een ver'keerde voorstelling geven van
miss juffrouw; misslaan; mislopen; missen; ver'zuimen
misshapen mis'vormd
missile projec'tiel
mission missie; zending
missionary zendeling(s-)

mistress me'vrouw; juffrouw, lera'res; mai'tresse
mistrust wantrouwen
misty nevelachtig, wazig; be'grijpen, be'slagen
misunderstand ver'keerd
misunderstanding misverstand
misuse misbruik; mis'bruiken; mis'handelen
mitigate ver'zachten, ver'lichten
mitre mijter; ver'stek
mitt(en) want
mix (ver')mengen; zich laten mengen; omgaan met **to – up** ver'warren
mixture mengsel, mengeling
moan ge'kerm; ge'jammer; kermen, suizen; jammeren
moat gracht
mob (mensen)massa; ge'peupel; bende; zich ver'dringen om, als één man te lijf gaan
mobile be'weeglijk, rondtrekkend, mo'biel; mo'bieltje, mo'biele teléfoon

Insight

A *mobile phone* is **een mobiele telefoon, een mobiel, een mobieltje** or **een gsm** in Dutch. A *mobile phone number* is **een mobiele telefoonnummer, een mobiel nummer** (note that **mobiel** can get an extra **-e**, for instance in: **dit is mijn mobiele nummer** *this is my mobile number*) or **gsm-nummer**, and in the Netherlands it is also very common to talk about **een o6-nummer** (**nul-zes-nummer**), since all mobile phone numbers there start with o6.

mist nevel, lage wolk; waas
mistake ver'gissing; fout; aanzien, ver'keerd be'grijpen, mis'kennen
to be mistaken zich ver'gissen; mis'plaatst zijn

mobilize mobili'seren
mock schijn-, kunst-; (be')spotten; be'spottelijk maken; naäpen
mockery spot; aanfluiting
mode mode; ma'nier

model mo'del; model'leren,
  boet'seren
moderate (ge')matig(d);
  matigen; be'daren
moderation matigheid **in –**
  met mate
modern(ize) mo'dern(i'seren)
modest be'scheiden; zedig
modification wijziging
modify wijzigen; matigen
moist(en) vochtig (maken)
moisture vocht(igheid)
mole mol; moedervlek
molecule mole'cule
molest lastig vallen
mollify ver'tederen
moment ogenblik; be'lang
momentarily voor een ogenblik
momentary kort'stondig
momentous ge'wichtig
momentum arbeidsvermogen
  van be'weging, vaart
monarch vorst('in)
monarchy monar'chie
monastery klooster
Monday maandag
monetary munt-, geldelijk
money geld
mongrel bastaard(hond)
monk monnik
monkey aap
monocle mo'nocle
monogram mono'gram
monologue al'leenspraak
monopolize monopoli'seren
monopoly mono'polie
monotonous een'tonig
monotony een'tonigheid
monsoon moesson
monster monster; ge'drocht
monstrosity wanproduct
monstrous monsterachtig
month(ly) maand(elijks)

monument monu'ment
monumental monumen'taal
mood stemming, hu'meur; wijs
moody hu'meurig; ont'stemd
moon(light) maan(licht);
  zwartwerken
moor hei(de); veenmoeras; meren
moorings meertouwen; ligplaats
moot be'twistbaar
mop zwabber; (afwas)kwast;
  dweilen, zwabberen; afgeven
mope mokken
moral zedelijk, zeden-, mo'reel;
  mo'raal **morals** zeden
morale mo'reel
morality zedelijke be'ginselen;
  zedelijkheid; morali'teit
moralize morali'seren
morbid ziekelijk; patho'logisch
more meer, nog (meer) **some –**
  nog wat **– or less** min of meer
moreover boven'dien
morning morgen, ochtend **in**
  the – 's ochtends **tomorrow –**
  morgenochtend
morose gemelijk
mortal sterfelijk; dodelijk,
  doods; sterveling
mortality sterfte(cijfer)
mortally dodelijk
mortar mor'tier; vijzel
mortgage hypo'theek (nemen op)
mortify diep ver'nederen; kas'tijden
mortuary lijkenhuis
mosaic moza''iek
mosque mos'kee
mosquito mus'kiet
moss mos
most meest; bij'zonder; het (or de)
  meeste **at the –** op zijn hoogst
  (or meest) **to make the – of** zoveel
  mogelijk profi'teren van
mostly groten'deels; meestal

MOT APK, verplichte jaarlijkse keuring
moth nachtvlinder, mot
mother moeder
motherly moederlijk
mother of pearl paarle'moer(en)
motif mo'tief
motion be'weging; motie; stoelgang; wenken
motionless onbe'weeglijk
motivate moti'veren
motive be'weegreden
motley bont
motor motor; rijden
motor cycle motorfiets
motorist automobi'list
motto motto
mould vorm(en); schimmel; boet'seren
mouldy be'schimmeld
moult ruien
mound wal, terp
mount berg; rijdier; (be')stijgen
mountain(eer) berg(beklimmer)
mountainous bergachtig
mourn (be')treuren
mourner rouwdrager
mournful treurig; droevig
mourning rouw
mouse muis
mousetrap muizeval
moustache snor
mouth mond(ing); opening
mouthful hapje
mouthpiece mondstuk; woordvoerder
movable be'weegbaar; ver'anderlijk
move zet; stap; ver'huizing; (zich) be'wegen; ver'huizen; ont'roeren
movement be'weging
moving roerend
mow maaien
much veel; zeer; vaak; vrijwel
muck drek, vuil
mud modder

muddle warboel; in de war brengen, door el'kaar gooien; scharrelen
muddy modderig
mudguard spatbord
muff mof; be'derven
muffle instoppen; dempen
mug mok, beker, kroes; sul; smoel
mulberry moerbei
mule muildier
multifarious veel'soortig
multiple veel'voudig; veelvoud
multiplex megabioscoop
multiplication vermenig'vuldiging
multiply (zich) vermenig'vuldigen
multitude menigte; groot aantal
mum: to keep – stilzwijgen
mumble mompelen
mummy mummie; mammie
mumps de bof
munch (hoorbaar) k(n)auwen (op)
mundane werelds
municipal ge'meente-, stedelijk, stads-
municipality ge'meente
munition krijgsvoorraad
mural muurschildering
murder moord; ver'moorden
murderer moordenaar
murderous moord'dadig
murky zwart, somber
murmur ge'murmel; murmelen; mopperen
muscle spier
muscular ge'spierd; spier-
muse muze; mijmeren
museum mu'seum
mush moes; ge'wauwel
mushroom champi'gnon
music mu'ziek
musical muzi'kaal; mu'ziek-
musician musicus; muzi'kant
muslin neteldoek
mussel mossel
must moet(en), moest(en)
mustard mosterd

muster monstering; monsteren; ver'zamelen

musty muf, schimmelig

mute stom; dempen

mutilate ver'minken

mutineer muiter

mutiny muite'rij, opstand

mutter mompelen, prevelen

mutton schapenvlees

mutual onderling, weder'zijds; weder'kerig

muzzle muil(band); mond

my mijn

myriad on'telbaar; tien'duizendtal

myself me('zelf), (ik')zelf

mysterious geheim'zinnig

mystery ge'heim; raadsel

mystic mysticus

mystic(al) ver'borgen; mys'tiek

mysticism mys'tiek

mystify ver'bijsteren

myth mythe; ver'dichtsel

mythical mythisch; ver'dicht

mythology mytholo'gie

N

nag zeuren; vitten

nail spijker; nagel; vastspijkeren

naïve na'ïef

naked naakt; bloot

name naam; (be')noemen; opnoemen; thuisbrengen

nameless onbe'kend; ano'niem, naamloos

namely namelijk

namesake naamgenoot

nap dutje; nop; dutten

nape nek

napkin ser'vet; luier

narcissus nar'cis

narcotic slaap'wekkend middel; ver'dovend

narrate ver'halen

narrative ver'haal; ver'halend

narrow smal, nauw; klein

narrow-minded klein'geestig

nasal na'saal, neus-

nasty akelig; smerig; naar, lelijk

nation volk, natie

national natio'naal; volks-, staats-

nationalist(ic) nationa'list(isch)

nationality nationali'teit

nationalize nationali'seren

native autoch'toon; aangeboren; in'heems

nativity ge'boorte (van Christus)

natural na'tuurlijk, na'tuur-

naturalist natura'list

naturalize naturali'seren

naturally na'tuurlijk; van na'ture

nature na'tuur; aard

naught nul; niets

naughty on'deugend

nausea misselijkheid; walging

nauseate misselijk maken

nautical zee(vaart'kundig)

naval ma'rine-, zee-

navel navel

navigable be'vaarbaar

navigate be'sturen

navigation stuurmanskunst, navi'gatie

navigator navi'gator

navy ma'rine, vloot

near dichtbij, na'bij

nearly bijna **not –** lang niet

neat net(jes); handig; puur

necessarily nood'zakelijk(erwijs)

necessary nood'zakelijk; be'hoefte

necessitate nood'zakelijk maken

necessity nood(zaak); be'hoefte

neck hals(stuk)

necklace (hals)ketting, (hals)snoer

necktie (strop)das

nectar nectar
need be'hoefte, nood(zaak); nodig hebben; hoeven, moeten **there is no –** het is niet nodig
needful nodig
needle naald
needless on'nodig
needlework naaiwerk, handwerk(en)
needy be'hoeftig
negation ont'kenning, ver'loochening
negative ont'kennend; negatief
neglect ver'zuim(en), ver'waarlozing; ver'waarlozen
negligence ver'waarlozing, on'achtzaamheid
negligent achteloos
negligible niet noemens'waard
negotiate onder'handelen
negotiation onder'handeling
neigh hinniken
neighbour buurman (or -vrouw); naaste
neighbourhood buurt, om'geving
neighbouring na'burig
neighbourly vriendelijk
neither geen van beide; even'min **– ... nor** noch ... noch
nephew neef(je)**nerve** zenuw; geestkracht; (bru'tale) moed; ver'mannen

nestle zich nestelen
net net; tule, vi'trage; met een net vangen
nether onder
Netherlands Nederland(s)
netting gaas
nettle (brand)netel
neurotic neu'rotisch; zenuwlijder, neu'root
neuter on'zijdig
neutral neu'traal (land)
neutralize neutrali'seren; neu'traal ver'klaren
never (nog) nooit; niet eens
nevertheless desondanks
new nieuw, vers
newborn pasgeboren
newcomer nieuweling
newly pas, opnieuw
news nieuws(berichten), be'richt; journal
newspaper krant
New Year's Day nieuwjaars'dag
New Year's Eve oudejaars'avond, oudejaars'dag
next volgend, aan'staande; daar'na **– door** hier'naast **– (door) to** naast
nib pen
nibble knabbelen
nice aardig; lekker; net(jes); fijn
nicety nauwge'zetheid; fi'nesse

Insight

Dutch makes no distinction between *nephew* and *(male) cousin*, since both are called **de neef**. The same goes for *niece* and *(female) cousin*, both of which are called **de nicht**. To make it clear that you are talking about your brother's or sister's children, you can use the diminutives **het neefje** and **het nichtje: ik heb vijf neefjes en nichtjes** *I have five nephews and nieces*.

nervous zenuw(achtig); bang
nest nest; (zich) nestelen

niche nis, hoekje
nickname bijnaam

nicotine nico'tine
niece nicht(je)
night nacht, avond **at (or in the) –** 's nachts
nightdress nachtjapon
nightfall het vallen van de avond
nightingale nachtegaal
nightmare nachtmerrie
nimble kwiek
nine(teen) negen(tien)
ninety negentig
nipple tepel
nitrogen stikstof
nitwit domoor
no neen; niet, geen **– one** niemand
nobility adel(stand)
noble edel(man), adelijk; groots; nobel
nobody niemand; nul
nocturnal nachtelijk, nacht-
nod knik(ken); knikkebollen
noise la'waai, ge'luid
noiseless ge'ruisloos
noisy luid'ruchtig, druk
nomad no'made; zwerver
nominal in naam; nomi'naal
nominate be'noemen; kandi'daat stellen
nomination be'noeming; kandi'daatstelling
nonchalant onver'schillig
non-committal (op'zettelijk) vaag
nondescript onbe'paald; onop'vallend
none geen (enkele), niemand, niets; geenszins
nonentity nul
nonsense onzin
nook hoekje, plekje
noon twaalf uur ('s middags)
noose strop, strik
nor noch, en … ook niet
normal nor'maal
normally ge'woonlijk

north (naar het) noorden; noord(en)-
northerly, northern noordelijk
Norway Noorwegen
Norwegian Noor(s)
nose neus
nostril neusgat
not niet
notable op'merkelijk, aan'zienlijk; no'tabele
notably met name, voor'al
notch kerf; kerven
note aantekening, no'titie; briefje; nota; toon, noot; be'tekenis; no'teren; opmerken
notebook no'titieboekje; notebook
noted be'kend, be'roemd
noteworthy opmerkens'waardig
nothing niets
notice aandacht; aankondiging; (op)merken **to give –** de dienst (or huur) opzeggen; kennis geven **to take – of** aandacht schenken aan
noticeable merkbaar
notification kennisgeving
notify ver'wittigen; be'kend maken
notion i'dee
notorious be'rucht
notwithstanding (des)ondanks
nought niets; nul
nourish voeden; koesteren
nourishment voeding, voedsel
novel ro'man; nieuw
novelist ro'manschrijver
novelty nieuwigheid
November november
novice nieuweling
now nu
nowadays tegen'woordig
nowhere nergens
noxious schadelijk
nozzle tuit
nuclear kern-, nucleair, atoom-
– waste kernafval
nucleus kern

nude naakt; naakstudie
nudge duwtje; zachtjes aanstoten
nugget (goud)klomp
nuisance: to be a – lastig zijn
null and void van nul en gener waarde
nullify nietig ver'klaren; opheffen
numb ver'kleumd, ver'doofd; ver'doven
number ge'tal; aantal; nummer(en); tellen, rekenen
numeral cijfer; telwoord
numerical nume'riek ·
numerous talrijk

nun non
nuptial huwelijks-
nurse ver'pleegster; kindermeisje; ver'plegen; zogen; ver'zorgen; koesteren
nursery crèche, kinder'dagverblijf; kinderkamer; kweke'rij
nurture (op)voeden; koesteren
nut noot; moer
nutcase mafkees
nutmeg nootmus'kaat
nutrition voeding(s'leer)
nutritional voedings
nutritive voedzaam
nymph nimf

O

oaf pummel
oak eik(enhout)(en)
oar riem
oasis o'ase
oath eed; vloek
oatmeal havermeel, havermout
oats haver
obedience ge'hoorzaamheid
obedient ge'hoorzaam
obese zwaar'lijvig
obey ge'hoorzamen
object voorwerp; doel; be'zwaar hebben (*or* maken) (tegen)
objection be'zwaar, tegenwerping
objectionable on'aangenaam, afkeurens'waardig
objective objec'tief
obligation ver'plichting
obligatory ver'plicht
oblige ver'plichten; ge'noegen doen
obliging voor'komend
oblique schuin; zijdelings
obliterate uitwissen
oblivion ver'getelheid
oblivious onbe'wust

oblong lang'werpig; rechthoek
obnoxious aan'stotelijk
oboe hobo
obscene on'zedelijk
obscure ob'scuur; onbe'kend; ver'borgen; on'duidelijk; on'zichtbaar maken; be'lemmeren; ver'doezelen
obscurity on'duidelijkheid; onbe'kendheid
observance in'achtneming
observant op'merkzaam
observation waarneming, obser'vatie; opmerking
observatory sterrenwacht
observe observeren, (op)merken, waarnemen; in acht nemen
obsess (ge'heel) ver'vullen
obsession ob'sessie
obsolete ver'ouderd
obstacle hindernis; be'letsel
obstetrics ver'loskunde
obstinate hard'nekkig
obstruct ver'sperren, be'lemmeren
obstruction hindernis, be'letsel; be'lemmering

obtain ver'krijgen, ver'werven, be'halen; gelden
obtainable ver'krijgbaar; haalbaar
obtuse stomp('zinnig)
obvious overduidelijk
occasion ge'legenheid; aanleiding (geven tot)
occasionally nu en dan
occult oc'cult
occupant be'woner, inzittende
occupation be'roep, bezigheid; be'zetting
occupy be'zetten, innemen; be'wonen
occur voorkomen; opkomen (bij)
occurrence voorval, ge'beurtenis
ocean oce'aan
o'clock uur

off van (... af); weg; af; vrij
offal afval
offence over'treding; aanstoot, be'lediging; aanval
offend be'ledigen, ergeren
offensive be'ledigend; on'aangenaam; aanval(s-)
offer (aan)bod; (aan)bieden; aanvoeren; zich voordoen
offering gift
offhand op het eerste ge'zicht
office kan'toor, ambt, functie; zorg
officer offi'cier; functio'naris
official offici'eel; ambtenaar, be'ambte
officiate dienst doen; de dienst leiden
officious be'moeiziek
offset (laten) opwegen tegen

Insight

English *o'clock* is Dutch **uur**: *it is twelve o'clock* translates as **het is twaalf uur**. However, **uur** is only used on the hour, not for any of the other times. For instance: **het is half elf** *it's ten thirty* (half before 11); **het is kwart over vier** *it's a quarter past four*; **het is tien voor acht** *it's ten to eight*.

octagonal acht'hoekig
octave oc'taaf
October oc'tober
octopus inktvis
odd on'even; los; over; vreemd
  – job kar'weitje – moment ver'loren ogenblik
oddity eigen'aardigheid, vreemde snuiter
oddment res'tant
odd oneven
odds kans; conflict; ver'schil
odious ver'foeilijk
odorous kwalijk (*or* wel')riekend
odour reuk; lucht(je)
of van, uit; met; over

offspring kroost
often vaak
ogle (toe)lonken
ogre boeman
oil olie, pe'troleum; smeren
oil painting schilde'rij in olieverf
oily olieachtig
ointment zalf
old oud
old-fashioned ouder'wets
olive o'lijf(boom)
omelet ome'let
omen voorteken
ominous onheil'spellend
omission ver'zuim, weglating
omit weglaten; nalaten

omnipotent al'machtig
omniscient al'wetend
on op; aan; bij; met; over; verder; aan de gang
once eens, één keer; eenmaal **at —** on'middellijk **— in a while** zo nu en dan **— or twice** een paar keer
one één; men
onerous zwaar
oneself (zich')zelf, zich
one-sided een'zijdig
onion ui
onlooker toeschouwer
only slechts, (al'leen) maar; pas, nog; enig **— too** maar al te
onset aanval; aanvang
onslaught woeste aanval
onto op
onus last, plicht, schuld
onward(s) voorwaarts
ooze (door)sijpelen
opal o'paal
opaque ondoor'schijnend
open open('baar); open'hartig; blootgesteld; openlucht; opengaan; opendoen
opening opening; be'gin; kans; inleidend
opera opera
operate ope'reren; werken; be'dienen
operation ope'ratie; handeling
operator telefo'nist(e); be'diener
opinion oordeel, mening **— poll** o'pinieonderzoek, o'piniepeiling
opinionated koppig, eigen'wijs
opium opium
opponent tegenstander
opportune gunstig
opportunist opportu'nist
opportunity ge'legenheid
oppose tegenwerken; stellen tegen'over
opposite tegen'over(gesteld)

opposition tegenstand; oppo'sitie
oppress (onder')drukken
oppression onder(or ver')drukking
oppressive drukkend
optic ge'zichts-, oog-
optical ge'zichts-
optimistic opti'mistisch
option keus
optional faculta'tief
opulence rijkdom
or of
oracle o'rakel
oral mondeling; mond-
orange sinaasappel; o'ranje
oration rede
orator redenaar
oratorio ora'torium
orb bol
orbit baan; kring
orchard boomgaard
orchestra(l) or'kest(-)
orchid orchi'dee
ordain voorschrijven; wijden
ordeal be'proeving, proef
order (volg)orde; stand; be'vel(en); be'stelling; ordenen; be'stellen **in — that** op'dat **in — to** om te **out of —** niet op volgorde; niet in orde
orderly ordelijk; ordon'nans
ordinance ver'ordening
ordinarily ge'woonlijk
ordinary ge'woon
organ orgel; or'gaan
organic or'ganisch
organism orga'nisme
organist orga'nist
organization organi'satie
organize organi'seren
orgy orgie, uitspatting
Orient Oosten
oriental oosters; oosterling
orientate oriën'teren
orifice opening
origin oorsprong; afkomst

original oor'spronkelijk; origi'neel
originate ont'staan (uit); in het leven roepen
ornament sieraad, ver'siersel
ornamental sier-
ornate sierlijk
orphan wees(-), ouderloos
orphanage weeshuis
orthodox ortho'dox; ge'bruikelijk
ostensible ogen'schijnlijk
ostentation uiterlijk ver'toon
ostentatious praalziek
ostracize doodverklaren
ostrich struisvogel
other ander; nog **the – day** onlangs
otherwise anders
otter otter
ought to (eigenlijk) moeten, zou (eigenlijk) moeten
　you – to go home je zou naar huis moeten gaan
ounce (approx.) kwart ons
our(selves) ons(zelf)
ours de (or het) onze, van ons
out (er')uit; (naar) buiten; weg **– and – door** en door **– of** uit; buiten; zonder
outbreak uitbarsting; oproer
outbuilding bijgebouw
outburst uitbarsting
outcast ver'stoteling
outcome resul'taat
outcry luid pro'test
outdoor openlucht-
outer buiten-
outfit uitrusting, uitzet
outgoing uitgaand, aftredend; uitgave
outgrow groeien uit; ont'groeien
outhouse bijgebouw, schuurtje
outing uitstapje
outlandish vreemd'soortig
outlaw banneling; vogel'vrij ver'klaren

outlay uitgave(n)
outlet uitlaat(klep), afvoerkanaal; vestiging, verkooppunt; markt, afzetgebied; con'tactdoos, stopcontact
outline omtrek; schets (en); aftekenen
outlive over'leven
outlook (voor')uitzicht; opvatting
outlying afgelegen
outnumber (in aantal) over'treffen
out-of-date ver'ouderd
out-of-the-way afgelegen; buite'nissig
outpost buiten(or voor)post
output opbrengst
outrage aanranding; schande, veront'waarding
outrageous schan'dalig
outright in'eens; rond'uit
outset be'gin
outside buiten(kant)
outsider buitenstaander
outskirts buitenkant
outspoken open'hartig
outstanding voor'treffelijk, onbe'taald, onbe'slist
outstrip achter zich laten; over'treffen
outward uit-, naar buiten **(to all) – appearances** uiterlijk
outwardly uiterlijk
outweigh zwaarder wegen dan
oval o'vaal
ovation o'vatie
oven oven
over boven; over('heen); door; meer dan; om **– again** nog eens
overalls over'all
overbearing aan'matigend
overboard over'boord
overcast be'trokken
overcharge te veel vragen
overcoat overjas

overcome over'stelpt, be'vangen; over'winnen
overcrowded over'vol
overdo te veel doen; over'drijven
overdue achter'stallig, te laat
overflow overloop; over'stromen, overlopen
overgrown over'woekerd
overhang uitstekende rand; overhangen
overhaul nakijken en repa'reren; inhalen
overhead boven (het hoofd); boven'gronds, lucht-
overheads algemene onkosten
overhear horen; afluisteren
overjoyed dolblij
overlap ten dele be'dekken, ge'deeltelijk samenvallen
overlook over'zien; over het hoofd zien
overnight in één nacht; de avond te'voren
overpower over'weldigen
overrate over'schatten
overrule ver'werpen
overrun over'stromen, over'woekeren

overseas over'zee(s)
overseer opzichter
overshadow over'schaduwen
oversight ver'gissing, onop'lettendheid; super'visie
oversleep zich ver'slapen
overstep over'schrijden
overtake inhalen
overthrow ten val brengen
overtime overwerk
overture voorstel; ouver'ture
overturn om'verwerpen, omslaan
overweight te zwaar, te dik; over (ge)wicht, te zware last
overwhelm over'stelpen
overwork zich over'werken
overwrought over'spannen
owe schuldig zijn
owing to dank zij
owl uil
own eigen(dom); be'zitten; er'kennen
owner eigenaar
ownership eigendom(srecht)
ox os
oxygen zuurstof
oyster oester
ozone ozone; frisse lucht

P

pace pas, tempo; stappen
pacific vrede'lievend
pacifist paci'fist
pacify tot be'daren brengen
pack pak(ken); hoop; spel; ver'(or in) pakken; proppen
package pak
packet pakje
packing ver'pakking
pact ver'drag
pad kussen(tje); blok; opvullen
paddle pootje baden
padlock hangslot

pagan heiden(s)
page bladzijde
pageant ver'toning; optocht
pager pieper, sema'foon
pail emmer
pain pijn (doen) **to take pains** moeite doen
painful pijnlijk
painstaking nauwge'zet
paint verf; verven; schilderen
paintbrush verfkwast, pen'seel
painter schilder
painting schilde'rij; schilderkunst

Insight

A *pair* is **een paar. Paar** can also mean *couple*. This seems
pretty straightfoward, but in practice there is one major point
to remember: in Dutch the verb form always has to agree
in number with the subject. In other words, since **het paar**
is a singular noun, the verb form that goes with it has to be
singular too. In English this is not necessarily the case: **het
paar is erg gelukkig** *the couple is/are very happy*. Don't forget
that this goes for all singular nouns describing more than one
person. A few examples: **het team, de regering** *the government*,
het management, de politie *the police*. **De politie heeft nog
niets gevonden** *the police haven't found anything yet*.

pair paar
pal maat
palace pa'leis
palatable smakelijk
palate ge'hemelte; smaak
palatial vorstelijk
palaver gewauwel
pale bleek, licht; paal; ver'bleken
Palestinian Pale'stijns; Pale'stijn
palette pa'let
paling om'heining
pallid bleek
pallor bleekheid
palm palm(tak) **to – off on**
  aansmeren
palpable voelbaar
palpitate snel kloppen; trillen
paltry nietig
pamper ver'wennen
pamphlet pam'flet
pan pan
panacea wondermiddel
pancake pannenkoek
pandemonium pande'monium
pane ruit
panel pa'neel, vak
pang steek; plotseling ge'voel
panic pa'niek; het hoofd ver'liezen
panic-stricken ver'lamd van schrik

panorama pano'rama
pansy vi'ooltje
pant hijgen; snakken (naar)
pantomime sprookjesvoorstelling;
  panto'mime
pantry pro'visiekast
pants: (pair of) – onderbroek
papal pauselijk
paper pa'pier(en); krant;
  ver'handeling; (e'xamen)opgave;
  be'hangen
par gelijkheid **on a –** ge'lijk
parable ge'lijkenis, pa'rabel
parachute para'chute
parade pa'rade; ap'pel; ver'toon;
  para'deren; aantreden; pronken
  met
paradise para'dijs
paradox para'dox
paraffin pe'troleum
paragraph a'linea
parallel paral'lel, even'wijdig;
  eve'naren
paralyse ver'lammen
paralysis ver'lamming
paramount hoogst
paranoid parano'ïde
paraphernalia spullen
parasite para'siet

parasol para'sol
parcel pakje, pak'ket
parch ver'dorren, uitdrogen
parchment perka'ment
pardon ver'giffenis; gratie
(ver'lenen); ver'geven; par'don!
parent ouder
parentage afkomst
parental ouder(lijk)
parenthood ouderschap
parish pa'rochie
park park('eren)
parking fine par'keerboete
parliament parle'ment
parliamentary parlemen'tair
parochial parochi'aal;
klein'burgerlijk
parody pa'rodie
parole erewoord, voor'waardelijke
vrijlating
paroxysm hevige aanval
parrot pape'gaai
parry afweren
parsley peter'selie
parson dominee
part deel, ge'deelte; rol;
stem; scheiden
partake deel hebben aan
partial ge'deeltelijk; par'tijdig;
ge'steld (op)
partially ten dele
participant deelnemer
participate deelnemen (aan)
particle deeltje, par'tikel
particular bij'zonder(heid);
kies'keurig, pre'cies **that – one**
die ene daar; die be'paalde **in**
particular in het bij'zonder
particularly (in het)
bij'zonder, voor'al
parting afscheid; scheiding
partisan aanhanger; par'tijdig
partition ver'deling;
tussenschot; vak; ver'delen

partly ge'deeltelijk, deels
partner partner
partnership ven'nootschap
partridge pa'trijs
part-time job deeltijdbaan,
parttimebaan
party ge'zelschap; par'tij(tje)
pass pas; stand van zaken; pas'seren,
voor'bijgaan; aangeven; slagen;
vellen (judgement); doorbrengen;
goedkeuren; ge'beuren; ermee
doorkunnen
passable redelijk; be'gaanbaar
passage (door)gang; pas'sage;
voor'bijgaan
passenger passa'gier
passer-by voor'bijganger
passing voor'bijgaand; over'lijden
in – ter'loops
passion hartstocht(elijke liefde);
lijden(sverhaal)
passionate harts'tochtelijk
passive pas'sief
passport paspoort
password wachtwoord
past voor'bij; ver'leden; vorig; over
pasta pasta
paste kleefpasta(or pap); pas'tei;
plakken
pastel pas'tel(tekening)
pastime tijdverdrijf
pastoral herderlijk,
herders-, landelijk
pastry korstdeeg; ge'bakje
pasture weide; gras
pat tikje; kluitje; zachtjes kloppen
patch lap(je); plek(je); oplappen
patent pa'tent; duidelijk
paternal vader(lijk)
path pad; baan
pathetic aan'doenlijk; zielig
pathology patholo'gie
pathos pathos
pathway pad

patience ge'duld
patient ge'duldig; pa'tient
patriarch patri'arch
patriot patri'ot
patriotic vaderlands'lievend, patriottisch
patrol pa'trouille; patroui'lleren
patron vaste klant; be'schermheer (*or* vrouw); be'scherm-
patronize be'schermen; uit de hoogte be'handelen; klei'neren; klant zijn van, vaak be'zoeken
patronizing neer'buigend
patter ge'kletter, ge'trippel; ge'babbel; kletteren, trippelen
pattern pa'troon; voorbeeld
paunch buik
pauper arme
pause rust, onder'breking; pau'seren, (even) wachten
pave pla'veien; banen
pavement trot'toir, rijweg (Am.)
pavilion pavil'joen
paw poot; krabben; aanraken
pawn pi'on; werktuig; pand; ver'panden
pay loon; (uit)be'talen; schenken (attention); maken (compliments); afleggen (visit); lonen **it does not –** het loont de moeite niet; het heeft geen zin
payment be'taling; loon
pea erwt
peace vrede; rust
peaceable vrede'lievend, vreedzaam
peaceful rustig; vreedzaam
peach perzik
peacock pauw
peak piek; klep; hoogtepunt
peanut (butter) pinda(kaas)
pear peer
pearl parel
peasant boer
pebble kiezelsteen

peculiar(ity) eigen'aardig(heid)
pedagogue peda'goog
pedal pe'daal; peddelen
pedant(ic) pe'dant
peddle venten
pedestal voetstuk
pedestrian voetganger; alle'daags
pedigree stamboom, ras-
pee plassen, een plas(je) doen; plas, u'rine
peek kijkje; gluren
peel schil(len)
peep gluren
peer turen; gelijke
peerage adelstand
peerless weergaloos
peeved gepi'keerd
peevish chag'rijnig
peg pen, haak, knijper, haring **to – away** ploeteren
pelican peli'kaan
pelt vel; be'kogelen; kletteren
pen pen; kooi
penal straf-, strafbaar
penalize straffen
penalty (geld/ge'vangenis)straf; (geld)boete; ge'volg, nadeel, schade; handicap, achterstand, strafpunt; strafschop
penance boete(doening)
pencil potlood
pendant hanger; luchter
pending hangend; in afwachting van
pendulum slinger
penetrate doodringen, door'boren
penetrating scherp('zinnig)
penguin pinguïn
peninsula schiereiland
penis penis
penitence be'rouw
penitent be'rouwvol; boeteling
penknife zakmes
penniless straat'arm
pension pen'sioen, uitkering

pensioner gepensio'neerde
pensive peinzend; somber
penthouse penthouse, dakappartement
pent-up opgekropt; opgesloten
people mensen; volk; fa'milie
pepper peper; paprika
peppermint peper'munt
per per
perceive waarnemen, be'merken
percent pro'cent
percentage percen'tage
perceptible waar'neembaar, merkbaar
perception waar'neming(svermogen)
perch stok(je), zitplaats; baars; gaan zitten
percussion slag(-)
perennial overblijvend; altijd durend, eeuwig
perfect perfect, vol'maakt, vol'slagen; perfectio'neren
perfection vol'maaktheid, per'fectie
perfectly vol'maakt, vol'komen
perforate perfo'reren
perform doen; opvoeren, ten beste geven, uitvoeren
performance opvoering, uitvoering; optreden; pres'tatie
perfume par'fum; geur
perfunctory noncha'lant, vluchtig
perhaps mis'schien
peril(ous) ge'vaar(lijk)
perimeter omtrek; perife'rie
period peri'ode, uur
periodical perio'diek; tijdschrift
periodically van tijd tot tijd
periphery omtrek; perife'rie
periscope peri'scoop
perish omkomen, ver'gaan
perishable aan be'derf onder'hevig; ver'gankelijk

perjure oneself meineed plegen
perjury meineed
perk up opleven
perky levendig, opgewekt, geest'driftig; ver'waand
permanent vast, perma'nent
permeate (door')dringen, (door') trekken
permissible ge'oorloofd
permission ver'lof
permit ver'gunning; toestaan
perpendicular loodrecht; loodlijn
perpetrate be'gaan
perpetual aan'houdend, eeuwig('durend)
perpetually con'stant
perpetuate ver'eeuwigen
perplex ver'warren; compli'ceren
perplexity ver'bijstering
persecute ver'volgen
perseverance vol'harding
persevere vol'harden
Persian Per'zisch; Pers
persist hard'nekkig doorgaan, volhouden
persistent hard'nekkig
person per'soon, mens
personal per'soonlijk
personality per'soonlijkheid
personally per'soonlijk; wat mij be'treft
personification verper'soonlijking
personnel perso'neel, staf, werknemers; perso'nele hulpmiddelen, troepen, manschappen; perso'neelsafdeling
perspective perspec'tief
perspiration transpi'ratie
perspire transpi'reren
persuade over'reden, over'tuigen
persuasion over'reding(skracht)
persuasive over'twigend
perturb veront'rusten

peruse bestu'deren; doorlezen
pervade ver'vullen, trekken door
perverse per'vers; dwars;
  eigen'zinnig
pervert per'vers per'soon; ver'storen;
  ver'draaien
pessimism pessi'misme
pessimist(ic) pessi'mist(isch)
pest plaag
pester plagen; lastig vallen
pet huisdier, lieveling; lievelings-;
  ver'troetelen
petal bloemblad
petite klein en tenger
petition ver'zoek(schrift), smeekbede
petrify ver'lammen
petrol ben'zine
petty klein, nietig
petulant kribbig
pew kerkbank
pewter tin(nen)
phantom spook; schijn; fan'toom
phase fase; stadium; schijngestalte
pheasant fa'zant
phenomenal fenome'naal
phenomenon ver'schijnsel; wonder
philanthropist filan'troop
philosopher filo'soof
philosophic(al) filo'sofisch
philosophy filoso'fie
phlegm slijm
phosphorescent fosfores'cerend
photograph foto(gra'feren)
photographer foto'graaf
photography fotogra'fie
phrase frase; uitdrukking; uitdrukken
physical li'chamelijk, lichaams-;
  na'tuur('kundig)
physician arts, dokter, inter'nist
physicist natuur'kundige
physics na'tuurkunde
physique lichaamsbouw, fy'siek
pianist pia'nist

piano pi'ano
pick keus; beste; hou'weel; kiezen,
  selec'teren; plukken; peuteren;
  uitzoeken **to – up** oprapen; op de
  kop tikken; oppikken; ophalen
pickaxe hou'weel
pickpocket zakkenroller
picnic picknick(en)
pictorial in beeld; geïllus'treerd
  tijdschrift
picture afbeelding, schilderij,
  foto; plaatje, iets beeldschoons;
  toonbeeld; (speel)film; beeld;
  afbeelden, schilderen, be'schrijven;
  zich voorstellen, zich inbeelden
  go to the pictures naar de
  bioscoop gaan **can you – it?** kun
  je het jezelf voorstellen?
picturesque schilderachtig
pie pas'tei, taart
piece stuk(je)
pier pier
pierce door'boren; door'zien
piercing door'dringend,
  onder'zoekend; scherp, snijdend
  (wind/cold), stekend (pain),
  snerpend (sound); piercing
piety vroomheid
pig varken
pigeon duif
pigeonhole (post)vak(je)
pig-headed eigen'wijs
pigtail vlecht
pike piek; snoek
pile stapel; hoop; aambei; nop;
  heipaal; (op)stapelen, ophopen
pilgrim(age) pelgrim(stocht)
pill pil
pillage plunderen
pillar (steun)pi'laar, zuil
pillow (hoofd)kussen
pillowcase kussensloop
pilot loods(en); pi'loot; be'sturen

pimple puistje
pin speld(en); pen; vastgekneld houden
pinafore schortje
pincers nijptang; schaar
pinch kneep; snuifje; nood; knijpen, klemmen; gappen
pine pijnboom; pijnhout; smachten (naar), kwijnen
pineapple ana'nas
pink roze; kleine anjer
pinnacle (berg)spits, torentje; toppunt
pint (approx) halve liter
pioneer pio'nier(en)
pious vroom
pip pit
pipe pijp, buis; fluit(en)
piper doedelzakspeler
piquant pi'kant
pique pi'keren; prikkelen
pirate zeerover(sschip), pi'raat
pistol pis'tool
piston zuiger
pit kuil; mijn, groeve **pitted** vol kuiltjes; pok'dalig
pitch pek; toonhoogte; graad; pik-; gooien; opslaan; stampen; storten
pitcher kan
pitchfork hooivork
piteous beklagens'waardig
pitfall val(strik)
pitiable, pitiful beklagen'swaardig; jammerlijk
pitiless mee'dogenloos
pittance schijntje
pity medelijden (hebben met) **what a –** wat jammer
pivot spil; draaien
pizza pizza
placard plak'kaat; re'clame maken voor, be'plakken
place plaats(en); thuisbrengen
  to take – plaatsvinden

placid kalm
plague pest; plaag; plagen; lastig vallen
plain duidelijk; een'voudig; effen; onaan'trekkelijk; vlakte
plaintiff aanklager
plait vlecht(en)
plan plan, platte'grond; ont'werpen, uitwerken, op touw zetten; van plan zijn
plane vlak; peil; vliegtuig; schaaf; pla'taan; schaven
planet pla'neet
plank plank
plant plant(en); instal'latie
plantation plan'tage
planter planter
plaque (ge'denk)plaat; tandaanslag; vlek
plasma plasma
plaster pleister(en); be'smeren
plastic plastic; plastisch
plate bord; plaat; goud en zilver
plateau pla'teau, hoogvlakte
platform platform; per'ron (at railway station); podium; bal'kon (in bus/tram); par'tijprogramma
platinum platina
platoon pelo'ton
platter schotel
plausible geloof'waardig
play spel(en); to'neelstuk; speling
player (to'neel)speler
playful speels, schertsend
playground speelplaats
playmate speelmakker
playpen box
plaything stuk speelgoed; speelbal
playwright to'neelschrijver
plea (dringend) ver'zoek; veront'schuldiging; pleit
plead aanvoeren; smeken; (be')pleiten
pleasant prettig, aardig

pleasantry geestigheid, aardigheid
please een ple'zier doen, be'hagen;
ver'kiezen; alstublieft **be pleased
to ...** met ge'noegen ...
pleasing aangenaam; in'nemend
pleasure ge'noegen, ple'zier
pleat plooi(en)
pledge ge'lofte; be'loven, ver'binden
plentiful overvloedig
plenty (of) ruim vol'doende, veel
pliable, pliant buigzaam; plooibaar
pliers buigtang
plight toestand
plod zwoegen
plop plons; plonzen
plot com'plot, in'trige; stukje
grond; be'ramen, samenspannen;
in kaart brengen
plough ploeg(en)
pluck moed; plukken; tokkelen
plucky flink
plug stop(contact), prop;
(dicht)stoppen
plum pruim
plumage ge'vederte
plumb loodrecht; pre'cies; peilen
plumber loodgieter
plumbing loodgieterswerk
plume pluim
plump mollig; (neer)ploffen
plunder buit; plunderen
plunge sprong; indompelen;
(zich) storten
plural meervoud
plus plus
ply han'teren; uitoefenen; over'laden
(met); ge'regeld rijden, be'varen
pneumonia longontsteking
poach stropen; po'cheren
pocket zak(-); in de zak steken;
(in)slikken
pock-marked pok'dalig
pod peul, co'con
poem ge'dicht

poet(ic) dichter(lijk)
poetry poëzie, dichtwerk, ge'dichten
poignant schrijnend; scherp;
aan'grijpend
point punt; zin; wissel; wijzen, richten
– of view ge'zichtspunt **to – out**
aanwijzen; er op wijzen
point-blank bot'weg, van dichtbij
pointed puntig; scherp; ad rem
pointer wijzer; aanwijzing
pointless zinloos
poise houding
poised in evenwicht
poison ver'gift(igen)
poisonous giftig
poke (op)por(ren); steken; slag
poker pook; poker
poky benauwd, klein
polar pool-
pole paal, stok; pool
police po'litie
policeman (po'litie)a'gent
policy be'leid; polis
polish was, smeerpoets; glans;
wrijven, poetsen; be'schaven,
opknappen
Polish Pools
polite be'leefd
political poli'tiek; staats-
politician po'liticus
politics poli'tiek, staatkunde
polka polka
poll stemming; opiniepeiling; aantal
stemmen; stemmen (ver'krijgen)
pollen stuifmeel
pollinate be'stuiven
pollute be'zoedelen, veront'reinigen
polo polo
pompous gewichtig; pompeus;
hoog'dravend
pond vijver
ponder (be')peinzen
ponderous zwaar'wichtig;
zwaar op de hand

pontifical pauselijk; pontifi'caal
pony pony
poo (vulg), poep; poepen
poodle poedel
pool plas; poel; zwembad; bij el'kaar doen
poor arm('zalig); slecht
poorly arm('zalig); niet lekker, minnetjes
pop knallen; wippen; puilen
pope paus
poplar popu'lier
poppy klaproos
popular popu'lair; volks-
populate be'volken
population be'volking
porcelain porse'lein(en)
porch por'tiek
pore porie; turen
pork varkensvlees
porn(ography) porno(gra'fie)
porous po'reus
porridge (havermout)pap
port haven; bakboord; port
portable koffer-, draagbaar
porter kruier; por'tier
portfolio porte'feuille, portfolio
portion deel, portie
portrait por'tret
portray (af)schilderen
pose houding; aanstelle'rij; po'seren; zich voordoen als; stellen
position po'sitie; houding; stelling
positive posi'tief; stellig
positively abso'luut
possess be'zitten
possession(s) be'zit(tingen)
possessive hebberig; be'zittelijk
possibility mogelijkheid
possible mogelijk
possibly mis'schien
post stijl, paal; post; be'trekking; op de post doen; (over)plaatsen; aanplakken

postage port; post-
postal post-
postcard briefkaart
post code postcode
poster poster
posterity nageslacht
posthumous pos'tuum
postman postbode
post mortem lijkschouwing
postpone uitstellen
posture houding
post-war naoorlogs
pot pot(ten); fuik; bom (duiten); inmaken
potato aardappel
potent krachtig
potential potenti'eel; potenti'aal
potter pottenbakker; aanrommelen
pottery aardewerk; pottenbakkerij
pouch zak, buidel
poultry pluimvee
pounce zich storten
pound (approx) half kilogram, pond; beuken (op); bonzen (op); fijnstampen
pour gieten, schenken; stromen
pout pruilen
poverty armoede
poverty-stricken arm(oedig)
powder poeier(en), (be')poeder (en); buskruit
power macht, kracht; mogendheid
powerful machtig, krachtig
powerless machteloos
power station elektrici'teitscentrale
practicable uit'voerbaar
practical praktisch
practically bijna, in de praktijk
practice oefening; prak'tijk; ge'woonte
practise (be')oefenen; (prak'tijk) uitoefenen
prairie prairie
praise lof; prijzen, loven

pram kinderwagen
prank streek, grap
prattle babbelen
prawn garnaal
pray bidden
prayer ge'bed
preach preken, prediken
preacher prediker
preamble inleiding
precarious hachelijk
precaution voorzorg(smaatregel)
precede voor('af)gaan
precedence voorrang, priori'teit,
  het voorgaan
precedent prece'dent
precinct ter'rein
precious kostbaar, dierbaar;
  edel; ge'wild
precipice hoge rotswand
precipitate plotseling; overijld,
  onbe'zonnen; neerslag; ver'haasten
precipitous zeer steil
precise juist, pre'cies
precision nauw'keurigheid, pre'cisie
preclude uitsluiten
precocious vroeg(njp)
preconceived voor'opgezet
precursor voorloper
predatory roof-
predecessor voorganger
predicament hachelijke po'sitie
predict voor'spellen
predominant over'heersend,
  over'wegend
pre-eminence superiori'teit
pre-eminent uitblinkend
pre-eminently bij uitstek
preen gladstrijken, (zich) mooimaken
preface voorwoord, inleiding; van
  een voorwoord voorzien, inleiden;
  leiden tot, het begin zijn van
prefer de voorkeur geven aan, liever
  willen
preferable beter (dan)

preferably bij voorkeur
preference voorkeur
pregnancy zwangerschap
pregnant zwanger; ge'laden
prehistoric voorhis'torisch
prejudice voor'oordeel;
  bevoor'oordelen
prejudicial schadelijk
preliminary voorbereidend;
  voorronde; inleidende
prelude voorspel; pre'lude
premature vroeg'tijdig, voor'barig
premeditated voor'opgezet
premier eerste minister, minister-
  presi'dent, pre'mier; eerste,
  voor'naamste
premise vooronderstellling,
  pre'misse; pand, per'ceel
premium premie
premonition voorgevoel
preoccupation af'wezige
  ge'dachten
preoccupy in be'slag nemen
preparation (voor)bereiding
preparatory voorbereidend
prepare (zich) voorbereiden,
  be'reiden
preposterous ab'surd
prescribe voorschrijven
prescription re'cept; voorschrift
presence aan'wezigheid
present aan'wezig, tegen'woordig;
  heden; ca'deau; schenken;
  presen'teren; ver'tonen; opvoeren;
  voorstellen **at —** op het ogenblik
presentable presen'tabel
presentation schenking; veerstelling;
  presen'tatie, uitreiking; opvoering
present-day heden'daags
presently straks
preservation be'houd; con'ditie
preserve wildpark; ge'bied;
  redden; be'waren, goedhouden,
  conser'veren

preserves con'serven
preside presi'deren,
de leiding hebben
presidency presi'dentschap
president presi'dent; voorzitter
press pers(en); drukken;
(aan)dringen; pressen
pressure druk(ken); drang; pressie
prestige pres'tige
presumably ver'moedelijk
presume veronder'stellen;
zo vrij zijn; ge'bruik maken (van)
presumption veronder'stelling;
aanmatiging
presumptuous aan'matigend
pretence voorwendsel; aanstelle'rij
pretend doen alsof; aanspraak
maken (op)
pretension pre'tentie
pretentious pretenti'eus
pretext voorwendsel
pretty lief, knap, mooi; nogal
prevail heersen; zegevieren
to – upon overhalen
prevalent heersend;
veel'voorkomend
prevent voor'komen, ver'hinderen
prevention préventie, voor'komen
preventive prevent'ief
previous voor'afgaand, vorig
previously vroeger; van te
voren, al eerder
pre-war voor'oorlogs
prey prooi
price prijs; prijzen
priceless on'schatbaar; kostelijk
prick prik; (inf) lul, eikel, schoft;
prikken, steken; (door)steken,
prikkelen
prickle stekel(tje); prikkel
prickly stekelig; kriebelig
pride trots, hoogmoed **to – oneself**
prat gaan
priest priester

prim stijf, preuts
primarily in de eerste plaats
primary pri'mair
prime eerst; bloei(tijd); voorbereiden
primeval oor'spronkelijk, oer-
primitive primi'tief
prince prins, vorst
princely vorstelijk
princess prin'ses
principal voor'naamst; hoofd(-)
principally voor'namelijk
principle prin'cipe
print druk(ken); prent; afdruk;
afdrukken; be'drukken; prenten
print-out uitdraai, print-out
printer drukker, printer
prior voor'afgaand, eerste; prior
priority voorrang
prism prisma
prison ge'vangenis
prisoner ge'vangene
privacy vrijheid; ge'heimhouding
private vrij, pri'vé, per'soonlijk;
particu'lier; ge'heim; sol'daat
privatize privati'seren
privilege voorrecht, privi'lege;
be'voorrechten
prize prijs; be'kroond; waar'deren
probability waar'schijnlijkheid
probable waar'schijnlijk,
ver'moedelijk
probation proef(tijd)
probe peilen; doordringen
problem pro'bleem, vraagstuk
problematic(al) proble'matisch;
twijfelachtig
procedure proce'dure,
me'thode, werkwijze
proceed doorgaan; voortkomen **he
proceeded to tell me** hij ver'telde
me ver'volgens
proceedings ge'beurtenissen;
no'tulen
proceeds opbrengst

process pro'ces, procédé;
be'handelen
procession stoet, optocht, pro'cessie
proclaim af(*or* ver')kondigen;
uitroepen tot
procrastinate talmen
procure (zich) ver'(*or* aan)schaffen
prod (aan)porren
prodigious ge'weldig
prodigy wonder
produce pro'ducten; produ'ceren,
opleveren, voortbrengen; te
voorschijn halen; aanvoeren;
opvoeren; ver'lengen
producer produ'cent; regis'seur
product pro'duct, voortbrengsel
production pro'ductie
productive produ'ctief
profane pro'faan; ont'heiligen
profess be'weren, be'tuigen,
be'lijden
profession be'roep;
be'tuiging, be'lijdenis
professional be'roeps(speler);
vak'kundig; professio'neel
professor pro'fessor
proffer aanbieden
proficiency be'kwaamheid
profile pro'fiel
profit winst; zijn voordeel doen (met)
profitable winst'gevend,
voor'delig, nuttig
profiteer woekeraar; woekerwinst
maken
profound diep('zinnig *or* gaand)
profuse over'vloedig, over'dadig
program (com'puter)pro'gramma;
program'meren
programme program'ma;
program'meren, een schema
opstellen voor
progress voor'uitgang, voortgang;
loop; vorderingen; vorderen,
voor'uitgaan, vorderingen maken

progressive progres'sief (per'soon)
prohibition ver'bod
prohibitive schrik'wekkend hoog
project plan, onderneming;
slingeren; projec'teren; ont'werpen
projectile projec'tiel
projection uitsteeksel; pro'jectie
proletariat proletari'aat
prolific zeer vruchtbaar
prologue pro'loog; inleiding
prolong ver'lengen, rekken
promenade prome'nade
prominence be'lang;
ver'hoging, uitsteeksel
prominent voor'aanstaand;
in het oog vallend; prominent
promise be'lofte; be'loven
promising veelbe'lovend
promote be'vorderen
promotion pro'motie; be'vordering
prompt on'middelijk, stipt; nopen
(tot); souf'fleren, voorzeggen
prone ge'neigd; languit voor'over
pronoun voornaamwoord
pronounce uitspreken;
uitspraak doen
pronunciation uitspraak
proof be'wijs; proef; be'stand
propaganda propa'ganda
propagate zich voortplanten;
ver'spreiden, propa'geren
propel voortdrijven
propeller propeller
proper juist; ge'past
properly op de juiste ma'nier, netjes,
goed; eigenlijk
property eigendom, bezit;
eigenschap
prophecy voor'spelling
prophet pro'feet
proportion (juiste) ver'houding;
deel; proportio'neren **proportions**
pro'porties
proportional even'redig

proposal voorstel; aanzoek
propose voorstellen; zich voornemen; een aanzoek doen
proposition voorstel; stelling; ge'val
propound opperen
proprietary pa'tent-, merk-, eigendoms-; eigenaars-
proprietor eigenaar
propriety goede vorm
propulsion stuwkracht·
prosaic pro'zaïsch
pros and cons voor en tegen
proscribe ver'bieden; ver'bannen
prose proza
prosecute ver'volgen; uitvoeren
prosecutor aanklager
prospect (voor')uitzicht; zoeken
prospective eventu'eel; aan'staande
prospector pros'pector
prosper ge'dijen
prosperity voorspoed, welvaart
prosperous voor'spoedig
prostitute prostitu'ée
prostitution prosti'tutie
prostrate voor'overliggend; ver'slagen; neerwerpen
protect be'schermen
protection be'scherming
protective be'schermend
protein eiwit, proteïne
protest pro'test('eren)
Protestant protes'tant(s)
prototype prototype
protract ver'lengen, rekken
protracted langge'rekt
protrude (voor')uitsteken; zich opdringen
proud trots (op); groot
prove be'wijzen; blijken
proverb spreekwoord
proverbial spreek'woordelijk
provide voor'zien; zorgen
provided (that) mits

providence (de) voor'zienigheid
province pro'vincie; ge'bied
provincial provinci'aal; pro'vincie-
provision voor'ziening; voorwaarde; be'paling; voorzorg(smaatregel); voorraad **provisions** levensmiddelen
provisional voor'lopig
proviso voorbehoud
provocation aanleiding
provocative provo'cerend
provoke uitdagen, uitlokken; tergen
prow voorsteven
prowess dapperheid; vaardigheid
prowl rondsluipen
proximity na'bijheid
proxy volmacht; gevol'machtigde
prudence voor'zichtigheid, be'leid
prudent be'dachtzaam, ver'standig
prudish preuts
prune pruime'dant; (be')snoeien
pry snuffelen; (open)breken
psalm psalm
pseudo(nym) pseudo('niem)
psychiatrist psychi'ater
psychic psychisch, geestelijk; paranor'maal, boven'natuurlijk; paranor'maal be'gaafd
psychological psycho'logisch
psychology psycholo'gie
pub ca'fé, bar, kroeg
puberty puber'teit
public open'baar, pu'bliek; volk **in —** in het open'baar
publication publi'katie
publicity publici'teit
publish uitgeven; be'kend maken
publisher uitgever
pudding pudding, toetje
puddle plas
puerile kinderachtig
puff wolkje, stoot; soes; puffen; opblazen

pugnacious strijd'lustig
pull ruk(ken); trek(ken) (aan) **to – up** uit(*or* op)trekken; stilhouden
pulley ka'trol
pullover slipover
pulp vruchtvlees; pap
pulpit preekstoel
pulsate kloppen; trillen
pulse pols(slag)
pulverize ver'brijzelen
pumice stone puimsteen
pump pomp(en); uithoren
pun woordspeling
punch stomp(en) drevel; punch; knipppen
Punch and Judy Jan Klaassen en Ka'trijn
punctual punctu'eel, stipt
punctuate onder'breken
punctuation inter'punctie
puncture lekke band, gaatje; (door) prikken
pungent scherp, prikkelend
punish straffen
punishment straf
puny nietig
pup jong(e hond)
pupil leerling; pu'pil
puppet mario'net; speelpop
purchase (aan)koop; houvast; (aan) kopen
pure zuiver, rein; louter

purgatory vagevuur
purify zuiveren
purity zuiverheid, reinheid
purple paars, purper
purport strekking; be'weren, be'doelen
purpose doel, be'doeling
purposely, on purpose op'zettelijk
purr spinnen; snorren
purse portemon'nee, beurs; samentrekken
pursue (achter')volgen
pursuit achter'volging; jacht; bezigheid
push duw(en), zetje; dringen
puss(y) poes(je)
put zetten, leggen; brengen; zeggen; doen **to – down** neerzetten; onder'drukken; opschrijven; toeschrijven (aan) **to – off** uitstellen; van zijn stuk brengen, afschrikken; uitdoen **to – on** aantrekken **to – out** uitsteken; uitdoen; blussen; lastig vallen **to – up** ophangen; opsteken; (aan) bieden; maken; bouwen; ver'hogen; bergen, lo'geren; aanpraten **to – up with** dulden
putty stopverf
puzzle (een) raadsel (zijn); piekeren
pyjamas py'jama
pyramid pira'mide

Q

quack kwak(en); kwakzalver
quadrangle binnenplein
quadruped vier'voetig (dier)
quail kwartel; (te'rug) schrikken
quaint typisch, eigen'aardig
quake beven
qualification kwalifi'catie; re'strictie
qualified be'voegd

qualify ge'schikt maken; de be'voegdheid ver'werven; kwalifi'ceren
quality kwali'teit; eigenschap
qualm onbe'haaglijk ge'voel; scru'pule
quandary lastig par'ket
quantity (grote) hoe'veelheid; grootheid

quarantine quaran'taine
quarrel (reden tot) twist, ruzie; twisten
quarrelsome twistziek
quarry wild, prooi; slachtoffer; steengroeve; (uit)graven
quarter kwart('aal); windstreek; wijk; ge'nade; in vieren delen; inkwartieren **– of an hour** kwar'tier
quarters kwar'tier(en); kringen
quarterly drie'maandelijks per kwar'taal
quartet kwar'tet
quartz kwartz
quasi quasi, zoge'naamd
quaver trilling; achtste noot; trillen
quay kaai, kade
queen koning'in; (in chess) koning'in, dame; (in cards) vrouw, dame; (inf) nicht, ver'wijfde flikker

query vraag(teken); twijfel; in twijfel trekken; een vraagteken zetten achter
quest: in – of op zoek naar
question vraag; kwestie; sprake; twijfel; onder'vragen; be'twijfelen
questionable twijfelachtig
queue rij; in de rij staan
quibble spits'vondigheid; haarkloven
quick vlug
quicken levend worden; sneller worden
quicksand drijfzand
quicksilver kwik(zilver)
quick-tempered op'vliegend
quiet rust(ig), stil
quieten sussen, be'daren
quilt gewat'teerde deken; wat'teren, doorstikken
quip geestigheid; steek

Insight

There are two queens in the Dutch language area: the Dutch head of state **koningin Beatrix** and the Belgian **koningin Paola**, wife of the Belgian head of state **koning Albert II (Albert de Tweede)**. The Dutch queen's official birthday is called **Koninginnedag** and is celebrated on 30 **April** (actually the birthday of her late mother **koningin Juliana**). The word **koninginnedag** is a compound noun made up of two words: **koningin** and **dag**. When forming a compound noun, often an **-s, -e** or **-en** is added between the two parts (**liefde** *love* and **verdriet** *sadness*, for instance, together make **liefdesverdriet** *love sickness*).

queer vreemd, raar, zonderling; ver'dacht, onbe'trouwbaar; onwel, niet lekker; (inf) homoseksu'eel; (inf) homo, flikker
quell onder'drukken
quench lessen; blussen
querulous knorrig, klagend

quit ophouden, stoppen; opgeven; ophouden met, stoppen met; ver'laten, ver'trekken/heengaan van **she has – her job** zij heeft haar baan opgegeven/opgezegd **I've had enough, I –** ik heb er genoeg van, ik stop/kap ermee **to be – of** af zijn van

quite helemaal; verreweg; vrij; juist, ja

quits quitte **we're –** we staan quitte

quiver peilkoker; trillen

quiz onder'vraging, ver'hoor; test, kort examen; quiz; onder'vragen, uithoren; mondeling exami'neren

R

rabbit ko'nijn

rabble ge'spuis

rabid dol

race wedloop, wedren; ras; racen; om het hardst lopen; rennen

racecourse renbaan

racehorse renpaard

racetrack renbaan, cir'cuit

racial raci'aal, ras-, rassen- **– discrimination** rassendiscriminatie

racing wedrennen

racist ra'cistisch; ra'cist

rack rek; pijnbank; folteren; afpijnigen

racket racket; herrie; afzette'rij

racketeer afzetter

radiance straling

radiant stralend

radiate (uit)stralen; straalsgewijs uitlopen

radiator radi'ator

radical radi'caal

radio radio(-)

radioactive radioac'tief

radish ra'dijs

radius straal; cirkel

raffle ver'loting; ver'loten

raft vlot

rafter dakspant

rag lapje, vod; jool; keet maken, te grazen nemen

rage woede; rage; tieren

ragged haveloos

raid in(or over)val (doen)

quota quota, aandeel; (maximum) aantal

quotation aanhaling(s-), ci'taat; no'tering

quote ci'teren, aanhalen; opgeven (a price); ci'taat, aanhaling; no'tering (on stock exchange, etc.)

rail stang, spaak; rail; spoor; uitvaren (tegen)

railing(s) hek

railway spoorweg, spoorbaan

rain regen(en)

rainbow regenboog

rainfall regenval

rainy regenachtig

raise oplichten; ver'heffen; ver'hogen; bij'eenbrengen, opbrengen; fokken; ver'wekken; grootbrengen

raisin ro'zijn

rake hark(en); losbol; doorzoeken

rally bij'eenkomst; (zich) ver'zamelen; bijkomen

ram ram(men)

ramble zwerftocht; zwerven; zich slingeren; bazelen, afdwalen

ramp helling, glooiing; oprit, afrit; verkeersdrempel

rampant: to be – woekeren; hoogtij vieren

rampart wal; bolwerk

ramshackle gammel

ranch (vee)fokke'rij

rancid ranzig

rancour wrok

random luk'raak **at random** op goed ge'luk

range ruimte, veld, kring; draagwijdte; baan; keten; for'nuis; vari'ëren; zwerven (over); (zich) opstellen

rank rij; ge'lid; rang, stand;
be'horen (tot)
rankle iemand dwars zitten
ransack plunderen
ransom losgeld
rant tekeer gaan
rap tik(ken); duit; gooien
rape ver'krachting; roof; ver'krachten
rapid snel
rapids stroomversnelling
rapt opgetogen, ver'rukt
rapture ver'voering
rapturous opgetogen, ver'rukkelijk
rare zeldzaam; niet gaar (meat)
rarely zelden
rarity zeldzaamheid
rascal schelm
rash onbe'zonnen; uitslag
rasp rasp(en)
raspberry fram'boos
rat rat; onderkruiper; overlopen
rate koers, cijfer, snelheid, prijs; klas;
plaatselijke be'lasting;
ge'val; schatten; be'rispen
rather liever, eerder; nog'al;
nou en of!
ratify be'krachtigen
ratio ver'houding
ration rant'soen('eren)
rational ratio'neel, redelijk
rattle rammelaar, ratel;
ge'kletter; rammelen, ratelen; van
streek brengen
raucous schor, rauw
ravage ver'woesten, ver'nietigen,
teisteren; leegplunderen, leegroven;
ver'woesting(en), ver'nietiging
rave razen (tegen, op), ijlen, (als een
gek) te'keergaan (tegen), lyrisch
worden (over), dwepen (met); zich
gek maken; juichende bespreking;
wild feest, dansfeest, rave
raven raaf
ravenous uitgehongerd

ravine ra'vijn
ravishing be'toverend
raw rauw; ruw; groen; guur —
materials grondstoffen
ray straal; rog (fish)
razor scheerapparaat(*or* mes)
razor-blade scheermesje
re- op'nieuw
reach be'reik(en); ge'deelte; (zich)
uitstrekken; reiken; er (bij) komen
react rea'geren
reaction re'actie
reactionary reactio'nair
read (voor)lezen; zeggen, aanwijzen;
stu'deren; opvatten
readily ge'makkelijk; gaarne
readiness ge'reedheid;
bereid'willigheid
reading lezen, lezing; stand;
interpre'tatie; lec'tuur; lees-
ready klaar; be'reid('willig);
ge'makkelijk
ready-made con'fectie,
pasklaar, kant-en-klaar
real werkelijk, echt
realism rea'lisme
realist(ic) rea'list(isch)
reality werkelijkheid
realization be'sef;
ver'wezenlijking, reali'satie
realize be'seffen; ver'wezenlijken;
reali'seren; opbrengen
really (in) werkelijk(heid)
realm (konink)rijk
reanimation reani'matie
reap maaien; oogsten
reappear op'nieuw ver'schijnen
rear achter-; achterhoede, achterkant
reason rede(n); (be)rede'neren
(with)in — redelijk(erwijs) **it stands
to —** het spreekt van'zelf
reasonable redelijk
reasoning rede'nering
reassurance ver'zekering

reassure ver'zekeren; ge'ruststellen

rebate korting; te'ruggave

rebel re'bel; in opstand komen, rebel'leren

rebellion opstand

rebellious op'standig

rebound te'rugstoot; te'rugstuiten

rebuff koude douche;   ·   voor het hoofd stoten

rebuke be'risping; be'rispen

recalcitrant weer'spannig

recant her'roepen; er van te'rugkomen

recapitulate recapitu'leren

recapture her'overen, op'nieuw ge'vangennemen; weer oproepen

recede te'rugwijken, te'ruglopen

receipt re'cu, kwi'tantie; ont'vangst; kwi'teren

receive ont'vangen

receiver ont'vanger hoorn

recent re'cent

recently on'langs, de laatste tijd

receptacle (ver'gaar)bak

reception ont'vangst; re'ceptie

receptive ont'vankelijk (voor)

recess re'ces; nis; schuilhoek

recipe re'cept

recipient ont'vanger

reciprocal weder'kerig; omgekeerde

reciprocate be'antwoorden; heen en weer gaan

recital voordracht; opsomming; re'cital

recite voordragen; opsommen

reckless roekeloos

reckon (be')rekenen; be'schouwen

reclaim her'winnen, droogleggen, redden

recline achter'over liggen

recluse kluizenaar

recognition (h)er'kenning; waar'dering

recognizable her'kenbaar

recognize (h)er'kennen

recoil te'rugloop; te'rugdeinzen; te'ruglopen

recollect zich her'innering

recollection her'innering

recommend aanbevelen; aanraden

recommendation aanbeveling; ad'vies

recompense be'loning; be'lonen; schadeloosstellen

reconcile ver'zoenen; over'eenbrengen

reconciliation ver'zoening

reconnaissance ver'kenning(s-)

reconstruct opbouwen, reconstru'eren

reconstruction weder'opbouw; recon'structie

record offici'ële ver'melding; no'titie; (grammo'foon)plaat; re'cord; repu'tatie; ongeëve'naard; optekenen; opnemen, te boek stellen

recount nieuwe telling; ver'halen

recover te'rugkrijgen; inhalen; her'stellen

recovery her'stel

recreation recre'atie, ont'spanning, hobby

recreational recrea'tief, recre'atie-, ont'spannings-

recrimination tegenbeschuldiging

recruit re'kruut, nieuweling; rekru'teren

rectangle rechthoek

rectangular recht'hoekig

rectify her'stellen

rector dominee; rector

rectory pasto'rie

recuperate her'stellen

recur te'rugkeren

recurrence her'haling

recurrent steeds te'rugkerend

red(den) rood (maken *or* worden)

reddish roodachtig

redeem aflossen; ver'vullen; ver'lossen; ver'zachten

red-handed op heter daad

red-hot rood'gloeiend

redouble ver'dubbelen

redoubtable ge'ducht

redress ver'goeding; weer goedmaken

reduce ver'minderen; ver'lagen

reduction afname, ver'mindering; korting; re'ductie

redundant over'bodig

reed riet

reek stinken

reel klos(je); duizelen, wankelen

refer ver'wijzen; zinspelen (op); be'trekking hebben (op); raadplegen

referee scheidsrechter

reference ver'wijzing; be'trekking; toespeling; ge'tuigschrift; hand-

refine raffi'neren

refined geraffi'neerd; be'schaafd

refinery raffinade'rij

reflect te'rugkaatsen; weer'spiegelen; weergeven; nadenken

reflection re'flectie, weer'spiegeling, weer'kaatsing; over'denking, over'weging **on —** bij nader inzien

reflector re'flector

reflex re'flex(-)

reform ver'betering; ver'beteren; (zich) beteren

reformation her'vorming; Refor'matie

refractory weer'barstig

refrain re'frein; zich ont'houden (van)

refresh ver'kwikken; opfrissen

refreshing ver'frissend; op'wekkend

refreshment ver'frissing, restau'ratie; con'sumptie

refrigerator koelkast

refuge toevlucht(soord)

refugee vluchteling

refund te'rugbetaling; te'rugbetalen

refusal weigering

refuse vuilnis; weigeren

refute weer'leggen

regain her'winnen; weer be'reiken

regal koninklijk

regard aandacht; achting; be'schouwen; in acht nemen; be'treffen **regards** groeten

regardless of ongeacht

regent re'gent('es)

regime re'gime

regiment regi'ment

region streek, ge'west, ge'bied

regional ge'westelijk

register re'gister; registeren; inschrijven; aangeven, te kennen geven; (laten) aantekenen

registration regis'tratie

regret spijt; be'treuren

regretfully met spijt

regrettable betreurens'waardig

regular ge'regeld, regel' matig, vast; echt; be'roeps(sol'daat)

regularity regelmaat

regulate regelen

regulation voorschrift, be'paling; regeling

rehabilitation rehabili'tatie

rehearsal repe'titie

rehearse repe'teren, instuderen

reign re'gering; be'wind

reimburse ver'goeden

rein teugel; inhouden; be'teugelen

reindeer rendier(en)

reinforce ver'sterken

reinforcement ver'sterking

reinstate her'stellen

reiterate her'halen

reject afgekeurd voorwerp;
afkeuren, van de hand wijzen
rejoice ver'heugd zijn
rejoin zich weer voegen bij
rejoinder re'pliek
rejuvenate ver'jongen
relapse instorting, te'rugval; weer
instorten, weer ver'vallen
relate ver'halen; in ver'band
brengen (met)
related ver'want
relation be'trekking, re'latie,
ver'houding; fa'milielid
relationship ver'wantschap;
ver'houding
relative fa'milielid; relatief,
be'trekkelijk; respec'tief
relax (zich) ont'spannen, re'laxen;
ver'slappen, ver'minderen,
ont'dooien
relaxation ont'spanning;
ver'slapping
release vrijlating; be'vrijding; vrij
(or los)laten; bevrijden; vrijgeven
relegate te'rugzetten; ver'bannen
relent zich laten ver'murwen
relentless mee'dogenloos
relevant van toepassing
(op), toe'passelijk
reliable be'trouwbaar
reliance ver'trouwen
relic reli'kwie; overblijfsel
relief ver'lichting; opluchting; hulp,
aflossing(sploeg); reli'ëf; extra
relieve ver'lichten; ont'lasten;
ont'zetten; aflossen; afwisselen
religion godsdienst, re'ligie
religious godsdienst-, gods'dienstig,
religi'eus; klooster-; plichtsgetrouw
relinquish opgeven; afstand doen van
relish smaak; pi'kante lekker'
nij; ge;nieten van
reluctance tegenzin

reluctant on'willig
rely ver'trouwen (op)
remain (over)blijven **remains**
overblijfselen
remainder rest
remark opmerking; opmerken
remarkable merk'waardig;
op'merkelijk
remedy (hulp)middel; ver'helpen
remember zich her'inneren;
ont'houden, denken om; de groeten
doen van
remembrance nagedachtenis
remind her'inneren (aan)
reminder (vriendelijke) aanmaning
reminiscent: to be – of
her'inneren aan
remiss na'latig
remit overmaken; kwijtschelden
remnant res'tant
remonstrate protes'teren
remorse wroeging
remorseless onbarm'hartig
remote afgelegen; ver; ge'ring
remotely in de verte, enigs'zins
removal ver'wijderen; ver'huizing
remove ver'wijderen, afnemen,
uittrekken; afzetten
remuneration ver'goeding
remunerative winst'gevend
Renaissance Renais'sance
rend (ver')scheuren
render geven; be'tuigen; maken;
ver'tolken; klaren
renegade af'vallig(e)
renew ver(or her)'nieuwen;
ver'lengen
renounce afstand doen van;
ver'stoten
renovate ver'nieuwen, opknappen,
reno'veren
renown ver'maardheid, roem
renowned ver'maard

Insight

To rent is **huren** in Dutch. **Een woning huren** *to rent accommodation* is very common, particularly in the Netherlands. *Rental accommodation* is called **een huurwoning**, whereas *owner-occupied accommodation* is called **een koopwoning**. *To let* (or *to rent to someone*) is **verhuren** in Dutch.

rent huur, pacht; scheur; huren, pachten

rental huur

renunciation afstand doen; ver'werping, ver'loochening

reopen her'openen; her'vatten

reorganize reorgani'seren

repair repar'atie; con'ditie; her'stellen

reparation schadeloosstelling

repartee puntigheid, ge'vatheid

repatriation repatri'ëring

repay te'rugbetalen

repeal afschaffing; her'roepen, afschaffen

repeat her'haling; her'halen; nazeggen, navertellen; opzeggen

repeated(ly) her'haald(elijk)

repel te'rug(*or* af)slaan; afstoten

repellent af'stotend

repent be'rouw hebben

repentance be'rouw

repentant be'rouwvol

repercussion re'actie, te'rugslag

repertoire reper'toire

repetition her'haling

replace ver'vangen, ver'nieuwen; te'rugzetten

replacement ver'vanging; nieuwe

replenish aan(*or* bij)vullen

replica ko'pie

reply antwoorden

report ver'slag (doen), rap'port, be'richt; rappor'teren; (zich) melden

reporter ver'slaggever

repose rust(en)

repository opslagplaats; schatkamer

represent voorstellen; vertegen'woordigen

representation voorstelling; vertegen'woordiging

representative vertegen'woordiger; representa'tief; typisch

repress onder'drukken

reprieve uitstel, gratie

reprimand be'risping; be'rispen

reprint herdruk; her'drukken

reprisal repre'saille

reproach ver'wijt(en); schande

reprobate onverlaat

reproduce weergeven; (zich) voortplanten, vermenig'vuldigen

reprove be'rispen

reptile rep'tiel

republic repu'bliek

republican republi'kein(s)

repudiate ver'werpen; niet er'kennen; ver'stoten

repugnant weerzin'wekkend

repulse afslaan; afwijzen

repulsive weerzin'wekkend

reputable respec'tabel

reputation repu'tatie; (goede) naam

repute aanzien; houden voor

request ver'zoek(en), aanvraag; vragen om

require nodig hebben; ver'langen

requirement be'hoefte, ver'eiste; eis
requisite ver'eist(e); be'hoefte
requisition vordering; vorderen
requite ver'gelden
rescind intrekken
rescue redding; redden **to come to the –** te hulp komen
research weten'schappelijk onderzoek
resemblance ge'lijkenis; over'eenkomst
resemble (ge)'lijken (op)
resent kwalijk nemen
resentful ge'belgd, boos
resentment wrevel
reservation middenberm, middenstrook; reser'vaat; reser'vering, plaatsbespreking; gereser'veerde plaats; re'serve, voorbehoud, be'denking
reserve re'serve; reser'vaat; gereser'veerdheid; be'waren, reser'veren
reserved gereser'veerd; te'rughoudend
reservoir reser'voir
reside woon'achtig zijn
residence woonplaats, woning; ver'blijf
resident inwoner; gast; resi'dent; inwonend
residential woon-
residue overschot; resi'du
resign aftreden; neerleggen **to – oneself to** be'rusten in
resignation ont'slag; be'rusting
resilience veerkracht
resin hars
resist zich ver'zetten, weerstand bieden; zich weer'houden (van); weer'staan
resistance ver'zet; weerstand(svermogen)
resolute vastbe'raden
resolution be'sluit, voornemen; voorstel; vastbe'radenheid

resolve be'sluit(en); vastbe'radenheid; (zich) oplossen
resonance reso'nantie
resonant reso'nerend
resort (va'kantie)oord; redmiddel; zijn toevlucht nemen (tot)
resound weer'galmen; weer'kaatsen
resource (red)middel, rijkdom, (hulp) bron
resourceful vindingrijk
respect eerbied, res'pect; opzicht; be'trekking; respec'teren, eer'biedigen
respectable fat'soenlijk; respec'tabel
respectful eer'biedig
respecting aan'gaande
respective respec'tief
respectively respec'tievelijk
respiration ademhaling
respite ver'ademing; uitstel
resplendent glansrijk, schitterend
respond rea'geren (op); be'antwoorden
response antwoord, weerklank; tegenzang
responsibility verant'woordelijkheid
responsible verant'woordelijk
responsive ont'vankelijk (voor)
rest rust (geven); steun; rest; (uit) rusten, liggen; leunen (met); be'rusten
restaurant restau'rant
restful rustig, kal'merend
restitution resti'tutie, ver'goeding
restive on'rustig
restless onge'durig, on'rustig, rusteloos
restoration restau'ratie; her'stel, te'ruggave
restore restau'reren; her'stellen, te'ruggeven, terug'zetten
restrain be'dwingen, in be'dwang houden
restrict be'perken

restriction be'perking; voorbehoud
resuscitate reani'meren, bijbrengen
result resul'taat, uitslag, ge'volg;
uitkomst; uitlopen (op); komen
resume her'vatten
resumption her'vatting
resurrection opstanding
retail klein(handel), de'tail (handel)
de'tailhandebar
retailer detail'list, leveran'cier
retain (vast or ont')houden
retaliate re'vanche nemen
retaliation wraak
retard achterlijke; tegen(or op)
houden
reticent terug'houdend
retina retina
retinue ge'volg
retire met pen'sioen gaan, aftreden;
naar bed gaan; (zich) te'rugtrekken
retired gepensio'neerd; afgelegen
retirement ont'slag; pensio'nering;
afzondering
retiring te'ruggetrokken
retort vinnig (or ge'wiekst)
antwoord(en); re'tort
retrace te'rugkeren op
retract her'roepen
retreat te'rug(or af)tocht;
a'siel; zich te'rugtrekken
retribution ver'gelding
retrieve te'rugvinden; her'stellen
retrospect: in – achter'af
be'schouwd
return te'rugkomst, te'rugkeer;
te'rugbrengen(or geven or zenden);
opbrengst; rap'port; re'tour-;
te'ruggaan(or keren or komen) **by
–** per omgaande **in –** in ruil **many
happy returns** nog vele jaren!
reunion her'eniging; reü'nie
reunite (zich) her'enigen
reveal ont'hullen, open'baren; aan
het licht brengen; kenbaar maken

revel zich ver'lustigen; feestvieren
revelation open'baring
revenge wraak(zucht) **to revenge
oneself, to be revenged** zich
wreken (op)
revenue (rijks)inkomsten
reverberate weer'galmen
reverberation nagalm
revere (ver')eren
reverence eerbied; buiging
reverent eer'biedig
reverie mijmering
reverse omgekeerd(e);
tegendeel; keerzijde; tegenslag,
nederlaag; omkeren; her'roepen;
achter'uitrijden
revert weer te'rugkeren; ver'vallen (in)
review re'visie; te'rugblik; re'censie;
op'nieuw in ogenschouw nemen;
te'rugzien op; her'zien; recen'seren
revile (be')schimpen
revise nazien; her'zien
revision repe'teren; her'ziening
revival opleving; weder'opvoering
revive (doen) her'leven, bijkomen;
op'nieuw invoeren/ingevoerd
worden
revoke her'roepen; niet be'kennen
revolt opstand; in opstand komen;
doen walgen
revolting walgelijk
revolution revo'lutie; omwenteling
revolutionary revolutio'nair
revolutionize een ommekeer
te'weegbrengen
revolve (om)wentelen
revolver re'volver
revulsion ommekeer; walging
reward be'loning; be'lonen
rhapsody rapso'die
rhetoric re'torica; reto'riek
rhetorical re'torisch
rheumatic reu'matisch
rheumatism reuma'tiek

rhinoceros neushoorn
rhubarb ra'barber
rhyme rijm(pje); rijmen
rhythm ritme
rhythmic ritmisch
rib rib(stuk); ba'lein; nerf
ribbon lint; flard
rice rijst
rich rijk; machtig, extra fijn; warm
riches rijkdom(men)
richly rijkelijk
rickety wankel
rid af; afhelpen **to get – of** kwijt
  raken, ver'drijven
riddle raadsel; grove zeef; door'zeven
ride rit(je), tocht(je); (paard)rijden
rider ruiter, be'rijder
ridge kam; nok; rug
ridicule spot; be'spotten
ridiculous be'lachelijk
rife wijdver'breid
riffraff uitschot
rifle ge'weer; plunderen
rift scheur, kloof
right juist; goed; in orde; vlak,
  helemaal; pre'cies; recht;
  rechterzijde; rechtzetten **to be**
  – ge'lijk hebben on the – rechts
  to the – aan de rechterkant;
  rechts('af) **– away** on'middellijk
righteous recht'schapen; (ge)
  recht'vaardig(d)
rightful recht'matig
right-hand rechter-
rightly te'recht; goed
rigid vast, stijf; star
rigmarole ge'klets
rigorous zeer streng
rigour strengheid
rim rand, velg
rime rijp
rind korst, zwoerd, schil
ring ring; piste; kliek; tele'foontje;
  luiden; bellen; weer'galmen

rink baan
rinse (om)spoelen
riot oproer (maken)
riotous op'roerig; los'bandig
rip scheur(en)
ripe rijp; be'legen
ripen rijp worden (or maken)
ripple golfje; lichte golfslag; kabbelen
rise stijgen; stijging; opkomst; opslag;
  toenemen; opstaan; opstijgen;
  om'hooglopen; stijgen; opkomen
  to give – to ver'oorzaken
risk ge'vaar, risico; wagen, ris'keren
risky ris'kant
rite rite
ritual ritu'eel
rival ri'vaal, mededinger;
  mededingend; concur'reren met;
  wedijveren met
rivalry rivali'teit wedijver;
  concur'rentie
river ri'vier
riverside oever
rivet klinknagel; klinken
rivulet beekje
road weg, straat
roadside (aan de) kant van de weg,
  berm
roadway rijweg
roam dwalen
roar ge'brul, ge'raas; brullen,
  bulderen; ronken
roast ge'braden; braden
rob (be')roven
robber(y) rover('ij)
robe toga, mantel
robin roodborstje
robust fors
rock rots, klip; schommelen; wiegen;
  schudden
rocket ra'ket, vuurpijl
rocky rotsachtig; wankel
rod roe(de)
rodent knaagdier

rogue schelm
roguish schalks
role rol
roll rol(len); roffel(en); lijst; broodje;
slingeren
roller rol, wals; zware golf
rollerblade skeeleren
Roman Ro'mein(s);
rooms(katho'liek)
romance liefdesgeschiedenis;
ro'mance; fanta'seren
romantic roman'tisch; ro'manticus
romp stoeipartij; stoeien
roof dak; ge'welf; ver'hemelte
rook roek
room kamer; ruimte; aanleiding
roomy ruim
root wortel (schieten); oorzaak;
wortelen; omwroeten **to – up**
(or out) uitroeien
rooted vastgegroeid; ingeworteld
rope touw, koord
rosary rozenkrans
rose roos
rosette ro'zet
rosy roze, blozend; roos'kleurig
rot ver'rotting; be'derf; larie;
(doen) ver'rotten
rotate ro'teren, (doen) draaien
rotation ro'tatie, (om)wenteling;
afwisseling **in – om** beurten
rotten (ver')rot; be'roerd; ge'meen
rotund kort en dik
rouge rouge
rough ruw, on'effen; ruig; hard
roughly onge'veer
round rond('om); om(-); ronde;
reeks; omgaan **to – off** afronden;
afmaken, vervol'maken
roundabout ro'tonde, ver'keersplein;
draaimolen; indi'rect, om'slachtig
rouse wakker maken; prikkelen
rout wilde vlucht; op de vlucht
drijven; snuffelen; opdiepen

route route
routine rou'tine; ge'bruikelijk
rove zwerven
row rij; herrie, rel, ruzie; roeien
rowdy la'waaierig
royal koninklijk; vorstelijk
royalty leden van het koninklijk huis;
iemand van koninklijken bloede;
royalty, aandeel in de opbrengst;
koningschap
rub wrijven; schuren **to – out**
uitgummen
rubber rubber; robber; gum
rubbish afval, vuilnis; rommel; klets
rubble puin
ruby ro'bijn(rood)
rudder roer(blad)
ruddy blozend
rude onbe'leefd; grof
rudiment(ary) rudi'ment('air)
ruff (plooi)kraag
ruffian woesteling
ruffle in de war brengen, rimpelen;
ver'storen
rug ta'pijt, vloerkleed
rugged fors en hoekig; stoer
ruin ru'ïne; ondergang; be'derven;
ruï'neren
ruinous ver'derfelijk; ruïneus
rule regel; heerschap'pij; be'slissen;
be'heren, re'geren; lini'ëren **as a –**
ge'woonlijk
ruler heerser, re'geerder; lini'aal
ruling be'slissing; re'gerend;
heersend
rum rum; raar
Rumania Roe'menië
Rumanian Roe'meens
rumble ge'rommel; rommelen
ruminate her'kauwen; be'peinzen
rummage snuffelen
rumour ge'rucht
rumple kreuken
rump steak biefstuk

run wedloop; reis; ritje; run; peri'ode;
  (hard)lopen, rennen; kruipen; raken;
  doorlopen; laten (vol)lopen; drijven
  in the long – op de lange duur **to**
  – down afnemen; opsporen;
  over'rijden; uitgeput raken;
  afkammen **to – into** tegenkomen;
  oprijden (or lopen) tegen **to –**
  out aflopen; opraken **to – out**
  of door ... heen raken **to – over**
  over'rijden; overlopen **to – through**
  door'steken; doorlezen
runaway op hol ge'slagen
rung sport
runner hardloper; bode; loper

running door'lopend; achter el'kaar
runway baan; startbaan/
  landingsbaan
rupture breuk
rural landelijk, platte'lands-
rush drukte, haast; toeloop; bies;
  rennen, vliegen; storten; zich haasten
Russia Rusland
rust roest; (ver')roesten
rustic boers; rus'tiek; lande'lijk
rustle ge'ritsel; (doen) ritselen
rusty roestig
rut wagenspoor; sleur
ruthless mee'dogenloos
rye rogge

S

sabotage sabo'tage
sabre sabel
sack zak; plundering; ontslaan; plunderen
sacrament sacra'ment
sacred heilig; ge'wijd
sacrifice offer(ande), opoffering;
  (op)offeren
sacrilege heiligschennis
sad be'droefd; droevig
saddle zadel(en); opschepen
sadness be'droefdheid
safe veilig; zeker; brandkast
safeguard waarborg(en)
safety veiligheid
safety belt veiligheidsgordel,
  veiligheidsriem
safety pin veiligheidsspeld
sag doorbuigen; (af or door)zakken
saga sage
sagacious schrander
sage wijze; salie
sail zeil(en); ver'trekken, varen
sailor ma'troos, zeeman
saint heilig(e); sint
sake: for the – of; ter wille van;
  om ... te

salad sla
salary sa'laris
sale (uit)verkoop, ver'koping
salesman be'diende; handelsreiziger
salient op'vallend; treffend
saliva speeksel
sallow ziekelijk (geel)
salmon zalm
saloon sa'lon; bar; zaal
salt zout; zouten
salutary heilzaam
salutation groet
salute sa'luut; salu'eren
salvage berging; bergloon;
  afval; bergen; redden
salvation ver'lossing; zaligheid
salve zalf; sussen; redden
salvo salvo
same zelfde **all the –** deson'danks;
  allemaal het'zelfde (or eender)
sample monster; staal(tje);
  voorproefje; keuren
sanatorium sana'torium; ziekenzaal
sanctimonious schijn'heilig
sanction sanctie; sanctio'neren
sanctity heiligheid

sanctuary sanctu'arium;
  reser'vaat; a'siel
sand zand
sands strand
sandal san'daal
sandpaper schuurpapier; schuren
sandpit zandgroeve; zandbak
sandwich sandwich, dubbele
  boterham; klemmen, vastzetten,
  plaatsen
sandy zandig, zand-
sane ge'zond van geest, ver'standig
sanguine opgewekt; blozend
sanitary ge'zondheids-
sanitation sani'tair
sanity ge'zond ver'stand
sap sap; uitputten
sapling jonge boom
sapphire saf'fier(blauw)
sarcasm sar'casme
sarcastic sar'castisch
sardine sar'dine
sardonic smalend
sash sjerp; schuifraamkozijn
satchel schooltas
satellite satel'liet
satiate (over)ver'zadigen
satin sa'tijn(en)
satire sa'tire
satiric(al) sa'tirisch
satirize hekelen
satisfaction vol'doening;
  ge'noegdoening
satisfactorily naar ge'noegen
satisfactory be'vredigend
satisfy vol'doen aan; be'vredigen,
  te'vreden stellen **to be satisfied
  with** te'vreden zijn over (or met)
saturate ver'zadigen; door'trekken;
  door'weken
satyr sater
sauce saus; brutali'teit
saucepan (steel)pan
saucer scholteltje

saucy bru'taal; vlot
saunter slenteren
sausage worst(je)
savage wild(e), woest
save redden; sparen; voor'komen
savings spaarpenningen
saviour redder, Heiland
savour smaak; smaken (naar);
  ge'nieten van
savoury smakelijk; pi'kant
saw zaag; zagen
sawdust zaagsel
saxophone saxo'foon
say zeggenschap; (op)zeggen;
  luiden **that is to –** dat wil zeggen
  it says ... er staat ...
saying ge'zegde
scaffold scha'vot; steiger
scaffolding stel'lage, steiger
scald met kokend water be'gieten,
  met stoom branden
scale schub; schilfer; ketelsteen;
  schaal; graadverdeling; (toon)
  ladder; be'klimmen
scales weegschaal
scallop schelp; schulp
scalp scalp('eren)
scaly ge'schubd; schilferig
scan afzoeken; een vluchtige blik
  werpen in (or op); scannen; (zich
  laten) scan'deren
scandal schan'daal, schande;
  lasterpraat
scandalize aanstoot geven
scandalous schandelijk; lasterlijk
Scandinavian Scandi'navisch;
  Scandi'naviër
scant schraal; karig (zijn met)
scanty spaarzaam, onvol'doende, dun
scapegoat zondebok
scar litteken; rotswand
scarce schaars
scarcely nauwelijks
scarcity schaarste

scare schrik('barend be'richt); bang maken
scarecrow vogelverschrikker
scarf sjaal; das
scarlet schar'laken
scathing bijtend
scatter (zich) ver'strooien; uit'eendrijven

schoolteacher onder'wijzer('es)
schooner schoener
science (na'tuur-)wetenschap
scientific weten'schappelijk
scientist ge'leerde
scintillate fonkelen
scissors schaar
scoff at spotten met

Insight

A number of nouns which are plural in English, such as *scissors*, are singular in Dutch: **de schaar**. Don't forget to use a singular verb form with these: **deze schaar is nieuw** *these scissors are new*. Other examples of plural nouns in English which are singular in Dutch are *trousers* **de broek (wil je een nieuwe broek?** *do you want a new (pair of) trousers?*), *glasses/spectacles* **de bril (mijn bril is kapot** *my glasses are broken*), *tweezers* **de pincet (waar ligt mij pincet?** *where are my tweezers?*).

scavenger opruimer; aasdier; scharrelaar
scene tafe'reel; scène
scenery décor; landschap, na'tuur(schoon)
scenic na'tuur-; toneel-
scent geur, o'deur; reuk(zin); spoor; ruiken; snuffelen
sceptic scepticus
sceptical sceptisch
sceptre scepter
schedule ta'bel; schema
scheme plan; schema; intri'geren
schism scheuring
scholar leerling; ge'leerde
scholarly ge'leerd, weten'schappelijk
scholarship (studie)beurs; wetenschap; ge'leerdheid
school school
schooling schoolopleiding
schoolmaster leraar
schoolroom schoollokaal

scold een uitbrander geven
scoop schoep, schep(pen); pri'meur
scooter autoped
scope be'stek; vrij spel
scorch schroeien
score score, stand, aantal punten; twintig(tal); partituur; maken, be'halen; tellen; krassen
scorn hoon; ver'smaden, het be'neden zich achten
scornful minachtend
scorpion schorpi'oen
Scot(ch) Schot(s)
scoundrel schurk
scour schuren; afzoeken
scourge gesel(en); teisteren
scout ver'kenner; padvinder; op zoek gaan
scowl dreigend kijken
scraggy mager
scramble ge'jakker; jachten; klauteren; zich ver'dringen

scrambled egg roerei
scrap stukje; oud; afdanken
scrapbook plakboek
scrape knel; schrappen; schuren, krabben; schrapen
scratch kras(sen), schram(men); krabben
scrawl ge'krabbel; krabbelen
scream gil(len)
screech ge'krijs; krijsen
screen scherm; koorhek; be'schermen, mas'keren
screw schroef; schroeven
screwdriver schroevedraaier
scribble ge'krabbel; krabbelen
scribe schrijver, schriftgeleerde
script schrift; tekst
scripture schrift
scroll rol; krul
scrounge (in)pikken; klaplopen
scrub schrobben
scruple scru'pule, ge'wetensbezwaar
scrupulous angst'vallig; nauwge'zet
scrutinize nauw'keurig onder'zoeken
scrutiny kritisch onderzoek
scuffle handgemeen
scullery bijkeuken
sculptor beeldhouwer
sculpture beeldhouwkunst(or werk); beeldhouwen
scum schuim; uitschot, schorem, afval
scurvy scheurbuik; ge'meen
scuttle bak; luik(gat); snellen
scythe zeis; maaien
sea zee
seafaring zeevarend
seal zeehond; zegel(en); ver(or be)'zegelen, sluiten
sea level zeespiegel
sealing-wax zegellak
seam naad; laag
seaman zeeman, ma'troos
sear ver'schroeien

search zoeken; fouil'lleren **in – of** op zoek naar
searching onder'zoekend, diep'gaand
searchlight zoeklicht
seashore kust
seaside kust
season sei'zoen, tijd; kruiden; drogen
seasonal sei'zoen-
seat (zit)plaats; bank; zetel
seaweed zeewier
secluded afgezonderd
seclusion afzondering
second tweede; se'conde; steunen
secondary secun'dair; middelbaar
second-hand tweede'hands; uit de tweede hand
secondly ten tweede
second-rate tweede'rangs
secrecy ge'heimhouding
secret ge'heim; heimelijk; ge'sloten
secretary secre'taris, secreta'resse
secrete afscheiden; ver'bergen, ver'duisteren
secretive ge'sloten
secretly in het ge'heim
sect sekte
section (onder)deel, afdeling; sectie; doorsnee; para'graaf; tra'ject
sector sector
secular secu'lier, wereldlijk
secure veilig; ver'zekerd; vast-(maken); zich ver'zekeren van
security veiligheid; veiligheidsmaatregel(en), veiligheidsvoorziening, ver'zekering; be'veiliging, (openbare) veiligheid; obli'gatie, ef'fect, aandeel; (waar) borg, onderpand **tight –** strenge veiligheidsmaatregelen **– check** veiligheidscontrole **– council** Veiligheidsraad
sedate be'zadigd, waardig
sedative pijnstillend (or kal'merend) (middel)

sedentary zittend
sediment be'zinksel
seduce ver'leiden
see zien, kijken (naar); zien, begrijpen, inzien; toezien (op), opletten, ervoor zorgen, zorgen voor; nadenken, be'kijken, zien; zich voorstellen; tegenkomen, ont'moeten; ont'vangen, spreken; be'zoeken, opzoeken, langs gaan bij; raadplegen; bege'leiden, (weg) brengen **we shall –** we zien wel/ wie weet **as far as I can –** volgens mij **I am seeing Joan next week** ik heb volgende week met Joan afgesproken **have you seen a doctor yet?** ben je al bij een dokter geweest? **– someone out** iemand uitlaten
seed zaad
seeing that aange'zien
seek zoeken; trachten
seem (toe)schijnen
seemingly ogen'schijnlijk
seemly be'tamelijk
seep sijpelen
seesaw wip
seethe zieden; gisten
segment seg'ment, partje
segregate (zich) afzonderen
seize pakken; nemen; aangrijpen
seizure nemen; be'slaglegging; aanval
seldom zelden
select uitgelezen; chic; se'lect; (uit) kiezen
selection se'lectie; keus
self zelf
self-assured zelfbe'wust
self-centred ego'centrisch
self-confidence zelfvertrouwen
self-conscious ver'legen
self-contained vrij; onafhankelijk
self-control zelfbeheersing

self-defence zelfverdediging
self-denial zelfverloochening
self-evident vanzelf'sprekend
self-government zelfbestuur
self-interest eigenbelang
selfish zelf'zuchtig, ego'ïstisch
selfless onbaat'zuchtig
self-pity zelfbeklag
self-preservation zelfbehoud
self-respect zelfrespect
self-righteous eigenge'rechtigd
self-sacrifice zelfopoffering
selfsame: the - pre'cies de(or het)'zelfde
self-satisfied zelfvol'daan
self-service zelfbediening
self-service restaurant zelfbedieningsrestaurant
self-supporting: to be – in eigen be'hoefte kunnen voor'zien
sell ver'kopen
semblance schijn, voorkomen
semicircle halve cirkel
semi-detached twee onder één kap
senate se'naat
senator se'nator
send sturen, zenden **to – for** laten komen
senile se'niel
senior oudste, ouder
sensation ge'voel, ge'waarwording; sen'satie
sensational opzien'barend; sensatio'neel
sense zin(tuig); ge'voel; ver'stand; (aan)voelen **in a –** in zekere zin **senses** ver'stand
senseless be'wusteloos; on'zinnig
sensible ver'standig, praktisch
sensitive ge'voelig (voor)
sensual sensuous zin'tuiglijk; sensueel, zinnelijk
sentence zin; vonnis; ver'oordelen
sentiment ge'voel(en)

sentimental sentimen'teel
sentinel, sentry schildwacht
separate af'zonderlijk; (af)scheiden
separation scheiding
September sep'tember
septic septisch
sequel ver'volg; ge'volg
sequence op'eenvolging, volgorde
serenade sere'nade (brengen)
serene kalm, se'reen
serenity vreedzaamheid
sergeant ser'geant
serial killer seriemoordenaar
series serie, reeks, op'eenvolging
serious ernstig; ge'wichtig
seriously ernstig, in alle ernst,
  au séri'eux
sermon preek
serpent slang
serrated ge'karteld
serum serum
servant be'diende; knecht,
  dienstmeisje; dienaar
serve (be')dienen; opscheppen;
  ser'veren
service dienst; strijdkracht; service;
  ser'vies
serviceable nuttig
servile slaafs, kruipend
servitude slaver'nij; dwangarbeid
session zitting
set[1] zetten, plaatsen, stellen,
  leggen; be'palen, voorschrijven;
  ge'lijkzetten (clock); opleggen,
  opdragen, opgeven, stellen; stijf
  worden; dekken (table); situ'eren;
  vestigen (a record); ondergaan
  (moon/sun)
set[2] stel, set, reeks; kring, groep;
  toestel, radio(toestel), tv(-toestel);
  ver'zameling; to'neelopbouw,
  scène, dé'cor, set

set[3] vast, be'paald, vastgesteld;
  vastbesloten; opgelegd,
  voorgeschreven; strak, koppig,
  hard'nekkig; klaar, ge'reed **– phrase**
  vaste uitdrukking **I'm all –** ik ben er
  helemaal klaar voor
set-back tegenslag
settee bank
setting zetting; (tijd en) plaats,
  om'geving
settle regelen; zich vestigen; gaan
  zitten; ver'zakken **to – down**
  tot rust komen
settlement schikking; ver'effening;
  nederzetting
settler kolo'nist
seven(teen)(th) zeven('tien)(de)
seventy zeventig
sever scheiden, ver'breken;
  doorsnijden
several ver'scheiden; af'zonderlijk
severe streng; ernstig; sober;
  hevig; zwaar
sew naaien
sewage afvalwater, rioolwater
sewer ri'ool
sewing naaien, naaiwerk
sex ge'slacht, sekse; seks,
  ero'tiek; seksu'ele omgang,
  geslachtsgemeenschap\ **have –
  with someone** met iemand
  naar bed gaan/vrijen
sexist sek'sistisch; sek'sist
sexual ge'slachts-, seksu'eel
sexuality seksuali'teit
sexy sexy, op'windend
shabby haveloos; min
shack keet
shackle boei(en)
shade schaduw; achtergrond;
  scherm, kap; tint; tikje, nu'ance;
  be'schutten, be'schaduwen

shadow schaduw(en); zweem
shadowy schaduwrijk, vaag
shady schaduwrijk; ver'dacht
shaft schacht; straal; pijl
shaggy ruig
shake schudden
shaky on'vast, wankel
shall zal, zullen
shallow on'diep; opper'vlakkig
sham namaak; schijn; voorwenden
shamble schuifelen
shambles troep, bende, zooi
shame schaamte; schande;
be'schaamd maken; te schande
maken **a –** jammer
shameful schandelijk
shape ge'daante; vorm(en);
zich ont'wikkelen
shapeless vormeloos
shapely goed ge'vormd
share (aan)deel; samen delen,
ver'delen
shark haai; oplichter
sharp scherp; bij de'hand;
pre'cies; kruis
sharpen slijpen
shatter ver'brijzelen; ver'nietigen
shave (zich) scheren
shaving krul; scheren
shawl sjaal, omslagdoek
she zij, ze
sheaf schoof; bundel
shear scheren
shears schaar
sheath schede
shed hok, schuur(tje); ver'gieten,
storten; afwerpen; ver'spreiden
sheen glans
sheep schaap, schapen
sheepish schaapachtig
sheer dun, door'schijnend;
kinkklaar; loodrecht

sheet laken; vel, plaat, vlak; schoot
shelf plank; platte rand
shell schaal, schelp, schil(d); huls;
ge'raamte; doppen; be'schieten
shellfish schelpdier
shelter schutting, schuilplaats;
be'schermen; schuilen
shelve op de lange baan schuiven;
op een plank zetten
shepherd herder; ge'leiden
sheriff sheriff
sherry sherry
shield schild; be'schermen
shift ploeg, werktijd; ver'schuiven
shimmer glinsteren
shin scheen
shindy herrie
shine glans; (laten) schijnen;
glimmen; uitblinken
shingle grint
shiny glimmend, blinkend
ship schip; in(*or* ver')schepen
shipbuilding scheepsbouw
shipment ver'scheping; zending
ship owner reder
shipping scheepvaart, schepen
shipwreck schipbreuk **to be**
shipwrecked schipbreuk lijden
shipyard werf
shirk zich ont'trekken aan
shirt (over)hemd
shit (vulg) stront, kak, poep;
rommel, rotzooi; ge'zeik, onzin;
hasj; schijten, poepen
shiver rilling; rillen
shoal on'diepte; school
shock schok (geven); shock; bos
(hair); aanstoot geven
shocking aan'stotelijk; gruwelijk;
schan'dalig
shoddy prul-, snert-
shoe schoen

shoot uitloper; (dood)schieten; afschieten; storten
shop winkel(en)
shopkeeper winke'lier
shoplifter winkeldief
shore kust, oever; stut(ten)
short kort; krap; bros **to cut –** onder'breken **in –** kort'om **to run –** opraken **to be – of** ge'brek hebben aan; te'kort komen
shortage te'kort
short circuit kortsluiting (ver'oorzaken)
shortcoming te'kortkoming
shorten (ver')korten
shorthand steno(gra'fie)
short-lived kort'stondig
shortly (binnen)kort
shorts korte broek
short-sighted bij'ziend; kort'zichtig
short-tempered prikkelbaar
shot schot; schroot; poging; kiekje; slag
shotgun jachtgeweer
should zou moeten; moest(en); be'horen; zou(den); mocht(en)
shoulder schouder; op zich nemen
shout schreeuw(en); brullen
shove schuiven
shovel schop; scheppen
show ver'toon, show, schijn; ten'toonstelling, amuse'ments-voorstelling, schouwspel, show; (ver')tonen; te zien zijn; laten zien; (be')wijzen; blijk geven van **to – off** zich aanstellen; pronken met
shower bui; douche; regen; over'stelpen
shrapnel gra'naatscherven
shred flard; schijn
shrew feeks
shrewd schrander
shriek gil(len)
shrill schel

shrimp gar'naal
shrine schrijn; heilige plaats
shrink (doen) krimpen, (doen) afnemen; wegkruipen, in'eenkrimpen; zielenknijper, psychi'ater
shrivel (doen) ver'schrompelen
shroud doodskleed; sluier; hullen
shrub heester
shrubbery struikgewas
shrug schoudersophalen
shudder huiveren; schudden
shuffle schuifelen; wassen
shun schuwen
shut dicht (doen); sluiten **to – up** (op)sluiten; zijn mond houden
shutter luik; sluiter
shuttle schietspoel; pendel-
shy ver'legen, schuw; schrikken
sick ziek(en); misselijk; beu **to be –** overgeven
sickening walgelijk; ver'velend
sickle sikkel
sickly ziekelijk; onge'zond
sickness ziekte; misselijkheid
side (zij)kant; zij(de); par'tij (kiezen) **– by –** naast el'kaar
sideboard buf'fet
sidetrack zijspoor; van zijn onderwerp afbrengen *or* afdwalen
sideways zijdelings
siding zijspoor
sidle up to schuchter be'naderen
siege be'leg
sieve zeef; zeven
sift zeven; ziften
sigh zucht(en)
sight ge'zicht; beziens'waardigheid; vi'zier; (in) zicht (krijgen) **at first –** op het eerste ge'zicht **to catch – of** in het oog krijgen
sign (uithang)bord; wenk, teken; (onder')tekenen; een teken geven

signal sein(en); een teken geven
signature handtekening
signet (ring) zegel(ring)
significance be'tekenis; be'lang
significant veelbe'tekenend;
  be'langrijk
signify be'tekenen; te kennen geven
signpost wegwijzer
silence stilte; stilwijgend;
  tot zwijgen brengen
silent stil(zwijgend), zwijgzaam;
  stom **to be –** zwijgen
silently in stilte, ge'ruisloos
silhouette silhou'et
silk zij(de); zijden
silky zijdeachtig
sill vensterbank, drempel
silly on'nozel, dwaas, flauw
silt slib; dichtslibben
silver zilver(werk); zilveren
similar ge'lijk, dergelijk
similarity over'eenkomst
simile verge'lijking
simmer zachtjes (laten)
  sudderen; pruttelen; gisten
simper meesmuilen
simple een'voudig; enkel'voudig;
  simpel; on'nozel
simpleton on'nozele hals
simplicity eenvoud
simplify vereen'voudigen
simply een'voudig; ge'woonweg,
  al'leen
simulate voorwenden; nabootsen
simultaneous gelijk'tijdig
sin zonde; zondigen
since sinds('dien), na'dien;
  van'af; daar
sincere op'recht
sincerity op'rechtheid
sinew pees
sinful zondig
sing zingen
singe (af)schroeien

singer zanger('es)
single enkel; eenpersoons-;
  onge'trouwd **to – out** uitpikken
singly af'zonderlijk; al'leen
singular bij'zonder; enkelvoud
sinister si'nister
sink gootsteen; (ver')zinken.
  ondergaan; tot zinken brengen
sinner zondaar
sinuous kronkelend, lenig
sip teugje; met teugjes drinken
sir mijnheer; sir **Dear Sir**
  Geachte Heer
sire (voor)vader; sire
siren si'rene
sister zusje; zuster
sit (gaan) zitten; zitting houden;
  po'seren **to – down** gaan zitten
  to – up rech'top (gaan) zitten;
  opblijven
site bouwgrond, (bouw)ter'rein;
  ligging
sitting room zitkamer
situated ge'legen
situation ligging; situ'atie;
  be'trekking
six(teen)(th) zes(tien)(de)
sixty zestig
size grootte, omvang; maat;
  lijmwater
sizeable flink
sizzle sissen
skate schaats(enrijden); vleet
skein streng
skeleton ske'let; ge'raamte
sketch schets(en)
skewer vleespen, spies; door'steken
ski ski(ën)
skid slippen
skilful be'kwaam, knap
skill be'kwaamheid, vaardigheid
skilled ge'schoold
skim afscheppen, afromen;
  scheren over; doorbladeren

skimp zuinig zijn (met)
skin huid; vel; pels; villen
skinny broodmager
skip afvalcon'tainer; springen; overslaan
skipper schipper
skirmish scher'mutseling
skirt rok; trekken (om)
skull schedel; doodskop
sky lucht, hemel
skyscraper wolkenkrabber
slab plak, plaat
slack slap; laks; stil; gruis
slacken ver'slappen; laten vieren
slam bons; dichtslaan
slander (be')laster(en)
slanderous lasterlijk
slang slang, zeer informele taal
slant helling; hellen
slap klap (geven); par'does; kwakken
slapdash noncha'lant
slash houw, jaap; (er'op los) maaien (or slaan); drastisch ver'minderen
slat lat, reep
slate lei(steen); leien; ervan langs geven
slaughter slachting; slachten; afmaken
slave slaaf; zich afbeulen
slavery slaver'nij
slavish slaafs
slay doodslaan
sledge slede; voorhamer; sleeën
sleek glanzig, glad
sleep slaap; slapen
sleeper slaper; slaapwagen; dwarsligger
sleeping slapen; slapend; slaap-
sleepless slapeloos
sleepy slaperig; doods; melig
sleet natte sneeuw
sleeve mouw
sleigh arreslee
slender slank, dun; karig, zwak, klein

slice snee(tje); snijden
slick vlot, glad
slide glijbaan; glijkoker; plaatje; glijden
slight ge'ring, licht; tenger; klei'nering; klei'neren
slightly iets; opper'vlakkig
slim slank
slime slijk, slijm
slimy slijmerig
sling slingerverband, mi'tella; lus; slinger(en); gooien
slink sluipen
slip sloop; onderjurk; ver'gissing; strookje; helling; (uit)glijden; uitschieten; schuiven; laten glijden; aan(or uit)doen; voor'bijgaan; ont'schieten
slipper pan'toffel
slippery glibberig, glad
slipshod slordig
slit spleet, scheur(en); snijden
slobber kwijlen
slogan leus
sloop sloep
slop morsen
slope helling; hellen, schuin lopen
sloppy drassig; dun; slordig; zoetelijk
slot gleuf
sloth luiheid; luiaard
slouch slungelen, hangen
slovenly slonzig, slordig
slow langzaam, traag; achter
  to – down ver'tragen, ophouden; vaart ver'minderen
slug slak
sluggish traag
sluice sluis; spoelen
slum slop, achterbuurt
slumber sluimering; sluimeren
slump ma'laise
slur vlek, smet; onduidelijk spreken
slush halfge'smolten sneeuw; bagger
slut slet

sly sluw

smack klap, smak, pats; bijsmaak; zweem; een klap geven; smakken met; zwemen naar

small klein

smallpox pokken

smart vinnig; flink; bijde'hand, handig; chic, keurig; zeer doen

smash botsing; cata'strofe; ver'pletteren, stukslaan; breken; botsen (tegen)

smattering mondjevol

smear veeg; (be')smeren; be'smeuren

smell reuk, lucht; ruiken (naar); rieken (naar)

smelt smelten

smile (glim)lach(en)

smirk grijns (or grijnzen) van vol'doening

smith smid

smithereens gruzele'menten

smoke rook; roken; walmen

smoky rokerig

smooth glad, vlak; kalm; vlot; gladstrijken

smother smoren; stikken; be'delven; doven

smoulder smeulen

smudge vlek(ken)

smug zelf'ingenomen

smuggle smokkelen

smut roetdeeltje; schunnigheden

snack hapje

snackbar snackbar

snag uitsteeksel; moeilijkheid

snail (huisjes)slak

snake slang

snap klap, krak; drukknoop; kiekje; knappen; happen; snauwen; pikken

snapshot kiekje; momentopname

snare (val)strik; (ver')strikken

snarl grauw(en); snauw(en)

snatch brokstuk; grissen

sneak klikspaan; klikken; sluipen; gappen

sneer schimplach; be'schimpen; smalen (op)

sneeze niezen

sniff snuiven; de neus ophalen (voor); snuffelen; ruiken aan

snigger grinniken

snip snipper; knip(pen)

snipe snip; ter'sluiks één voor één neerschieten

sniper sluipschutter

snob snob

snooze dutje; dutten

snore snurken

snort snuiven

snout snuit

snow sneeuw(en)

snowdrift sneeuwbank

snowflake sneeuwvlok

snowy sneeuw-

snub brute afwijzing; bits afwijzen
  – nose mopneus

snuff snuif; snuiven; snuiten

snug knus

snuggle (zich) nestelen

so zo; dus; ook **or –** onge'veer **– that** zodat; opdat

soak (door')weken; in de week zetten (or staan); (laten) trekken
  to – up opnemen, absor'beren

soap zeep

soapsuds zeepsop

soar om'hoogvliegen; de hoogte invliegen

sob snik(ken)

sober nuchter; sober; ont'nuchteren

so-called zoge'naamd

soccer voetbal

sociable soci'aal; ge'zellig

social soci'aal

socialism socia'lisme

society ver'eniging; maatschap'pij; ge'zelschap

sock sok
socket gat, kas, holte
sod zode
soda soda
sodden doornat
sofa sofa
soft zacht; week
soften zacht maken (*or* worden);
ver'zachten
software software, (com'puter)
programma(tuur)
soggy door'weekt, drassig, klef
soil grond, bodem; vuil maken
solace troost
solar zonne-, zons-
solder sol'deersel; sol'deren
soldier sol'daat; mili'tair
sole enig; zool; tong (fish)
solely al'leen
solemn ernstig; plechtig
solemnity plechtigheid
solicit ver'zoeken om
solicitor rechts'kundig advi'seur,
procu'reur
solicitous be'zorgd; ver'langend
solid vast (lichaam); mas'sief stevig;
soli'dair
solidarity saam'horigheidsgevoel,
solidari'teit
solidify mas'sief (doen) worden
soliloquy al'leenspraak, mono'loog
solitary eenzaam
solitude eenzaamheid
solo solo
soluble op'losbaar
solution oplossing
solve oplossen
solvent sol'vent; oplossend;
oplosmiddel
sombre somber
some sommige; enige; (er) wat
(van); een (of ander); onge'veer
– such een dergelijk, zo'n **– day**
weleens

somebody (een zeker) iemand
somehow op de een of andere
ma'nier; hoe dan ook
someone iemand
somersault buiteling, salto mortale
something iets
sometime wel eens
sometimes soms
somewhat enigs'zins; iets, wat
somewhere ergens; een plaats
(waar)
son zoon
sonata so'nate
song lied
sonnet son'net
sonorous diepklinkend; weids
soon spoedig, vroeg; lief **as –
as** zo'dra **no sooner ... than**
nauwelijks ... of **I would sooner**
ik zou liever
soot roet
soothe sussen; ver'zachten
sophisticated mon'dain
soporific slaap'wekkend
sopping wet drijfnat
soprano so'praan
sorcerer tovenaar
sorcery tovena'rij
sordid vuil; on'smakelijk
sore zeer; gepi'keerd; teer; zere plek
sorrow smart; treuren
sorrowful droevig
sorry treurig **I am –** het spijt me
sort soort; sor'teren
soul ziel; sterveling
soul-destroying geest'dodend
sound ge'luid, klank; zeeëngte;
degelijk, gaaf, ge'zond,
be'trouwbaar; flink, vast; (doen)
klinken; peilen; polsen
sounding klinkend; peiling
soup soep
sour zuur
source bron

south zuid(er), zuiden(-), naar
het zuiden, ten zuiden van
southerly zuidelijk
souvenir souve'nir
sovereign vorst; soeve'rein
sovereignty soevereini'teit
sow zeug; (be')zaaien
soy soja
space (tijd)ruimte; spatie; spati'
ëren, ver'delen
space bar spatiebalk
spacecraft ruimtevaartuig
spaced out zweverig, high, onder
invloed; wereld'vreemd, excen'triek
spacious ruim
spade schop
span spanwijdte; spanne
spangle lovertje; be'zaaien
spaniel spaniël
spank voor zijn broek geven; patsen
spanner moersleutel
spar rondhout; (oefenend)
boksen; redetwisten
spare vrij; re'serve; schraal; (re'serve)
onderdeel; sparen; missen; ont'zien
spark vonk(en); greintje
sparkle vonken schieten; fonkelen;
tintelen; mous'seren
sparrow mus
sparse dun(ge'zaaid)
spasm kramp('achtige
be'weging); vlaag
spasmodic kram'pachtig; bij vlagen
spate stroom, vlaag, hoop
spatter spatten; plassen (tegen)
speak spreken; uitdrukken
speaker spreker; voorzitter
spear speer
special bij'zonder, speci'aal
specialism specia'lisme,
speciali'satie
specialist specia'list
specialization speciali'satie
specialize speciali'seren

specially in het bij'zonder, voor'al
species soort(en), ge'slacht(en)
specific be'paald; uit'drukkelijk;
speci'fiek
specification specifi'catie
specify specifi'ceren; ver'melden
specimen proef; staaltje
speck spikkel; vuiltje
speckle spikkel, stippel, vlekje;
be'spikkelen, stippelen
spectacle schouwspel
spectacles bril
spectacular spectacu'lair,
groots, grandi'oos
spectator toeschouwer
spectre spook; schim
spectrum spectrum
speculate be'spiegelingen
houden; specu'leren
speculation be'spiegeling;
specu'latie
speculator specu'lant
speech (toe)spraak
speechless sprakeloos
speed vaart; snelheid;
ver'snelling; snel rijden **– bump**
verkeers'drempel
speed(il)y spoedig
spell beurt; peri'ode; be'tovering;
spellen; be'tekenen
spend uitgeven; be'steden,
doorbrengen; uitputten
spew (uit)braken
sphere bol; hemellichaam;
ge'bied, sfeer
spherical bol'vorming
spice spece'rij
spicy ge'kruid; pi'kant
spider spin
spike (ijzeren) punt; stekel
spill doen overlopen, laten
overstromen, morsen, omgooien,
ver'spillen; ver'gieten (blood);
overlopen, over'stromen

spin ritje; spinnen; draaien
spinach spi'nazie
spinal ruggegraats-
spindle klos; spil
spine ruggegraat; stekel
spinster ongetrouwde vrouw
spiral spi'raal(vormig)
spire torenspits
spirit geest; fut **spirits** stemming;
  levenslust; sterke drank
spirited vurig; geani'meerd
spiritual geestelijk (lied)
spit spuug; spit; landtong;
  spuwen; druppelen
spite kwaa'daardigheid; ergeren
spiteful hatelijk
splash spat; be'spatten; plassen;
  uit el'kaar spatten; natmaken
spleen milt; gal
splendid schitterend, prachtig
splendour pracht
splice splitsen; lassen
splint spalk(en)
splinter splinter
split spleet; scheuring; splijten;
  splitsen; (ver')delen
splitting barstend
splutter sputteren
spoil buit; be'derven; ver'wennen
spoilsport spelbreker
spoke spaak; sport
spokesman woordvoerder
sponge spons; mos'covisch
  ge'bak; sponzen; klaplopen
sponsor sponsor; peet; op touw
  zetten
spontaneous spon'taan; zelf-
spool spoel
spoon(ful) lepel
sporadic spo'radisch
spore spoor
sport sport; grap; sportieve vent
  (*or* meid); spelen
sporting sport-; spor'tief; aardig

sportsman sportliefhebber
spot vlek; stip(pelen); plek; scheutje;
  in de gaten krijgen
spotless smetteloos; brandschoon
spotlight zoeklicht
spouse gade
spout tuit; straal; spuiten
sprain ver'stuiken
sprawl uitgestrekt (gaan) liggen;
  wijd uit'eenlopen, zich wan'orderlijk
  ver'spreiden
spray spuitbus; takje; (be')sproeien
spread wijdte; ont'haal;
  (zich) (uit)spreiden; (zich)
  ver'spreiden; (be')smeren
sprig twijgje
sprightly opgewekt
spring veer(kracht); lente; bron;
  springen; ont'staan (uit);
  (uit de grond) schieten
sprinkle (be')sprenkelen, strooien
sprint sprint(en)
sprout spruit(en)
spruce spar(rehout); keurig;
  opknappen
spry kwiek
spur spoor; uitloper; prikkel; de
  sporen geven; aansporen **on the**
  – of the moment in de eerste
  opwelling
spurious on'echt
spurn ver'smaden
spurt guts; vlaag; spuiten (met);
  spurten
sputter sputteren, spatten
spy spi'on; (be)spio'neren;
  be'speuren
squabble ge'kibbel; kibbelen
squad (sport)ploeg
squadron eska'dron; es'kader
squalid vuil en ar'moedig
squall (wind)vlaag; schreeuwen
squalor vuile armoede
squander ver'spillen

square vierkant; plein; kwa'draat; recht('hoekig); quitte; eerlijk; in het kwa'draat brengen; afrekenen

squash pletten, platdrukken; ge'plet worden; squash; siroop ge'drang, oploop

squat ge'drongen; neerhurken; kraakpand; kraken

squawk krijsen

squeak piepen

squeal gillen

squeamish overdreven ge'voelig

squeeze ge'drang; knijpen, uitpersen; bijstoppen; afpersen

squint scheel kijken; gluren; (vluchtige) blik

squirm zich in allerlei bochten wringen; in el'kaar kruipen

squirrel eekhoorn

squirt spuiten

stab steek(wond); (door)steken

stability stabili'teit

stabilize stabili'seren

stable stal(len); sta'biel, vast

stack stapel; opstapelen

stadium stadion

staff staf, stok

stag mannetjeshert **stag-night** vrijge'zellenavond

stage e'tappe, stadium; to'neel; tra'ject; ten to'nele brengen; op touw zetten

stagger (doen) wankelen; ver'bijsteren; spreiden

stagnant stilstaand

stagnation stilstand; stremming

staid be'zadigd

stain (be')vlek(ken); smet; beits(en); kleurstof; afgeven; brandschilderen

stainless smetteloos; roestvrij

stair trede; trap-

staircase, stairs trap

stake paal; brandstapel; inzet(ten); staken **at —** op het spel

stale oud('bakken), ver'schaald, muf; suf

stalk stengel, steel; stronk; be'sluipen; achter'volgen

stall stal(letje); (laten) afslaan

stallion hengst

stalwart stevig, stoer; flink; stand'vastig, trouw

stamen meeldraad

stamina uithoudingsvermogen

stammer ge'stamel; stamelen, stotteren

stamp (post)zegel; stempel(en); fran'keren; stampen

stampede pa'niek; stormloop; stormlopen; op hol slaan

stand standard, voet, stel; tri'bune; plaats; (gaan *or* blijven) staan; liggen; zetten; ver'dragen, uitstaan; van kracht blijven; zijn **to — back** achter'uitgaan; (van …) af liggen **to — out** uitsteken; opvallen

standard standaard; maatstaf; vaandel

standardize standaardi'seren

stand-by re'serve, steun

standing aanzien; permanent; (stil)staand

standpoint standpunt

standstill stilstand

stanza vers, strofe

staple hoofd-; kram, niet(je)

stapler nietmachine

star ster

starboard stuurboord

starch zetmeel; stijfsel; stijven

stare (aan)staren

stark grimmig; stijf, on'buigzaam; schril; kaal **— contrast** schril contrast

starling spreeuw

starry sterren-

start be'gin(nen); start(en); schok; ver'trekken; aanzetten, aanslaan; opschrikken

startle doen schrikken
startling verbazing'wekkend;
  ont'stellend
starvation ver'hongering
starve (laten) ver'hongeren
state staat, toestand; staatsie;
  staats-; mededelen, uit'eenzetten,
  consta'teren
stated ge'noemd; vastgesteld
stately statig
statement ver'klaring
statesman staatsman
statesmanship staatkunde
static statisch
station sta'tion; stand(plaats);
  plaatsen
stationary stilstaand; statio'nair
stationer kan'toorboekhandel(aar)
stationery schrijfbehoeften
statistic sta'tistisch
statistics statis'tiek(en)
statue standbeeld
stature ge'stalte; ge'halte
status status
statute swet, sta'tuut
staunch trouw; stelpen
stave duig; staaf; inslaan **to – off**
  afwenden
stay ver'blijf; stut; (ver')blijven;
  lo'geren
steadfast stand'vastig
steady stevig, vast; so'lide;
  stand'vastig; kalm; vasthouden
steak runderlapje, biefstuk; moot
steal stelen; sluipen
steam stoom; dampen; stomen
steamer stoomboot; stomer
steed ros
steel staal; stalen
steep steil; sterk; (in)dompelen
steeple toren(spits)
steer sturen
steering wheel stuur

stem stengel, steel; (voor)steven;
  stuiten
stench stank
stencil stencil(en)
stenographer steno'graaf
step stap(pen); pas; trede,
  stoep, step-, stief-
step- stief-
stereo stereo
stereotype stereo'tiep
sterile ste'riel; on'vruchtbaar
sterilize sterili'seren
sterling sterling; recht'schapen
stern achtersteven; streng
stew stoofschotel; stoven
steward hofmeester; official,
  be'diende
stick stok; plakken; (blijven)
  steken; volhouden
sticky kleverig
stiff stijf, stroef; stevig; moeilijk
stiffen stijver (*or* moeilijker)
  maken
stifle (ver')stikken; onder'drukken
stigma brandmerk, (schand)
  vlek, stigma
stile overstap
still stil(te); distil'leerketel; nog
  (al'tijd); toch; kal'meren
stillness stilte
stilt stelt
stilted hoog'dravend; stijf
stipend be'zoldiging
stipulate be'dingen
stipulation voorwaarde
stir ophef; (be')roeren, zich
  ver'roeren; aanzetten
stirfry roerbakken; roergebakken
  ge'recht/eten
stirring veelbe'wogen; op'windend
stirrup stijgbeugel
stitch steek, hechting; stikken,
  hechten

stock voorraad; ef'fecten; afkomst;
bouil'lon; standaard, voor'zien (van),
voorraad inslaan; in voorraad hebben
stockade palis'sade
stockbroker ef'fectenmakelaar
stocking kous
stodgy onver'teerbaar; zwaar
stoic(al) stoï'cijns
stoke stoken
stolid standvastig
stomach maag; ver'dragen
stone (edel)steen; pit; 6,35 kilo;
stenen; stenigen; ont'pitten
stone-deaf stokdoof
stony steenachtig; steenhard;
doods, koud
stool kruk; stoelgang
stoop ronde rug; bukken; zich
ver'lagen
stop oponthoud; halte; re'gister;
(dicht)stoppen; blijven (staan);
stilstaan; ophouden (met);
stopzetten; stelpen **to put a – to**
een eind maken aan
stoppage oponthoud; opstopping
stopper stop
storage opslaan; bergruimte; opslag-
store warenhuis; ba'zaar; voorraad;
maga'zijn; opslaan; opbergen
to lay in a – of inslaan
storeroom bergruimte, pro'visiekamer
stork ooievaar
storm storm, (flinke) bui, onweer;
razen; stuiven; be'stormen
stormy stormachtig, onweersachtig
story ver'haal, ge'schiedenis;
ver'dieping
stout ge'zet; stevig; flink
stove kachel, for'nuis
stow stouwen; opbergen
stowaway ver'stekeling
straddle schrijlings staan (or zitten);
spreiden over

straight recht; eerlijk; in orde;
puur **– away** di'rect
straighten rechttrekken(or zetten);
in orde brengen
straightforward op'recht;
een'voudig
strain (in)spanning; toon; afkomst;
trek; (over' or in)spannen; (ver')
rekken; afgieten
strained ge'dwongen, gefor'
ceerd, onna'tuurlijk
strainer ver'giet, zeefje
straits zee'ëngte, Straat;
moeilijkheden
strand streng; stranden **to be**
stranded stranden; hulpeloos staan
strange vreemd
stranger vreemde; onbe'kende
strangle wurgen; onder'drukken,
smoren
strap riem, band; vastmaken
(met een riem)
strapping potig, flink
strategic stra'tegisch
strategy strate'gie
straw stro(otje); rietje
strawberry aardbei
stray afgedwaald (dier); (af)dwalen
streak streep; straal; strepen; streaken
stream stroom; stromen
streamer serpen'tine, wimpel
streamline(d) (ge')stroomlijn(d)
street straat
strength kracht(en); sterkte; ge'halte
strengthen (ver')sterken
strenuous inspannend
stress spanning, druk, stress,
be'lasting; klem(toon), nadruk,
ac'cent; spanning, druk;
be'nadrukken, de nadruk leggen
op; be'lasten, onder druk zetten **be**
under – onder druk staan **lay – on**
benadrukken

stretch uitge'strektheid; (zich) (uit)rekken; spannen; uitsteken
  at a – achter el'kaar
stretcher bran'card
strew strooien; be'zaaien
stricken ge'troffen
strict streng; pre'cies; strikt
stride schrede; schrijden
strident krassend
strife twist, strijd
strike staking; slaan; aansteken; (toe)schijnen, opkomen bij; treffen; staken; doorhalen
striking treffend
string touw; snoer; snaar; file; strijkinstrument; (aan'een)rijgen
stringent streng
strip strook; (af)stropen; (zich) uitkleden; ont'doen; afhalen
  – lighting tl-verlichting
stripe streep; strepen
strive streven (naar); worstelen
stroke slag; haal; be'roerte; zet; strelen
stroll wandeling; kuieren; trekken
strong sterk
stronghold bolwerk
structure struc'tuur, (ge')bouw; samenstelling
struggle strijd; krachtsinspanning; vechten; strompelen
strum trommelen
strut stijl; trots stappen
stub stomp, stronk, peukje
stubble stoppels
stubborn hard'nekkig, hals'starrig
stud (sier)spijker, sierknopje; knoop(je); (ren)stal, fokbedrijf; fokhengst, dekhengst (also figuratively); nop
student stu'dent(e)
studied welover'wogen
studio atel'ier, studio
studious leer'gierig

study studie; stu'deerkamer; (be)stu'deren
stuff materi'aal, (grond)stof; spul; troep, rommel; (op)vullen, volstoppen; proppen, stoppen, steken; opzetten **all that – can go** al die troep kan wel weg **I'm stuffed** ik zit vol **you can – it!** je kan de pot op!
stuffy be'nauwd
stumble struikelen, strompelen
stump stomp, stronk; stommelen
stun wezenloos slaan; ver'bluffen
stunt stunt; be'lemmeren
stupefy ver'stomd doen staan
stupendous over'weldigend, machtig
stupid dom, on'zinnig
stupor ver'doving
sturdy fors
stutter stotteren
sty hok; strontje
style stijl
stylish stijlvol; deftig
subconscious onderbe'wust(zijn)
subdivision onderverdeling; onderafdeling
subdue onder'werpen; onder'drukken; dempen
subject onderwerp; vak; onderdaan; onder'hevig (aan); onder'werpen; blootstellen (aan)
subjection onder'werping; onder'worpenheid
subjective subjec'tief
subjugate onder'werpen
sublime su'bliem
submarine onder'zeeboot
submerge over'stromen, ver'zwelgen
submission onder'werping; onder'danigheid; be'wering
submissive onder'danig
submit (zich) onder'werpen; overleggen; zou(den) naar voren willen brengen; voorleggen

subordinate onderge'schikt(e)
subscribe tekenen voor;
  onder'schrijven; zich
  abon'neren (op)
subsequent later
subservient onderge'schikt;
  onder'danig
subside zakken; afnemen; zinken
subsidiary dochter-, bij('komstig)
subsidize subsidiëren
subsidy sub'sidie
subsist be'staan; leven
subsistence be'staan; onderhoud
substance stof; hoofdzaak;
  wezen; sub'stantie
substantial substan'ti'eel,
  aan'zienlijk; so'lide **substantially**
  in wezen
substantiate be'wijzen
substitute plaatsver'vanger,
  surro'gaat; in de plaats stellen
substitution substi'tutie
subterfuge uitvlucht
subterranean onderaards
subtle sub'tiel, fijn, spits'vondig
subtract aftrekken
suburb voorstad, buitenwijk
suburban fo'renzen-, van de
  voorstad
succeed slagen; (op)volgen
success suc'ces
successful suc'cesr ÿk/vol, ge'slaagd;
  ge'lukkig
succession op(een)volging;
  suc'cessie **in –** achter el'kaar
successive opeen'volgend
successor opvolger
succinct kort en bondig
succulent sappig
succumb be'zwijken
such zulk; zo('n); zo'danig
  – as zo'als; wat
suck zuigen (op) **to – up** vleien;
  opzuigen

suckle zogen
suction zuiging; zuig-
sudden plotseling
sue ge'rechtelijk ver'volgen; smeken
suede suède
suffer lijden; boeten
suffering lijden
suffice vol'doende zijn
sufficient vol'doende
suffocate (doen) stikken
suffocation ver'stikking
suffrage kiesrecht
sugar suiker(en)
suggest doen denken aan;
  voorstellen; sugge'reren
suggestion voorstel;
  sug'gestie; spoor
suggestive sugge'rerend; sugges'tief
suicide zelfmoord
suit pak; kleur; huwelijksaanzoek;
  (aan)passen; ge'schikt zijn voor;
  schikken; goed staan (bij)
suitable ge'schikt
suitcase (hand)koffer
suite ge'volg; ameuble'ment;
  aparte'menten
suitor minnaar; eiser
sulk mokken, chag'rijnig zijn;
  boze/chag'rijnige bui
sullen stuurs; somber
sully be'zoedelen
sulphur zwavel
sultan sultan
sultana rozijn
sultry zwoel
sum som **to – up** samenvatten;
  opsommen
summarize samenvatten
summary samenvatting; sum'mier
summer zomer **– time** zomertijd
summertime zomerseizoen, zomer
summit top(punt)
summon ont'bieden, bij'eenroepen;
  ver'zamelen

summons dagvaarding
sumptuous weelderig
sun zon(ne-)
sunbeam zonnestraal
sunbed zonnebank, zonnehemel
sunburn zonnebrand
sunburnt ver'brand
Sunday zondag
sundial zonnewijzer
sundown zons'ondergang
sundry di'vers(en)
sunken blind; ingevallen
sunlight zonlicht
sunny zonnig
sunrise zons'opgang
sunset zons'ondergang
sunshine zonneschijn
sunstroke zonnesteek
super machtig
superb groots, schitterend
supercilious hoog'hartig
superficial opper'vlakkig
superfluous over'tollig
superhuman boven'menselijk
superintend toezicht houden op
superintendent inspec'teur
superior superi'eur, hoger; arro'gant
superlative van de hoogste
  graad; superlatief
supermarket supermarkt
supernatural bovenna'tuurlijk(e)
supersede ver'vangen
supersonic super'sonisch, sneller dan
  het geluid
superstition bijgeloof
superstitious bijge'lovig
supervise toezicht hebben op;
  survei'lleren
supervision toezicht
supper (avond)eten, avondmaal,
  sou'per
supplant ver'dringen
supple soepel, buigzaam

supplement supple'ment;
  aanvullen
supplementary aanvullend
supply voorraad; voor'ziening;
  ver'schaffen; vol'doen (aan)
support steun; (onder')steunen;
  onder'houden; staven
supporter aanhanger, sup'porter
suppose (ver)onder'stellen,
  aannemen **I – so** ik neem aan van
  wel **– he isn't there?** stel dat hij er
  niet is?
supposed ver'meend; aangenomen
supposing (that) stel dat
supposition veronder'stelling
suppress onder'drukken; ver'bieden
supremacy oppermacht
supreme opper-, uiterste
surcharge toeslag
sure zeker **to make –** contro'leren
surely (toch) zeker
surety borg
surf branding; surfen **– the net**
  internetten/op het net surfen
surface oppervlak(te), vlak
surfboard surfplank
surfeit overdaad
surge opwelling; golven,
  storten; stuwen; zwellen
surgeon chi'rurg
surgery chirur'gie; spreekkamer
surly nors
surmise ver'moeden
surmount be'kronen; over'winnen
surname achternaam
surpass over'treffen
surplus overschot; over('tollig)
surprise ver'rassing, ver'bazing;
  ver'rassen; ver'wonderen, ver'bazen
surprising ver'wonderlijk, ver'bazend
surrender overgave; (zich) overgeven
surround om'ringen, om'singelen
surroundings om'geving

surveillance toezicht
survey in'spectie; overzicht; opmeting; inspec'teren; over'zien; opmeten
surveyor ex'pert; opzichter; landmeter
survival leven, voortbestaan; overblijfsel
survive over'leven; blijven be'staan
survivor over'levende
susceptible vatbaar, ge'voelig (voor)
suspect ver'dacht(e); ver'moeden; ver'denken
suspend staken; schorsen; opschorten **to be suspended** hangen
suspenders jarre'telles
suspense spanning
suspicion ver'moeden; achterdocht; ver'denking; schijnte
suspicious ver'dacht; achter'dochtig
sustain staande houden; voeden; doorstaan; lijden
sustenance voedsel; onderhoud
swagger zeilen; opscheppen
swallow zwaluw; (door or in)slikken, ver'zwelgen
swamp moe'ras; over'spoelen; over'stelpen
swampy moe'rassig
swan zwaan
swap rail; (ver')ruilen
swarm zwerm(en); wemelen
swarthy donker
sway invloed; schommelen, ervan afbrengen
swear zweren; vloeken
sweat zweet; zweten
sweater trui
Swedish Zweeds
sweep zwaai; schoorsteenveger; (op)vegen; voeren; schrijden
sweeping wijds; ver'strekkend

sweet zoet; lief; fris; snoepje
sweeten suiker doen in
sweetheart liefje, schat
swell deining; (aan or op)zwellen; toenemen
swelling zwelling, ver'dikking
swerve zwenken
swift snel; gierzwaluw
swill afval; (uit)spoelen
swim zwemmen; duizelen
swindle oplichte'rij; oplichten
swine zwijn(en)
swing zwaai(en); schommel; animo; swing; slingeren
swirl (doen) warrelen
swish zoevend geluid, ge'ruis; chic, modi'eus; zoeven, suizen, ruizen
Swiss Zwitser(s)
switch schakelaar; wissel; ommezwaai, ver'andering; (om)schakelen, ver'anderen (van), overgaan (op) **– off** uitschakelen, uitdoen
swoon flauwte; be'zwijmen
swoop zich storten
sword zwaard
syllable lettergreep
symbol sym'bool
symbolic(al) sym'bolisch
symbolize symboli'seren
symmetrical sym'metrisch
symmetry symme'trie
sympathetic vol medeleven; wel'willend
sympathize meevoelen
sympathy sympa'thie
symphony symfo'nie
symptom symp'toom
synagogue syna'goge
synchronize (doen) samenvallen; ge'lijkzetten
syndicate syndi'caat
synod sy'node

synonym(ous) syno'niem
synopsis sy'nopsis
syntax syn'taxis
synthesis syn'these
synthetic syn'thetisch

syringe spuit(je); uitspuiten
syrup stroop, si'roop
system sys'teem; stelsel; net;
  lichaam
systematic syste'matisch

T

tab label; lus; rekening
table tafel; ta'bel
tablespoon eetlepel
table tennis tafeltennis
tablet ta'blet(je); ge'denkplaat
taboo ta'boe (ver'klaren)
tacit stil'zwijgend
taciturn zwijgzaam
tack kopspijker; spoor; koers;
  rijgen; toevoegen; van koers
  veranderen
tackle tuig; takel; aanpakken;
  tekkelen
tact(ful) tact(vol)
tactical tac'tisch
tactics tac'tiek
tactless tactloos
taffeta tafzij
tag eti'ketje; eindje, bandje **to – on**
  to zich aansluiten bij
tail staart; pand; achter-
tailor kleermaker
taint smet; be'derven

take (aan, in, mee *or* op)nemen;
  brengen; kosten (time) **to –**
  down opschrijven **to – for**
  houden voor **to – in** herbergen;
  innemen; in zich opnemen;
  beetnemen **to – off** uittrekken;
  opstijgen **to – on** aannemen; op
  zich nemen **taken aback** van zijn
  stuk ge'bracht
takings ont'vangsten
talc(um) talk
tale ver'haal; praatje
talent(ed) ta'lent(vol)
talk ge'sprek; sprake; be'spreking;
  praten, spreken **to – over**
  be'spreken, be'praten
talkative praatziek
tall lang, hoog
tally eti'ket; kloppen
talon klauw
tame tam; temmen
tamper with knoeien met
tampon tampon

Insight

Tan can be difficult to translate into Dutch. *Tan* is simply a brown colour, i.e. **bruin**, and *to tan* is **(zich) bruinen**, but there is not really an easy translation for *a tan* which is the result of sunbathing. This tan is usually described as **een bruine kleur** *a brown colour* or **een bruin kleurtje** (the diminutive indicating a positive attitude towards the colour). The expression **er bruin uitizien** (literally, *to look brown*) can also be used in some contexts: **je ziet er lekker bruin uit** *you have a great tan*.

tan (geel)bruin; tanen; bruinen; jongebruind

tandem tandem **in** – achter elkaar

tang scherpe smaak

tangerine manda'rijn

tangible tastbaar

tangle knoop, war; in de war raken (or maken)

tank tank, bak

tannin looizuur

tantalize tantali'seren

tantamount: to be – to neerkomen op

tantrum driftbui

tap kraan; tik(ken), kloppen; (af)tappen

tape band

taper waspit; taps toelopen

tapestry tapisse'rie; wandtapijt

tar teer; teren

tardy traag

target schietschijf; mikpunt, doel

tariff ta'rief

tarnish be'slaan, aantasten; be'zoedelen

tarpaulin zeil(doek)

tarry (ver')toeven

tart taart; slet; wrang

tartar tandsteen; driftkop; Ta'taar

task taak

tassel kwast(je)

taste smaak(je), proefje; proeven, smaken (naar)

tasteful smaakvol

tasteless smaakeloos

tasty smakelijk

tattoo tatoe'age; taptoe; tatoe'ëren

tattered haveloos

tatters flarden

taunt schimpscheut; schimpen op

taut strak

tavern herberg

tawdry op'zichtig, prullig

tawny vaalgeel

tax be'lasting; veel vergen van; be'schuldigen **– cut** be'lastingverlaging **– evasion** be'lastingontduiking **to be taxed** be'lasting be'talen, onder'hevig zijn aan be'lasting

taxation be'lasting

taxi taxi(ën)

tax-free belasting'vrij

taxpayer be'lastingbetaler

tea thee **– towel** theedoek

teach onder'wijzen, les geven, leren

teacher onder'wijzer('es), leraar, lera'res

team elftal; ploeg; span

teamwork teamwork, samenwerking, samenspel

teapot theepot

tear traan; scheur(en); vliegen

tease plagen

teaspoon theelepeltje

teat tepel; speen

technical technisch, ambachts-

technicalities tech'niek; formali'teiten

technically technisch; strikt ge'nomen

technician technicus

technique tech'niek

tedious ver'velend

teem wemelen (van)

teetotaller ge'heelonthouder

telecommunications telecommunicatie; telecommuni'catietechniek

telegram tele'gram

telegraph tele'graaf; telegra'feren

telephone tele'foon; telefo'neren

telephone box tele'fooncel

telephone call tele'foongesprek

telephone directory tele'foongids, tele'foonboek

teleshopping (het) telewinkelen, (het) teleshoppen

telescope tele'scoop; in el'kaar schuiven
television tele'visie
television commercial re'clamespot(je)
tell (het) ver'tellen, (het) zeggen; onder'scheiden
telling raak; veel'zeggend
temper aard, hu'meur; drift(bui); hardheid; ver'zachten; harden
temperament aard; tempera'ment
temperamental tempera'mentvol, vol kuren
temperance matigheid; ont'houding
temperate ge'matigd, matig
temperature tempera'tuur; ver'hoging
tempest hevige storm
tempestuous stormachtig, on'stuimig
temple tempel; slaap
temporal tijdelijk; wereldlijk
temporary tijdelijk, voor'lopig
tempt ver'leiden; lokken
temptation ver'leiding; aanvechting
tempting ver'leidelijk
tenth tiende
tenable ver'dedigbaar
tenacious vast'houdend; hard'nekkig
tenant huurder, pachter
tend ge'neigd zijn; lopen; overhellen; (licht) kunnen; passen op
tendency neiging
tender mals; te(d)er; ge'voelig; of'ferte; be'taalmiddel; tender; aanbieden
tendon pees
tendril rank
tenement pachtgoed; (huur)kamer, apparte'ment
tennis (court) tennis(baan)
tenor te'nor; loop; strekking
tense strak; ge'spannen, spannend; tijd

tension spanning
tent tent
tentacle voelhoorn; vangarm
tentative voorlopig; aarzelend
tenterhooks: on – op hete kolen (zitten)
tenuous ijl, schraal
tenure be'zit; tijd
tepid lauw
term tri'mester, se'mester, onderwijsperiode; ter'mijn, peri'ode; (vak)term, woord
terminal eind('station); terminal; terminaal
terminate (be')ëindigen, aflopen; opzeggen
terminology terminolo'gie
terminus eindstation (*or* punt)
terms voorwaarden, con'dities, be'palingen **come to – with** zich verzoenen met, zich neerleggen bij
terrace ter'ras; huizenrij
terrestrial aard-; land-
terrible vreselijk, ver'schrikkelijk
terrier terriër
terrific ge'weldig
terrify schrik aanjagen **to be terrified** in doodsangst ver'keren, zich doodschrikken
territorial territori'aal
territory (grond)gebied
terror schrik, angst
terrorism terro'risme
terrorist terro'ristisch, ter'reur; terro'rist
terrorize terrori'seren, schrik aanjagen
terse kort en bondig
test proef(werk), e'xamen; be'proeving; testen, exami'neren; op de proef stellen **– tube** rea'geerbuis
testament testa'ment

testify ge'tuigen (van); onder ede ver'klaren

testimonial ge'tuigschrift, ver'klaring

testimony ge'tuigenis

text tekst

textbook leerboek, studieboek, schoolboek

textile tex'tiel

texture weefsel; samenstel, bouw

than dan

thank (be')danken **thanks** be'dankt; dank

thankful dankbaar

thankless on'dankbaar

thanksgiving dankbétuiging; Thanksgiving

that dat; die; wat; daar-

thatch(ed roof) riet(en dak)

thaw dooi(en); (doen) ont'dooien

the de, het

theatre the'ater, schouwburg; to'neel; zaal

theatrical to'neel-; thea'traal

thee U

theft diefstal

their hun

theirs (die or dat) van hun

them hen, ze

theme onderwerp; thema

themselves zich(zelf), zelf

then toen('malig); dan; boven'dien **by –** tegen die tijd **but –** maar … (dan ook) **– and there** on'middellijk

thence van'daar; daaruit

theologian theo'loog

theological theo'logisch

theology godge'leerdheid

theoretical theo'retisch

theory theo'rie

there daar('heen); er

thereabouts daar in de buurt; daarom'trent

therefore daarom

thermometer thermometer

these deze; hier-

thesis stelling; disser'tatie

they zij

thick dik; dicht

thicken dikker worden; binden

thicket struikgewas

thickness dikte; laag

thick-skinned dik'huidig

thief dief

thieve stelen

thigh dij

thimble vingerhoed

thin dun; mager; ijl; ver'dunnen

thing ding **a –** iets **the – that** wat **things** spullen; (de) dingen

think denken (aan or over); nadenken; ge'loven; een i'dee hebben; vinden

thinnish vrij dun

third derde; terts

thirdly ten derde

thirst dorst(en); zucht (naar)

thirsty: to be – dorst hebben; dorstig zijn

thirteen(th) dertien(de)

thirty dertig

this deze, dit; hier-

thistle distel

thorn doorn

thorny doornig; netelig

thorough grondig; echt

those die; de'genen; er; daar-

though hoe'wel; al (… ook); (ja) maar, (en) toch **as –** als'of

thought i'dee, ge'dachte; (na)denken; at'tentie

thoughtful in ge'dachten ver'zonken; at'tent

thoughtless onbe'zonnen; onat'tent

thousand duizend

thrash geselen, aframmelen; ver'slaan, niets heel laten van

thread garen; draad; de draad steken door; zich (een weg) banen

threadbare kaal; afgezaagd
threat be'dreiging
threaten dreigen met; be'dreigen
three drie
thresh dorsen
threshold drempel
thrice driemaal
thrift zuinigheid
thrifty spaarzaam
thrill sen'satie; aangrijpen; ver'rukken
thrilling aan'grijpend; (erg) op'windend
thrive ge'dijen; bloeien
throat keel
throb bonzen, kloppen
throne troon
throng ge'drang; (zich ver')dringen (op)
throttle smoorklep; smoren
through door('heen); doorgaand
throughout door heel **– the day** de hele dag door
throw worp; werpen; (toe *or* af) gooien; gooien met
thrust stoot, steek; stoten, steken; werpen
thud plof
thug misdadiger, moordenaar
thumb duim; be'duimelen
thump bons; stomp(en); bonken (op), bonzen (op)
thunder donder(en), onweer **– storm** onweer(sbui)
thunderbolt bliksemflits; donderslag
thundercloud onweerswolk
thunderous daverend
Thursday donderdag
thus (al')dus; zo
thwart dwarsbomen, ver'ijdelen
tick tik(ken); streepje; ogenblikje; teek; tijk; aftekenen
ticket kaartje, ticket
tickle kietelen; jeuken; amu'seren

ticklish kietelig; netelig
tidal ge'tij-, vloed-
tide ge'tij, stroom; helpen
tidings nieuws
tidy net(jes); flink; opruimen
tie (strop)das; band; onbesliste wedstrijd; (vast)binden; strikken, knopen; ge'lijkstaan, ge'lijk aankomen
tier rang, ver'dieping
tiger tijger
tight vast; dicht op el'kaar; strak; kachel
tighten strakker aanhalen; ver'scherpen
tile tegel; dakpan; be'tegelen
till tot(dat); geldlade; be'ploegen **up –** tot (aan) **not ... –** pas
tilt overhellen; kantelen; schuinhouden (*or* zetten) **full –** met volle vaart
timber timmerhout; balk
time (de) tijd; keer; ge'legenheid; maat, tempo; de tijd opnemen van; uitrekenen **at the same –** tege'lijkertijd; desondanks **for the – being** voor'lopig **in –** op tijd; op den duur; in de maat
timely tijdig
timid, timorous schuchter
tin tin; blik(ken); bus, trommel
tinge tint(en); tikje
tingle tintelen
tinker ketellapper; prutsen
tinkle tingelen
tinned in blik
tinsel klatergoud
tint tint(en)
tiny heel klein
tip punt, top; (een) fooi (geven); wenk, optillen, kantelen; storten
tipsy aangeschoten
tiptoe: on – op de tenen; in spanning
tire band; ver'moeien; moe (*or* beu) worden

tired moe; beu
tireless onvermoeid
tiresome ver'velend
tissue weefsel; vloei-
tit mees; (inf) tiet; tepel; sukkel, klier
titbit lekker hapje
title titel; aanspraak (op); be'titelen
titled adellijk
titter giechelen
to naar; tot (aan); (om) te; in; aan; dicht **— and fro** heen en weer
toad pad
toadstool paddestoel
toast ge'roosterd brood; toost; roosteren; drinken op
tobacco ta'bak
tobacconist si'garenhandelaar
today van'daag; tegen'woordig
toddle dribbelen
toe teen
toffee toffee
together samen; tege'lijk
toil arbeid; zwoegen; zich slepen
toilet toi'let **— bag** toi'lettas
token teken, blijk, bewijs; bon, ca'deaubon; munt, fiche, penning; aandenken
tolerable draaglijk; redelijk
tolerance ver'draagzaamheid
tolerant ver'draagzaam
tolerate dulden
toll tol; luiden
tomato to'maat **— juice** to'matensap **— ketchup** (to'maten)ketchup
tomb graftombe
tombstone grafsteen
tomorrow morgen
tom-tom tam-tam
ton ton
tone toon, klank; tint; harmoni'ëren
tongs tang
tongue tong; taal; klepel
tonic ver'sterkend middel

tonight van'avond, van'nacht
tonsil a'mandel
too ook (nog); (al) te
tool ge'reedschap, werktuig
tooth tand, kies
toothache kiespijn
toothbrush tandenborstel
toothpaste tandpasta
toothpick tandenstoker
top top; tol; bovenste, bovenaan
topic onderwerp
topical actu'eel
topography topogra'fie
topple (bijna) omvallen/kantelen; (bijna) doen omvallen/kantelen
topsy-turvy op zijn kop
torch zaklantaren; fakkel
torment foltering; kwellen
tornado tor'nado, wervelstorm
torpedo tor'pedo; torpe'deren
torrent (berg)stroom; stortvloed
torrential stort-
torrid heet
torso torso, romp
tortoise schildpad
tortuous kronkelend; draaiend
torture foltering; kwelling; folteren; kwellen
toss toss; opgooien; slingeren; de lucht in gooien
tot peuter **— up** optellen
total to'taal; be'dragen
totally vol'komen
totter wankelen
touch aanraking; con'tact; tikje; trekje; aanslag; (aan)raken; el'kaar raken; (aan)roeren
touching roerend
tough taai; zuur; hard; moeilijk; ruwe klant
tour (rond)reis; rondtoer; (op) tour'nee (zijn); (af)reizen
tourist toe'rist
tournament toer'nooi

tousle ver'fomfaaien
tow sleeptouw; slepen
toward(s) naar ... toe, in de richting van; jegens; tegen
towel handdoek
tower toren; zich torenhoog ver'heffen
town stad
townhall stad'huis
toxic ver'giftig
toy (stuk) speelgoed; speelbal; spelen
trace spoor; tikje; opsporen, vinden; overtrekken, schetsen
track spoor; pad; baan; opsporen
tracksuit trainingspak
tractor tractor
trade handel(en); vak; zaken; handeldrijven
trademark handelsmerk
trader handelaar; handelsvaartuig
tradesman leveran'cier
trades union (vak)bond, vakvereniging
tradition tra'ditie
traditional traditio'neel
traffic ver'keer; handel(en) **— jam** (ver'keers)opstopping, file **— lane** rijstrook **— sign** ver'keersteken, ver'keersbord
tragedy treurspel; trage'die
tragic treurspel; trage'die
trail spoor; nasleep; pad; (laten) slepen; kruipen; opsporen **to — off** (*or* **away**) wegsterven
trailer kruipplant; aanhangwagen
train trein; sleep; ge'volg; reeks; opleiden; trainen; (af)richten
trainee stagi'air(e)
trainer trainer
training opleiding; training
trait trek
traitor(ous) ver'rader(lijk)
tram tram
tramp landloper; wandeling; sjouwen; lopen; trappen

trample trappen
trance trance; geestvervoering
tranquil rustig
tranquillity rust
transact doen, sluiten
transaction trans'actie; ver'richten
transcend te boven gaan
transfer overplaatsing; overdruk; overdragen, overbrengen, over(*or* ver')plaatsen; transfer (sport)
transfigure een andere ge'daante geven
transfix door'steken; aan de grond nagelen
transform (ge'heel) ver'anderen; transfor'meren
transgress over'treden; te buiten gaan
transient kort'stondig
transit: in — onder'weg
transition(al) overgang(s-)
transitory ver'gankelijk
translate ver'talen; omzetten
translation ver'taling
translucent door'schijnend
transmission trans'missie; overbrengen; gangwissel
transmit overbrengen; uitzenden
transparent door'zichtig, transpa'rant
transpire blijken; zich voordoen
transplant ver'planten, overplanten; transplan'teren; getransplan'teerd orgaan, transplan'taat; transplan'tatie
transport ver'voer, trans'port; ver'voeren
transport café wegrestaurant
transpose ver'wisselen; transpo'neren
transsexual transseksu'eel
transverse dwars
transvestite traves'tiet

trap val(strik), hinderlaag; sjees;
in de val laten lopen; opsluiten
trapdoor valluik
trash prullen, prul'laria; afval; rotzooi
travel reizen; zich voortplanten
  – agency reisbureau
traveller reiziger **– cheque**
reischeque
traverse dwars; doortrekken
travesty tra'vestie; aanfluiting
trawler treiler
tray blad; bak
treacherous ver'raderlijk; vals
treachery ver'raad
tread tred(en); loopvlak; be'treden;
trappen
treason (land)verraad
treasure schat(ten); ju'weel;
hoogschatten; angst'vallig
be'waren
treasurer penningmeester
treasury schatkist; minis'terie van
fi'nanciën
treat trak'tatie; feestje; be'handelen;
trak'teren
treatise ver'handeling
treatment be'handeling
treaty ver'drag
treble drie'voudig; so'praan;
verdrie'voudigen
tree boom; leest
trek trek(ken)
trellis latwerk
tremble beven
tremendous e'norm
tremor trilling
trench loopgraaf; voor
trenchant snijdend; krachtig
trend neiging; loop, richting
trepidation schroom, beven
trespass op ver'boden ter'rein zijn
(*or* komen); be'slag leggen
tress lok
trestle schraag

trial ver'hoor; proef(neming);
be'proeving; lastpost
triangle driehoek; tri'angel
triangular drie'hoekig
triathlon triatlon
tribe stam
tribulation be'proeving
tribunal rechtbank; tribu'naal
tributary zijrivier; bij-
tribute hulde(blijk); schatting
trick truc; kunstje; streek; slag;
be'driegen
trickle straaltje; sijpelen, biggelen;
druppelen
tricky lastig, netelig
tricycle driewieler
trifle kleinigheid; klein beetje; fruit en
cake met custard en room; spotten
trifling onbe'duidend
trigger trekker
trim net(jes); con'ditie; bijwerken,
bijknippen; gar'neren
trimming gar'nering, versiering
Trinity drie'ëenheid
trinket kleinood
trip tocht(je); (doen) struikelen;
trippelen **to – up** struikelen;
zich in de vingers snijden
triple drie'delig; drie'dubbel
tripod drievoet
trite afgezaagd
triumph tri'omf; zegevieren
triumphal tri'omf-
triumphant zegevierend,
triom'fantelijk
trivial onbe'duidend
trolley trolley; rolwagen(tje),
theewagen
troop troep; pelo'ton; zich scharen;
allen (tege'lijk) gaan
trophy prijs, tro'fee; zegeteken
tropics tropen
tropical tropisch
trot draf; draven

trouble zorg; moeite (nemen);
hinderen; lastig vallen
troublesome lastig
trough trog; dal
trousers broek
trout fo'rel(len)
trowel troffel; schopje
truant: to play – spijbelen
truce wapenstilstand
truck vrachtauto; (goederen)wagen
trudge sjokken
true waar; echt; (ge')trouw; zuiver
truism afgezaagde waarheid
truly heus
trump troef; troeven **to – up**
ver'zinnen
trumpet trom'pet(ten)
truncheon stok
trundle rollen
trunk stam, romp; hutkoffer;
slurf; interlo'kaal
truss bundel, spant; (vast)binden
trust ver'trouwen (op); be'waring;
trust; hopen
trustee execu'teur; gevol'machtigde
trustful goed van ver'trouwen
trustworthy be'trouwbaar
trusty trouw
truth waarheid
truthful eerlijk
try poging; pro'beren; be'proeven;
op de proef stellen; ver'horen
trying moeilijk
T-shirt t-shirt
tub kuip, ton
tube buis, slang; (binnen)band;
tube; onder'grondse
tuberculosis tubercu'lose
tuck plooi; stoppen
Tuesday dinsdag
tuft bosje
tug ruk(ken); sleepboot; trekken
tuition onderwijs
tulip tulp

tumble tuimelen
tumbledown bouw'vallig
tumble dryer droogtrommel
tumbler (limo'nade)glas
tumour tumor
tumult tumult
tumultuous tumultu'eus, ru'moerig
tune wijsje, melo'die; stemmen
tuneful wel'luidend
tunic overgooier; tu'niek
tunnel tunnel (maken)
turban tulband
turbine tur'bine
turbulent woelig, wild, turbu'lent
turf zode(n), gras; renbaan
turkey kal'koen; Tur'kije
turmoil be'roering
turn draai; bocht; ommekeer; beurt;
dienst; kunstje; (om)draaien;
omslaan; omkeren; worden;
ver'anderen; omzetten; wenden **to
– down** om'vouwen; afwijzen **to –
out** uitdraaien; aantreden, opstaan;
(er) uitzetten; produ'ceren; aflopen;
blijken **to – over** omslaan; (zich)
omkeren; overdragen; over'denken
to – to overgaan op; zich wenden
tot; aanpakken **to – up** omslaan,
optrekken; opdraaien; ver'schijnen
turnip knol, raap
turnover omzet
turnpike tolhek
turpentine terpen'tijn
turquoise tur'koois
turret torentje; ge'schuttoren
turtle zeeschildpad
tusk slagtand
tussle worsteling; worstelen
tutor pri'véleraar
tut tut nou nou
twaddle ge'wauwel; wauwelen
twang ping; neusgeluid; tingelen
tweed tweed
tweezers pin'cet

twelve twaalf
twenty twintig
twice tweemaal
twiddle draaien
twig twijgje
twilight schemering
twin tweeling
twinge steek
twinkle fonkelen
twirl (rond)draaien
twist kromming; (ver')draaien; zich slingeren; ver'trekken
twitch zenuwtrekking; trekken

twitter tjilpen
two twee
twofold twee'voudig
type type; letter(type); tikken
typewriter schrijfmachine, typemachine
typhoid tyfus
typhoon ty'foon
typical typisch
typify ty'peren
tyrannical tiran'niek
tyranny tiran'nie
tyrant ti'ran

U

ubiquitous alomheersend
udder uier
UFO ufo, vliegende schotel
ugly lelijk

un- on-
unable niet in staat
unaccompanied zonder bege'leiding; a-ca'pella

Insight

Ugly is easily translated as **lelijk**. However, when learning a language, the exact translation of a word or expression might escape you, and you won't always have your dictionary at hand. As a language learner, it is a good to train yourself in saying things in a different way if it proves hard to find certain words. Opting for the opposite of the word you're saying, for instance, can be a handy way of expressing what you mean. In the case of *ugly* you can say that something is **niet mooi** *not beautiful*, or **helemaal niet mooi** *really not beautiful*.

ulcer zweer
ulterior heimelijk, bij-
ultimate laatste; uit'eindelijk; essen'tieel, grond-; ul'tiem
ultimatum ulti'matum
ultra-violet ultravio'let
umbrella para'plu; tuinparasol
umpire scheidsrechter
UN VN (Verenigde Naties)

unaccountable onver'klaarbaar
unaccustomed niet ge'wend
unanimous een'stemmig, eensge'zind
unassuming be'scheiden
unattended onbe'heerd
unauthorized onbe'voegd
unavailing ver'geefs
unavoidable onver'mijdelijk
unaware niet be'wust

unawares onbe'wust; onver'hoeds
unbearable on'draaglijk
unbelievable onge'looflijk
unbound niet ge'bonden
unbroken onver'broken;
on'afgebroken
unbutton losknopen
uncalled-for onge'vraagd; mis'plaatst
uncanny griezelig, onge'looflijk,
geheim'zinnig
uncertain on'zeker
unchecked onbe'lemmerd
uncle oom
uncommon onge'woon
uncompromising on'buigzaam,
rotsvast
unconcerned onver'schillig;
onbe'kommerd
unconditional onvoor'waardelijk
unconquerable onover'winnelijk
unconscious be'wusteloos; onbe'wust
uncontrollable onbe'dwingbaar,
onbe'daarlijk
uncork ont'kurken
uncouth lomp
uncover ont'bloten; aan het licht
brengen
undaunted onver'saagd
undecided onbe'slist; in dubio
undeniable ontegen'zeggelijk,
onbe'twistbaar
under onder(-)
undercurrent onderstroom;
ver'borgen stroming
underdone on'gaar
undergraduate stu'dent
underground onder de grond;
onder'gronds(e)
undergrowth kreupelhout
underhand onder'hands
underlying grond-,
undermine onder'mijnen
underneath onder, be'neden;
onderkant

understand be'grijpen; horen;
aannemen
understanding be'grip;
ver'standhouding; sympa'thiek
undertake onder'nemen;
op zich nemen
undertaker be'grafenisondernemer
undertaking onder'neming; be'lofte
undertone ge'dempte stem;
grondkleur; ondergrond
underwear ondergoed
undesirable onge'wenst
undo los(or open)maken;
onge'daan maken
undoing ondergang
undoubtedly onge'twijfeld
undress (zich) uitkleden
undue over'matig
undulate golven
unearth opgraven; aan het licht
brengen
unearthly boven'aards; on'mogelijk
uneasy onge'rust, on'rustig
uneducated onge'schoold
unemployed werkloos
unemployment werk'loosheid
unemployment benefit
werk'loosheidsuitkering
unending eindeloos
unequal onge'lijk; niet opgewassen
(tegen)
unerring on'feilbaar
uneven on'effen; onge'lijk; on'even
uneventful onbe'wogen, saai
unexpected(ly) onver'wacht(s),
onvoor'zien
unfailing on'feilbaar; onuit'puttelijk;
zeker
unfamiliar onbe'kend; niet op de
hoogte
unfasten los(or open)maken
unfathomable ondoor'grondelijk
unfeeling onge'voelig
unfetter ont'ketenen

unfinished onvol'tooid
unfit onge'schikt
unfold ont'vouwen, (zich) ont'plooien
unforgettable onver'getelijk
unforgivable onver'geeflijk
unfortunately jammer ge'noeg, he'laas
unfounded onge'grond
unfurl (zich) ont'plooien
ungainly lomp
ungodly goddeloos
ungovernable on'tembaar
ungracious on'hoffelijk
unhappiness ver'driet
unharmed onge'deerd, onbe'schadigd
unheard-of onge'kend; onge'hoord
unheeded on'opgemerkt; onge'merkt, ver'waarloosd
unholy goddeloos; heidens
unicorn eenhoorn
uniform ge'lijk('matig); uni'form
unify ver'enigen
unimaginative zonder fanta'sie; fanta'sieloos
unimpaired on'aangetast
uninformed niet op de hoogte, on'wetend
uninhabitable onbe'woonbaar
unintelligent dom
unintelligible onver'staanbaar, onbe'grijpelijk
uninvited onge'nood
union ver'bond, unie; (vak)bond; stu'dentenvereniging
unique u'niek
unison: in – een'stemmig; tege'lijk
unit eenheid; afdeling
unite (zich) ver'enigen
united ver'enigd; saam'horig; ge'zamenlijk
United Kingdom Ver'enigd Koninkrijk
United States of America Ver'enigde Staten van A'merika

unity eenheid; eensge'zindheid
universal univer'seel; alge'meen
universe heel'al
university universi'teit
unkempt onver'zorgd
unkind on'aardig
unknown onbe'kend(e)
unless ten'zij
unlike ver'schillend, anders dan
  it is – him to forget het is niets voor hem het te ver'geten
unload ont'laden, lossen
unlock ont'sluiten
unmanageable on'handelbaar
unmask ont'maskeren, onthullen
unmistakable onmis'kenbaar
unmitigated onver'minderd; onver'valst
unnerve ont'zenuwen
unobtrusive be'scheiden
unoccupied onbe'zet; onbe'woond; niet bezig
unofficial niet offi'cieel
unpack uitpakken
unpalatable on'smakelijk; on'aangenaam
unparalleled weergaloos, ongeëve'naard
unpardonable onver'geeflijk
unpleasant on'aangenaam
unprecedented onge'hoord
unpredictable onbe'rekenbaar
unprincipled ge'wetenloos
unprofitable on'vruchtbaar
unquestionable onbe'twistbaar
unquestionably onge'twijfeld
unravel ont'warren
unreasoned onberede'neerd
unreservedly zonder voorbehoud
unrestrained onbe'teugeld; onge'dwongen
unrivalled ongeëve'naard
unruly on'ordelijk, on'handelbaar

unsavoury smakeloos; on'smakelijk; onver'kwikkelijk
unscathed onge'deerd
unscrew losschroeven
unscrupulous ge'wetenloos
unselfish onbaat'zuchtig
unsettled on'zeker
unsightly on'ooglijk
unsparing kwistig, mild; mee'dogenloos
unspeakable onbe'schrijf(e)lijk
unsuccessful ver'geefs **to be –** geen suc'ces hebben
unsuspicious argeloos
untangle ont'warren
untenable on'houdbaar
unthinkable on'denkbaar
untidy slordig, wan'ordelijk
untie losmaken
until tot(dat)
untimely on'tijdig; onge'legen
untiring onver'moeid
unto tot (aan)
untold onver'teld; on'telbaar
untoward on'gunstig
unused onge'bruikt; niet ge'wend (aan)
unusual onge'woon, onge'bruikelijk
unutterable onuit'sprekelijk
unvaried unvarying onver'anderlijk
unveil ont'hullen; ont'sluieren
unwarranted ongerecht'vaardigd
unwavering stand'vastig
unwieldy log
unwind afwinden; (zich) ont'rollen
unwittingly onop'zettelijk, onbe'wust
unwonted onge'woon
unwrap uitpakken
unyielding onver'zettelijk
up (verder) op; (naar) boven; om'hoog; over'eind; ver'streken
to be – to in staat zijn; in de zin hebben, uitvoeren; zijn aan

upbringing opvoeding
upheaval opschudding
uphill de heuvel op, opwaarts; zwaar
uphold hooghouden; steunen
upholstery be'kleding
upkeep onderhoud
uplift ver'heffen
upon op
upper boven(ste); superieur
uppermost hoogst; bovenst; op de voorgrond
upright recht'op; op'recht
uprising opstand
uproar tu'mult
uproarious ru'moerig; stormachtig
uproot ont'wortelen; uitroeien
upset om'verwerpen; in de war sturen; van streek maken
upshot resul'taat
upside down onderste'boven
upstairs (naar) boven
upstart parve'nu(achtig); poen(ig)
upstream stroom'opwaarts
up-to-date bijgewerkt, op de hoogte; mo'dern, heden'daags
upturn verbetering, ommekeer
upward(s) opwaarts, naar boven; (en) hoger, (en) ouder
uranium u'ranium
urban stedelijk, stads-, steeds
urchin kwa'jongen
urge (aan)drang; aanzetten; aandringen (op)
urgent dringend
urn urn
us ons
usable bruikbaar
usage ge'bruik; be'handeling
use ge'bruik(en); toepassing; nut; ver'bruiken **to be used to** ge'wend zijn (aan) **it used to be** het was vroeger
useful nuttig, handig
useless nutteloos

usher plaatsaanwijzer; leiden
usual ge'bruikelijk, ge'woon **as –** zoals ge'woonlijk
usually ge'woonlijk
usurp usur'peren
utensils ge'rei; werktuigen, ge'reedschap

utility (openbare) voorziening, nut(tigheids-)
utilize be'nutten
utmost uiterste, hoogste
utter vol'slagen; uiten
utterance uiting; uitspraak
uttermost uiterst

V

vacancy vaca'ture, leemte
vacant va'cant; onbe'woond; wezenloos
vacate ont'ruimen
vacation va'kantie
vaccinate inenten
vacuum vacuüm, leegte; stofzuigen
vacuum cleaner stofzuiger
vagabond vagebond
vagrant ronddolend
vague vaag
vain ijdel; ver'geefs **in –** tever'geefs
vale dal
valet be'diende
valid (rechts')geldig
validity (rechts)geldigheid
valley dal
valour moed
valuable waardevol; kostbaar(heid)
valuation ta'xatie
value waarde; ta'xeren; op prijs stellen
valve klep, ven'tiel
van (be'stel)wagen; voorhoede
vandalism vanda'lisme
vane vaantje; wiek, schoep
vanguard voorhoede
vanilla va'nille
vanish (spoorloos) ver'dwijnen; uitsterven
vanity ijdelheid
vanquish over'winnen
vantage voorsprong; gunstig
vapour damp
variable ver'anderlijk; ver'stelbaar

variation afwisseling; ver'andering; vari'atie
variety ver'scheidenheid afwisseling; soort; varié'té
various ver'scheiden
varnish ver'nis(sen)
vary vari'ëren
vase vaas
vast on'metelijk, kolos'saal
vastly e'norm
VAT btw (be'lasting op de toegevoegde waarde)
vat vat
Vatican Vati'caan
vault ge'welf, kluis; sprong; springen
veal kalfsvlees
veer draaien; vieren; van richting ver'anderen
vegetable groente(-); plant'aardig
vegetarian vegetariër; vege'tarisch
vegetation vege'tatie, plantengroei
vehement hevig
vehicle voertuig; drager
veil sluier(en)
vein ader; neiging, trek; stemming
velocity snelheid
velvet flu'weel; flu'welen
vendor ver'koper
veneer fi'neer(hout); ver'nisje; fi'neren
venerable eerbied'waardig; eer'waard
venerate diep ver'eren
venereal ge'slachts-
Venetian Vene'tiaans
venetian blind jaloe'zie

vengeance wraak
vengeful wraak'gierig
Venice Venetië
venom(ous) ve'nijn(ig)
vent opening, luchtgaatje; uitweg; luchten
ventilate venti'leren
ventilation venti'latie
ventriloquist buikspreker
venture onder'heming; waagstuk; (het) wagen
venturesome, venturous stout'moedig
verb werkwoord
verbal in woorden; mondeling; werk'woordelijk
verbatim woordelijk
verdict uitspraak; oordeel, vonnis; be'slissing
verge rand; grenzen (aan)
verify verifi'ëren
veritable waar
vermilion vermil'joen
vermin ongedierte
vernacular moedertaal
versatile veel'zijdig
verse poëzie; cou'plet
versed be'dreven
version ver'taling, versie, lezing, be'werking
vertebrate ge'werveeld (dier)
vertical verti'caal; loodlijn
very zeer, erg; pre'cies; al'leen al
vessel vaartuig; vat
vest hemd; vest; (be')kleden
vestry sacris'tie
veteran vete'raan; er'varen
vet(erinary) veearts(e'nij)
veto veto; ver'werpen
vex ergeren
vexation ergernis
viaduct via'duct
vial flesje
vibrate vi'breren

vibration trilling
vicar dominee, pas'toor
vice ondeugd; bankschroef; vice-
vice versa vice versa, omgekeerd
vicinity na'bijheid, buurt
vicious boos'aardig; vici'eus
victim slachtoffer
victor over'winnaar
victorious zegevierend
victory over'winning
video video; videorecorder; op (de) video opnemen
video recorder videorecorder
videotape videoband
vie wedijveren
Vienna Wenen
Viennese Weens
view uitzicht, ge'zicht; mening; be'schouwen **in —** in het ge'zicht; voor ogen **in — of** ge'zien
viewpoint uitzichtpunt; ge'zichtspunt
vigil wacht, waken, wake
vigilance waakzaamheid
vigorous krachtig, ener'giek
vigour kracht, ener'gie
vile af'schuwelijk
villa villa
village dorp
villain schurk
villainous schurkachtig, heel slecht, ge'meen
vindicate wrekend, handhaven, recht'-vaardigen, zuiveren (van blaam)
vindictive wraak'gierig
vine wijnstok; wingerd
vinegar a'zijn
vineyard wijngaard
vintage jaar; wijnoogst
viola altviool; vi'ooltje
violate schenden
violation schennis
violence ge'weld
violent hevig, heftig, geweld'dadig
violet vi'ooltje; vio'let

violin vi'ool
violinist vio'list
viper adder
virgin maagd(elijk); onge'rept
virile man'moedig, krachtig
virtual eigenlijk
virtually praktisch
virtue deugd; ver'dienste
virtuous deugdzaam
virulent kwad'aardig; ve'nijnig
visa visum
visibility zicht
visible zichtbaar
visibly zienderogen
vision ge'zicht; vérziende blik; visi'oen
visit be'zoek(en)
visitor be'zoeker, gast
visual ge'zichts-
vital essen'tieel; vi'taal; levens-
vitality vitali'teit
vitamin vita'mine
vivacious levendig
vivid helder; levendig
vocabulary woordenlijst; woordenschat, vocabu'laire
vocal stem-, zang-
vocation roeping; be'roep

vogue zwang; populari'teit
voice stem; uiten
void on'geldig; ont'bloot; leegte
volatile vluchtig; wispel'turig
volcano vul'kaan
volley regen, stroom; volley
volt(age) volt('age)
volume (boek)deel; vo'lume, omvang; massa
voluminous volumi'neus
voluntary vrij'willig; wille'keurig; lief'dadigheids-
volunteer vrij'williger; vrij'willig in dienst treden; aanbieden
voluptuous wel'lustig; weelderig
vomit overgeven, (uit)braken; braaksel, overgeefsel
vote stem(recht); motie; stemmen; toestaan
voter kiezer
vouch instaan
vow ge'lofte; plechtig be'loven
vowel klinker
voyage reis
vulgar vul'gair, plat
vulgarity vulgari'teit, platheid
vulnerable kwetsbaar
vulture gier

Insight

Vulgar can be **vulgair** or **plat** in Dutch, but also **ordinair**. **Ordinair** can be – and is – used in many different contexts, but as a speaker of English you should be aware that it is what is known as 'a false friend': it closely resembles a word from your own language, *ordinary*, but it means something different. And as you can see, in the case of **ordinair** you could make a pretty big faux pas by using it in the sense of *ordinary*. There are quite a few of these false friends. A few examples: **stoel**, which doesn't mean *stool* but *chair*; **een eekhoorn**, which is not *an acorn* but *a squirrel*; **de benzine**, which doesn't mean *benzene* but *petrol/gas*; and **sectie**, which is pronounced the same as **sexy** – also a Dutch word – but which means *section*.

W

wad prop; pakje
waddle waggelen
wade waden
wafer wafel; hostie
waft drijven, zweven
wag kwispelen (tail)
wage loon; voeren
wager weddenschap; wedden om
wagon wagen, wa'gon
wail weeklagen; loeien
waist taille
waistcoat vest
wait wachten; dienen
waiter kelner
waiting room wachtkamer
waitress ser'verster
waive afstand doen van, afzien van
wake kielzog; spoor to – up wakker
worden (or maken)
walk wandeling, eind lopen; loop;
laan; sfeer; lopen, wandelen to go
for a – gaan wandelen
wall muur, wand, wal
wallet porte'feuille, portemon'nee
wallpaper be'hang
walnut walnoot; notenhout(en)
waltz wals(en)
wan bleek; flets
wand toverstaf
wander zwerven; dwalen
wane afnemen
wangle klaarspelen; knoeien met
want be'hoefte; ge'brek, nood;
willen (hebben); nodig hebben,
moeten worden
wanton bal'dadig; wild
war oorlog; strijden
ward pu'pil; zaal; stadswijk
to – off afweren
warden direc'teur
warder ci'pier
wardrobe klerenkast; garde'robe

ware waar, goed
warehouse pakhuis
warlike oorlogs'zuchtig
warm warm; (ver')warmen
warmth warmte
warn waarschuwen
warning waarschuwing
warp kromtrekken; ver'draaien
warrant be'vel; waarborgen
warrior krijgsman
wart wrat
wartime oorlogs(tijd)
wary voor'zichtig
wash was; golfslag; (zich) wassen;
spoelen to – up afwassen
washable wasbaar
wash basin wastafel
washer wasser; sluitring, leertje
washing was(goed); was-
washing machine wasautomaat,
wasmachine
washing up afwas, vaat
wasp wesp
wastage ver'spilling
waste ver'spilling; afval(-);
woeste'nij; ver'spillen; (weg)
kwijnen to lay – ver'woesten
wasteful ver'kwistend
wastepaper basket prullenmand
watch wacht; hor'loge; uitkijken;
gadeslaan; opletten
watchful waakzaam
watchman waker
water water (geven); wateren
watercolour waterverf; aqua'rel
waterfall waterval
watertight, waterproof waterdicht
watery water(acht)ig; regen-
wave golf; wuiven (met);
watergolven, perma'nenten
waver flikkeren; weifelen; beven
wavy golvend

wax was(sen); wassen; worden
way ma'nier, wijze; opzicht; kant,
weg, eind; zin; vaart **by the –**
tussen haakjes **to give –** toegeven;
wegzakken **in a –** in zekere zin **to
make one's own –** zijn weg vinden;
voor'uitkomen
wayfarer reiziger, zwerver
waylay aanranden; aanklampen
wayside (aan de) kant van de weg
wayward eigen'zinnig
we wij, we
weak zwak; slap
weaken ver'zwakken; ver'slappen
weakling zwakkeling
weakness zwakte; zwak (punt)
wealth rijkdom; schat
wealthy rijk
weapon wapen
wear dracht, kleding; slij'tage;
dragen; slijten; zich houden **to – out**
(ver')slijten, afdragen; afmatten
weariness ver'moeidheid
weary moe
weather weer; ver'weren;
door'staan
weather-beaten door storm
ge'teisterd; ver'weerd
weathercock weerhaant
weave weven; (samen)vlechten; zich
slingerend banen
web web; weefsel
website website
wedding huwelijk(splechtigheid),
bruiloft
wedge wig; vastzetten
wee heel klein
weed onkruid; ta'bak, marihu'ana,
hasj; lange slapjanus; wieden,
ver'wijderen, schoffelen; zuiveren
weedy vol onkruid; spichtig
week week
weekend weekend, weekeinde
weekly wekelijks, week-

we
wei
wei
wei
wei
wel
ver
weld
welf
wet

wherever
wherever waar (...
overal waar
whether of
whewl oef
which w
whif

well goed; ver; wel; put, bron; wellen
as – ook; even'goed; zo'wel
well-bred wel'opgevoed
well-known be'kend
well-nigh nage'noeg
well-off welge'steld; goed'af
well-read be'lezen
west west(en), west(waards) **– of**
ten westen van
westerly westelijk, wester-
western westers, westelijk
wet nat (maken)
whack mep; slaan
whale walvis
wharf kade, aanlegsteiger
what wat (voor (een)), welk; waar-
– is the time? hoe laat is het?
– is it called? hoe heet het?
whatever wat (*or* welk) dan ook; wat
… toch
wheat tarwe
wheel wiel, rad; zwenken; duwen
wheelbarrow kruiwagen
wheel clamp wielklem
wheeze piepen, hijgen
whelp welp; kwa'jongen
when wan'neer; (en) toen
whence van'waar
whenever wan'neer ook; telkens
wan'neer
where waar (naar toe)
whereabouts waar onge'veer;
ver'blijfplaats, ligging
whereas ter'wijl

... ook or toch);

...elk, wat; die, dat; wie

... vleugje, wolkje

...hile tijd; ter'wijl; hoe'wel
to – away ver'slijten

whilst ter'wijl; alhoe'wel

whim(sical) gril(lig)

whimper grienen, janken

whine jengelen, janken

whinny hinniken

whip zweep; (met de zweep) slaan;
wippen, schieten; kloppen

whir ge'snor; snorren

whirl roes; dwarrelen; tollen,
slingeren, stormen

whirlpool draaikolk

whirlwind wervelwind

whisk klopper; (weg)wippen

whiskers bakkebaarden; snor

whisky whisky

whisper ge'fluister; fluisteren

whistle fluit(je); fluiten

white wit; blank

whitewash witkalk; witten

Whitsun Pinksteren

whittle down ge'leidelijk
ver'minderen

whiz suizen, zoeven

who wie; die

whoever wie ... ook; al wie

whole (ge')heel; vol'ledig **on the –**
over het ge'heel ge'nomen, in het
algemeen

wholesale groothandel; inkoops-;
op grote schaal

wholesome ge'zond

wholly to'taal

whoop kreet; schreeuwen

whooping cough kinkhoest

whore hoer

whose wiens, wier; van wie

why waarom; wel

wick pit, ka'toentje

wicked slecht; on'deugend;
schan'dalig; cool

wicker rieten

wide breed, wijd **wide-awake**
klaar wakker

widely wijd en zijd; zeer

widen (zich) ver'wijden

widespread uitgestrekt; wijd ver'spreid

widow weduwe

widower weduwnaar

width breedte, wijdte

wield zwaaien; uitoefenen

wife vrouw

wig pruik

wiggle wiebelen met

wild wild; woest

wilderness wildernis

wilful eigen'zinnig; moed'willig

will wil(len); testa'ment; zal, zult,
zullen; kunnen

Insight

One of the most important false friends – some are discussed
under V – is the Dutch **wil**, from the verb **willen**. **Willen**
doesn't mean *will* but *want*, so **Gerda wil een auto kopen**
doesn't mean that *Gerda will buy a car* but that *Gerda wants
to buy a car*. Note also that **willen** is an irregular verb with
the singular forms **ik wil, jij/u wilt, hij/zij wil**, and the plural
form **willen**, in the present tense.

willing be'reid('willig), ge'willig
willow wilg
wilt ver'leppen
wily slim, sluw
wimp doetje, lulletje
win winnen, be'halen
wince in'eenkrimpen, zijn
  ge'zicht ver'trekken
wind wind; blaas-; kronkelen; winden
windfall afgewaaide vrucht;
  buitenkansje
window raam
window pane ruit
windowsill vensterbank
windscreen voorruit
windshield voorruit
windshield wiper ruitenwisser
windsurfing windsurfen
windy winderig
wine wijn
wing vleugel; cou'lisse; flank
wink knipoogje; knipogen
winner winnaar
winning winnend; in'nemend
winter winter(-)
wintry winters
wipe (af)vegen
wire (ijzer)draad; tele'gram
wireless radio; draadloos
wisdom wijsheid
wise wijs, ver'standig; wijze
wish ver'langen; wens(en); **I – that
  you were here** ik wou dat je hier
  was **I – to speak to him** ik zou
  hem willen spreken
wistful ver'langend, wee'moedig
wit ver'nuft, ver'stand; geest(igheid)
  at one's wits' end ten einde raad
witch heks
witchcraft tovena'rij
with met, bij; van
withdraw (zich) te'rugtrekken
wither ver'welken; ver'nietigen
withhold ont'houden

within binnen(in)
without zonder; buiten
withstand weer'staan
witness ge'tuige(nis); ge'tuige
  zijn van; ge'tuigen (van)
witticism geestigheid
witty geestig
wizard tovenaar
wobble wiebelen
woeful ramp'zalig
wolf wolf; opschrokken
woman vrouw; mens
womb baarmoeder; schoot
wonder wonder; ver'wondering;
  (zich) ver'wonderen; zich afvragen
wonderful wonder'baarlijk; prachtig
woo het hof maken
wood hout; bos
wooded be'bost
wooden houten; houterig
woodland bosland; bos-
woodwork houtwerk; houtbe'werking
woody bosrijk
wool(len) wol(len)
woolly wollig
word woord; be'richt **– processor**
  tekstverwerker
wording re'dactie, woordkeus
work werk(en); han'teren **–
  experience** werkervaring
worker arbeider, werker
working werking
workmanship vakmanschap
workout training
workshop werkplaats
world(ly) wereld(s)
world record wereldrecord
world war wereldoorlog
worldwide wereldwijd, over de hele
  wereld
worm wurm(en); kruipen; indringen
worn-out ver'sleten; uitgeput
worry zorg; (zich) be'zorgd maken;
  lastig vallen

worse erger, slechter
worship aan'bidding;
  godsdienst(oefening); aan'bidden;
  ver'eren
worst ergst, slechtst
worth waard(e) **– while – doing**
  (seeing etc.), de moeite waard
worthless waardeloos; ver'achtelijk
worthy (achtens')waardig, waard
would zou(den) (willen); wilde(n);
  wou
would-be zoge'naamd; toe'komstig,
  poten'tieel, mogelijk **a – buyer** een
  mogelijke koper
wound wond(en)
wrangle ruzie (maken)
wrap sjaal, cape; wikkelen, inpakken;
  hullen, ver'zinken **to – around**
  omslaan
wrapping ver'pakking
wrath(ful) toorn(ig)
wreak uit'storten; ver'oorzaken,
  aanrichten
wreath krans
wreck wrak; ver'nielen

wrench ruk(ken); schroefsleutel
wrest ont'wringen, afpersen
wrestle worstelen
wretch stakker
wretched el'lendig; be'roerd
wriggle draaien, wriemelen;
  zich wringen
wring (uit)wringen; afdwingen;
  omdraaien
wrinkle rimpel(en)
wrist pols
writ (be'vel)schrift, dagvaarding
write schrijven
writer schrijver
writhe (zich ver')wringen
writing (ge')schrift,
  schrijven; schrijf-
wrong ver'keerd; on'juist; niet in
  orde; kwaad, onrecht (aandoen)
  what is –? wat man'keert eraan?
  wat is er? **to go –** misgaan;
  ver'keerd gaan; de'fect raken; de
  ver'keerde weg opgaan
wrought iron smeedijzer
wry zuur

X

X-ray röntgenfoto, doorlichten

xenophobia vreemdelingen- haat

Y

yacht jacht; zeilen
yap keffen; snauwen
yard plaats(je), erf; kleine meter
  (91,44 cm)
yarn garen; ver'haal
yawn geeuw(en); gapen
year jaar
yearly jaarlijks
yearn vurig ver'langen (naar)
yeast gist

yell gil(len)
yellow geel
yelp janken
yes ja
yesterday gisteren
yet nog; al; toch **as –** tot nu toe
yield opbrengst; (zich) overgeven;
  (be'z)wijken (voor); opleveren
yogurt yoghurt
yoke juk; schouder(*or* heup)stuk

yolk dooier
you u; jij, je, jou; jullie
young jong(en); jeugd

yours (die *or* dat) van u,
(die *or* dat) van jou, (die *or* dat)
van jullie

Insight

There is no single Dutch word which expresses the meaning
of *yours*. In Dutch, possession is usually expressed with the
preposition **van**, literally meaning *of*. *Remco's iPhone* is **de
iPhone van Remco;** *my parent's house* is **het huis van mijn
ouders.** Like the English *'s* you can also express possession in
Dutch using a simple **-s** (**mijn moeders auto** *my mother's car*),
but this is not possible in all contexts, and in any case the
structure with **van** is much more common: **de auto van mijn
moeder.**

youngster jong'mens, jonge'man;
jochie
your uw; je, jouw; jullie

yourself (u')zelf, zich; je('zelf)
youth jeugd; tiener
youthful jeugdig

Z

zeal vuur; lijver
zealot dweper
zealous ijverig; vurig
zenith zenit; toppunt
zero nul(punt)
zest animo
zigzag zigzag
zinc zink

zip rits(sluiting); ritsen; zoeven,
scheuren; snel gaan
ZIP code postcode
zipper rits(sluiting)
zodiac dierenriem
zone zone
zoo dierentuin
zoological zoö'logisch

Credits